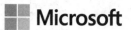

Microsoft Excel 2019
Inside Out

Bill Jelen
MrExcel

Microsoft Excel 2019 Inside Out
Published with the authorization of Microsoft Corporation by:
Pearson Education, Inc.

ISBN-13: 978-1-5093-0769-2
ISBN-10: 1-5093-0769-9

Library of Congress Control Number: 2018959530

1 18

Trademarks

Microsoft and the trademarks listed at http://www.microsoft.com on the "Trademarks" webpage are trademarks of the Microsoft group of companies. All other marks are property of their respective owners.

Warning and Disclaimer

Every effort has been made to make this book as complete and as accurate as possible, but no warranty or fitness is implied. The information provided is on an "as is" basis. The author, the publisher, and Microsoft Corporation shall have neither liability nor responsibility to any person or entity with respect to any loss or damages arising from the information contained in this book.

Special Sales

For information about buying this title in bulk quantities, or for special sales opportunities (which may include electronic versions; custom cover designs; and content particular to your business, training goals, marketing focus, or branding interests), please contact our corporate sales department at corpsales@pearsoned.com or (800) 382-3419. For government sales inquiries, please contact governmentsales@pearsoned.com.
For questions about sales outside the U.S., please contact intlcs@pearson.com.

Editor-in-Chief: Brett Bartow
Executive Editor: Loretta Yates
Assistant Editor: Charvi Arora
Development Editor: Rick Kughen
Managing Editor: Sandra Schroeder
Senior Project Editor: Tracey Croom
Project Editor: Charlotte Kughen
Copy Editor: Rick Kughen
Indexer: Cheryl Lenser
Proofreader: Sarah Kearns
Technical Editor: Bob Umlas
Editorial Assistant : Cindy J. Teeters
Cover Designer: Twist Creative, Seattle
Compositor: Bronkella Publishing LLC
Graphics: TJ Graham Art

To Robert F. Jelen, World War II veteran, former POW, and a great dad to four kids.

Contents at a Glance

Table of Contents

Chapter 20   More Tips and Tricks for Excel 2019 505

Part IV   Excel Visuals

Chapter 21   Formatting Worksheets. 515

About the Author

Bill Jelen, Excel MVP and the host of MrExcel.com, has been using spreadsheets since 1985, and he launched the MrExcel.com website in 1998. He loves performing his live Power Excel seminars around the United States. He has produced more than 2,200 episodes of his daily video podcast, *Learn Excel from MrExcel*. He is the author of 57 books about Microsoft Excel and writes the monthly Excel column for *Strategic Finance* magazine. He has created the Data Analytics—Leveraging Excel video-on-demand course for the Institute of Managerial Accountants. Before founding MrExcel.com, Bill Jelen spent 12 years in the trenches—working as a financial analyst for finance, marketing, accounting, and operations departments of a $500 million public company. When he is not geeking out about Excel, you will find him photographing rocket launches at Cape Canaveral Air Force Station. Check out his photography at WeReportSpace.com. He lives in Merritt Island, Florida, with his wife, Mary Ellen.

Inside OUT

You can find my favorite tricks in the Inside Out sidebars throughout this book.

If you have a favorite Excel trick or technique that is not in this book, consider sending it via email to *InsideTips@MrExcel.com*. Anyone sending in a tip that is new to me will win bragging rights and a collectible Excel Guru patch, designed by the same people who design the NASA mission patches.

Introduction

Excel 2019 is a roll-up of most of the features introduced to Office 365 subscribers in the three years since Excel 2016 was released. Although this book title is *Excel 2019 Inside Out*, I don't actually expect that many readers will be using the perpetual version of Excel 2019. Instead, most customers have switched over to Office 365, where new features are introduced monthly.

The Excel team has been responsive to items requested through the Excel.UserVoice.com website, and many small features and improvements happened in Excel 2019. Here are the new features as of the official release of Office 2019:

- Co-authoring has been massively improved. If you have several people who must access the same workbook at the same time, you'll have no issue as long as you save your workbook to OneDrive. Read more in Chapter 1, "What's New in Excel 2019."

- The charting team introduced two new chart types: Funnel and Filled Map Charts. The May 2018 announcement that Excel charts would soon support custom visuals from Power BI did not make it to Excel 2019, but the update will likely roll out to Office 365 in early 2019. Read about these charts in Chapter 23, "Graphing Data Using Excel Charts."

- There are new features in Power Query (found in the Get & Transform group on the Data tab). You can now Split By Delimiter to Rows instead of columns, and you can create new columns by typing examples. Read about Power Query in Chapter 13, "Transforming Data."

- Pivot tables will not Sum instead of Count if your data has a mix of numbers and empty cells. Another great improvement in pivot tables is the Pivot Table Defaults feature. If you want every new pivot table to start in tabular layout instead of compact layout, this feature is for you. Read more in Chapter 15, "Using Pivot Tables to Analyze Data."

- Data types debut with support for Geography and Stock Quotes. It seems likely that more data types will be introduced for Office 365 subscribers. See Chapter 5, "Understanding Formulas."

- Ideas is a new artificial intelligence feature. Excel analyzes up to 250,000 cells of data and uses artificial intelligence to provide more than 30 charts. For now, this feature is exclusive to Office 365. See Chapter 15, "Using Pivot Tables to Analyze Data."

- Excel 2019 offers six new calculation functions. `CONCAT`, `TEXTJOIN`, `MAXIFS`, and `MINIFS` are covered in Chapter 8, "Using Everyday Functions: Math, Date and Time, and Text Functions." The new `SWITCH` and `IFS` functions are covered in Chapter 9, "Using Powerful Functions: Logical, Lookup, and Database Functions."

- Power Pivot is now freely available to anyone who uses Office 2019. You can insert new calculated fields using the DAX formula language. DAX improvements include the ability to add medians to pivot tables or report text in the values field of pivot tables. Read about Power Pivot in Chapter 17, "Mashing Up Data with Power Pivot."

- Office 365 is getting a new ribbon interface. The icons have been redrawn, and the selected tab is now denoted with an underline instead of an outline. However, Excel 2019 is still sporting the old ribbon.

- Excel 2019 adds support for icons and 3D objects. The icon feature offers 180 icons that you can insert. Support for 3D objects lets you rotate and view various objects in Excel.

- Office 365 offers seven new array formulas: SEQUENCE, RANDARRAY, SORT, SORTBY, UNIQUE, FILTER, and SINGLE. A single formula can now spill into adjacent cells, eliminating the need to press Ctrl+Shift+Enter to generate an array. These are covered in Chapter 1, "What's New in Excel 2019."

- The Keep The Copy feature keeps copied cells on the Clipboard until you remove them by pressing Esc. In the past, it was often frustrating that simple tasks such as inserting one extra row would cause the Clipboard to clear. Now there's a solution for that problem.

- Excel will no longer nag you when you close or save a CSV file. There used to be warnings that you would lose your formulas and formatting. These were particularly annoying when you only needed to open the CSV file to check something without making changes. Excel always threw a warning when you tried to close the file.

- Insert Data From Picture is a new image-recognition capability in Excel that lets you quickly convert a picture of a data table into an Excel file.

- Forms.Office.Com allows you to design an online survey, collect answers in real time, and then download the results to Excel. This is covered in Chapter 1, "What's New in Excel 2019."

- Although this book covers VBA as the macro language, there is one new interesting feature in programmability: Any user-defined functions written in JavaScript now work in both the desktop version of Excel *and* in Excel Online. JavaScript is still slow and clunky compared to VBA, but it could be the hint of what's coming in the future.

- Microsoft has a new focus on accessibility. The new Modern Sound Scheme provides gentle audible feedback for a number of actions in Excel. See Chapter 1, "What's New in Excel 2019."

- Power BI Desktop and Power BI allow you to share your Excel workbooks and dashboards over the Internet or to a tablet or phone. Chapter 28, "Sharing Dashboards with Power BI," introduces this new functionality.

- Picture transparency has been added to Office 365. Now you can see the values in cells behind your picture.

- The algorithm for VLOOKUP has been improved. If you are doing repetitive lookups, VLOOKUP speed could be ten times faster.

Who This Book Is For

This book is for anyone who uses Excel twenty hours a week or more. Whether you use Excel for organizing your to-do list or to analyze 5 million rows of call center data every day, this book includes the information you need to solve problems quickly and easily.

Assumptions About You

I like to believe most of my readers use Excel 40 hours a week, and those are the weeks you are on vacation. At the very least, I'm assuming you regularly use Excel for your job. You are comfortable using Excel formulas beyond AutoSum. You likely know and use VLOOKUP and Pivot Tables regularly. You are looking for the fastest and most efficient ways to finish tasks in Excel.

How This Book Is Organized

This book gives you a comprehensive look at the various features you will use. This book is structured in a logical approach to all aspects of using the Windows-based versions of Excel 2019 or Excel in Office 365.

Part I, "The Excel Interface," covers the ribbon, customizing Excel, and keyboard shortcuts.

Part II, "Calculating with Excel," covers all Excel calculation functions.

Part III, "Data Analysis with Excel," covers Power Query, Pivot Tables, and other features that help you perform data analysis.

Part IV, "Excel Visuals," covers charting, 3D Map, and Power BI.

About the Companion Content

I have included the Excel workbooks I used to create the screenshots in this book to enrich your learning experience. You can download this book's companion content from the following page:

microsoftpressstore.com/Excel2019InsideOut/downloads

The companion content includes the following:

- Workbooks used to create the examples in the workbook

- Sample data that you can use to practice the concepts in the book

- VBA macros from Chapter 19

Acknowledgments

Thanks to all the Excel project managers who were happy to take the time to discuss the how or why behind a feature. At various times, Ash Sharma, Sam Radakovitz, David Gainer, Johnnie Thomas, Sangeeta Mudnal, Joe McDaid, Urmi Gupta, and Prash Shirolkar pitched in to help with a particular issue. Thanks to former Excel project managers Rob Collie and Dany Hoter for their assistance. Thanks to Tracy Syrstad, Barb Jelen, Jeannie Muncy, Zeke Jelen, and Suat Ozgur for making up the MrExcel.com team.

Other Excel MVPs often offered their take on potential bugs. I could send a group email over a weekend, and someone like Ken Puls, Roger Govier, Liam Bastick, Jon Peltier, Jan-Karel Pieterse, Charles Williams, Brad Yundt, or Ingeborg Hawighorst would usually respond. I particularly loved launching a missive just after the Microsoft crew in Building 36 went home on Friday evening, knowing they would return on Monday morning with 40 or 50 responses to the conversation. Without any Excel project managers to temper the discussion, we would often have designed massive improvements that we would have liked to have implemented in Excel. Someone would show up on Monday and tell us why that could never be done.

Thanks to my fellow YouTube Excel MVPs: Mynda Treacy, Oz Du Soleil, Jon Acompora, Leila Gharani, and Mike Girvin. Check out our creative and funny #ExcelHash competitions on YouTube.

Bob Umlas is the smartest Excel guy that I know, and I was thrilled to have him as the technical editor for this book.

Putting together a book requires careful coordination with editors, proofreaders and compositors. My sincere thanks to Charlotte and Rick Kughen, Sarah Kearns, and Tricia Bronkella.

Indexing is a tough job that requires attention to detail. The index created by Cheryl Lenser gets two thumbs up from Nellie Jay.

I've been writing books for Loretta Yates since 2004. If my spreadsheet is correct, this is our 27th project. Thanks for 15 years of trusting me with your books.

Thanks to Master Chief Rusty Pedersen for all of the fiberglass and carburetor knowledge that went in to this book. When I am not dealing with Excel, Mary Ellen Jelen and I photograph rocket launches at Cape Canaveral Air Force Station. Thanks to my associates at WeReportSpace.com: Michael Seeley and Jared Haworth. Robert F. Jelen, my 96-year-old father, lives next door to us. I enjoy our daily lunches. I apologize that I had to miss a few when deadlines for this book were looming.

I wrote this book at the Kola Mi Writing Camp. The staff there was fantastic.

Mary Ellen Jelen did a great job of keeping me on track with this book.

Support and Feedback

The following sections provide information on errata, book support, feedback, and contact information.

Stay in Touch

Let's keep the conversation going! We're on Twitter:

http://twitter.com/MicrosoftPress

http://twitter.com/MrExcel

Errata, Updates, and Book Support

We've made every effort to ensure the accuracy of this book and its companion content. You can access updates to this book—in the form of a list of submitted errata and their related corrections—at:

microsoftpressstore.com/Excel2019InsideOut/errata

If you discover an error that is not already listed, please submit it to us at the same page.

If you need additional support, email Microsoft Press Book Support at:

microsoftpresscs@pearson.com.

Please note that product support for Microsoft software and hardware is not offered through the previous addresses. For help with Microsoft software or hardware, go to http://support.microsoft.com.

This chapter explains the new features in Excel 2019 and a few important features that you might have missed if you upgraded directly from Excel 2013 to Excel 2019.

Office 365 Is the Future

Although this book is titled *Excel 2019 Inside Out*, it is far more likely that you are using Office 365 instead. During the Excel 2016 product cycle, subscriptions to Office 365 far outpaced people who purchased the traditional Office 2016.

Those people who mistakenly paid $400 for a perpetual license to Office 2016 sat on the sidelines as the people paying $10 a month for five licenses of Office 365 received new features month after month.

For Office 2019, it is even worse: Microsoft has said that Office 2019 is for the last holdouts—the people who refuse to switch to a subscription. As I write this in the summer of 2018, there are already new features coming out in the Office 365 version of Excel that will not be in Excel 2019.

If you are one of those holdouts, here is the guide to Office 365. First, Office 365 has nothing to do with using Excel in the cloud. You will still be running Excel from your computer just like the perpetual version of Excel. You can choose how often you want to get updates. I, as the author of this book, have one beta computer signed up for the Office Insider program, and it gives me new updates every Tuesday. These bits frequently break something. When the Insider Fast subscribers find a problem, we report it to Microsoft, so the bugs can be fixed when it rolls out to the Monthly channel in four weeks. Most people are on the Semi-Annual plan. You get updates twice times a year, and those updates have been thoroughly vetted by millions of others.

I've encouraged the Microsoft marketing department to offer an amnesty program. There should be a way for someone to say, "Gee, I made a mistake by giving you $400 for a perpetual license to Excel. Could I please convert this to an Office 365 subscription, so I start getting the exciting new updates like everyone else?"

Every feature mentioned in this chapter as being new in Excel 2019 has reached the Office 365 subscriber months or years ago.

Office 2019 Requires Windows 10

Microsoft used to support any version of Office for ten years. This is broken down into five years of mainstream support and five years of extended support. During extended support, you would get bug fixes, but no problem fixes unless your company pays for Premier support. Starting with Office 2019, the extended support period is being reduced to two years, which means that Office 2016 and Office 2019 will both lose extended support in October 2025.

In 2020, Windows 7 and Windows 8.1 will no longer be supported. Microsoft has decided Office 2019 will not run on Windows 7 or Windows 8.1. You will have to use a supported release of Windows 10. All Windows 10 releases are supported for 24 months, which means the original unpatched version of Windows 10 is no longer supported and would not be able to run Office 2019.

The reason for the change is to reduce the testing matrix that Microsoft must perform for each release of Office.

Forward-Looking Features in Excel 2019

The computing world is becoming increasingly a mobile workforce. You spend a lot of time doing tasks on your phone that you used to do on a desktop computer. Checking email can easily be done on a mobile phone. Spreadsheets can easily be viewed in mobile, but it is still difficult to author a spreadsheet on a phone. However, Microsoft is counting on spreadsheet use on mobile devices to increase.

A certain subset of people using Excel will extend the functionality of Excel by using macros and user-defined functions written in Visual Basic for Applications (VBA). This language is 30 years old and will never run in Excel Online, Excel for Android, or Excel for iOS. With Excel 2019, Microsoft announced support for user-defined functions written in JavaScript, which opens the possibility for a custom function to work both on your PC and in Excel online. There is still no support for Android or iOS, and the JavaScript functions are super-slow compared to their VBA counterparts. However, this is a step in the right direction.

Artificial Intelligence in Office 365

In early 2018, Microsoft began rolling out the Artificial Intelligence feature to Office 365 subscribers. If you enable Artificial Intelligence, you will be able to select up to 250,000 cells of data and ask Excel to analyze the data, looking for interesting patterns. Your data is sent to a Microsoft server where some routines written by Microsoft Research look for trends and patterns.

TROUBLESHOOTING

The Artificial Intelligence feature has appeared with two different names and in different locations.

In early 2018, "Insights" debuted on the Insert tab, just to the left of the Charts group. By September 2018, Microsoft was running a test in which the feature is called "Ideas" and appears on the far-right side of the Home tab.

The final name and location will depend on metrics during the test, but Ideas on the Home tab seems to be the eventual winner.

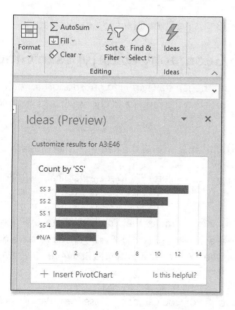

The Ideas icon is a lightning bolt and appears to the right of Find & Select in the Home tab of the ribbon.

Artificial Intelligence for Office uses the same engine used to power Insights in Power BI, but the Excel team did extra work to fine-tune the results. You will often get back 24 to 36 results—each one would insert a chart, pivot table, or pivot chart in your workbook (see Figure 1.1).

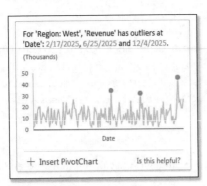

For 'Region: West', 'Revenue' has outliers at
'Date': 2/17/2025, 6/25/2025 and 12/4/2025.

Figure 1.1   The Artificial Intelligence server is looking for outliers and other interesting points.

Microsoft's initial decision is that Ideas will not be supported in Excel 2019. They've drawn a line that Ideas is a service that happens online, and if you are not paying the monthly fee for Office 365, you don't qualify for the service. This seems like yet another policy designed to prevent people from buying the perpetual licenses of Office.

Read more about Ideas in Chapter 15, "Using Pivot Tables to Analyze Data."

Support for Stocks and Geography Data Types in Office 365

During the summer of 2018, Microsoft began slowly rolling out support for data types in Excel. Type some ticker symbols in a range. Select the range and choose Stocks as the Data type on the Data tab of the ribbon.

The stock symbols will be replaced with an icon and the name of the company.

Click on any icon (or select the cell and Ctrl+Shift+F2) to see a data card with information about the company.

Far more interesting, though, are the new formulas that you can create. In Figure 1.2, the formula =B2.Exchange, =B2.Employees, =B2.[Ticker Symbol] will retrieve data from the Internet and return it to your worksheet. You can also use =FIELDVALUE(B2,"Volume") instead of the dot notation.

Once you have formulas in C2:G2 for Roku, you can copy those formulas down, and the results change to return values from Netflix, Amazon, Twitter, and so on.

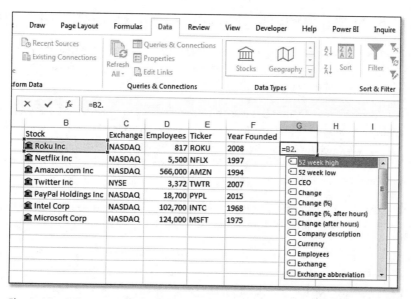

Figure 1.2   Column B contains linked data types. The formulas in C:G refer to the symbol in column B.

If the data item is a single word, you can write a formula without the square brackets: =B2.CEO. However, if the data item contains a space or other special characters, use square brackets: =B2.[Price (after hours)].

All data such as Price and Price After Hours is delayed by 15 minutes.

These new Linked Data Types do not automatically refresh with every workbook refresh. You can either right-click B2 and choose Data Type, Refresh to refresh the entire block of B2:G8 or use Data, Refresh All (Ctrl+Alt+F5).

If you apply Filters to the data, a new drop-down menu appears at the top of the Filter menu. You can choose to sort the data by any field in the data card. In Figure 1.3, the data is sorted ascending by employee. You can even sort by a field that is not returned to the spreadsheet.

Figure 1.3   The Filter drop-down menu allows you to choose a field by which you want to sort.

CHAPTER 1

Power Query Is Still the Best New Feature in Excel 2019

That heading you just read seems like an anomaly. Power Query is not new. It was introduced as an add-in for Excel 2013, and it was made a full part of Excel in Excel 2016. How can a feature that is five years old be the best new feature?

I still consider it a "new" feature because most people have not discovered it. Because of a series of branding missteps by the Microsoft Marketing team, the name "Power Query" was removed from the feature when it was quietly added as the third group on the Data tab of the Excel 2016 ribbon. Later, in Office 365, the Power Query icons were moved to the first group on the Data tab, replacing nearly similar icons from Excel 2013.

Consider the two versions of the ribbon shown in Figure 1.4. It is very easy to assume that the icons in the Excel 2019 ribbon are just a rearrangement of the icons from Excel 2013.

Figure 1.4   The same place and names are completely new and improved.

Although the icons look similar, the logic behind the icons is completely new and far more powerful than the legacy versions of the same icons.

Here are the improvements:

- The data cleansing tools are new and offer all types of transformations that were difficult in previous versions of Excel. You can unpivot, and you can group and summarize. You can do the equivalent of a VLOOKUP, returning an item description when the CSV file only has an item number. You can split by delimiter to new rows. You can convert a date field to months or quarters or years during an import. New transformations are added frequently. While the Power Query ribbon offers 50+ transformations, there are hundreds of transformations available with a couple of lines of code in the M programming language.

I estimate that you can save 20 percent of your time spent cleaning data on the first day of your Power Query usage. If you have something that used to take 20 minutes, you can do it in 16 minutes on the first day.

- Power Query is self-documenting. As you do steps in Power Query, those steps are remembered and documented. When the internal auditor shows up and wants to know how you produced this data that made its way into the packet you handed out, you will have the steps documented.

- Although Power Query is 20 percent faster right away, it is 99 percent faster going forward. Once you have cleaned a data set using Power Query, you simply re-open the workbook containing the query results and click Refresh to have Power Query re-apply all of the transformations to the new data.

- Power Query can work on an entire folder of files. If you must combine all the CSV or Excel files from a folder, Power Query makes it easy.

Read more about Power Query in Chapter 13, "Transforming Data."

Co-Authoring Allows Multiple People to Edit the Same Workbook at the Same Time

In the past, shared workbooks were a hassle. As soon as you shared a workbook to allow multiple people to edit the workbook, many basic features in Excel were deactivated. The ability to have everyone in a department edit the same file has been rewritten and works very well.

Google Sheets is an online spreadsheet competitor to Excel. Because everyone using Google Sheets is online, they were the first spreadsheet app to market with a usable interface where multiple people could edit a workbook.

Microsoft's implementation requires your workbook to be saved online. You can save it in One-Drive, OneDrive for Business, or SharePoint Online. Once the workbook is saved in those locations, you can have multiple people on multiple endpoints editing the workbook.

For example, right now, I am editing the same workbook in Excel 2019, Excel 2016, Excel for the iPad, and Excel Online for an old machine that only offers Excel 2013.

When I look at the workbook, I see four cell pointers. The cell pointer with the fill handle is the active cell on my computer. The other cell pointers indicate the active cell on every other computer. When one of the other people are editing a cell, that cell temporarily becomes shaded. See Figure 1.5.

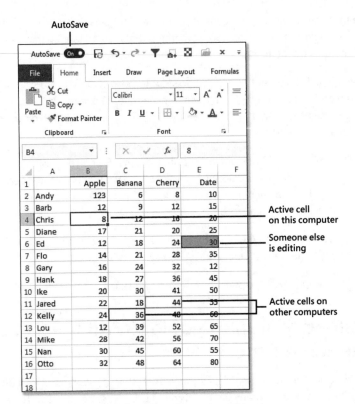

Figure 1.5 Four people editing the same workbook.

Setting Up Co-Authoring

To set up a workbook for co-authoring, you need to use File, Save As and choose a OneDrive location or a SharePoint Online location.

After saving the workbook, you will see the AutoSave icon at the top left of the screen light up. A Sharing icon appears at the top right of the screen.

When you click Sharing, you can enter email addresses of specific people, or you can use the Get A Sharing Link tool to generate a link where others can edit. The Sharing Link tool is at the bottom of the Share panel.

When other people open the workbook, their initials should appear in a colored circle at the top right of the worksheet. Hover over the initials to see the name of the person. The color of the circle will match the color of the extra cell pointers.

You can hover over one of the extra cell pointers to see the name of the person who is editing that cell.

The delay for updating the cell pointer from all computers is very short. The delay for updating values can be longer. For example, imagine that you are looking at Computer A and someone is changing a cell on Computer B. The person using Computer B selects A1, types **123**, and presses Enter. That person's cell pointer will generally move to A2. On the other computer, you will see A1 be selected, then you will see A2 be selected. One to two seconds later, you will see the 123 appear in A1. For some reason, the synchronization of the cell pointers happens faster than the value updates.

Etiquette for Co-Authoring

You won't have any trouble if you do not select any cells that other people are editing. Wait until they finish editing the cell and for the cell to update. You are then free to edit the cell.

If two people edit the same cell at the same time, Excel will choose one who wins. In general, the last person to change the cell "wins," but not in all cases. Different endpoints support co-authoring in different ways. Sometimes, a person with an older version of Excel won't have full support for co-authoring, and that person will always win.

There are some features that are not supported in co-authoring. If someone tries to use one of those features, the others might get "Refresh Recommended" or "Upload Failed" errors. In my opinion, once you get one of these messages, you start over. Microsoft says it is not that bad. Their advice:

- If you don't have any unsaved changes, simply click Refresh.

- If you have unsaved changes that you were not particularly fond of, click Discard.

- If you have unsaved changes that you need to keep, click Save A Copy and save the file with a different name. Select and copy the changes you need to keep. Reopen the original file and paste the changes back in.

The Bad Side of AutoSave

In my workday, I very rarely need to share workbooks. I will say that only one out of 200 workbooks requires co-authoring. Most of the time, I am not co-authoring.

AutoSave is great when everyone needs to see every change that you make, but AutoSave is horrible if you are the only person using the workbook.

How often do you do steps like this?

1. You need to create a February report.

2. Rather than start from nothing, you open the January report.

3. Then, you change the title.

4. You change the headings.

5. You clear out the January data.

6. Finally, you click File, Save As to save the workbook with "February" in the name.

With AutoSave, you destroy the January workbook after every step of the process.

Here's another scenario: You have a great forecast model. Your manager has a crazy idea and wants to see the impact on profit if you do X. You know this idea will never work, but you need to give the manager the results. So, you open the forecast file, make the crazy changes, print, and then close the workbook without saving. This ability to close the workbook without saving is gone with AutoSave. Every change gets saved automatically.

In 99.5 percent of the cases, AutoSave is really bad. If you regularly save your workbooks to OneDrive, AutoSave will be enabled by default. The Excel MVPs complained loudly to the Excel team on your behalf, and we were able to get a setting added to Excel Options. Choose File, Options, Save, and unselect AutoSave OneDrive and SharePoint Online Files By Default On Excel, as shown in Figure 1.6.

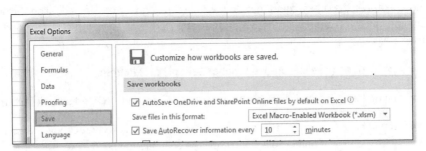

Figure 1.6   Turn this feature off.

Improvements to PivotTables

Way back in Excel 2007, a new Compact Layout was introduced, and it was the default for all future pivot tables. There are a lot of people who preferred the old Tabular layout. For six years, I lobbied the Excel team to give us a check box to make all future pivot tables start in Tabular layout instead of Compact layout. In Excel 2019, that function is finally available, but it is much better than I requested.

I am pretty excited that the release of this new feature led to the creation of an entirely new category in Excel Options. Because this feature has been slowly rolling out to Office 365 subscribers, there is a simple test to see if you have it. Open Excel Options, and if you have the brand-new "Data" category on the left, then you have the feature.

The first choice in the new Data category is Make Changes To The Default Layout Of PivotTables (the button reads, Edit Default Layout). Microsoft brought all the other pivot table options from the Advanced category to this new Data category.

Click the Edit Default Layout button (see Figure 1.7) to open the Edit Default Layout dialog box shown in Figure 1.8.

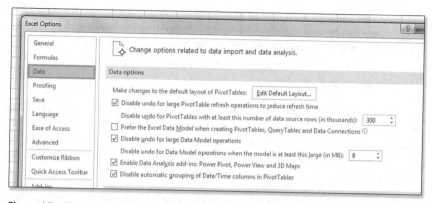

Figure 1.7   The new default pivot table layout feature leads off a new Data category in Excel Options.

Once in the Edit Default Layout dialog box, you can control six settings right in the dialog box. You could also import settings from an existing pivot table using the Import button. Or, you can click the PivotTable Options button to change any settings.

Figure 1.8   There are six settings available in the Edit Default Layout dialog box. Use the Import or PivotTable Options buttons to change other defaults.

More PivotTable Improvements

Pivot tables will no longer count if your data contains a mix of numbers and empty cells. You will still get a Count of Revenue if someone types some spaces where the revenue should be. However, if the cells are simply empty, Excel will treat them as numeric, and you will get a sum instead of a count.

In Excel 2016, adding a Date field to a pivot table would cause the pivot table to AutoGroup the dates. There was no way to turn this off except for editing the Windows Registry. You now have a way to turn it off. Use the Disable Automatic Grouping Of Date/Time Columns In PivotTables setting found in the Data category of Excel Options. Read more about PivotTables in Chapter 15, "Using Pivot Tables to Analyze Data."

You can format individual cells in a pivot table, and that formatting will persist after a Refresh. Say that you need the East region Gadget revenue to be red. Right-click the revenue cell for East Gadget and choose Format Cells. Apply any formatting from the Format Cells dialog box. You can rearrange the pivot table, and provided you do not remove Product, Region, or Revenue from the pivot table, the formatting will persist.

The Power Pivot tab is now available in all SKUs of Excel 2019 for Windows. Back in Excel 2016, people with the Home, University, or Small Business versions did not have the full Power Pivot tab.

The Data Model version of PivotTables has new DAX calculations, such as Median or even ConcatenateX to allow you to report text in the values section of a pivot table. Read more about the Data Model in Chapter 17, "Mashing Up Data with Power Pivot."

Power BI Desktop is a new way to share your pivot table and pivot charts. Read about Power BI in Chapter 28, "Sharing Dashboards with Power BI."

New Calculation Functions in Excel 2019

Excel 2019 includes six new calculation functions.

In the Text category, CONCAT and TEXTJOIN are new. While CONCAT lets you specify a range of cells, TEXTJOIN is better because you can specify a delimiter between each cell and indicate if empty cells should be ignored. Read more in Chapter 8, "Using Everyday Functions: Math, Date and Time, and Text Functions."

In the Statistics category, MAXIFS and MINIFS join the existing AVERAGEIF, SUMIFS, and COUNTIFS. Read more in Chapter 8, "Using Everyday Functions: Math, Date and Time, and Text Functions."

Two new functions in the Logical category will simplify complex nested IF statements. The SWITCH function will let you test a single value for many possible values. The IFS function will let you specify many possible conditions without introducing new IF functions in the

Value_If-False argument. Read more in Chapter 9, "Using Powerful Functions: Logical, Lookup, and Database Functions."

Faster VLOOKUP When Multiple Columns

Say that you must do twelve columns of VLOOKUPs, one for each month. Every VLOOKUP starts out with =VLOOKUP($A2 and uses the same lookup table.

Formula gurus would tell you it would be faster to do one column with MATCH and twelve columns of INDEX.

New since Excel 2016, Excel will detect this situation and automatically speed up the VLOOKUP recalculation time. When Excel starts to look up the value for February, it will remember the location of the matching row for January.

Two New Charts in 2019

Excel 2019 adds two new chart types—a funnel chart as shown in Figure 1.9 and a filled map chart as shown in Figure 1.10.

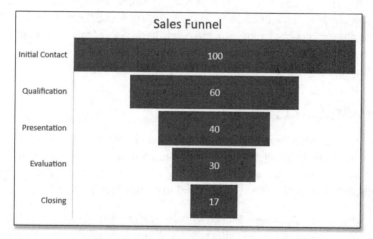

Figure 1.9   Funnel charts are new since Excel 2016.

The important word in filled map charts is the word "Filled." You can color code countries, states, provinces, counties, and zip code boundaries. However, you cannot plot individual points for each city. I never quite understood why Excel downloads the shape of a county but not the shape of a city.

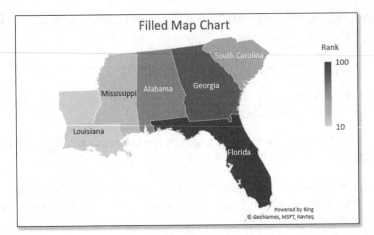

Figure 1.10   A filled map chart showing six states in the southeastern United States.

Read more about both chart types in Chapter 23, "Graphing Data Using Excel Charts."

One of the biggest improvements in charting is not out yet, but it has been promised soon for Office 365 customers. For the Power BI product, Microsoft allowed anyone to create an open-source visualization type. At the Build Conference in May 2018, Microsoft announced that you would soon be able to import custom visuals to Excel. Because this feature did not make it to Excel 2019, it is another example of exclusive content for Office 365 subscribers. Take a look at the custom visuals in Chapter 28.

Inserting Icons and 3D Models

A new Icons feature appears next to Shapes on the Insert tab of the ribbon. The Shapes feature debuted in Excel 97. The 175 available shapes included a few interesting pictures, such as a heart or a lightning bolt. The new Icons feature offers 185 graphics divided into logical categories such as People, Communication, Arts, Apparel, and so on (see Figure 1.11).

Once you insert an icon into your worksheet, a new Graphics Tools tab appears in the ribbon. You can re-color, re-size, rotate, or add effects. The only apparent difference between an icon and a shape is that a shape can contain a text box. If you need to add text to your icon, you can use the Convert To Shape icon on the left side of the Graphics Tools tab in the ribbon.

Figure 1.11   The Icons feature adds 185 new shapes to Excel.

Inserting and Exploring 3D Models

Almost half of all manufacturing companies are using 3D printing as a tool for rapid prototyping. Forbes estimates that 3D printing is a 12 billion dollar industry, and it is growing. Excel now allows you to import and rotate 3D printing files.

Specifically, Excel supports these file types: Filmbox (*.fbx), Object (*.obj), 3D Manufacturing Format (*.3mf), Polygon (*.ply), StereoLithography (*.stl), and Binary GL Transmission (*.glb).

On the Insert tab, choose 3D Models. There are a few sample files provided by Microsoft, or you can import any file you have. One great resource for free 3D models is NASA; browse for royalty-free models at https://nasa3d.arc.nasa.gov/models/printable.

Figure 1.12 shows a 3D model of the Hubble Space Telescope.

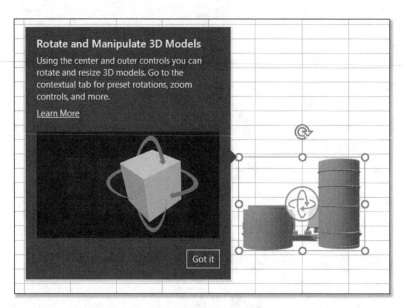

Figure 1.12   Notice the 3D rotation icon in the center of the model.

Click the center rotation icon and drag your mouse in any direction to rotate the model. Figure 1.13 reveals that the side view of Figure 1.12 is actually several pieces that you could print on a 3D printer and assemble.

Figure 1.13   After rotating the 3D model, you can see all seven pieces.

Using the Inking Tools in Excel 2019

With the proliferation of touch screens, the Draw tab of the ribbon is now a permanent part of Excel 2019. Microsoft made a big deal about the ability to customize the pens used while drawing. As shown in Figure 1.14, the built-in pen types are either fine-point markers for drawing lines or wide-tipped highlighters. The highlighters are semi-transparent so that you can see the underlying text.

To add a new pen, use the New Pen icon. Choose Pen or Highlighter, then choose a thickness and a color.

To draw on the worksheet, click on a pen and then either drag with the mouse or draw with the touchscreen. To stop inking, use the Stop Inking icon on the right side.

I never like the results of me trying to draw a circle. If I wanted to circle something, I would use the built-in Shape tools to draw a perfect oval. However, if you need something quick, the tools on the Draw tab could work.

By the way, for those of you who use Microsoft Word, the similar feature in Word offers a pencil in addition to pens and highlighters. Also, there are a variety of gel-pen effects, such as Sparkles.

One oddity is the ability to play back your drawing. If you've highlighted five cells, clicking Ink Replay will highlight those cells in an animated fashion. I have no idea when you would use this; if you could add each highlight one at a time like a PowerPoint slide, I would get it. However, this feature is like blowing through the entire PowerPoint deck in one second.

Figure 1.14   The Ink tools have improved since Excel 2016.

Suggesting Ideas to the Excel Team

A new website has gained popularity since Excel 2016. Microsoft is billing Excel.UserVoice.com as "Excel's Suggestion Box." They encourage you to visit the site and tell them what changes you would like to see in Excel. The ideas are posted publicly, and other customers can vote for your idea. Each idea shows the title, description, and current vote count.

You can find a link to this website by using the new Help tab in the ribbon. Choose Suggest A Feature, and Excel will launch a browser for Excel.UserVoice.com.

The Excel team says they will personally respond to any idea with more than 20 votes. Just submitting an idea doesn't mean they will implement it. In many cases, they will tell you the idea has already been implemented, or that they can't implement your idea for one reason or another. However, if they encourage you to keep collecting votes, then your idea is actually under consideration.

I will attest that this works. Since Excel 2007, I've been lobbying for the Excel team not to have pivot tables default to Compact layout. I posted an idea and started encouraging viewers of my podcast to vote for my idea. After I collected 200–300 votes, I received a call from someone on the Excel team saying they were going to add the Defaults feature to Excel. They actually implemented something far more encompassing.

Each of the following features are new since Excel 2016 and were the result of the ideas getting a lot of votes on Excel.UserVoice.com.

Keeping the Copied Cells on the Clipboard

This new feature is a great example of what happens when you listen to people posting ideas on Excel.UserVoice.com. The original idea was posted and then received 224 votes. The Excel team implemented the idea, but then a lot of people did not like the side-effect of the idea.

The person who suggested the idea noted that they would frequently select some cells and choose Copy, click New Sheet, type a heading, and finally, choose Paste. However, the act of typing something in a cell would clear the Clipboard. This would cause some extra steps, such as screaming in your head, going back to the original sheet, pressing Ctrl+C to Copy again, moving to the new worksheet, and pressing Ctrl+V to Paste.

In my experience, the problem was slightly different. I would insert seven blank rows, then copy eight rows of data. I would want to insert one extra row, so I had room for the paste. Inserting rows caused the Clipboard to clear.

Excel 2019 will now keep the dotted marquee active even if you type something in a cell or if you insert some rows. (By the way, the "marquee" is the official Microsoft name for what a lot of people call the "marching ants" or "dancing ants"—the flashing animation around a selection that looks like a line of ants marching or the chaser lights on a movie marquee.)

TROUBLESHOOTING

Keeping the copied cells on the clipboard can trip up people using legacy hotkeys to Insert Cells.

In Excel 2019, Insert Copied Cells and Insert Cells are two different commands with two different hotkey sequences.

Excel speedsters have often memorized hotkeys for common tasks. In Excel 2019, you can choose Alt, H, I, E versus Alt, H, I, I to differentiate whether you want to insert empty cells or insert the clipboard contents.

The trouble is for people using the legacy Office 2003 hotkeys. Back in Office 2003, the same hotkeys would intelligently invoke one command or the other. If you press Alt+I, E when the clipboard is empty, Excel invokes Insert Cells to insert empty cells. If you press Alt+I, E with something on the clipboard, Excel invokes Insert Copied Cells, which inserts the contents of the clipboard in the newly inserted cells.

If you pressed Alt+I, E when the clipboard was empty, the Insert Cells dialog would open. If you press D and Enter, you would shift the data down, inserting new blank cells.

If you pressed Alt+I, E when there was something on the clipboard, the Insert Copied Cells would open. Pressing D (for Down) and Enter would complete the command.

People who frequently use these hotkeys do not slow down to notice which dialog box opens. Press Alt+I, E, D, Enter will complete the command and close the dialog box.

Because the Clipboard now does not get cleared, you might frequently be pasting the cells from the Clipboard instead of inserting empty cells. If you are experiencing this problem, there are four possible solutions:

- Stop using hotkeys and use the commands on the ribbon.
- Start using the new Alt, H, I, I, D, Enter sequence when you want to insert blank cells.
- Start pressing the Esc key to clear the Clipboard before you begin the Alt+I, E, D, Enter sequence. With an empty Clipboard, pressing Alt+I, E, D, Enter will always insert empty cells.
- Stop using Ctrl+V to paste. If you press Enter to paste, the clipboard will automatically get cleared.

I experience this problem frequently, and I have settled on the third option—pressing the Esc key to clear the Clipboard—as the easiest.

Speaking from experience, I like the new Keep The Copy feature. It saves me time a couple of times a week. I also hate the new feature because it causes me to choose Undo about ten times a week. It sounded really good on paper, but I never realized how frequently I would Insert Cells using the legacy hotkeys. And now that my Insert Cells process is sometimes broken, this one change is my leading cause of spreadsheet errors.

CHAPTER 1

Here are the common options after you copy cells:

- Press Ctrl+V to paste. This keeps the items on the Clipboard so that you can select another range and Ctrl+V again.

- Press Enter to paste. This pastes the content from the Clipboard and clears the Clipboard.

- Use Home, Insert, Insert Copied Cells to open the Insert Paste dialog box. Figure 1.15 shows an example just before this command. One cell with the text, "NEW" has been copied to the clipboard. Six cells have been selected in the midst of some data. Selecting Insert Copied Cells will paste the word "NEW" six times and shift the remaining data down. You will get the result shown in Figure 1.16.

B	C	D	E	F
NEW				
	Apple	Banana	Cherry	Dill
	Apple	Banana	Cherry	Dill
	Apple	Banana	Cherry	Dill
	Apple	Banana	Cherry	Dill
	Apple	Banana	Cherry	Dill
	Apple	Banana	Cherry	Dill

Figure 1.15   Copying one cell and preparing to paste it to six cells while shifting the data.

Figure 1.16   After selecting Insert Copied Cells from the ribbon, the Insert Paste dialog appears. You can choose Shift Cells Down or Shift Cells Right.

Inside OUT

Even simple things in Excel can be difficult for the Excel team to program. Take the simple act of selecting some cells.

If you have black text on a white background and select those cells, Excel marks the selection with a border and applies a 30-percent gray to the cells. That seems really simple to program.

However, what if the cells have a fill color, and you have 30 orange cells and select 10 of them? Excel must add gray to the existing orange. The programmer has some code to make the orange darker. That code has to work with 16 million possible fill colors. I am not sure how I would begin to program that.

If you still have a copy of Excel 2013 installed on a PC, try this experiment:

1. Select some cells, such as B2:E10, as shown in the following figure.

2. In Excel 2013, it was impossible to deselect one of those cells. However, let's say you tried the logical step of holding Ctrl while clicking the cell that you wanted to remove from the selection. When you Ctrl+click the cell, nothing happens.

3. If you thought you had mis-clicked, and you try to Ctrl+click again, rather than unselecting the cell, a bug causes the additional gray color to get applied to the selected cell a second time! The gray becomes darker gray. Likely, this is both annoying because Excel does not offer a way to unselect and amusing because you found a weird bug in Excel. If you continue Ctrl+clicking the cell, it gets progressively darker and darker. After Ctrl+clicking eight times, the cell will be almost completely black.

In the figure below, I have Ctrl+clicked eight cells in B7:E8 anywhere from one to eight times to show you the progression.

This bug is fascinating to me because this process is one the Excel team never thought you would do, and it reveals a little bit of the logic behind how Microsoft shades the selected cells.

I typically would shake my head and go about re-selecting the cells correctly.

Thankfully, someone out there decided to do something about Excel's inability to unselect a cell and wrote up a great suggestion at Excel.UserVoice.com. Then, hundreds of other people voted. And now, in Excel 2019, Ctrl+clicking will remove a cell from the selection as described in this chapter.

Unselecting a Cell with Ctrl+Click

You can select multiple ranges in Excel by using the Ctrl key. In Figure 1.17, click and drag the mouse to select the first six cells. Hold the Ctrl key while dragging the mouse to select the eight Yes cells in columns C and D. In real life, you might have many more regions to select, and if you accidentally selected an extra cell, such as the "No" cell, there was no way to remove one cell from the selection in Excel 2016.

To remove the cell from the selection, you had to start all over again, carefully selecting one region at a time.

An improvement in Excel 2019 allows you to Ctrl+click a cell to remove it from the selection. This feature is new since Excel 2016, thanks to 327 votes at Excel.UserVoice.com.

Figure 1.17   Ctrl+click the No in column C to remove it from the selection.

Formatting Superscripts and Subscripts

It was previously possible to format characters in a cell as superscript or subscript, but it required a trip to the Format Cells dialog box while you were in Edit mode. After 372

Excel.UserVoice.com votes for Superscript and Subscript icons on the Quick Access Toolbar, they have been added to Excel.

They aren't on the Quick Access Toolbar by default, but you can add them:

1. Right-click the Quick Access Toolbar and choose Customize Quick Access Toolbar.

2. Scroll to the bottom of the popular commands.

3. Click Subscript, then click the Add>> button in the center of the dialog box.

4. Click Superscript, then click the Add>> button.

5. Click OK.

To actually format a character in a cell, you can do it while you are typing in the cell. In Figure 1.18, type **You should drink H**. Click the Subscript icon to toggle to Subscript mode. Type a **2**. Click the Subscript icon again to leave Subscript mode. Type **O per day**. Click the Superscript icon. Type **citation needed**. When you press Enter to accept the cell, you automatically exit Superscript mode.

What if you need to format part of an existing cell? Select those characters in the formula bar, and then click either the Subscript or Superscript icon. You will not see the results in the formula bar, but they will appear in the cell.

Figure 1.18   Add Superscript and Subscript icons to the Quick Access Toolbar to apply the formatting as you type.

Less Nagging About CSV Files

Using Comma Separated Values (CSV) is a very common way to move data between systems. Excel natively opens CSV files. CSV files are great for storing values and text, but they don't handle storing formulas or formatting or charts or pivot tables.

If you open a CSV file, the Excel team is afraid you might add some formulas and formatting and then forget to save as an Excel file. When you save as CSV, Excel would routinely nag you that you were about to lose formulas and formatting. Even if you acknowledged that warning and that you want to save as CSV, Excel would nag you again when you closed the file.

One passionate request at Excel.UserVoice.Com was from someone who had to deal with CSV files all day. This person pointed out that she understood CSV files don't support formulas, but her job was to produce CSV files all day, every day, and she did not appreciate the constant nagging. There were 1,196 votes for this idea. Excel 2019 now makes nagging optional.

The first time you try to save as a CSV file, this message appears in the information bar above the formula bar:

> *POSSIBLE DATA LOSS: Some features might be lost if you save this workbook in the comma-delimited (*.csv) format. To preserve these features, save it in an Excel file format.*

Because the message appears in the information bar instead of a dialog box, you can simply ignore it. The information bar still offers the Save As button, but it also offers the Don't Show Again button, which when clicked, means you will never be nagged about CSV files again.

If you choose Don't Show Again and decide that you would like to be reminded about CSV files, choose File, Options, Save, and select Show Data Loss Warning When Editing Comma Delimited Files (*.csv).

Accessibility Improvements Across Office

Microsoft is committed to improving the Office experience for people with disabilities. There is a dedicated project manager for each product who makes sure that new features are possible to use if you are using a screen reader or other adaptive technologies.

Microsoft wants everyone to consider that some people might be reading their Excel worksheets with a screen reader. Your hilarious cartoon pasted in the worksheet might not make any sense to someone who is using a screen reader. You will see many instances in which you can add alternate text to any object in Excel. Alt Text is a short description of the art, which is helpful to those with visual difficulties and/or are using a screen reader program.

A new Check Accessibility icon is available in the Review tab that is useful with a couple of simple rules. First, give worksheets meaningful names instead of "Sheet1," "Sheet2," and so on. Provide Alt Text for charts and images/graphics.

NOTE

Although there are 28 chapters in this book, I always write Chapter 1 last because it encompasses the new features that are discussed in the other chapters. So, even though you might be reading this chapter first, I wrote it last. All Microsoft Press books contain Alt Text for every figure, which allows someone with a screen reader to follow along. With my recent experience of having written 800 Alt Text entries, I can tell you that adding Alt Text is easy. Adding the Alt Text forces me to think about the key elements of the image that need to be explained to someone who cannot see the image. Each Alt Text entry just takes a minute or two, and it will help you focus the message in the surrounding text while helping the reader understand the point of the image, chart, or graphic.

Inside OUT

Microsoft is promoting awareness of accessibility issues. When you see "Recommendations Available" in the Status Bar, click the notifier to open the Accessibility Checker pane.

In the figure below, there are several issues that are easy to correct:

- The dark blue font on a black background in cell I3 is hard to read, but it is the result of the default table style. Thankfully, it is easy to fix.

- Sheet1 is not a helpful sheet name, unlike the other sheets with descriptive names. Someone using Narrator will not have any idea what is on the first worksheet without a more descriptive name.

- The shape in column H has no alternative text. The checker suggests adding "Lightning Bolt" as alternative text for the shape.

Other accessibility improvements include the following:

- The "Tell Me" feature introduced in Excel 2013 now actually works and works well. Press Alt+Q in any Office application to jump to the Tell Me box. If you know that you want to use the Sort Smallest To Largest command on the Data tab of the ribbon, you can press Alt+Q, type Sort Smallest, and press Enter to run the Sort Ascending command.

- A new Modern sound scheme is available by selecting Options, Ease Of Access. Choose Provide Feedback With Sound and choose either Modern or Classic. Microsoft doesn't explicitly explain this, but I think "Classic" apparently stands for "Super Annoying," and "Modern" stands for "Soothing." I can see just fine, but I have this feature turned on to provide a gentle audio response to certain tasks.

- Provide Feedback With Animation is now an option in the Ease Of Access group. If the animations annoy you, you can easily turn them off.

- It used to be impossible to rename a worksheet tab without using the mouse. The sheet tabs have been added to the F6 loop. Press F6 until a sheet tab is selected. Press Shift+F10 to display the context menu, and use the arrow to Rename.

- The Windows Narrator has been improved with Excel. For example, say that you selected a pivot table slicer in Excel 2016. As you use the arrow keys to move up and down through the slicer, Narrator would endlessly call out "Slicer Item," "Slicer Item," "Slicer Item." In the improved version, Narrator will announce, "Slicer Items List with Eight Items." Use the down arrow to move from Apple to Banana and Narrator will announce, "Down Arrow. Banana." Press the up arrow. Narrator will announce, "Up Arrow. Apple." It is still not perfect because it will not announce whether a tile is selected.

Changes to the Ribbon and Home Screen

A new Home screen appears when you start Excel or open the File menu. The first three commands in the left navigation bar are Home, New, and Open. Without clicking anything, you will be on the Home screen of the File menu. The Home screen has been added for Excel 2019, and you will find it combines a few elements from both the New screen and the Open screen.

At the top of the Home screen, you will notice a message that reads, "Good Morning," "Good Afternoon," or "Good Evening."

Below that message are tiles normally shown when you select New. The first tile is Blank Workbook. Next are a few tiles offering Excel tutorials and then some tiles of popular templates. A hyperlink at the far right offers more templates in the New screen.

Below the row of tiles, three tabs offer Recent Files, Pinned, and Shared With Me. This is a subset of the options on the Open screen. Note that if you recently opened a pinned file, it will be in both the Recent and Pinned tabs. If you scroll all the way to the bottom of this section, a hyperlink for "Find More in Open" appears (although it would be easier to click Open in the left navigation bar).

Figure 1.19 shows the new Home screen. When you open Excel, the new Home screen replaces the 2016 Excel Start screen. If you prefer Excel open to a blank workbook, you can turn off the Home screen. Go to File, Options, General. Scroll to the bottom and clear the check box for Show The Start Screen When This Application Starts.

Figure 1.19   A new Home category at the top of the File menu combines some elements from the New and Open categories.

New Look for the Office 365 Ribbon

In Excel 2016, the selected tab on the ribbon had a thin line on the left, top, and bottom of the tab. This selection indicator made the selected tab appear as a tab on a file folder.

In the summer of 2018, Microsoft began rolling out a new feature to Office 365 subscribers, which placed a thick border along the bottom of the selected tab name. In Figure 1.20, the Page Layout tab has a thick green underline. I neither hate nor love this; it is consistent with other items throughout Excel. For example, the Active and All tabs in the PivotTable Fields list have used this indicator for some time.

Figure 1.20   The three lines that used to surround the left, top, and right of the selected ribbon tab have been replaced by a thick underline.

You will also notice that the icons in Figure 1.20 appear a little less crisp. The Office User Interface team says this is an improvement. The current direction from Microsoft is that Excel 2019 will not have these new icons.

Collecting Survey Data in Excel Using Office 365

Microsoft introduced an online survey tool at Forms.Office.com that has been integrated with the Office 365 versions of Excel. To create a survey, start with a blank Excel workbook, and choose Insert, Forms, New Form, as shown in Figure 1.21.

Figure 1.21   Select the workbook cell where you want the results to appear.

Excel will prompt you to save your workbook to a OneDrive for Business account. As you type a name in the Workbook Name dialog box, remember that this name is the default title of the form. For this survey, you could use **Excel 2019 Reader Survey**.

A new form opens in your default web browser at Forms.Office.com. The name of the workbook appears as the default title. Customize the survey using these optional steps (see Figure 1.22):

1. Click the Title field to reveal new elements such as a subtitle and a form picture.

2. Click the Subtitle field and describe the form.

3. Click the picture icon at the right side of the title and choose Upload. Upload a small image or company logo, which will appear near the form title.

4. In the top-right corner of the screen, click Themes and choose a built-in theme or upload your own image. The theme provides a whimsical background and will only appear when the survey is viewed on a computer. When the survey is viewed on a phone, no space is available for the theme.

See responses here

Build questions here   Preview   Theme   Share

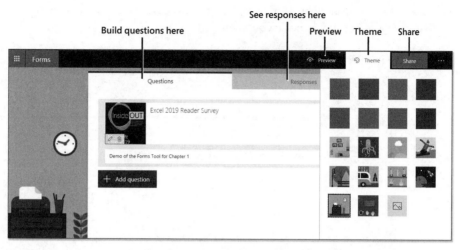

Figure 1.22   Add a subtitle, image, and theme to customize your form.

Click the Add Question button. Four question types are shown: Choice, Text, Rating, and Date. If you choose the ellipsis icon (...) after Date, you can choose Ranking or Likert. You will see an example of a Likert scale as question 2.

Select "Choice" as the type of question. The form will change to give you a space to type the question text and two choices. A button lets you add more choices. Another button lets you add "Other" as a choice. When you choose Other, the people taking the survey will be allowed to type a different value in the form.

Several options at the bottom of the question allow customization of the question:

- Choose Multiple Answers to allow people to choose more than one answer.

- Choose Required to add an asterisk to the question. The person taking the survey will have to answer the question before submitting the form.

- Use the ellipsis (...) icon to optionally add a subtitle to the question.

- If you choose Shuffle Options, the choices will be offered in a different order each time. Shuffling options is meant to prevent bias from someone who is bored and chooses the first answer for each question.

- If you choose Drop-down, the person taking the survey will have to open a drop-down menu.

CHAPTER 1

When you are done with the first question, click Add Question to move on to the next question. Figure 1.23 shows the first question.

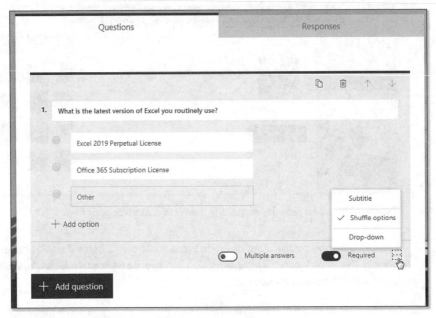

Figure 1.23   Build a question by filling out the fields.

Figure 1.24 shows a Likert scale. Named after psychologist Rensis Likert, this question type allows different ratings across the top and questions down the side.

Although Likert is not shown as one of the four main question types, you can choose Likert by using the ellipsis (...) icon in the Question Type menu.

When you type a question such as, "How often....," the form suggests choices for Daily, Weekly, Monthly, Seasonally, and Never. You can click Add All, or you can add just the ones that you want. Or, you can ignore those suggestions and type new option names.

When you are done building your questions, click the Preview button shown at the top right of Figure 1.22. You can see how the form will look on a computer or on a mobile device (see Figure 1.25). When you are done with the Preview, click the <- Back icon above the Preview (not the Back button in your browser).

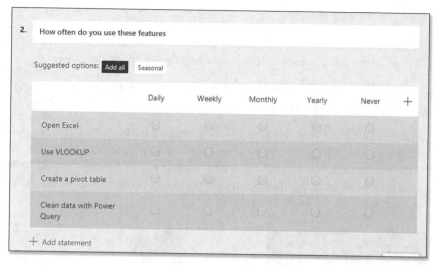

Figure 1.24 In a Likert scale, you can choose ratings for a series of statements. Ratings are shown across the top and statements are down the side.

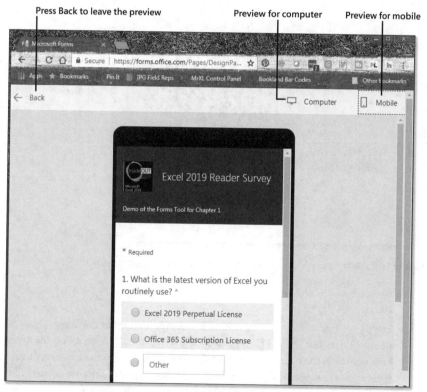

Figure 1.25 Preview the form before publishing it.

When you are ready to publish the survey, click the Share button (see top right of Figure 1.22).

The form defaults to only allowing people from your organization to participate. Open the top drop-down menu to choose to allow anyone with the link to use the survey.

There are four ways to share the survey. You can create a link, get the code to embed the survey in a web page, or generate an email. However, my favorite way is to use a QR code.

QR stands for Quick Response and is a two-dimensional barcode. Try this experiment right now with this book or e-book. Open the Camera application on your smartphone. Focus the camera on the barcode shown in Figure 1.26. You do not have to take a picture. Simply hover on the barcode for a few seconds, and a box should pop up asking if you want to open a web page. Click that box, and you will be taken to the survey.

Figure 1.26 After completing your survey, you can share it via this QR code.

NOTE

Every year, I fly to 35 seminars around the country. Whether there are 40 people or 400 people, I start out with a PowerPoint slide that has the QR code filling the entire slide. I ask people in the room to take out their phones and point the cameras at the screen. Except for a few people using flip phones or people in the extreme corners of the room, this is a very easy way to get people to participate in the survey.

As people finish your survey, the Responses tab updates to show a summary of the results. If you are conducting a live survey, like I do in my seminars, it is fun to watch the answers from the audience appear on the screen (see Figure 1.27).

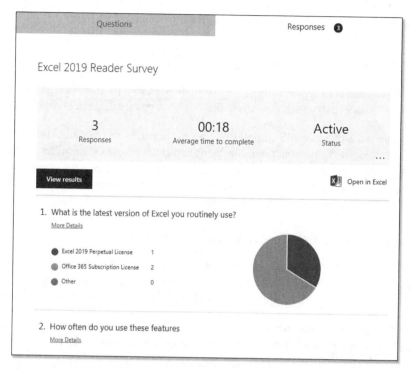

Figure 1.27　Results from the survey are summarized on the Responses tab.

While all this is great, here is the payoff: After your staff meeting or after tweeting your survey, the answers automatically appear in your Excel workbook, as you can see in Figure 1.28. Additional system fields tell you the date and time that each item was submitted. If the workbook is sent to your organization, the respondents' names appear (this does not happen with public surveys). Then, the answers to all the questions appear. You can now do any analysis you desire, such as sorting, filtering, charting, or creating a pivot table.

	B	E	F	G
1	Completion time	What is the latest version of i	Open Excel	Use VLOOKUP
2	7/27/18 5:59:48	Office 365 Subscription License	Daily	Daily
3	7/27/18 6:04:56	Office 365 Subscription License	Daily	Daily
4	7/27/18 6:13:12	Excel 2019 Perpetual License	Weekly	Never
5				

Figure 1.28　Results from the survey appear in Excel.

Note that the Forms.Office.Com website also offers the ability to create a quiz in Excel. The functionality is similar, although you can assign a certain number of points to each question. When you share a quiz, you will want to choose Only People In My Organization Can Respond. That way, each quiz answer will have the name and e-mail of the student in columns C & D. In a public survey, those columns are blank (so I hid them in Figure 1.28).

Future Features Coming to Office 365

If the Office team repeats the same pattern from three years ago, I predict that about a month after Excel 2019 ships to customers, the Office team will release a bunch of new features.

This happened with Excel 2016; the new features made my books seem out of date a month after it came out. However, this time, I have one computer on the Office Insider track that is getting the early test of upcoming features. The remainder of this chapter discusses features that are likely to appear in Office 365 by the end of 2018. There is a chance some of the interface will change slightly by the time the feature is released.

New Threaded Comments and Chat

It used to be that a single cell could have a single comment. With collaboration today, you might have multiple people from a company editing the same workbook at the same time. It would make sense that those people might want to have a conversation about one cell.

Office 365 will offer threaded comments. Instead of a single comment, the comments appear in a panel. You can see each person's comment in sequence (see Figure 1.29).

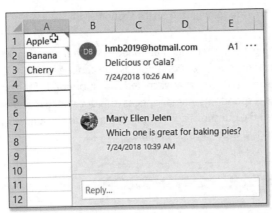

Figure 1.29   A threaded comment allows people to have a conversation about a cell.

CAUTION

Excel tricksters have long used various cool tricks to alter the formatting of comments. For example, the late David Hawley showed how you could change the shape of a comment to a star in his 2007 book, *Excel Hacks: Tips & Tools for Streamlining Your Spreadsheets*. I remember doing a segment for Leo Laporte on TechTV where I used comments to hold a photo that would pop-up when you hovered over the comment indicator. Others will color-code comments so that pink comments are warnings and yellow icons are cautions.

If you want to continue to use any of the legacy commenting tricks to format or display comments, you need to switch to using Notes instead of Comments. The Excel team added a Notes drop-down menu next to Comments, and the new menu includes all the old legacy comment functionality. The legacy comments are now called Notes. Actually, if you go back 20 years, the first version of comments were originally called Notes, so they are simply going back to the old name.

New threaded comments and old Notes can coexist in the same worksheet. Notes will have a red triangle indicator. Comments will have a purple thought-bubble-shaped indicator.

The threaded comments become a permanent part of the workbook. There have been requests to have a less-permanent form of comments, such as a Chat panel. This would allow people to collaborate on a workbook to discuss the workbook without the chat becoming a permanent part of the workbook.

Workbooks Statistics and Smart Lookup

Two new icons will appear on the Review tab of Office 365. The Workbook Statistics opens a panel showing the number of cells and formulas in the workbook (see Figure 1.30).

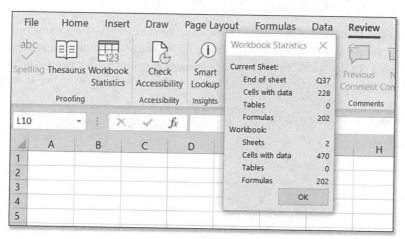

Figure 1.30   The Workbook Statistics panel identifies the number of active cells and formulas in this sheet and the entire workbook.

The Smart Lookup feature is branded as an "Insights" feature and using it requires you to opt in to the artificial intelligence features. Click on any cell and ask for a Smart Lookup by clicking the large Smart Lookup icon in the Review tab (see Figure 1.30). In Figure 1.31, if you click Smart Lookup for the word "Hypergolic," it returns a definition and some links to pages about rockets. This does not seem like "artificial intelligence," but I guess it is just as easy as opening a browser.

Figure 1.31   The only thing new about Smart Lookup tool is that it is branded as Insights.

Dynamic Array Functions in Office 365

Excel Project Manager Joe McDaid has been working on a bevy of new dynamic array functions for Excel. People using Office 365 will see these by the end of 2018 or early 2019. The functions are entered in a single cell but return a large range of answers. This is much easier than the old array formulas. You won't have to remember Ctrl+Shift+Enter anymore to use an Array formula.

The dynamic array functions are FILTER, RANDARRAY, SEQUENCE, SORT, SORTBY, and UNIQUE.

Inside OUT

This improvement represents new engineering to the Calculation engine in Excel. Excel now understands how to deal with a formula that spills into multiple answers.

The possible combinations of these new function stretch far beyond the six functions. You will be able to use SEQUENCE inside just about any other Excel formula function to generate several answers where you would have previously seen just one answer.

In the image below, the rarely-used ROMAN function returns an array of answers thanks to SEQUENCE.

	=ROMAN(SEQUENCE(10,5,1,1))			
H	**I**	**J**	**K**	**L**
I	II	III	IV	V
VI	VII	VIII	IX	X
XI	XII	XIII	XIV	XV
XVI	XVII	XVIII	XIX	XX
XXI	XXII	XXIII	XXIV	XXV
XXVI	XXVII	XXVIII	XXIX	XXX
XXXI	XXXII	XXXIII	XXXIV	XXXV
XXXVI	XXXVII	XXXVIII	XXXIX	XL
XLI	XLII	XLIII	XLIV	XLV
XLVI	XLVII	XLVIII	XLIX	L

`=ROMAN(SEQUENCE(10,5,1,1))` generates 50 cells of Roman numerals from 1 to 50 (or I, II, III, IV, to XLIX, L). The new calculation engine makes every function potentially an array function.

Even without using an array function, you can simply refer to a range from a single cell. `=A1:C10` entered in E2 will return 30 cells. Because this new syntax breaks the behavior of implicit intersection, a SINGLE function has been added for cases where you want to use intersection.

Entering One Formula and Returning Many Results

This is amazing. Take a look at Figure 1.32. A formula of **=A2:A9** is typed in cell C5. Excel spills the answers into C5:C12. If you select any cell in C5:C12, the formula appears in the formula bar, and a blue outline appears around the results range. Think of the blue outline as indicating that this one formula is returning all of the answers inside the outline.

Here is an important distinction: The formula only exists in one cell: C5. When you select C6 or C7 or C12, the formula appears in the formula bar in a light gray font. But you can only edit the formula if you select C5. A formula of =FORMULATEXT(C5) will work. A formula of =FORMULATEXT(C6) will fail.

If A1:A9 happens to be a table and you add new rows to the table, the results from this one formula will automatically expand. Or if you delete row 4, the results will contract.

Figure 1.32 A single formula returns many results.

The first time that this happens to you in Excel, you will see a message shown in Figure 1.33. Once you click Got It, they won't bother you again.

Formula spilled

Your formula returned multiple values so we spilled them into the neighboring blank cells.

Learn more

Got it

Figure 1.33 Excel tries to explain this new spill feature.

If you use Excel a lot, you realize two problems with this new functionality. The first problem: What happens if C6 through C12 are not blank? If Excel cannot return all the answers, then you get none of the answers. A brand new #SPILL function will appear, and the on-grid drop-down menu explains "Spill Range Isn't Blank" (see Figure 1.34).

Figure 1.34   If there is not room for the results, a #SPILL error appears.

The second problem will only be apparent to hard-core Excellers. There is a concept called implicit intersection. If you enter =**A2:A9** anywhere in rows 2 through 9, Excel will only return the value from A2:A9 that intersects the formula. In other words, =A2:A9 in C5 will return Nectarine from A5. Enter that same formula in C7, and you will get Lemon.

This is a bizarre trick that I've never used in real life. The only time that I've ever used implicit intersection is when trying to win a bar bet. However, someone out there is using it. Some modeler is taking advantage of this trick. Microsoft can't take this feature away, so if you want to do what implicit intersection used to do, use the SINGLE function. If you enter =SINGLE(A2:A9) when in rows 2 through 9, the value from that row will be returned (see Figure 1.35).

	A	B	C	D	E
			C9		=SINGLE($A$2:$A$9
1	**Product**				
2	Watermelon				
3	Orange				
4	Apple				
5	Nectarine				
6	Lime				
7	Lemon		Lemon	=SINGLE($A$2:$A$9)	
8	Zucchini				
9	Star fruit		Star fruit	=SINGLE($A$2:$A$9)	
10				(Ctrl) ▾	
11					

Figure 1.35   The new SINGLE function must be used when someone needs to do implicit intersection.

Text appears in A2:A9, and cell A7 contains Lemon. A formula of =SINGLE($A$2:$A$9) entered anywhere in row 7 will return Lemon. Copy that formula to row 9, and it will return Star fruit because A9 contains Star fruit.

Note that implicit intersection and SINGLE also work for columns. If you had values in B1:J1 and enter =SINGLE(B1:J1) anywhere in column C, the formula will return just the value from C1.

The Excel team did a great job with backward compatibility on this feature: If you have an old workbook that is already doing implicit intersection, Excel will wrap that formula in the SINGLE function for you. If you create a SINGLE function and send it to someone who does not have SINGLE, Excel will rewrite the formula as implicit intersection.

Sorting with a Formula

Sorting with a formula is easier thanks to the new SORT and SORTBY array functions.

In Figure 1.36, you have a two-column range of results in A2:B16. Those results are constantly changing because of formulas that sum daily sales. You would like a formula to sort the results.

Sorting might be easy for you, but you can't trust your manager's manager to click the AZ button. That is why you used to go to crazy lengths with RANK, SMALL, MATCH, and INDEX to sort with a formula. All that goes away with the introduction of SORT.

The SORT function is a dynamic array function that returns a sorted list. The syntax is:

```
SORT( Array, [Sort_Index], [Sort_Order], [By_Column])
```

In Figure 1.36, the data in A2:B16 is sorted by name. You would like the results to be sorted by score, with the highest scores at the top. To sort that data with a formula, you would follow these steps:

1. Start by selecting where you want the results to appear. In Figure 1.36, this is cell D4.

2. Begin typing a formula: **=SORT(A2:B16,**

3. If you want to sort based on the score in column B, use **2** as the Sort_index because column B is the second column of the A2:B9 range. Type **2** and a comma.

4. For the Sort_Order, use **1** for ascending or **-1** for descending. Choose **-1**.

5. The fourth argument is rarely used. There is an obscure version of sorting where you don't sort the rows, but you sort the columns. Use **True** for the fourth argument if you want to sort by column. In most cases, you will leave this blank.

6. Type the closing parenthesis.

7. Press Enter. The results will spill into D4:E16.

| D4 | ▾ | ⋮ | × | ✓ | *fx* | =SORT(A4:B16,2,-1) |

	A	B	C	D	E	F
1	Original Data					
2						
3	**Name**	Score				
4	Amanda	559		Daniela	903	
5	Bernardo	291		Carol	808	
6	Carol	808		Thiago	693	
7	Daniel	200		Eduardo	656	
8	Daniela	903		Amanda	559	
9	Eduardo	656		Isabella	559	
10	Gabriel	404		Helena	526	
11	Helena	526		Joao Pedro	485	
12	Isabella	559		Gabriel	404	
13	Joao Pedro	485		José	354	
14	José	354		Bernardo	291	
15	Stephanie	270		Stephanie	270	
16	Thiago	693		Daniel	200	
17						

Figure 1.36   A formula sorts the data from A2:B16 in a new location.

Convert the original range to a table using Ctrl+T. Type a new row at the bottom of the table with a high score. The SORT function automatically expands, and the new high score appears at the top of the results (see Figure 1.37).

| D4 | ▾ | ⋮ | × | ✓ | *fx* | =SORT(A4:B17,2,-1) |

	A	B	C	D	E
1	Original Data				
2					
3	**Name** ▾	**Score** ▾			
4	Amanda	559		Zeke	999
5	Bernardo	291		Daniela	903
6	Carol	808		Carol	808
7	Daniel	200		Thiago	693
8	Daniela	903		Eduardo	656
9	Eduardo	656		Amanda	559
10	Gabriel	404		Isabella	559
11	Helena	526		Helena	526
12	Isabella	559		Joao Pedro	485
13	Joao Pedro	485		Gabriel	404
14	José	354		José	354
15	Stephanie	270		Bernardo	291
16	Thiago	693		Stephanie	270
17	Zeke	999		Daniel	200

Figure 1.37   Add new data to the original data set, and the SORT results expand.

Inside OUT

What if you only want the top three results and just the names, not the scores?

The SORT function is very flexible. What if you only wanted to return the top three scores and you only needed to see the names? Select G3:G5. Type the SORT formula and press Ctrl+Shift+Enter. The formula wants to return all fifteen sales rows and two columns. However, because you selected three cells, you are only seeing the first column and first three rows.

The SORT function is fine for simple situations. But sometimes you need to do more complex sorting. In Figure 1.38, the original data in A2:C16 contains Name, Team, and Score. You want to present the results sorted by Team ascending and Score descending. You only want to show the names, not the teams or the scores. The SORTBY function offers this flexibility.

1.   You want to sort the names from A4:A16. The formula in E4 starts out
     =SORTBY(A4:A16,

2.   You want to first sort by team name. Type **B4:B16,**.

3.   You want the teams to sort ascending, so type **1**, as the third argument.

4.   SORTBY allows a multi-level sort. The second key is C4:C16. Type **C4:C16**, as the fourth argument.

5.   The scores from C4:C16 should be sorted descending. Type **-1** as the last argument. Close the formula with a right parenthesis and press Enter.

The results shown in E4:E16 has Eduardo at the top. Just to make sure it is working, I copied the data to G4:I16 and performed the sort using the Sort dialog. The results match.

E4				fx	=SORTBY(A4:A16,B4:B16,1,C4:C16,-1)			
	A	B	C	D	E	F	G	H	I
1								
2								
3	Name	Team	Score				Name	Team	Score
4	Amanda	Red	559		Eduardo		Eduardo	Blue	656
5	Bernardo	Blue	291		Helena		Helena	Blue	526
6	Carol	Red	808		Joao Pedro		Joao Pedr	Blue	485
7	Daniel	Blue	200		Bernardo		Bernardo	Blue	291
8	Daniela	Red	903		Stephanie		Stephanie	Blue	270
9	Eduardo	Blue	656		Daniel		Daniel	Blue	200
10	Gabriel	Red	404		Daniela		Daniela	Red	903
11	Helena	Blue	526		Carol		Carol	Red	808
12	Isabella	Red	559		Thiago		Thiago	Red	693
13	Joao Pedro	Blue	485		Amanda		Amanda	Red	559
14	José	Red	354		Isabella		Isabella	Red	559
15	Stephanie	Blue	270		Gabriel		Gabriel	Red	404
16	Thiago	Red	693		José		José	Red	354
17								

Figure 1.38   A formula performs a multi-level sort.

TROUBLESHOOTING

There might be times when you need a multi-level SORT, but you cannot use SORTBY to refer to ranges.

In the example below, you want to sort the results of a UNIQUE function. Those results live only in memory and do not have a cell address.

In this case, you can force a multi-level sort with the SORT function by passing an array constant as the Sort_index and another array constant as the Sort_order.

If you want to sort by the second column ascending and the first column descending, use:

```
=SORT(UNIQUE(B4:C29,FALSE,FALSE),{2,1},{1,-1})
```

F5	▼ :	× ✓	fx	=SORT(UNIQUE(B4:C29,FALSE,FALSE),{2,1},{1,-1})					
⊿	A	B	C	D	E	F	G	H	I	J
1										
2										
3	Team	Name	Product	Score		Sorted Unique Combination of Name/Product				
4	Red	Amanda	Apple	559						
5	Blue	Bernardo	Orange	291		Thiago	Apple			
6	Red	Carol	Lemon	808		Isabella	Apple			
7	Blue	Daniel	Lime	200		Helena	Apple			
8	Red	Daniela	Apple	903		Daniela	Apple			
9	Blue	Eduardo	Orange	656		Daniel	Apple			
10	Red	Gabriel	Lemon	404		Amanda	Apple			
11	Blue	Helena	Lime	526		Thiago	Kiwi			
12	Red	Isabella	Apple	559		José	Lemon			
13	Blue	Joao Pedro	Orange	485		Joao Pedro	Lemon			

Inside OUT

A classic question is how to randomly sort a list of people. This is popular in Human Resources where they do random drug testing.

You can use the new RANDARRAY function as the second argument of the SORTBY function. In the figure below, use:

```
=SORT(A4:A16,RANDARRAY(13)).
```

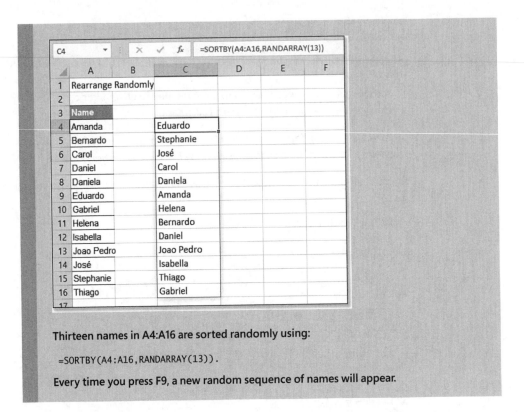

Thirteen names in A4:A16 are sorted randomly using:

```
=SORTBY(A4:A16,RANDARRAY(13)).
```

Every time you press F9, a new random sequence of names will appear.

Filtering with a Formula

In Figure 1.39, you have a database in A3:C16. You want to use a formula to extract all records where the person is on the Red team. Use the new `FILTER` function.

The syntax is `=FILTER(array,include,[if_empty])`.

In this case, the array to filter is A4:C16. The include argument is `B4:B16="Red"`. The optional third argument will prevent an error in the case where no one is assigned to the Red team. You could specify None, None Found, or 0 here.

Figure 1.39 shows the results of a `FILTER` function. The beauty of this single formula solution is that you don't need to know how many Red team records there will be. The old array formula solution required you to pre-plan the largest possible number of matches. This formula is so much easier.

Figure 1.39 Extract all red team records.

The example in Figure 1.39 has the Red team hard-coded in the formula. It is simple to change this to have the team name in another cell. In Figure 1.40, the team name is stored in cell F1. Change the formula to:

```
=FILTER(A4:C16,B4:B16=F1,"None")
```

When you change from Red to Blue, the output range returns the records for the Blue team. This may be the same number of rows, it might be more, or it might be less.

If you type **Yellow** in F1, because there are no people assigned to the Yellow team, the result will be the word **None** in E4. This is because the last argument in the formula is None. If you leave this optional argument off, you will get an #N/A error instead.

Figure 1.40 Instead of hard coding Red in the formula, point to cell F1 instead.

TROUBLESHOOTING

How can you use FILTER to get all of the cells with a red font? Can you SORT by color or cell icon?

No. The FILTER, SORT, and SORTBY are operating on values in the cell. You cannot sort by font color, cell color, or icon.

Extracting Unique Values with a Formula

Getting a unique list of values has always been difficult in Excel. Excel MVP Mike "Excelisfun" Girvin spends two entire chapters of his *Ctrl+Shift+Enter: Mastering Excel Array Formulas: Do the Impossible with Excel Formulas Thanks to Array Formula Magic* book explaining how you can write a formula to return a unique list of values. This becomes dramatically simpler using the UNIQUE array function. The syntax is:

```
=UNIQUE(Array, [by_col], [occurs_once])
```

The By_Col argument will usually be False. The Filter command in Excel operates on a row-by-row basis. I've occasionally heard of people who want to filter by columns and setting this argument to True would allow you to filter sideways from normal.

The Occurs_Once choice in this argument makes me smile because to me it proves that the Excel team's definition of "unique" is out of step with the rest of the world. Say that you have a list in A2:A5. The list is Apple, Butter, Cherry, Apple, Butter. If you used the Excel Conditional Formatting command to mark the "unique" values, Excel would only mark Cherry. Their twisted rationale is that Cherry is the only item in the list to appear exactly once. This is never what I need when I want a list of unique values. I expect to get a list of Apple, Butter, Cherry.

The default value for Occurs_Once is True to return the nearly useless list of items that occur only once in the list. I think most people will be choosing False for this argument for "occurs one or more times."

Consider Figure 1.41. A list of products and customers appears in A2:B116. The silly formula in D3 shows that Lemon is the only product to be ordered exactly once:

```
=UNIQUE(A2:A116,FALSE,TRUE)
```

Who would ever need to know this? The person charged with figuring out the list of One-Hit Wonders might be the only case.

The far more common formula shown in D7 returns a list of every product that has been ordered one or more times. Change the third argument from TRUE to FALSE to switch to the common-sense situation of any product that has been ordered one or more times. The formula is:

```
=UNIQUE(A2:A116,FALSE,FALSE)
```

Going beyond the simple example, you could ask for all unique combinations of product and customer by entering the formula in two columns and specifying an array of A2:B116. A partial list of the results appear in H7:I17 of Figure 1.41.

CHAPTER 1

	A	B	C	D	E	F	G	H	I	J
					fx	=UNIQUE(A2:A116,FALSE,FALSE)				
1	Product	Customer		*=UNIQUE(A2:A116,FALSE,TRUE)*						
2	Watermelon	Diane		**Products that appear exactly once**						
3	Orange	Barb		Lemon						
4	Apple	Otto								
5	Apple	Otto		*=UNIQUE(A2:A116,FALSE,FALSE)*				*=UNIQUE(A2:B116,FALSE,FALSE)*		
6	Nectarine	Gary		**Unique list of products**				**Unique Combinations**		
7	Watermelon	Diane		Watermelon				Watermelon	Diane	
8	Lime	Diane		Orange				Orange	Barb	
9	Lemon	Diane		Apple				Apple	Otto	
10	Zucchini	Fred		Nectarine				Nectarine	Gary	
11	Star fruit	Tracy		Lime				Lime	Diane	
12	Apple	Otto		Lemon				Lemon	Diane	
13	Apple	Otto		Zucchini				Zucchini	Fred	
14	Watermelon	Diane		Star fruit				Star fruit	Tracy	
15	Orange	Quenten		Plum				Orange	Quenten	
16	Star fruit	Sam						Star fruit	Sam	
17	Star fruit	Ike						Star fruit	Ike	

Figure 1.41   The UNIQUE function dramatically simplifies returning a unique list of products.

The UNIQUE function does not sort the results. They appear in the same sequence they are found in the original data, just as the Advanced Filter command would do.

What if you need the results sorted? Simply wrap the FILTER or UNIQUE function inside of SORT. Figure 1.42 shows an example.

Figure 1.42   Combine SORT and UNIQUE to get a sorted unique list.

TROUBLESHOOTING

The previous example used two array functions nested inside each other. The limit is 32 functions nested.

Although the array functions are more powerful than regular functions, they support the same limit of up to 32 levels of nesting.

In the following figure, FILTER is wrapped in UNIQUE and then wrapped in SORT. Excel has no problem dealing with these complex combinations.

Note, however, that you cannot use 3-D references in the new array functions. There will also never be support for sorting by color or icon.

Generating a Sequence of Numbers

The new SEQUENCE function will generate a sequence of numbers. This function can be very simple: =SEQUENCE(10) entered in A1 will generate the numbers 1 through 10 in A1:A10. However, the syntax allows for a lot of flexibility:

=SEQUENCE([Rows],[Columns],[Start],[Stop])

In Figure 1.43, the formula =SEQUENCE(10,3) returns a 10-row by 3-column array with the numbers 1 to 30. A formula of =SEQUENCE(10,1,7,3) in G1 returns a 10-row by 1-column range with numbers starting with the number 7 and incrementing by 3.

C1	▾	⋮	✕	✓	*fx*	=SEQUENCE(10,3)		
	A	B	C	D	E	F	G	H
1	1		1	2	3		7	
2	2		4	5	6		10	
3	3		7	8	9		13	
4	4		10	11	12		16	
5	5		13	14	15		19	
6	6		16	17	18		22	
7	7		19	20	21		25	
8	8		22	23	24		28	
9	9		25	26	27		31	
10	10		28	29	30		34	
11	=SEQUENCE(10)		=SEQUENCE(10,3)				=SEQUENCE(10,1,7,3)	
12								

Figure 1.43   Generate a sequence of numbers.

You might be thinking that SEQUENCE is the most boring new function. I don't think Microsoft intended SEQUENCE to be used as shown in Figure 1.43. They did not give us SEQUENCE just to save us the hassle of Ctrl+dragging the fill handle or using =A1+1.

The power of SEQUENCE is when you need to return a sequence of numbers to another formula.

My favorite example in this realm is the IPMT and PPMT functions that are often used to calculate amortization tables for a loan. These functions are discussed in Chapter 10. But you can see the power of SEQUENCE in the examples in Figure 1.44.

In Figure 1.44, you are planning on borrowing $772,000 for 30 years. A PMT function in B4 calculates the monthly payment.

But to create an amortization table, you need the IPMT and PPMT functions. A sequence of 5 numbers in A7:A11 is used to calculate the interest portion of the payment in B7:B11. As you would expect, the interest portion of the payment goes down a little bit in each month. Say that you need to know the total interest paid in months 1 through 5. A SUM function in B12 calculates the total as $13,633.03. It took 11 cells to calculate that value.

Can we shorten this by using SEQUENCE as the Period Number inside of IPMT? The formula in D7 is =IPMT($B$3/12,SEQUENCE(5),$B$2,$B$1). Press Enter and Excel returns the five monthly answers. That is fine, but you want the answer in one formula.

The formula in F7 wraps the IPMT inside a SUM function. Amazingly, there is no need to press Ctrl+Shift+Enter to make this work: =SUM(IPMT($B$3/12,SEQUENCE(5),$B$2,B$B1)) returns the same answer that required 11 cells over in B12.

What if you want to know the total interest paid in each year of the loan for tax planning purposes? The formula in G10 uses a SEQUENCE function to return 12 consecutive numbers starting from the month number in F10. Copy this down for each row of the loan.

Couldn't you do this with CUMIPMT? Sure, but it requires an extra argument. The point of the example is that you will be able to insert the SEQUENCE function inside of other functions to generate array functions.

D7		▾ ⋮ ✕ ✓	fx	=IPMT($B$3/12,SEQUENCE(5),$B$2,$B$1)				

◢	A	B	C	D	E	F	G	H	I
1	Price	772000		B7	=IPMT($B$3/12,A7,$B$2,$B$1)				
2	Term	360		D7	=IPMT($B$3/12,SEQUENCE(5),$B$2,$B$1)				
3	Rate	4.25%		F7	=SUM(IPMT($B$3/12,SEQUENCE(5),$B$2,$B$1))				
4	Payment	($3,797.78)		G10	=SUM(IPMT($B$3/12,SEQUENCE(12,1,F10,1),$B$2,$B$1))				
5									
6	Month	Interest				Interest Months 1-5			
7	1	($2,734.17)		($2,734.17)		($13,633.03)			
8	2	($2,730.40)		-2730.3997					
9	3	($2,726.62)		-2726.6194		Interest in 12 months starting			
10	4	($2,722.83)		-2722.8257		1	($32,558.42)		
11	5	($2,719.02)		-2719.0186		13	($31,994.39)		
12		($13,633.03)				25	($31,405.91)		
13						37	($30,791.92)		
14						349	($1,032.02)		

Figure 1.44   Use SEQUENCE inside of other functions to generate new array formulas.

TROUBLESHOOTING

The format of the spill range will not be updated by the formula. The answers can spill, but the spill cells will remain unformatted.

If you know that your formula is going to return currency or dates, you should pre-format the range. In the following image, you would format B3:B12 as a date before entering =SEQUENCE(10,1,$C$1) in B3.

Generating an Array of Random Numbers with a Formula

The new RANDARRAY function will return a range of any number of rows and columns of random numbers.

The syntax is
=RANDARRAY([Rows],[Columns])

A trivial example shown in Figure 1.45 generates five rows and three columns of random numbers. Just like the RAND function, the results will be a decimal between 0 and 1.

Figure 1.45   Use RANDARRAY to generate an array of random numbers.

CHAPTER 1

The power of RANDARRAY will be in building simulations and Monte-Carlo models where you need to multiply a range of numbers by a series of random numbers.

Refer to the Entire Array

To refer to the entire spilled dynamic array in another formula, use the new Spilled Range Operator. =AVERAGE(E1#) would average all the numbers returned by the formula in E1 in Figure 1.45.

Learning About New Functions and Features

The funny thing about Office 365 is that any book will become just a little more obsolete on any given Tuesday as the Excel team pushes new features out to the Office 365 subscribers. Once a year, Microsoft invites me to a non-disclosure session and shows me what they are working on. Some of those new features are in the product now. But there are other notes in my notebook about features that will be coming sometime in the future.

There are more functions and features that may have been released by the time you are reading this book. As new features are released, I will update this web page: http://mrx.cl/newafterexcel2019.

Using the Excel Interface

Using the Ribbon

The mantra of the ribbon is to use pictures and words. Many people noticed the little whisk broom icon in previous versions of Excel but never knew what it did. In the ribbon, the same icon has the words "Format Painter" next to it. When you hover, the ToolTip offers paragraphs explaining what the tool does. The ToolTip also offers a little-known trick: You can double-click the Format Painter to copy the formatting to many places.

The Look of the Ribbon Is Changing

In early 2007, all of Office moved from a menu bar to the ribbon. At first, the ribbon was super confusing. You would constantly be hunting from ribbon tab to ribbon tab trying to find where the command you needed was hiding. For example:

- In Excel 2003, Insert Rows was on the Insert menu, but in Excel 2007, Insert Rows was on the far-right side of the Home tab.

- Pivot Tables, which had been on the Data menu, were moved to the Insert tab.

- The ribbon was taller than the combination of the menu, the Standard Toolbar, and the Formatting Toolbar, which meant that you could see a few less rows in your Excel worksheet.

After 20 minutes of struggling with the new ribbon in 2007, you were finally ready to Print, Save, or Send, but the File tab was not there. Microsoft had replaced the word "File" with an Office logo that few people thought to click. When you clicked the Office logo, the File menu opened.

Most who used Excel 2003 for 40 hours a week hated the new ribbon at first. I remember dedicating every Wednesday of my MrExcel Podcast to a new feature called "Where Is It Wednesday." A new theme song for the Wednesday podcast had a lyric that said, "It's a great feature, I just can't find it anymore."

Even Bill Gates asked, "You are going to offer a classic mode, right?" But somehow, Jensen Harris and the Office User Interface team convinced Bill Gates that there should be no classic mode.

The ribbon improved slightly in Office 2010. The Office logo in the top left was replaced with the word "File." Hardcore Excel users eventually figured out where their favorite features were located.

And now, Microsoft is talking about changing the ribbon again. They say the ribbon is too tall and it gets in the way. They are talking about a special mode where the ribbon will be a single row. Also, they want to use less color in the ribbon.

The great news for Excel users is that the new ribbon is first being added to Outlook, and then it will be added to the online version of Excel. The core Excel, Word, and PowerPoint running on client computers will not get the one-row ribbon until Microsoft gauges the reaction to the shorter ribbon in Outlook and Excel Online.

Most people do not use Excel online, so the new ribbon won't bother us.

Even if we don't get the one-row ribbon soon, Microsoft is still changing the look of the tall ribbon, but only for Office 365 customers.

Figure 2.1 shows the new ribbon that started rolling out to Office 365 customers in the Summer of 2018. One big change is the active ribbon tab is denoted with a horizontal line instead of a block of color. In Figure 2.1, the word "Formulas" is underlined. Also, the new ribbon uses less color. The icons look like line art instead of the rich illustrations of the past.

Figure 2.1   In the summer of 2018, the Office 365 ribbon switched to this style.

Contrast the new ribbon above with the Excel 2019 ribbon in Figure 2.2.

Figure 2.2   Excel 2019 uses the same ribbon from Excel 2016.

Many people hate change; I like the old ribbon better. In the old ribbon, the Logical icon looked like a purple hard-bound book; the book's spine was on the left, and the icon had some depth, which made it look like a book. Because the icons now use less color, the same icon in Office 365 uses black lines to try to indicate a book. The spine is not obvious, the depth is fainter, and it doesn't look as much like a book anymore.

Microsoft started using the new ribbon in Office 365 in mid-2018, which means anyone who purchases the perpetual Excel 2019 will be stuck with the old ribbon. I do not understand the hostile attitude of Microsoft Marketing to their perpetual edition customers. It is as if they are saying, "Thank you for your $400. We are going to give you an inferior, out-of-date product to punish you for refusing to switch to our $10-a-month subscription plan."

If someone bought the perpetual Office 2016 on January 30, 2016, they would have paid $400. Another customer purchasing Office 365 on January 20, 2016 would have paid $10 a month or about $320 by the time Office 2019 is released in the fall of 2018. The perpetual edition customers are paying more than the Office 365 customers, and Microsoft is blatantly treating them like second-class citizens.

The title on the front cover of this book is "Excel 2019 Inside Out," so I will be using the old-style Excel 2019 ribbon in the screenshots for this book. But there is a good chance that you are using Office 365 and have the new style ribbon. Luckily, the same commands appear in the same sequence. Your icons simply have less color.

Using Flyout Menus and Galleries

One element in the ribbon is the gallery control. Galleries are used when there are dozens of options from which you can choose. The gallery shows you a visual thumbnail of each choice. A gallery starts out showing a row or two of choices in the ribbon. (For an example, open the Cell Styles gallery on the Excel 2019 Home tab.) The right side of the gallery offers icons for Up, Down, and Open. If you click Up or Down, you scroll one row at a time through the choices.

If you click the Open control at the bottom-right side of the gallery, the gallery opens to reveal all choices at once.

Rolling Through the Ribbon Tabs

With Excel as the active application, move the mouse anywhere over the ribbon and roll the scroll wheel on top of the mouse. Excel quickly flips from tab to tab on the ribbon. Scroll away from you to roll toward the Home tab on the left. Scroll toward you to move to the right.

Revealing More Commands Using Dialog Box Launchers, Task Panes, and "More" Commands

The ribbon holds perhaps 20 percent of the available commands. The set of commands and options available in the ribbon will be enough 80 percent of the time, but you will sometimes have to go beyond the commands in the ribbon. You can do this with dialog box launchers, More commands, and the task pane.

A *dialog box launcher* is a special symbol in the lower-right corner of many ribbon groups. Click the dialog box launcher to open a related dialog box with many more choices than those offered in the ribbon.

Figure 2.3 shows details of the Alignment group of the Home tab. In the lower-right corner of the group is the dialog box launcher. It looks like the top-left corner of a dialog box, with an arrow pointing downward and to the right.

Figure 2.3   The dialog box launcher takes you to additional options.

When you click the dialog box launcher, you go to a dialog box that often offers many more choices than those available in the ribbon. In Figure 2.4, you see the Alignment tab of the Format Cells dialog box.

Figure 2.4   After clicking the dialog box launcher, you get access to many more choices.

Many menus in the ribbon end with an entry for finding more rules and option; these entries end with an ellipsis (...). Clicking a More item takes you to a dialog box or task pane with more choices than those available in the ribbon.

Resizing Excel Changes the Ribbon

The ribbon modifies as the size of the Excel application window changes. You should be aware of this when you are coaching a co-worker over the phone. You might be looking at your screen and telling him to "look for the big Insert drop-down menu to the right of the orange word *Calculation*." Although this makes perfect sense on your widescreen monitor, it might not make sense on his monitor. Figure 2.5 shows some detail of the Home tab on a widescreen monitor. The Cell Styles gallery shows ten thumbnails, and Insert, Delete, and Format appear side-by-side.

Figure 2.5   On a widescreen monitor, you see ten choices in the Cell Styles gallery.

Figure 2.6 shows the typical view on a laptop. The Cell Styles gallery is collapsed to a single drop-down menu. The Insert, Delete, and Format icons are now arranged vertically.

Figure 2.6   On a normal monitor, the Cell Styles gallery is collapsed.

As you resize the Excel screen to a smaller width, more items collapse. Soon, the three icons for Insert, Delete, and Format are collapsed into a single drop-down menu called Cells. Eventually, the Excel ribbon gets too small, and Excel hides it completely.

Activating the Developer Tab

If you regularly record or write macros, you might be looking for the VBA tools in the ribbon. They are all located on the Developer tab, which is hidden by default. However, it is easy to make the Developer tab visible. Follow these steps:

1. Right-click the ribbon and choose Customize The Ribbon. Excel displays the Customize Ribbon category of the Excel Options dialog box.

2. A long list box of ribbon tabs is shown on the right side of the screen. Every one of them is checked except for Developer. Check the box next to Developer.

3. Click OK. The Developer tab displays.

Activating Contextual Ribbon Tabs

The ribbon tabs you see all the time are called the *main tabs*. Another 23 tabs come and go, depending on what is selected in Excel. In Figure 2.7, you can see two contextual tabs that appear only when a chart is selected.

Figure 2.7   Two chart tools tabs appear temporarily while a chart is selected.

TROUBLESHOOTING

Your worksheet often has a pivot table or a chart, yet you cannot see the contextual tabs in the ribbon.

When you insert a new pivot table using the default settings, the pivot table will be the only data on a newly inserted worksheet. I've suggested to the Excel team that if the person using Excel is looking at a new worksheet that only contains a pivot table, then clearly, the customer is looking at the pivot table. However, if you accidentally click outside of the pivot table, both of the pivot table contextual tabs are deleted. To get them back, click any cell inside the pivot table.

Here is the frustrating thing: As soon as you click outside of the object (that is, the chart), it is no longer selected, and the Chart Tools tabs disappear.

If you need to format an object and you cannot find the icons for formatting it, try clicking the object to see if the contextual tabs appear.

Two other tabs occasionally appear, although Excel classifies them as main tabs instead of contextual tabs. If you add the Print Preview Full Screen icon to the interface, you arrive at a Print Preview tab. Also, from the Picture Tools Design tab, you can click Remove Background to end up at the Background Removal tab.

Finding Lost Commands on the Ribbon

Often, the command you need is front and center on the Home tab, and everything is fine. However, there are times when you cannot find an obscure command that you know is somewhere in Excel.

Microsoft introduced a new Tell Me What You Want to Do search box on the Office 2016 ribbon. The functionality of that box has improved for Excel 2019.

Type Validation in the box. The results are shown in Figure 2.8. They define the term for you. They tell you how to pronounce the word. They offer the Data Validation command. They offer Help on the command. It works well. For some reason, they offer the Find & Select command as well, but you can overlook that.

Figure 2.8   The new Search box works great.

This feature works okay if you know the name of the command that you are searching for. If you try to answer the Tell Me What You Want To Do box with an English language phrase, such as **Choose from a list**, the search box has little chance of returning the command (see Figure 2.9). I've tested many phrases and never get the command that I am describing.

Figure 2.9   It fails if you try to describe the feature.

One great improvement since Excel 2016: If you know the name of the command but the command falls into the dreaded "commands not in ribbon" category, the Search box will successfully return the command and offer you a way to invoke it (see Figure 2.10).

Figure 2.10   If the feature is in Excel but not in the ribbon, the search box will find it.

Here is my strategy for finding those commands that aren't on the ribbon:

1. Right-click the ribbon and select Customize Quick Access Toolbar. Excel displays the Quick Access Toolbar category of the Excel Options dialog box.

2. Open the top-left drop-down menu and change Popular Commands to All Commands. You now have an alphabetical list of more than 2,000 commands.

3. Scroll through this alphabetical list until you find the command you are trying to locate in the ribbon.

4. Hover over the command in the left list box. A ToolTip appears, showing you where you can find the command. If the ToolTip shows Command Not In Ribbon, click the Add button in the center of the screen to add the command to the Quick Access Toolbar.

Shrinking the Ribbon

The ribbon takes up four vertical rows of space. This won't be an issue on a big monitor, but it could be an issue on a tiny laptop.

To shrink the ribbon, you can right-click it and choose Collapse The Ribbon. Or, use the carat (^) icon on the far-right side of the ribbon. The ribbon collapses to show only the ribbon tabs. When you click a tab, the ribbon temporarily expands. To close the ribbon, choose a command or press Esc.

TIP

The ribbon often stays open after certain commands. For example, I frequently click the Increase Decimal icon three times in a row. When the ribbon is minimized, you can click Home and then click Increase Decimal three times without having the ribbon close.

To permanently bring the ribbon back to full size, right-click a ribbon tab and uncheck Collapse The Ribbon. Or, click any tab and then click the pushpin icon in the lower-right corner of the ribbon. You can also toggle between minimized and full size by double-clicking any ribbon tab.

Using the Quick Access Toolbar

A problem with the ribbon is that only one-seventh of the commands are visible at any given time. You will find yourself moving from one tab to another. The alternative is to use the Quick Access Toolbar (QAT) to store your favorite commands.

The QAT starts out as a tiny toolbar with AutoSave, Save, Undo, and Redo. It is initially located above the File tab in the ribbon.

If you start using the QAT frequently, you can right-click the toolbar and choose Show Quick Access Toolbar Below The Ribbon to move the QAT closer to the grid.

Adding Icons to the QAT

The drop-down menu at the right side of the QAT, shown on the right side in Figure 2.11, offers 12 popular commands you might choose to add to the Quick Access Toolbar. Choose a command from this list to add it to the QAT.

CHAPTER 2

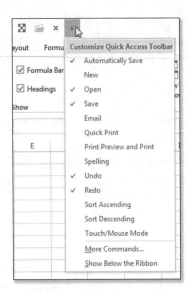

Figure 2.11   Use the drop-down menu at the right side of the QAT to add 13 popular commands.

When you find a command in the ribbon you are likely to use often, you can easily add the command to the QAT. To do so, right-click any command in the ribbon and select Add To Quick Access Toolbar. Items added to the Quick Access Toolbar using the right-click method are added to the right side of the QAT.

The right-click method works for many commands, but not with individual items within commands. For example, you can put the Font Size drop-down menu on the QAT, but you cannot specifically put size 16 font in the QAT.

Removing Commands from the QAT

You can remove an icon from the QAT by right-clicking the icon and selecting Remove from Quick Access Toolbar.

Customizing the QAT

You can make minor changes to the QAT by using the context menus, but you can have far more control over the QAT if you use the Customize command. Right-click the QAT and select Customize Quick Access Toolbar to display the Quick Access Toolbar section of the Excel Options dialog box, as shown in Figure 2.12.

Figure 2.12   You can customize the QAT using the Excel Options dialog box.

The Excel Options dialog box offers many features for customizing the Quick Access Toolbar:

- You can choose to customize the QAT for all documents on your computer or just for the current workbook by using the top-right drop-down menu.

- You can add separators between icons to group the icons logically. A separator icon is available at the top of the left menu. Click the separator icon in the left list box and then click the Add icon in the center of the screen.

- You can resequence the order of the icons on the toolbar. Select an icon in the right list box, and then click the up/down arrow icons on the right side of the dialog box.

- You can access 2,000+ commands, including the commands from every tab and commands that are not available in the ribbon. Although the dialog box starts with just 53 popular commands in the left list box, use the left drop-down menu to choose All Commands or Commands Not In The Ribbon. When you find a command in the left list box, select the command and then click Add in the center of the dialog box to add that command to the QAT.

- You can reset the QAT to its original default state using the Reset button in the lower right.

- You can export your custom QAT icons from your computer and import on another computer.

CHAPTER 2

- You can move the QAT to appear above or below the ribbon using the check box in the lower left.

Using the Full-Screen File Menu

Open the File menu to see the Backstage view. Here is the logic: When you are working on most ribbon tabs, you are working in your document. When you are about to change the font or something like that, you want to see the results of the change for the "in" commands. However, the Excel team thinks that after you move to the File menu, you are done working in your document, and you are about to do something with the whole document, such as send the workbook, print the workbook, post the workbook to Twitter, and so on. Microsoft calls these the "out" commands. The theory is that you don't need to see the worksheet for the "out" commands, so Microsoft fills the entire screen with the File menu.

To open the Backstage view, click the File menu. The Backstage view fills the screen, as shown in Figure 2.13. Backstage is split into three sections: the narrow left navigation panel and two wider sections that provide information.

Figure 2.13   The Backstage view fills the entire screen.

The left navigation panel includes these commands:

- **Home**—New in Excel 2019, it combines elements of New and Open. At the top, you can see tutorials from Microsoft and popular templates. In the middle, recent and pinned files. Both sections have a link to "Find More in New" or "Find More in Open."

- **Info**—Provides information about the current workbook. This is discussed later in the "Getting Information About the Current Workbook" section.

- **New**—Used to create a new workbook or start from a template.

- **Open**—Used to access a file stored on your computer or the OneDrive. See Chapter 1.

- **Save**—Saves the file in the same folder as it was previously stored. Note that Save is a command instead of a panel in Backstage.

- **Save As**—Stores the file on your computer or in OneDrive. See Chapter 1.

- **Print**—Used to choose print settings and print. Includes Print Preview. See Chapter 27, "Printing."

- **Share**—Changed in Excel 2019. This is now the entry point for sharing a workbook with your co-workers. See Chapter 1.

- **Export**—Used to create a PDF or change the file type.

- **Publish**—Used to upload your workbook to Power BI.

- **Close**—Closes the current workbook. Like Save, this entry is a pure command.

- **Account**—Sign in to Office. Choose a color theme and a background. See if updates are available. Learn your version of Excel. This and the next two items have been moved to the bottom left of the screen, below the area shown shown in Figure 2.13.

- **Feedback**—Send a smile or send a frown to the Excel team. Also contains a link to the Excel.UserVoice.com website where you can suggest new ideas for Excel.

- **Options**—Contains pages of Excel settings. See Chapter 3, "Customizing Excel," for details.

- **Recent File List**—This list appears only if you've changed a default setting in Excel Options. Visit File, Options, Advanced Display and choose Quickly Access This Number Of Recent Workbooks.

Pressing the Esc Key to Close Backstage View

To get out of Backstage and return to your worksheet, you can either press the Esc key or click the back arrow in the top-left corner of Backstage.

Recovering Unsaved Workbooks

As in previous versions of Excel, the AutoRecover feature can create copies of your workbook every *n* minutes. If you close the workbook without saving, you might be able to get the file back, provided it was open long enough to go through an AutoRecover.

CHAPTER 2

If the workbook was new and never saved, scroll to the bottom of the Recent Workbooks List and choose Recover Unsaved Workbooks.

If the workbook had previously been saved, open the last saved version of the workbook. Go to the File menu, and the last AutoSave version from before you closed the file will be available.

Clearing the Recent Workbooks List

If you need to clear out the Recent Workbooks list, you should visit File, Options, Advanced, Display. Set the Show This Number Of Recent Documents list to zero. You can then set it back to a positive number, such as 10.

Getting Information About the Current Workbook

When a workbook is open, and you go to the File, Info, you see the Info gallery for that workbook. The Info pane lists all sorts of information about the current workbook:

- The workbook path is shown at the top of the center panel.

- You can see the file size.

- You can see when the document was last modified and who modified it.

- If any special states exist, these will be reported at the top of the middle pane. Special states might include the following:

  - Macros Not Enabled

  - Links Not Updated

  - Checked Out From SharePoint

- You can see if the file has been AutoRecovered and recover those versions.

- You can mark the document as final, which will cause others opening the file to initially have a read-only version of the file.

- You can edit links to other documents.

- You can add tags or categories to the file.

- Using the Check For Issues drop-down menu, you can run a compatibility checker to see if the workbook is compatible with legacy versions of Excel. You can run an accessibility checker to see if any parts of the document will be difficult for people with disabilities. You can run a Document Inspector to see if any private information is hidden in the file.

Marking a Workbook as Final to Prevent Editing

Open the Protect Workbook icon in the Info gallery to access a setting called Mark As Final. This marks the workbook as read-only. It prevents someone else from making changes to your final workbook.

However, if the other person visits the Info gallery, that person can re-enable editing. This feature is designed to warn the other people that you've marked it as final and no further changes should happen.

If you can convince everyone in your workgroup to sign up for a Windows Live ID, you can use the Restrict Permission By People setting. This layer of security enables you to define who can read, edit, and/or print the document.

Finding Hidden Content Using the Document Inspector

The Document Inspector can find a lot of hidden content, but it is not perfect. Still, finding 95 percent of the types of hidden content can protect you a lot of the time.

CAUTION

The Document Inspector is not foolproof. Do you frequently hide settings by changing the font color to white or by using the ;;; custom number format? These types of things won't be found by the Document Inspector. The Document Inspector also won't note that you scrolled over outside the print area and jotted your after-work grocery list in column X.

To run the Document Inspector, select File, Info, Check For Issues, Inspect Document, and click OK. The results of the Document Inspector show that the document has personal information stored in the file properties (author's name) and perhaps a hidden worksheet.

Adding Whitespace Around Icons Using Touch Mode

If you are trying to use Excel on a tablet or a touch screen, you want to try touch mode. Follow these steps:

1. Go to the right side of the QAT and open the drop-down menu that appears there.

2. The twelfth command is called Touch/Mouse Mode. The icon is a blue dot with a ring of whitespace and then dashed lines around the whitespace. Choose this command to add it to the QAT.

3. Click the icon on the QAT. You see whitespace added around all the icons.

Using the New Sheet Icon to Add Worksheets

The Insert Worksheet icon is a circle with a plus sign that appears to the right of the last sheet tab.

When you click this icon, a new worksheet is added to the right of the active sheet. This is better than Excel 2010, where the new worksheet was added as the last worksheet in the workbook and then had to be dragged to the correct position.

Navigating Through Many Worksheets Using the Controls in the Lower Left

Older versions of Excel had four controls for moving through the list of worksheet tabs. The worksheet navigation icons are now a left and right arrowhead in the lower left.

The controls are active only when you have more tabs than are visible across the bottom of the Excel window. Click the left or right icon to scroll the tabs one at a time. Ctrl+click either arrow to scroll to the first or last tab. Note that scrolling the tabs does not change the active sheet. It just brings more tabs into view, so you can then click the selected tab.

Just as in prior versions of Excel, you can right-click the worksheet navigation arrows to see a complete list of worksheets. Click any item in the list to move to that worksheet.

In certain circumstances, an ellipsis (...) icon appears to the left of the worksheet navigation arrows. This icon selects the worksheet to the left of the active sheet.

Using the Mini Toolbar to Format Selected Text

When you select some text in a chart title or within a cell, the mini toolbar appears above the selected text. If you move away from the mini toolbar, it fades away. However, if you move the mouse toward the mini toolbar, you see several text formatting options.

To use the mini toolbar, follow these steps:

1. Select some text. If you select text in a cell, you must select a portion of the text in the cell by using Cell Edit mode. In a chart, SmartArt diagram, or text box, you can select any text. As soon as you release the mouse button, the mini toolbar appears above and to the right of the selection.

2. Move the mouse pointer toward the mini toolbar. The mini toolbar stays visible if your mouse is above it. If you move the mouse away from the mini toolbar, it fades away.

3. Make changes in the mini toolbar to affect the text you selected in step 1.

4. When you are done formatting the selected text, you can move the mouse away from the mini toolbar to dismiss it.

Expanding the Formula Bar

Formulas range from very simple to very complex. As people started writing longer and longer formulas in Excel, an annoying problem began to appear: If the formula for a selected cell was longer than the formula bar, the formula bar would wrap and extend over the worksheet. In many cases, the formula would obscure the first few rows of the worksheet. This was frustrating, especially if the selected cell was in the top few rows of the spreadsheet.

Excel 2016 includes a formula bar that prevents the formula from obscuring the spreadsheet. For example, in Figure 2.14, cell F1 contains a formula that is longer than the formula bar. Notice the down-arrow icon at the right end of the formula bar. This icon expands the formula bar.

Figure 2.14   Initially, Excel shows only the first row of the formula.

Press Ctrl+Shift+U or click the down-arrow icon at the right side of the formula bar to expand the formula bar. The formula bar expands to the last manually resized height, and the entire worksheet moves down to accommodate the larger formula bar.

The formula, in this example, is too long for the default larger formula bar. You must hover your mouse near the bottom of the formula bar until you see the up/down white arrow cursor. Click and drag down until you can see the entire formula (see Figure 2.15).

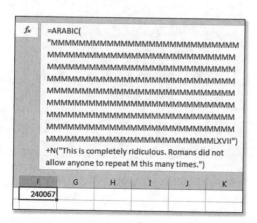

Figure 2.15   The worksheet moves down to accommodate the formula.

NOTE

Excel guru Bob Umlas keeps suggesting that the formula bar should change color when you are not seeing the entire formula. That is a great suggestion that perhaps the Excel team will one day add to Excel.

Zooming In and Out on a Worksheet

In the lower-right corner of the Excel window, a zoom slider enables you to zoom from 400 percent to 10 percent with lightning speed. You simply drag the slider to the right to zoom in and to the left to zoom out. The Zoom Out and Zoom In buttons on either end of the slider enable you to adjust the zoom in 10 percent increments.

Clicking the % indicator to the right of the zoom slider opens the legacy Zoom dialog box.

Inside OUT

If you decrease the zoom below 40%, Microsoft assumes that you are looking for an overview of the entire spreadsheet.

An interesting feature appears when you decrease the zoom to 39% or less. Any regions that have been assigned a name will appear as boxes with the name super-imposed. This is great for getting an overview of the named ranges created by someone else.

Using the Status Bar to Add Numbers

If you select several cells that contain numeric data and then look at the status bar, at the bottom of the Excel window, you can see that the status bar reports the average, count, and sum of the selected cells (see Figure 2.16).

270	229	242	236
294	228	247	224
282	263	232	266
278	226	235	289
222	221	262	267
280	258	254	224
241	295	247	269
291	261	260	265
258	280	302	267

Average: 257.3611111   Count: 36   Max: 302   Sum: 9265

Figure 2.16   The status bar shows the sum, average, and count of the selected cells.

If you need to quickly add the contents of several cells, you can select the cells and look for the total in the status bar. This feature has been in Excel for a decade, yet very few people realized it was there. In legacy versions of Excel, only the sum would appear, but you could right-click the sum to see other values, such as the average, count, minimum, and maximum.

You can customize which statistics are shown in the status bar. Right-click the status bar and choose any or all of Min, Max, Numerical Count, Count, Sum, and Average.

Switching Between Normal View, Page Break Preview, and Page Layout View Modes

Three shortcut icons to the left of the zoom slider enable you to quickly switch between three view modes:

- **Normal view**—This mode shows worksheet cells as normal.

- **Page Break preview**—This mode draws the page breaks in blue. You can actually drag the page breaks to new locations in Page Break preview. This mode has been available in several versions of Excel.

- **Page Layout view**—This view was introduced in Excel 2007. It combines the best of Page Break preview and Print Preview modes.

CHAPTER 2

In Page Layout view mode, each page is shown, along with the margins, header, and footer. A ruler appears above the pages and to the left of the pages. You can make changes in this mode in the following ways:

- To change the margins, drag the gray boxes in the ruler.

- To change column widths, drag the borders of the column headers.

- To add a header, select Click To Add Header.

Customizing Excel

The Excel Options dialog box offers dozens of changes you can make in Excel. This chapter walks you through examples of customizing the ribbon and discusses some of the important option settings available in Excel.

Performing a Simple Ribbon Modification

Suppose that you generally like the ribbon, but there is one icon that seems to be missing. You can add icons to the ribbon to make it customized to your preference. If you feel the Data tab would be perfect with the addition of a pivot table icon, you can add it (see Figure 3.1).

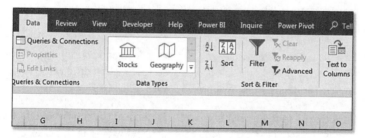

Figure 3.1 Decide where the new command should go on the ribbon.

To add the pivot table command to the Data tab, follow these steps:

1. Right-click the ribbon and select Customize The Ribbon.

2. In the right list box, expand the Data tab by clicking the + sign next to Data.

3. Click the Sort & Filter entry in the right list box. The new group will go after this entry.

4. Click the New Group button at the bottom of the right list box. A New Group (Custom) item appears after Sort & Filter, as shown in Figure 3.2.

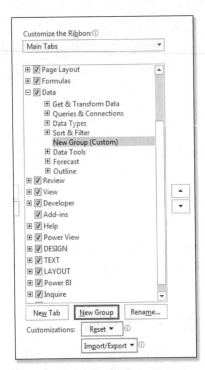

Customize the Ribbon: ⓘ

Main Tabs

- ☐ ☑ Page Layout
- ☐ ☑ Formulas
- ☐ ☑ Data
  - ☐ Get & Transform Data
  - ☐ Queries & Connections
  - ☐ Data Types
  - ☐ Sort & Filter
  - New Group (Custom)
  - ☐ Data Tools
  - ☐ Forecast
  - ☐ Outline
- ☐ ☑ Review
- ☐ ☑ View
- ☐ ☑ Developer
  - ☑ Add-ins
- ☐ ☑ Help
- ☐ ☑ Power View
- ☐ ☑ DESIGN
- ☐ ☑ TEXT
- ☐ ☑ LAYOUT
- ☐ ☑ Power BI
- ☐ ☑ Inquire

New Tab | New Group | Rename...

Customizations: Reset ▼ ⓘ

Import/Export ▼ ⓘ

Figure 3.2   Commands have to be added to a new group.

5. While the New Group is selected, click the Rename button at the bottom of the list box. The Rename dialog box appears.

6. The Rename dialog box offers to let you choose an icon and specify a name for the group. The icon is shown only when the Excel window is too small to display the whole group. Choose any icon and type a display name of **Pivot**. Click OK.

7. The left list box shows the popular commands. You could change Popular Commands to All Commands and scroll through 2,400 commands. However, in this case, the commands you want are on the Insert tab. Choose All Tabs from the top-left drop-down menu. Expand the Insert tab, and then expand Tables. Click PivotTable in the left list box. Click the Add button in the center of the dialog box to add PivotTable to the new custom Pivot group on the ribbon. Excel automatically advances to the next icon of Recommended PivotTables. Click Add again.

8. In the drop-down menu above the left list box, select All Commands. The left list box changes to show an alphabetical list of all commands.

9. Scroll through the left list box until you find PivotTable And PivotChart Wizard. This is the obscure entry point to create Multiple Consolidation Range pivot tables. Select that item

in the left list box. Click Add. At this point, the right side of the dialog box should look like Figure 3.3.

Figure 3.3   Three new icons have been added to a new custom group on the Data tab.

10. Click OK.

Figure 3.4 shows the new group in the Data tab of the ribbon.

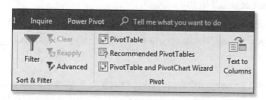

Figure 3.4   The results appear in the ribbon.

Adding a New Ribbon Tab

To add a new ribbon tab, follow these basic steps:

1. Right-click the ribbon and select Customize The Ribbon.

2. Click New Tab and rename the tab.

3. Add New Group(s) to the new tab.

4. Add commands to the new groups.

As you go through the steps to add a new ribbon tab, you will discover how absolutely limiting the ribbon customizations are. You have no control over which items appear with large icons and which appear with small icons. This applies even to galleries. If you add the Cell Styles gallery to a group on the ribbon, it always appears as an icon instead of a gallery, even if it is the only thing on the entire ribbon tab (see the left icon in Figure 3.5). The workaround is to add an entire built-in group to the tab. On the right of Figure 3.5, the entire Styles group was added. The Cell Styles gallery is now allowed to appear as a gallery.

Figure 3.5   When added to a custom group, a gallery is reduced to a single icon with a drop-down menu.

TROUBLESHOOTING

When customizing the ribbon using this interface, you cannot control which icons appear large and which appear small in the ribbon.

The Excel ribbon contains a logical mix of large icons for important features and small icons for minor features. If you would like to create a new group, you cannot control which icons will be small and which will be large.

You can either learn RibbonML or use a third-party tool such as Ribbon Commander to create custom ribbon tabs. Try a free trial of Ribbon Commander at https://mrx.cl/ribboncommander.

Sharing Customizations with Others

If you have developed the perfect ribbon customization and you want everyone in your department to have the same customization, you can export all the ribbon customizations.

To export the changes, follow these steps:

1. Right-click the ribbon and select Customize The Ribbon.

2. Below the right list box, select Import/Export, Export All Customizations.

3. Browse to a folder and provide a name for the customization file. The file type will be .exportedUI. Click OK.

4. In Windows Explorer, find the .exportedUI file. Copy it to a co-worker's computer.

5. On the co-worker's computer, repeat step 1. In step 2, select Import Customization File. Find the file and click OK.

NOTE

This is an all-or-nothing proposition. You cannot export your changes to one custom tab without exporting your changes to the Data and Home tabs.

Questions About Ribbon Customization

Can the customizations apply only to a certain workbook?

No. The Customize The Ribbon command in Excel 2019 applies to all workbooks.

Can I reset my customizations and go back to the original ribbon?

Right-click the ribbon and select Customize The Ribbon. Below the right list box, select Reset, Reset All Customizations.

How can I get complete control over the ribbon?

Learn RibbonX and write some VBA to build your own ribbon.

➤ For more information on building your own ribbon, **see** *RibbonX: Customizing the Office 2007 Ribbon*, by Robert Martin, Ken Puls, and Teresa Hennig (Wiley, ISBN 0470191112).

These ribbon customizations are really lacking. Is there another option that doesn't require me to write a program?

Yes, some third-party ribbon customization programs are available. For example, check out a free one from Excel MVP Andy Pope at www.andypope.info/vba/ribboneditor.htm.

Using the Excel Options Dialog Box

Open the File menu and select Options from the left navigation pane to open the Excel Options dialog box. The dialog box has categories for General, Formulas, Data, Proofing, Save, Language, Ease Of Access, Advanced, Customize Ribbon, Quick Access Toolbar, Add-Ins, and Trust Center. The Trust Center leads to another 12 categories.

To the Excel team's credit, they tried to move the top options to the General category. Beyond those 15 settings, though, are hundreds of settings spread throughout 21 categories in the Excel Options and Trust Center. Table 3.1 gives you a top-level view of where to start looking for settings.

Table 3.1 Excel Options Dialog Box Settings

Category	Types of Settings
General	The most commonly used settings, such as user interface settings, the default font for new workbooks, number of sheets in a new workbook, customer name, and Start screen.
Formulas	All options for controlling calculation, error-checking rules, and formula settings. Note that options for multithreaded calculations are currently considered obscure enough to be on the Advanced tab rather than on the Formulas Tab.
Data	The data category is new in 2017. It offers the new Edit Default Layout for pivot tables, several other pivot table options, and then a series of checkboxes to bring back the legacy Get Data categories. When Power Query replaced Get Data on the Data tab of the ribbon, the old legacy icons were removed.
Proofing	Spell-check options and a link to the AutoCorrect dialog box.
Save	The default method for saving, AutoRecovery settings, legacy colors, and web server options.
Language	Choose the editing language, ToolTip language, and Help language.
Ease of Access	Options available are Provide Feedback With Sound, Provide Feedback With Animation, Screen Tip Style, and the default document font size.
Advanced	All options that Microsoft considers advanced, spread among 14 headings.
Customize Ribbon	Icons to customize the ribbon.
Quick Access Toolbar	Icons to customize the Quick Access Toolbar (QAT).
Add-Ins	A list of available and installed add-ins. New add-ins can be installed from the button at the bottom of this category.
Trust Center	Links to the Microsoft Trust Center, with 12 additional categories.

Getting Help with a Setting

Many settings appear with a small *i* icon. If you hover the mouse near this icon, Excel displays a super ToolTip for the setting. The ToolTip explains what happens when you choose the setting. It also provides some tips about what you need to be aware of when you turn on the setting. For example, the ToolTip in Figure 3.6 shows information about the calculation settings. It also explains that you should use the F9 key to invoke a manual calculation.

Figure 3.6   The i button explains many settings.

CHAPTER 3

Inside OUT

The Excel team is actively listening to ideas suggested by their customers. Several of the settings in the following section were suggested by customers.

If you have a great idea that would make Excel easier, post your idea to Excel.UserVoice .com. Create a good title and use a slightly sarcastic tone when writing up how your idea would make the work life of millions of people easier.

After posting your idea, ask others in your organization to vote for your idea. Once you get 20 votes, you've reached the threshold where the Excel team will respond to your idea. As others browsing Excel.UserVoice.com read your idea, they can vote. If you get above the 200-vote level, it is likely that your idea will be added to a future release of Office 365.

New Options in Excel 2019

Excel 2019 offers several new settings:

- Office Intelligent Services is found on the General category. This Office-365 exclusive feature will send up to 250,000 cells of your worksheet to a Microsoft Artificial Intelligence application for analysis. You must opt-in to use this feature in Options and then invoke the feature using the Insights command on the Insert menu.

- Enable LinkedIn Features is found in the General category. Microsoft purchased LinkedIn, and they added features to allow LinkedIn profile information to appear in Outlook and

Word. There are not any LinkedIn features available in Excel (yet), so you must wonder why they added this option in Excel.

- Default PivotTable Layout is found in the new Data category. Change the default layout for all future pivot tables. Several items in the new Data category were moved to the Data category from the Advanced category.

- Disable Automatic Grouping Of Date/Time Columns In A Pivot Table is found in the Data category. One of the highly touted features in Excel 2016 was that any date field added to a pivot table would be rolled up to years and months. Some people hated it, and so now there is a checkbox to turn it off.

- Show Legacy Data Import Wizards is a series of seven choices in the new Data category. The Power Query tools debuted in Excel 2016 on the Data tab of the ribbon. These tools became so popular, Microsoft decided to remove the old Get External Data group from the ribbon, but some people had specific reasons why they liked the old icons. You can now add those old icons back by choosing From Access, From Web, From Text, From SQL Server, From OData Data Feed, From XML Data Import, or From Data Connection. If you choose something from this area, it will appear hidden on the ribbon. Look in Data, Get Data, Legacy Wizards.

- AutoSave OneDrive And SharePoint Online Files By Default On Excel is the first item in the Save category of Excel Options. A small percentage of people need to have many people work in the same workbook at the same time. A large percentage of people who don't need this feature quickly hated that Excel was saving their file after every change. You can globally turn AutoSave Off or On using this setting. I recommend leaving it off. Then, for the workbooks that you need to edit with other people, you can turn it on.

- Show Data Loss Warning When Editing Comma Delimited Files (*.csv) is found in the Save category. Excel used to nag you whenever you opened a file in CSV format. If you did not save the file as XLSX, it would warn you that you are about to lose formulas and format-ting. A lot of people were tired of the nagging, and Microsoft turned off the nagging by default. If you need to be nagged, you can turn it back on here.

- The ability to save Checked Out files To Server Drafts was removed from the Save cat-egory. A Learn More hyperlink in Excel Options explains why.

- The Ease Of Access category is new in Excel 2019. You can choose to Provide Feedback With Sound and choose a Modern or Classic sound scheme. The new part is the Modern sound scheme. The annoying Classic Sound Scheme was previously the only choice in the Advanced category. You can turn off Animations. The choice to control if Screen Tips are shown is repeated here from the General category. You can set the Default Font Size used in the document. You can choose to turn off the calculation Function Screen Tips.

- Use Pen To Select and Interact By Default is new in the Advanced category. If you prefer using a touchscreen, you can change the default behavior of touch.

Using AutoRecover Options

For many versions, Excel periodically saves a copy of your work every 10 minutes. If your computer crashes, the recovery pane offers to let you open the last AutoRecovered version of the file. This feature is sure to save you from retyping data that might have otherwise been lost.

Another painful situation occurs when you do not save changes and then close Excel. Yes, Excel asks if you want to save changes for each open document, but this question usually pops up at 5:00 p.m. when you are in a hurry to get out of the office. If you are thinking about what you need to do after work and not paying attention to which files are still open, you might click No to the first document and then click No again and again without noticing that the fifth open document was one that should have been saved.

Another scenario involves leaving an Excel file open overnight only to discover that Windows Update decided to restart the computer at 3 a.m. After being burned a dozen times, you can change the behavior of Windows Update to stop doing this. However, if Windows Update closed Excel without saving your documents, you can lose those AutoRecovered documents.

A setting introduced in Excel 2010 has Excel save the last AutoRecovered version of each open file when you close without saving. This setting is on the Save category of Excel Options and is called Keep The Last AutoSaved Version If I Close Without Saving.

Controlling Image Sizes

An Image Size & Quality section appears in the Advanced category. Most people add a photo to dress up the cover page of a document. However, you probably don't need an 8-megapixel image being saved in the workbook. By default, Excel compresses the image before saving the file. You can control the target output size using the drop-down menu in Excel options. Choices include 96ppi, 150ppi, and 220ppi. The 96ppi setting will look fine on your display. Use 220ppi for images you will print. If you want to keep your images at the original size, you can select the Do Not Compress Images In File setting.

You should also understand the Discard Editing Data check box. Suppose that you insert an image in your workbook and then crop out part of the photograph. If you do not enable Discard Editing Data, someone else can come along and uncrop your photo. This can be an embarrassing situation—just ask the former TechTV co-host who discovered certain bits of photographs were still hanging around after she cropped them out.

Working with Protected View for Files Originating from the Internet

Starting in Excel 2010, files from the Internet or Outlook initially open in protected mode. This mode gives you a chance to look at the workbook and formulas without having anything malicious happen. Unfortunately, you cannot view the macro code while the workbook is in protected view.

If you only want to view or print the workbook, protected mode works great. One statistic says that 40% of the time, people simply open a document and never make changes to it.

After you click Enable Editing, Excel will skip protected mode the next time you open the file.

Working with Trusted Document Settings

By default, Excel warns you about all sorts of things. If you open a workbook with macros, links, external data connections, or even the new WEBSERVICE function, a message bar appears above the worksheet to let you know that Excel disabled those "threats."

If you declare a folder on your hard drive to be a trusted folder, you can open those documents without Excel warning you about the items. Visit File, Options, Trust Center, Trust Center Settings, Trusted Locations to set up a trusted folder.

Starting in Excel 2010, if you open a file from your hard drive and enable the content, Excel automatically enables that content next time. The inherent problem here is that if you open a file and discover the macros are bad, you will not want those macros to open the next time automatically. There is no way to untrust a single document other than deleting, renaming, or moving it. Instead, you have to go to the Trusted Documents category of the Trust Center where you can choose to clear the entire list of trusted documents.

Options to Consider

Although hundreds of Excel options exist, this section provides a quick review of options that might be helpful to you:

- Save File In This Format in the Save category. If you regularly create macros, choose the Excel Macro-Enabled Workbook as the default format type.

- Update your Default File Location in the Save tab. Excel always wants to save new documents in your My Documents folder. However, if you always work in the C:\Accounting-Files\ folder, update the default folder to match your preferred location.

- Show This Number Of Recent Workbooks has been enhanced dramatically since Excel 2003. Whereas legacy versions of Excel showed up to nine recent workbooks at the bottom of the File menu, Excel 2019 allows you to see up to 50 recent workbooks in the Open category of the File menu. You can change this setting by visiting the Display section of the Advanced category.

- Edit Custom Lists has been moved to the Display section of the Advanced category. Custom lists add functionality to the fill handle, allow custom sort orders, and control how fields are displayed in the label area of a pivot table. Type a list in the correct sequence in a worksheet. Edit Custom Lists and click Import. Excel can now automatically extend items from that list, the same as it can extend January into February, March, and so on.

- Make Excel look less like Excel by hiding interface elements in the three Display sections of the Advanced category. You can turn off the formula bar, scrollbars, sheet tabs, row and column headers, and gridlines. You can customize the ribbon to remove all main tabs except the File menu. The point is that if you design a model to be used by someone who never uses Excel, the person can open the model, plug in a few numbers, and get the result without having to see the entire Excel interface.

- Show A Zero in Cells That Have Zero Value is in the Display Options For This Worksheet section of the Advanced category. Occasionally people want zeros to be displayed as blanks. Although a custom number format of 0;-0;; will do this, you can change the setting globally by clearing this option.

- Group Dates in the AutoFilter Menu is in the Display Options For This Workbook section of the Advanced category. Starting with Excel 2007, date columns show a hierarchical view of years, months, and days in the AutoFilter drop-down menu. If you like the old behavior of showing each date, turn off this setting.

- Add a folder on your local hard drive as a trusted location. Files stored in a trusted location automatically have macros enabled and external links updated. If you can trust that you will not write malicious code, then define a folder on your hard drive as a trusted location. From Excel Options, select the Trust Center category and then Trust Center Settings. In the Trust Center, select Trusted Locations, Add New Location.

Five Excel Oddities

You might rarely need any of the features presented in this section. However, in the right circumstance, they can be time-savers.

- Adjust the gridline color in the Display section of the Advanced category. If you are tired of gray gridlines, you can get a new outlook with bright red gridlines. I've met people who have changed the gridline color and can attest that nothing annoys an old accountant more than seeing bright red gridlines.

- Allow negative time by switching to the 1904 date system in the General section of the Advanced category. Excel never allows a time to return a negative time. However, if you are tracking comp time and you allow people to borrow against future comp time, it might be nice to allow negative time. In this case, switch to the 1904 date system to have up to four years of negative time. Use caution when changing this setting. All existing dates in the workbook will shift by approximately four years.

- Put an end to the green triangles on your account numbers stored as text. Most of the green triangle indicators are useful. However, if you have a column of text account numbers in which most values are numbers, seeing thousands of green triangles can be annoying. Also, the green triangles can hide other, more serious problems. Clear the Numbers Formatted As Text or Preceded By An Apostrophe in the Error Checking Rules check box in the Formulas category.

- Automatically Insert A Decimal Point replicates the antique adding machines that were office fixtures in the 1970s. When working with a manual adding machine, it was frustrating to type decimal points. You could type **123456**, and the adding machine would interpret the entry as 1,234.56. If you find that you are doing massive data entry of numbers in dollars and cents, you can have Excel replicate the old adding machine functionality. After enabling this setting, you can indicate how many digits of the number should be interpreted as being after the decimal point. The only hassle is that you need to enter $5 as **500**. The old adding machines actually had a 00 key, but those are long since gone.

- Change *Dwight* to *Diapers* using AutoCorrect Options. If you were a fan of the NBC sitcom *The Office*, you might remember the 2007 episode in which Jim allegedly put a macro on Dwight's computer that automatically changed the typed word *Dwight* to *Diapers*. However, this doesn't require a macro. From Excel Options, choose the Proofing Category and then click the AutoCorrect Options button. On the AutoCorrect tab, you can type new correction pairs. In this example, you would type **Dwight** into the Replace box and **Diapers** into the With box. The next time someone types *Dwight* and then a space, the word will automatically change to *Diapers*. You can also remove correction pairs by selecting the pairs and then pressing Delete. For example, if you hate that Microsoft converts (c) to ©, you can delete that entry from the list.

CHAPTER 4

Keyboard Shortcuts

If you do a lot of typing, being able to access commands from the ...
ing your hand to the mouse. Excel 2019 still uses many of the old Alt keyboard s...
Excel 2003. All the old Ctrl shortcut keys are still functional. For instance, Ctrl+C still copies a
selection, Ctrl+X cuts a selection, and Ctrl+V pastes a selection.

This chapter points out which of the old Excel 2003 keyboard shortcuts still work, shows you
some new shortcuts, and introduces you to the keyboard accelerators.

Learning the right ten shortcuts from this chapter can make you twice as fast in Excel.

Using Keyboard Accelerators

The goal of the Excel 2019 keyboard accelerators is to enable you to access every command by
using only the keyboard. In legacy versions of Excel, many popular commands had keyboard
accelerators, but other commands did not. Excel 2019 tries to ensure that every command can
be invoked from the keyboard.

To access the new accelerators, press and release the Alt key. Notice that Excel places a KeyTip
above each command. Also, numeric KeyTips appear over each icon in the Quick Access Toolbar
(QAT; see Figure 4.1). Press the F10 key to display or hide the KeyTips.

Figure 4.1   Type the letters in the KeyTips along the top to open various tabs.

It is possible to memorize the KeyTips for the ribbon tabs. Pressing Alt+F accesses the File menu
in all Office 2019 applications. Alt+H accesses the Home tab in all Office 2019 applications.

the cursor inside the Tell Me What You Want To Do box. The accelerator definitions tab remain constant even if new ribbon tabs are displayed. When you activate a pivot the original KeyTip letters remain, and two new KeyTips appear for the contextual tabs: JT PivotTable Tools Options and JY for PivotTable Tools Design (see Figure 4.2).

Figure 4.2 New ribbon tabs have new letters, so the old letters remain constant.

Unfortunately, the KeyTips for the Quick Access Toolbar change every time you add new buttons or rearrange buttons on the Quick Access Toolbar. If you want to memorize those KeyTips, you need to make sure you do not add a new Quick Access Toolbar icon at the beginning of the list.

Selecting Icons on the Ribbon

After you press the Alt key, you can press one of the KeyTip letters to bring up the appropriate tab. You now see that every icon on the ribbon has a KeyTip.

When you choose a ribbon tab, the KeyTips on the Quick Access Toolbar disappear, so Microsoft is free to use the letters A through Z and the numbers 0 through 9.

On very busy ribbon tabs, some commands require two keystrokes: for example, A+C for Align Center in the Alignments group of the Home tab, as shown in Figure 4.3. Note that after you press Alt to display the accelerators in the ToolTips, you do not have to continue holding down the Alt key.

Figure 4.3 After pressing the letter to switch to the ribbon, type the letter or letters to invoke a particular command.

Some shortcut keys seem to make sense: AT for Align Top, AM for Align Middle, AB for Align Bottom, AL for Align Left, W for Wrap Text, and M for Merge. Other shortcut keys seem to be assigned at random. Some take a little pondering: FA for the dialog box launcher in Figure 4.3 makes sense in that it opens the legacy Format dialog box and moves to the Alignment tab. Others have a historical precedent. In Excel 2003, F was used for File, so O was used for Format.

Similarly, in the Home tab, O now opens the Format drop-down menu. However, because Microsoft no longer underlines the accelerator key in the menu name, O will never make sense to someone new to Excel. There might be some arcane, logical reason why 5 and 6 are used for increase and decrease indent, but it is unknown by most people.

Selecting Options from a Gallery

Figure 4.4 shows the results of pressing Alt+H+J, which is the equivalent of selecting Home, Cell Styles. This opens the gallery of cell styles. As you can see in Figure 4.4, you can invoke the New Cell Style and Merge Styles commands at the bottom of the gallery by pressing N and M, respectively. However, there are no letters on the table style choices in the gallery.

Figure 4.4   After opening a gallery, you use the arrow keys to navigate through the gallery and press Enter to select a style.

To select a cell style using the keyboard, use the arrow keys to move through the gallery. Because this gallery is two dimensional, you can use the up arrow, down arrow, right arrow, left arrow, Page Down, Page Up, Home, and End keys to navigate through the gallery. When you have the desired table style highlighted, press the Enter key to select it.

Navigating Within Drop-Down Menu Lists

If you press Alt+H+F+S, which is the equivalent of selecting Home, Font Size, the font size in the drop-down menu is selected. You can either type a font size and press Enter or press the down-arrow key to open the drop-down menu. You can then use the down arrow, up arrow, Page Down, Page Up, Home, and End keys to navigate to a choice in the list. When you have the desired item highlighted, press Enter to select that item.

Backing Up One Level Through a Menu

Suppose you press Alt+H to access the Home tab and then realize you are in the wrong tab. You can press the Esc key to move back to display the ToolTips for the main menu choices. If you want to clear the ToolTips completely, press Alt again.

Dealing with Keyboard Accelerator Confusion

If you want to select something on the Home tab (previously shown in Figure 4.2), you might be frustrated because you can see the menu choices but no ToolTips appear for most commands. For icons in the top of the ribbon, it appears that the main KeyTips apply to the menu items. For example, you might think that the H KeyTip applies to Cut. Even though you are already on the Home tab, you need to press the H key to force Excel to show the ToolTips for the individual menu items on the Home tab.

TROUBLESHOOTING

There are some parts of the Excel window that seem impossible to access using keyboard shortcuts. For example, how can you rename a worksheet using only the keyboard?

It is extremely subtle, but there is something called the F6 Loop. When you press F6, the focus will move from the worksheet to the sheet tabs. Press F6 again to jump to any task pane, then to the zoom controls, and then back to the worksheet.

Once you use F6 to activate an area, you can use Tab or arrow keys to activate different controls within that area.

Say that you have cell A1 selected on Sheet1 and you want to rename Sheet2. Press F6 to move focus to the sheet tabs. Press the right arrow to move from Sheet1 to Sheet2. Press Shift+F10 (or the Program key) to open the right-click menu. Use the up arrow eight times to move to Rename. Press Enter to select the Rename command.

Inside OUT

It seems particularly tricky to use keyboard shortcuts to access a slicer.

The solution is not perfect, but you can select all objects using Alt, H, FD, O. Once you have selected all objects, you can cycle between the slicers although the indicators are very subtle.

Refer to the following figure while reading these keyboard steps.

1. Starting from cell B5, press Alt, H, FD, O to begin Select Objects mode.

2. Press Tab once to activate the Rep slicer. At this point, you can use the arrow keys to reposition the slicer.

3. Press Tab a second time to move to the Multi-Select icon inside the Rep slicer. Press Spacebar to toggle multi-select on or off.

4. Press Tab again to move to the Clear Filter icon. Press Spacebar to clear the filter.

5. Press Tab again to move into the slicer items. This step is really subtle because exactly one slicer will have a dotted line. A black dotted line on a field of dark blue is really hard to see. Plus, while you would think that the selected slicer tile would always be Andy, it is not. Excel remembers your last selected slicer and starts there. Perhaps using arrows to move to the next slicer tile will allow your eye to see what is changing. Spacebar will toggle the slicer tile on or off if the Multi-Select is enabled. If Multi-Select is off, then pressing Spacebar on one slicer tile will turn all the others off and turn that tile on. By the way, you can use Shift+Tab to move back to the Clear Filter and then Shift+Tab again to move back to Multi-Select.

6. Pressing Tab from the Slicer Items of the Rep slicer will move to the next object in the worksheet, the Oval.

7. Press Tab again to move to the Star.

8. Press Tab again to move to the Product slicer. At this point, you are essentially at Step 2 for the next slicer.

9. When you are done accessing the slicers, use the Escape key to exit Select Objects mode and return to cell B5.

CHAPTER 4

Selecting from Legacy Dialog Boxes

Some commands lead to legacy dialog boxes like the ones in previous editions of Excel. These dialog boxes do not display the Excel 2019 KeyTips. However, most of the dialog boxes do use the convention of having one letter of each command underlined, which is called a *hotkey* in Microsoft parlance. In this case, you can press the underlined letter to select the command.

For example, press Alt+H+V+S instead of selecting Home, Paste, Paste Special. You are then presented with the Paste Special dialog box, as shown in Figure 4.5. To select Values and Transpose in this dialog box, press V for Values and E for Transpose, because those are the letters underlined in the dialog box. You can then press Enter instead of clicking the default OK button.

Figure 4.5   In a legacy dialog box, type the underlined letters to select options.

Using the Shortcut Keys

The following five tables provide what I believe to be a comprehensive list of shortcut keys. I have collected these over the many versions of Excel. For some reason, Excel Help no longer lists all the shortcut keys. I count 75 shortcut keys in the following tables that are no longer documented in Excel Help. I realize this is a mind-numbingly long list, but I want to include it here because the Excel team no longer provides a complete list.

If you decide to learn and start using one new shortcut key every week, you will quickly become very fast at using Excel. After Table 4.5, I identify my favorite shortcut keys from this list.

Table 4.1 lists the common Windows Ctrl shortcut keys.

Table 4.1 Windows Shortcut Keys

Key Combination	Action
Ctrl+C	Copy.
Ctrl+X	Cut.
Ctrl+V	Paste.
Ctrl+Alt+V	Paste Special.
Ctrl+Z	Undo.
Ctrl+Y or F4	Redo.
Ctrl+A or Ctrl+Shift+spacebar	Select all. If the active cell contains data and is adjacent to other cells with data, Ctrl+A initially selects the current region. Pressing Ctrl+A again selects all.
Ctrl+S or Shift+F12 or Alt+Shift+F2	Save.
Alt+2 or F12	Save As.
Ctrl+O or Ctrl+F12	Open.
Ctrl+W or Ctrl+F4	Close workbook window.
Ctrl+N	New workbook.
Ctrl+P or Ctrl+F2 or Ctrl+Shift+F12	Display Print tab in File menu.
Ctrl+B	Bold.
Ctrl+U	Underline.
Ctrl+I	Italic.
Ctrl+F	Find.
Ctrl+H	Replace.
Ctrl+Shift+F or Ctrl+Shift+P	Font tab of Format Cells dialog box.

CHAPTER 4

Ctrl+G or F5	Go To dialog.
Ctrl+T or Ctrl+L	Format as Table.
Ctrl+E	Flash Fill.
Ctrl+Q	Quick Analysis options.

Table 4.2 illustrates the shortcut keys you use to navigate in Excel.

Table 4.2   Shortcut Keys for Navigation

Shortcut Key	Action
Ctrl+Home	Moves to cell A1 or the top-left unhidden cell in the worksheet.
Ctrl+End	Moves to the last cell in the used range of the worksheet. If the cursor is in the formula bar, it moves to the end of the formula text.
Page Down	Moves one screen down in the worksheet.
Page Up	Moves one screen up in the worksheet.
Alt+Page Down	Moves one screen right in the worksheet.
Alt+Page Up	Moves one screen left in the worksheet.
Ctrl+Page Up	Moves to the previous worksheet.
Ctrl+Page Down	Moves to the next worksheet.
Ctrl+Shift+F6	Moves to the previous window.
Shift+F11	Inserts a new worksheet.
Ctrl+F11	Inserts an Excel 4 macro sheet.
Alt+Tab	Switches to the next program.
Alt+Shift+Tab	Switches to the previous program.
Ctrl+Esc	Displays the Windows Start menu.
Ctrl+F5	Restores the window size of the current workbook.
F6	Switches between the worksheet, ribbon, task pane, and zoom controls. If the workbook has been split, this also switches between panes.
Ctrl+F6	Switches to the next open workbook window when more than one workbook is open.
Ctrl+Shift+F6	Switches to the previous workbook window.
Ctrl+F9	Minimizes the window.
Ctrl+F10	Maximizes the window.

End	Toggles into End mode. Displays End Mode in the status bar. When in End mode, press an arrow key to move to the edge of the current region. If the active cell is already at the edge of a current region or is a blank cell, this jumps to the next nonblank cell or to the edge of the worksheet.
End Home	Moves to the last used range in the worksheet. Similar to Ctrl+End.
Ctrl+arrow key or End followed by an arrow key	Moves to the edge of the current region. If the active cell is at the edge of a current region or is a blank cell, this jumps to the next non-blank cell or to the edge of the worksheet.
Home	Moves to the beginning of the row.
Ctrl+backspace	Scrolls to display the active cell.
F5	Displays the Go To dialog box.
Shift+F5	Displays the Find dialog box.
Shift+F4	Find Next.
Ctrl+. (period)	Moves to the next corner of the selected range.

Table 4.3 shows the shortcut keys you use to select data and cells.

Table 4.3   Shortcut Keys for Selecting Data and Cells

Shortcut Key	Action
Ctrl+spacebar	When an object is selected, this selects all objects on the worksheet.
Ctrl+spacebar	If used outside a table, this selects the entire column. If used inside a table, it toggles between selecting the data, the data and headers, and the entire column.
Shift+spacebar	Selects the entire row. If inside a table, this toggles between selecting the table row and the entire row.
Ctrl+Shift+spacebar or Ctrl+A	Selects the entire worksheet, unless the active cell is a region of two or more nonblank cells, in which case it selects the current region. Repeat the keystroke to select the entire worksheet. When the active cell is in a table, the first press selects the data rows of the table. The second press expands to include the headings and total row. The third press selects the entire worksheet.
Shift+backspace	With multiple cells selected, this reverts the selection to only the active cell.
Ctrl+ *	Selects the current region. In a pivot table, this selects the entire table.
Ctrl+/	Selects the array containing the active cell.
Ctrl+Shift+O (letter O)	Selects all cells that contain comments.

CHAPTER 4

Ctrl+\	In a selected row, this selects the cells that do not match the formula in the active cell.
Ctrl+Shift+|	In a selected column, this selects the cells that do not match the formula in the active cell.
Ctrl+[(opening square bracket)	Selects all cells directly referenced by formulas in the selection.
Ctrl+Shift+{ (opening brace)	Selects all cells directly or indirectly referenced by formulas in the selection.
Ctrl+] (closing square bracket)	Selects cells that contain formulas that directly reference the active cell.
Ctrl+Shift+} (closing brace)	Selects cells that contain formulas that directly or indirectly reference the active cell.
Alt+; (semicolon)	Selects the visible cells in the current selection.
Ctrl+Shift+Page Down	Adds the next worksheet to the selected sheets and makes the next worksheet the active sheet. This puts the workbook in group mode if it is not already in group mode. Pressing Ctrl+Shift+Page Down three times puts the current sheet and the next three sheets in group mode. Any changes made to the visible sheet are also made to all sheets in group mode. To exit group mode, right-click a sheet tab and choose Ungroup Sheets.
Ctrl+Shift+Page Up	Adds the previous worksheet to the selected sheets. This puts the workbook in group mode if it was not already in group mode.

Table 4.4 shows the shortcut keys you use to extend a selection. In extend mode, clicking any cell selects from the active cell to the clicked cell.

Table 4.4   Shortcut Keys for Extending Selections

Shortcut Key	Action
F8	Turns extend mode on or off. In extend mode, EXT appears in the status line, and the arrow keys extend the selection.
Shift+F8	Adds another range of cells to the selection. You can use the arrow keys to move to the start of the range you want to add. Then press F8 and the arrow keys to select the next range.
Shift+arrow key	Extends the selection by one cell.
Ctrl+Shift+arrow key	Extends the selection to the last nonblank cell in the same column or row as the active cell.
Shift+Home	Extends the selection to the beginning of the row.
Ctrl+Shift+Home	Extends the selection to the beginning of the worksheet.

CHAPTER 4

Ctrl+Shift+End	Extends the selection to the last used cell on the worksheet in the lower-right corner. If the cursor is in the formula bar, this selects to the end of the formula.
Shift+Page Down	Extends the selection down one screen.
Shift+Page Up	Extends the selection up one screen.
End Shift+arrow key	Extends the selection to the last nonblank cell in the same column or row as the active cell.
End+Shift+Home	Extends the selection to the last used cell on the worksheet in the lower-right corner.
End Shift+Enter	Extends the selection to the last cell in the current row.
Scroll Lock+Shift+Home	Extends the selection to the cell in the upper-left corner of the window.
Scroll Lock+Shift+End	Extends the selection to the cell in the lower-right corner of the window.

Table 4.5 shows the shortcut keys you use for entering, editing, formatting, and calculating data.

Table 4.5   Shortcut Keys for Data Entry, Formatting, and Calculating Data

Shortcut	Key Action
Enter	Completes a cell entry and selects the next cell. Often moves down one cell, but you can override this with File, Options, Advanced. In a data form, this moves to the first field in the next record. In a dialog box, this performs the action for the default button (often OK). After F10 is used to activate the menu bar, Enter selects the chosen menu item.
Alt+Enter	Starts a new line in the same cell.
Ctrl+Enter	Fills the selected cell range with the current entry.
Shift+Enter	Completes a cell entry and selects the previous cell. Often the cell above, but you can override with File, Options, Advanced. If the Move Selection Direction is set to the right, then pressing Shift+Enter will move to the left.
Tab	Completes a cell entry and selects the next cell to the right. Moves between unlocked cells in a protected worksheet. Moves to the next option in a dialog box. In a multicell selection, selects the next cell.
Shift+Tab	Completes a cell entry and selects the previous cell to the left. In a dialog box, this moves to the previous option.
Esc	Cancels a cell entry. Closes Full-Screen mode. Closes an open menu dialog box or message window.
Arrow keys	Moves one cell up, down, left, or right. If in edit mode, this moves one character up, down, left, or right.

Home	Moves to the beginning of the line. Moves to the cell in the upper-left corner of the window when Scroll Lock is turned on. Selects the first command on the menu when a menu is visible.
F4 or Ctrl+Y	Repeats the last action. When a cell reference is selected in a formula, F4 toggles between the various combinations of relative and absolute references.
Ctrl+Alt+L	Reapplies the Filter and re-sorts the data if you used any sort commands in the filter drop-down menus. Use when you are filtering a column of formulas whose value might have changed.
Ctrl+Shift+F3	Displays the Create Names from Selection dialog box to enable you to create names from row and column labels.
Ctrl+D	Fills down.
Ctrl+R	Fills to the right.
Ctrl+F3	Displays the Name Manager.
Ctrl+K	Inserts a hyperlink or enables you to edit the selected hyperlink.
Ctrl+; (semicolon)	Enters the date.
Ctrl+Shift+: (colon)	Enters the time.
Alt+down arrow	When a drop-down menu is selected, this opens the drop-down menu. Otherwise, it displays a drop-down menu of the values in the current column of a range to enable you to select a cell value from the menu.
Ctrl+Z or Alt+backspace	Undoes the last action.
= (equal sign)	Starts a formula.
Backspace	In the formula bar or while you're editing a cell, this deletes one character to the left. When you're not in edit mode, this clears the contents of the current cell and puts the cell in edit mode.
Enter	Completes a cell entry from the cell or formula bar.
Ctrl+Shift+Enter	Enters a formula as an array formula.
Shift+F3	In a formula, this displays the Insert Function dialog box.
Ctrl+A	When the insertion point is to the right of a function name in a formula, this displays the Function Arguments dialog box. See also Select All in Table 4.1.
Ctrl+Shift+A	When the insertion point is to the right of a function name in a formula, this inserts the argument names and parentheses.
F3	Pastes a defined name into a formula.
Alt+= (equal sign)	Inserts an AutoSum formula with the SUM function.
Ctrl+Shift+" (quotation mark)	Copies the value from the cell above the active cell into the cell or the formula bar.

Ctrl+' (apostrophe)	Copies a formula from the cell above the active cell into the cell or the formula bar and places the cell in edit mode. Note that the formula is an exact copy; any references are not moved down by a row.
Ctrl+` (backtick)	Alternates between displaying cell values and displaying formulas.
F9	Calculates all worksheets in all open workbooks. When a portion of a formula is selected, calculate the selected portion and then press Enter or Ctrl+Shift+Enter (for array formulas) to replace the selected portion with the calculated value.
Shift+F9	Calculates the active worksheet.
Ctrl+Alt+F9	Calculates all worksheets in all open workbooks, regardless of whether they have changed since the last calculation.
Ctrl+Alt+Shift+F9	Rechecks dependent formulas and then calculates all cells in all open workbooks, including cells not marked as needing to be calculated.
F1	Displays Help.
F2	Edits the active cell and positions the insertion point at the end of the cell contents. If in-cell editing is turned off, this moves the insertion point to the formula bar. When you're editing a formula or a reference in a dialog box, F2 toggles between Point and Enter modes. If pressing backspace starts inserting cell references instead of moving back a character, press F2 and try again.
Delete	Removes cell contents (data and formulas) from selected cells without affecting cell formats or comments. In editing mode, this deletes the character to the right of the insertion point or deletes the selection.
Ctrl+Delete	Deletes text to the end of the line.
F7	Displays the Spelling dialog box.
Shift+F2	Adds or edits a cell comment.
Ctrl+– (minus sign)	Displays the Delete dialog box.
Ctrl+Shift++ (plus sign)	Displays the Insert dialog box to insert blank cells.
Alt+' (apostrophe)	Displays the Style dialog box.
Ctrl+1	Displays the Format Cells dialog box when cells are selected. When a chart element or object is selected, this displays the Format task pane for that object.
Alt+'	Displays the Style dialog box.
Ctrl+2 or Ctrl+B	Toggles bold formatting.
Ctrl+3 or Ctrl+I	Toggles italic formatting.
Ctrl+4 or Ctrl+U	Toggles underline formatting.
Ctrl+Shift+~	Applies the General number format.

CHAPTER 4

Ctrl+Shift+$	Applies the Currency format with two decimal places (negative numbers in parentheses).
Ctrl+Shift+%	Applies the Percentage format with no decimal places.
Ctrl+Shift+^	Applies the Scientific number format with two decimal places.
Ctrl+Shift+#	Applies the Date format with the day, month, and year.
Ctrl+Shift+@	Applies the Time format with the hour and minute as well as AM or PM.
Ctrl+Shift+!	Applies the Number format with two decimal places, thousands separator, and a minus sign (–) for negative values.
Ctrl+5	Applies or removes strikethrough.
Ctrl+9	Hides the selected rows.
Ctrl+Shift+((opening parenthesis)	Unhides any hidden rows within the selection.
Ctrl+0 (zero)	Hides the selected columns.
Ctrl+Shift+) (closing parenthesis)	Unhides any hidden columns within the selection. Although this shortcut key is shown as a ToolTip in the Home tab, it has not worked since Excel 2010, and the Excel team has no immediate plans to fix it.
Ctrl+Shift+&	Applies the outline border to the selected cells.
Ctrl+Shift+_ (underscore)	Removes the outline border from the selected cells.
Ctrl+U	Toggles the formula bar between collapsed and expanded.
Ctrl+6	Toggles between hiding and displaying objects.
Ctrl+8	In group and outline mode, this toggles the display of outline symbols.
Ctrl+F1	Collapses or expands the ribbon.
Alt or F10	Displays KeyTips.
Shift+F10	Opens the right-click menu for the selection.
Alt+Shift+F10	Displays the menu or message for an Error Checking button.
Alt+F11	Opens the Visual Basic for Applications Editor.
Alt+F8	Opens the Macros dialog box.
Spacebar	In a dialog box, this selects or clears a check box or performs the action for a selected button.
Ctrl+Tab	In a dialog box, this switches to the next tab.
Ctrl+Shift+Tab	In a dialog box, this switches to the previous tab.
Arrow keys	In a dialog box or open menu, this moves between options in an open drop-down menu or between options in a group of options.
End	When a menu is open, this selects the last item in the menu.
Alt+Shift+F1	Inserts a new worksheet to the left of the current worksheet.

F11	Creates a chart of the data in the current range in a new chart sheet.
Alt+F1	Creates a chart of the data in the current range in the current worksheet.
Alt+spacebar	Opens the Control menu for the Excel window. The Control menu is attached to the XL logo in the top left of the window.
Ctrl+F4	Closes the selected workbook window.
Alt+F4	Closes Excel.
Ctrl+F10	Maximizes or restores the selected workbook window.
Ctrl+F7	When a workbook is not maximized, this moves the entire workbook window. Press Ctrl+F7. Use the arrow keys to move the window. Press Enter when you're finished or Esc to cancel.
Ctrl+F8	Performs the Size command when a workbook is not maximized. Press Ctrl+F8. Using the left or right arrow key expands the width of the window by moving the right edge of the window. Using the up or down arrow key moves the bottom edge of the window to shrink or stretch the window.
Shift+F6	Moves focus between the worksheet, ribbon, status bar, and task pane. For example, when the focus is on the status bar, you can use the arrows to move between the Record Macro, Normal, Page Layout, Page Break Preview, and Zoom icons.
Ctrl+F6	Moves between windows of a workbook. This would apply only if you used View, New Window.

CHAPTER 4

Using My Favorite Shortcut Keys

The problem with a list of hundreds of shortcut keys is that it is overwhelming. You cannot possibly absorb 238 new shortcut keys and start using them. The following sections cover some of my favorite shortcuts. Try to incorporate one new shortcut key every week into your Excel routine.

Quickly Move Between Worksheets

Ctrl+Page Down jumps to the next worksheet. Ctrl+Page Up jumps to the previous worksheet. Suppose that you have 12 worksheets named Jan, Feb, Mar, ..., Dec. If you are currently on the Jan worksheet, hold down Ctrl and press Page Down five times to move to Jun.

Jumping to the Bottom of Data with Ctrl+Arrow

Provided there are no blank cells in your data, press Ctrl+down arrow to move to the last row in the data set. Use Ctrl+up arrow to move to the first row in the data set.

Add the Shift key to select from the current cell to the bottom. If you have data in A2:J987654 and are in A2, you can hold down Ctrl+Shift while pressing the down arrow and then the right arrow to select all the data rows but exclude the headings in row 1.

Selecting the Current Region with Ctrl+*

Press Ctrl+* to select the current range. The current range is the whole data set, in all directions from the current cell until Excel hits the edge of the worksheet or a completely blank row and column. On a desktop computer, pressing Ctrl and the asterisk on the numeric keypad does the trick.

Jumping to the Next Corner of a Selection

You've just selected A2:J987654, but you are staring at the bottom-right corner of your data. Press Ctrl+period to move to the next corner of your data. Because you are at the bottom-right corner, it takes two presses of Ctrl+period to move to the top-left corner. Although this moves the active cell, it does not undo your selection.

Inside OUT

You might frequently run into a situation where the active cell is no longer in view.

This can happen when you use the scroll bars or if you select A2:J10000 by using Ctrl+Shift+Down Arrow and Ctrl+Shift+Right Arrow.

To bring the active cell back in to view, press Ctrl+Backspace.

Pop Open the Right-Click Menu Using Shift+F10

When I do my seminars, people always ask why I don't use the right-click menus. I don't use them because my hand is not on the mouse! Pressing Shift+F10 opens the right-click menu. Use the up/down arrow keys to move to various menu choices and the right-arrow key to open a fly-out menu. When you get to the item you want, press Enter to select it.

Crossing Tasks Off Your List with Ctrl+5

I love to make lists, and I love to cross stuff off my list. It makes me feel like I've gotten stuff done. Select a cell and press Ctrl+5 to apply strikethrough to the cell.

Date Stamp or Time Stamp Using Ctrl+; or Ctrl+:

Here is an easy way to remember this shortcut. What time is it right now? It is 11:21 here. There is a colon in the time. Press Ctrl+colon to enter the current time in the active cell.

Need the current date? Same keystroke, minus the Shift key. Pressing Ctrl+semicolon enters the current time.

Note that this is not the same as using =NOW() or =TODAY(). Those functions change over time. These shortcuts mark the time or date that you pressed the key, and the value does not change.

Repeating the Last Task with F4

Suppose that you just selected a cell and did Home, Delete, Delete Cells, Delete Entire Row, OK. You need to delete 24 more rows in various spots throughout your data set.

Select a cell in the next row to delete and press F4, which repeats the last command but on the currently selected cell.

Select a cell in the next row to delete and press F4. Before you know it, all 24 rows are deleted without your having to click Home, Delete, Delete Cells, Delete Entire Row, OK 24 times.

The F4 key works with 92 percent of the commands you will use. Try it. You'll love it. It'll be obvious when you try to use one of the unusual commands that cannot be redone with F4.

Adding Dollar Signs to a Reference with F4

That's right—two of my favorites in a row use F4. When you are entering a formula, and you need to change A1 to $A$1, click F4 while the insertion point is touching A1. You can press F4 again to freeze only the row with A$1. Press F4 again to freeze the column with $A1. Press again to toggle back to A1.

Choosing Items from a Slicer

It is somewhat bizarre, but you can now use shortcut keys to jump into a slicer. Using the new Multi-Select icon, you can then select or deselect items in the slicer. To get to the slicer, use Ctrl+G to display the Go To dialog box. Press S to open Go To Special. Type **B** for Objects and press Enter to select the first object on the worksheet. You might have to press Tab to get to the slicer, but then you can navigate through the slicer using the arrow keys. Pressing Enter or the spacebar on an item toggles that item. To exit the slicer, use Ctrl+G, type a cell address such as A1, and press Enter.

Finding the One Thing That Takes You Too Much Time

The shortcuts in this section are the ones I learned over the course of 20 years. They were all for tasks that I had to do repeatedly. In your job, watch for any tasks you are doing over and over, especially things that take several mouse clicks. When you identify one, try to find a shortcut key that will save you time.

TIP

When you perform commands with the mouse, do all the steps except the last one. Hover over the command until the ToolTip appears. Many times, the ToolTip tells you of the keyboard shortcut.

Using Excel 2003 Keyboard Accelerators

In legacy versions of Excel, most menu items included one underlined letter. In those versions, you could hold down the Alt key while pressing the underlined letter to invoke the menu item. In the Excel 2003 screen shown in Figure 4.6, you can display the Edit menu by pressing Alt+E, and you can select Edit, Fill, Justify by pressing Alt+E+I+J.

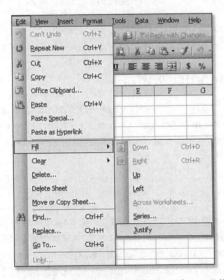

Figure 4.6   Pressing Alt+E+I+J performs Edit, Fill, Justify.

Instead of pressing Alt+E+I+J all at once, when the Edit menu is displayed, you can display the Fill fly-out menu by pressing I. Then you can perform the Justify command by pressing J.

If you have advanced Excel skills, you probably have a few of these commands memorized, such as Alt+E+I+J for Edit, Fill, Justify; Alt+E+S+V for Edit, Paste Special, Values; and Alt+D+L for

Data Validation. If you have some of these commands memorized, when you hear that the ribbon has replaced the legacy menu, you might be worried that you have to relearn all the shortcut keys. However, there is good news for the power Excel gurus who have favorite Alt shortcut keys burned into their minds—most of them still work as they did in Excel 2003.

If you regularly use the Excel 2003 keyboard accelerators but have to look at the screen to use them, you should start using the new keyboard accelerators discussed at the beginning of this chapter.

Invoking an Excel 2003 Alt Shortcut

In Excel 2003, the main menus are File, Edit, View, Insert, Format, Tools, Data, Window, and Help. The keyboard accelerator commands in Excel 2003 are Alt+F, Alt+E, Alt+V, Alt+I, Alt+O, Alt+T, Alt+D, Alt+W, and Alt+H.

If you are moving from Excel 2003 to Excel 2019, you will have the best success when trying to access commands on the Edit, View, Insert, Format, Tools, and Data menus. None of the keyboard accelerators associated with Window or Help work in Excel 2019. Alt+H takes you to the Home tab instead of the few commands on the Help menu, and Alt+W takes you to the View tab.

Some of the keyboard shortcuts associated with the File menu in Excel 2003 continue to work in Excel 2019. Pressing Alt+F opens the File menu. In Excel 2003, pressing Alt+F+O performs File, Open. It happens that O is the shortcut on the File menu for Open, so pressing Alt+F+O in Excel 2019 also performs File, Open.

TIP

You will have to train yourself to pause briefly after typing the first letter in the legacy shortcut key sequence. For example, press Alt+E, pause for a brief moment to allow Excel to display the Office Access Key window, and then press S, V for Edit, Paste Special, Values. If you do not pause, the second letter is lost because Excel displays the pop-up Office Key Sequence window.

For the shortcut keys Alt+E, Alt+V, Alt+I, Alt+O, Alt+T, and Alt+D, Excel switches into Office 2003 Access Key mode. In this mode, a ToolTip appears over the ribbon, indicating which letters you have typed so far (see Figure 4.7). When you have entered enough letters, the command is invoked. If you have forgotten the sequence, you can press Esc to exit the Excel 2003 Access Key mode.

Figure 4.7   The Office 2003 access key ToolTip shows which keys you have used so far while entering a legacy shortcut.

Determining Which Commands Work in Legacy Mode

If you try a command that no longer works in Excel 2019, nothing happens. Several commands don't make sense in the framework of Excel 2019, so they have been deprecated.

Table 4.6 lists the legacy keyboard commands and indicates which of them continue to work in Excel 2019.

Table 4.6   Excel Legacy Keyboard Commands

Legacy Shortcut	Excel 2019?	Command
Alt+F+N	Yes	File, New
Alt+F+O	Yes	File, Open
Alt+F+C	Yes	File, Close
Alt+F+S	Yes	File, Save
Alt+F+A	Yes	File, Save As
Alt+F+G	No	File, Save as Web Page
Alt+F+W	No	File, Save Workspace
Alt+F+H	No	File, File Search
Alt+F+M	No	File, Permission
Alt+F+E	No	File, Check Out or Check In (toggle)
Alt+F+R	No	File, Version History
Alt+F+B	No	File, Web Page Preview
Alt+F+U	No	File, Page Setup
Alt+F+T+S	No	File, Print Area, Set Print Area
Alt+F+T+C	No	File, Print Area, Clear Print Area
Alt+F+V	No	File, Print Preview
Alt+F+P	Yes as Alt+F+P+P	File, Print
Alt+F+D+M	No	File, Send To, Mail Recipient
Alt+F+D+S	No	File, Send To, Original Sender

Alt+F+D+C	No	File, Send To, Mail Recipient (for Review)
Alt+F+D+A	No	File, Send To, Mail Recipient (As Attachment)
Alt+F+D+R	No	File, Send To, Routing Recipient
Alt+F+D+E	No	File, Send To, Exchange Folder
Alt+F+D+O	No	File, Send To, Online Meeting Participant
Alt+F+D+X	No	File, Send To, Recipient Using Internet Fax Service
Alt+F+I	No	File, Properties
Alt+F+1	Yes	File, 1
Alt+F+2	Yes	File, 2
Alt+F+3	Yes	File, 3
Alt+F+4	Yes	File, 4
Alt+F+5	Yes	File, 5
Alt+F+6	Yes	File, 6
Alt+F+7	Yes	File, 7
Alt+F+8	Yes	File, 8
Alt+F+9	Yes	File, 9
Alt+F+T	No	File, Options
Alt+F+X	Yes	File, Exit
Alt+E+U	Yes	Edit, Undo
Alt+E+R	Yes	Edit, Repeat
Alt+E+T	Yes	Edit, Cut
Alt+E+C	Yes	Edit, Copy
Alt+E+B	Yes	Edit, Office Clipboard
Alt+E+P	Yes	Edit, Paste
Alt+E+S	Yes	Edit, Paste Special
Alt+E+H	No	Edit, Paste as Hyperlink
Alt+E+I+D	Yes	Edit, Fill, Down
Alt+E+I+R	Yes	Edit, Fill, Right
Alt+E+I+U	Yes	Edit, Fill, Up
Alt+E+I+L	Yes	Edit, Fill, Left
Alt+E+I+A	Yes	Edit, Fill, Across Worksheets
Alt+E+I+S	Yes	Edit, Fill, Series
Alt+E+I+J	Yes	Edit, Fill, Justify
Alt+E+A+A	Yes	Edit, Clear, All
Alt+E+A+F	Yes	Edit, Clear, Formats

CHAPTER 4

Alt+E+A+C	Yes	Edit, Clear, Contents
Alt+E+A+M	Yes	Edit, Clear, Comments
Alt+E+D	Yes	Edit, Delete
Alt+E+L	Yes	Edit, Delete Sheet
Alt+E+M	Yes	Edit, Move or Copy Sheet
Alt+E+F	Yes	Edit, Find
Alt+E+E	Yes	Edit, Replace
Alt+E+G	Yes	Edit, Go To
Alt+E+K	Yes	Edit, Links
Alt+E+O	No	Edit, Object
Alt+E+O+V	No	Edit, Object, Convert
Alt+V+N	Yes	View, Normal
Alt+V+P	Yes	View, Page Break Preview
Alt+V+K	No	View, Task Pane
Alt+V+T+C	No	View, Toolbars, Customize
Alt+V+F	Yes	View, Formula Bar
Alt+V+S	No	View, Status Bar
Alt+V+H	Yes	View, Header and Footer
Alt+V+C	Yes	View, Comments
Alt+V+V	Yes	View, Custom Views
Alt+V+U	Yes	View, Full Screen (Caution: Use the maximize button to return.)
Alt+V+Z	Yes	View, Zoom
Alt+I+E	Yes	Insert, Cells
Alt+I+R	Yes	Insert, Rows
Alt+I+C	Yes	Insert, Columns
Alt+I+W	Yes	Insert, Worksheet
Alt+I+H	Yes	Insert, Chart
Alt+I+S	Yes	Insert, Symbol
Alt+I+B	Yes	Insert, Page Break
Alt+I+A	Yes	Insert, Reset All Page Breaks
Alt+I+F	Yes	Insert, Function
Alt+I+N+D	Yes	Insert, Name, Define
Alt+I+N+P	Yes	Insert, Name, Paste
Alt+I+N+C	Yes	Insert, Name, Create
Alt+I+N+A	Yes	Insert, Name, Apply

Alt+I+N+L	Yes	Insert, Name, Label
Alt+I+M	Yes	Insert, Comment (Legacy)
Alt+I+A	Yes	Insert, Ink Annotations
Alt+I+P+C	Yes	Insert, Picture, Clip Art
Alt+I+P+F	Yes	Insert, Picture, From File
Alt+I+P+S	Yes	Insert, Picture, From Scanner or Camera
Alt+I+P+D	Yes	Insert, Picture, Ink Drawing and Writing
Alt+I+P+A	No	Insert, Picture, AutoShapes
Alt+I+P+W	No	Insert, Picture, WordArt
Alt+I+P+O	No	Insert, Picture, Organization Chart
Alt+I+G	No	Insert, Diagram
Alt+I+O	Yes	Insert, Object
Alt+I+I	Yes	Insert, Hyperlink
Alt+O+E	Yes	Format, Cells
Alt+O+R+E	Yes	Format, Row, Height
Alt+O+R+A	Yes	Format, Row, AutoFit
Alt+O+R+H	Yes	Format, Row, Hide
Alt+O+R+U	Yes	Format, Row, Unhide
Alt+O+C+W	Yes	Format, Column, Width
Alt+O+C+A	Yes	Format, Column, AutoFit Selection
Alt+O+C+H	Yes	Format, Column, Hide
Alt+O+C+U	Yes	Format, Column, Unhide
Alt+O+C+S	Yes	Format, Column, Standard Width
Alt+O+H+R	Yes	Format, Sheet, Rename
Alt+O+H+H	Yes	Format, Sheet, Hide
Alt+O+H+U	Yes	Format, Sheet, Unhide
Alt+O+H+B	Yes	Format, Sheet, Background
Alt+O+H+T	Yes	Format, Sheet, Tab Color
Alt+O+A	No	Format, AutoFormat
Alt+O+D	Yes	Format, Conditional Formatting
Alt+O+S	Yes	Format, Style
Alt+T+S	Yes	Tools, Spelling
Alt+T+R	Yes	Tools, Research
Alt+T+K	Yes	Tools, Error Checking
Alt+T+H+H	No	Tools, Speech, Speech Recognition

CHAPTER 4

Alt+T+H+T	No	Tools, Speech, Show Text to Speech Toolbar
Alt+T+D	Yes	Tools, Shared Workspace
Alt+T+B	Yes	Tools, Share Workbook
Alt+T+T+H	Yes	Tools, Track Changes, Highlight Changes
Alt+T+T+A	Yes	Tools, Track Changes, Accept or Reject Changes
Alt+T+W	Yes	Tools, Compare and Merge Workbooks
Alt+T+P+P	Yes	Tools, Protection, Protect Sheet
Alt+T+P+A	Yes	Tools, Protection, Allow Users to Edit Ranges
Alt+T+P+W	Yes	Tools, Protection, Protect Workbook
Alt+T+P+S	Yes	Tools, Protection, Protect and Share Workbook
Alt+T+N+M	Yes	Tools, Online Collaboration, Meet Now
Alt+T+N+S	Yes	Tools, Online Collaboration, Schedule Meeting
Alt+T+N+W	Yes	Tools, Online Collaboration, Web Discussions
Alt+T+N+N	Yes	Tools, Online Collaboration, End Review
Alt+T+G	Yes	Tools, Goal Seek
Alt+T+E	Yes	Tools, Scenarios
Alt+T+U+T	Yes	Tools, Formula Auditing, Trace Precedents
Alt+T+U+D	Yes	Tools, Formula Auditing, Trace Dependents
Alt+T+U+E	Yes	Tools, Formula Auditing, Trace Error
Alt+T+U+A	Yes	Tools, Formula Auditing, Remove All Arrows
Alt+T+U+F	Yes	Tools, Formula Auditing, Evaluate Formula
Alt+T+U+W	Yes	Tools, Formula Auditing, Show Watch Window
Alt+T+U+M	Yes	Tools, Formula Auditing, Formula Auditing Mode
Alt+T+U+S	No	Tools, Formula Auditing, Show Formula Auditing Toolbar
Alt+T+V	Yes	Tools, Solver
Alt+T+M+M	Yes	Tools, Macro, Macros
Alt+T+M+R	Yes	Tools, Macro, Record New Macro
Alt+T+M+S	Yes	Tools, Macro, Security
Alt+T+M+V	Yes	Tools, Macro, Visual Basic Editor
Alt+T+M+E	No	Tools, Macro, Microsoft Script Editor
Alt+T+I	Yes	Tools, Add-Ins
Alt+T+C	No	Tools, COM Add-Ins
Alt+T+A	Yes	Tools, AutoCorrect Options
Alt+T+C	No	Tools, Customize
Alt+T+O	No	Tools, Options

Alt+T+D	No	Tools, Data Analysis
Alt+D+S	Yes	Data, Sort
Alt+D+F+F	Yes	Data, Filter, AutoFilter
Alt+D+F+S	Yes	Data, Filter, Show All
Alt+D+F+A	Yes	Data, Filter, Advanced Filter
Alt+D+O	Yes	Data, Form
Alt+D+B	Yes	Data, Subtotals
Alt+D+L	Yes	Data, Validation
Alt+D+T	Yes	Data, Table
Alt+D+E	Yes	Data, Text to Columns
Alt+D+N	Yes	Data, Consolidate
Alt+D+G+H	Yes	Data, Group and Outline, Hide Detail
Alt+D+G+S	Yes	Data, Group and Outline, Show Detail
Alt+D+G+G	Yes	Data, Group and Outline, Group
Alt+D+G+U	Yes	Data, Group and Outline, Ungroup
Alt+D+G+A	Yes	Data, Group and Outline, Auto Outline
Alt+D+G+C	Yes	Data, Group and Outline, Clear Outline
Alt+D+G+E	Yes	Data, Group and Outline, Settings
Alt+D+P	Yes	Data, PivotTable and PivotChart Report
Alt+D+D+D	Yes	Data, Import External Data, Import Data
Alt+D+D+W	Yes	Data, Import External Data, New Web Query
Alt+D+D+N	Yes	Data, Import External Data, New Database Query
Alt+D+D+E	Yes	Data, Import External Data, List
Alt+D+I+D	No	Data, List, Discard Changes and Refresh
Alt+D+I+B	No	Data, List, Hide Border of Inactive Lists
Alt+D+X+I	Yes	Data, XML, Import
Alt+D+X+E	Yes	Data, XML, Export
Alt+D+X+R	Yes	Data, XML, Refresh XML Data
Alt+D+X+X	Yes	Data, XML, XML Source
Alt+D+X+P	Yes	Data, XML, XML Map Properties
Alt+D+X+Q	Yes	Data, XML, Edit Query
Alt+D+X+A	Yes	Data, XML, XML Expansion Packs Edit Query
Alt+D+D+A	Yes	Data, Import External Data, Data Range Properties
Alt+D+D+M	Yes	Data, Import External Data, Parameters
Alt+D+I+C	Yes	Data, List, Create List

CHAPTER 4

Alt+D+I+R	Yes	Data, List, Resize List
Alt+D+I+T	Yes	Data, List, Total Row
Alt+D+I+V	Yes	Data, List, Convert to Range
Alt+D+I+P	Yes	Data, List, Publish List
Alt+D+I+L	No	Data, List, View List on Server
Alt+D+I+U	No	Data, List, Unlink List
Alt+D+I+Y	No	Data, List, Synchronize
Alt+D+R	Yes	Data, Refresh Data
Alt+W+N	No	Window, New Window
Alt+W+A	No	Window, Arrange
Alt+W+B	No	Window, Compare Side by Side with Filename
Alt+W+H	No	Window, Hide
Alt+W+U	No	Window, Unhide
Alt+W+S	No	Window, Split
Alt+W+F	No	Window, Freeze Panes
Alt+W+1	No	Window, 1
Alt+W+2	No	Window, 2
Alt+W+3	No	Window, 3
Alt+W+4	No	Window, 4
Alt+W+5	No	Window, 5
Alt+W+6	No	Window, 6
Alt+W+7	No	Window, 7
Alt+W+8	No	Window, 8
Alt+W+9	No	Window, 9
Alt+W+M	No	Window, More Windows
Alt+H+H	No	Help, Microsoft Excel Help
Alt+H+O	No	Help, Show the Office Assistant
Alt+H+M	No	Help, Microsoft Office Online
Alt+H+C	No	Help, Contact Us
Alt+H+L	No	Help, Lotus 1-2-3 Help
Alt+H+K	No	Help, Check for Updates
Alt+H+R	No	Help, Detect and Repair
Alt+H+V	No	Help, Activate Product
Alt+H+F	No	Help, Customer Feedback Options
Alt+H+A	No	Help, About Microsoft Office Excel

Some people liked using Alt+F+T+S in Excel 2003 for File, Print Area, Set Print Area. If you are one of those people, you will be unhappy to hear that your favorite shortcut key is not supported in Excel 2019. Instead, use Alt+P+R+S. However, most of the powerful and common shortcut keys are still available, so there is a good chance that your knowledge of past shortcut keys will help when you upgrade to Excel 2019.

CHAPTER 4

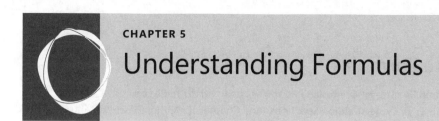

Understanding Formulas

Excel's forté is performing calculations. When you use Excel, you typically use a combination of cells with numbers and cells with formulas. After you design a spreadsheet to calculate something, you can change the numbers used in the assumption cells and then watch Excel instantly calculate new results.

Getting the Most from This Chapter

Even if you think you know about formulas, you should review these points:

- Everyone should read the "Double-Click the Fill Handle to Copy a Formula" section. Somehow, most people have learned to drag the fill handle to copy a formula. This leads to horrible frustration on long data sets, as they go flying past the end of the data. This simple but powerful trick is the one that universally amazes attendees of my seminar.

- Honestly answer this question: Do you really understand the difference between cell H1 and cell $H$1? If you think the latter has anything to do with currency, you need to review the "Overriding Relative Behavior: Absolute Cell References" section thoroughly. This isn't a trick, but one of the fundamental building blocks to creating Excel worksheets. Roughly 5 percent of the people in a Power Excel seminar do not understand this concept, and about 70 percent of the people in a community computer club presentation do not understand it. If you don't know when and why to use the dollar signs, you are in good company with 20 million other people using Excel. It is worth taking time to learn this essential technique.

- There are three ways to enter formulas, and I believe my preferred way is the best. I probably will not convince you to change, but when you understand my way, you can enter formulas far faster than by using the other two ways. To get a good understanding of the alternatives, read the "Three Methods of Entering Formulas" section later in this chapter.

Introduction to Formulas

This chapter and Chapter 6, "Controlling Formulas," deal with formula basics. The chapters between Chapter 7, "Understanding Functions," and Chapter 10, "Other Functions," introduce adding functions to your formulas. Chapter 11, "Connecting Worksheets and Workbooks," introduces formulas that calculate data found on other worksheets or in other workbooks. Chapter 12, "Array Formulas and Names in Excel," provides interesting examples such as 3D formulas and the all-powerful array formulas.

Because of the record-oriented nature of spreadsheets, you can generally build a formula once and then copy that formula to hundreds or thousands of cells without changing anything in the formula.

Formulas Versus Values

When looking at an Excel grid, you cannot tell the difference between a cell with a formula and one that contains numbers. To see if a cell contains a number or a formula, select the cell. Look in the formula bar. If the formula bar contains a number, as shown in Figure 5.1, you know that it is a static value. If the formula bar contains a formula, you know that the number shown in the grid is the result of a formula calculation (see Figure 5.2). Keep in mind that formulas start with an equal sign.

Figure 5.1   The formula bar reveals whether a value is a static number or a calculation. In this case, cell E2 contains a static number.

Figure 5.2   In this case, cell E2 contains the result of a formula calculation. A formula starts with an equal sign.

Entering Your First Formula

Your first formula was probably a SUM function, entered with the AutoSum button. However, this discussion is talking about a pure mathematical formula that uses a value in a cell that's added, subtracted, divided, or multiplied by a number or another cell.

> ## TROUBLESHOOTING
>
> **Although your first formula was likely a sum function, many people mistakenly believe that every formula must include the sum function.**
>
> **If you need to multiply A2 by B2 and subtract C2, the formula should simply be =A2*B2-C2. There is no need to wrap this formula in the SUM function like this: =SUM(A2*B2-C2).**

Billions of variations of formulas can be used. Everyday life throws situations at you that can be solved with a formula. Keep these important points in mind as you start tinkering with your own formulas:

- Every formula starts with an equal sign.

- Entering formulas is just like typing an equation in a calculator with one exception (see the next point).

- If one of the terms in your formula is already stored in a cell in Excel, you can point to that cell's address instead of typing the number into that cell. Using this method enables you to change the value in one cell and then watch all the formulas recalculate.

To illustrate these points, see the steps to building a basic formula included in the following example.

Building a Formula

You want to enter a formula to calculate a target sales price, as shown in Figure 5.3. Cell D2 shows the product cost. In column E, you want to calculate the list price as two times the cost plus $3.

Figure 5.3   The formula in cell E2 recalculates if the value in cell D2 changes.

To enter a formula, follow these steps:

1. Select cell E2.

2. Type an equal sign. The equal sign tells Excel that you are starting a formula.

3. Type **2*D2** to indicate that you want to multiply two times the value in cell D2.

4. Type **+3** to add three to the result. If your formula reads =2*D2+3, proceed to step 5. Otherwise, use the backspace key to correct the formula.

5. Press Enter. Excel calculates the formula in cell E2.

By default, Excel usually moves the cell pointer down or to the right after you finish entering a formula. You should move the cell pointer back to cell E2 to inspect the formula, as shown in Figure 5.3. Note that Excel shows a number in the grid, but the formula bar reveals the formula behind the number.

The Relative Nature of Formulas

The formula =2*D2+3 really says, "multiply two by the cell immediately to the left of me and then add three." If you need to put this formula in cells E3 to E999, you do not need to re-enter the formula 997 times. Instead, copy the formula and paste it to all the cells. When you do, Excel copies the essence of the formula: "Multiply two by the cell to the left of me and add three." As you copy the formula to cell E3, the formula becomes =2*D3+3. Excel handles all this automatically. Figure 5.4 shows the formula after it is copied.

	A	B	C	D	E
1			SKU	Mfg Cost	List Price
2			J41	16.4	35.8
3			J20	14.47	31.94
4			I51	16.14	35.28

E3   fx   =2*D3+3

Figure 5.4   After you paste the formula, Excel automatically updates the cell reference to point to the current row.

Excel's capability to change D2 to D3 in the formula is called *relative referencing*. This is the default behavior of a reference. Sometimes, you do not want Excel to change a reference as the formula is copied, as explained in the next section.

Overriding Relative Behavior: Absolute Cell References

Relative referencing, which is Excel's ability to change a formula as it is copied, is what makes spreadsheets so useful. At times, however, you need part of a formula to always point at one particular cell. This happens a lot when you have a setting at the top of the worksheet, such as a growth rate or a tax rate. It would be nice to change this cell once and have all the formulas use the new rate.

The following example sets up a sample worksheet that exhibits this problem and shows how to use an arcane notation style to solve the problem. When you see a reference with two dollar signs, such as $G$1, this indicates an absolute reference to G1. An absolute reference is a cell or range address in which the row numbers and the column letters are locked and do not change during copying. Absolute references have a dollar sign before each column letter and each row number. Examples include $G$1 and $T$2:$W$99.

Suppose that you have a sales tax factor in a single cell at the top of a worksheet. After you enter the formula =C2*G1, it accurately calculates the tax in cell D2, as shown in Figure 5.5.

D2		×	✓	fx	=C2*G1		
	A	B	C	D	E	F	G
1	SKU	Mfg Cost	List Price	Sales Tax		Tax Factor	6.25%
2	J41	16.4	35.8	2.24			
3	J20	14.47	31.94				
4	I51	16.14	35.28				

Figure 5.5   This formula works fine in row 2.

However, when you copy the same formula to cell D3, you get a zero as the result. As you can see in Figure 5.6, Excel correctly changed cell C2 to C3 in the copied formula. However, Excel also changed G1 to G2. Because there is nothing in G2, the formula calculates a zero.

The formula now points to empty cell G2.

SUM		×	✓	fx	=C3*G2		
	A	B	C	D	E	F	G
1	SKU	Mfg Cost	List Price	Sales Tax		Tax Factor	6.25%
2	J41	16.4	35.8	2.24			
3	J20	14.47	31.94	=C3*G2			
4	I51	16.14	35.28	0.00			

Figure 5.6   This formula fails in row 3.

Because the sales tax factor is only in G1, you want Excel to always point to G1. To make this happen, you need to build the original formula as =C2*$G$1. The two dollar signs tell Excel that you do not want to have the reference change as the formula is copied. The $ before the G freezes the reference to always point to column G. The $ before the 1 freezes the reference to always point to row 1. Now, when you copy this formula from cell D2 to other cells in column D, Excel changes the formula to =C3*$G$1, as shown in Figure 5.7.

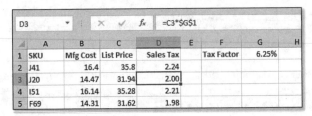

Figure 5.7   The dollar signs in the formula make sure that the copied formula always points to cell G1.

To recap, a reference with two dollars signs is called an *absolute reference*.

If you are never going to copy the formula to the left or right, you can safely use =C2*G$1. This formula freezes only the row number. Given the shape of the current data, it is likely that using a single dollar sign will be valid.

Using Mixed References to Combine Features of Relative and Absolute References

In some situations, you might want to build a reference that has only one dollar sign. For example, in Figure 5.8, you want to use the monthly bonus rate in row 3, but you want to allow the column to change. In this case, the formula for cell B13 would be =B6*B$3.

B13			fx	=B6*B$3		
	A	B	C	D	E	F	G
1	**Widget Sales Bonus Calculation**						
2							
3	Bonus	3%	2%	0%	2%	3%	1%
4							
5	$ Sold	Jan	Feb	Mar	Apr	May	Jun
6	Rob	6237	9009	5247	9207	7029	6435
7	Matt	7722	5544	6138	5445	9603	5544
8	Ken	8712	7524	6237	6336	8415	7623
9	Miguel	5148	7524	9603	5049	5643	5445
10	Kasper	5841	6534	8118	8910	9009	9405
11							
12	Bonus	Jan	Feb	Mar	Apr	May	Jun
13	Rob	187.11	180.18	0.00	184.14	210.87	64.35
14	Matt	231.66	110.88	0.00	108.90	288.09	55.44
15	Ken	261.36	150.48	0.00	126.72	252.45	76.23
16	Miguel	154.44	150.48	0.00	100.98	169.29	54.45
17	Kasper	175.23	130.68	0.00	178.20	270.27	94.05

Figure 5.8   By having the dollar sign before the 3 in B$3, you lock the reference to row 3 but allow the formula to point to columns D, E, and so on as you copy the formula.

When you copy this formula, it always points to the bonus amount in row 3, but the remaining elements of the formula are relative. For example, the formula in E15 is =E8*E$3, which multiplies Ken's April sales by the April bonus rate.

There are two kinds of mixed references. One mixed reference freezes the row number and allows the column letter to change, as in A$1. The other mixed reference freezes the column letter but allows the row number to change, as in $A1. No one has thought up clever names to distinguish between these references, so they are simply called *mixed references*.

To illustrate the other kind of mixed reference, as shown in Figure 5.9, suppose you want a single formula to multiply the daily rate from column A by the number of days in row 4. This formula requires both kinds of mixed references.

Figure 5.9   You can create a formula by using a combination of dollar signs to allow cell C6 to be copied to all cells in the table.

In this case, you want the cell A6 reference to always point to column A, even when the formula is copied to the right. Therefore, the A6 portion of the formula should be entered as $A6. You also want the C5 portion of the formula to always point to row 5, even when the formula is copied down the rows. Therefore, the C5 portion of the formula should be entered as C$5.

Using the F4 Key to Simplify Dollar Sign Entry

In the preceding section, you entered quite a few dollar signs in formulas. The good news is that you do not have to type the dollar signs! Instead, immediately after entering a reference, press the F4 key to toggle the reference from a relative reference to an absolute reference, which automatically has the dollar signs before the row and column. If you press F4 again, the reference toggles to a mixed reference with a dollar sign before the row number. When you press F4 once again, the reference toggles to a mixed reference with a dollar sign before the column letter. Pressing F4 one more time returns the reference to a relative reference. You might find it easier to choose the right reference by looking at the various reference options offered by the F4 key.

The following sequence shows how the F4 key works while you are entering a formula. This particular example was included because it requires two types of mixed references.

The important concept is that you start pressing F4 after typing a cell reference but before you type a mathematical operator.

1. Type =**A6**.

2. Before typing the asterisk to indicate multiplication, press the F4 key. On the first press of F4, the reference changes to =$A$6.

3. Press the F4 key again. The reference changes to A$6 to freeze the reference to row 6. This still isn't right because freezing the reference to row 6 will not help.

4. Press F4 one more time. Excel locks just the column, changing the reference to =$A6. This is the version of the reference you want. As you copy the formula across, the formula always points back to column A. As you copy the formula down, the row number in this reference is allowed to change to point to other rows.

5. To continue the formula, type an asterisk to indicate multiplication and then click cell C5 with the mouse. Press F4 twice to change C5 to a reference that locks only the row (that is, C$5).

6. Press Enter to accept the formula.

7. When you copy the formula from cell C6 to the range C6:G28, the formula automatically multiplies the rate in column A by the number of days in row 5. Figure 5.10 shows the copied formula in cell E9. The formula correctly multiplies the 10-dollar rate in cell A9 by the 24 hours figure in cell E5.

SUM	▾ :	✕ ✓ fx	=$A9*E$5			
	A	B	C	D	E	F	G
1		**XYZ Tool Rental**					
2		**Price List**					
3							
4			-------- Number of Hours ---->				
5	Per Hour	Item	4	8	24	48	72
6	13.50	Aerator TA-17D Split Drive	$54.00	$108.00	$324.00	$648.00	$972.00
7	18.00	Aerator TA-25D Split Drive	$72.00	$144.00	$432.00	$864.00	$1,296.00
8	10.75	Aerator Tow Behind 36" w/weight canisters	$43.00	$86.00	$258.00	$516.00	$774.00
9	10.00	Auger One Man	$40.00	$80.00	=$A9*E$5	$480.00	$720.00

Figure 5.10   By using the correct combination of row and column mixed references, you can enter this formula once and successfully copy it to the entire rectangular range.

Using F4 After a Formula Is Entered

The F4 trick described in the preceding section works immediately after you enter a reference. If you try to change cell A6 after you type the asterisk, pressing the F4 key has no effect.

However, you can still use F4 by clicking somewhere in the formula bar adjacent to the characters A6. Pressing F4 now adds dollar signs to that reference.

> ### NOTE
>
> **After you press F4 again, Excel returns the reference to the relative state A6. As you continue to press F4, Excel toggles between the four modes. It is fine to toggle between them all and then choose the correct one. If you accidentally toggle past the $A6 version, just keep pressing F4 until the correct mode comes up again.**

Using F4 on a Rectangular Range

Some functions allow you to specify a rectangular range. For example, in Figure 5.11, you would like to enter a formula to calculate year-to-date sales. Although =SUM(B2:B13) works for cell C13, you cannot copy this formula to the other cells in the column. To copy this formula, you need to change the formula to =SUM(B$2:B13).

Figure 5.11   Using F4 at this point never produces the desired result of B$2:B13.

At this point in the figure, you might be tempted to press the F4 key. This does not work. If you select B2:B13 with the mouse or arrow keys, pressing F4 now converts the reference to the fully absolute range $B$2:$B$13. Continuing to press F4 toggles to B$2:B$13, then $B2:$B13, and then B2:B13. Excel does not even attempt to go through the other 12 possible combinations of dollar signs to offer B$2:B13 eventually. If you typed B2:B13, pressing F4 adjusts only the B13 reference.

In this case, you need to click the insertion point just before, just after, or in the middle of the characters B2 in the formula. If you then press F4, toggle through the various dollar sign combinations on the B2 reference. Pressing F4 twice results in the proper combination, as shown in Figure 5.12.

11	Oct	55770	
12	Nov	30420	
13	Dec	48240	=SUM(B$2:B13
14			SUM(**number1**, [number2], …)
15			

Figure 5.12   Using F4 is tricky when your reference is a rectangular range—you must click into the formula.

TROUBLESHOOTING

Avoid referring to many cells when you need to refer to a single cell.

In the screenshot below, a formula of =B$2:B$9 brings the value from B4 to the formula in D4. While the formula works, it is taking advantage of an arcane concept called Implicit Intersection. Instead, simply enter =B2 in cell E2 and copy down.

With the introduction of Modern Array formulas in Office 365, the bad habit of entering =B2:B9 when you really need only B4 will lead to Excel spilling the formula into adjacent cells.

	A	B	C	D
1	Product	Revenue		
2	Apple	4504		4504
3	Banana	2767		2767
4	Cherry	4066		4066
5	Date	1050		1050
6	Elderberry	4523		4523
7	Fig	1810		1810
8	Guava	4726		4726
9	Honeydew	1428		1428

D4 = =B$2:B$9

Three Methods of Entering Formulas

In the examples in the previous sections, you entered a formula by typing it. You generally need to start a formula by typing the equal sign (or the plus sign); after that point, you have three options:

- Type the complete formula as described in the previous sections.

- Type the operator keys, but use the mouse to touch cell references. In this book, this is referred to as the *mouse method*.

TIP

If you use the mouse method to ente[r] border with the mouse, ignore the formula bar and
(QAT) to icons for Equal Sign, Plus Si[gn]
Exponentiation Sign, and Dollar Sign
ing back to the keyboard. There isn't
mark to the left of the formula bar f[or]

should try this method for half a day. When you get a
ow keys, you can enter formulas much faster by using

Entering Formulas Using the

The arrow key method is popular with peo[ple]
Lotus 1-2-3 release 2.2. It is worthwhile to
all formula entry can be accomplished usi[ng]
it works:

F
6.25%

1. In cell C2, type + using the numeric
   keypad, then press the equal sign o[r]

2. Press the left-arrow key to move th[e] to the original cell. Thus, you only have to press the right
   cell, which is the one with a green s of four times to arrive at cell F2.
   second cell pointer that you can us[e]
   in Figure 5.14, the temporary formu[la] e flashing cell border to the correct location, cell F1.
   ula bar now shows +B2*F1.

   to the F1 reference.

	A	B	C	D	E
	Invoice	Merch $	Tax		Rate
1					
2	1701	116.7	+B2		
3	1702	134.71			
4	1703	129.56			
5	1704	119.81			

B2 × ✓ fx +B2

ula and keep the cell pointer in cell C2.

s, with no trips to the mouse. You can enter formulas
eferences, parentheses, or exponents by using just the

Figure 5.14 By using the arrow keys durin[g] eypad.
used to navigate to a cell refe[rence]

3. To accept cell B2 as the correct refe[rence]
   example, * or +), a parenthesis, or

4. Note that the dashed cell pointer [is on] just the arrow keys and the number keypad.
   cell, C2. rkers mad with formulas that start with =+.

   ith an equal sign. However, to make former Lotus
5. Press the right-arrow key three tim llows you to start a formula with a plus sign. Power
   F2. With each key press, the tempo t using a plus sign enables them to start a formula
   formula (+B2*D2, +B2*E2, and +B2 cause I routinely start formulas with the plus sign,
   you press the right-arrow key thre instead of just =. Even though the formulas appear

that way onscreen, I don't actually enter the equal sign. When a formula starts with a plus sign, Excel adds an equal sign and does not remove the plus sign, so you end up with a formula that looks like =+B2*$F$1. I tell people that I am not going to work more slowly in Excel just to allay their irrational fears of =+.

Entering the Same Formula in Many Cells

So far in this chapter, you have entered a formula in one cell and then copied and pasted to get the formula in many cells. To enter the same formula in many cells, you can use three alternatives:

- Preselect the entire range where the formulas need to go. Enter the formula for the first cell and press Ctrl+Enter to enter the formula in the entire selection simultaneously.

- Enter the formula in the first cell and then use the fill handle to copy the formula.

- Beginning with Excel 2007, the method is to define the range as a table. When you use this method, the new formulas are copied down a column automatically.

Copying a Formula by Using Ctrl+Enter

This strategy works when you are entering formulas for one or more screens that are full of data:

1. If you have just a few cells, select them before entering the formula.

2. Click in the first cell and drag down to the last cell, as shown in Figure 5.16. Notice from the name box that the active cell is the first cell.

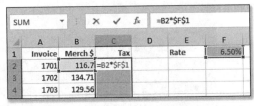

Figure 5.16   Even with a large range selected, the formula is built only in the active cell.

3. Enter the formula by using any of the three methods described earlier in this chapter. Even if you use the arrow key method, Excel keeps the entire range selected. Figure 5.16 shows a formula after you press F4 to convert the F1 reference to $F$1.

4. At this point, you would normally press Enter to complete the formula. Instead, press Ctrl+Enter to enter this formula in the entire selected range. Note that Excel does not enter =B2*$F$1 in each cell. Instead, it converts the formula as if it were copied to each cell.

Copying a Formula by Dragging the Fill Handle

If you want to enter a formula in one cell and then copy it to the other cells in a range, you can use the fill handle, which is the square dot in the lower-right corner of the cell pointer. There are two ways to use the fill handle:

- Drag the fill handle.

- Double-click the fill handle.

The dragging method works fine when you have less than one screen full of data:

1. Enter the formula in cell B2.

2. Press Ctrl+Enter to accept the formula and keep the cell pointer in cell B2.

3. Click the fill handle. You know that you are above the fill handle when the mouse pointer changes to a thick plus sign, as shown in Figure 5.17. Drag the mouse down to the last row of data.

Fill Handle

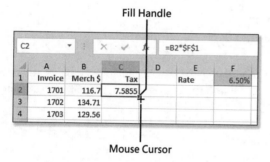

Mouse Cursor

Figure 5.17   You can copy a formula by double-clicking or dragging the fill handle.

4. When you release the mouse button, the original cell is copied to all the cells in the selected range.

This method is fine for copying a formula to a few cells. However, if you have thousands or hundreds of thousands of cells, it is annoying to drag to the last row. You invariably end up flying past the last row. Note that Excel 2016 automatically slows down and briefly pauses at the last row. However, it is far easier to copy a formula by double-clicking the fill handle.

Double-Click the Fill Handle to Copy a Formula

In most data sets, double-clicking the fill handle is the fastest way to copy the formula.

Instead of dragging the fill handle, double-click the fill handle. Provided one of the cells to the left, right, or below the active cell is nonblank, Excel fills to the bottom of the current region.

CHAPTER 5

Before Excel 2010, using this method would fail if there were a few blank cells in the column to the left. Starting in Excel 2010, the logic was improved, and the technique almost always finds the correct number of rows based on the adjacent data.

Use the Table Tool to Copy a Formula

When you define your current data set as a table, Excel automatically copies new formulas down to the rest of the cells in the table.

Figure 5.18 shows an Excel worksheet that has headings at the top and many rows of data below the headings.

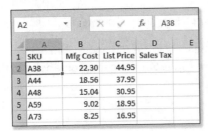

Figure 5.18   This is a typical worksheet in Excel.

To define a range as a table, select a cell within the data set and press Ctrl+T. Excel uses its IntelliSense to guess the edges of the table. If its guess is correct, click OK in the Create Table dialog box, as shown in Figure 5.19.

Figure 5.19   The Create Table dialog box.

Ctrl+T is one of four entry points for creating a table. You can still use the Excel 2003 shortcut of Ctrl+L (because the feature was called a List in Excel 2003). You can choose Format as Table on the Home tab. You can choose the Table icon from the Insert tab.

As shown in Figure 5.20, after Excel recognizes the range as a table, several changes occur:

- The table is formatted with the default formatting. Depending on your preferences, this might include banded rows or columns.

- AutoFilter drop-down menus are added to the headings.

- Any formulas you enter use the headings to refer to cells within the table.

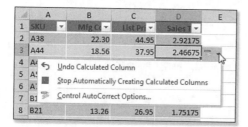

Figure 5.20   Defining a range as a table provides formatting and powerful features such as Auto-filters and natural language formulas.

Now when you enter a formula in the table, Excel automatically copies that formula down to all rows of the table.

NOTE

As shown in Figure 5.21, a lightning bolt drop-down menu appears to the right of cell D3. This drop-down menu offers you the opportunity to stop Excel from automatically copying the formula down.

Figure 5.21   Thanks to the Table tool in Excel, a new formula entered anywhere in column D is copied automatically to all the cells in column D.

CHAPTER 5

Although you can go a long way with simple formulas, it is also possible to build extremely powerful formulas. The topics in this chapter explain the finer points of formula operators, date math, and how Excel distinguishes between cutting and copying cells referenced in formulas.

Formula Operators

Excel offers the mathematical operators shown in Table 6.1.

Table 6.1   Mathematical Operators

Operator	Description
+	Addition
-	Subtraction
*	Multiplication
/	Division or fractions
^	Exponents
()	Overriding the order of operations
-	Unary minus (for negative numbers)
&	Joining text (concatenation)
>	Greater than
<	Less than
>=	Greater than or equal to
<=	Less than or equal to
<>	Not equal to
=	Equal to

CHAPTER 6

,	Union operator, as in SUM(A1,B2)
:	Range operator, as in SUM(A1:B2)
\<space\>	Intersection operator, as in SUM(A:J 2:4)
#	Formula Spill Operator, as in =AVERGAGE(#E1)

Order of Operations

When a formula contains many calculations, Excel evaluates the formula in a certain order. Rather than calculating from left to right as a calculator might, Excel performs certain types of calculations, such as multiplication, before calculations such as addition.

You can override the default order of operations with parentheses. If you do not use parentheses, Excel uses the following order of operations:

> NOTE
>
> To see how Excel calculates the formulas you enter, first, enter a formula in a cell. Next, from the Formulas tab, select Formulas, Formula Auditing, Evaluate Formula to open the Evaluate Formula dialog box. Repeatedly click the Evaluate button and watch the formula calculate in slow motion.

1. Unary minus is evaluated first.

2. Exponents are evaluated next.

3. Multiplication and division are handled next, in a left-to-right manner.

4. Addition and subtraction are handled next, in a left-to-right manner.

The following sections provide some examples of order of operations.

Unary Minus Example

The unary minus is always evaluated first. Think about when you use exponents to raise a number to a power. If you raise –2 to the second power, Excel calculates (–2) × (–2), which is +4. Therefore, the formula =–2^2 evaluates to 4.

If you raise –2 to the third power, Excel calculates (–2) × (–2) × (–2). Multiplying –2 by –2 results in +4, and multiplying +4 by –2 results in –8. Therefore, the simple formula =–2^3 generates –8.

You need to understand a subtle but important distinction. When Excel encounters the formula =–2^3, it evaluates the unary minus first. If you want the exponent to happen first and then have the unary minus applied, you have to write the formula as =–(2^3). However, in a formula such as =100–2^3, the minus sign is considered to be a subtraction operator and not a unary minus sign. In this case, 2^3 is evaluated as 8, and then 8 is subtracted from 100. To indicate a unary minus, use =100–(–2^3).

Addition and Multiplication Example

The order of operations is important when you are mixing addition/subtraction with multiplication/division. For example, if you want to add 20 to 30 and then multiply by 1.06 to calculate a total with tax, the following formula leads to the wrong result:

=20+30*1.06

The result you are looking for is 53. However, the Evaluate Formula dialog box shows that Excel calculates the formula =20+30*1.06 like so (see Figure 6.1):

1.06 × 30 = 31.8
31.8 + 20 = 51.8

Figure 6.1   The underline indicates that Excel does the multiplication first.

Excel's answer is $1.20 less than expected because the formula is not written with the default order of operations in mind.

To force Excel to do the addition first, you need to enclose the addition in parentheses:

=(20+30)*1.06

The addition in parentheses is done first, and then 50 is multiplied by 1.06 to get the correct answer of $53.

Stacking Multiple Parentheses

If you need to use multiple sets of parentheses when doing math by hand, you might write math formulas with square brackets and curly braces, like this:

{3-[6*4*3-(3-6)+2]/27}*14

In Excel, you use multiple sets of parentheses, as follows:

=(3-(6*4*3-(3-6)+2)/27)*14

Formulas with multiple parentheses in Excel are confusing. Excel does two things to try to improve this situation:

- As you type a formula, Excel colors the parentheses in a set order: black, red, purple, green, violet, topaz, aquamarine, blue. The colors then repeat starting with red. By far, the most common problem is having one too few or one too many parentheses. By using red as the second color, the last parenthesis in most unbalanced equations is red. Excel uses black only for the first parenthesis and for the closing match to that parenthesis. This means if your last parenthesis in the formula is not black, you have the wrong number of parentheses.

- When you type a closing parenthesis, Excel shows the opening parenthesis in bold for a fraction of a second. This would be more helpful if Excel kept the opening parenthesis in bold for 5 seconds or 20 seconds.

Understanding Error Messages in Formulas

Don't be frustrated when a formula returns an error result. This eventually happens to everyone. The key is to understand the difference between the various error values so that you can begin to troubleshoot the problem.

As you enter formulas, you might encounter some errors, including those listed next:

- **#VALUE!**—This error indicates that you are trying to do math with nonnumeric data. For example, the formula =4+"apple" returns a #VALUE! error. This error also occurs if you try to enter an array formula but fail to use Ctrl+Shift+Enter, as described in Chapter 12, "Array Formulas and Names in Excel."

- **#DIV/0!**—This error occurs when a number is divided by zero—that is, when a fraction's denominator evaluates to zero.

- **#REF!**—This error occurs when a cell reference is not valid. For example, this error can occur if one of the cells referenced in the formula has been deleted. It can also occur if you cut and paste another cell over a cell referenced in this formula. You may also get this error if you are using Dynamic Data Exchange (DDE) formulas to link to external systems and those systems are not running.

- **#N/A!**—This error occurs when a value is not available to a function or a formula. #N/A! errors most often occur because of key values not being found during lookup functions. They can occur as a result of HLOOKUP, LOOKUP, MATCH, or VLOOKUP. They can also result when an array formula has one argument that is not the same shape as the other arguments or when a function omits one or more required arguments. Interestingly, when an #N/A! error enters a range, all subsequent calculations that refer to the range have a value of #N/A!.

- **NULL!**—This error usually indicates that two cell references by a formula are separated by a space instead of a colon or comma. The space operator is the intersection operator. If there are no cells in common between the two references, a NULL! error appears.

- **SPILL!**—This error is new in Office 365 after the summer of 2018. If you use one of the new =A1:A100 formulas in cell C1 and some non-blank cells appear in the 100 cells needed for the response, you will see a SPILL! error in all cells. Other causes of the SPILL error include the formula spilling beyond the edge of the worksheet or running out of memory.

- **#FIELD!**—This error is new in 2018 and indicates a problem with a Linked Data Type. The error occurs if the referenced field is not available in a linked data type or if the formula is referencing a cell that does not contain a linked data type. Here is an example: Type **Florida** in cell A1 and use the Data Types gallery on the Data tab to mark that cell as geography. You can use **=A1.Population** to retrieve the population. However, if you change cell **A1** to **Apple**, the #FIELD! error will appear because Excel does not have a geography definition for Apple.

- **#CALC**—New as of late 2018 or early 2019 for Office 365 customers. The calculation engine can't resolve the formula yet, but the syntax might be supported in the future. The Excel team has plans for a series of new functions that will roll out over several releases, and the #CALC error is needed if they plan on rolling out part of a two-function solution.

- **######**—This is not really an error. Instead, it means that the result is too wide to display in the current column width, so you need to make the column wider to see the actual result. Although ###### usually means the column is not wide enough, it can also appear if you are subtracting one date or time from another and end up with a negative amount. Excel does not allow negative dates or times unless you switch to the 1904 Date System.

In Figure 6.2, cell E17 is a simple SUM function. It is returning an #N/A error because cell E11 contains the same error. Cell E11 contains the formula =D11*C11. The root cause of the problem is the VLOOKUP function in cell D11. Because Fig cannot be found in the product table in $G$7:$H$9, the VLOOKUP function returns #N/A.

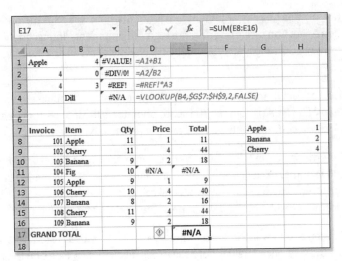

Figure 6.2   The error in E17 is actually caused by an error two calculations earlier.

Figure 6.2 shows only a small table, so it is relatively easy to find the earlier #N/A errors. How-ever, when you're totaling 100,000 rows, it can be difficult to find the one offending cell. To track down errors, follow these steps:

1.   Select the cell that shows the final error. To the left of that cell, you should see an exclamation point in a yellow diamond.

2.   Hover the cursor over the yellow diamond to reveal a drop-down menu arrow.

3.   From the drop-down menu, select Trace Error. Excel draws in red arrows pointing back to the source of the error, as shown in Figure 6.3. For example, from the original #N/A! error in cell D11, blue arrows demonstrate what cells were causing the error. To remove the arrows, use the Remove Arrows command on the Formulas tab.

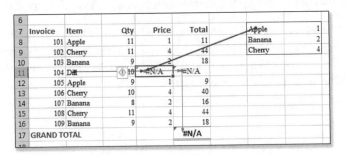

Figure 6.3   Selecting Trace Error reveals the cells leading to the error.

Using Formulas to Join Text

You use the ampersand (&) operator when you need to join text. In Excel, the & operator is known as the concatenation operator.

When using the & operator, you often need to include a space between the two items that are combined to improve the appearance of the output. For example, if the cells contain first name and last name, you want to have a space between the names. To include a space between cells, you follow the & with a space enclosed in quotes, as in &" ". As shown in Figure 6.4, the formula =A2&" "&B2 joins the first name and last name with a space in between.

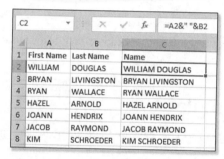

Figure 6.4   You can join cells with any text in quotation marks.

> ## NOTE
>
> Excel 2019 now features a TEXTJOIN function. There are cases where TEXTJOIN will be easier than using the ampersand operator. To read more about TEXTJOIN, see "Joining Text with TEXTJOIN" in Chapter 8.

Joining Text and a Number

In many cases, you can use the & operator to join text with a number or a date. In Figure 6.5, the formula in cell E2 joins the words "The price is $" with the result of the calculation in cell D2. Although D2 is formatted to show only two decimal places, the underlying answer has more decimal places. The regular concatenation formula in E2 shows the extra decimal places. To fix the problem, use the TEXT() function around D2 in the formula. Specify any valid numeric formatting code in quotes as the second argument. The corrected formula in E6 uses TEXT(D6,"#,##0.00").

When you join text to a date or time, you see the serial number that Excel stores behind the scenes instead of the date. Cell E3 in Figure 6.5 shows the result of joining text with a date. Use the TEXT() function around the date to format it as shown in cell E7.

Figure 6.5   When joining numbers or dates, use the TEXT() function to control the format of the number.

Copying Versus Cutting a Formula

In Figure 6.6, the formula in cell C4 references A4+B4. Because there are no dollar signs within the formula, those are relative references.

Figure 6.6   The formula in cell C4 adds the two numbers to the left of the formula.

If you *copy* cell C4 and paste it to cell G2, the formula works perfectly, adding the two numbers to the left of G2. However, if you *cut* C4 and paste to F6, the formula continues to point to cells A4+B4, as shown in Figure 6.7. Whereas cutting and copying are relatively similar in applications such as Word, they are very different in Excel. It is important to understand the effect of cutting a formula in Excel in contrast to copying the formula. When you cut a formula, the formula continues to point to the original precedents, no matter where you paste it.

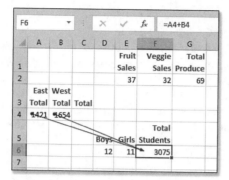

Figure 6.7 Copying C4 to G2 works. Cutting C4 to F6 fails.

A similar rule applies to the references mentioned in a formula. For example, in Figure 6.6, the formula in cell C4 points to A4 and B4. As long as you copy cell A4, you can paste it anywhere without changing the formula in C4. But if you would cut A4 and paste it elsewhere, the formula in C4 would update to reflect the new location.

Inside OUT

Sometimes you need to do a combination of a Cut and a Copy. You need the formulas to keep pointing to the original cells, but you need to copy the formulas to a new spot.

The common approach is to convert the formulas to text, copy and paste, and then convert from text back to formulas. Follow these steps:

1. Select the range of formulas to cut/copy.
2. Press Ctrl+H to display the Replace dialog.
3. Replace each = with ^=.
4. Copy the cells.
5. Paste to a new place.
6. Use Replace to change each ^= to =.

Automatically Formatting Formula Cells

The rules for formatting the result of a formula seem to be inconsistent. Suppose that you have $1.23 in cell A1. All cells in the worksheet have the general format except cell A1.

If you enter **=A1+3** in another cell with general format, the result automatically inherits the currency format of cell A1.

CHAPTER 6

When you are referring to multiple cells in a formula, the resulting automatic format does not appear to follow a pattern. When you start the formula with an equal sign, either the format is copied from the first or the last cell referenced. When you use a plus sign, the format sometimes comes from the second, first, or last reference, and sometimes the format is a mix of two references.

If your formula is going to refer to multiple cells with different formatting, start the formula with an equal sign. Refer to the cell with the desired cell format first, but accept that you might have to explicitly format the resulting cell.

Using Date Math

Dates in Excel are stored as the number of days since January 1, 1900. For example, Excel stores the date Feb-17-2021 as 44244. In Figure 6.8, cell E1 contains the date. Cell E2 contains the formula =E1 and has been formatted to show a number.

Figure 6.8   Although cell E1 is formatted as a date, Excel stores the date as the number of days since January 1, 1900.

This convenient system enables you to do some pretty simple math. For example, Figure 6.9 shows a range of invoice dates in column B. The payment terms for the invoice are in column D. You can calculate the due date by adding cells B2 and D2. Here is what actually happens in Excel's calculation engine:

1.   The date in cell B2—2/1/2018—is stored as 43132.

2.   Excel adds 10 to that number to get the answer 43142.

3.   Excel formats this number as a date, to yield 2/11/2018.

Figure 6.9   When the answer is formatted correctly, Excel's date math is very cool.

However, a frustrating problem can occur if the cell containing the formula has the wrong numeric format. For example, in Figure 6.10, the WORKDAY function in column D did not automatically convert the result to a date. It is important to recognize that dates in 2019–2021 fall in the range of 43,466 to 44,561. So, if you are expecting a date answer as the result of a formula and get a number in this range, the answer probably needs to have a date format applied.

Figure 6.10   The formula appears to give the wrong answer. However, this is a formatting problem.

To apply a date format, on the Home tab use the Number drop-down menu to choose the Date format. The answer in column D now appears correctly.

In general, most formulas that refer to a date cell are automatically formatted as a date. Most formulas that contain functions from the Date category are formatted as a date. (The WORKDAY function is one annoying exception.)

Troubleshooting Formulas

It is difficult to figure out worksheets that were set up by other people. When you receive a worksheet from a co-worker, use the information in the following sections to find and examine the formulas.

Seeing All Formulas

For a long time, Excel has given customers the capability to see all the formulas in a worksheet. The mode that provides this functionality is called *Show Formulas mode*.

To toggle into Show Formulas mode for a worksheet, select the Formulas tab, and then choose the Show Formulas icon in the Formula Auditing group. Alternatively, you can press Ctrl+` (the acute accent) to toggle into this mode. On U.S. keyboards, the acute accent is usually just below the Esc key, on the same key with the tilde (~).

To hide the formulas and return to normal mode, choose the Show Formulas icon again.

Highlighting All Formula Cells

These steps apply a cell color to all formula cells in the worksheet:

1. Ensure that you have a single cell selected.

2. Select Home, Find & Select, Formulas.

3. Use the Paint Bucket icon in the Home tab to apply a color to all the formula cells.

Editing a Single Formula to Show Direct Precedents

It is helpful to identify cells that are used to calculate a formula. These cells are called the *precedents* of the cell.

A cell can have several levels of precedents. In a formula such as =D5+D7, there are two direct precedents: D5 and D7. However, all the direct precedents of D5 and D7 are second-level precedents of the original formula.

If you are interested in visually examining the direct precedents of a cell, follow these steps:

1. Select a cell that has a formula.

2. Press F2 to put the cell in Edit mode. In this mode, each reference of the formula is displayed in a different color. For example, the formula in cell H5 in Figure 6.11 refers to three cells. The characters F5 in the formula appear in blue and correspond to the blue box around cell F5.

3. Visually check the formula to ensure that it is correct.

Figure 6.11   Editing a single formula lights up the direct precedent cells.

Using Formula Auditing Arrows

If you have a complicated formula, you might want to identify direct precedents and then possibly second- or third-level precedents. You can have Excel draw arrows from the current cells to all cells that make up the precedents for the current cell. To have Excel draw arrows, follow these steps:

1. From the Formula Auditing group on the Formulas tab, click Trace Precedents. Excel draws arrows from the current cell to all the cells that are directly referenced in the formula. For example, in Figure 6.12, an arrow is drawn to a worksheet icon near cell B30. This indicates that at least one of the precedents for this cell is on another worksheet.

Figure 6.12   The results of Trace Precedents for cell D32.

2. Click Trace Precedents again. Excel draws arrows from the precedent cells to the precedents of those cells. These are the second-level precedents of the original cell. Continue clicking Trace Precedents to see additional levels. In this case, practically every cell on the worksheet is a precedent of cell D32.

3. To remove the arrows, use the Remove Arrows icon in the Formula Auditing group.

Tracing Dependents

The Formula Auditing section provides another interesting option besides the ones discussed so far in this chapter. You can use the Formula Auditing section to trace dependents, so you can find all the cells on the current worksheet that depend on the active cell. Before deleting a cell, consider clicking Trace Dependents to determine whether any cells on the current sheet refer to this cell. This prevents many #REF! errors from occurring.

CAUTION

Even if tracing dependents does not show any cells that are dependent on the current cell, other cells on other worksheets or on other workbooks might rely on this cell.

Using the Watch Window

If you have a large spreadsheet, you might want to watch the results of some distant cells. You can use the Watch Window icon in the Formula Auditing section of the Formulas tab to open a floating box called the Watch Window screen. To use the Watch Window screen, follow these steps:

1. Click the Add Watch icon. The Add Watch dialog box appears.

2. In the Add Watch dialog box, specify a cell to watch, as shown in Figure 6.13. After you add several cells, the Watch Window screen floats above your worksheet, showing the current value of each cell that was added to it. The Watch Window screen identifies the current value and the current formula of each watched cell.

In theory, this feature can be used to watch a value in a far-off section of the worksheet.

TIP

To jump to a watched cell quickly, you can double-click the cell in the Watch Window screen. You can resize the watch window and resize the columns as necessary.

Figure 6.13   Adding a watch to the Watch Window screen.

Evaluate a Formula in Slow Motion

Most of the time, Excel calculates formulas in an instant. It can help your understanding of the formula to watch it being calculated in slow motion. If you need to see exactly how a formula is being calculated, follow these steps:

1. Select the cell that contains the formula in which you are interested.

2. On the Formulas tab, in the Formula Auditing group, select Evaluate Formula. The Evaluate Formula dialog box appears, showing the formula. The following component of the formula is highlighted: It is the next section of the formula to be calculated.

3. If desired, click Evaluate to calculate the highlighted portion of the formula.

4. Click Step In to begin a new Evaluate section for the cell references in the underlined portion of the formula. Figure 6.14 shows the Evaluate Formula dialog box after stepping in to the E30 portion of the formula.

Figure 6.14 The Evaluate Formula dialog box enables you to calculate a formula in slow motion.

Evaluating Part of a Formula

When you do not need to evaluate an entire formula, use the F9 feature. Follow these steps to evaluate part of a formula:

1. Use the mouse to select just the desired portion of the formula in the formula bar, as shown in Figure 6.15.

Figure 6.15 You can select a portion of the formula in the formula bar.

CHAPTER 6

2. Press F9. Excel calculates just the highlighted portion of the formula, as shown in Figure 6.16.

Figure 6.16   Press F9 to calculate just the highlighted portion of the formula.

Be sure to press the Esc key to exit the formula after you use this method. If you press Enter instead to accept the formula, that portion of the formula permanently stays in its calculated form, such as 0.407407.

TROUBLESHOOTING

You might need to use Excel as a calculator without overwriting any cells.

If you must do a calculation without entering the result in a cell, follow these steps:

1. Choose any cell (regardless of whether it contains data).

2. Type an equal sign and the calculation. For example, **=14215469*5**. Do not press Enter. Instead, press F9.

3. The answer, 71077345, appears in both the formula bar and in the cell. The characters are already selected, so you can easily press Ctrl+C to copy the answer to the Clipboard.

4. Press Esc to clear the temporary calculation and go back to the original cell contents.

Understanding Functions

Excel is used on 750 million desktops around the world. People in all career types use Excel, as do many home users who take advantage of Excel's powerful features to track their finances, investments, and more. Part of Excel's versatility is its wide range of built-in functions.

Excel 2019 offers 474 built-in calculation functions. This number grows with each new release. Excel 2019 debuts six new functions: CONCAT, IFS, MAXIFS, MINIFS, SWITCH, and TEXTJOIN. By the end of 2018, Office 365 introduced SORT, SORTBY, FILTER, UNIQUE, and SINGLE, bringing the function count to 479.

Working with Functions

To use functions successfully in a worksheet, you need to follow the function syntax. Keep in mind that a formula that makes use of a function needs to start with an equal sign. You type the function name, an opening parenthesis, function arguments (separated by commas), and the closing parenthesis.

The general syntax of a function looks like this:

```
=FunctionName(Argument1,Argument2,Argument3)
```

Parentheses are needed with every function, including functions that require no arguments. For example, these functions still require the parentheses:

```
=NOW()
=DATE()
=TODAY()
=PI()
```

The arguments for a function should be entered in the correct order, as specified in this book or Excel Help. For example, the PMT() function expects the arguments to have the interest rate first, followed by the number of periods, followed by the present value. If you attempt to send the arguments in the wrong order, Excel happily calculates the wrong result.

In many cases, you can enter arguments as numbers or as cell references. For example, all these formulas are valid:

```
=SUM(1,2,3^2,4/5,6*7)
=SUM(A1:A9,C1,D2,Sheet2!E3:M10)
=SUM(A1:A9,100,200,B3*5)
```

NOTE

Chapters 8, "Using Everyday Functions: Math, Date and Time, and Text Functions," and 9, "Using Powerful Functions: Logical, Lookup, Web, and Database Functions," cover many interesting functions. This chapter covers a number of the most commonly used functions.

NOTE

Excel functions can return some errors. This happens most frequently when one of the arguments passed to the function is outside the range of what the function expects. When you receive a #NUM!, #VALUE!, or #N/A error, you should look in Excel Help for the function. The Remarks section usually indicates exactly what problems can cause each type of error.

The Formulas Tab in Excel 2019

One way to find functions in Excel 2019 is on the Formulas tab. This tab offers the Insert Function, AutoSum, Recently Used, Financial, Logical, Text, Date & Time, Lookup & Reference, Math & Trig, and More Functions icons.

As shown in Figure 7.1, when you click the More Functions icon, a drop-down menu with six additional function groups—Statistical, Engineering, Cube, Information, Compatibility, and Web—appears.

Figure 7.1   The Formulas tab contains icons for finding functions.

The Formulas tab is designed to make it easier to find the right function. You select an icon from the ribbon, and an alphabetical list of functions in that group appears. If you hover your mouse over a function in the list, Excel displays a description of what the function does, as shown in Figure 7.2.

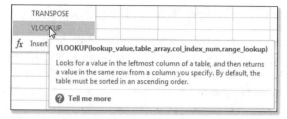

Figure 7.2   Hover over a function, and Excel displays a tip explaining what the function does.

Finding the Function You Need

The inherent problem with the Formulas tab is that you often have to guess where your desired function might be hiding. The function categories have been established in Excel for a decade, and in some cases, functions are tucked away in strange places.

For example, the SUM() function is a Math & Trig function. This makes sense because adding numbers is clearly a mathematical process. However, the AVERAGE() function is not available in the Math & Trig icon. (It is under More Functions, Statistical.) The COUNT() function could be math, reference, or information, but it is found under More Functions, Statistical.

By dividing the list of functions into categories, Microsoft has made it rather difficult to find certain functions. Fortunately, as described in the following sections, you can use some tricks to make this process simpler.

Using Tab to AutoComplete Functions

One feature in Excel 2019 is Formula AutoComplete. Sometimes you might remember part of the function name but not the name. For example, if you type =**LOOK**, Excel will offer LOOKUP, HLOOKUP, and VLOOKUP. Rather than trying to figure out which category on the Formulas tab contains your function, you can just start typing =**LOOK** into a cell. Excel displays a pop-up window with all the functions that contain LOOK, as shown in Figure 7.3. This feature has been changed since Excel 2016. Previously, typing =**LOO** would not have returned VLOOKUP or HLOOKUP because the AutoComplete only matched from the beginning of a word.

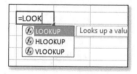

Figure 7.3   Rather than use the icons on the Formulas tab, you can type =**LOOK** to display a list of the Lookup functions.

To accept a function name from the list, you can either double-click the function name or select the name and press Tab.

Using the Insert Function Dialog Box to Find Functions

A large Insert Function icon appears on the Formula tab of the ribbon. This command is repeated at the bottom of every function category. These 14 new entry points for Insert Function were added in Excel 2007, but it is easier to use the fx icon located to the left of the formula bar. Click the fx, and the Insert Function dialog box appears.

Use the Search for a Function box to locate the function. For example, if you typed **loan payment** and then clicked Go, Excel would suggest PMT (the correct function) as well as PPMT, ISPMT, RATE, and others.

When you choose a function in the Insert Function dialog box, the dialog box displays the syntax for the function, as well as a one-sentence description of the function, as shown in Figure 7.4. If you need more details, you can click the Help On This Function hyperlink in the lower-left corner of the Insert Function dialog box.

Figure 7.4   The Insert Function dialog box enables you to browse the syntax and descriptions. The Help On This Function hyperlink leads to more help.

Getting Help with Excel Functions

Every Excel function has three levels of help:

- On-grid ToolTip

- Function Arguments dialog box

- Excel Help

TIP

If you type =FunctionName(in a cell, you can press Ctrl+A anytime after the opening parenthesis to display the Function Arguments dialog box.

Insert Function

Search for a function:

loan payment   Go

Or select a category: Recommended

Select a function:

PMT
PPMT
RATE
ISPMT
PV
CUMIPMT
IPMT

PMT(rate,nper,pv,fv,type)
Calculates the payment for a loan based on constant payments and a constant interest rate.

Help on this function   OK   Cancel

The following sections discuss these levels of help. However, you are sure to find the Function Arguments dialog box to be one of the best ways of getting help.

Using On-Grid ToolTips

In any cell, you can type an equal sign, a function name, and the opening parenthesis. Excel displays a ToolTip that shows the expected arguments. In many cases, this ToolTip is enough to guide you through the function. For example, I can usually remember that the function for figuring out a car loan payment is =PMT(), but I can never remember the order of the arguments. The ToolTip, as shown in Figure 7.5, is enough to remind me that rate comes first, followed by the number of periods, and then the principal amount or present value. Any function arguments displayed in square brackets are optional, so in the example shown in Figure 7.5, you know that you may not have to enter anything for fv or type.

Click any argument name to jump to that argument.
Click the function name for Help.

Figure 7.5   The ToolTip assists you in remembering the proper order for the arguments.

As you type each comma in the function, the next argument in the ToolTip lights up in boldface. This way, you always know which argument you are entering.

TIP

By the way, you can click the formula ToolTip and drag it to a new location on the worksheet. This can be useful if the ToolTip is covering cells that you need to click when building the function.

If you click the function name in the ToolTip, Excel opens Help for that function.

Using the Function Arguments Dialog Box

When you access a function through the Function Wizard or a drop-down menu, Excel displays the Function Arguments dialog box. This dialog box is one of the best features in Excel. If you've started to type the function and typed the opening parenthesis, then pressing Ctrl+A or clicking the fx icon to the left of the formula bar displays the Function Arguments dialog box.

As shown in Figure 7.6, the Function Arguments dialog box has many elements:

- The one-sentence description of the function appears in the center of the dialog box.

- As you tab into the text box for each argument, the description of the argument is shown in the dialog box. This description guides you as to what Excel is expecting. For example, in the dialog box shown in Figure 7.6, Excel reminds you that the interest rate needs to be divided by four for quarterly payments. This reminds you to divide the rate in cell B3 by 12 for monthly payments.

- To the right of each argument in the dialog box is a reference button. You can click this button to collapse the dialog box so you can point to the cells for that argument.

- To the right of each text box is a label that shows the result of the entry for that argument.

- Any arguments in bold are required. Arguments not in bold are optional.

- After you enter the required arguments, the dialog box shows the preliminary result of the formula. This is on the right side, just below the last argument text box. It appears again in the lower-left corner, just above the Help On This Function hyperlink.

- A Help On This Function hyperlink to the Help topic for the function appears in the lower-left corner of the dialog box.

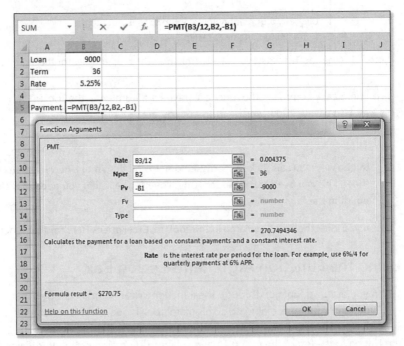

Figure 7.6   The Function Arguments dialog box helps you build a function, one step at a time.

TROUBLESHOOTING

How can you use the Function Arguments dialog when you have a nested function? For example, if you are using MATCH inside of INDEX.

Start by typing the =INDEX(function and press Ctrl+A to display the Function Arguments.

In the second Row_Num box of the Function Arguments dialog box, type MATCH(.

Using your mouse, reach up to the formula bar and click inside of the word MATCH. The Function Arguments dialog will switch to display the arguments for MATCH. When you complete the MATCH function and you want to return to the INDEX version of the Function Arguments dialog box, use the mouse to click on INDEX in the Formula Bar.

Using Excel Help

The Excel Help topics for the functions are incredibly complete. Each function's Help topic includes the following sections:

- The function syntax appears at the top of the topic. This includes a description of each function that might be more complete than the description in the Function Arguments dialog box.

- The Remarks section helps troubleshoot possible problems with the function. It discusses specific limits for each argument and describes the meaning of each possible error that could be returned from the function.

- Each function has an example section composed of an embedded Excel Web App worksheet. You can click the XL icon in the footer of the example to download the example to your computer.

- The See Also section at the bottom of a Help topic enables you to discover related functions. The logical groupings suggested by See Also are far more useful than the category groupings in the Formulas tab.

Using AutoSum

Microsoft realizes that the most common function is the SUM() function. It is so popular that Excel provides one-click access to the AutoSum feature.

The AutoSum icon is the large Greek letter sigma that is the second icon on the Formulas tab or a small icon on the right side of the Home tab. You can click this icon to use AutoSum, or you can use the drop-down menu at the bottom of the icon to access AutoSum versions of Average, Count Numbers, Max, and Min, as shown in Figure 7.7.

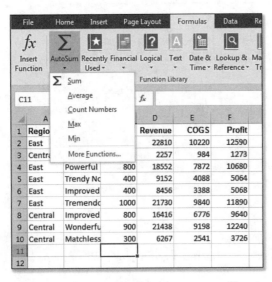

Figure 7.7   The AutoSum drop-down menu offers the capability to average and more.

TIP

Pressing Alt+= is equivalent to clicking the AutoSum icon.

When you click the AutoSum button, Excel seeks to add up the numbers that are above or to the left of the current cell. In general, when you click the AutoSum icon, Excel guesses which cells you are trying to sum. Excel automatically types the SUM() formula. You should review Excel's guess to make sure that Excel chose the correct range to sum. In Figure 7.8, for example, Excel correctly guesses that you want to sum the column of quantities above the cell.

Figure 7.8   The AutoSum feature is proposing a formula to sum C2:C10.

Potential Problems with AutoSum

Although you should always check the range proposed by the AutoSum feature, in some cases you should be especially wary. If the headings above the data are numeric, for example, this will fool AutoSum. In Figure 7.9, the 2019 heading in B1 is numeric. This causes Excel to include the heading incorrectly in the total for column B.

Figure 7.9   Numeric headings confuse AutoSum.

When Excel proposes the wrong range for a sum, use your mouse to highlight the correct range before pressing Enter.

Excel avoids including other SUM() functions in an AutoSum range. If a range contains a SUM() function that references other cells, Excel prematurely stops just before the SUM() function. This problem happens only when the SUM() function references other cells. If the cell contained =7000+1878 or =H3+H4 or =SUM(7000,1878), AutoSum would include the cell.

Excel prefers to sum a column of numbers instead of a row of numbers. Figure 7.10 shows a strange anomaly. If you place the cell pointer in cell F2 and click AutoSum, Excel correctly guesses that you want to total B2:E2. Cell F3 works fine. However, when you get to cell F4, Excel has a choice. There are two numbers above F4 and four numbers to the left of F4. Because there are two numbers directly above, Excel tries to total those two numbers. This problem seems to happen only in the third row of the data set. After that, Excel sees that the three cells above are all summing across the rows, and AutoSum works perfectly in F5:F10.

Figure 7.10   Excel can choose between summing two numbers above or four numbers to the left. Excel chooses incorrectly.

Special Tricks with AutoSum

There is an amazing trick you can use with AutoSum. If you select a range of cells before clicking the AutoSum button, Excel does a much better job of predicting what to sum.

In Figure 7.10, for example, you could select B11:E11 before clicking the AutoSum button, and Excel would know to sum each column. Be careful, though, because Excel does not preview its guess before entering the formula. You should always check a formula after using AutoSum to make sure the correct range was selected.

If your selection contains a mix of blank cells and nonblank cells, Excel adds the AutoSum to only the blank cells. In Figure 7.11, for example, you select the range B2:F11 before clicking the AutoSum button.

Figure 7.11   If your selection contains a mix of blank and nonblank cells, AutoSum writes only to the blank cells.

After you click the AutoSum button, Excel correctly fills in totals for all the rows and columns, as shown in Figure 7.12.

▲	A	B	C	D	E	F
1	Customer	2019	2020	2021	2022	Total
2	Functional Eggbeater Co	84093	91661	101744	113953	391451
3	Vivid Edger Co	64853	68096	70820	71528	275297
4	Powerful Edger Supply	61312	63151	70098	78510	273071
5	Trendy Notebook Corp	52486	56160	62338	63585	234569
6	Improved Vegetable Inc.	66694	69362	70749	73579	280384
7	Tremendous Thermostat Partners	69840	77522	84499	92949	324810
8	Improved Vegetable Inc.	61326	62553	66306	70284	260469
9	Wonderful Kettle Corp	73658	77341	81208	90141	322348
10	Matchless Hardware Traders	72129	77178	81809	87536	318652
11	Total	606391	643024	689571	742065	2681051

Cell reference B2 contains the value 84093.

Figure 7.12   By using AutoSum, you can add 14 SUM() formulas with one click.

Inside OUT

Can you AutoSum from the top of a column of numbers?

There is no secret way to make the AutoSum add the numbers below the active cell.

However, if you must do this frequently, follow these steps:

1. Select the blank cell above a column of numbers.

2. Press Alt+= to start the AutoSum.

3. If Excel filled in any cell reference as the beginning formula, press the Delete key.

4. Press the down arrow once to move to the first number in the range.

5. Press Ctrl+Shift+Down Arrow to select to the end of the range.

6. Press Enter.

Using AutoAverage or AutoCount

The AutoSum button includes a drop-down menu arrow with choices for Average, Count, Max, and Min. If you find yourself frequently using the choices in this drop-down menu, you can add an icon to the Quick Access Toolbar that will AutoAverage, AutoCount, and so on. Open the AutoSum drop-down menu. Right-click Average and choose Add To Quick Access Toolbar to have one-click access to an icon that works similar to AutoSum but uses the AVERAGE calculation instead (see Figure 7.13).

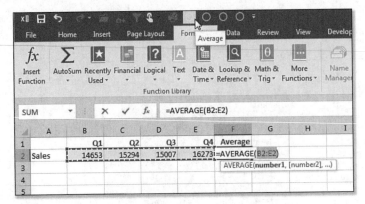

Figure 7.13   Add icons to the Quick Access Toolbar to get one-click access to AutoAverage, AutoMin, AutoMax, and AutoCount.

CAUTION

Microsoft uses the same green circle icon to represent Average, Count, Max, and Min. If you are going to add all four icons to the Quick Access Toolbar, add them in alphabetical order to help you remember the sequence in which they appear.

Function Reference Chapters

Chapters 8 and 9 provide a fairly comprehensive reference for the common functions in Excel. Chapter 10, "Other Functions," provides a reference of the remaining functions.

Function coverage is broken out as follows:

- Chapter 8 describes functions that many people encounter in their everyday lives: some of the math functions, date functions, and text functions.

- Chapter 9 describes functions that are a bit more difficult, but that should be a part of your everyday arsenal. These include a series of functions for making decisions in a formula. They include the IF function and are known collectively as the *logical functions*. Chapter 9 also describes the information, lookup, and database functions.

- Chapter 10 provides a reference for financial, statistical, trigonometry, and engineering functions.

Using Everyday Functions: Math, Date and Time, and Text Functions

Excel offers many functions for dealing with basic math, dates and times, and text. This chapter describes the functions that you can access with the Formulas tab using the Text icon, the Date & Time icon, and the Math portion of the Math & Trig icon.

Math Functions

Table 8.1 provides an alphabetical list of the math functions in Excel 2019. Detailed examples of these functions are provided later in this chapter.

Table 8.1 Alphabetical List of Math Functions

Function	Description
ABS(number)	Returns the absolute value of a number. The absolute value of a number is the number without its sign.
AGGREGATE(function, options, array, [k])	Performs one of 17 functions with the capability to ignore error values, other subtotals, or rows hidden by a filter.
ARABIC(text)	Converts a Roman numeral to Arabic.
AVERAGEIF(range, criteria, [average_range])	Finds average (arithmetic mean) for the cells specified by a given condition or criteria.
AVERAGEIFS(average_range, criteria_range1, criteria1, [criteria_range2, criteria2 ...])	Returns the average value among cells specified by a given set of conditions or criteria.
CEILING(number, significance)	Returns the number rounded up, away from zero, to the nearest multiple of significance. For example, if you want to avoid using pennies in your prices and your product is priced at $4.42, you can use the formula =CEILING(4.42,0.05) to round the price up to the nearest nickel. Note that Excel calculates =CEILING(-2.1,-1) as –3, which is different from the ISO standard. See CEILING.MATH for an alternative.

Function	Description
CEILING MATH(number, [significance],[mode])	Rounds a number up to the nearest multiple of significance. (Before Excel 2013, this function was named CEILING.PRECISE.) Provides compatibility with the ISO standard for computing the ceiling of a negative number.
COMBIN(number,number_ chosen)	Returns the number of combinations for a given number of items. You use COMBIN to determine the total possible number of groups for a given number of items.
COMBINA(number,number_chosen)	Returns the number of combinations with repetitions for a given number of items.
COUNTIF(range,criteria)	Counts the number of cells within a range that meet the given criteria.
COUNTIFS(criteria_range1, criteria1, [criteria_range2,criteria2]...)	Counts the number of cells within a range that meet the given set of conditions or criteria.
EVEN(number)	Returns the number rounded up to the nearest even integer. You can use this function for processing items that come in twos. For example, suppose a packing crate accepts rows of one or two items. The crate is full when the number of items, rounded up to the nearest two, matches the crate's capacity.
EXP(number)	Returns e raised to the power of a number. The constant e equals 2.718281828459045, the base of the natural logarithm. Note that Excel 2016 began returning a 16th digit of precision, potentially causing different answers than Excel 2013.
FACT(number)	Returns the factorial of a number. The factorial of a number is equal to $1 \times 2 \times 3 \times ... \times$ number.
FACTDOUBLE(number)	Returns the double factorial of a number.
FLOOR(number, significance)	Rounds the number toward zero, to the nearest multiple of significance.
FLOOR.MATH(number, [significance],[mode])	Rounds the number down to the nearest multiple of significance. (Before Excel 2013, this function was known as FLOOR.PRECISE.) Differs from FLOOR when you have negative numbers. Whereas FLOOR(-1.2,-1) rounds toward zero to produce –1, the new FLOOR.MATH(-1.2) rounds to the lower number, which is –2.
GCD(number1,number2,...)	Returns the greatest common divisor of two or more integers. The greatest common divisor is the largest integer that divides each number without a remainder.
INT(number)	Rounds a number down to the nearest integer.
LCM(number1,number2,...)	Returns the least common multiple of integers. The least common multiple is the smallest positive integer that is a multiple of all integer arguments number1, number2, and so on. You use LCM to add fractions that have different denominators.
MAXIFS(max_range, criteria_range1, criteria1, [criteria_range2, criteria2...])	Returns the maximum value among cells specified by a given set of conditions or criteria.

Function	Description
MINIFS(min_range, criteria_range1, criteria1, [criteria_range2, criteria2...])	Returns the minimum value among cells specified by a given set of conditions or criteria.
MOD(number,divisor)	Returns the remainder after a number is divided by the divisor. The result has the same sign as the divisor.
MROUND(number,multiple)	Returns a number rounded to the desired multiple.
MULTINOMIAL(number1, number2,...)	Returns the ratio of the factorial of a sum of values to the product of factorials.
ODD(number)	Returns a number rounded up to the nearest odd integer.
PI()	Returns the number 3.14159265358979, the mathematical constant pi, accurate to 15 digits.
POWER(number, power)	Returns the result of a number raised to a power.
PRODUCT(number1, number2,...)	Multiplies all the numbers given as arguments and returns the product.
QUOTIENT(numerator, denominator)	Returns the integer portion of a division operation. You use this function when you want to discard the remainder of a division.
RAND()	Returns an evenly distributed random number greater than or equal to 0 and less than 1. A new random number is returned every time the worksheet is calculated.
RANDARRAY([rows],[columns])	Returns an array of random numbers. Office 365 exclusive.
RANDBETWEEN(bottom, top)	Returns a random number between the numbers specified. A new random number is returned every time the worksheet is calculated.
ROMAN(number, form)	Converts an Arabic numeral to Roman, as text.
ROUND(number, num_ digits)	Rounds a number to a specified number of digits.
ROUNDDOWN(number, num_digits)	Rounds a number down, toward zero.
ROUNDUP(number,num_ digits)	Rounds a number up, away from zero.
SEQUENCE(rows,[columns],[start], [step])	Returns a sequence of numbers. Office 365 exclusive.
SIGN(number)	Determines the sign of a number. Returns 1 if the number is positive, 0 if the number is 0, and −1 if the number is negative.
SQRT(number)	Returns a positive square root.
SQRTPI(number)	Returns the square root of (number × pi).
SUBTOTAL(function_num, ref1,ref2,...)	Returns a subtotal in a list or database. It is generally easier to create a list with subtotals by using the Subtotals command (from the Data menu). After the subtotal list is created, you can modify it by editing the SUBTOTAL function.
SUM(number1,number2,...)	Adds all the numbers in a range of cells.
SUMIF(range,criteria,sum_range)	Adds the cells specified by the given criteria.

CHAPTER 8

SUMIFS(sum_range, criteria_range1, criteria1, [criteria_range2, criteria2 ...]	Adds the cells specified by a given set of conditions or criteria.
SUMPRODUCT(array1,array2, array3,...)	Multiplies corresponding components in the given arrays and returns the sum of those products.
TRUNC(number,num_digits)	Truncates a number to an integer by removing the fractional part of the number.

Date and Time Functions

Table 8.2 provides an alphabetical list of the date and time functions in Excel 2019. Detailed examples of these functions are provided later in this chapter.

Table 8.2   Alphabetical List of Date and Time Functions

Function	Description
DATE (year, month, day)	Returns the serial number that represents a particular date.
DATEDIF (start_date, end_date, unit)	Calculates the number of days, months, or years between two dates. This function is provided for compatibility with Lotus 1-2-3.
DATEVALUE (date_text)	Returns the serial number of the date represented by date_text. You use DATEVALUE to convert a date represented by text to a serial number.
DAY (serial_number)	Returns the day of a date, represented by a serial number. The day is given as an integer ranging from 1 to 31.
DAYS (end_date, start_date)	Calculates the difference in days between two dates. Works even if one or both dates are stored as text instead of as a date.
DAYS360 (start_date, end_date, method)	Returns the number of days between two dates, based on a 360-day year (that is, twelve 30-day months), which is used in some accounting calculations. You use this function to help compute payments if your accounting system is based on twelve 30-day months.
EDATE (start_date, months)	Returns the serial number that represents the date that is the indicated number of months before or after a specified date (that is, the start_date). You use EDATE to calculate maturity dates or due dates that fall on the same day of the month as the date of issue.
EOMONTH (start_date, months)	Returns the serial number for the last day of the month that is the indicated number of months before or after start_date. You use EOMONTH to calculate maturity dates or due dates that fall on the last day of the month.
HOUR (serial_number)	Returns the hour of a time value. The hour is given as an integer, ranging from 0 (12:00 a.m.) to 23 (11:00 p.m.).

Function	Description
ISOWEEKNUM (date)	Returns the ISO week number of the given date.
MINUTE (serial_number)	Returns the minutes of a time value. The minutes are given as an integer, ranging from 0 to 59.
MONTH (serial_number)	Returns the month of a date represented by a serial number. The month is given as an integer, ranging from 1 (for January) to 12 (for December).
NETWORKDAYS (start_date, end_date, holidays)	Returns the number of whole working days between start_date and end_date. Working days exclude weekends and any dates identified in holidays. You use NETWORKDAYS to calculate employee benefits that accrue based on the number of days worked during a specific term. Weekdays are defined as Saturday and Sunday. To handle other calendars, see NETWORKDAYS.INTL.
NETWORKDAYS.INTL (start_date, end_date, weekend, holidays)	Returns the number of whole working days between the start date and the end date. Added in Excel 2010 to support calendars in which the weekend is a pair of days other than Saturday and Sunday.
NOW ()	Returns the serial number of the current date and time.
SECOND (serial_number)	Returns the seconds of a time value. The seconds are given as an integer in the range 0 to 59.
TIME (hour, minute, second)	Returns the decimal number for a particular time. The decimal number returned by TIME is a value ranging from 0 to 0.99999999, representing the times from 0:00:00 (12:00:00 a.m.) to 23:59:59 (11:59:59 p.m.).
TIMEVALUE (time_text)	Returns the decimal number of the time represented by a text string. The decimal number is a value ranging from 0 to 0.99999999, representing the times from 0:00:00 (12:00:00 a.m.) to 23:59:59 (11:59:59 p.m.).
TODAY ()	Returns the serial number of the current date. The serial number is the date/time code that Microsoft Excel uses for date and time calculations.
WEEKDAY (serial_number, return_type)	Returns the day of the week corresponding to a date. The day is given as an integer, ranging from 1 (for Sunday) to 7 (for Saturday), by default.
WEEKNUM (serial_num, return_type)	Returns a number that indicates where the week falls numerically within a year. See also ISOWEEKNUM.
WORKDAY (start_date, days, holidays)	Returns a number that represents a date that is the indicated number of working days before or after a date (the starting date). Working days exclude weekends and any dates identified as holidays. You use WORKDAY to exclude weekends and holidays when you calculate invoice due dates, expected delivery times, or the number of days of work performed. To view the number as a date, format the cell as a date. Weekends are defined as Saturday and Sunday. For alternative calendars, see WORKDAY.INTL.

CHAPTER 8

WORKDAY.INTL (start_date, days, weekend, holidays)	Returns a number that represents a date that is the indicated number of working days before or after a starting date. Added to Excel 2010 to accommodate calendar systems where the weekend is a pair of days other than Saturday and Sunday.
YEAR (serial_number)	Returns the year corresponding to a date. The year is returned as an integer in the range 1900 through 9999.
YEARFRAC (start_date, end_date, basis)	Calculates the fraction of the year represented by the number of whole days between two dates (start_date and end_date). You use the YEARFRAC worksheet function to identify the proportion of a whole year's benefits or obligations to assign to a specific term.

Text Functions

Table 8.3 provides an alphabetical list of the text functions in Excel 2019. Detailed examples of these functions are provided later in this chapter.

Table 8.3   Alphabetical List of Text Functions

Function	Description
ASC (text)	Changes full-width (double-byte) English letters or katakana within a character string to half-width (single-byte) characters.
BAHTTEXT (number)	Converts a number to Thai text and adds the suffix Baht.
CHAR (number)	Returns the character specified by number. You use CHAR to translate code page numbers you might get from files on other types of computers into characters. See also UNICHAR.
CLEAN (text)	Removes all nonprintable characters from text. You use CLEAN on text imported from other applications that contains characters that might not print with your operating system. For example, you can use CLEAN to remove some low-level computer code that frequently appears at the beginning and end of data files and cannot be printed.
CODE (text)	Returns a numeric code for the first character in a text string. The returned code corresponds to the character set used by your computer. See also UNICODE.
CONCAT (Text1, [Text2...])	Concatenates a list or range of text strings.
CONCATENATE (text1, text2,...)	Joins several text strings into one text string.
DOLLAR (number, decimals)	Converts a number to text using currency format, with the decimals rounded to the specified place. The format used is $#,##0.00_);($#,##0.00).

EXACT (text1, text2)	Compares two text strings and returns TRUE if they are the same and FALSE otherwise. EXACT is case-sensitive but ignores formatting differences. You use EXACT to test text being entered into a document.
FIND (find_text, within_text, start_num)	Finds one text string (find_text) within another text string (within_text) and returns the number of the starting position of find_text, from the first character of within_text. You can also use SEARCH to find one text string within another, but unlike SEARCH, FIND is case sensitive and doesn't allow wildcard characters.
FINDB (find_text, within_text, start_num)	Finds one text string (find_text) within another text string (within_text) and returns the number of the starting position of find_text, based on the number of bytes each character uses, from the first character of within_text. You use FINDB with double-byte characters. You can also use SEARCHB to find one text string within another.
FIXED (number, decimals, no_commas)	Rounds a number to the specified number of decimals, formats the number in decimal format using a period and commas, and returns the result as text.
LEFT (text, num_chars)	Returns the first character or characters in a text string, based on the number of characters specified.
LEFTB (text, num_bytes)	Returns the first character or characters in a text string, based on the number of bytes specified. You use LEFTB with double-byte characters.
LEN (text)	Returns the number of characters in a text string.
LENB (text)	Returns the number of bytes used to represent the characters in a text string. You use LENB with double-byte characters.
LOWER (text)	Converts all uppercase letters in a text string to lowercase.
MID (text, start_num, num_chars)	Returns a specific number of characters from a text string, starting at the position specified, based on the number of characters specified.
MIDB (text, start_num, num_bytes)	Returns a specific number of characters from a text string, starting at the position specified, based on the number of bytes specified. You use MIDB with double-byte characters.
NUMBERVALUE (text, [decimal_separator], [group_separator])	Converts text to a number, allowing for different punctuation for thousands separators and decimal separators.
PHONETIC (reference)	Extracts the phonetic (furigana) characters from a text string. Furigana are a Japanese reading aid. They consist of smaller kana printed next to a kanji to indicate its pronunciation.
PROPER (text)	Capitalizes the first letter in a text string and any other letters in text that follow any character other than a letter. Converts all other letters to lowercase.

CHAPTER 8

REPLACE (old_text, start_num, num_chars, new_text)	Replaces part of a text string, based on the number of characters specified, with a different text string.
REPLACEB,(old_text, start_num, num_bytes, new_text)	Replaces part of a text string, based on the number of bytes specified, with a different text string. You use REPLACEB with double-byte characters.
REPT (text, number_times)	Repeats text a given number of times. You use REPT to fill a cell with some instances of a text string.
RIGHT (text, num_chars)	Returns the last character or characters in a text string, based on the number of characters specified.
RIGHTB (text, num_bytes)	Returns the last character or characters in a text string, based on the number of bytes specified. You use RIGHTB with double-byte characters.
SEARCH (find_text, within_text, start_num)	Returns the number of the character at another a specific character or text string is first found, beginning with start_num. You use SEARCH to determine the location of a character or text string within another text string so that you can use the MID or REPLACE function to change the text.
SEARCHB (find_text, within_text, start_num)	Finds one text string (find_text) within another text string (within_text) and returns the number of the starting position of find_text. The result is based on the number of bytes each character uses, beginning with start_num. You use SEARCHB with double-byte characters. You can also use FINDB to find one text string within another.
SUBSTITUTE (text, old_text, new_text, instance_num)	Substitutes new_text for old_text in a text string. You use SUBSTITUTE when you want to replace specific text in a text string; you use REPLACE when you want to replace any text that occurs in a specific location in a text string.
T (value)	Returns the text referred to by value.
TEXT (value, format_text)	Converts a value to text in a specific number format.
TEXTJOIN (delimiter, ignore_empty, text1, [text2...])	Concatenates a list of range of text strings using a delimiter.
TRIM (text)	Removes all spaces from text except for single spaces between words. You use TRIM on text that you have received from another application that might have irregular spacing.
UNICHAR (number)	Returns the Unicode character references by the given number.
UNICODE (text)	Returns the number (code point) of the first character of the text.
UPPER (text)	Converts text to uppercase.
VALUE (text)	Converts a text string that represents a number to a number.

Examples of Math Functions

The most common formula in Excel is a formula to add a column of numbers. In addition to *SUM*, Excel offers a variety of mathematical functions.

Using SUM to Add Numbers

The *SUM* function is by far the most commonly used function in Excel. This function can add numbers from one or more ranges of data.

Syntax:

=SUM(number1,number2,...)

The *SUM* function adds all the numbers in a range of cells. The arguments *number1, number2,...* are 1 to 255 arguments for which you want the total value or sum.

A typical use of this function is =SUM(B4:B12). It is also possible to use =SUM(1,2,3). In the latter example, you cannot specify more than 255 individual values. In the former example, you can specify up to 255 ranges, each of which can include thousands or millions of cells.

In Figure 8.1, cell B25 contains a formula to sum three individual cells: =SUM(B17,B19,B23).

Figure 8.1   A variety of *SUM* formulas.

CHAPTER 8

It is unlikely that you will need more than 255 arguments in this function, but if you do, you can group arguments in parentheses. For example, *=SUM((A10,A12),(A14,A16))* would count as only two of the 255 allowed arguments.

If a text value that looks like a number is included in a range, the text value is not included in the result of the sum. Strangely enough, if you specify the text value directly as an argument in the function, Excel adds it to the result. For example, *=SUM(1,2,"3")* is 6, yet *=SUM(D4:D6)* in cell D7 of Figure 8.1 results in 3.

The comma is treated as a union operator. If you replace the comma with a space, Excel finds the cells that fall in the intersection of the selected ranges. In cell E17, the formula of *=SUM(F13:H14 G12:G15)* adds up the two cells that are in common between the two ranges.

If one cell in a referenced range contains an error, the result of the *SUM* function is an error. To add numbers while ignoring error cells, use the *AGGREGATE* function.

It is valid to create a spearing formula. This type of formula adds the identical cell from many worksheets. For example, *=SUM(Jan:Dec!B20)* adds cell B20 on all 12 sheets between Jan and Dec. If the sheet names contain spaces or other nonalphabetic characters, surround the sheet names with apostrophes: *=SUM('Jan 2018:Dec 2018'!B20)*.

Using AGGREGATE to Ignore Error Cells or Filtered Rows

Added in Excel 2010, the *AGGREGATE* function lets you perform 17 functions on a range of data while selectively ignoring error cells or rows hidden by a filter.

Syntax:

=AGGREGATE(*function_num, options, array,* [k])

The *options* argument is the interesting feature of the function. You can choose to ignore any, all, or none of these categories:

- Error values

- Hidden rows

- Other *SUBTOTAL* and *AGGREGATE* functions

The capability to ignore filtered rows and other *AGGREGATE* functions is similar to the *SUBTOTAL* function. The capability of *AGGREGATE* to ignore error values solves a common Excel problem. For most Excel functions, a single #N/A error cell in a range causes most functions to return an #N/A error. The options in *AGGREGATE* enable you to ignore any error cells in the range.

The *options* argument controls which values are ignored. This is a simple binary system, as follows:

- To ignore other subtotals, add 0. To include subtotals, add 4.

- To ignore hidden rows, add 1.

- To ignore error values, add 2.

- Thus, to ignore other subtotals, hidden rows, and error values, you specify *3 (0+1+2)* as the *options* argument.

- To ignore error values but include other *SUBTOTAL* values, you specify *5 (1+4)* as the argument.

This calculation works out as shown in Table 8.4.

Table 8.4   Arguments for the *AGGREGATE* Function

Option	Meaning
0	Ignore other subtotals
1	Ignore hidden rows and subtotals
2	Ignore error cells and subtotals
3	Ignore all three
4	Ignore nothing
5	Ignore hidden rows
6	Ignore error cells
7	Ignore hidden rows and error cells

In Figure 8.2, the *#N/A* error in cell F13 causes the *SUM* function in F18 to also return an *#N/A*. If you use a *2, 3, 5,* or *7* as the second argument of *AGGREGATE*, you can easily sum all the other numbers as in cell F1. You can also use other function numbers to calculate *MIN, MAX, COUNT, MEDIAN, MODE, PERCENTILE,* and *QUARTILE* values.

You can also use the function to ignore cells hidden by a filter. Whereas the old *SUBTOTAL* function enabled you to do this for 11 calculation functions, the *AGGREGATE* function adds 8 new functions to the list.

CHAPTER 8

| B20 | ▼ | : | × | ✓ | fx | {=AGGREGATE(14,6,(D9:D16)/((B9:B16="East")*(C9:C16="R1")),2)} |

▲	A	B	C	D	E	F	G	H	I	J
1	SUM Ignoring Errors:			255000		4530	=AGGREGATE(9,2,F9:F16)			
2	MIN Ignoring Errors:			1000		10	=AGGREGATE(5,2,F9:F16)			
3	3rd Smallest Ignoring Errors:			4000		80	=AGGREGATE(15,3,F9:F16,3)			
4	Value at 30th Percentile.exc:			4400		72	=AGGREGATE(16,3,F9:F16,0.3)			
5	Value at 30th Percentile.inc:			3400		56	=AGGREGATE(18,3,F9:F16,0.3)			
6	Value at 3rd Quartile:			40000		880	=AGGREGATE(17,3,F9:F16,3)			
7										
8	Customer	Region	Rep	Sales	Rate	Bonus				
9	Astonishing Raft Inc.	West	R3	16000	3%	480				
10	Excellent Sandal Company	East	R1	1000	1%	10				
11	Fabulous Shoe Corporation	East	R2	2000	2%	40				
12	Mouthwatering Hardware Supply	West	R4	64000	4%	2560				
13	Paramount Umbrella Corporation	West	R5	128000	#N/A	#N/A				
14	Powerful Vise Company	West	R4	32000	4%	1280				
15	Rare Barometer Company	East	R1	8000	1%	80				
16	Stunning Door Corporation	East	R2	4000	2%	80				
17										
18	SUM			255000		#N/A	=SUM(F9:F17)			
19										
20	2nd largest East R1 sale:	1000	{=AGGREGATE(14,6,(D9:D16)/((B9:B16="East")*(C9:C16="R1")),2)}							
21										

Figure 8.2   Using a *2* or *3* as the *options* argument for *AGGREGATE* allows the function to ignore error cells in a range.

Table 8.5 shows the 19 functions available in the *AGGREGATE* function. This list mirrors the 11 functions available in *SUBTOTAL* (arranged alphabetically to match those in the *SUBTOTAL* function) and then 8 new functions arranged in order of popularity.

Table 8.5   Functions Available in *AGGREGATE*

Fx #	Function
1	AVERAGE
2	COUNT
3	COUNTA
4	MAX
5	MIN
6	PRODUCT
7	STDDEV.S
8	STDDEV.P
9	SUM
10	VAR.S
11	VAR.P
12	MEDIAN
13	MODE.SNGL
14	LARGE

15	SMALL
16	PERCENTILE.INC
17	QUARTILE.INC
18	PERCENTILE.EXC
19	QUARTILE.EXC

The last six functions in this list require you to specify a value for *k* as the fourth argument. *LARGE* and *SMALL* typically return the kth largest or smallest value from a list. Use the fourth argument in *AGGREGATE* to specify the value for *k*. The last six functions allow for a calculated array instead of a range of cells. After September 2018, customers using Office 365 will be able to specify arrays for all 19 functions within aggregate. Excel 2019 and earlier will allow arrays only for the last six functions.

In cell F3 of Figure 8.2, the final argument of *3* specifies that you want the third smallest number in the array. For *LARGE*, *SMALL*, and *QUARTILE*, you should specify an integer for *k*. For *PERCEN-TILE*, specify a decimal between *0* and *1*.

When you are trying to return results from the visible rows of a filtered data set, you can use either *SUBTOTAL* or *AGGREGATE*. In Figure 8.3, the *SUM* function in D1 returns the sum of the visible and hidden rows. The *SUBTOTAL* function in D2 returns the sum of the visible rows, the same as the *AGGREGATE* function in D3. The advantage of *AGGREGATE* is that it can return *MEDIAN*, *LARGE*, *SMALL*, *PERCENTILE*, and *QUARTILE* on the visible rows as well.

Figure 8.3 *AGGREGATE* performs calculations on the visible items of a filtered data set.

Choosing Between COUNT and COUNTA

The key to choosing between *COUNT* and *COUNTA* is to analyze the data you want to count. In Figure 8.4, someone has used the letter X in column B to indicate that training has been started. In this case, you would use *COUNTA* to get an accurate count. Column C contains dates (which are treated as numeric). In column C, either *COUNT* or *COUNTA* returns the correct result. Column D has a mix of text and numeric entries. If you want to count how many people took the test, use *COUNTA*. If you want to count how many people received a numeric score, use *COUNT*.

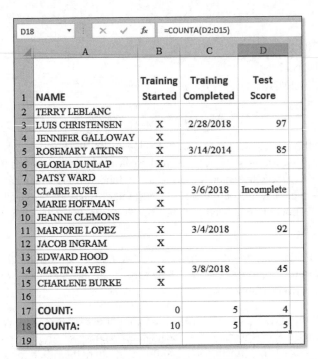

Figure 8.4 Whether you use *COUNT* or *COUNTA* depends on whether your data is numeric. *COUNT* counts only dates and numeric entries. *COUNTA* counts anything that is nonblank.

Rounding Numbers

You can use a variety of functions—including *ROUND, ROUNDDOWN, ROUNDUP, INT, TRUNC, FLOOR, FLOOR.MATH, CEILING, CEILING.MATH, EVEN, ODD,* and *MROUND*—to round a result or to remove decimals from a result. The most common function is *ROUND.*

- *ROUND(number, num_digits)* rounds the number. To round to the nearest dollar, use 0 as the second argument. To round to the nearest penny, use 2 as the second argument. To round to the nearest thousand dollars, use –3 as the third argument.

- *ROUNDUP(number, num_digits)* always rounds away from zero. Although this usually makes the number larger, the behavior for negative numbers is unusual. *=ROUNDUP(-1.1,0)* rounds away from zero to –2. If you want that to round to –1, use *TRUNC(number)* instead.

- ROUNDDOWN(number, num_digits) always rounds toward zero. Although this makes sense for positive numbers, the result for negative numbers might not make sense. =ROUNDDOWN(-3.1,0) rounds toward zero and produces –3. If you expect this to produce –4, use =INT(-3.1) instead.

- MROUND(number, multiple) rounds to the nearest multiple. Use for rounding to the nearest 5 or 25. =MROUND(115,25) rounds to 125. There are some unusual variants. =EVEN(number) always rounds up to an even number, for the unusual situation in which items are packed two to a case. =ODD(number) rounds up to an odd integer.

Figure 8.5 illustrates several rounding options.

Figure 8.5   Rounding is easy in Excel using these functions.

The last four functions in this group—*CEILING, CEILING.MATH, FLOOR*, and *FLOOR.MATH*—round a number in a certain direction to a certain number of digits. They require you to enter the number and the number of decimals to which to round. The behavior of the functions when a number was negative caused complaints from the mathematics community, so the Excel team reversed the behavior with the *.MATH* versions of the functions.

For example, =CEILING(5.1,1) rounds the 5.1 up to 6. Originally, Excel would always round away from zero: =CEILING(-5.1,-1) would round to –6. Mathematicians pointed out that –6 is actually lower than 5.1 and the correct answer should be –5. Thus, *CEILING.MATH(-5.1,1)* rounds up to –5.

The older CEILING function required the second argument to have the same sign as the first argument. The *.MATH* versions can deal with a negative number and a positive significance. Microsoft added an optional third Mode argument that allows *CEILING.MATH* to round away from zero. Figure 8.6 illustrates *CEILING*.

Figure 8.6   For negative numbers, *CEILING.MATH* rounds toward zero.

Using SUBTOTAL Instead of SUM with Multiple Levels of Totals

Consider the data set shown in Figure 8.7. This report shows a list of invoices for each customer. Someone has manually inserted rows and used the *SUM* function to total each customer. Cells C70 and C75 contain a *SUM* function.

	A	B	C	D	E	F	G	H
					=SUBTOTAL(9,E2:E75)			
1	Customer	Invoice	Revenue	Revenue	Revenue			
67	Supreme Washer S	1133	562.94	562.94	562.94			
68	Supreme Washer S	1126	629.79	629.79	629.79			
69	Supreme Washer S	1148	341.13	341.13	341.13			
70	Supreme Washer : Total		1533.86	1533.86	1533.86			
71								
72	Well-Suited Utensi	1120	709.41	709.41	709.41			
73	Well-Suited Utensi	1153	224.07	224.07	224.07			
74	Well-Suited Utensi	1122	690.03	690.03	690.03			
75	Well-Suited Utens Total		1623.51	1623.51	1623.51			
76								
77	GRAND TOTAL		20598.01	20598.01	20598.01			
78								
79	Row 70 formulas:							
80	Column C	=SUM(C67:C69)						
81	Column D	=SUM(D67:D69)						
82	Column E	=SUBTOTAL(9,E67:E69)						
83								
84	Row 77 formulas:							
85	Column C	=C5+C10+C15+C20+C25+C30+C35+C40+C45+C50+C55+C60+C65+C70+C75						
86	Column D	=SUM(D2:D75)/2						
87	Column E	=SUBTOTAL(9,E2:E75)						
88								

Figure 8.7   When you use *SUBTOTAL* instead of *SUM* for the customer totals, the problem of creating a grand total becomes simple.

It becomes incredibly difficult to total the data when it has intermediate *SUM* functions. The original formula in C77 must point to each subtotal cell.

Many accountants can teach you the old accounting trick whereby you total the entire column and divide by two to get the grand total. This is based on the assumption that every dollar is in the column twice: once on the detail row and once on the summary row. The formula in D77 is far shorter than the formula in C77 and produces the same answer. This trick does work, but it is hard to explain to your manager why it works.

A better solution is to use the *SUBTOTAL* function. Instead of =SUM(D2:D75), use =SUBTOTAL(9,D2:D75). The function totals all numbers in D2:D75 but ignores other subtotal functions.

While you are summing in this case, the *SUBTOTAL* function offers 11 arguments, numbered from 1 to 11: *AVERAGE, COUNT, COUNTA, MAX, MIN, PRODUCT, STDEV, STDEVP, SUM, VAR,* and *VARP*. It just happens that *SUM* is the ninth item in this list when these functions are arranged alphabetically in the English language, so *9* became the function number for *SUM*.

Totaling Visible Cells Using SUBTOTAL

If you are using a filter to query a data set, you can use the *SUBTOTAL* function instead of the *SUM* function to show the total of the visible rows. In Figure 8.8, cell E1 contains a *SUM* function, which totals rows whether they are visible or not. Cell E2 contains a *SUBTOTAL* function. As you use the Filter drop-down menus to show just rows for sales of J730 by Jamie, the *SUBTOTAL* function updates to reflect the total of the visible rows. This makes the *SUBTOTAL* function a great tool for ad-hoc reporting.

Figure 8.8   The *SUBTOTAL* function in cell E2 ignores rows hidden as the result of a filter.

NOTE

Although the function in Figure 8.8 uses the function number *109*, the *Subtotal* command always ignores rows hidden as the result of a filter. =SUBTOTAL(9,E5:E5090) would return an identical result when the rows are hidden through a filter, as in this case. If you have rows hidden by the Hide command, you should use *109* to ignore the manually hidden rows.

Using RAND, RANDARRAY, and RANDBETWEEN to Generate Random Numbers and Data

In some situations, you might want to generate random numbers. Excel offers three functions to assist with this process: *RAND, RANDARRAY,* and *RANDBETWEEN.*

The *RAND* function returns an evenly distributed random number greater than or equal to 0 and less than 1. A new random number is returned every time the worksheet is calculated.

=*RAND()* generates a random decimal between 0 and 0.999999999999999. Whether you are a teacher trying to randomly assign the order for book report presentations or the commissioner of a fantasy football league trying to figure out the draft sequence, =*RAND()* can help.

Starting in late 2018, Office 365 customers can use the new RANDARRAY([Rows],[Columns] to generate an array of results similar to RAND(). To generate a random number greater than or equal to 0 but less than 100, you can use *RAND()*100.*

To generate a random sequence for a list, you select a blank column next to your data and enter **=RAND()** in the column. Every time you press the F9 key, the column generates a new set of random numbers. You might want to agree up front with the draft participants that you will press F9 three times to randomize the list and then convert the formulas to values. To do so, follow these steps:

1. Enter the heading **Random** in row 1 next to your data.

2. Enter **=RAND()** in cell B2.

3. Move the cell pointer to cell B2 and double-click the fill handle.

4. Turn off automatic calculation by using Formulas, Calculation Options, Manual. This prevents the *RAND()* functions from recalculating after you sort in step 7.

5. Press the F9 key three times.

6. Choose one cell in column B.

7. From the Data tab, click the AZ button to sort ascending. The new sequence of items in column A is random (see Figure 8.9).

You can also use this technique to select a random subset from a data set. If your manager wants you to contact every 20th customer, you can select all the customers in which =*RAND()* is 0.05 or less.

Whereas =*RAND()* returns a random decimal, =*RANDBETWEEN* generates an integer between two integers.

Figure 8.9 Kristina gets to draft first in this season's fantasy football league, thanks to the *RAND* function.

The *RANDBETWEEN* function returns a random integer between the numbers you specify. A new random number is returned every time the worksheet is calculated. This function takes the following arguments:

- *bottom*—This is the smallest integer *RANDBETWEEN* can return.

- *top*—This is the largest integer *RANDBETWEEN* can return.

To generate random numbers between 50 and 59, inclusive, you use =RANDBETWEEN(50,59). *RANDBETWEEN* is easier to use than =RAND to achieve random integers; with =RAND, you would have to use =INT(RAND()*10)+50 to generate this same range of data.

Even though *RANDBETWEEN* generates integers, you can use it to generate sales prices or even letters. =RANDBETWEEN(5000,9900)/100 generates random prices between $50.00 and $99.00, including prices with cents, such as $76.54.

The capital letter A is also known as character 65 in the ASCII character set. B is 66, C is 67, and so on up through Z, which is character 90. You can use =CHAR(RANDBETWEEN(65,90)) to generate random capital letters.

Choosing a Random Item from a List

In Figure 8.10, you want to randomly assign employees to certain projects. The list of projects is in column A. The list of employees is in E2:E6. As shown in Figure 8.10, the function for B2:B11 is =INDEX($E$2:$E$6,RANDBETWEEN(1,5)).

Figure 8.10   I wonder whether Dilbert's pointy-haired boss assigns projects this way.

Using =ROMAN to Finish Movie Credits and =ARABIC to Convert Back to Digits

Excel can convert numbers to Roman numerals. If you stay in the theater after a movie until the end of movie credits, you see that the copyright date is always expressed in Roman numerals. If you are the next J.J. Abrams, you can use *=ROMAN(2022)* or *=ROMAN(YEAR(Now()))* to generate such a numeral.

NOTE

Romans did have a way to represent 5,000 and 10,000, but the format cannot be typed on a modern keyboard; hence, the programmers behind *ARABIC* are apparently allowing nonsensical numbers like MMMMMIV.

The *=ARABIC()* function can convert a Roman numeral back to a regular number. Whereas *=ROMAN()* works only with the numbers 1 through 3,999, the *ARABIC* function deals with invalid Roman numerals from –255,000 through 255,000. Leviculus!

Using ABS to Figure Out the Magnitude of Error

Suppose that you work for a local TV station, and you want to prove that your forecaster is more accurate than those at the other stations in town. The forecaster at the rival station in town is horrible—some days he misses high, and other days he misses low. The rival station uses Figure 8.11 to say that his average forecast is 99 percent accurate. All those negative and positive errors cancel each other out in the average.

Figure 8.11   ABS measures the size of an error, ignoring the sign.

The *ABS* function measures the size of the error. Positive errors are reported as positive, and negative errors are reported as positive as well. You can use *=ABS(A2-B2)* to demonstrate that the other station's forecaster is off by 20 degrees on average.

Using GCD and LCM to Perform Seventh-Grade Math

My seventh-grade math teacher, Mr. Irwin, taught me about greatest common denominators and least common multiples. For example, the least common multiple of 24 and 36 is 72. The greatest common denominator of 24 and 36 is 12. I have to admit that I never saw these concepts again until my son Josh was in seventh grade. This must be permanently part of the seventh-grade curriculum.

If you are in seventh grade or you are assisting a seventh grader with his or her math lesson, you will be happy to know that Excel can calculate these values for you.

Syntax:

`=GCD(number1,number2,...)`

The *GCD* function returns the greatest common divisor of two or more integers. The greatest common divisor is the largest integer that divides both *number1* and *number2*, and so on, without a remainder.

The arguments *number1, number2, . . .* are 1 to 255 values. If any value is not an integer, it is truncated. If any argument is nonnumeric, *GCD* returns a *#VALUE!* error. If any argument is less than zero, *GCD* returns a *#NUM!* error. The number 1 divides any value evenly. A prime number has only itself and 1 as even divisors.

Syntax:

=LCM(*number1,number2,...*)

The *LCM* function returns the least common multiple of integers. The least common multiple is the smallest positive integer that is a multiple of all integer arguments—*number1, number2*, and so on. You use *LCM* to add fractions with different denominators.

The arguments *number1, number2, . . .* are one to 255 values for which you want the least common multiple. If the value is not an integer, it is truncated. If any argument is nonnumeric, *LCM* returns a *#VALUE!* error. If any argument is less than 1, *LCM* returns a *#NUM!* error.

Using MOD to Find the Remainder Portion of a Division Problem

The *MOD* function is one of the obscure math functions that I find myself using quite frequently. Have you ever been in a group activity in which everyone in the group was to count off by sixes? This is a great way to break up a group into six subgroups. It makes sure that friends who were sitting together get put into disparate groups.

Using the *MOD* function is a great way to perform this concept with records in a database. Perhaps for auditing, you need to check every eighth invoice. Or you need to break up a list of employees into four groups. You can solve these types of problems by using the *MOD* function.

Think back to when you were first learning division. If you had to divide 43 by 4, you would have written that the answer was 10 with a remainder of 3. If you divide 40 by 4, the answer is 10 with a remainder of 0.

The *MOD* function divides one number by another and reports back just the remainder portion of the result. You end up with an even distribution of remainders. If you convert the formulas into values and sort, your data is broken into similar-sized groups.

The *MOD* function returns the remainder after *number* is divided by *divisor*. The result has the same sign as *divisor*. This function takes the following arguments:

- *number*—This is the number for which you want to find the remainder.

- *divisor*—This is the number by which you want to divide *number*. If *divisor* is 0, *MOD* returns a *#DIV/0!* error.

NOTE

MOD is short for modulo, the mathematical term for this operation. You would normally say that 17 modulo 3 is 2.

The *MOD* function is good for classifying records that follow a certain order. For example, the SmartArt gallery contains 84 icons arranged with 4 icons per row. To find the column for the 38th icon, use *=MOD(38,4)*.

The example in Figure 8.12 assigns all employees to one of four groups.

Figure 8.12 To organize these employees into four groups, use *=MOD(ROW(),4)*. Then paste the values and sort by the remainders.

Inside OUT

The MOD function can be used to create green bar formatting.

Back in the 1980s, many computer reports were printed on green bar paper. Two rows would have a white background followed by two rows with a green background. This allowed your eye to follow the data across the row easily.

Green bar effects are available when you format a range as a table using Ctrl+T. However, many people don't like tables because they eliminate the ability for custom views and subtotals.

A workaround is to apply conditional formatting to a range. Specify a formula, such as =MOD(ROW(),4)<=1, for a light green background. The MOD function, in this case, returns 0, 1, 2, or 3. Anything with a MOD of 0 or 1 will be formatted in green.

Using SQRT and POWER to Calculate Square Roots and Exponents

Most calculators offer a square root button, so it seems natural that Excel would offer a *SQRT* function to do the same thing. To square a number, you multiply the number by itself, ending up with a square. For example, 5×5 = 25.

A square root is a number that, when multiplied by itself, leads to a square. For example, the square root of 25 is 5, and the square root of 49 is 7. Some square roots are more difficult to calculate. The square root of 8 is a number between 2 and 3—somewhere close to 2.828. You can calculate the number with =*SQRT(8)*.

A related function is the *POWER* function. If you want to write the shorthand for 6×6×6×6×6, you would say "six to the fifth power," or 6^5. Excel can calculate this with =*POWER(6,5)*.

> **NOTE**
>
> *SQRTPI* is a specialized version of *SQRT*. This function is handy for converting square shapes to equivalent-sized round shapes.

Figuring Out Other Roots and Powers

The *SQRT* function is provided because some math people expect it to be there. There are no equivalent functions to figure out other roots.

If you multiply 5×5×5 to get 125, then the third root of 125 is 5. The fourth root of 625 is 5. Even a $30 calculator offers a key to generate various roots beyond a square root. Excel does not offer a cube root function. In reality, even the *POWER* and the *SQRT* functions are not necessary.

- =*6^3* is 6 raised to the third power, which is 6×6×6, or 216.
- =*2^8* is 2 to the eighth power, which is 2×2×2×2×2×2×2×2, or 256.

For roots, you can raise a number to a fractional power:

- =*256^(1/8)* is the eighth root of 256. This is 2.
- =*125^(1/3)* is the third root of 125. This is 5.

Thus, instead of using =*SQRT(25)*, you could just as easily use =*25^(1/2)*. However, people reading your worksheets are more likely to understand =*SQRT(25)* than =*25^(1/2)*.

Using SUMIFS, AVERAGEIFS, COUNTIFS, MAXIFS, and MINIFS to Conditionally Calculate

The *COUNTIF* and *SUMIF* functions debuted in Excel 97. They would let you sum or count records that met a single condition. Microsoft dramatically improved those functions with updated functions SUMIFS and AVERAGEIFS. The plural version of the functions can handle up to 127 conditions.

In February 2017, Microsoft added MAXIFS and MINIFS to find the smallest or largest value for records that meet one or more conditions.

Figure 8.13 shows a database. You want to examine all of the Central region sales where the product is Widget. If column B says Widget and column C says Central, you want to perform calculations on the revenue in column D. In this figure, the text values Widget and Central are stored in F1 and G1 respectively.

The SUMIFS function starts with a reference to the revenue amounts in D2:D16. After that first argument, you will provide anywhere from 1 to 127 pairs of arguments. In each pair, the first argument is the range to examine. The second argument is the value to match. For example, to find records in the Central region, you could specify C2:C16,F1. To find records where the product is Widget, you would use B2:B16,G1.

Thus, for a formula to test two conditions, you will have five arguments. The SUMIFS, AVERAGEIFS, MINIFS, and MAXIFS all follow the same syntax. The difference is the COUNTIFS function, which omits the initial argument to specify the numeric column.

	A	B	C	D	E	F	G	H	I	J	K	L
1	Customer	Product	Region	Revenue		Central	Widget					
2	Wonderful l	Widget	East	76,906								
3	Forceful Fla	Widget	East	32,297		277,591	Total					
4	Best Paint Ir	Gadget	East	59,761		=SUMIFS($D$2:$D$16,$C$2:$C$16,$F$1,$B$2:$B$16,$G$1)						
5	Guarded Rai	Widget	East	66,858								
6	Rare Quilt Ir	Widget	Central	99,613		69,398	AVERAGE					
7	Rare Juicer (	Widget	Central	47,138		=AVERAGEIFS($D$2:$D$16,$C$2:$C$16,$F$1,$B$2:$B$16,$G$1)						
8	Improved R	Gadget	Central	61,763								
9	Different Tu	Widget	Central	47,363		47,138	Smallest					
10	Best Paint Ir	Widget	Central	83,477		=MINIFS($D$2:$D$16,$C$2:$C$16,$F$1,$B$2:$B$16,$G$1)						
11	Fascinating	Widget	West	73,950								
12	Crisp Eggbe	Gadget	West	46,113		99,613	Largest					
13	Different Ac	Widget	West	22,334		=MAXIFS($D$2:$D$16,$C$2:$C$16,$F$1,$B$2:$B$16,$G$1)						
14	Rare Vise In	Widget	West	70,064								
15	Rare Oven C	Gadget	West	63,138		4	Count					
16	Effortless Cl	Widget	West	55,642		=COUNTIFS($C$2:$C$16,$F$1,$B$2:$B$16,$G$1)						

Figure 8.13   *SUMIFS, AVERAGEIFS, MINIFS, MAXIFS,* and *COUNTIFS* calculate only the records that fall in the Central region for product Widget.

Syntax:

SUMIFS(*sum_range,criteria_range1,criteria1[,criteria_range2, criteria2...]*)

The *SUMIFS()* function adds the cells in a range that meet multiple criteria.

Note the following in this syntax:

- *sum_range* is the range to sum.

- *criteria_range1, criteria_range2, . . .* are one or more ranges in which to evaluate the associated criteria.

- *criteria1, criteria2, ...* are one or more criteria in the form of a number, an expression, a cell reference, or text that define which cells will be added. For example, they can be expressed as *32, "32", ">32", "apples",* or *B4*.

- Each cell in *sum_range* is summed only if all the corresponding criteria specified are true for that cell.

- You can use the wildcard characters question mark (?) and asterisk (*) in *criteria*. A question mark matches any single character; an asterisk matches any sequence of characters. If you want to find an actual question mark or asterisk, you need to type a tilde (~) before the character.

- Unlike the range and criteria arguments in *SUMIF*, the size and shape of each *criteria_range* and *sum_range* must be the same.

In Figure 8.14, you want to build a table that shows the total by region and product. *sum_range* is the revenue in H11:H5011. The first criteria pair consists of the regions in $C$11:$C$5011 being compared to the word East in B$1. The second criteria pair consists of the divisions in $B$11:$B$5011 being compared to G854 in $A2. The formula in B2 is *=SUMIFS($H$11:$H$5011, $C$11:$C$5011,B$1,$B$11:$B$5011,$A2)*. You can copy this formula to B2:D6.

B2			× ✓ *fx*	=SUMIFS($H$11:$H$5011,$C$11:$C$5011,B$1,$B$11:$B$5011,$A2)					
	A	B	C	D	E	F	G	H	I
1		East	Central	West					
2	G854	18,931K	17,327K	13,339K					
3	A105	18,440K	21,199K	12,636K					
4	V937	17,574K	18,157K	13,660K					
5	I543	19,488K	21,257K	13,246K					
6	H833	19,065K	19,484K	12,843K					
7		=SUMIFS($H$11:$H$5011,$C$11:$C$5011,B$1,$B$11:$B$5011,$A2)							
8									
9									
10	Customer	Product	Region	District	Rep	Date	Qty	Revenue	Profit
11	Wonderful Faucet C	V937	East	Southeast	ADAM DU	2/3/14	730	76,906	41,529
12	Forceful Flagpole C	H833	East	Southeast	ADAM DU	12/19/14	804	32,297	16,794

Figure 8.14   The *SUMIFS()* function is used to create this summary by region and product.

Dates and Times in Excel

Date calculations can drive people crazy in Excel. If you gain a certain confidence with dates in Excel, you will be able to quickly resolve formatting issues that come up.

Here is why dates are a problem. First, Excel stores dates as the number of days since January 1, 1900. For example, June 30, 2021, is 44,377 days since 1/1/1900. When you enter 6/30/2021 in a cell, Excel secretly converts this entry to 44,377 and formats the cell to display a date instead of the value. So far, so good. The problem arises when you try to calculate something based on the date.

When you try to perform a calculation on two cells when the first cell is formatted as currency and the second cell is formatted as fixed numeric with three decimals, Excel has to decide if the new cell inherits the currency format or the fixed with three decimals format. These rules are hard to figure out. In any given instance, you might get the currency format or the fixed with three decimals format, or you might get the format previously assigned to the cell with the new formula. With numbers, a result of $80.52 or 80.521 looks about the same. You can probably understand either format.

However, imagine that one of the cells is formatted as a date. Another cell contains the number 30. If you add the 30 to the date, which format does Excel use? If the cell containing the new formula happened to be previously assigned a numeric format, the answer suddenly switches from a date format to the numeric equivalent. This is frustrating and confusing. You start with June 30, 2021, add 30 days, and get an answer of 44,407. This makes no sense to an Excel novice. It forces many people to give up on dates and start storing dates as text that looks like dates. This is unfortunate because you can't easily do calculations on text cells that look like dates.

Here is a general guideline to remember: If you work with dates in the range of the years 2017 to 2028, those numeric equivalents are from 42,736 through 47,118. If you do some date math and get a strange answer in the 40,000–50,000 range, Excel probably has the right answer, but the numeric format of the answer cell is wrong. You need to select Short Date from the Number drop-down menu on the Home tab to correct the format.

The Excel method for storing dates is simple when you understand it. If you have a date cell and need to add 15 days to it, you add the number 15 to the cell. Every day is equivalent to the number 1, and every week is equivalent to the number 7. This is very simple to understand.

When you see 44,377 instead of June 30, 2021, Excel calls the 44,377 a serial number. Some of the Excel functions discussed here convert from a serial number to text that looks like a date, or vice versa.

For time, Excel adds a decimal to the serial number. There are 24 hours in a day. The serial number for 6:00 a.m. is 0.25. The serial number for noon is 0.5. The serial number for 6:00 p.m. is 0.75. The serial number for 3:00 p.m. on June 30, 2021 is 44,377.625. To see how this works, try this out:

1. Create a blank Excel workbook.

2. In any cell, enter a number in the range of 40,000 to 45,000.

3. Add a decimal point and any random digits after the decimal.

4. Select that cell.

CHAPTER 8

5. From the Home tab, select the dialog box launcher in the lower-right corner of the Number group.

6. In the Date category, scroll down and select the format 3/14/01 1:30 PM. Excel displays your random number as a date and time. If the decimal portion of your number is greater than 0.5, the result is in the p.m. portion of the day.

7. Go to another cell and enter the date you were born, using a four-digit year.

8. Again, select the cell and format it as a number. Excel converts it to show how many days after the start of the last century you were born. This is great trivia but not necessarily useful.

CAUTION

Although most Excel date issues can be resolved with formatting, you should be aware of some real date problems:

- On a Macintosh, Excel dates are stored since January 1, 1904. If you are using a Mac, your serial number for a date in 2021 will be different from that on a Windows PC. Excel handles this conversion when files are moved from one platform to another.

- Excel cannot handle dates in the 1800s or before. This really hacks off all my friends who do genealogy. If your Great-Great-Great Uncle Felix was born on February 17, 1895, you are going to have to store that as text.

- Around Y2K, someone decided that 1930 is the dividing line for two-digit years. If you enter a date with a two-digit year, the result is in the range of 1930 through 2029. If you enter 12/31/29, this will be interpreted as 2029. If you enter 1/1/30, it will be interpreted as 1930. If you need to enter a mortgage ending date of 2040, for example, be sure to use the four-digit year, 6/15/2040. If you are regularly entering dates in the 2030–2040 range, you can change the dividing line for two-digit years. Go to Region And Language settings in the Control Panel. Click Additional Settings. Click the Date tab. The When A Two Digit Year Is Entered setting allows you to change the dividing line.

The point is that Excel dates are nothing to be afraid of. You need to understand that behind the scenes, Excel is storing your dates as serial numbers and your times as decimal serial numbers. Occasionally, circumstances cause a date to be displayed as a serial number. Although this freaks some people out, it is easy to fix using the Format Cells dialog box. Other times, when you want the serial number (for example, to calculate elapsed days between two dates), Excel converts the serial number to a date, indicating, for example, that an invoice is past due by "February 15, 1900" days. When you get these types of nonsequiturs, you can visit the Format Cells dialog box. Or press the shortcut key—Ctrl+Shift+tilde—to format the cell as General.

TROUBLESHOOTING

For compatibility with ancient spreadsheet programs, Excel includes the date of February 29, 1900—a date that does not exist.

Leap day is not added to the years 1700, 1800, 1900, 2100, 2200, 2300, and 2500. Lotus 1-2-3 erroneously included February 29, 1900. To allow Lotus files to convert to Excel, Microsoft repeated the error. The result is that any weekdays from January 1, 1900, to February 28, 1900, are off by one day.

Saturday, March 03, 1900	Saturday is correct
Friday, March 02, 1900	Friday is correct
Thursday, March 01, 1900	Thursday is correct
Wednesday, February 29, 1900	No such day!
Tuesday, February 28, 1900	Really Wednesday
Monday, February 27, 1900	Really Tuesday
Sunday, February 26, 1900	Really Monday
Saturday, February 25, 1900	Really Sunday
Sunday, January 01, 1900	Really Monday

A table of dates formatted as a long date spans from March 3, 1900, back to February 25, 1900. Excel shows that March 1, 1900, is a Thursday, and this is correct. However, Microsoft says the Wednesday before this day is February 29, 1900—a day that does not exist. This causes all weekdays from January 1, 1900, to February 28, 1900, to be wrong in Excel. When Excel says that February 28, 1900, was on a Tuesday, that is incorrect; February 28, 1900, really was a Wednesday.

Understanding Excel Date and Time Formats

It is worthwhile to learn the various Excel custom codes for date and time formats. Figure 8.15 shows a table of how March 5, 2021, would be displayed in various numeric formats. The codes in A4:A17 are the possible codes for displaying just date, month, or year. Most people know the classic *mm/dd/yyyy* format, but far more formats are available. You can cause Excel to spell out the month and weekday by using codes such as *dddd, mmmm d, yyyy*. Here are the possibilities:

- mm—Displays the month with two digits. Months before October are displayed with a leading zero (for example, January is 01).

- m—Displays the month with one or two digits, as necessary.

- mmm—Displays a three-letter abbreviation for the month (for example, Jan, Feb).

- mmmm—Spells out the month (for example, January, February).

- mmmmm—First letter of the month, useful for creating "JFMAMJJASOND" chart labels.

CHAPTER 8

- **dd**—Displays the day of the month with two digits. Dates earlier than the 10th of the month are displayed with a leading zero (for example, the 1st is 01).

- **d**—Displays the day of the month with one or two digits, as needed.

- **ddd**—Displays a three-letter abbreviation for the name of the weekday (for example, Mon, Tue).

- **dddd**—Spells out the name of the weekday (for example, Monday, Tuesday).

- **yy or y**—Uses two digits for the year (for example, 15).

- **yyyy or yyy**—Uses four digits for the year (for example, 2015).

	A	B	C
1	3/5/2021		
2			
3	FORMAT	DISPLAYS AS	NOTE
4	m	3	*1 or 2 digit month as needed*
5	mm	03	*Always 2 digits for month*
6	mmm	Mar	*3 letter month abbreviation*
7	mmmm	March	*Spell out the month*
8	mmmmm	M	*1st text - for JFMAMJJASOND*
9	d	5	*1 or 2 digit day as needed*
10	dd	05	*Always 2 digits for day*
11	ddd	Fri	*3 letter day abbreviation*
12	dddd	Friday	*Spell out the weekday*
13	yy	21	*2 digits for year*
14	yyyy	2021	*4 digits for year*
15	mm/dd/yyyy	03/05/2021	
16	mmm d, yy	Mar 5, 21	
17	d-mmmm-yyyy	5-March-2021	

Figure 8.15 Any of these custom date format codes can be typed in the Custom Numeric Format box.

You are allowed to string together any combination of these codes with a space, comma, slash, or dash. It is valid to repeat a portion of the date format. For example, the format *dddd, mmmm d, yyyy* shows the day portion twice in the date and would display as Thursday, March 5, 2018.

Although the date formats are mostly intuitive, several difficulties exist in the time formats. The first problem is the *M* code. Excel has already used *M* to mean month. In a time format, you cannot use *M* alone to mean minutes. The *M* code must either be preceded or followed by a colon.

There is another difficulty: When you are dealing with years, months, and days, it is often perfectly valid to mention only one of the portions of the date without the other two. It is common to hear any of these statements:

- "I was born in 1965."

- "I am going on vacation in July."

- "I will be back on the 27th."

If you have a date such as March 5, 2018, and use the proper formatting code, Excel happily tells you that this date is March or 2018 or the 5th. Technically, Excel is leaving out some really important information—the 5th of what? As humans, we can often figure out that this probably means the 5th of the next month. Thus, we aren't shocked that Excel is leaving off the fact that it is March 2018.

TIP

Custom number formats are entered in the Format Cells dialog box. There are three ways to display this dialog:

- **Press Ctrl+1.**
- **From the Home tab, in the Number group, select the drop-down menu and select More Number Formats from the bottom of the drop-down menu.**
- **Click the expand icon in the lower-right corner of the Number group on the Home tab.**

When the Format Cells dialog box is displayed, you select the Number tab. In the Category list, you select Custom. In the Type box, you enter your custom format. The Sample box displays the active cell with the format applied.

Imagine how strange it would be if Excel did this with regular numbers. Suppose you have the number 352. Would Excel ever offer a numeric format that would display just the tens portion of the number? If you put 352 in a cell, would Excel display 5 or 50? It would make no sense.

Excel treats time as an extension of dates and is happy to show you only a portion of the time. This can cause great confusion. To Excel, 40 hours really means 1 day and 16 hours. If you create a timesheet in Excel and format the total hours for the week as *H:MM*, Excel thinks that you are purposefully leaving off the day portion of the format! Excel presents 45 hours as just 21 hours because it assumes you can figure out there is 1 day from the context. But our brains don't work that way; 21 hours means 21 hours, not 1 day and 21 hours.

To overcome this problem in Excel, you use square brackets. Surrounding any time element with square brackets tells Excel to include all greater time/date elements in that one element, as in the following examples:

- 5 days and 10 hours in *[H]* format would be 130.

- 5 days and 10 hours in *[M]* format would be 7800, to represent that many minutes.

- 5 days and 10 hours in *[S]* format would be 468000, to represent that many seconds.

As shown in Figure 8.16, the time formatting codes include various combinations of *h, hh, s, ss, :mm,* and *mm:,* all of which can be modified with square brackets.

	A	B	C	D	E
B4			=TEXT($A$1,A4)		
1	20:05:07				
2					
3	**FORMAT**	**DISPLAYS AS**	**NOTE**		
4	h	20	*1 or 2 digit hour as needed*		
5	hh	20	*Always 2 digits for hour*		
6	h:mm	20:05	*1 or 2 digit hour as needed*		
7	hh:mm	20:05	*Always 2 digits for hour*		
8	h:mm:ss	20:05:07	*Hours, minutes, seconds in military time*		
9	h:m:s	20:5:7	*Strange looking, but a valid code*		
10	s	7	*Seconds, using 1 or 2 digits*		
11	ss	07	*Seconds, using 2 digits*		
12	h:mm AM/PM	8:05 PM	*Hours and minutes with AM or PM*		
13	[h]:mm	44:05	*Include any full days as hours*		
14	[m]	2645	*Include any hours or days as minutes*		
15	[s]	158707	*Include any days, hours or minutes as seconds*		
16	mm.ss.00	05.07.00	*Show decimal portions of seconds*		

Figure 8.16   Custom time format codes.

To display date and time, you enter the custom date format code, a space, and then the time format code.

Examples of Date and Time Functions

In all the examples in the following sections, you should use care to ensure that the resulting cell is formatted using the proper format, as discussed in the preceding section.

Using NOW and TODAY to Calculate the Current Date and Time or Current Date

There are a couple of keyboard shortcuts for entering date and time. Pressing Ctrl+; enters the current date in a cell. Pressing Ctrl+: enters the current time in a cell. However, both of these hotkeys create a static value; that is, the date or time reflects the instant that you typed the hotkey, and it never changes in the future.

Excel offers two functions for calculating the current date: *NOW* and *TODAY*. These functions are excellent for figuring out the number of days until a deadline or how late an open receivable might be.

CAUTION

It would be nice if *NOW()* would function like a real-time clock, constantly updating in Excel. However, the result is calculated when the file is opened, with each press of the F9 key, and when an entry is made elsewhere in the worksheet.

Syntax:

=NOW()
=TODAY()

NOW returns the serial number of the current date and time. *TODAY* returns the serial number of the current date. The *TODAY* function returns today's date, without a time attached. The *NOW* function returns the current date and time.

Both of these functions can be made to display the current date, but there is an important distinction when you are performing calculations with the functions. In Figure 8.17, column A contains *NOW* functions, and column C contains *TODAY* functions. Row 2 is formatted as a date and time. Row 3 is formatted as a date. Row 4 is formatted as numeric. Cell A3 and C3 look the same. If you need to display the date without using it in a calculation, *NOW* or *TODAY* work fine.

	A	B	C	D
1	NOW()		TODAY()	Comment
2	6/20/18 5:01 PM		6/20/18 12:00 AM	*Formatted as Date/Time*
3	6/20/18		6/20/18	*Formatted as Date*
4	43271.7096		43271.0000	*Formatted as Serial Number*
5				
6				
7	9/7/2018		9/7/2018	*Deadline*
8	78.2904		79.0000	*Days Until Deadline*

Figure 8.17   *NOW* and *TODAY* can be made to look alike, but you need to choose the proper one if you are going to be using the result in a later calculation.

CHAPTER 8

Row 8 calculates the number of days until a deadline approaches. Although most people would say that tomorrow is one day away, the formula in A8 would tend to say that the deadline is 0.2904 days away. This can be deceiving. If you are going to use the result of *NOW* or *TODAY* in a date calculation, you should use *TODAY* to prevent Excel from reporting fractional days. The formula in A8 is *=A7–A3*, formatted as numeric instead of a date.

Using YEAR, MONTH, DAY, HOUR, MINUTE, and SECOND to Break a Date/Time Apart

If you have a column of dates from the month of July 2018, you can easily make them all look the same by using the *MMM-YY* format. However, the dates in the actual cells are still different. The July 2018 records are not sorted as if they were a tie. Excel offers six functions that you can use to extract a single portion of the date: *YEAR, MONTH, DAY, HOUR, MINUTE,* and *SECOND*.

In Figure 8.18, cell A1 contains a date and time. Functions in A3 through A8 break out the date into components:

- *=YEAR(date)* returns the year portion as a four-digit year.

- *=MONTH(date)* returns the month number, from 1 through 12.

- *=DAY(date)* returns the day of the month, from 1 through 31.

- *=HOUR(date)* returns the hour, from 0 to 23.

- *=MINUTE(date)* returns the minute, from 0 to 59.

- *=SECOND(date)* returns the second, from 0 to 59.

	A	B
1	7/14/21 7:18:29 PM	
2		
3	2021	=YEAR(A1)
4	7	=MONTH(A1)
5	14	=DAY(A1)
6	19	=HOUR(A1)
7	18	=MINUTE(A1)
8	29	=SECOND(A1)

Figure 8.18   These six functions allow you to isolate any portion of a date or time.

In each case, *date* must contain a valid Excel serial number for a date. The cell containing the date serial number may be formatted as a date or as a number.

Using DATE to Calculate a Date from Year, Month, and Day

The *DATE* function is one of the most amazing functions in Excel. Microsoft's implementation of this function is excellent, allowing you to do amazing date calculations.

Syntax:

=DATE(*year*,*month*,*day*)

The *DATE* function returns the serial number that represents a particular date. This function takes the following arguments:

- *year*—This argument can be one to four digits. If *year* is between 0 and 1899 (inclusive), Excel adds that value to 1900 to calculate the year. For example, *=DATE(100,1,2)* returns January 2, 2000 (1900+100). If *year* is between 1900 and 9999 (inclusive), Excel uses that value as the year. For example, *=DATE(2000,1,2)* returns January 2, 2000. If *year* is less than 0 or is 10,000 or greater, Excel returns a *#NUM!* error.

- *month*—This is a number representing the month of the year. If *month* is greater than 12, *month* adds that number of months to the first month in the year specified. For example, *=DATE(1998,14,2)* returns the serial number representing February 2, 1999. If zero, it represents December of the previous year. If negative, returns prior months, although –1 represents November, –2 is October, and so on.

- *day*—This is a number representing the day of the month. If *day* is greater than the number of days in the month specified, it adds that number of days to the first day in the month. For example, *=DATE(2018,1,35)* returns the serial number representing February 4, 2018. Zero represents the last day of the previous month. Negative numbers return days earlier, just as with month. In a trivial example, *=DATE(2018,3,5)* returns March 5, 2018.

The true power in the *DATE* function occurs when one or more of the year, month, or day are calculated values. Here are some examples:

- If cell A2 contains an invoice date and you want to calculate the day one month later, you use *=DATE(Year(A2),Month(A2)+1,Day(A2))*.

- To calculate the beginning of the month, you use *=DATE(Year(A2),Month(A2),1)*.

- To calculate the end of the month, you use *=DATE(Year(A2),Month(A2)+1,1)-1*.

The *DATE* function is amazing because it enables Excel to deal perfectly with invalid dates. If your calculations for Month cause it to exceed 12, this is no problem. For example, if you ask

Excel to calculate =*DATE(2018,16,45)*, Excel considers the 16th month of 2018 to be April 2019. To find the 45th day of April 2018, Excel moves ahead to May 15, 2018.

Figure 8.19 shows various results of the *DATE* and *TIME* functions.

	A	B	C	D	E	F
1	Year	Month	Day	DATE		
2	2021	16	45	5/15/2022	=DATE(A2,B2,C2)	
3	2022	1	60	3/1/2022	=DATE(A3,B3,C3)	
4	2021	1	60	3/1/2021	=DATE(A4,B4,C4)	
5	2021	3	5	3/5/2021	=DATE(A5,B5,C5)	
6						
7						
8	Hour	Minute	Second	TIME		
9	1	12	23	1:12:23 AM	=TIME(A9,B9,C9)	
10	13	12	23	1:12:23 PM	=TIME(A10,B10,C10)	
11	12	72	23	1:12:23 PM	=TIME(A11,B11,C11)	
12	37	12	23	1:12:23 PM	=TIME(A12,B12,C12)	
13						

Figure 8.19   The formulas in column *D* use *DATE* or *TIME* functions to calculate an Excel serial number from three arguments.

Using TIME to Calculate a Time

The *TIME* function is similar to the *DATE* function. It calculates a time serial number given a specific hour, minute, and second.

Syntax:

=TIME(*hour,minute,second*)

The *TIME* function returns the decimal number for a particular time. The decimal number returned by *TIME* is a value ranging from 0 to 0. 999988425925926, representing the times from 0:00:00 (12:00:00 a.m.) to 23:59:59 (11:59:59 p.m.). This function takes the following arguments:

- *hour*—This is a number from 0 to 23, representing the hour.
- *minute*—This is a number from 0 to 59, representing the minute.
- *second*—This is a number from 0 to 59, representing the second.

As with the *DATE* function, Excel can handle situations in which the minute or second argument calculates to more than 60. For example, =*TIME(12,72,120)* evaluates to 1:14 p.m.

Additional examples of *TIME* are shown in the bottom half of Figure 8.19.

Using DATEVALUE to Convert Text Dates to Real Dates

It is easy to end up with a worksheet full of text dates. Sometimes this is due to importing data from another system. Sometimes it is caused by someone not understanding how dates work.

If your dates are in many conceivable formats, you can use the *DATEVALUE* function to convert the text dates to serial numbers, which can then be formatted as dates.

Syntax:

=DATEVALUE(*date_text*)

The *DATEVALUE* function returns the serial number of the date represented by *date_text*. You use *DATEVALUE* to convert a date represented by text to a serial number. The argument *date_text* is text that represents a date in an Excel date format. For example, *"3/5/2018"* and *"05-Mar-2018"* are text strings within quotation marks that represent dates. Using the default date system in Excel for Windows, *date_text* must represent a date from January 1, 1900, to December 31, 9999. *DATEVALUE* returns a *#VALUE!* error if *date_text* is out of this range. If the year portion of *date_text* is omitted, *DATEVALUE* uses the current year from your computer's built-in clock. Time information in *date_text* is ignored.

Any of the text values in column A of Figure 8.20 are successfully translated to a date serial number. In this instance, Excel should have been smart enough to automatically format the resulting cells as dates. By default, the cells are formatted as numeric. This leads many people to believe that *DATEVALUE* doesn't work. You have to apply a date format to achieve the desired result.

> ### CAUTION
> The DATEVALUE function must be used with text dates. If you have a column of values in which some values are text, and some are actual dates, using DATEVALUE on the actual dates causes a #VALUE error. You could use =IF(ISNUMBER(A1),A1,DATEVALUE(A1)). Also consider the =DAYS(*end*,*start*) function, which deals with either text dates or real dates.

> ### CAUTION
> There are a few examples of text that DATEVALUE cannot recognize. One common example is when there is no space after the comma. For example, "January 21,2011" returns an error. To solve this particular problem, use Replace to change a comma to a comma space.

	A	B
1	**TEXT**	**DATEVALUE**
2	3/5/2021	44260
3	03/05/2021	44260
4	3/5/2021	44260
5	5-Mar-21	44260
6	Mar 5, 2021	44260
7	March 05, 2021	44260
8	03-05-2021	44260
9	3-5-2021	44260

Figure 8.20   The formulas in column B use *DATEVALUE* to convert the text entries in column A to date serial numbers.

Using TIMEVALUE to Convert Text Times to Real Times

It is easy to end up with a column of text values that look like times. Similar to using *DATEVALUE*, you can use the *TIMEVALUE* function to convert these to real times.

Syntax:

=TIMEVALUE(*time_text*)

The *TIMEVALUE* function returns the decimal number of the time represented by a text string. The decimal number is a value ranging from 0 to 0. 999988425925926, representing the times from 0:00:00 (12:00:00 a.m.) to 23:59:59 (11:59:59 p.m.). The argument *time_text* is a text string that represents a time in any one of the Microsoft Excel time formats. For example, *"6:45 PM"* and *"18:45"* are text strings within quotation marks that represent time. Date information in *time_text* is ignored.

The *TIMEVALUE* function is difficult to use because it is easy for a person to enter the wrong formats. In Figure 8.21, many people would interpret cell A8 as meaning 45 minutes and 30 seconds. Excel, however, treats this as 45 hours and 30 minutes. This misinterpretation makes *TIMEVALUE* almost useless for a column of cells that contain a text representation of minute and seconds.

CAUTION

There are a few examples of text that *TIMEVALUE* cannot recognize. One common example is when there is no space before the AM or PM. For example, "11:00PM" returns an error. To solve this particular problem, use Replace to change "PM" to " PM" and to change "AM" to " AM."

	A	B	C
1	**TEXT**	**TIMEVALUE**	**FORMATTED**
2	1:10	0.048611111	1:10:00 AM
3	1:10 AM	0.048611111	1:10:00 AM
4	1:10 PM	0.548611111	1:10:00 PM
5	13:10	0.548611111	1:10:00 PM
6	1:10:30	0.048958333	1:10:30 AM
7	1:45:30	0.073263889	1:45:30 AM
8	45:30	0.895833333	9:30:00 PM
9	0:45:30	0.031597222	12:45:30 AM
10			

Cell B2 = =TIMEVALUE(A2)

Figure 8.21   The formulas in column B use *TIMEVALUE* to convert the text entries in column A to times. If there is no leading zero before entries with minutes and seconds, the formula produces an unexpected result.

Frustratingly, Excel does not automatically format the results of this function as a time. Column B shows the result as Excel presents it. Column C shows the same result after a time format has been applied.

Using WEEKDAY to Group Dates by Day of the Week

The *WEEKDAY* function would not be so intimidating if people could just agree how to number the days. This one function can give eight different results, just for Monday.

Syntax:

=WEEKDAY(*serial_number*, *return_type*)

The *WEEKDAY* function returns the day of the week corresponding to a date. The day is given as an integer, ranging from 1 (Sunday) to 7 (Saturday), by default. This function takes the following arguments:

- *serial_number*—This is a sequential number that represents the date of the day you are trying to find. Dates may be entered as text strings within quotation marks (for example, *"1/30/2018"*, *"2018/01/30"*), as serial numbers (for example, 43130, which represents January 30, 2018), or as results of other formulas or functions (for example, *DATEVALUE("1/30/2018")*).

- *return_type*—This is a number that determines the type of return value:

  - If *return_type* is *1* or omitted, *WEEKDAY* works like the calendar on your wall. Typically, calendars are printed with Sunday on the left and Saturday on the right. The default version of *WEEKDAY* numbers these columns from 1 through 7.

- If *return_type* is *2*, you are using the biblical version of *WEEKDAY*. In the biblical version, Sunday is the seventh day. Working backward, Monday must occupy the 1 position.

- If *return_type* is *3*, you are using the accounting version of *WEEKDAY*. In this version, Monday is assigned a value of *0*, followed by *1* for Tuesday, and so on. This version makes it very easy to group records by week. If cell A2 contains a date, then *A2-WEEKDAY(A2,3)* converts the date to the Monday that starts the week.

- *return_type*s of *11* through *17* were added in Excel 2010. *11* returns Monday as 1 and Sunday as 7 (the same as using 2). *12* returns Tuesday as 1, *13* returns Wednesday as 1, and so on, up to *17* returning Sunday as 1.

Figure 8.22 shows the results of *WEEKDAY* for all ten return types.

	A	B	C	D	E	F	G	H	I	J	K
1	WEEKDAY()	Return_Type ----->									
3	Date	1	2	3	11	12	13	14	15	16	17
4	Sunday, April 04, 2021	1	7	6	7	6	5	4	3	2	1
5	Monday, April 05, 2021	2	1	0	1	7	6	5	4	3	2
6	Tuesday, April 06, 2021	3	2	1	2	1	7	6	5	4	3
7	Wednesday, April 07, 2021	4	3	2	3	2	1	7	6	5	4
8	Thursday, April 08, 2021	5	4	3	4	3	2	1	7	6	5
9	Friday, April 09, 2021	6	5	4	5	4	3	2	1	7	6
10	Saturday, April 10, 2021	7	6	5	6	5	4	3	2	1	7
11	Sunday, April 11, 2021	1	7	6	7	6	5	4	3	2	1

Figure 8.22   Columns B:K compare the *WEEKDAY* function for the ten different *return_type* values shown in row 3.

Using WEEKNUM or ISOWEEKNUM to Group Dates into Weeks

For many versions, Excel did not calculate weeks to match the ANSI standard. The *return_type* of *21* or the *ISOWEEKNUM* function returns the week number to match the ANSI standard. In this system, weeks always start on Monday. The first week of the year must have four days that fall into this year. Another way to say this is that the week containing the first Thursday of the month is numbered as Week 1.

In the ANSI system, you might have Week 1 actually starting as early as December 29 or as late as January 4. The last week of the year is numbered 52 in most years but is 53 every fourth year. This system ensures that a year is made up of whole seven-day weeks. This is better than the old results of *WEEKNUM*.

In the old system with *WEEKNUM*, the week containing the first of the year was always labeled as Week 1. If the first fell on a Sunday, and your weeks started on Monday, then Sunday, January 1 is Week 1 and Monday, January 2 is Week 2. The possibility of having weeks that last for one day made it difficult to compare one week to the next. Nonetheless, the Excel team added new *return_type*s for this system as well. In the past, *1* meant weeks started on Sunday, and *2* meant weeks started on Monday. Now, you can specify weeks should start on Monday (*11*), Tuesday (*12*), and so on, up to Sunday (*17*).

Syntax:

`=WEEKNUM(serial_num,[return_type])`

The *WEEKNUM* function returns a number that indicates where the week falls numerically within a year. This function takes the following arguments:

- *serial_num*—This is a date within the week.

- *return_type*—This is a number that determines on what day the week begins. The default is *1*. If *return_type* is *1* or omitted, the week begins on Sunday. If *return_type* is *2*, the week begins on Monday. *return_type*s of *11* through *17* were added to Excel 2013 and specify that the week should start on Monday (*11*) through Sunday (*17*). The new *return_type* of *21* ensures that every week has exactly seven days. Weeks always start on Monday, but the first Thursday of the year is the middle of Week 1.

Calculating Elapsed Time

If you work in a human resources department, you might be concerned with years of service to calculate a certain benefit. Excel provides one function, *YEARFRAC*, that can calculate decimal years of service in five ways. An old function, *DATEDIF* (pronounced Date Dif), has been hanging around since Lotus 1-2-3; it can calculate the difference between two dates in complete years, months, or days. Excel 2013 added the *DAYS* function, which can calculate elapsed days even if one or both of the values are text dates.

Syntax:

`=DATEDIF(start_date,end_date,unit)`

The *DATEDIF* function calculates complete years, months, or days. This function calculates the number of days, months, or years between two dates. It is provided for compatibility with Lotus 1-2-3. This function takes the following arguments:

- *start_date*—This is a date that represents the first, or starting, date of the period.

- *end_date*—This is a date that represents the last, or ending, date of the period.

- *unit*—This is the type of information you want returned. The various values for *unit* are shown in Table 8.6.

Table 8.6 Unit Values Used by the *DATEDIF* Function

Unit Value	Description
Y	The number of complete years in the period. A complete year is earned on the anniversary date of the employee's start date.
M	The number of complete months in the period. This number is incremented on the anniversary date. If the employee was hired on January 18, that person has earned 1 month of service on the 18th of February. If an employee is hired on January 31, then she earns credit for the month when she shows up for work on the 1st after any month with fewer than 31 days.
D	The number of days in the period. This could be figured out by simply subtracting the two dates.
MD	The number of days, ignoring months and years. You could use a combination of two DATEDIF functions—one using M and one using MD—to calculate days.
YM	The number of months, ignoring years. You could use a combination of two DATEDIF functions—one using Y and one using YM—to calculate months.
YD	The number of days, ignoring complete years.

Figure 8.23 compares the six unit values of *DATEDIF*. Each cell uses $A$1 as the start date and that row's column A as the end date.

	A	B	C	D	E	F	G	H
1	1/1/21	Unit - for DATEDIF ---->						
2			Y	M	D	D^2	M^3	D^4
3								
5	DATE		Y	M	D	MD	YM	YD
367	12/28/21		0	11	361	27	11	361
368	12/29/21		0	11	362	28	11	362
369	12/30/21		0	11	363	29	11	363
370	12/31/21		0	11	364	30	11	364
371	1/1/22		1	12	365	0	0	0
372	1/2/22		1	12	366	1	0	1
373								
374		D^2 = days in excess of months						
375		M^3 = months in excess of full years						
376		D^4 = days in excess of full years						

Figure 8.23 *DATEDIF* is great for calculating elapsed years, months, and days.

CAUTION

DATEDIF has been in Excel forever, but it was only documented in Excel 2000. Why doesn't Microsoft reveal *DATEDIF* in Help? Probably because of the strange anomaly when you try to calculate the gap from the 31st of January to the 1st of March in a non-leap year.

- The *"D"* version of *DATEDIF* reports this as 29 days. This is correct.

- The *"M"* version of *DATEDIF* reports this as one full month. This must be correct because the dates span the entire month of February.

- The *"MD"* version of *DATEDIF* reports this as a negative two days more than a full month. See cell D7 in Figure 8.24. This is the downside of trying to express a measurement in months when the length of a month is not constant. Negative values for this version of *DATEDIF* happen only when the end date is March 1 or March 2.

Despite this problem, for 363 days a year, *DATEDIF* remains an effective way to express a date delta as a certain number of years, months, and days.

Figure 8.24   In rare cases, *DATEDIF* will report 1 month and –2 days.

Syntax:

```
=DAYS(end_date, start_date,)
```

The *DAYS* function always calculates elapsed days between two dates. Introduced in Excel 2013, the function offers one new trick: It works with text dates as well as real dates. This function takes the following arguments:

- *end_date, start_date*—The two dates between which you want to know the number of days. If either argument is text, that argument is passed through *DATEVALUE()* to return a date.

Using EOMONTH to Calculate the End of the Month

Syntax:

=EOMONTH(*start_date,months*)

The *EOMONTH* function returns the serial number for the last day of the month that is the indicated number of months before or after *start_date*. You use *EOMONTH* to calculate maturity dates or due dates that fall on the last day of the month. This function takes the following arguments:

- *start_date*—This is a date that represents the starting date.

- *months*—This is the number of months before or after *start_date*. A positive value for *months* yields a future date; a negative value yields a past date. If *months* is not an integer, it is truncated.

  =EOMONTH(A2,0) converts any date to the end of the month.

CAUTION
You must format the result of the *EOMONTH* formula to be a date to see the expected results.

Using WORKDAY or NETWORKDAYS or Their International Equivalents to Calculate Workdays

The functions *WORKDAY* and *NETWORKDAYS* are pretty cool. They calculate days by excluding weekends and holidays. Weekends can be any two-day period, such as Saturday/Sunday or Thursday/Friday, or any one day, such as only Sunday. As of Excel 2013, you can specify odd work weeks such as Monday, Thursday, Friday, Saturday.

These functions are great for calculating shipping days when you ship with FedEx or UPS. They are also great for making sure your result doesn't fall on a bank holiday. Here's how you do it:

1. In an out-of-the-way section of a spreadsheet, enter any holidays that will fall during the workweek. This might be federal holidays, floating holidays, company holidays, and so on. The list of holidays can either be entered down a column or across a row. In the top portion of Figure 8.25, the holidays are in E2:E11.

	A	B	C	D	E
1	Start Date:	Saturday, April 17, 2021			Holidays
2	# Work Days	65			1/1/2021
3	End Date:	Tuesday, July 20, 2021			1/18/2021
4		=WORKDAY(B1,B2,E2:E11)			2/15/2021
5					5/31/2021
6	Start Date:	Saturday, April 14, 2018			7/5/2021
7	End Date:	Sunday, June 17, 2018			9/6/2021
8	# Work Days	45			10/11/2021
9		=NETWORKDAYS(B6,B7,E2:E11)			11/11/2021
10					11/25/2021
11					12/24/2021

Figure 8.25 *WORKDAY* and *NETWORKDAYS* can calculate the number of Monday-through-Friday days, exclusive of a range of holidays.

2.   Enter a starting date in a cell, such as B1.

3.   In another cell, enter the number of workdays that the project is expected to take, such as B2.

4.   Enter the ending date formula as =**WORKDAY(B1,B2,E2:E7)**.

The *NETWORKDAYS* function takes two dates and figures out the number of workdays between them. For example, you might have a project that is due on June 17, 2018. If today is April 14, 2018, *NETWORKDAYS* can calculate the number of workdays until the project is due.

Syntax:

=WORKDAY(*start_date,days,holidays*)

Syntax:

=NETWORKDAYS(*start_date,end_date,holidays*)

The *NETWORKDAYS* function returns the number of whole workdays between *start_date* and *end_date*. Workdays exclude weekends and any dates identified in holidays. You use *NETWORKDAYS* to calculate employee benefits that accrue based on the number of days worked during a specific term. This function takes the following arguments:

- *start_date*—This is a date that represents the start date.

- *end_date*—This is a date that represents the end date.

CHAPTER 8

- *holidays*—This is an optional range of one or more dates to exclude from the working calendar, such as state and federal holidays and floating holidays. The list can be either a range of cells that contain the dates or an array constant of the serial numbers that represent the dates. If any argument is not a valid date, *NETWORKDAYS* returns a *#NUM!* error.

Both of the functions described in this section assume that Saturday and Sunday are weekends and are not workdays. If you have any other weekend system, you can use *WORKDAY.INTL* or *NETWORKDAYS.INTL*, as described in the next section.

In Figure 8.25, the current date is entered in cell B6. The project due date is entered in cell B7. The holidays range is in E2:E11, as in the previous example. The formula in cell B8 to calculate workdays is =*NETWORKDAYS(B6,B7,E2:E11)*.

Using International Versions of WORKDAY or NETWORKDAYS

Two functions introduced in Excel 2010 expand the *WORKDAY* and *NETWORKDAYS* functions for situations in which the work week is not Monday through Friday. The most common example is a weekend on Friday and Saturday, which has become popular in Qatar, Bahrain, Kuwait, United Arab Emirates, and Algeria. It also handles the situation in which a manufacturing plant is working six days and the weekend is only Sunday. A new form of the *weekday* argument introduced in Excel 2013 allows for a nonstandard workweek, such as those found at farm markets or barbershops.

Syntax:

=WORKDAY.INTL(*start_date*,*days*,*weekend*,*holidays*)

Syntax:

=NETWORKDAYS.INTL(*start_date*,*end_date*,*weekend*,*holidays*)

Both functions work as their noninternational equivalents, with the addition of having the weekend specified as shown below. (Note that there are no noninternational equivalents for 8, 9, and 10.)

1—Weekend on Saturday and Sunday

2—Weekend on Sunday and Monday

3—Weekend on Monday and Tuesday

4—Weekend on Tuesday and Wednesday

5—Weekend on Wednesday and Thursday

6—Weekend on Thursday and Friday

7—Weekend on Friday and Saturday

11—Sunday only

12—Monday only

13—Tuesday only

14—Wednesday only

15—Thursday only

16—Friday only

17—Saturday only

You can specify any nonstandard workweek by using a seven-digit binary text as the weekend argument. The seven digits correspond to Monday through Sunday in order. A 1 indicates the company is closed that day (that is, it is a weekend), and a 0 indicates the company is open.

For example, the Hartville Marketplace is open Monday, Thursday, Friday, and Saturday. The weekend argument would be "0110001", as shown in Figure 8.26.

	A	B	C	D	E	F	G	H
1	**Farm Market Days**							
2								
3	Open Monday, Thursday, Friday, Saturday, even on holidays							
4								
5	Start	End	Days Open					
6	5/31/2021	9/6/2021	57					
7								
8	*7-digit Weekend argument: 1 means closed, 0 means open.*							
9	*7 digits, starting on Monday, ending on Sunday*							
10	*0110001 means open Monday, closed Tue-Wed, open Thu-Sat, closed Sun*							

Figure 8.26 Use the seven-digit binary text as the *weekday* argument to handle nonstandard work weeks.

Examples of Text Functions

When they think of Excel, most people think of numbers. Excel is great at dealing with numbers, and it lets you write formulas to produce new numbers. Excel offers a whole cadre of formulas for dealing with text.

CHAPTER 8

You might sometimes be frustrated because you receive data from other people, and the text is not in the format you need. Or the mainframe might send customer names in uppercase, or the employee in the next department might put a whole address into a single cell. Excel provides text functions to deal with all these situations and more.

Joining Text with TEXTJOIN

Microsoft introduced two new functions for joining text in February 2017. The CONCAT function will join text in several cells. While CONCAT is better than the legacy CONCATENATE, it is not as flexible as the amazing TEXTJOIN function.

In Figure 8.27, CONCAT successfully joins a long list of names. However, there is no space or comma between each item. The TEXTJOIN function lets you specify a delimiter. In D6 of the figure, =TEXTJOIN(", ",True,A2:A24) joins all of the names, and each name is separated by a comm and a space.

Further, the third argument of TEXTJOIN can be an array or a 3-D reference. That means you can make choices about whether to include each name or not. To join only the names where column B indicates the RSVP is Yes, you could use =TEXTJOIN(", ",True,IF(B2:B24="Yes",A2:A24,"")) entered with Ctrl+Shift+Enter.

	A	B	C	D	E	F	G	H	I
1	**Name**	**RSVP**		Join All					
2	Ellen Atkins	Yes		Ellen AtkinsErnest BullockSandra CarrollSonia DavidJason Eve
3	Ernest Bullock	No		*=CONCAT(A2:A24)*
4	Sandra Carroll	Yes		
5	Sonia David	Yes		Join All with Commas
6	Jason Everett	No		Ellen Atkins, Ernest Bullock, Sandra Carroll, Sonia David, Jaso
7	Gary Hammond	Yes		*=TEXTJOIN(", ",TRUE,A2:A24)*
8	Jacqueline Kemp	No		
9	Stacy King	Yes		Join only where RSVP=Yes
10	Bradley Marks	No		Ellen Atkins, Sandra Carroll, Sonia David, Gary Hammond, Sta
11	Madeline Martinez	Yes		*{=TEXTJOIN(", ",TRUE,IF(B2:B24="Yes",A2:A24,""))}*
12	Bertha Moreno	Yes		Do not type { or }, and use Ctrl+Shift+Enter
13	Delores Peck	No		
14	Mattie Pierce	Yes		Old Way
15	Vera Powers	No		Ellen Atkins, Ernest Bullock, Sandra Carroll
16	Kay Quinn	Yes		*=A2&", "&A3&", "&A4*
17	Lindsay Rhodes	No		

Figure 8.27   TEXTJOIN offers new ways to a range of names.

Syntax:

=TEXTJOIN(*delimiter*,*ignore_empty*,*text1*,[*text2*,...])

The TEXTJOIN function joins a list or a range of text using a delimiter.

Before the introduction of TEXTJOIN in 2017, you would have had to use =A2&" "&A3&" "&A4& and so on. Even the legacy CONCATENATE function could not accept a range of cells. The formula would have been =CONCATENATE("A2"," ",A3," ",A4," ",...).

Using LOWER, UPPER, or PROPER to Convert Text Case

Three functions—*LOWER*, *UPPER*, and *PROPER*—convert text to or from capital letters. In Figure 8.28, the products in column B were entered in a haphazard fashion. Some products used lowercase, and some products used uppercase. Column C uses *=UPPER(B2)* to make all the products a uniform uppercase.

	A	B	C	D	E	F	G
	F2 ▾ : ✕ ✓ *fx*		=PROPER(E2)				
1	Quantity	Product	Upper		NAME	Proper	
2	2	q754	Q754		ERIN RICHMOND	Erin Richmond	
3	1	g644	G644		JACK O'RASI	Jack O'Rasi	
4	5	G644	G644		KEITH MCCARTNEY	Keith Mccartney	
5	4	q754	Q754		ERNEST CURTIS	Ernest Curtis	
6	7	Q754	Q754		LEAH HARRISON	Leah Harrison	
7	7	d350	D350		ALLISON BRIGGS	Allison Briggs	
8	1	Q754	Q754		STEVEN CARR	Steven Carr	
9	1	g644	G644		TERRI HARDY	Terri Hardy	
10	3	G644	G644		KYLE SANCHEZ	Kyle Sanchez	
11	2	n870	N870		RYAN PITTS	Ryan Pitts	
12	3	q754	Q754				
13	4	d350	D350		MY MANAGER TYPES IN ALL CAPITALS		
14	8	q754	Q754		my manager types in all capitals		
15	5	I175	I175				
16	2	i175	I175				
17	3	i175	I175				
18							
19	C2: =UPPER(B2)						
20	E14: =LOWER(E13)						
21							

Figure 8.28   *UPPER*, *LOWER*, and *PROPER* can convert text to and from capital letters.

In cell E13, the text was entered by someone who never turns off Caps Lock. You can convert this uppercase to lowercase with *=LOWER(E13)*.

In column E, you see a range of names in uppercase. You can use *=PROPER(E2)* to convert the name to the proper case, which capitalizes just the first letter of each word. The *PROPER* function is mostly fantastic, but there are a few cells that you have to manually correct. *PROPER* correctly capitalizes names with apostrophes, such as O'Rasi in cell F3. It does not, however, correctly capitalize the interior *c* in McCartney in cell F4. The function is also notorious for creating company names such as Ibm, 3m, and Aep.

> **NOTE**
>
> If you want to keep the data only in column C, you have to convert the formulas to values before deleting columns A and B. To do this, select the data in column C and then press Ctrl+C to copy. Then select Home, Paste, Paste Values to convert the formulas to values.

Syntax:

`=LOWER(text)`

The *LOWER* function converts all uppercase letters in a text string to lowercase. The argument *text* is the text you want to convert to lowercase. *LOWER* does not change characters in *text* that are not letters.

Syntax:

`=PROPER(text)`

The *PROPER* function capitalizes the first letter in a text string and any other letters in text that follow any character other than a letter. It converts all other letters to lowercase letters.

The argument *text* is text enclosed in quotation marks, a formula that returns text, or a reference to a cell containing the text you want to capitalize partially.

Syntax:

`=UPPER(text)`

The *UPPER* function converts text to uppercase. The argument *text* is the text you want to be converted to uppercase. *text* can be a reference or text string.

Using TRIM to Remove Leading and Trailing Spaces

If you frequently import data, you might be plagued with a couple of annoying situations. This section and the next one deal with those situations.

You may have trailing spaces at the end of text cells. Although " *ABC*" and "*ABC* " might look alike when viewed in Excel, they cause functions such as *MATCH* and *VLOOKUP* to fail. *TRIM* removes leading and trailing spaces.

In Figure 8.29, you can see a simple *VLOOKUP* in column B. The formula in cell B2 is `=VLOOKUP(A2,$F$2:$G$5,2,FALSE)`. Even though you can clearly see that *M40498* is in the lookup table, *VLOOKUP* returns an *#N/A!* error, which indicates that the product ID is missing from the lookup table.

	A	B	C	D	E	F	G
1	ITEM	VLOOKUP				Item	Description
2	M40498	#N/A				M40498	10" GOLD WEAVE
3	M40583	#N/A				M40583	12" GOLD WEAVE
4	M40485	#N/A				M40584	14" GOLD FLORENTINE
5						M40485	16" SILVER WEAVE
6							

Figure 8.29 This *VLOOKUP* should work, but in this instance, it fails.

To diagnose and correct this problem, follow these steps:

1. Select one of the data cells in column F. Press the F2 key to put the cell in Edit mode. A flashing insertion character appears at the end of the cell. Check to see if the flashing cursor is immediately after the last character.

2. Select one of the data cells in column A. Press the F2 key to put the cell in Edit mode. Note whether the flashing insertion character is immediately after the last character. Figure 8.30 shows that the products in column A have several trailing spaces after them. The products in the lookup table do not have any trailing spaces.

Figure 8.30 Spaces are padding the right side of the products in column A.

3. If the problem is occurring in the values being looked up, you could modify the formula in cell B2 to use the *TRIM* function. The new formula would be *=VLOOKUP(TRIM(A2),$F$2:$G$5,2,FALSE)*. Figure 8.31 shows how this solves the problem.

Figure 8.31 Using *TRIM* to remove leading spaces allows *VLOOKUP* to work.

4. If the problem is occurring in the first column of the lookup table, insert a new temporary column. Enter the function **=TRIM(F2)** in the temporary column. Copy this formula down to all rows of the lookup table. Copy the new formulas. Select F2. Select Home, Paste, Values to paste the new values. Although the old and new values look the same, the *TRIM* function has removed the trailing spaces, and now the products match.

NOTE

It is not necessarily efficient to calculate, but you can solve the trailing spaces in column F by using *=VLOOKUP(A2,TRIM(F$2:G$5),2,FALSE)* if you press Ctrl+Shift+Enter to accept the formula.

Syntax:

=TRIM(*text*)

The *TRIM* function removes all spaces from text except for single spaces between words. You use *TRIM* on text that you have received from another application that might have irregular spacing. The argument *text* is the text from which you want spaces removed.

In Figure 8.32, cell C1 contains six letters: ABC DEF. You might assume that the cell is set to be centered. However, the formula in cell C2 appends an asterisk to each end of the value in cell C1. This formula shows that there are several leading and trailing spaces in the value.

	A	B	C
1		Original Value:	ABC DEF
2		="*"&C1&"*"	* ABC DEF *
3		Length(C1)	15
4		TRIM(C1)	ABC DEF
5		="*"&C4&"*"	*ABC DEF*
6		LENGTH(C4)	7
7			

Figure 8.32   *TRIM* removes leading spaces and extra interior spaces.

Using *=LEN(C1)* shows that the text actually contains 15 characters instead of six characters. The *TRIM(C1)* formula removes any leading spaces, any trailing spaces, and any extra interior spaces. The function still leaves one space between ABC and DEF because you want to continue to have words separated by a single space.

The formulas in cells C5 and C6 confirm that the leading and trailing spaces are removed and that the length of the new value is only seven characters.

Inside OUT

Sometimes TRIM appears to not remove spaces. This is particularly true when the data originated from a web page.

Look at your keyboard. By far, the largest key on the keyboard is the space bar. Press that space bar, and you will type an ASCII Character 32—also known as a space. However, there at least 20 varieties of space characters, such as the Unicode 200A hair space. The problem—since the rise of the web—is that the ASCII Character 160 is a nonbreaking space.

A web browser will always render "space space space" as "space," which causes problems when people try to get words to line up or VBA code to be indented. The solution is to change the space to a   or a nonbreaking space.

TRIM was written long before the web became common, and TRIM only operates on Character 32 spaces. If you have data with nonbreaking spaces or Mongolian vowel separators, TRIM will not remove those spaces.

Use the CHAR or UNICHAR functions to discover the character code behind your spaces. Then use SUBSTITUTE to change those back to regular spaces.

	=SUBSTITUTE(D1,CHAR(160),CHAR(32))						
	B	C	D	E	F	G	H
Original Text	ABC	ABC					
TRIM	ABC	ABC	=TRIM(D1)				
CODE of LEFT	32	160	=CODE(LEFT(D1,1))				
REPLACE	ABC	ABC	=SUBSTITUTE(D1,CHAR(160),CHAR(32))			
TRIM	ABC	ABC	=TRIM(D4)				

Two identical-looking cells contain two spaces followed by ABC. In the first column, the TRIM function correctly removes the leading spaces. However, in the second column, the spaces stay even after using TRIM. Formulas in the next row use the CODE from the LEFT of each original cell. In the first column, the ASCII code for the space is 32. In the second column, the ASCII code is 160. A workaround of =SUBSTITUTE(D1,CHAR(160),CHAR(32)) is shown to change the non-breaking spaces to regular spaces. After that formula, the TRIM works as expected.

Using the CHAR or UNICHAR Function to Generate Any Character

Early computers used a character set of 128 ASCII characters. Any computer that you've had in your home offered at least an 8-bit processor and could easily display 255 characters. Thus, computers sold in the United States offered the original 128 ASCII characters and an extended 128 characters with accented characters needed for German, French, and some other European languages. The *CHAR()* function makes it possible to display any of these 255 characters.

Today, the Unicode character set includes more than 137,000 characters, covering most written languages used on Earth. Unicode includes glyphs used in languages from Aboriginal to Yijing. You will find glyphs from Braille, Burmese, Cherokee, Greek, Old Persian, and many languages that you have not heard of. There are also map symbols, playing card symbols, emoticons, dice, domino, and mahjong markings. Unfortunately, the Unicode organization officially rejected including Klingon in 2001. Also, although the Calibri font will render chess, dice, and playing card symbols, it does not support domino or mahjong.

All versions of Excel supported *CHAR()* to generate symbols 0 through 255. Excel 2013 added support for *UNICHAR()* to render the 100,000+ symbols defined by Unicode.

You might have ventured into Start, All Programs, Accessories, System Tools, Character Map to find a particular character in the Wingdings character set. Also, if you have a favorite symbol, you might have memorized that you can insert the symbol by using a hotkey. For example, if you hold down Alt, type 0169 on the numeric keypad, and then release Alt, an Office program inserts the copyright symbol (©).

TIP

Although I know a few characters off the top of my head, I usually take a look at all characters in a set by entering =CHAR(ROW()) in cells A1:A255. This returns character A in row 65, and so on. In Excel 2019, you can use =UNICHAR(ROW()) in column A1:A1048576 to browse for symbols. To find something in particular, check out https://unicode-table.com/en/#control-character.

Syntax:

=CHAR(*number*)

The *CHAR* function returns the character specified by a number. You use *CHAR* to translate code page numbers you might get from files on other types of computers into characters.

The argument *number* is a number between 1 and 255 that specifies which character you want. The character is from the character set used by your computer.

Syntax:

=UNICHAR(*number*)

The *UNICHAR* function returns the Unicode character specified by a number.

Figure 8.33 shows some symbols available from *CHAR* and *UNICHAR*.

Figure 8.33   This figure shows examples of *CHAR* and *UNICHAR* results.

If you see a strange character in your data, you can learn the character number by using the *CODE* or *UNICODE* function, as described in the following section.

Using the CODE or UNICODE Function to Learn the Character Number for Any Character

If you can't remember that a capital A is character code 65, you can use the *CODE* function to learn the code associated with the character. The function returns the ASCII code for the first character in the text. *=CODE("A")* returns 65.

The old *CHAR* function did not work with characters beyond the first 255 characters. Starting in Excel 2013, the Excel team added the *UNICODE* function to return the Unicode character number for a character.

Syntax:

```
=CODE(text)
=UNICODE(text)
```

The *CODE* function returns a numeric code for the first character in a text string. The returned code corresponds to the character set used by your computer. The argument *text* is the text for which you want the code of the first character. This is an important distinction. *CODE* returns the code for only the first character in a cell. =CODE("A") and =CODE("ABC") return only 65 to indicate the capital letter A.

The *UNICODE* function returns the character code for the 100,000+ characters currently defined.

Using LEFT, MID, or RIGHT to Split Text

One of the newer rules in information processing is that each field in a database should contain exactly one piece of information. Throughout the history of computers, there have been millions of examples of people trying to cram many pieces of information into a single field. Although this works great for humans, it is pretty difficult to have Excel sort a column by everything in the second half of a cell.

Column A in Figure 8.34 contains part numbers. As you might guess, the Part Number field contains two pieces of information: a three-character vendor code, a dash, and a numeric part number.

	A	B	C	D	E	F	G
1	PART NUMBER	OH	OO	LEFT	MID		
2	RPM-104020	1	2	RPM	104020		Alternate choices for MID
3	BOR-21862	1	0	BOR	21862		=MID(A2,5,100)
4	LUK-04-158	3	1	LUK	04-158		=TRIM(MID(A2,5,100))
5	BOR-10294E	1	0	BOR	10294E		=MID(A2,5,LEN(A2)-5)
6	BOR-10643	3	2	BOR	10643		=RIGHT(A2,LEN(A2)-FIND("-",A2))
7	BOR-10625B	1	2	BOR	10625B		
8	BOR-10635	1	0	BOR	10635		If the Vendor code was not always 3 letters:
9	BOR-22816	3	1	BOR	22816		=LEFT(A2,FIND("-",A2)-1)
10	BWW-BC42TF	0	0	BWW	BC42TF		

Figure 8.34   *LEFT* makes quick work of extracting the vendor code. Several varieties of *MID* or *RIGHT* extract the part number.

When a customer comes in to buy a part, he probably doesn't care about the vendor. So the real question is, "Do you have anything in stock that can fix my problem?"

Excel offers three functions—*LEFT*, *MID*, and *RIGHT*—that enable you to isolate just the first or just the last characters, or even just the middle characters, from a column.

Syntax:

=LEFT(*text*,*num_chars*)

The *LEFT* function returns the first character or characters in a text string, based on the number of characters specified. This function takes the following arguments:

- *text*—This is the text string that contains the characters you want to extract.

- *num_chars*—This specifies the number of characters you want *LEFT* to extract. *num_chars* must be greater than or equal to zero. If *num_chars* is greater than the length of the text, *LEFT* returns all the *text*. If *num_chars* is omitted, it is assumed to be *1*.

Syntax:

=RIGHT(*text*,*num_chars*)

The *RIGHT* function returns the last character or characters in a text string, based on the number of characters specified. This function takes the following arguments:

- *text*—This is the text string that contains the characters you want to extract.

- *num_chars*—This specifies the number of characters you want *RIGHT* to extract. *num_chars* must be greater than or equal to zero. If *num_chars* is greater than the length of text, *RIGHT* returns all of *text*. If *num_chars* is omitted, it is assumed to be *1*.

Syntax:

=MID(*text*,*start_num*,*num_chars*)

MID returns a specific number of characters from a text string, starting at the position specified, based on the number of characters specified. This function takes the following arguments:

- *text*—This is the text string that contains the characters you want to extract.

- *start_num*—This is the position of the first character you want to extract in the text. The first character in the text has *start_num* *1*, and so on. If *start_num* is greater than the length of the text, *MID* returns *""* (that is, empty text). If *start_num* is less than the length of the text, but *start_num* plus *num_chars* exceeds the length of the text, *MID* returns the characters up to the end of the text. If *start_num* is less than *1*, *MID* returns a *#VALUE!* error.

- *num_chars*—This specifies the number of characters you want *MID* to return from the text. If *num_chars* is negative, *MID* returns a *#VALUE!* error.

In Figure 8.34, it is easy to extract the three-character vendor code by using *=LEFT(A2,3)*. It is a bit more difficult to extract the part number. As you scan through the values in column A, it is clear that the vendor code is consistently three letters. With the dash in the fourth character of the text, it means that the part number starts in the fifth position. If you are using *MID*, you, therefore, use *5* as the *start_num* argument.

However, there are a few thousand part numbers in the data set. Right up front, in cell A4, is a part number that breaks the rule. LUK-04-158 contains six characters after the first dash. This might seem to be an isolated incident, but in row 10, BWW-BC42TF also contains six characters after the dash. Because this type of thing happens in real life, two errors in the first nine records are enough to warrant a little extra attention. The four possible strategies for extracting the part number are listed in G2:G6. They are as follows:

- Ask *MID* to start at the fifth character and return a large enough number of characters to handle any possible length (that is, *=MID(A2,5,100)*).

- Ask *MID* to start at the fifth character but use *TRIM* around the whole function to prevent any trailing spaces from being included (that is, *=TRIM(MID(A2,5,100))*).

- Ask *MID* to start at the fifth character, but calculate the exact number of characters by using the *LEN* function (that is, *=MID(A2,5,LEN(A2)-4)*).

- Skip *MID* altogether and ask *RIGHT* to return all the characters after the first dash. This requires you to use the *FIND* function to locate the first dash—that is, *=RIGHT(A2,LEN(A2)-FIND("-",A2))*.

Using LEN to Find the Number of Characters in a Text Cell

It seems pretty obscure, but you will find the *LEN* function amazingly useful. The *LEN* function determines the length of characters in a cell, including any leading or trailing spaces.

Syntax:

=LEN(*text*)

The *LEN* function returns the number of characters in a text string. The argument *text* is the text whose length you want to find. Spaces count as characters.

There are instances in which you can use *LEN* along with *LEFT*, *MID*, or *RIGHT* to isolate a portion of text.

You can also use *LEN* to find records that are longer than a certain limit. Suppose you are about to order nameplates for company employees. Each nameplate can accommodate 15 characters. In Figure 8.35, you add the *LEN* function next to the names and sort by the length, in descending order. Any problem names appear at the top of the list.

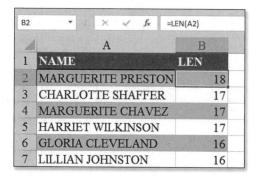

Figure 8.35 *LEN* identifies the number of characters in a cell.

Using SEARCH or FIND to Locate Characters in a Particular Cell

Two nearly identical functions can scan through a text cell, looking for a particular character or word. Many times, you just want to know if the word appears in the text. These functions go further than telling you if the character exists in the text; they tell you at exactly which character position the character or word is found. The character position can be useful in subsequent formulas with *LEFT*, *RIGHT*, or *REPLACE*.

First, let's look at an example of using *FIND* to determine whether a word exists in another cell. Figure 8.36 shows a database of customers. The database was created by someone who doesn't know Excel and jammed every field into a single cell.

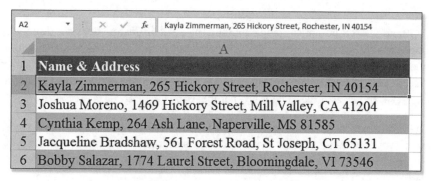

Figure 8.36 When the manager asked an employee to type this in Excel, she didn't realize that the employee had never used Excel before.

Here is how to make this work properly:

1. To find all the customers in California, in cell B2, enter **=FIND(", CA",A2)**. When you enter the formula, you get a *#VALUE!* error. This is okay. In fact, it is useful information: It tells you that CA is not found in the first record.

2. Copy the formula down to all rows.

NOTE

Like all the other data sets in this book, these names and addresses are randomly generated from lists of the most popular first name, last name, street name, and city names. Don't try to send Christmas cards to these people, because none of the addresses exist. And don't think that the ZIP Codes are real; everything here is completely random.

3. Sort low to high by column B. You'll see that 98% of the records have a *#VALUE!* error and sort to the bottom of the list. The few California records have a valid result for the formula in column B and sort to the top of the list, as shown in Figure 8.37.

	A	B
	fx =FIND(", CA",A2)	
1	Name & Address	California?
2	Marilyn Atkins, 1581 Twelfth Avenue, Oak Grove, CA 69942	47
3	Joshua Moreno, 1469 Hickory Street, Mill Valley, CA 41204	48
4	Kayla Zimmerman, 265 Hickory Street, Rochester, IN 40154	#VALUE!
5	Cynthia Kemp, 264 Ash Lane, Naperville, MS 81585	#VALUE!
6	Jacqueline Bradshaw, 561 Forest Road, St Joseph, CT 65131	#VALUE!
7	Bobby Salazar, 1774 Laurel Street, Bloomingdale, VI 73546	#VALUE!

Figure 8.37   You don't care where *FIND* found the text; you simply want to divide the list into records with valid values versus errors.

FIND and *SEARCH* are similar to one another. The *SEARCH* function does not distinguish between uppercase and lowercase letters. *SEARCH* identifies CA, ca, Ca, and cA as matches for CA. If you need to find a cell with exactly AbCdEf, you need to use the *FIND* command instead of *SEARCH*. Also, *SEARCH* allows for wildcard characters in `find_text`. A question mark (*?*) finds a single character, and an asterisk (*) finds any number of characters.

The *FIND* function makes it easy to find the first instance of a particular character in a cell. However, if your text values contain two instances of a character, your task is a bit more difficult. In Figure 8.38, the part numbers in column A really contain three segments, each separated by a dash:

1. To find the first dash, enter =**FIND("-",A2)** in column B.

CAUTION

The trick with this application of FIND is to look for something that is likely to be found only in California records. If you had customers in Cairo, Illinois, they would have also been found by the FIND command you just used. The theory with this sort of search is that you can quickly check through the few matching records to find false positives.

C2	▼	:	×	✓	fx	=FIND("-",A2,B2+1)		

◢	A	B	C	D	E	F	G	H
1	**Part Number**	**First Dash**	**Second Dash**	**First Part**	**2nd Part**	**3rd Part**		*Formulas:*
2	37767-33-385568	6	9	37767	33	385568		*B2: =FIND("-",A2)*
3	632-6-43	4	6	632	6	43		*C2: =FIND("-",A2,B2+1)*
4	10-13-5656	3	6	10	13	5656		*D2: =LEFT(A2,B2-1)*
5	9-671672-119067	2	9	9	671672	119067		*E2: =MID(A2,B2+1,C2-B2-1)*
6	41-50555-51	3	9	41	50555	51		*F2: =RIGHT(A2,LEN(A2)-C2)*
7	568-536-177914	4	8	568	536	177914		

Figure 8.38 Formulaically isolating data between the first and second dashes can be done, but it helps to break each number down into small parts.

2. To find the second dash, use the optional *start_num* parameter to the *FIND* function. The *start_num* parameter is a character position. You want the function to start looking after the first instance of a dash. This can be calculated as the result of the first *FIND* in column B plus one. Thus, the formula in cell C2 is *=FIND("-",A2,B2+1)*.

3. After you find the character positions of the dashes, isolate the various portions of the part number. In column D, for the first part of the number, enter **=LEFT(A2,B2-1)**. This basically asks for the left characters from the part number, stopping at one fewer than the first dash.

4. In column E, for the middle part of the number, enter **=MID(A2,B2+1,C2-B2-1)**. This asks Excel to start at the character position one after the first dash and then continue for a length that is one fewer than the first dash subtracted from the second dash.

5. In column F, for the final part of the number, enter **=RIGHT(A2,LEN(A2)-C2)**. This calculates the total length of the part number, subtracts the position of the second dash, and returns those right characters.

Syntax:

=FIND(*find_text,within_text,start_num*)

FIND finds one text string (*find_text*) within another text string (*within_text*) and returns the number of the starting position of *find_text* from the first character of *within_text*. You can also use *SEARCH* to find one text string within another, but unlike *SEARCH*, *FIND* is case sensitive and doesn't allow wildcard characters.

CHAPTER 8

The *FIND* function takes the following arguments:

- *find_text*—This is the text you want to find. If *find_text* is "" (that is, empty text), *FIND* matches the first character in the search string (that is, the character numbered *start_num* or *1*). *find_text* cannot contain wildcard characters.

- *within_text*—This is the text that contains the text you want to find.

- *start_num*—This specifies the character at which to start the search. The first character in *within_text* is character number 1. If you omit *start_num*, it is assumed to be 1.

Syntax:

=SEARCH(*find_text*,*within_text*,*start_num*)

SEARCH returns the number of the character at which a specific character or text string is first found, beginning with *start_num*. You use *SEARCH* to determine the location of a character or text string within another text string so that you can use the *MID* or *REPLACE* function to change the text.

The *SEARCH* function takes the following arguments:

- *find_text*—This is the text you want to find. You can use the wildcard characters question mark (*?*) and asterisk (*) in *find_text*. A question mark matches any single character; an asterisk matches any sequence of characters. If you want to find an actual question mark or asterisk, you type a tilde (~) before the character. If you want to find a tilde, you type two tildes. If *find_text* is not found, a *#VALUE!* error is returned.

- *within_text*—This is the text in which you want to search for *find_text*.

- *start_num*—This is the character number in *within_text* at which you want to start searching. If *start_num* is omitted, it is assumed to be 1. If *start_num* is not greater than zero or is greater than the length of *within_text*, a *#VALUE!* error is returned.

CAUTION

If *find_text* **does not appear in** *within_text*, FIND **returns a** #VALUE! **error. If** *start_num* **is not greater than zero,** FIND **returns a** #VALUE! **error. If** *start_num* **is greater than the length of** *within_text*, FIND **returns a** #VALUE! **error.**

Using SUBSTITUTE to Replace Characters

When you have the capability to find text, you might want to replace text. Excel offers two functions for this: *SUBSTITUTE* and *REPLACE*. The *SUBSTITUTE* function is easier to use and should be your first approach.

Syntax:

`=SUBSTITUTE(text,old_text,new_text,instance_num)`

The *SUBSTITUTE* function substitutes *new_text* for *old_text* in a text string. You use *SUBSTITUTE* when you want to replace specific text in a text string; you use *REPLACE* when you want to replace any text that occurs in a specific location in a text string.

The *SUBSTITUTE* function takes the following arguments:

- *text*—This is the text or the reference to a cell that contains text for which you want to substitute characters.

- *old_text*—This is the text you want to replace.

- *new_text*—This is the text you want to replace *old_text* with.

- *instance_num*—This specifies which occurrence of *old_text* you want to replace with *new_text*. If you specify *instance_num*, only that instance of *old_text* is replaced. Otherwise, every occurrence of *old_text* in text is changed to *new_text*.

Using REPT to Repeat Text Multiple Times

The *REPT* function repeats a character or some text a certain number of times.

Syntax:

`=REPT(text,number_times)`

The *REPT* function repeats text a given number of times. You use *REPT* to fill a cell with a number of instances of a text string. This function takes the following arguments:

- *text*—This is the text you want to repeat.

- *number_times*—This is a positive number that specifies the number of times to repeat text. If *number_times* is *0*, REPT returns "" (that is, empty text). If *number_times* is not an integer, it is truncated. The result of the *REPT* function cannot be longer than 32,767 characters.

In Microsoft Word, it is easy to create a row of periods between text and a page number. In Excel, you have to resort to clever use of the *REPT* function to do this.

In Figure 8.39, column A contains a page number. Column B contains a chapter title. The goal in column C is to join enough periods between columns B and A to make all the page numbers line up.

CHAPTER 8

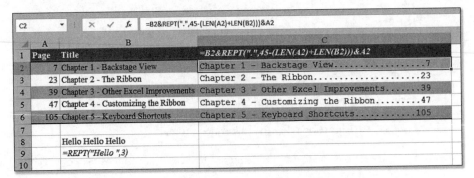

Figure 8.39   The *REPT* function can be used to calculate a certain number of repeated entries.

The number of periods to print is the total desired length, less the length of columns A and B. The formula for cell C2 is *=B2&REPT(". ",45-(LEN(A2)+LEN(B2)))&A2*.

NOTE

To make this work, you must change the font in column C to be a fixed-width font, such as Courier New.

TIP

An alternative solution is to format column A with the custom format of *"@*. "*. This shows the text in the cell and follows it with a series of periods, enough to fill the current width of the column.

Using EXACT to Test Case

For the most part, Excel isn't concerned about the case. To Excel, ABC and abc are the same things. In Figure 8.40, cells A1 and B1 contain the same letters, but the capitalization is different.

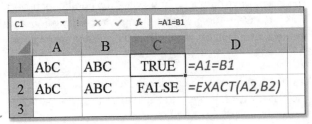

Figure 8.40   Excel usually overlooks differences in capitalization when deciding whether two values are equal. You can use *EXACT* to find out whether they are equal and the same case.

The formula in cell C1 tests whether these values are equal. In the rules of Excel, AbC and ABC are equivalent. The formula in cell C1 indicates that the values are equal. To some people, these two text cells might not be equivalent. If you work in a store that sells the big plastic letters that go on theater marquees, your order for 20 letter *a* figures should not be filled with 20 letter *A* figures.

Excel forces you to use the *EXACT* function to compare these two cells to learn that they are not the same.

Syntax:

=EXACT(*text1*, *text2*)

The *EXACT* function compares two text strings and returns *TRUE* if they are the same and *FALSE* otherwise. *EXACT* is case sensitive but ignores formatting differences. You use *EXACT* to test text being entered into a document. This function takes the following arguments:

- *text1*—This is the first text string.

- *text2*—This is the second text string.

Using TEXT to Format a Number as Text

Excel is great at numbers. Put a number in a cell, and you can format it in a variety of ways. However, when you join a cell containing text with a cell containing a number or a date, Excel falls apart.

Consider Figure 8.41. Cell A11 contains a date and is formatted as a date. When you join the name in cell B11 with the date in cell A11, Excel automatically converts the date back to a numeric serial number. This is frustrating.

	A	B	C	D	E	F	G	H
B1		f_x =DOLLAR(A1)						
1	1234.56	$1,234.56	=DOLLAR(A1)					
2	1234.56	$1,235	=DOLLAR(A2,0)					
3	1234.56	$1,234.56	=DOLLAR(A3,2)					
4								
5	1234.56	1,234.56	=FIXED(A5)					
6	1234.56	1,235	=FIXED(A6,0)					
7	1234.56	1235	=FIXED(A7,0,TRUE)					
8								
9	3/5/2015	Thursday, March 5, 2015						
10								
11	12/1/1989	Joe	Joe was born on 32843	=B11&" was born on "&A11				
12	12/1/1989	Joe	Joe was born on 12/1/89	=B12&" was born on "&TEXT(A12,"m/d/y")				
13								

Figure 8.41 *TEXT* can be used to format a number as text.

Today, the *TEXT* function is the most versatile solution to this problem. If you understand the basics of custom numeric formatting codes, you can easily use *TEXT* to format a date or a number in any conceivable format. For example, the formula in cell C12 uses =*TEXT(A12, "m/d/y")* to force the date to display as a date.

The *TEXT* function gives you a lot of versatility. To learn the custom formatting codes for a cell, you can select the cell, display the Format Cells dialog box (by pressing Ctrl+1), and select the Custom category on the Number tab. Excel shows you the codes used to create that format.

If you don't care to learn the number formatting codes, you can use either the *DOLLAR* or *FIXED* function to return a number as text, with a few choices regarding the number of decimals and whether Excel should use the thousands separator. The formulas shown in C1:C7 in Figure 8.41 return the formatted text values shown in column B.

Syntax:

=TEXT(*value*, *format_text*)

The *TEXT* function converts a value to text in a specific number format. Formatting a cell with an option on the Number tab of the Format Cells dialog box changes only the format, not the value. Using the *TEXT* function converts a value to formatted text, and the result is no longer calculated as a number.

The *TEXT* function takes the following arguments:

- *value*—This is a numeric value, a formula that evaluates to a numeric value, or a reference to a cell that contains a numeric value.

- *format_text*—This is a number format in text form from the Category box on the Number tab in the Format Cells dialog box. *format_text* cannot contain an asterisk (*) and cannot be the general number format.

Inside OUT

If you are exporting data to text for importing to another system, you might need numbers to appear with leading zeroes. While a combination of TEXT with LEN or RIGHT has been used in the past, a hack with the new BASE function solves the problem.

The BASE function introduced in Excel 2013 expands upon the old DEC2OCT, DEC2BIN, and DEC2HEX functions. If you want to express 25 in binary, the formula of =BASE(25,2) will return 11001. If you need 25 in hexadecimal, use =BASE(25,16). If an alien race takes over Earth and they use a Base 5 numbering scheme, we could use Excel to communicate using =BASE(25,5).

However, no self-respecting computer would ever write 11001. Binary systems are going to want an eight-digit number of 00011001. So, the BASE function allows an optional third argument for a minimum number of digits. In cell E4 below, the 00011001 result is from =BASE(A4,B4,8).

Astute reader Mordechai Steinfeld in Toronto realized that he could hack the BASE function to take advantage of its ability to add leading zeroes to a number. Mordechai takes any number in Base 10 and converts it to Base 10 just to add the leading zeroes. See rows 11 through 16 to see several examples.

By the way, a hat tip to the awesome Debra Dalgleish of Contextures.com. Debra recognized the brilliance of Mordechai's idea and communicated it in her weekly Excel newsletter in September 2017. I definitely recommend signing up for her free newsletter for great weekly Excel tips.

	A	B	C	D	E
1	Hacking the BASE function to add leading zero				
2					
3	Number		Radix	Result	Min digits	Result
4	25	2	11001	8	00011001
5	25	8	31	4	0031
6	25	16	19	4	0019
7					
8	Show numbers with leading zeroes				
9					
10	Desired Width	Number	Result		
11	5	25	00025	=BASE(B11,10,A11)	
12	5	1234	01234	=BASE(B12,10,A12)	
13	7	25	0000025	=BASE(B13,10,A13)	
14	7	12345	0012345	=BASE(B14,10,A14)	
15	9	25	000000025	=BASE(B15,10,A15)	
16	9	12345	000012345	=BASE(B16,10,A16)	

The binary representation of 25 is 11001. However, if you need to show that with eight digits, you would use =BASE(25,2,8) to produce 00011001. To convert a number to hexadecimal with four digits, use =BASE(25,16,4) to produce 0019. To pad a decimal number with leading zeroes, use =BASE(25,10,5) to convert 25 to 00025. Use =BASE(25,10,8) to produce 00000025.

Using the T and VALUE Functions

The *T* and *VALUE* functions are left over from Lotus days.

=T("text") returns the original text. If cell B1 contains the number 123, =T(B1) will return empty text. Basically, T() returns the value in the cell only if it is text.

=VALUE() converts text that looks like a number or a date to the number or the date.

CHAPTER 8

Using Powerful Functions: Logical, Lookup, and Database Functions

This chapter covers four groups of workhorse functions. If you process spreadsheets of medium complexity, you turn to logical and lookup functions regularly.

- The logical functions, including the ubiquitous IF function, help make decisions.

- The information functions might be less important than they once were because Microsoft has added the IFERROR function, but INFO, CELL, and TYPE still come in handy. The lookup functions include the powerful VLOOKUP, MATCH, and INDIRECT functions. These functions are invaluable, particularly when you are doing something in Excel when it would be better to use Access 2019.

- The database functions provide the D functions, such as DSUM and DMIN. Even though these functions fell out of favor with the introduction of pivot tables, they are a powerful set of functions that are worthwhile to master.

- Linked Data Types debuted in 2018 with support for Stock Quotes and Geography. Over time, expect Excel to support more data types. This chapter ends with a discussion of formulas to pull data from Linked Data Types.

Table 9.1 provides an alphabetical list of all the logical functions in Excel 2019. Detailed examples of these functions are provided later in this chapter.

Table 9.1 Alphabetical List of Logical Functions

Function	Description
AND(logical1, logical2,...)	Returns TRUE if all its arguments are TRUE; returns FALSE if one or more arguments are FALSE.
FALSE()	Returns the logical value FALSE. This function is useless, considering that typing FALSE without the parentheses returns the same value.
IF(logical_test, value_if_true, value_if_false)	Returns one value if a condition specified evaluates to TRUE and another value if it evaluates to FALSE.

IFERROR(value, value_if_error)	Returns value_if_error if the expression is an error; otherwise, returns the value itself.
IFNA(value, value_if_na)	Returns value_if_na if the expression resolves to #N/A; otherwise, returns the result of the expression.
IFS(logical_test1, value_if_true1, [logical_test2, value_if_true2…])	Checks whether one or more conditions are met and returns a value corresponding to the first TRUE condition.
NOT(logical)	Reverses the value of its argument. You use NOT when you want to make sure a value is not equal to another particular value.
OR(logical1, logical2,…)	Returns TRUE if any argument is TRUE; returns FALSE if all arguments are FALSE.
SWITCH(Expression, Value1, Result1, [Default_or_value2], [Result2]…)	Evaluates an expression against a list of values and returns the result corresponding to the first matching value. If there is no match, an optional default value is returned.
TRUE()	Returns the logical value TRUE. Equivalent to typing **TRUE**.
XOR()	Returns the logical Exclusive Or of the arguments. However, to be compatible with an XOR chip frequently used in electrical engineering, this function actually measures if an odd number of arguments are TRUE. People who don't make their living designing electrical circuits will wonder why =XOR(True,True,True) is True.

Table 9.2 provides an alphabetical list of the information functions in Excel 2019. Detailed examples of these functions are provided in the remainder of the chapter.

Table 9.2   Alphabetical List of Information Functions

Function	Description
CELL(info_type, reference)	Returns information about the formatting, location, or contents of the upper-left cell in a reference.
ERROR.TYPE(error_val)	Returns a number corresponding to one of the error values in Microsoft Excel or returns an #N/A error if no error exists. You can use ERROR.TYPE in an IF function to test for an error value and return a text string, such as a message, instead of the error value.
INFO(type_text)	Returns information about the current operating environment.
ISBLANK(value)	Returns TRUE if value refers to an empty cell. Note that if a cell contains "blanks" or spaces, this function will not return TRUE.

ISERR(value)	Returns TRUE if value refers to any error value except #N/A.
ISERROR(value)	Returns TRUE if value refers to any error value (that is, #N/A, #VALUE!, #REF!, #DIV/0!, #NUM!, #NAME?, or #NULL!).
ISEVEN(number)	Returns TRUE if number is even and FALSE if number is odd.
ISFORMULA(reference)	Checks whether a reference is to a cell containing a formula and returns TRUE or FALSE.
ISLOGICAL(value)	Returns TRUE if value refers to a logical value.
ISNA(value)	Returns TRUE if value refers to the #N/A (value not available) error value.
ISNONTEXT(value)	Returns TRUE if value refers to any item that is not text. (Note that this function returns TRUE if value refers to a blank cell.)
ISNUMBER(value)	Returns TRUE if value refers to a number.
ISODD(number)	Returns TRUE if the number is odd and FALSE if the number is even.
ISREF(value)	Returns TRUE if value refers to a reference.
ISTEXT(value)	Returns TRUE if value refers to text.
N(value)	Returns a value converted to a number.
NA()	Returns the error value #N/A, which means "no value is available." You use NA to mark empty cells or cells that are missing information to avoid the problem of unintentionally including empty cells in your calculations. When a formula refers to a cell containing #N/A, the formula returns the #N/A error value.
SHEET([value])	Returns the sheet number of the referenced sheet.
SHEETS([reference]	Returns the number of sheets in a reference.
TYPE(value)	Returns the type of value. You use TYPE when the behavior of another function depends on the type of value in a particular cell.

Table 9.3 provides an alphabetical list of the lookup functions in Excel 2019. Detailed examples of these functions are provided later in this chapter.

Table 9.3 Alphabetical List of Lookup Functions

Function	Description
ADDRESS(row_num, column_num, abs_num, a1, sheet_text)	Creates a cell address as text, given specified row and column numbers.
AREAS(reference)	Returns the number of areas in a reference. An area is a range of contiguous cells or a single cell.

CHOOSE(index_num, value1, value2,...)	Uses index_num to return a value from the list of value arguments. You use CHOOSE to select one of up to 254 values, based on the index number. For example, if value1 through value7 are the days of the week, CHOOSE returns one of the days when a number between 1 and 7 is used as index_num.
COLUMN(reference)	Returns the column number of the given reference.
COLUMNS(array)	Returns the number of columns in an array or a reference.
FILTER(Array,Include, [If_Empty])	Filter a range or array. Office 365 exclusive.
FORMULATEXT(reference)	Returns a formula as a string.
GETPIVOTDATA(data_field, pivot_table,[field1], [item1],...)	Returns data stored in a pivot table report. You can use GETPIVOTDATA to retrieve summary data from a pivot table report if the summary data is visible in the report.
HLOOKUP(lookup_value, table_array, row_index_num, range_lookup)	Searches for a value in the top row of a table or an array of values, and then returns a value in the same column from a row you specify in the table or array. You use HLOOKUP when your comparison values are located in a row across the top of a table of data, and you want to look down a specified number of rows. You use VLOOKUP when your comparison values are located in a column to the left of the data you want to find.
HYPERLINK(link_location, friendly_name)	Creates a shortcut or jump that opens a document stored on a network server, an intranet, or the Internet. When you click the cell that contains the HYPERLINK function, Excel opens the file stored at link_location.
INDEX(array, row_num, column_num)	Returns the value of a specified cell or array of cells within the array.
INDEX(reference, row_num, column_num, area_num)	Returns a reference to a specified cell or cells within the reference.
INDIRECT(ref_text, a1)	Returns the reference specified by a text string. References are evaluated immediately to display their contents. You use INDIRECT when you want to change the reference to a cell within a formula without changing the formula itself.
LOOKUP(lookup_value, lookup_vector, result_vector)	Returns a value from either a one-row or one-column range. This vector form of LOOKUP looks in a one-row or one-column range, known as a vector, for a value and returns a value from the same position in a second one-row or one-column range. This function is included for compatibility with other worksheets. You should use VLOOKUP instead.

LOOKUP(lookup_value, array)	Returns a value from an array. The array form of LOOKUP looks in the first row or column of an array for the specified value and returns a value from the same position in the last row or column of the array. This function is included for compatibility with other spreadsheet programs. You should use VLOOKUP instead. However, unlike VLOOKUP, the LOOKUP function can process an array of lookup_values.
MATCH(lookup_value, lookup_array, match_type)	Returns the relative position of an item in an array that matches a specified value in a specified order. You use MATCH instead of one of the LOOKUP functions when you need the position of an item in a range instead of the item itself.
OFFSET(reference, rows, cols, height, width)	Returns a reference to a range that is a specified number of rows and columns away from a cell or range of cells. The reference that is returned can be a single cell or a range of cells. You can specify the number of rows and the number of columns to be returned.
ROW(reference)	Returns the row number of a reference.
ROWS(array)	Returns the number of rows in a reference or an array.
RTD(progid, server, topic, [to pic2], ...)	Retrieves real-time data from a program that supports COM automation.
SINGLE(Value)	Returns a single value when given a value, range or array. Used instead of implicit intersection. Office 365 exclusive.
SORT(Array, Sort_index, Sort_order, By_col)	Sorts a range or array. Office 365 exclusive.
SORTBY(Array, by_array1, sort_order1, ...)	Sorts a range or array based on the values in a corresponding range or array. Office 365 exclusive.
TRANSPOSE(array)	Returns a vertical range of cells as a horizontal range, or vice versa. TRANSPOSE must be entered as an array formula in a range that has the same number of rows and columns, respectively, because the array has columns and rows. You use TRANSPOSE to shift the vertical and horizontal orientation of an array on a worksheet. For example, some functions, such as LINEST, return horizontal arrays. LINEST returns a horizontal array of the slope and y-intercept for a line. Use TRANSPOSE to convert the LINEST result to a vertical array.
UNIQUE(array, [by_col], [occurs_once])	Returns the unique values from a range or array. Office 365 exclusive.
VLOOKUP(lookup_value, table_array, col_index_num, range_lookup)	Searches for a value in the leftmost column of a table and then returns a value in the same row from a column you specify in the table. You use VLOOKUP instead of HLOOKUP when your comparison values are located in a column to the left of the data you want to find.

CHAPTER 9

Table 9.4 provides an alphabetical list of all the database functions in Excel 2019. Detailed examples of these functions are provided later in this chapter.

Table 9.4   Alphabetical List of Database Functions

Function	Description
DAVERAGE(database, field, criteria)	Averages the values in a column in a list or database that match the conditions specified.
DCOUNT(database, field, criteria)	Counts the cells that contain numbers in a column in a list or database that match the conditions specified.
DCOUNTA(database, field, criteria)	Counts all the nonblank cells in a column in a list or database that match the conditions specified.
DGET(database, field, criteria)	Extracts a single value from a column in a list or database that matches the conditions specified. If multiple matches are found, returns #NUM! error.
DMAX(database, field, criteria)	Returns the largest number in a column in a list or database that matches the conditions specified.
DMIN(database, field, criteria)	Returns the smallest number in a column in a list or database that matches the conditions specified.
DPRODUCT(database, field, criteria)	Multiplies the values in a column in a list or database that match the conditions specified.
DSTDEV(database, field, criteria)	Estimates the standard deviation of a population based on a sample, using the numbers in a column in a list or database that match the conditions specified.
DSTDEVP(database, field, criteria)	Calculates the standard deviation of a population based on the entire population, using the numbers in a column in a list or database that match the conditions specified.
DSUM(database, field, criteria)	Adds the numbers in a column in a list or database that match the conditions specified.
DVAR(database, field, criteria)	Estimates the variance of a population based on a sample, using the numbers in a column in a list or database that match the conditions specified.
DVARP(database, field, criteria)	Calculates the variance of a population based on the entire population, using the numbers in a column in a list or database that match the conditions specified.

Examples of Logical Functions

With only eight functions, the logical function group is one of the smallest in Excel. The IF function is easy to understand, and it enables you to solve a variety of problems.

Using the IF Function to Make a Decision

Many calculations in our lives are not straightforward. Suppose that a manager offers a bonus program if her team meets its goals. Or perhaps a commission plan offers a bonus if a certain profit goal is met. You can solve these types of calculations by using the IF function.

Syntax:

```
IF(logical_test,value_if_true,value_if_false)
```

There are three arguments in the IF function. The first argument is any logical test that results in a TRUE or FALSE. For example, you might have logical tests such as these:

```
A2>100
B5="West"
C99<=D99
```

All logical tests involve one of the comparison operators shown in Table 9.5.

Table 9.5   Comparison Operators

Comparison Operator	Meaning	Example
=	Equal to	C1=D1
>	Greater than	A1>B1
<	Less than	A1<B1
>=	Greater than or equal to	A1>=0
<=	Less than or equal to	A1<=99
<>	Not equal to	A2<>B2

The remaining two arguments are the formula or value to use if the logical test is TRUE and the formula or value to use if the logical test is FALSE.

When you read an IF function, you should think of the first comma as the word *then* and the second comma as the word *otherwise*. For example, =IF(A2>10,25,0) would be read as "If A2>10, then 25; otherwise, 0."

Figure 9.1 calculates a sales commission. The commission rate is 1.5 percent of revenue. However, if the gross profit percentage is 50% or higher, the commission rate is 2.5 percent of revenue.

NOTE

Mathematicians would correctly note that in both the second and third arguments of the formula =IF(H2>=50%,0.025*F2,0.015*F2), you are multiplying by F2. Therefore, you could simplify the formula by using =IF(H2>=50%,0.025,0.015)*F2.

Figure 9.1   In rows 2, 4, and 5, the commission is 1.5%. In rows 3 and 6 through 9, the commission is 2.5%.

In this case, the logical test is H2>=50%. The formula for whether that test is true is 0.025*F2. Otherwise, the formula is 0.015*F2. You could build the formula as =IF(H2>=50%,0.025*F2,0.015*F2).

Using the AND Function to Check for Two or More Conditions

The previous example had one simple condition: If the value in column H was greater than or equal to 50%, the commission rate changed.

However, in many cases, you might need to test for two or more conditions. For example, suppose that a retail store manager offers a $25 bonus for every leather jacket sold on Fridays this month. In this case, the logical test requires you to determine whether both conditions are true. You can do this with the AND function.

Syntax:

AND(logical1,logical2,...)

The arguments logical1,logical2,... are from one to 255 expressions that evaluate to either TRUE or FALSE. The function returns TRUE only if all arguments are TRUE.

In Figure 9.2, the function in cell F2 checks whether cell E2 is a jacket and whether the date in cell D2 falls on a Friday:

=AND(E2="Jacket",WEEKDAY(D2,2)=5)

Figure 9.2   The AND function is TRUE only when every condition is met.

Using OR to Check Whether One or More Conditions Are Met

In the earlier examples, all the conditions had to be met for the IF function to be true. In other cases, you might need to identify when exactly one condition is true, or when one or more conditions are true.

For example, a sales manager may want to reward big orders and orders from new customers. The manager may offer a commission bonus if the order is more than $50,000 or if the customer is a new customer this year. The bonus is awarded if either condition is true. But only one bonus is paid; you do not give two bonuses if a customer is both new and the order is large. In this case, you would use the OR function with logical tests to check whether the customer is new or if the order is large.

To test whether a particular sale meets either condition, use the OR function. The OR function returns TRUE if any condition is TRUE and returns FALSE if none of the conditions are TRUE.

Syntax:

```
OR(logical1,logical2,...)
```

The OR function checks whether any of the arguments are TRUE. It returns a FALSE only if all the arguments are FALSE. If any argument is TRUE, the function returns TRUE.

The arguments `logical1,logical2,...` are 1 to 255 conditions that can evaluate to TRUE or FALSE.

Nesting IF Functions Versus IFS SWITCH or CHOOSE

The IF function offers only two possible values: Either the logical test is TRUE, and the first formula or value is used, or the logical test is FALSE and the second formula or value is used.

Many situations have a series of choices. For example, in a human resources department, annual merit raises might be given based on the employee's numeric rating in an annual review in which employees are ranked on a five-point scale. The rules for setting the raise are as follows:

- 5: 8% raise
- 4: 7% raise
- 3: 5% raise
- 2: 3% raise
- 1: No raise

Traditionally, you would test for five conditions by nesting four IF functions:

```
=IF(D2=5,8%,IF(D2=4,7%,IF(D2=3,5%,IF(D2=2,3%,0%))))
```

You only needed four IF functions to test for five conditions. After testing for the first four conditions, the fifth answer would be provided in the `Value_If_False` for the last IF function.

In February 2017, Office 365 customers were offered two alternatives:

`=IFS(D2=5,8%,D2=4,7%,D2=3,5%,D2=2,3%,TRUE,0%)`

`=SWITCH(D2,5,8%,4,7%,3,5%,2,3%,0%)`

Syntax:

`IFS(logical_test1, value_if_true1, [logical_test2, value_if_true2…])`

Syntax:

`SWITCH(Expression, Value1, Result1,[Default_or_value2],[Result2]…)`

In the IFS function, you can handle multiple conditions without nesting new functions. The IFS means that you have multiple IF conditions. The IFS formula above reads, "If D2 is 5, then return 8%. Otherwise, if D2=4, then return 7%. Otherwise, if D2=3, then return 5%. Otherwise, if D2=2, then return 3%." The last two arguments in IFS are a little bizarre. You essentially want to have a value to return if none of the previous conditions are true. You need to put a logical test that is always True. Explicitly typing **TRUE** solves the problem.

Inside OUT

The Excel team had two choices of how to handle the final Else in IFS. The solution is a tiny bit nerdy.

For decades, people using Excel were used to a syntax in which the final argument in an IF or a nested IF is the "value if false" or the "else" clause.

You are likely very used to the `=IF(Something is True,Do This,Or That)` construct, even if you had to nest IF statements with `=IF(A2 is high,then this,IF(A2 is medium,then this,otherwise that))`. The last argument of the function outlines what to do if none of the other tests are true.

There is a guy on the Excel team who had to decide how IFS would work. For ease, let's refer to him as Joe. Well, Joe is facing a dilemma. The IF function will always have three arguments. Excel had it easy because the Else clause was always in the last position.

However, for IFS, the Else clause could come after 4 arguments or 6 arguments or 120 arguments. Joe does not know where to look for the Else clause.

As a long-time fan of IF, I would have expected that the Else clause would be the fifth, seventh, or 121st argument in the function, but that is harder to program.

Joe wants to know that every odd-numbered argument is a logical test, and every even-numbered argument outlines what to do if the logical test is true.

There was a suggestion to use =IFS(A2>10,"*****",A2>7,"***",Else,"*"), but this causes language problems. Joe finally opted for having the next to last argument be TRUE. This makes it easier for Excel because there is already logic to convert True to a local language.

So, the Else clause if the IFS function is a bit unusual, but it is not impossible to deal with. If you leave off the Else clause and if nothing else was True, then IFS will return FALSE, just like this function: =IF(5<4,"Miracle").

The SWITCH function is better, in this case, because you only specify cell D2 once. You tell the SWITCH function that you want to return a value based on the value of D2. If it is 5, then 8%. If it is 4, then 7%. If it is 3, then 5%. If it is 2, then 3%. For any other value, use 0%. Note that SWITCH does not require you to enter the TRUE argument as the second-to-last argument.

In this particular case, because the five possible scores are 1 through 5, the CHOOSE function will be shortest:

=CHOOSE(D2,0,3%,5%,7%,8%)

The CHOOSE function points to a single value and then expects the value to return if the answer is 1, 2, 3, 4, 5, and so on.

Note that Excel classifies CHOOSE as a Lookup and Reference function instead of a Logical function.

➤ Read more about CHOOSE in "Examples of Lookup and Reference Functions" on page 244.

Figure 9.3 compares the four formulas. In this case, CHOOSE is the shortest.

CAUTION

These IF formulas are hard to read. There is a temptation to use them for situations with very long lists of conditions. Whereas Excel 2003 prevented you from nesting more than seven levels of IF functions, Excel 2007 and later allow you to nest up to 64 IF statements. Before you start nesting that many IF statements, you should consider using VLOOKUP, which is explained later in this chapter.

CHAPTER 9

Raise Calculation		Nested IF (51 Characters)
		=IF(D2=5,8%,IF(D2=4,7%,IF(D2=3,5%,IF(D2=2,3%,0%))))
Score	Raise	Using IFS (45 Characters)
5	8%	=IFS(D2=5,8%,D2=4,7%,D2=3,5%,D2=2,3%,TRUE,0%)
4	7%	Using SWITCH (34 Characters)
3	5%	=SWITCH(D2,5,8%,4,7%,3,5%,2,3%,0%)
2	3%	Using CHOOSE (25 Characters)
1	0%	=CHOOSE(D2,0,3%,5%,7%,8%)

Figure 9.3   Four different ways to calculate the raise percentage.

CHOOSE will not always be the shortest formula. SWITCH will win if you have to look for values that are not sequential or don't have to start with 1:

```
=SWITCH(A2,30,"CURRY",35,"DURANT",23,"GREEN",11,"THOMPSON","OTHER")
```

IFS will be better if you need to look for ranges of values:

```
=IFS(A2>80,"Top Tier",A2>50,"Group 2",A2>20,"Group 3",TRUE,"Bottom Tier")
```

Nested IF will be better if there is any chance the workbook will be opened in Excel 2016, Excel 2013, Excel 2010, or an earlier version. The new IFS and SWITCH functions will return #NAME? error if opened in a prior version of Excel.

Using the NOT Function to Simplify the Use of AND and OR

In the language of Boolean logic, there are typically NAND, NOR, and XOR functions, which stand for Not And, Not Or, and Exclusive Or. To simplify matters, Excel offers the NOT function.

Syntax:

```
NOT(logical)
```

Quite simply, NOT reverses a logical value. TRUE becomes FALSE, and FALSE becomes TRUE when processed through a NOT function.

For example, suppose you need to find all flights landing outside Oklahoma. You can build a massive OR statement to find every airport code in the United States. Alternatively, you can build an OR function to find Tulsa and Oklahoma City and then use a NOT function to reverse the result: =NOT(OR(A2="Tulsa",A2="Oklahoma City")).

Using the IFERROR or IFNA Function to Simplify Error Checking

The IFERROR function, which was introduced in Excel 2007, was added at the request of many customers. To better understand the IFERROR function, you need to understand how error checking was performed during the 22 years before Excel 2007 was released.

Consider a typical spreadsheet that calculates a ratio of sales to hours. A formula of =B2/C2 returns the #DIV/0 error in the records when column C contains a zero. The typical workaround is to test for the error condition: =IF(C2=0,0,B2/C2).

In legacy versions of Excel, it was typical to use this type of IF formula on thousands of rows of data. The formula is more complex and takes longer to calculate than the new IFERROR function. However, this particular formula is tame compared to some of the formulas needed to check for errors.

A common error occurs when you use the VLOOKUP function to retrieve a value from a lookup table. In Figure 9.4, the VLOOKUP function in cell D2 asks Excel to look for the rep number S07 from cell B2 and find the corresponding name in the lookup table of F2:G9. This works great, returning JESSE from the table. However, a problem arises when the sales rep is not found in the table. In row 7, rep S09 is new and has not yet been added to the table, so Excel returns the #N/A result.

	A	B	C	D	E	F	G
				fx	=VLOOKUP(B2,$F$2:$G$9,2,FALSE)		
1	Invoice	Rep	Amount	Name		Rep	Name
2	15100	S07	128.59	JESSE		S01	GRACE
3	15101	S06	144.67	ERIN		S02	JULIE
4	15102	S05	121	JEREMY		S03	CHRISTY
5	15103	S04	169.47	THELMA		S04	THELMA
6	15104	S04	169.62	THELMA		S05	JEREMY
7	15105	S09	172.55	#N/A		S06	ERIN
8	15106	S08	112.68	MARION		S07	JESSE
9	15107	S02	145.44	JULIE		S08	MARION
10	15108	S01	101.05	GRACE			

Figure 9.4   An #N/A error means that the value is not in the lookup table.

If you want to avoid #N/A errors, the generally accepted workaround in legacy versions of Excel was to write this horrible formula:

```
=IF(ISNA(VLOOKUP(B7,$F$2:$G$9,2,FALSE)),"New Rep", VLOOKUP(B7,$F$2:$G$9,2,FALSE))
```

In English, this formula says first to find the rep name in the lookup table. If the rep is not found and returns the #N/A error, then use some other text, which in this case is the words *New Rep*. If the rep is found, then perform the lookup again and use that result.

Because VLOOKUP was one of the most time-intensive functions, it was horrible to have Excel perform every VLOOKUP twice in this formula. In a data set with 50,000 records, it could take minutes for the VLOOKUP to complete. Microsoft wisely added the new IFERROR function in Excel 2010 to handle all these error-checking situations.

CHAPTER 9

Starting in Excel 2013, Microsoft has added the IFNA function. It works just like the IFERROR function, but the second argument is used only when the first argument results in an #N/A error. You might be able to imagine a situation in which you want to replace the #N/A errors but allow other errors to appear.

Syntax:

`IFERROR(value,value_if_error)`

The advantage of the IFERROR function is that the calculation is evaluated only once. If the calculation results in any type of an error value, such as #N/A, #VALUE!, #REF!, #DIV/0!, #NUM!, #NAME?, or #NULL!, Excel returns the alternative value. If the calculation results in any other valid value, whether it is numeric, logical, or text, Excel returns the calculated value.

Syntax:

`IFNA(value,value_if_na)`

If the expression evaluates to a value of #N/A, then IFNA returns value_if_na instead of the expression. Added in Excel 2013, this function replaces only #N/A errors and allows other errors to appear as the result.

The formula from the preceding section can be rewritten as =IFERROR(VLOOKUP(B7, $F$2:$G$9,2,FALSE),"New Rep") or as =IFNA(VLOOKUP(B7, $F$2:$G$9,2,FALSE),"New Rep"). Although IFNA is a bit shorter than IFERROR, the new IFNA function fails for anyone using Excel 2010 or earlier. This makes IFERROR a safer function to use for the next several years. Either IFERROR or IFNA calculates much more quickly than putting two VLOOKUPs in an IF function.

Examples of Information Functions

Found under the More Function icon, the 20 information functions return eclectic information about any cell. Eleven of the 20 functions are called the IS functions because they test for various conditions.

Using the ISFORMULA Function with Conditional Formatting to Mark Formula Cells

The Excel team introduced the ISFORMULA function in Excel 2013 to identify whether a cell contains a formula. A hack had been floating around for years to mark formula cells using an old XL4 Macro Language function. Being able to use ISFORMULA is a great improvement.

Syntax:

`ISFORMULA(reference)`

Checks whether reference contains a formula. Returns TRUE or FALSE.

Figure 9.5 shows a worksheet in which all the cells have a conditional formatting formula that uses =ISFORMULA. Any cells that contain a formula are shown in white text on black fill.

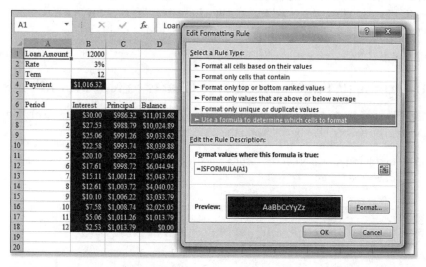

Figure 9.5   Use the ISFORMULA function with conditional formatting to mark all the formula cells.

Using IS Functions to Test for Types of Values

The remaining IS functions enable you to test whether a cell contains numbers, text, or various other data types.

Figure 9.6 shows a common solution. Column C contains a mix of text and numeric ZIP Codes. The formula in column D, =IF(ISNONTEXT(C5),RIGHT("0000"&C5,5),C5), replaces numeric ZIP Codes with text ZIP Codes. If the value in column C is nontext, the program pads the left side of the ZIP Code with zeros and then takes the five rightmost digits.

	A	B	C	D	E	F
				=IF(ISNONTEXT(C2),RIGHT("0000"&C2,5),C2)		
1	City	ST	Zip Code	Zip Fixed		
2	Salem	OH	44460	44460		
3	Uniontown	OH	44685	44685		
4	Merritt Island	FL	32953	32953		
5	Portland	ME	4123	04123		
6	Portland	ME	04123	04123		
7	St Thomas	VI	801	00801		
8	St Thomas	VI	00801	00801		
9						

Figure 9.6   The formula in column D detects nontext ZIP Codes and converts to text with five digits.

Using the N Function to Add a Comment to a Formula

You can call Excel's N function a creative use for an obsolete function. Lotus 1-2-3 used to offer an N() function that converted True to 1 and False to 0. The N of any text is zero. Some have figured they could use this function to add a comment to a formula:

```
=VLOOKUP(A2,MyTable,2,False)+N("The False ensures an exact match. Don't omit False")
```

Using the NA Function to Force Charts to Not Plot Missing Data

Suppose that you are in charge of a school's annual fund drive. Each day, you mark the fundraising total on a worksheet by following these steps:

1. In column A, you enter the results of each day's collection through nine days of the fund drive (see Figure 9.7).

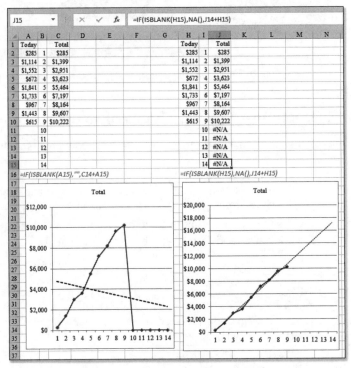

Figure 9.7   Using NA in the chart on the right allows the trendline to ignore future missing data points and project a reasonable ending result.

2. You enter a formula in column C to keep track of the total collected throughout the fund drive.

3. To avoid making it look like the fund drive collected nothing in days 10 through 14, you enter a formula in column C to check whether column A is blank. If it is, then the IF function inserts a null cell in column C. For example, the formula in cell C15 is =IF(ISBLANK(A15),"",A15+C14).

4. You build a line chart based on B1:C15. You then add a trendline to the chart to predict future fundraising totals.

5. As shown in columns A:C of Figure 9.7, this technique fails. Even though the totals for days 10 through 14 are blank, Excel charts those days as zero. The linear trendline predicts that your fundraising will go down, with a projected total of just over $2,000.

6. You try the same chart again, but this time you use the NA function instead of "" in the IF statement in step 3. The formula is shown in cell H16, and the results are in cell J15. Excel understands that NA values should not be plotted. The trendline is calculated based on only the data points available and projects a total just under $18,000.

In many cases, you are trying to avoid #N/A! errors. However, in the case of charting a calculated column, you might want to have #N/A! produce the correct look to the chart.

Using the CELL Function to Return the Worksheet Name

The CELL function can tell you information about a specific cell. Although the function can return many ancient bits of information (Excel 2003 color index, for example), it has one argument that allows you to put the worksheet name in a cell.

=CELL("filename",A1) returns the complete path, filename, and worksheet name. The technique is to locate the right square bracket at the end of the filename. Everything after that character is the worksheet tab name.

Figure 9.8 shows an example.

Figure 9.8   The CELL function returns the full path, filename, and tab name to a cell.

CHAPTER 9

Examples of Lookup and Reference Functions

The Lookup & Reference icon contains 18 functions. The all-star of this group is the venerable VLOOKUP function, which is one of the most powerful and most used functions in Excel. As database people point out, a lot of work done in Excel should probably be done in Access. The VLOOKUP function enables you to perform the equivalent of a join operation in a database.

This lookup and reference group also includes several functions that seem useless when considered alone. However, when combined, they allow for some very powerful manipulations of data. The examples in the following sections reveal details on how to use the lookup functions and how to combine them to create powerful results.

Using the CHOOSE Function for Simple Lookups

Most lookup functions require you to set up a lookup table in a range on the worksheet. However, the CHOOSE function enables you to specify up to 254 choices right in the syntax of the function. The formula that requires the lookup should be able to calculate an integer from 1 to 254 to use the CHOOSE function.

Syntax:

CHOOSE(index_num,value1,value2,...)

The CHOOSE function chooses a value from a list of values, based on an index number. The CHOOSE function takes the following arguments:

- index_num—This specifies which value argument is selected. index_num must be a number between 1 and 254 or a formula or reference to a cell containing a number between 1 and 254:

  - If index_num is 1, CHOOSE returns value1; if it is 2, CHOOSE returns value2; and so on.

  - If index_num is a decimal, it is rounded down to the next lowest integer before being used.

  - If index_num is less than 1 or greater than the number of the last value in the list, CHOOSE returns a #VALUE! error.

- value1,value2,...—These are 1 to 254 value arguments from which CHOOSE selects a value or an action to perform based on index_num. The arguments can be numbers, cell references, defined names, formulas, functions, or text.

The example in Figure 9.9 shows survey data from some respondents. Columns B:F indicate their responses on five measures of your service. Column G calculates an average that ranges from 1 to 5. Suppose that you want to add words to column H to characterize the overall rating from the respondent. The following formula is used in cell H4:

```
=CHOOSE(G4,"Strongly Disagree","Disagree","Neutral","Agree","Strongly Agree")
```

Figure 9.9   CHOOSE is great for simple choices in which the index number is between 1 and 254.

Using VLOOKUP with TRUE to Find a Value Based on a Range

VLOOKUP stands for *vertical lookup*. This function behaves differently, depending on the fourth parameter. This section describes using VLOOKUP in which you need to choose a value based on a table that contains ranges.

Suppose that you have a list of students and their scores on a test. The school grading scale is based on these ranges:

- 92–100 is an A.

- 85–91 is a B.

- 70–84 is a C.

- 65–69 is a D.

- Below 65 is an F.

Follow these steps to set up a VLOOKUP for this scenario:

1. Because in this version of VLOOKUP you do not have to list every possible grade, build a table showing the scores where the grading scale changes from one grade to the next.

2. Although the published grading scale starts with the higher values, your lookup table must be sorted in ascending sequence. This requires a bit of translation as you set up the table. Although the grading scale says that below 65 is an F, you need to set up the table to show that an F corresponds to any grade at 0 or higher. Therefore, in cell E2 enter **0**, and in cell F2, enter **F** (see Figure 9.10).

Figure 9.10   The VLOOKUP formula in column C finds the correct grade from the table in columns E and F.

3. Continue building the grading scale in successive rows of columns E and F. Anything above a 65 is given a D. Anything above 70 is given a C. Note that this is somewhat counterintuitive because it is the opposite order that you would use if you were building a grading scale using nested IF functions.

4. Ensure that the numeric values are the leftmost column in your lookup table. In Figure 9.10, the lookup table range is E2:F6. When you use VLOOKUP, Excel searches the first column of the lookup table for the appropriate score.

5. When using this version of VLOOKUP with ranges, sort the list in ascending order. If you are not sure of the proper order, use the Sort command from the Home tab to sort the table.

6. Because the first argument in the VLOOKUP function is the student's score, in cell C2, enter **=VLOOKUP(B2,**.

7. Because the next argument is the range of the lookup table, be sure to press the F4 key after entering E2:F6 to change to an absolute reference of $E$2:$F$6.

8. Ensure that the third argument specifies which column of the lookup table should be returned. Because the letter grade is in the second column of E2:F6, use 2 for the third argument.

9. Ensure that the final argument is either TRUE or simply omitted. This tells Excel that you are using the sorted range variety of lookup.

10. After you enter the formula in cell C2, again select cell C2 and double-click the fill handle to copy the formula down to all students.

Using VLOOKUP with FALSE to Find an Exact Value

In some situations, you do not want VLOOKUP to return a value based on a close match. Instead, you want Excel to find the exact match in the lookup table.

Figure 9.11 shows a table of sales. The original table had columns A through C: Rep, Date, and Sale Amount. Although a data analyst might have all the rep numbers memorized, the manager who is going to see the report prefers to have the rep names on the report.

D2	▼ : × ✓ ƒx	=VLOOKUP(A2,$F$2:$G$7,2,FALSE)				
	A	B	C	D	E	F	G
1	Rep	Date	Sale Amt	Rep Name			
2	R5	2/17/2006	151.67	Manny		R4	Amar
3	R7	2/17/2006	168.89	Michael		R8	Jerry
4	R5	2/17/2006	106.78	Manny		R6	Linda
5	R3	2/17/2006	152.93	Marc		R5	Manny
6	R6	2/18/2006	109.02	Linda		R3	Marc
7	R3	2/18/2006	141.96	Marc		R7	Michael
8	R8	2/18/2006	136.05	Jerry			

Figure 9.11   In this case, VLOOKUP needs to find the exact rep number from the table in columns E and F.

To fill in the rep names from a lookup table, you follow these steps:

1. In columns F and G, enter a table of rep numbers and rep names. Note that it is not important for this table to be sorted by the rep number field. It is fine that the table is sorted alphabetically by name.

2. Use FALSE as the fourth parameter in VLOOKUP. You need to do this because close matches are not acceptable here. If something was sold by a new rep with number R9, you do not want to give credit to the name associated with R8 just because it is a close match. Either Excel finds an exact match and returns the result, or Excel does not give you a result.

3. For cell D2, you want Excel to use the rep number in A2, so in cell D2, enter =VLOOKUP(A2,.

4. The lookup table is in F2:G7, so enter F2:G7 and then press the F4 key to make the reference absolute. This enables you to copy the formula in step 7. After pressing F4, type a comma.

5. In the lookup table, the rep name is in column 2 of the table, so type 2 to specify that you want to return the second column of the lookup table.

CHAPTER 9

6. Finish the function with **FALSE)**. Press Ctrl+Enter to accept the formula and keep the cursor in cell D2.

7. Double-click the fill handle to copy the formula down to all the rows.

8. VLOOKUP is a very time-intensive calculation. Having thousands of VLOOKUP formulas significantly affects your recalculation times. In this particular case, you have successfully added rep names. It would be appropriate to convert these live formulas to their current values. Therefore, press Ctrl+C to copy. Then, from the Home tab, select Paste, Paste Values to convert the formulas to values.

NOTE

If your lookup table is arranged sideways, with going across a row, you should use HLOOKUP. If your data is vertical, but the key field is not the leftmost column, you can use a combination of INDEX and MATCH, also explained later in this chapter.

9. Look through the results. If a sale was credited to a new rep who is not in the table, the name appears as #N/A. Manually fix these records, if needed.

To recap, the two versions of the VLOOKUP formula behave very differently. VLOOKUP with FALSE as the fourth parameter looks for an exact match, whereas VLOOKUP with TRUE as the fourth parameter looks for the closest (lower) match. In the TRUE version, the lookup table must be sorted. In the FALSE version, the table can be in any sequence. In every case, the key field must be in the left column of the lookup table.

Syntax:

VLOOKUP(lookup_value,table_array,col_index_num,range_lookup)

VLOOKUP searches for a value in the leftmost column of a table and then returns a value in the same row from a column you specify in the table. The VLOOKUP function takes the following arguments:

- lookup_value—This is the value to be found in the first column of the table. lookup_value can be a value, reference, or text string.

- table_array—This is the table of information in which data is looked up. You can use a reference to a range, such as E2:F9, or a range name such as RepTable.

- col_index_num—This is the column number in table_array from which the matching value must be returned. A col_index_num value of 1 returns the value in the first column in table_array; a col_index_num value of 2 returns the value in the second column in table_array, and so on. If col_index_num is less than 1, VLOOKUP returns the #VALUE! error value; if col_index_num is greater than the number of columns in table_array, VLOOKUP returns the #REF! error value.

- range_lookup—This is a logical value that specifies whether VLOOKUP should find an exact match or an approximate match. If it is TRUE or omitted, an approximate match is returned. In other words, if an exact match is not found, the next largest value that is less than lookup_value is returned. If it is FALSE, VLOOKUP finds an exact match. If one is not found, the error value #N/A is returned. If VLOOKUP cannot find lookup_value and if range_lookup is TRUE, it uses the largest value that is less than or equal to lookup_value. If lookup_value is smaller than the smallest value in the first column of table_array, VLOOKUP returns an #N/A error. If VLOOKUP cannot find lookup_value, and range_lookup is FALSE, VLOOKUP returns an #N/A error.

Using VLOOKUP to Match Two Lists

If Excel is used throughout your company, you undoubtedly have many lists in Excel. People use Excel to track everything. How many times are you faced with a situation in which you have two versions of a list and you need to match them up?

In Figure 9.12, the worksheet has two simple lists. Column A shows last week's version of who was coming to an event. Column C shows this week's version of who is coming to an event. Follow these steps if you want to find out quickly if anyone is new:

1. Add the heading **There?** to cell D2.

	A	B	C	D
	D3		fx	=VLOOKUP(C3,$A$3:$A$15,1,FALSE)
1	RSVP's LAST WEEK		RSVP's THIS WEEK	
2				There?
3	VERONICA HAHN		ARTHUR FLETCHER	ARTHUR FLETCHER
4	ELLEN LINDSAY		BARBARA BERGER	BARBARA BERGER
5	CECILIA HARMON		CANDICE GLENN	CANDICE GLENN
6	DONALD TYLER		CECILIA HARMON	CECILIA HARMON
7	NICOLE KELLY		CHRIS PAGE	CHRIS PAGE
8	MARCIA ERICKSON		CHRISTOPHER DONOVAN	#N/A
9	BARBARA BERGER		JOANN BROOKS	#N/A
10	CHRIS PAGE		ELLEN LINDSAY	ELLEN LINDSAY
11	CANDICE GLENN		JACOB MCINTYRE	#N/A
12	STACY DUNLAP		JOHN GARRISON	JOHN GARRISON
13	ARTHUR FLETCHER		KATHLEEN RICHARD	KATHLEEN RICHARD
14	KATHLEEN RICHARD		MARCIA ERICKSON	MARCIA ERICKSON
15	JOHN GARRISON		MYRTLE MOON	#N/A
16			NICOLE KELLY	NICOLE KELLY
17			STACY DUNLAP	STACY DUNLAP
18			VERONICA HAHN	VERONICA HAHN
19				

Figure 9.12 An #N/A error as the result of VLOOKUP tells you that the person is new to the list.

2. Because the formula in cell D3 should look at the value in cell C3 to see whether that person is in the original list in column A, start the formula with **=VLOOKUP(C3,$A$3:$A$15,**.

3. Because your only choice for the column number is to return the first column from the original list, finish the function with **1,FALSE)**. Then press Ctrl+Enter to accept the formula and stay in cell D3.

4. Double-click the fill handle to copy the formula down to all rows.

For any cells in which column D contains a name, it means that the person was on the RSVP list from last week. If the result of the VLOOKUP is #N/A, you know that this person is new since the previous week.

TIP

If you study the data in Figure 9.12, you see that three more names are in the column C list than in the column A list, yet four people were reported as being new this week. This means that one of the people from last week has dropped off the list. To quickly find who dropped off the list, use the formula =VLOOKUP(A3,$C$3:$C$18,1,FALSE) in B3:B15 to find that Donald Tyler has dropped off the list.

Note that you can also use MATCH to solve this problem.

Using the MATCH Function to Locate the Position of a Matching Value

At first glance, MATCH seems like a function that would rarely be useful. MATCH returns the relative position of an item in a range that matches a specified value in a specified order. You use MATCH instead of one of the lookup functions when you need the position of an item in a range instead of the item itself.

Suppose that your manager asks, "Can you tell me on which row I would find this value?" The manager wants to know the value or some piece of data on that record. However, rarely would the manager want to know that XYZ is found on the 111th relative row within the range A99:A11432.

MATCH comes in handy in several instances. In the first instance, consider a situation in which you are using VLOOKUP to find whether an item is in a list. In this case, you do not care what value is returned. You are interested in seeing either whether a valid value is returned, meaning that the entry is in the old list, or whether an #N/A is returned, meaning that the entry is new. In this case, using MATCH is a slightly faster way to achieve the same result.

Another handy way to use MATCH is with the INDEX function. MATCH has two features that make it more versatile than VLOOKUP. MATCH allows for wildcard matches. MATCH also allows for a search based on an exact match, based on the number just below the value, or based on a value greater than or equal to the lookup value. This third option is not available in the VLOOKUP or HLOOKUP functions.

Syntax:

MATCH(lookup_value,lookup_array,match_type)

The MATCH function returns the relative position of an item in a column or row of values. It is useful for determining if a certain value exists in a list.

The MATCH function takes the following arguments:

- lookup_value—This is the value you use to find the value you want in a table. lookup_value can be a value, which is a number, text, or logical value or a cell reference to a number, text, or logical value.

- lookup_array—This is a contiguous range of cells that contains possible lookup values. lookup_array can be an array or an array reference.

- match_type—This is the number –1, 0, or 1. Note that you can use TRUE instead of 1 and FALSE instead of 0. match_type specifies how Microsoft Excel matches lookup_value with values in lookup_array. If match_type is 1, MATCH finds the largest value that is less than or equal to lookup_value. lookup_array must be placed in ascending order, such as –2, –1, 0, 1, 2,...; A–Z; or FALSE, TRUE. If match_type is 0, MATCH finds the first value that is exactly equal to lookup_value. lookup_array can be in any order. If match_type is –1, MATCH finds the smallest value that is greater than or equal to lookup_value. lookup_array must be placed in descending order, such as TRUE, FALSE; Z–A; or 2, 1, 0, –1, –2,... If match_type is omitted, it is assumed to be 1.

MATCH returns the position of the matched value within lookup_array, not the value itself. For example, MATCH("b",{"a","b","c"},0) returns 2, the relative position of b within the array {"a","b","c"}.

MATCH does not distinguish between uppercase and lowercase letters when matching text values. If MATCH is unsuccessful in finding a match, it returns an #N/A error.

If match_type is 0 and lookup_value is text, lookup_value can contain the wildcard characters asterisk (*) and question mark (?). An asterisk matches any sequence of characters; a question mark matches any single character.

Using MATCH to Compare Two Lists

You might face situations in which you have two versions of a list, and you need to match them up.

CHAPTER 9

In Figure 9.13, the worksheet has two simple lists. Column A shows last week's list. Column C shows this week's version of the list. You want to find out quickly which items are new. Here's how you do it:

1. Add the heading **There?** to cell D2.

	A	B	C	D
	D3		fx =MATCH(C3,$A$3:$A$11,0)	
1	ENTRIES LAST WEEK		ENTRIES THIS WEEK	
2				There?
3	PILGRIM		COLUMBIA	2
4	COLUMBIA		CONSTELLATION	8
5	MAYFLOWER		COURAGEOUS	#N/A
6	VOLUNTEER		DEFENDER	5
7	DEFENDER		FREEDOM	#N/A
8	RELIANCE		INTREPID	9
9	RANGER		MAYFLOWER	3
10	CONSTELLATION		PILGRIM	1
11	INTREPID		RANGER	7
12			RELIANCE	6
13			STARS AND STRIPES	#N/A
14			VOLUNTEER	4
15			WEATHERLY	#N/A
16			YOUNG AMERICA	#N/A
17				

Figure 9.13   MATCH operates slightly more quickly than VLOOKUP and achieves the same result in this special case in which you are trying to figure out whether a value is in another list.

2. Because the formula in cell D3 looks at the value in cell C3 to see if that value is in the original list in column A, start the formula with =**MATCH(C3,$A$3:$A$11,**.

3. Because you want an exact match, use **0** as the third parameter. Finish the function with a **)**. Press Ctrl+Enter to accept the formula and stay in cell C3.

4. Double-click the fill handle to copy the formula down to all rows.

For any cells in which column D contains a number, it means that the entry was on the original list from last week. If the result of MATCH is #N/A, you know that this item is new since the previous week.

Using INDEX and MATCH for a Left Lookup

INDEX is another function that does not immediately seem to have many great uses. In its basic form, INDEX returns the value from a particular row and column of a rectangular range. It returns a value from a particular position of a vertical or horizontal vector.

Typically, you specify a rectangular range and then indicate the row number and column number of the value that you want to return. In Figure 9.14, the formula in C3 returns the third row and second column of B5:D9. Certainly, this is a needlessly complicated way to point to cell C7.

C3			× ✓ *fx*	=INDEX(B5:D9,C1,C2)								
	A	B	C	D	E	F	G	H	I	J	K	L	M
1		Row:	3										Andy
2		Column:	2										Betty
3		Index:	31	=INDEX(B5:D9,C1,C2)									Charley
4		Random:	Andy	=INDEX(M1:M7,RANDBETWEEN(1,7))									Dale
5		10	11	12									Eddie
6		20	21	22									Flo
7		30	31	32			Total						Gabby
8		40	41	42	Row:	4	123	=SUM(INDEX(B5:D9,G8,0))					
9		50	51	52	Column:	3	160	=SUM(INDEX(B5:D9,0,G9))					
10													
11			47	=INDEX(A14:L14,MONTH(TODAY()))									
12													
13	Jan	Feb	Mar	Apr	May	Jun	Jul	Aug	Sep	Oct	Nov	Dec	
14	45	46	28	37	10	47	14	17	26	40	41	19	
15													

Figure 9.14   INDEX can be used in a variety of situations without the MATCH function.

INDEX becomes interesting when you have a formula calculating the position argument. Still in Figure 9.14, a list of people is in M1:M7. You can randomly select from the list by using INDEX and RANDBETWEEN(1,7), as shown in C4.

If you specify zero as the row or column argument, INDEX returns the entire row or column. The INDEX in H8 is returning all three values from row 4 of the table, so you have to wrap the index function in a SUM or COUNT or AVERAGE function.

The data in row 14 illustrates an undocumented feature of INDEX. When the reference contains data in a single row, you can specify the column number as the second argument. To get the data for September, you can use the correct =INDEX(A14:L14,0,9) or the shortened =INDEX(A14:L14,9). In Figure 9.14, the formula in C11 returns the value from the current month by using =MONTH(TODAY()) to return a 9 as the second argument of the INDEX function. (This was written in September, hence the 9.0.)

You've reached Excel guru status when you start combining INDEX and MATCH. On its own, neither INDEX nor MATCH seems particularly useful. Used together, though, they become a powerful combination that is more flexible than VLOOKUP and often faster to calculate than VLOOKUP.

In Figure 9.15, a customer number is in cell B1. The customer lookup table appears in columns F, G, and H. The main problem is that the customer table does not have the customer number on the left side.

Figure 9.15 This combination of INDEX and MATCH enables you to look up data that is to the left of a key field.

In many cases, you would copy column H to column E and use column E as the key of the table. However, the table in F:H is likely to be repopulated every day from a web query or an OLAP query. Therefore, it might become monotonous to move the data after every refresh. The solution is to use a combination of INDEX and MATCH. Here's what you do:

1. Use the formula =MATCH(B1,H2:H89,0) to search through column H to find the row with the customer number that matches the one in cell B1. In this case, C499 is in row 9, which is the eighth row of the table.

2. Be sure to use exactly the same shape range as the first argument in the INDEX function: =INDEX(F2:F89,WhichRow,WhichColumn) searches through the customer names in column F.

3. For the second parameter of the INDEX function, specify the relative row number. This information was provided by the MATCH function in step 1.

4. Ensure that the third parameter of the INDEX function is the relative column number. Because the range F2:F89 has only one column, this is either 1 or can simply be omitted.

5. Putting the formula together, the formula in cell B2 is =INDEX(F2:F89,MATCH(B1,H2:H89,0),1).

Syntax:

```
INDEX(array,row_num,[column_num])
INDEX(reference,row_num,[column_num],[area_num])
```

The INDEX function returns the value at the intersection of a particular row and column within a range. This function takes the following arguments:

- array—This is a range of cells or an array constant. If array contains only one row or column, the corresponding row_num or column_num argument is optional. If array has more than one row and more than one column, and if only row_num or column_num is used, INDEX returns an array of the entire row or column in array.

- row_num—This selects the row in array from which to return a value. If row_num is omitted, column_num is required.

- column_num—This selects the column in array from which to return a value. If column_num is omitted, row_num is required.

If both the row_num and the column_num arguments are used, INDEX returns the value in the cell at the intersection of row_num and column_num.

If you set row_num or column_num to 0, INDEX returns the array of values for the entire column or row, respectively. To use values returned as an array, you use the INDEX function as an array formula in a horizontal range of cells for a row and in a vertical range of cells for a column. To enter an array formula, you press Ctrl+Shift+Enter. Thanks to modern arrays introduced in September 2018, customers using Office 365 will not need to press Ctrl+Shift+Enter.

row_num and column_num must point to a cell within array; otherwise, INDEX returns a #REF! error.

Using MATCH and INDEX to Fill a Wide Table

The lookup functions VLOOKUP, HLOOKUP, and MATCH can be very processor intensive when the lookup table contains hundreds of thousands of rows. The problem is worse when you have to return multiple columns from the same row of the lookup table. If it takes Excel 3 seconds to find the matching row for column 2 of the table, it will take another 3 seconds to find the matching row for column 3 of the table. If you hope to return 12 monthly columns, it could take 36 seconds.

Instead, you could find the matching row once using a MATCH function in a helper column. After the MATCH identifies the correct row, 12 INDEX functions can return the values for each month. INDEX is incredibly fast. The 13 formulas will run in 12% of the time it takes to run 12 VLOOKUP formulas.

Figure 9.16 illustrates the technique. A MATCH function in column C figures out which row contains the match. INDEX functions in D5:O12 return the monthly numbers.

CHAPTER 9

D5	▼	:	×	✓	fx	=INDEX(B$17:B$14056,$C5)						

	A	B	C	D	E	F	G	H	I	J	K	L	M
1	Order Fulfillment Decision Tool												
2	Enter Customer Order in A&B, check stock in D:O												
3													
4	Qty	Item	Match	WH1	WH2	WH3	WH4	WH5	WH6	WH7	WH8	WH9	WH10
5	2	C529	8005	0	5	0	81	96	5	5	0	2	0
6	10	F708	3635	1	2	0	88	1	0	53	2	0	0
7	9	X291	452	0	80	0	0	0	50	29	33	0	87
8	1	E890	6335	2	87	0	1	2	0	5	0	95	4
9	5	C299	12192	0	2	4	0	48	0	2	0	89	66
10	4	S323	7450	4	5	3	69	5	0	4	102	97	0
11	1	V600	9038	131	48	129	1	0	1	0	105	67	117
12	9	P765	8596	3	0	70	2	1	3	0	0	0	0
13			C12: =MATCH(B12,$A$17:$A$14056,0)					H12: =INDEX(F$17:F$14056,$C12)					
14	Inventory By Warehouse												
15													
16	Item	WH1	WH2	WH3	WH4	WH5	WH6	WH7	WH8	WH9	WH10	WH11	WH12
17	G245	36	2	71	1	96	83	0	34	81	59	0	0
18	J535	0	3	0	0	0	85	5	137	0	32	0	5

Figure 9.16   This performs eight relatively slow MATCH functions and then 96 relatively fast INDEX functions.

Inside OUT

There are people who study formula speed. Using the Fast Excel tools written by Excel MVP Charles Williams, you can compare the formula speed of one method to another.

In the summer of 2018, Office 365 customers will notice that 12 columns of VLOOKUP are calculating as quickly as one MATCH and 12 INDEX functions. The calculation engine in Excel was tweaked to remember the location that the first VLOOKUP found the answer and re-uses that information for the other VLOOKUPs in that row.

Performing Many Lookups with LOOKUP

Even Excel Help tells you to avoid the old LOOKUP function. However, LOOKUP can do one useful trick that VLOOKUP and HLOOKUP cannot do—it can process many lookups in one single array formula. LOOKUP can also deal with a lookup range that is vertical and a return range that is horizontal, or vice versa.

One additional superpower of the old LOOKUP function is the capability to look up several values at once. You have to use Ctrl+Shift+Enter to accept the formula, and because LOOKUP will be returning an array of answers, you should enclose the LOOKUP in a wrapper function such as SUM to add all the results from the function.

In Figure 9.17, a series of invoices appear in rows 4 through 17. A GP% (gross profit percentage) is associated with each invoice. The sales rep will earn a bonus depending on the GP% of each invoice, as shown in E6:F10. Instead of calculating a bonus for each row, you can calculate a bonus for all the rows at once. The formula in B1 of Figure 9.17 specifies an array of B4:B17 as the lookup value. This causes Excel to perform the LOOKUP 14 times, once for each value in the range B4:B17. The formula wraps the LOOKUP results in a SUM function to add up all the bonus results. To calculate correctly, you must hold down Ctrl+Shift while pressing Enter after typing this formula. When you press Ctrl+Shift+Enter, Excel adds the curly braces around the formula. You do not type the curly braces manually. Typing the curly braces will not work.

Figure 9.17   Unlike VLOOKUP and HLOOKUP, the aging LOOKUP function can process many lookups in a single array formula.

As of late 2018, any Office 365 customers will have access to modern arrays. This is a major change to how Excel calculates. You will no longer have to use Ctrl+Shift+Enter in the example above. Also, with the introduction of modern arrays, every Excel function can accept an array, so you can use =SUM(VLOOKUP(B4:B17,E6:F10,2,False)), and it will calculate correctly. Modern arrays are not in Excel 2019, so those customers will still have to use LOOKUP and Ctrl+Shift+Enter.

Using FORMULATEXT to Document a Worksheet

Quiz: Which Excel function is used the most in this book? It is FORMULATEXT. The FORMULATEXT function was added in Excel 2013. If you ask for the =FORMULATEXT(A1), Excel shows the formula that is in cell A1 as text. All the formulas shown in this book (such as cell C1 in Figure 9.17) are generated with the FORMULATEXT function.

You can use FORMULATEXT to document the formulas used in your worksheet. Normally, you can either print your worksheet with formulas showing or with the results from the formulas. By using FORMULATEXT, you can show both the formula and the result.

If you use FORMULATEXT on a cell with an array formula, the resulting text will be wrapped in curly braces that would be shown in the formula bar.

In Figure 9.18, the text of the formula shown in C3 comes from a FORMULATEXT function.

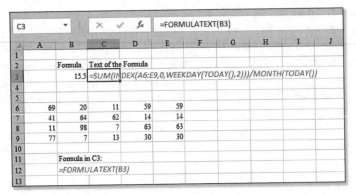

Figure 9.18   A FORMULATEXT function in C3 shows the formula used in B3.

Syntax:

FORMULATEXT(reference)

This function returns a formula as text.

> ### TROUBLESHOOTING
>
> **FORMULATEXT fails when your reference does not contain a formula.**
>
> There are people who had written their own versions of FormulaText as a VBA function before Excel 2013 added FormulaText. The version that was made popular on the Internet would return the formula as text if the cell contained a formula. Otherwise, it would return the value in the cell.
>
> However, Excel's built-in version of FORMULATEXT returns a #N/A error if the cell does not contain a formula.
>
> One workaround is to wrap FORMULATEXT in IFNA. Instead of =FORMULATEXT(C2), use =IFNA(FORMULATEXT(C2),C2).

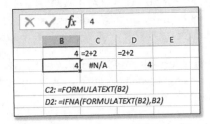

> Two cells show an answer of 4. Next to each cell, a FORMULATEXT function attempts to show the formula in the adjacent cell. This works for the first cell, where the formula is =2+2. However, in the second cell, the FORMULATEXT returns a #N/A error because the cell simply contains the number 4 instead of a formula. A workaround of =IFNA(FORMULATEXT(B2),B2) will work for either formulas or values.

Using Numbers with OFFSET to Describe a Range

The language of Excel is numbers. There are functions that count the number of entries in a range. There are functions that can tell you the numeric position of a looked-up value. You might know that a particular value is found in row 20, but what if you want to perform calculations on other cells in row 20?

The OFFSET function handles this very situation. You can use OFFSET to describe a range using mostly numbers. OFFSET is flexible: It can describe a single cell, or it can describe a rectangular range.

Although INDEX can return a single cell, row, or column from a rectangular range, it has limitations. If you specify C5:Z99 as the range for an INDEX function, you can select only cells below and/or to the right of C5. The OFFSET function can move up and down or left and right from the starting cell, which is C5.

Syntax:

`OFFSET(reference,rows,cols,height,width)`

The OFFSET function returns a reference to a range that is a given number of rows and columns from a given reference. This function takes the following arguments:

- reference—This is the reference from which you want to base the offset. reference must be a reference to a cell or range of adjacent cells; otherwise, OFFSET returns a #VALUE! error.

- rows—This is the number of rows, up or down, that you want the upper-left cell to refer to. Using 5 as the rows argument, for example, specifies that the upper-left cell in the reference is five rows below reference. rows can be positive, which means below the starting reference, or negative, which means above the starting reference.

- cols—This is the number of columns to the left or right that you want the upper-left cell of the result to refer to. For example, using 5 as the cols argument specifies that the upper-left cell in the reference is five columns to the right of reference. cols can be positive, which means to the right of the starting reference, or negative, which means to the left of the starting reference. If rows and cols offset reference over the edge of the worksheet, OFFSET returns a #REF! error. Figure 9.19 demonstrates various combinations of rows and cols from a starting cell of cell C5.

- height—This is the height, in number of rows, that you want the returned reference to be. height must be a positive number.

- width—This is the width, in number of columns, that you want the returned reference to be. width must be a positive number. If height or width is omitted, Excel assumes it is the same height or width as reference.

| C10 | ▼ | : | × | ✓ | fx | =OFFSET($C$5,A10,B10,1,1) |

▲	A	B	C	D	E	F
1	Examples of 1-cell ranges returned by Offset					
2						
3	1	2	4	8	16	
4	32	64	128	256	512	
5	1024	2048	4096	8192	16384	
6	32768	65536	131072	262144	524288	
7	1048576	2097152	4194304	8388608	16777216	
8						
9	Row	Column	Offset			
10	-2	0	4	=OFFSET($C$5,A10,B10,1,1)		
11	0	-2	1024	=OFFSET($C$5,A11,B11,1,1)		
12	0	2	16384	=OFFSET($C$5,A12,B12,1,1)		
13	2	0	4194304	=OFFSET($C$5,A13,B13,1,1)		
14	-2	-2	1	=OFFSET($C$5,A14,B14,1,1)		
15	2	2	16777216	=OFFSET($C$5,A15,B15,1,1)		
16						

Figure 9.19 These OFFSET functions return a single cell that is a certain number of rows and columns away from cell C5.

OFFSET enables you to specify a reference. It does not move a cell. It does not change the selection. It is just a numeric way to describe a reference. OFFSET can be used in any function that is expecting a reference argument.

Excel Help provides a trivial example of =SUM(OFFSET(C2,1,2,3,1)), which sums E3:E5. However, this example is silly because no one would ever write such a formula! If you were to write such a formula, you would just write =SUM(E3:E5) instead. The power of OFFSET comes when at least one of the four numeric arguments is calculated by the COUNT function or a lookup function.

In Figure 9.20, you can use COUNT(A5:A99) to count how many entries are in column A. If you assume that there are no blanks in the range of data, you can use the COUNT result as the height argument in OFFSET to describe the range of numbers. Here's what you do:

1. There is nothing magical about the reference, so write it as **=OFFSET(A5,**.

2. Do not move the starting position any rows or columns from cell A5. The starting position is A5, so you always use 0 and 0 for rows and columns. Therefore, the formula is now **=OFFSET(A5,0,0,**.

A3	▼	:	×	✓	*fx*	=SUM(OFFSET(A5,0,0,COUNT(A5:A999),1))

	A	B	C	D	E	F	G	H	I	J	K
1	Example of Dynamic Range Generated by Offset										
2	=SUM(OFFSET(A5,0,0,COUNT(A5:A999),1))										
3	3				15		31		63		255	1023
4											
5	1				1		1		1		1	1
6	2				2		2		2		2	2
7					4		4		4		4	4
8					8		8		8		8	8
9							16		16		16	16
10							32		32		32	32
11									64		64	64
12									128		128	128
13											256	256
14											512	512
15												

Figure 9.20 Every argument except `height` is hard-coded in these functions. The `height` argument comes from a COUNT function to allow the range to expand as more entries are added.

3. If you want to include only the number of entries in the list, use COUNT(A5:A999) as the height of the range. The formula is now **=OFFSET(A5,0,0,COUNT(A5:A999),**.

4. The width is one column, so make the function **=OFFSET(A5,0,0,COUNT(A5:A999),1)**.

5. Use your OFFSET function anywhere you would normally specify a reference. You can use =SUM(OFFSET(A5,0,0,COUNT(A5:A999),1)) or specify that formula as the series in a chart. This creates a dynamic chart that grows or shrinks as the number of entries changes.

TROUBLESHOOTING

OFFSET is a volatile function and will slow recalculation of your worksheet. Avoid OFFSET using a little-known version of INDEX.

Normally, =INDEX(A1:A10,5) will return the value stored in the fifth row of A1:A12. Excel guru Dan Mayoh discovered an alternate use for INDEX. If the INDEX function is placed adjacent to a colon, the INDEX function returns the cell address instead of the value stored in the cell. =SUM(A1:INDEX(A1:A12,5)) will sum A1:A5.

Of course, you would not hard-code the 5 in the INDEX function. You might use MONTH(TODAY()) to dynamically choose the number corresponding to the current month.

=SUM(A1:INDEX(A1:A12,MONTH(TODAY()))) is not volatile and does the same thing as =SUM(OFFSET(A1,0,0,MONTH(TODAY()),1)).

Using INDIRECT to Build and Evaluate Cell References on the Fly

The INDIRECT function is deceivingly powerful. Consider this trivial example: In cell A1, enter the text **B2**. In cell B2, enter a number. In cell C3, enter the formula **=INDIRECT(A1)**. Excel returns the number that you entered in cell B2 in cell C3. The INDIRECT function looks in cell A1 and expects to find something that is a valid cell or range reference. It then looks in that address to return the answer for the function.

The reference text can be any text that you can string together using various text functions. This enables you to create complex references that dynamically point to other sheets or to other open workbooks.

The reference text can also be a range name. You could have a validation list box in which someone selects a value from a list. If you have predefined a named range that corresponds to each possible entry on the list, INDIRECT can point to the various named ranges on the fly.

When you use traditional formulas, even absolute formulas, there is a chance that someone might insert rows or columns that will move the reference. If you need a formula to always point to cell J10, no matter how someone rearranges the worksheet, you can use =INDIRECT("J10") to handle this.

Syntax:

```
INDIRECT(ref_text,a1)
```

The INDIRECT function returns the reference specified by a text string. This function takes the following arguments:

- ref_text—This is a reference to a cell that contains an A1-style reference, an R1C1-style reference, a name defined as a reference, or a reference to a cell as a text string. If ref_ text is not a valid cell reference, INDIRECT returns a #REF! error. If ref_text refers to an external workbook, the other workbook must be open. If the source workbook is not open, INDIRECT returns a #REF! error.

- a1—This is a logical value that specifies what type of reference is contained in the cell ref_text. If a1 is TRUE or omitted, ref_text is interpreted as an A1-style reference. If a1 is FALSE, ref_text is interpreted as an R1C1-style reference.

Figure 9.21 is a monthly worksheet in a workbook that has 12 similar sheets. In each worksheet, the data headings are in row 6, and the total for the worksheet appears in cell D2. To build a summary sheet that points to D2 on the individual worksheets, you can concatenate the month name from column A with "!D2" to build a reference.

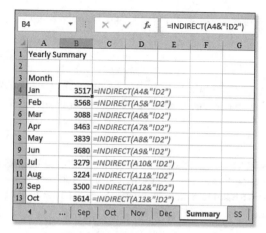

Figure 9.21   Cell D4 dynamically builds a text formula to reference the previous sheet,

Using the HYPERLINK Function to Add Hyperlinks Quickly

Excel enables you to add a hyperlink by using the Excel interface. On the Insert tab, select the Hyperlink icon. Next, you specify text to appear in the cell and the underlying address. Building links in this way is easy, but it is tedious to build them one at a time. If you have hundreds of links to add, you can add them quickly by using the HYPERLINK function.

Syntax:

HYPERLINK(link_location,friendly_name)

The HYPERLINK function creates a shortcut that opens a document stored on your hard drive, a network server, or the Internet. This function takes the following arguments:

- link_location—This is the URL address on the Internet. It could also be a path, filename, location in the same workbook, and location in another file. For example, you could link to "[C:\files\Jan2018.xls]!Sheet1!A15". Note that link_location can be a text string enclosed in quotes or a cell that contains the link.

- friendly_name—This is the underlined text or numeric value that is displayed in the cell. friendly_name is displayed in blue and is underlined. If friendly_name is omitted, the cell displays the link_location value as the jump text. friendly_name can be a value, a text string, a name, or a cell that contains the jump text or value. If friendly_name returns an error (for example, #VALUE!), the cell displays the error instead of the jump text.

Figure 9.22 shows a list of web pages in column A. Column B contains the titles of those web pages. To quickly build a table of hyperlinks, you use =HYPERLINK(A2,B2) in cell C2 and copy the formula down the column. Unfortunately, you must keep columns A and B intact for the

CHAPTER 9

hyperlink to keep working. You can hide those columns, but there is no Paste Special option to convert the formula to values that will keep the hyperlink.

NOTE

Note that Excel does not check whether the link location is valid at the time you created the link. If the link is not valid when someone clicks it, the person encounters an error.

TIP

It is difficult to select a cell that contains a HYPERLINK function. If you click the cell, Excel attempts to follow the hyperlink. Instead, click the cell and hold the mouse button until the pointer changes from a hand to a plus. Alternatively, click a nearby cell and use the arrow keys to move to the cell with the hyperlink.

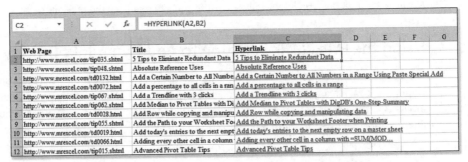

Figure 9.22   The formulas in column C enable you to create hundreds of hyperlinks in seconds.

To keep only the hyperlinks, copy column C and paste to a blank Word document. Open a new workbook. Copy from Word and paste back to the new Excel document.

Alternatively, use ="#HYPERLINK("""&A2&""""&", "&""""&B2&""""&")" in C2. Copy down and paste special values. Use Find and Replace to change # to =.

Using the TRANSPOSE Function to Formulaically Turn Data

With many people using Excel in a company, there are bound to be different usage styles from person to person. Some people build their worksheets horizontally, and other people build their worksheets vertically. For example, in Figure 9.23, the monthly totals stretch horizontally across row 80. However, for some reason, you need these figures to be arranged going vertically down from cell B84.

The typical method is to copy C80:N80 and then use Home, Paste, Transpose. This copies a snapshot of the totals in row 80 to a column of data.

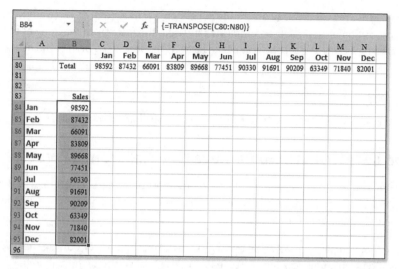

Figure 9.23   One TRANSPOSE function occupies 12 cells, from B84:B95.

This is fine if you need only a snapshot of the totals. However, what if you want to see the totals continually updated in column B? Excel provides the TRANSPOSE function for such situations.

Because the function returns several answers, you need to use special care when entering the formula. Here's how:

1. Note that C80:N80 contains 12 cells.

2. Select an identical number of cells starting in B84. Select B84:B95.

3. Even though you have 12 cells selected, type the formula, **=TRANSPOSE(C80:N80)**, as if you had only one cell selected.

4. To tell Excel 2019 that this is a special type of formula called an array formula, hold down Ctrl+Shift while you press Enter. Pressing Ctrl+Shift+Enter is not required in Office 365 thanks to modern array formulas introduced in September 2018.

Excel shows the formula surrounded by curly braces in the formula bar. This is one single formula entered in 12 cells. Therefore, you cannot delete or change one cell in the range. If you want to change the formula, you need to delete all 12 cells in B84:B95 in a single command.

Syntax:

TRANSPOSE(array)

The TRANSPOSE function transposes a vertical range into a horizontal array or vice versa.

CHAPTER 9

The argument `array` is an array or a range of cells on a worksheet that you want to transpose. The transposition of an array is accomplished by using the first row of the array as the first column of the new array, the second row of the array as the second column of the new array, and so on.

NOTE

You can also use TRANSPOSE to turn a vertical range into a horizontal range.

Using GETPIVOTDATA to Retrieve One Cell from a Pivot Table

You might turn to this book to find out how to use most of the Excel functions. However, for the GETPIVOTDATA function, you are likely to turn to this book to find out why the function is being automatically generated for you.

Suppose that you have a pivot table on a worksheet. You should click outside the pivot table. Next, you type an equal sign and then use the mouse to click one of the cells in the data area of the pivot table. Although you might expect this to generate a formula such as =E9, instead, Excel puts in the formula =GETPIVOTDATA("Sales",$B$5,"Customer","Astonishing Glass Company","Region","West"), as shown in Figure 9.24.

H9		× ✓ fx	=GETPIVOTDATA("Sales",$B$5,"Customer","Astonishing Glass Company","Region","West")					
	B	C	D	E	F	G	H	I
5	Sum of Sales	Region						
6	Customer	East	Central	West	Grand Total			
7	Alluring Ink Company	0	170	0	170			
8	Alluring Quilt Company	289	0	0	289			
9	Astonishing Glass Company	0	0	314	314		314	
10	Astonishing Shovel Inc.	190	0	0	190			
11	Bright Shoe Company	0	246	0	246			
12	Brilliant Luggage Inc.	0	307	0	307			
13	Different Belt Corporation	0	0	249	249			

Figure 9.24   Excel inserts this strange function in the worksheet.

This function is annoying. As you copy the formula down to more rows, the function keeps retrieving sales to Astonishing Glass in the West region. By default, Excel is generating this function instead of a simple formula such as =E9. This happens whether you use the mouse or the arrow keys to specify the cell in the formula.

To avoid this behavior, you can enter the entire formula by manually typing it on the keyboard. Typing **=E9** in a cell forces Excel to create a relative reference to cell E9. You are then free to copy the formula to other cells.

There is also a way to turn off this behavior permanently:

1. Select a cell inside an active pivot table.

2. The Pivot Table Tools tabs are displayed. Select the Analyze tab. From the PivotTable group, select the Options drop-down menu and then select the Generate GetPivotData icon. The behavior turns off.

3. Enter formulas by using the mouse, arrow keys, or keyboard without generating the GETPIVOTDATA function.

Microsoft made GETPIVOTDATA the default behavior because the function is pretty cool. Now that you have learned how to turn off the behavior, you might want to understand exactly how it works in case you ever need to use the function.

Syntax:

GETPIVOTDATA(data_field,pivot_table,field1,item1,field2,item2,...)

The GETPIVOTDATA function returns data stored in a pivot table report. You can use GETPIVOTDATA to retrieve summary data from a pivot table report, provided that the summary data is visible in the report. This function takes the following arguments:

- data_field—This is the name, enclosed in quotation marks, for the data field that contains the data you want to retrieve.

- pivot_table—This is a reference to any cell, range of cells, or named range of cells in a pivot table report. This information is used to determine which pivot table report contains the data you want to retrieve.

- field1, item1, field2, item2,...—These are 1 to 126 pairs of field names and item names that describe the data you want to retrieve. The pairs can be in any order. Field-names and names for items other than dates and numbers are enclosed in quotation marks. For OLAP pivot table reports, items can contain the source name of the dimension as well as the source name of the item.

Calculated fields or items and custom calculations are included in GETPIVOTDATA calculations.

- If pivot_table is a range that includes two or more pivot table reports, data is retrieved from whichever report was created in the range most recently.

- If the field and item arguments describe a single cell, the value of that cell is returned, regardless of whether it is a string, a number, an error, and so on.

- If an item contains a date, the value must be expressed as a serial number or populated by using the DATE function so that the value is retained if the spreadsheet is opened in a different locale. For example, an item referring to the date March 5, 2015, could be entered as 42068 or DATE(2015,3,5). Times can be entered as decimal values or by using the TIME function.

- If pivot_table is not a range in which a pivot table report is found, GETPIVOTDATA returns #REF!. If the arguments do not describe a visible field, or if they include a page field that is not displayed, GETPIVOTDATA returns #REF!.

Examples of Database Functions

If you were a data analyst in the 1980s and the early 1990s, you would have been enamored with the database functions. I used @DSUM every hour of my work life for many years. It was one of the most powerful weapons in any spreadsheet arsenal. Combined with a data table, the DSUM, DMIN, DMAX, and DAVERAGE functions got a serious workout when people performed data analysis in a spreadsheet.

Then, in 1993, Microsoft Excel added the pivot table to the Data menu in Excel. Pivot tables changed everything. Those powerful database functions seemed tired and worn out. Since that day in 1993, I had never used DSUM again until I created the example described in the following section. As far as I knew, the database functions had been living in a cave in South Carolina.

Maybe it is like the nostalgia of finding a box of photos of an old girlfriend, but I realized that the database functions are still pretty powerful. Customers whined enough to have Microsoft add AVERAGEIF to the COUNTIF and SUMIF arsenal. This was unnecessary: Customers could have done this easily by setting up a small criteria range and using DAVERAGE.

Inside OUT

The database functions would be far more popular if they did not require headings for the criteria range.

The DSUM is ultra-powerful to return all records in which a specific criteria range appears (such as the region is East). However, in real life, your manager is going to want to see the records where the region is Central and West instead of East. When you start to copy the DSUM function for other regions, you realize that you need an additional two cells to hold each criteria range.

If you wanted 100 rows of DSUM to return the sales for 100 employees, you would need 200 cells of criteria range. Arranging those cells vertically would make it difficult to point to the correct criteria range. In the figure here, a blend of horizontal criteria ranges, OFFSET, and MATCH provide a method, but it will be slow to calculate. This is why you don't see DSUM functions everywhere.

As shown in the figure, modern functions, such as SUMIFS or FILTER, provide easier ways than DSUM to arrive at the results.

⊿	A	B	C	D	E	F	G	H	I	J
1	Employee	Sales		Helper Cells with Many Criteria Ranges						
2	Jared	1277		Employee	Employee	Employee	Employee	Employee	Employee	Employee
3	Andy	1099		Andy	Barb	Chris	Diane	Ed	Flo	Gary
4	Jared	1356		Use OFFSET in E7 so criteria range moves to the right as you copy down						
5	Kelly	1830								
6	Gary	1119			DSUM	SUMIFS	FILTER			
7	Jared	1086		Andy	99621	99621	99621			
8	Barb	1444		Barb	105899	105899	105899			
9	Ike	1674		Chris	92882	92882	92882			
10	Flo	1383		Diane	89747	89747	89747			
11	Barb	1590		Ed	98890	98890	98890			
12	Gary	1567		Flo	135856	135856	135856			
13	Ed	1199		Gary	95926	95926	95926			
14	Barb	1934		Hank	96658	96658	96658			
15	Chris	1041		Ike	77656	77656	77656			
16	Flo	1684		Jared	102762	102762	102762			
17	Jared	1680		Kelly	90389	90389	90389			
18	Diane	1190		E7: =DSUM($A$1:$B$726,"Sales",OFFSET($C$2,0,MATCH(D7,$D$3:$N$3,0),2,1))						
19	Gary	1916		F7: =SUMIFS($B$2:$B$726,$A$2:$A$726,D7)						
20	Flo	1293		G7: =SUM(FILTER($B$2:$B$726,$A$2:$A$726=D7))						
21	Gary	1330								

Eleven of the 12 database functions are similar. DSUM, DAVERAGE, DCOUNT, DCOUNTA, DMAX, DMIN, DPRODUCT, DSTDEV, DSTDEVP, DVAR, and DVARP all perform the equivalent operation of their non-D equivalents, but they allow for complex criteria to include records that meet certain criteria. See examples of each of these in Figure 9.25.

| B1 | ▼ | : | × | ✓ | fx | =DSUM($A$23:$I$5024,H$23,$A$17:$I$18) | | | |

⊿	A	B	C	D	E	F	G	H	I
1	DSUM	657,028	=DSUM($A$23:$I$5024,H$23,$A$17:$I$18)						
2	DAVERAGE	59,730	=DAVERAGE($A$23:$I$5024,H$23,$A$17:$I$18)						
3	DCOUNT	11	=DCOUNT($A$23:$I$5024,H$23,$A$17:$I$18)						
4	DCOUNTA	11	=DCOUNTA($A$23:$I$5024,H$23,$A$17:$I$18)						
5	DMAX	89,898	=DMAX($A$23:$I$5024,H$23,$A$17:$I$18)						
6	DMIN	26,058	=DMIN($A$23:$I$5024,H$23,$A$17:$I$18)						
7	DPRODUCT	2.048E+52	=DPRODUCT($A$23:$I$5024,H$23,$A$17:$I$18)						
8	DSTDEV	17,960	=DSTDEV($A$23:$I$5024,H$23,$A$17:$I$18)						
9	DSTDEVP	17,124	=DSTDEVP($A$23:$I$5024,H$23,$A$17:$I$18)						
10	DVAR	322,545,029	=DVAR($A$23:$I$5024,H$23,$A$17:$I$18)						
11	DVARP	293,222,753	=DVARP($A$23:$I$5024,H$23,$A$17:$I$18)						
13									
17	Customer	Product		Region	District	Rep	Date	Qty	Revenue	Profit
18	Best Paint Inc.								
19									
23	Customer	Product		Region	District	Rep	Date	Qty	Revenue	Profit
24	Wonderful Faucet C	G854		East	Southeast	ADAM DU	2/3/15	730	76,906	41,529
25	Forceful Flagpole C	A105		East	Southeast	ADAM DU	12/19/15	804	32,297	16,794
26	Best Paint Inc.	V937		Central	Chicago	PETER WA	12/5/15	414	59,761	31,673

Criteria Range   Database

Figure 9.25 A simple criteria range specifies to limit DSUM to only records for Best Paint Inc. as a customer.

CHAPTER 9

To save you the hassle of looking up the confusing few, DCOUNT counts numeric cells, and DCOUNTA counts nonblank cells. DSTDEV and DVAR calculate the standard deviation and variance of a sample of a population, respectively. DSTDEVP and DVARP calculate the standard deviation and variance of the entire population, respectively. The 12th database function, DGET, has the same arguments, but it acts a bit differently, as explained later in this chapter.

Using DSUM to Conditionally Sum Records from a Database

There are three arguments to every database function. It is very easy to get your first DSUM working. The `criteria` argument is the one that offers vast flexibility. The following section explains the syntax for DSUM. The syntax for the other 11 database functions is identical to this.

Syntax:

`DSUM(database,field,criteria)`

The DSUM function adds records from one field in a data set, provided that the records meet some criteria that you specify. The DSUM function takes the following arguments:

- database—This is the range of cells that make up the list or database, including the heading row. A `database` is a list of related data in which rows of related information are records, and columns of data are fields. In Figure 9.25, the database is the 5,002 rows of data located at A23:I5024.

- field—This indicates which column is used in the function. You have three options when specifying a field:

  - You can point to the cell with the `fieldname`, such as H23 for Revenue.

  - You can include the word Revenue as the `field` argument.

  - You can use the number 8 to indicate that Revenue is the eighth field in the database.

- criteria—This is the range of cells that contains the conditions specified. You can use any range for the `criteria` argument. The criteria range typically includes at least one column label and at least one cell below the column label for specifying a condition for the column. You can also use the computed criteria discussed in "Using the Miracle Version of a Criteria Range," later in this chapter. Learning how to create powerful criteria ranges enables you to unlock the powerful potential of the database functions. Several examples are provided in the following sections.

NOTE

To conserve space, the remaining examples in the following sections show only the DSUM result. You can compare the various results to the $657,028 of revenue for the current example.

Creating a Simple Criteria Range for Database Functions

Although a criteria range needs only one field heading from the database, it is just as easy to copy the entire set of headings to a blank section of the worksheet. In Figure 9.25, for example, the headings in A17:I17, along with at least one additional row, create a criteria range.

In Figure 9.25, you see results of the 11 database functions for a simple criteria in which the customer is Best Paint Inc. Each formula specifies a database of $A$23:$I$5024. The field is H23, which is the heading for Revenue. The criteria range is A17:I18. In this example, the criteria range could have easily been A17:A18, but the A17:I18 form enables you to enter future criteria without specifying the criteria range again.

Using a Blank Criteria Range to Return All Records

This is a trivial example, but if the second row of the criteria range is completely blank, the database function returns the total of all rows in the data set. As shown in Figure 9.26, this is $256.6 million. This is equivalent to using the SUM function.

B1		×	✓	f_x	=DSUM($A$23:$I$5024,H23,$A$17:$I$18)			
	A		B	C	D	E	F	G
1	DSUM		256,645,202	=DSUM($A$23:$I$5024,H23,$A$17:$I$18)				
13								
17	Customer	Product		Region	District	Rep	Date	Qty
18								
19								
23	Customer	Product		Region	District	Rep	Date	Qty
24	Wonderful Faucet Cc	G854		East	Southeast	ADAM DU	2/3/15	730
25	Forceful Flagpole Cc	A105		East	Southeast	ADAM DU	12/19/15	804
26	Best Paint Inc.	V937		Central	Chicago	PETER WA	12/5/15	414

Figure 9.26   If the second row of the criteria is blank, the result reflects all rows.

Using AND to Join Criteria

Many people who have used SUMIF in Excel 2003 and earlier are likely to want to know how to conditionally sum based on two conditions. This is simple to do with DSUM. If two criteria are placed on the same row of the criteria range, they are joined by an AND. In Figure 9.27, for example, the $123,275 is the sum of records in which the customer is Best Paint Inc. and the product is V937.

CHAPTER 9

B1	▼	:	×	✓	fx	=DSUM($A$23:$I$5024,H$23,$A$17:$I$18)		

▲	A	B	C	D	E	F	G
1	**DSUM**	123,275	*=DSUM($A$23:$I$5024,H$23,$A$17:$I$18)*				
13							
17	**Customer**	**Product**	**Region**	**District**	**Rep**	**Date**	**Qty**
18	Best Paint Inc.	V937					
19							
23	**Customer**	**Product**	**Region**	**District**	**Rep**	**Date**	**Qty**
24	Wonderful Faucet Cc	G854	East	Southeast	ADAM DU	2/3/15	730

Figure 9.27   When two criteria are on the same line, they are joined by an AND function; rows must meet both criteria to be included in the DSUM.

Using OR to Join Criteria

When two criteria are placed on separate rows of the criteria range, they are joined by an OR function. In Figure 9.28, the $2.1 million represents records for either Improved Radio Traders or Best Paint Inc.

B1	▼	:	×	✓	fx	=DSUM($A$23:$I$5024,H$23,$A$17:$I$19)		

▲	A	B	C	D	E	F	G
1	**DSUM**	2,106,524	*=DSUM($A$23:$I$5024,H$23,$A$17:$I$19)*				
13							
17	**Customer**	**Product**	**Region**	**District**	**Rep**	**Date**	**Qty**
18	Improved Radio Traders						
19	Best Paint Inc.						
20							
23	**Customer**	**Product**	**Region**	**District**	**Rep**	**Date**	**Qty**
24	Wonderful Faucet Cc	G854	East	Southeast	ADAM DU	2/3/15	730
25	Forceful Flagpole Cc	A105	East	Southeast	ADAM DU	12/19/15	804
26	Best Paint Inc.	V937	Central	Chicago	PETER WA	12/5/15	414

Figure 9.28   When two criteria are on different rows, they are joined by an OR function; rows can meet either criterion to be included in the DSUM.

You can use OR to join criteria from different fields. The criteria range in Figure 9.29 shows a Region value of West joined by an OR with a District value of Texas. This pulls a superset of all the West records plus just the Texas records, which happen to fall in the Central region.

B1	▾	:	×	✓	fx	=DSUM($A$23:$I$5024,H$23,$A$17:$I$19)		

	A	B	C	D	E	F	G
1	DSUM	65,724,062	=DSUM($A$23:$I$5024,H$23,$A$17:$I$19)				
13							
17	Customer	Product	Region	District	Rep	Date	Qty
18			West				
19				Texas			
20							
23	Customer	Product	Region	District	Rep	Date	Qty
24	Wonderful Faucet C(	G854	East	Southeast	ADAM DU	2/3/15	730
25	Forceful Flagpole C(	A105	East	Southeast	ADAM DU	12/19/15	804
26	Best Paint Inc.	V937	Central	Chicago	PETER W/	12/5/15	414

Figure 9.29   The criteria to be joined with OR can be in separate columns.

Using Dates or Numbers as Criteria

The example in Figure 9.30 finds records with a date after 2017 and with revenue under $50,000. The criteria in F18 for the date could have used any of these formats:

```
>12/31/2017
>=1/1/2018
>31-Dec-2017
```

B1	▾	:	×	✓	fx	=DSUM($A$23:$I$5024,H$23,$A$17:$I$18)		

	A	B	C	D	E	F	G	H
1	DSUM	37,035,431	=DSUM($A$23:$I$5024,H$23,$A$17:$I$18)					
13								
17	Customer	Product	Region	District	Rep	Date	Qty	Revenue
18						>12/31/2017		<50000
20								
23	Customer	Product	Region	District	Rep	Date	Qty	Revenue
24	Wonderful Faucet C(	G854	East	Southeast	ADAM DU	2/3/15	730	76,906
25	Forceful Flagpole C(	A105	East	Southeast	ADAM DU	12/19/15	804	32,297

Figure 9.30   Using dates or numbers in criteria.

Using the Miracle Version of a Criteria Range

Using the criteria ranges in the preceding examples, you could easily build any complex criteria with multiple AND or OR operators.

However, this could get complex. Imagine if you wanted to pull all the records for five specific customers and five specific products. You would have to build a criteria range that is 26 rows tall. Basically, the first row is the headings for customer and product. The second row indicates that you want to see records for Customer1 and Product1. The third row indicates that you want to see records for Customer1 and Product2. The fourth row indicates that you want to see records for `Customer1` and `Product3`. The seventh row indicates `Customer2` and `Product1`. The 26th row indicates `Customer5` and `Product5`.

If you need to pull the records for seven customers and seven products from five districts, your criteria range would grow to 246 rows tall and would probably never finish calculating.

There is a miraculous version of the criteria range that completely avoids this problem. Here's how it works:

- The criteria range consists of a range that is two cells tall and one or more cells wide.

- Contrary to instructions in Excel Help, the top cell of the criteria range cannot contain a field heading. The top cell must be blank or contain anything that does not match the database header row. For example, you could use a heading of "Computed Criteria."

- The second row in the criteria range can contain any formula that evaluates to TRUE or FALSE. This formula must point to cells in the first data row of the database. The formula can be as complex as you want provided the formula returns TRUE or FALSE. You can combine AND, OR, VLOOKUP, NOT, MATCH, and any other functions.

For a simple example, suppose you want to find records that match one of 15 customers. You copy the customers to K24:K38. In the second row of the criteria field, write the formula `=NOT(ISNA( MATCH(A24,$K$24:$K$38,0)))`. This formula does a MATCH on the first customer in the database to see if it is in the list in K. The ISNA and NOT functions make sure that the criteria cell returns a TRUE when the customer is one of the 15 customers.

Very quickly and without complaint, Excel compares the 5,000 rows of your database with this complex formula, and the DSUM produces the correct value, as shown in Figure 9.31.

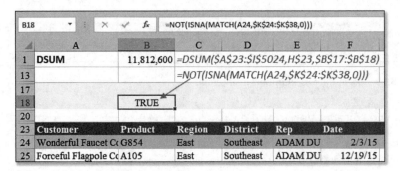

Figure 9.31   The formula version of the criteria range is rare but incredibly powerful.

Using the DGET Function

The DGET function returns a single cell from a database. The problem is that this function is picky. If your criteria range matches zero records, DGET returns a #VALUE error. If your criteria range returns more than one row, DGET returns a #NUM! error.

To have DGET work, you need to write a criteria record that causes one and only one row to be evaluated as TRUE.

Syntax:

DGET(database,field,criteria)

The DGET function returns a single cell matching criteria from a data set.

Examples of Linked Data Types

Microsoft debuted linked data types in 2018. The first two data types are stock market data and geographic data.

Enter a list of states, cities, or countries in some cells. Select those cells and choose Geography from the Data Types gallery on the Data tab. As shown in Figure 9.32, a Map icon appears next to each value to tell you that the cells contain a geography data type.

Figure 9.32   Mark cells as the Geography data type.

If you click the map icon for a cell, a data card appears with information from Wikipedia about the state listed in the cell.

However, the more interesting feature is the new formulas that can point to the linked cell. In this example, Ohio is in H2. Go to any cell and type **=H2** followed by a period. A list of fields

CHAPTER 9

appears. You can choose any of these fields to retrieve information about the geography. For example, =H2.Capital or =H2.Population. As shown in Figure 9.33, if the field name contains a space, wrap the name in square brackets: =H2.[Building Permits].

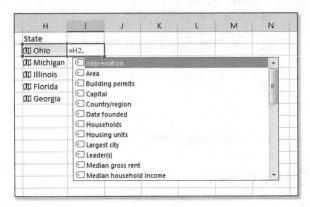

Figure 9.33   Build a formula to return a property of the state.

After entering the formula for the first state, you can copy the formula to pull similar data for each state. Figure 9.34 shows the largest city in each state.

Figure 9.34   Once you've entered a formula, copy it down to other states.

If you type a different state name in a cell, the formulas will update. In Figure 9.35, Hawaii replaced Illinois. In a second or so, Chicago is replaced with Honolulu.

What if you mistype a name? You will see a brand-new error value called #FIELD!.

Figure 9.35 Change a state name and the calculated fields update.

Given that this is a new feature, there are some odd limitations:

- The cell containing the Linked Data cannot be a formula. It must be a value. In Figure 9.35, once you have Columbus in I2, it would be nice to mark Columbus as geography and get the Columbus Ohio population with =I2.Population. However, this will not work.

- My computer always includes a custom list with the U.S. states from Alabama to Wyoming. This allows me to type **Alabama** and drag the fill handle to get the other state names. You must be careful to drag the states before marking Alabama as a Geography type. Once the cell is marked as Geography, the fill handle will not fill from custom lists.

- Your computer will have to be connected to the Internet to retrieve fields associated with a Linked Data Type.

Inside OUT

Microsoft Labs offer a free Fuzzy Lookup add-in for Excel.

Doing a VLOOKUP is impossible when you have names like "ABC Corp." and "ABC Incorporated" and "A B C". Back in Excel 2010, the research team at Microsoft Labs created a Fuzzy Lookup add-in for Excel. The technology was cool, but Microsoft ended up adding the functionality to SQL Server instead of to Excel.

However, the add-in still works in Excel 2019 and is free from Microsoft Labs. Download from https://www.microsoft.com/en-us/download/details.aspx?id=15011.

CHAPTER 9

Set the tool to return the two best matches. In the figure below, there were two valid matches for Coca-Cola and a human will do a better job of knowing which one is your customer.

Original Company	Matched Company	Similarity
AMAZON COM INC STK	Amazon.com Inc.	94%
MOTOROLA	Motorola Solutions, Inc.	90%
MOTOROLA	Motorola Mobility Holdings, Inc.	87%
ATT CORP	AT&T, Inc.	81%
ATT CORP	ITT Corporation	51%
BERSHIER HATHWAY	Berkshire Hathaway Inc.	91%
MICROSOFT	Microsoft Corporation	95%
COCACOLA	The Coca-Cola Company	91%
COCACOLA	Coca-Cola Enterprises Inc.	90%
DR PEPPER CORP	Dr Pepper Snapple Group, Inc.	79%
AUTO DESK INC COM STK NPV	Autodesk, Inc.	85%
MELLON BANK	The Bank of New York Mellon Corporation	87%

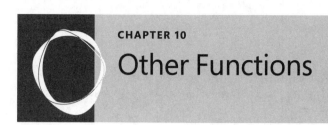

Other Functions

This chapter provides a reference to functions from the Web, Financial, Statistical, Trigonometry, Matrix, and Engineering functions.

Web Functions

Table 10.1 provides an alphabetical list of all the Web functions from Excel 2019.

Table 10.1   Alphabetical List of Web Functions

Function	Description
ENCODEURL(*text*)	Returns a URL-encoded string.
FILTERXML(*xml*, *xpath*)	Returns specific data from the XML content by using the xpath.
WEBSERVICE(*url*)	Returns data from a web service.

Inside OUT

These three functions are designed to work together, and they pre-date the new tools in Power Query. The main function is the WEBSERVICE function. Provide a URL to a web service that will return the results as an ATOM feed or a JSON feed. One free example is search.twitter.com. Specify a URL with q=vlookup and the function will return the last ten Tweets about VLOOKUP.

Before using WEBSERVICE, you might have to run the URL through ENCODEURL(). This function replaces all illegal characters with their &20 equivalents. For example, pivot table will become pivot&20table after using ENCODEURL.

You might put the Twitter search term in A2 and then URL prefix in A1. Entering **=WEBSERVICE(ENCODEURL(A1&A2))** in cell A3 will return somewhere around 20,000 characters of results to a single cell.

To select specific fields from the ATOM or JSON feed, use the FILTERXML function. The returned results can be described using XPATH. For example, if you select B1:B25 and type **=FILTERXML(A3,"//title")** followed by Ctrl+Shift+Enter, Excel will return the 15 tweets parsed out of cell A4.

TROUBLESHOOTING

Excel allows 32,768 characters in a cell but will not show you more than the first 1,000 characters.

In the WEBSERVICE example, the result of the WEBSERVICE function is more than 20,000 characters. Excel can store them, and FILTERXML can parse the data, but you cannot look at the data. One strategy: Copy the results in A4 and paste to Notepad. This will help you to find the various XPATH field names being used.

Financial Functions

Although the bulk of Excel's financial functions are for professional financiers and investors, a few functions are useful for anyone planning to use a loan to purchase a car or house.

Table 10.2 provides an alphabetical list of the Financial functions in Excel 2019.

Table 10.2   Alphabetical List of Financial Functions

Function	Description
ACCRINT(issue, first_ interest, settlement, rate, par, frequency, basis)	Returns the accrued interest for a security settlement that pays periodic interest.
ACCRINTM(issue, settlement, rate, par, basis)	Returns the accrued interest for a security that pays interest at maturity.
AMORDEGRC(cost, date_ purchased, first_period, salvage, period, rate, basis)	Returns the depreciation for each accounting period. This function is provided for the French accounting system. If an asset is purchased in the middle of the accounting period, the prorated depreciation is taken into account. The function is similar to AMORLINC, except that a depreciation coefficient is applied in the calculation, depending on the life of the assets.

AMORLINC(*cost, date_purchased, first_period, salvage, period, rate, basis*)	Returns the depreciation for each accounting period. This function is provided for the French accounting system. If an asset is purchased in the middle of the accounting period, the prorated depreciation is taken into account.
COUPDAYBS(*settlement, maturity, frequency, basis*)	Returns the number of days from the beginning of the coupon period to the settlement date.
COUPDAYS(*settlement, maturity, frequency, basis*)	Returns the number of days in the coupon period that contains the settlement date.
COUPDAYSNC(*settlement, maturity, frequency, basis*)	Returns the number of days from the settlement date to the next coupon date.
COUPNCD(*settlement, maturity, frequency, basis*)	Returns a number that represents the next coupon date after the settlement date. To view the number as a date, you select Date in the Number Format drop-down menu on the Home tab.
COUPNUM(*settlement, maturity, frequency, basis*)	Returns the number of coupons payable between the settlement date and maturity date, rounded up to the nearest whole coupon.
COUPPCD(*settlement, maturity, frequency, basis*)	Returns a number that represents the previous coupon date before the settlement date. To view the number as a date, choose a date from the Number Format drop-down menu on the home tab.
CUMIPMT(*rate, nper, pv, start_period, end_period, type*)	Returns the cumulative interest paid on a loan between *start_period* and *end_period*.
CUMPRINC(*rate, nper, pv, start_period, end_period, type*)	Returns the cumulative principal paid on a loan between *start_period* and *end_period*.
DB(*cost, salvage, life, period, month*)	Returns the depreciation of an asset for a specified period, using the fixed-declining balance method.
DDB(*cost, salvage, life, period, factor*)	Returns the depreciation of an asset for a specified period, using the double-declining-balance method or some other specified method.
DISC(*settlement, maturity, pr, redemption, basis*)	Returns the discount rate for a security.
DOLLARDE(*fractional_dollar, fraction*)	Converts a dollar price expressed as a fraction into a dollar price expressed as a decimal number. Use DOLLARDE to convert fractional dollar numbers, such as securities prices, to decimal numbers.
DOLLARFR(*decimal_dollar, fraction*)	Converts a dollar price expressed as a decimal number into a dollar price expressed as a fraction. Use DOLLARFR to convert decimal numbers to fractional dollar numbers, such as securities prices.

CHAPTER 10

Function	Description
DURATION(*settlement, maturity, coupon yld, frequency, basis*)	Returns the Macaulay duration for an assumed par value of $100. The duration is defined as the weighted average of the present value of the cash flows and is used as a measure of a bond price's response to changes in yield.
EFFECT(*nominal_rate, npery*)	Returns the effective annual interest rate, given the nominal annual interest rate and the number of compounding periods per year.
FV(*rate, nper, pmt, pv, type*)	Returns the future value of an investment, based on periodic, constant payments and a constant interest rate.
FVSCHEDULE(*principal, schedule*)	Returns the future value of an initial principal after applying a series of compound interest rates. Use FVSCHEDULE to calculate the future value of an investment with a variable or adjustable rate.
INTRATE(*settlement, maturity, investment, redemption, basis*)	Returns the interest rate for a fully invested security.
IPMT(*rate, per, nper, pv, fv, type*)	Returns the interest payment for a given period for an investment, based on periodic, constant payments and a constant interest rate. For a more complete description of the arguments in IPMT and more information about annuity functions, see PV.
IRR(*values, guess*)	Returns the internal rate of return for a series of cash flows represented by the numbers in values. These cash flows do not have to be even, as they would be for an annuity. However, the cash flows must occur at regular intervals, such as monthly or annually. The internal rate of return is the interest rate received for an investment consisting of payments (negative values) and income (positive values) that occur at regular periods.
ISPMT(*rate, per, nper, pv*)	Calculates the interest paid during a specific period of an investment. This function is provided for compatibility with Lotus 1-2-3.
MDURATION(*settlement, maturity, coupon, yld, frequency, basis*)	Returns the modified duration for a security coupon with an assumed par value of $100.
MIRR(*values, finance_rate, reinvest_rate*)	Returns the modified internal rate of return for a series of periodic cash flows. MIRR considers both the cost of the investment and the interest received on reinvestment of cash.
NOMINAL(*effect_rate, npery*)	Returns the nominal annual interest rate, given the effective rate and the number of compounding periods per year.
NPER(*rate, pmt, pv, fv, type*)	Returns the number of periods for an investment, based on periodic, constant payments and a constant interest rate.

NPV(*rate, value1, value2, ...*)	Calculates the net present value of an investment by using a discount rate and a series of future payments (negative values) and income (positive values).
ODDFPRICE(*settlement, maturity, issue, first_coupon, rate, yld, redemption, frequency, basis*)	Returns the price per $100 face value of a security having an odd (short or long) first period.
ODDFYIELD(*settlement, maturity, issue, first_coupon, rate, pr, redemption, frequency, basis*)	Returns the yield of a security that has an odd (short or long) first period.
ODDLPRICE(*settlement, maturity, last_interest, rate, yld, redemption, frequency, basis*)	Returns the price per $100 face value of a security having an odd (short or long) last coupon period.
ODDLYIELD(*settlement, maturity, last_interest, rate, pr, redemption, frequency, basis*)	Returns the yield of a security that has an odd (short or long) last period.
PDURATION(*rate, pv, fv*)	Returns the number of periods required by an investment to reach a specified value.
PMT(*rate, nper, pv, fv, type*)	Calculates the payment for a loan based on constant payments and a constant interest rate.
PPMT(*rate, per, nper, pv, fv, type*)	Returns the payment on the principal for a given period for an investment based on periodic, constant payments and a constant interest rate.
PRICE(*settlement, maturity, rate, yld, redemption, frequency, basis*)	Returns the price per $100 face value of a security that pays periodic interest.
PRICEDISC(*settlement, maturity, discount, redemption, basis*)	Returns the price per $100 face value of a discounted security.
PRICEMAT(*settlement, maturity, issue, rate, yld, basis*)	Returns the price per $100 face value of an issue security that pays interest at maturity.
PV(*rate, nper, pmt, fv, type*)	Returns the present value of an investment. The present value is the total amount that a series of future payments is worth now. For example, when you borrow money, the loan amount is the present value to the lender.

CHAPTER 10

RATE(nper, pmt, pv, fv, type, guess)	Returns the interest rate per period of an annuity. RATE is calculated by iteration and can have zero or more solutions. If the successive results of RATE do not converge to within 0.0000001 after 20 iterations, RATE returns a NUM! error.
RECEIVED(settlement, maturity, investment, discount, basis)	Returns the amount received at maturity for a fully invested security.
RRI(nper, pv, fv)	Returns an equivalent interest rate for the growth of an investment.
SLN(cost, salvage, life)	Returns the straight-line depreciation of an asset for one period.
SYD(cost, salvage, life, per)	Returns the sum-of-years'-digits depreciation of an asset for a specified period.
TBILLEQ(settlement, maturity, discount)	Returns the bond-equivalent yield for a Treasury bill (T-bill).
TBILLPRICE(settlement, maturity, discount)	Returns the price per $100 face value for a T-bill.
TBILLYIELD(settlement, maturity, pr)	Returns the yield for a T-bill.
VDB(cost, salvage, life, start_period, end_period, factor, no_switch)	Returns the depreciation of an asset for any specified period, including partial periods, using the double-declining-balance method or some other specified method. VDB stands for variable declining balance.
XIRR(values, dates, guess)	Returns the internal rate of return for a schedule of cash flows that is not necessarily periodic. To calculate the internal rate of return for a series of periodic cash flows, use the IRR function.
XNPV(rate, values, dates)	Returns the net present value for a schedule of cash flows that is not necessarily periodic. To calculate the net present value for a series of cash flows that is periodic, use the NPV function.
YIELD(settlement, maturity, rate, pr, redemption, frequency, basis)	Returns the yield on a security that pays periodic interest. You use YIELD to calculate bond yield.
YIELDDISC(settlement, maturity, .pr, redemption, basis)	Returns the annual yield for a discounted security.
YIELDMAT(settlement, maturity, issue, rate, pr, basis)	Returns the annual yield of a security that pays interest at maturity.

Statistical Functions

Table 10.3 provides an alphabetical list of the Statistical functions in Excel 2019.

Table 10.3   Alphabetical List of Statistical Functions

Function	Description
AVEDEV(*number1, number2, ...*)	Returns the average of the absolute deviations of data points from their mean. AVEDEV is a measure of the variability in a data set.
AVERAGE(*number1, number2, ...*)	Returns the average (arithmetic mean) of the arguments.
AVERAGEA(*value1, value2, ...*)	Calculates the average (arithmetic mean) of the values in the list of arguments. In addition to numbers, text and logical values, such as TRUE and FALSE, are included in the calculation.
BETA.DIST(*x, alpha, beta, cumulative, A, B*)	Returns the cumulative beta probability density function. The cumulative beta probability density function is commonly used to study variation in the percentage of something across samples, such as the fraction of the day people spend watching television.
BETA.INV(*probability, alpha, beta, A, B*)	Returns the inverse of the cumulative beta probability density function. That is, if probability is equal to BETADIST(x,...), then BETA.INV(*probability*,...) is equal to x. You can use the cumulative beta distribution in project planning to model probable completion times, given an expected completion time and variability.
BINOM.DIST(*number_s, trials, probability_s, cumulative*)	Returns the individual term binomial distribution probability. You use BINOM.DIST in problems with a fixed number of tests or trials, when the outcomes of any trial are only success or failure, when trials are independent, and when the probability of success is constant throughout the experiment. For example, BINOM.DIST can calculate the probability that two of the next three babies born will be male.
BINOM.DIST.RANGE(*trials, probability_s, number_s, [number_s2]*)	Returns the probability of a trial result using a binomial distribution.
BINOM.INV(*trials, probability_s, alpha*)	Returns the smallest value for which the cumulative binomial distribution is greater than or equal to a criterion value. You use this function for quality assurance applications. For example, you can use BINOM.INV to determine the greatest number of defective parts that are allowed to come off an assembly line run without having to reject the entire lot.

CHAPTER 10

CHISQ.DIST(x, degrees_freedom, cumulative)	Returns the one-tailed probability of the chi-squared distribution. The chi-squared distribution is associated with a chi-squared test. You use the chi-squared test to compare observed and expected values. For example, in a genetic experiment, you might hypothesize that the next generation of plants will exhibit a certain set of colors. By comparing the observed results with the expected ones, you can decide whether your original hypothesis is valid.
CHISQ.DIST.RT(x, degrees_freedom)	Returns the right-tailed probability of the chi-squared distribution.
CHISQ.INV(probability, degrees_freedom)	Returns the inverse of the one-tailed probability of the chi-squared distribution. If the probability is equal to CHISQ.DIST(x,...), then CHISQ.INV(probability,...) is x. You use this function to compare observed results with expected ones to decide whether your original hypothesis is valid.
CHISQ.INV.RT(probability, degrees_freedom)	Returns the inverse of the right-tailed probability of the chi-squared distribution.
CHISQ.TEST(actual_range, expected_range)	Returns the test for independence. CHISQ.TEST returns the value from the chi-squared distribution for the statistic and the appropriate degrees of freedom. You can use chi-squared tests to determine whether hypothesized results are verified by an experiment.
CONFIDENCE.NORM(alpha, standard_dev, size)	Returns the confidence interval for a population mean. The confidence interval is a range on either side of a sample mean. For example, if you order a product through the mail, you can determine, with a particular level of confidence, the earliest and latest the product will arrive. Uses standard normal distribution.
CONFIDENCE.T(alpha, standard_dev, size)	Returns the confidence interval based on the student's t-distribution.
CORREL(array1, array2)	Returns the correlation coefficient of the array1 and array2 cell ranges. You use the correlation coefficient to determine the relationship between two properties. For example, you can examine the relationship between a location's average temperature and the use of air conditioners.
COVARIANCE.P(array1, array2)	Returns covariance, the average of the products of deviations for each data point pair. You use covariance to determine the relationship between two data sets. For example, you can examine whether greater income accompanies greater levels of education. Based on a population.
COVARIANCE.S(array1, array2)	Returns covariance, the average of the products of deviations for each data point pair. You use covariance to determine the relationship between two data sets. For example, you can examine whether greater income accompanies greater levels of education. Based on a sample.

CHAPTER 10

DEVSQ(*number1, number2, ...*)	Returns the sum of squares of deviations of data points from their sample mean.
EXPON.DIST(*x, lambda, cumulative*)	Returns the exponential distribution. You use EXPON.DIST to model the time between events, such as how long a bank's automated teller machine takes to deliver cash. For example, you can use EXPON.DIST to determine the probability that the process takes, at most, 1 minute.
F.DIST(*x, degrees_ freedom1, degrees_ freedom2, cumulative*)	Returns the F probability distribution. You can use this function to determine whether two data sets have different degrees of diversity. For example, you can examine test scores given to men and women entering high school and determine whether the variability in the females is different from that found in the males.
F.DIST.RT(*x, degrees_freedom1, degrees_freedom2*)	Returns the right-tailed F probability distribution.
F.INV(*probability, degrees_freedom1, degrees_freedom2*)	Returns the inverse of the F probability distribution. If the probability is equal to F.DIST($x, ...$), then F.INV(*probability, ...*) is equal to x.
F.INV.RT(*probability, degrees_freedom1, degrees_freedom2*)	Returns the inverse of the right-tailed F probability distribution.
F.TEST(*array1, array2*)	Returns the result of an F-test. An F-test returns the one-tailed probability that the variances in *array1* and *array2* are not significantly different. You use this function to determine whether the two samples have different variances. For example, given test scores from public and private schools, you can test whether those schools have different levels of diversity.
FISHER(*x*)	Returns the Fisher transformation at x. This transformation produces a function that is approximately normally distributed rather than skewed. You use this function to perform hypothesis testing on the correlation coefficient.
FISHERINV(*y*)	Returns the inverse of the Fisher transformation. You use this transformation when analyzing correlations between ranges or arrays of data. If y is equal to FISHER(x), then FISHERINV(y) is equal to x.
FORECAST(*x, known_y's, known_x's*)	Calculates, or predicts, a future value by using existing values. The predicted value is a y value for a given x value. The known values are existing x values and y values, and the new value is predicted by using linear regression. You can use this function to predict future sales, inventory requirements, or consumer trends.

CHAPTER 10

FORECAST.ETS(*target_date, values, timeline, seasonality, data_completion*)	Returns the forecasted value for a specific future target date using the exponential smoothing method. New in Excel 2019.
FORECAST.ETS.CONFINT(*target_date, values, timeline, confidence_level, seasonality*)	Returns a confidence interval for the forecast value at the specified target date. New in Excel 2019.
FORECAST.ETS.SEASONALITY(*values, timeline, data_completion, aggregation*)	Returns the length of the repetitive pattern Microsoft Excel detects for the specified time series. New in Excel 2019.
FORECAST.ETS.STAT(*values, timeline, statistic_type, seasonality, data_completion*)	Returns the requested statistic for the forecast. The eight available statistics are Alpha, Beta, Gamma, mean absolute scaled error (MASE), symmetric mean absolute percentage error (SMAPE), mean absolute percentage error (MAE), root mean squared error metric (RMSE), and step size. New in Excel 2019.
FORECAST.LINEAR(*x, known_y's, known_x's*)	Calculates, or predicts, a future value by using existing values. The predicted value is a y value for a given x value. The known values are existing x values and y values, and the new value is predicted by using linear regression. You can use this function to predict future sales, inventory requirements, or consumer trends. This is a new name for FORECAST in Excel 2019.
FREQUENCY(*data_array, bins_array*)	Calculates how often values occur within a range of values and returns a vertical array of numbers. For example, you can use FREQUENCY to count the number of test scores that fall within ranges of scores. Because FREQUENCY returns an array, it must be entered as an array formula.
GAMMA(*x*)	Returns the gamma function value.
GAMMA.DIST(*x, alpha, beta, cumulative*)	Returns the gamma distribution. You can use this function to study variables that might have a skewed distribution. The gamma distribution is commonly used in queuing analysis.
GAMMA.INV(*probability, alpha, beta*)	Returns the inverse of the gamma cumulative distribution. If the *probability* is equal to GAMMA.DIST(*x, ...*), then GAMMA.INV (*probability, ...*) is equal to x.
GAMMALN(*x*)	Returns the natural logarithm of the gamma function.
GAUSS(*x*)	Returns 0.5 less than the standard normal curve distribution.
GEOMEAN(*number1, number2, ...*)	Returns the geometric mean of an array or a range of positive data. For example, you can use GEOMEAN to calculate average growth rate given compound interest with variable rates.

GROWTH(*known_y's, known_x's, new_x's, const*)	Calculates predicted exponential growth by using existing data. GROWTH returns the y values for a series of new x values that you specify by using existing x values and y values. You can also use the GROWTH worksheet function to fit an exponential curve to existing x values and y values.
HARMEAN(*number1, number2, ...*)	Returns the harmonic mean of a data set. The harmonic mean is the reciprocal of the arithmetic mean of reciprocals.
HYPGEOM.DIST(*sample_s, number_sample, population_s, number_population*)	Returns the hypergeometric distribution. HYPGEOM.DIST returns the probability of a given number of sample successes, given the sample size, population successes, and population size. You use HYPGEOM.DIST for problems with a finite population, in which each observation is either a success or a failure, and each subset of a given size is chosen with equal likelihood.
INTERCEPT(*known_y's, known_x's*)	Calculates the point at which a line will intersect the y-axis by using existing x values and y values. The intercept point is based on a best-fit regression line plotted through the known x values and known y values. You use the intercept when you want to determine the value of the dependent variable when the independent variable is 0. For example, you can use the INTERCEPT function to predict a metal's electrical resistance at 0 degrees Celsius when your data points were taken at room temperature or higher.
KURT(*number1, number2, ...*)	Returns the kurtosis of a data set. Kurtosis characterizes the relative peakedness or flatness of a distribution compared with the normal distribution. Positive kurtosis indicates a relatively peaked distribution. Negative kurtosis indicates a relatively flat distribution.
LARGE(*array, k*)	Returns the kth largest value in a data set. You can use this function to select a value based on its relative standing. For example, you can use LARGE to return a highest, runner-up, or third-place score.
LINEST(*known_y's, known_x's, const, stats*)	Calculates the statistics for a line by using the least-squares method to calculate a straight line that best fits the data and returns an array that describes the line. Because this function returns an array of values, it must be entered as an array formula.
LOGEST(*known_y's, known_x's, const, stats*)	In regression analysis, calculates an exponential curve that fits the data and returns an array of values that describes the curve. Because this function returns an array of values, it must be entered as an array formula.
LOGNORM.DIST(*x, mean, standard_dev, cumulative*)	Returns the cumulative lognormal distribution of x, in which LN(x) is normally distributed with the parameters *mean* and *standard_dev*. You use this function to analyze data that has been logarithmically transformed.

LOGNORM.INV(*probability, mean, standard_dev*)	Returns the inverse of the lognormal cumulative distribution function of x, where LN(x) is normally distributed with the parameters *mean* and *standard_dev*. If the *probability* is equal to LOGNORM.DIST(x,...), LOGNORM.INV (*probability*,...) is equal to x.
MAX(*number1, number2, ...*)	Returns the largest value in a set of values.
MAXA(*value1, value2, ...*)	Returns the largest value in a list of arguments. Text and logical values such as TRUE and FALSE are compared, as are numbers.
MEDIAN(*number1, number2, ...*)	Returns the median of the given numbers. The median is the number in the middle of a set of numbers; that is, half the numbers have values that are greater than the median and half have values that are less.
MIN(*number1, number2, ...*)	Returns the smallest number in a set of values.
MINA(*value1, value2, ...*)	Returns the smallest value in a list of arguments. Text and logical values such as TRUE and FALSE are compared, as are numbers.
MODE.MULT(*number1, number2, ...*)	Returns a vertical array of the most frequently occurring, or repetitive, values in an array or a range of data. MODE.MULT was new in Excel 2010 and handles the specific case when there are two or more values that are tied for the most frequently occurring value. Whereas MODE.SNGL returns only the first mode value, MODE.MULT returns all the mode values.
MODE.SNGL(*number1, number2, ...*)	Returns the most frequently occurring, or repetitive, value in an array or a range of data. Like MEDIAN, MODE.SNGL is a location measure. If there are two values that are tied for the most frequently occurring value, only the first one will be returned by MODE.SNGL. If you need to return all of the tied values, use the new MODE.MULT.
NEGBINOM.DIST(*number_f, number_s, probability_s, cumulative*)	Returns the negative binomial distribution. NEGBINOM.DIST returns the probability that there will be *number_f* failures before the *number_s*th success when the constant probability of a success is *probability_s*. This function is similar to the binomial distribution function, except that the number of successes is fixed and the number of trials is variable. As with the binomial distribution function, trials are assumed to be independent.
NORM.DIST(*x, mean, standard_dev, cumulative*)	Returns the normal cumulative distribution for the specified mean and standard deviation. This function has a wide range of applications in statistics, including hypothesis testing.
NORM.INV(*probability, mean, standard_dev*)	Returns the inverse of the normal cumulative distribution for the specified mean and standard deviation.

Function	Description
NORM.S.DIST(*z*)	Returns the standard normal cumulative distribution function. The distribution has a mean of zero and a standard deviation of one. You use this function in place of a table of standard normal curve areas.
NORM.S.INV(*probability*)	Returns the inverse of the standard normal cumulative distribution. The distribution has a mean of zero and a standard deviation of one.
PEARSON(*array1, array2*)	Returns the Pearson product–moment correlation coefficient, r, a dimensionless index that ranges from –1.0 to 1.0, inclusive, and reflects the extent of a linear relationship between two data sets.
PERCENTILE.EXC(*array, k*)	Returns the *k*th percentile of values in a range. You can use this function to establish a threshold of acceptance. For example, you can decide to examine candidates who score above the 90th percentile. PERCENTILE.EXC assumes the percentile is between 0 and 1, exclusive.
PERCENTILE.INC(*array, k*)	Returns the *k*th percentile of values in a range. PERCENTILE.INC assumes the percentile is between 0 and 1, inclusive.
PERCENTRANK.EXC(*array, x, significance*)	Returns the rank of a value in a data set as a percentage of the data set. You can use this function to evaluate the relative standing of a value within a data set. PERCENTRANK.EXC is renamed from PERCENTRANK. It assumes the percentile is between 0 and 1, exclusive.
PERCENTRANK.INC(*array, x, significance*)	Returns the rank of a value in a data set as a percentage of the data set. You can use this function to evaluate the relative standing of a value within a data set. For example, you can use PERCENTRANK.INC to evaluate the standing of an aptitude test score among all scores for the test. PERCENTRANK.INC assumes percentiles from 0 to 1, inclusive.
PERMUT(*number, number_chosen*)	Returns the number of permutations for a given number of objects that can be selected from number objects. A permutation is any set or subset of objects or events in which internal order is significant. Permutations are different from combinations, for which the internal order is not significant. You use this function for lottery-style probability calculations.
PERMUTATIONA(*number, number_chosen*)	Returns the number of permutations for a given number of objects (with repetitions) that can be selected from the total objects.
PHI(*x*)	Returns the value of the density function for a standard normal distribution.
POISSON.DIST(*x, mean, cumulative*)	Returns the Poisson distribution. A common application of the Poisson distribution is predicting the number of events over a specific time, such as the number of cars arriving at a toll plaza in 1 minute.

CHAPTER 10

`PROB(x_range, prob_range, lower_limit, upper_limit)`	Returns the probability that values in a range are between two limits. If `upper_limit` is not supplied, returns the probability that values in `x_range` are equal to `lower_limit`.
`QUARTILE.EXC(array, quart)`	Returns the quartile of a data set. Quartiles are often used in sales and survey data to divide populations into groups. For example, you can use `QUARTILE.EXC` to find the top 25% of incomes in a population. This function assumes percentiles run from 0 to 1, exclusive.
`QUARTILE.INC(array, quart)`	Returns the quartile of a data set. Quartiles are often used in sales and survey data to divide populations into groups. This function assumes percentiles run from 0 to 1, inclusive.
`RANK.AVG(number, ref, order)`	Returns the rank of a number in a list of numbers. The rank of a number is its size relative to other values in a list. (If you were to sort the list, the rank of the number would be its position.) When two or more items are tied, `RANK.AVG` averages their ranks.
`RANK.EQ(number, ref, order)`	Returns the rank of a number in a list of numbers. When two or more items are tied, `RANK.EQ` assigns the lower rank to all items in the tie. Renamed from RANK in Excel 2010.
`RSQ(known_y's, known_x's)`	Returns the square of the Pearson product–moment correlation coefficient through data points in `known_y's` and `known_x's`. The r-squared value can be interpreted as the proportion of the variance in y attributable to the variance in x.
`SKEW(number1, number2, ...)`	Returns the skewness of a distribution. Skewness characterizes the degree of asymmetry of a distribution around its mean. Positive skewness indicates a distribution with an asymmetric tail extending toward more positive values. Negative skewness indicates a distribution with an asymmetric tail extending toward more negative values.
`SKEW.P(number1, number2, ...)`	Returns the skewness of a distribution based on a population. Skewness characterizes the degree of asymmetry of a distribution around its mean. Positive skewness indicates a distribution with an asymmetric tail extending toward more positive values. Negative skewness indicates a distribution with an asymmetric tail extending toward more negative values.
`SLOPE(known_y's, known_x's)`	Returns the slope of the linear regression line through data points in `known_y's` and `known_x's`. The `slope` is the vertical distance divided by the horizontal distance between any two points on the line, which is the rate of change along the regression line.
`SMALL(array, k)`	Returns the kth smallest value in a data set. You use this function to return values with a particular relative standing in a data set.
`STANDARDIZE(x, mean, standard_dev)`	Returns a normalized value from a distribution characterized by `mean` and `standard_dev`.

STDEV.P(*number1, number2, ...*)	Calculates standard deviation based on the entire population given as arguments. The standard deviation is a measure of how widely values are dispersed from the average value (that is, the mean).
STDEV.S(*number1, number2, ...*)	Estimates standard deviation based on a sample. The standard deviation is a measure of how widely values are dispersed from the average value (that is, the mean).
STDEVA(*value1, value2, ...*)	Estimates standard deviation based on a sample. The standard deviation is a measure of how widely values are dispersed from the average value (that is, the mean). Text and logical values such as TRUE and FALSE are included in the calculation.
STDEVPA(*value1, value2, ...*)	Calculates standard deviation based on the entire population given as arguments, including text and logical values. The standard deviation is a measure of how widely values are dispersed from the average value (that is, the mean).
STEYX(*known_y's, known_x's*)	Returns the standard error of the predicted y value for each x in the regression. The standard error is a measure of the amount of error in the prediction of y for an individual x.
SUMSQ(*number1, number2, ...*)	Returns the sum of the squares of the arguments.
SUMX2MY2(*array_x, array_y*)	Returns the sum of the difference of squares of corresponding values in two arrays.
SUMX2PY2(*array_x, array_y*)	Returns the sum of the sum of squares of corresponding values in two arrays. The sum of the sum of squares is a common term in many statistical calculations.
SUMXMY2(*array_x, array_y*)	Returns the sum of squares of differences of corresponding values in two arrays.
T.DIST(*x, degrees_freedom, tails, cumulative*)	Returns the percentage points (that is, probability) for the Student t-distribution, where a numeric value (x) is a calculated value of t for which percentage points are to be computed. The t-distribution is used in the hypothesis testing of small sample data sets. You use this function in place of a table of critical values for the t-distribution.
T.DIST.2T(*x, degrees_freedom*)	Returns the two-tailed probability for the Student t-distribution.
T.DIST.RT(*x, degrees_freedom*)	Returns the right-tailed probability for the Student t-distribution.
T.INV(*probability, degrees_freedom*)	Returns the t-value of the Student's t-distribution as a function of the probability and the degrees of freedom.
T.INV.2T(*probability, degrees_freedom*)	Returns the right-tailed t-value of the Student's t-distribution as a function of the probability and the degrees of freedom.
T.TEST(*array1, array2, tails, type*)	Returns the probability associated with a Student's t-test. You use T.TEST to determine whether two samples are likely to have come from the same two underlying populations that have the same mean.

CHAPTER 10

TREND(*known_y's, known_x's, new_x's ,const*)	Returns values along a linear trend. Fits a straight line (using the method of least squares) to the arrays *known_y's* and *known_x's*. Returns the y values along that line for the array of *new_x's* that you specify.
TRIMMEAN(*array, percent*)	Returns the mean of the interior of a data set. TRIMMEAN calculates the mean taken by excluding a percentage of data points from the top and bottom tails of a data set. You can use this function when you want to exclude outlying data from your analysis.
VAR.P(*number1, number2, ...*)	Calculates variance based on the entire population.
VAR.S(*number1, number2, ...*)	Estimates variance based on a sample.
VARA(*value1, value2, ...*)	Estimates variance based on a sample. In addition to numbers, text and logical values such as TRUE and FALSE are included in the calculation.
VARPA(*value1, value2, ...*)	Calculates variance based on the entire population. In addition to numbers, text and logical values such as TRUE and FALSE are included in the calculation.
WEIBULL.DIST(*x, alpha, beta, cumulative*)	Returns the Weibull distribution. You use this distribution in reliability analysis, such as to calculate a device's mean time to failure.
Z.TEST(*array, x, sigma*)	Returns the two-tailed p value of a z-test. The z-test generates a standard score for x with respect to the data set, *array*, and returns the two-tailed probability for the normal distribution. You can use this function to assess the likelihood that a particular observation is drawn from a particular population.

Trigonometry Functions

Table 10.4 provides an alphabetical list of the Trigonometry functions in Excel 2019.

Table 10.4   Alphabetical List of Trig Functions

Function	Description
ACOS(*number*)	Returns the arccosine of a number. The arccosine is the angle whose cosine is *number*. The returned angle is given in radians in the range 0 to π.
ACOSH(*number*)	Returns the inverse hyperbolic cosine of a *number*, which must be n greater than or equal to 1. The inverse hyperbolic cosine is the value whose hyperbolic cosine is *number*, so ACOSH(COSH(*number*)) equals number.

ACOT(*number*)	Returns the arccotangent of a number in radians, in the range of 0 to π.
ACOTH(*number*)	Returns the inverse hyperbolic cotangent of a number.
ASIN(*number*)	Returns the arcsine of a number. The arcsine is the angle whose sine is *number*. The returned angle is given in radians in the range –π / 2 to π / 2.
ASINH(*number*)	Returns the inverse hyperbolic sine of a number. The inverse hyperbolic sine is the value whose hyperbolic sine is *number*, so ASINH(SINH(*number*)) equals *number*.
ATAN(*number*)	Returns the arctangent of a number. The arctangent is the angle whose tangent is *number*. The returned angle is given in radians in the range –π / 2 to π / 2.
ATAN2(*x_num*, *y_num*)	Returns the arctangent of the specified x- and y-coordinates. The arctangent is the angle from the x-axis to a line containing the origin (0, 0) and a point with coordinates (*x_num*, *y_num*). The angle is given in radians between –π and π, excluding –π.
ATANH(*number*)	Returns the inverse hyperbolic tangent of a number. *number* must be between –1 and 1 (excluding –1 and 1). The inverse hyperbolic tangent is the value whose hyperbolic tangent is *number*, so ATANH(TANH(*number*)) equals number.
COS(*number*)	Returns the cosine of the given angle.
COSH(*number*)	Returns the hyperbolic cosine of a number.
COT(*number*)	Returns the cotangent of an angle.
COTH(*number*)	Returns the hyperbolic cotangent of a number.
CSC(*number*)	Returns the cosecant of a number.
CSCH(*number*)	Returns the hyperbolic cosecant of a number.
DEGREES(*angle*)	Converts radians into degrees.
LN(*number*)	Returns the natural logarithm of *number*. Natural logarithms are based on the constant e (2.71828182845904).
LOG(*number*, *base*)	Returns the logarithm of *number* to the specified base.
LOG10(*number*)	Returns the base-10 logarithm of *number*.
RADIANS(*angle*)	Converts degrees to radians.
SEC(*number*)	Returns the secant of an angle.
SECH(*number*)	Returns the hyperbolic secant of an angle.
SIN(*number*)	Returns the sine of the given angle.
SINH(*number*)	Returns the hyperbolic sine of *number*.
TAN(*number*)	Returns the tangent of the given angle.
TANH(*number*)	Returns the hyperbolic tangent of *number*.

CHAPTER 10

Matrix Functions

Table 10.5 provides an alphabetical list of the Matrix functions in Excel 2019.

Table 10.5 Alphabetical List of Matrix Functions

Function	Description
MDETERM(*array*)	Returns the matrix determinant of an array.
MINVERSE(*array*)	Returns the inverse matrix for the matrix stored in an array.
MMULT(*array1, array2*)	Returns the matrix product of two arrays. The result is an array with the same number of rows as *array1* and the same number of columns as *array2*.
MUNIT(*dimension*)	Returns the unit matrix for the specified dimension.
SERIESSUM(*x, n, m, coefficients*)	Returns the sum of a power series based on the formula $\text{SERIES}(x,n,m,a) \approx a_1 x n + a_2 x^{(n+m)} + a_3 x^{(n+2m)} + \ldots + a_i x^{(n+(i-1)m)}$
SUMPRODUCT(*array1, array2, array3,...*)	Multiplies corresponding components in the given arrays and returns the sum of those products.

Engineering Functions

Table 10.6 provides an alphabetical list of the Engineering functions in Excel 2019.

Table 10.6 Alphabetical List of Engineering Functions

Function	Description
BASE(*number, radix, min_length*)	Converts a number into a text representation with the given radix (base).
BESSELI(*x, n*)	Returns the modified Bessel function, which is equivalent to the BESSELJ function evaluated for purely imaginary arguments.
BESSELJ(*x, n*)	Returns the Bessel function of the first kind.
BESSELK(*x, n*)	Returns the modified Bessel function of the second kind, which is equivalent to the BESSELY functions evaluated for purely imaginary arguments.
BESSELY(*x, n*)	Returns the Bessel function of the second kind. This is the most commonly used form of the Bessel functions. This function provides solutions of the Bessel differential equation and are infinite at x=0. This function is sometimes called the Neumann function.
BIN2DEC(*number*)	Converts a binary number to decimal.
BIN2HEX(*number, places*)	Converts a binary number to hexadecimal.
BIN2OCT(*number, places*)	Converts a binary number to octal.

BITAND(*number1, number2*)	Returns a bitwise AND of two numbers.
BITLSHIFT(*number, shift_amount*)	Returns a number shifted left by *shift_amount* bits.
BITOR(*number1, number2*)	Returns a bitwise OR of two numbers.
BITRSHIFT(*number, shift_amount*)	Returns a number shifted right by *shift_amount* bits.
BITXOR(*number1, number2*)	Returns a bitwise Exclusive OR of two numbers.
COMPLEX(*real_num, i_num, suffix*)	Converts real and imaginary coefficients into a complex number in the form x + yi or x + yj. Use *suffix* to control whether "i" or "j" is used.
CONVERT(*number, from_unit, to_unit*)	Converts a number from one measurement system to another. For example, CONVERT can translate a table of distances in miles to a table of distances in kilometers.
DEC2BIN(*number, places*)	Converts a decimal number to binary.
DEC2HEX(*number, places*)	Converts a decimal number to hexadecimal.
DEC2OCT(*number, places*)	Converts a decimal number to octal.
DECIMAL(*number, radix*)	Converts a text representation of a number with a given base into a decimal number.
DELTA(*number1, number2*)	Tests whether two values are equal. Returns 1 if *number1* = *number2*; returns 0 otherwise. You use this function to filter a set of values. For example, by summing several DELTA functions, you can calculate the count of equal pairs. This function is also known as the Kronecker Delta function.
ERF(*lower_limit, upper_limit*)	Returns the ERROR function integrated between *lower_limit* and *upper_limit*.
ERFC(*x*)	Returns the complementary ERF function integrated between x and infinity.
GESTEP(*number, step*)	Returns 1 if *number* is greater than or equal to *step*; otherwise, returns 0. You use this function to filter a set of values. For example, by summing several GESTEP functions, you can calculate the count of values that exceed a threshold.
HEX2BIN(*number, places*)	Converts a hexadecimal number to binary.
HEX2DEC(*number*)	Converts a hexadecimal number to decimal.
HEX2OCT(*number, places*)	Converts a hexadecimal number to octal.
IMABS(*inumber*)	Returns the absolute value (modulus) of a complex number in x + yi or x + yj text format.
IMAGINARY(*inumber*)	Returns the imaginary coefficient of a complex number in x + yi or x + yj text format.
IMARGUMENT(*inumber*)	Returns the argument 0 (theta), an angle expressed in radians.

IMCONJUGATE(*inumber*)	Returns the complex conjugate of a complex number in x + yi or x + yj text format.
IMCOS(*inumber*)	Returns the cosine of a complex number in x + yi or x + yj text format.
IMCOSH(*inumber*)	Returns the hyperbolic cosine of a complex number.
IMCOT(*inumber*)	Returns the cotangent of a complex number.
IMCSC(*inumber*)	Returns the cosecant of a complex number.
IMCSCH(*inumber*)	Returns the hyperbolic cosecant of a complex number.
IMDIV(*inumber1, inumber2*)	Returns the quotient of two complex numbers in x + yi or x + yj text format.
IMEXP(*inumber*)	Returns the exponential of a complex number in x + yi or x + yj text format.
IMLN(*inumber*)	Returns the natural logarithm of a complex number in x + yi or x + yj text format.
IMLOG10(*inumber*)	Returns the common logarithm (base-10) of a complex number in x + yi or x + yj text format.
IMLOG2(*inumber*)	Returns the base-2 logarithm of a complex number in x + yi or x + yj text format.
IMPOWER(*inumber, number*)	Returns a complex number in x + yi or x + yj text format raised to a power.
IMPRODUCT(*inumber1, inumber2, ...*)	Returns the product of 2 to 255 complex numbers in x + yi or x + yj text format.
IMREAL(*inumber*)	Returns the real coefficient of a complex number in x + yi or x + yj text format.
IMSEC(*inumber*)	Returns the secant of a complex number.
IMSECH(*inumber*)	Returns the hyperbolic secant of a complex number.
IMSIN(*inumber*)	Returns the sine of a complex number in x + yi or x + yj text format.
IMSINH(*inumber*)	Returns the hyperbolic sin of a complex number.
IMSQRT(*inumber*)	Returns the square root of a complex number in x + yi or x + yj text format.
IMSUB(*inumber1, inumber2*)	Returns the difference of two complex numbers in x + yi or x + yj text format.
IMSUM(*inumber1, inumber2,...*)	Returns the sum of two or more complex numbers in x + yi or x + yj text format.
IMTAN(*inumber*)	Returns the tangent of a complex number.
OCT2BIN(*number, places*)	Converts an octal number to binary.
OCT2DEC(*number*)	Converts an octal number to decimal.
OCT2HEX(*number, places*)	Converts an octal number to hexadecimal.

Connecting Worksheets and Workbooks

CHAPTER 11

In Chapter 7, "Understanding Functions," and Chapter 8, "Using Everyday Functions: Math, Date and Time, and Text Functions," you find out how to set up formulas that calculate based on values within one worksheet. You can also easily connect a worksheet to several other worksheets or connect various workbooks. Excel 2019 offers easier-than-ever ways to connect a worksheet to data from the Web, data from text files, or data from databases such as Access.

In this chapter, you discover how to do the following:

- Connect two worksheets

- Connect two workbooks

- Manage links between workbooks

Connecting Two Worksheets

Although Excel 2019 offers 17 billion cells on every worksheet, it is fairly common to separate any model onto several worksheets. You might choose to have one worksheet for each month in a year or to have one worksheet for each functional area of a business. For example, Figure 11.1 shows a workbook with worksheets for revenue and expenses. Because different departments might be responsible for the functional areas, it makes sense to separate them into different worksheets. Eventually, though, you will want to pull information from the various worksheets into a single summary worksheet.

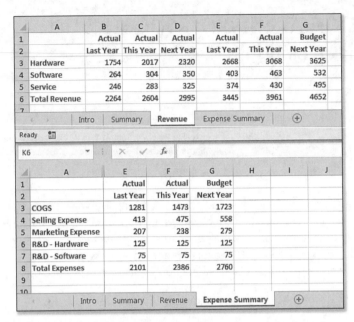

	A	B	C	D	E	F	G
1		Actual	Actual	Actual	Actual	Actual	Budget
2		Last Year	This Year	Next Year	Last Year	This Year	Next Year
3	Hardware	1754	2017	2320	2668	3068	3625
4	Software	264	304	350	403	463	532
5	Service	246	283	325	374	430	495
6	Total Revenue	2264	2604	2995	3445	3961	4652

Intro   Summary   **Revenue**   Expense Summary   ⊕

Ready

K6

	A	E	F	G	H	I	J
1		Actual	Actual	Budget			
2		Last Year	This Year	Next Year			
3	COGS	1281	1473	1723			
4	Selling Expense	413	475	558			
5	Marketing Expense	207	238	279			
6	R&D - Hardware	125	125	125			
7	R&D - Software	75	75	75			
8	Total Expenses	2101	2386	2760			
9							
10							

Intro   Summary   Revenue   **Expense Summary**   ⊕

Figure 11.1   Different functional areas need to work on budgets for revenue and expenses, so revenue and expenses are kept on separate worksheets.

Excel in Practice: Seeing Two Worksheets of the Same Workbook Side by Side

The workbook in Figure 11.1 illustrates a useful trick—seeing two worksheets of the same workbook side by side. Follow these steps to see two worksheets of the same workbook side by side:

1. Open the first worksheet that you want to view.

2. On the View tab, click New Window. If your workbook is in full-screen mode, it appears that nothing happened. However, when you look in the title bar, you see your workbook title has ":2" after the title.

3. On the View tab, click Arrange All and then click either Vertical or Horizontal. Click the Windows of Active Workbook check box. The arrangement in Figure 11.1 is horizontal, whereas the arrangement in Figure 11.2 is vertical. Note that the Arrange All command will not work if you have any hidden workbooks open, such as the Solver add-in or a Personal Macro Workbook. In those cases, you have to resize and arrange the Excel windows manually.

Figure 11.2   Set up a link to get information from the Revenue tab to appear on the Summary tab.

4.   In the second window, click the second worksheet tab that you want to view. You can now see both worksheets of the same workbook side by side. In Excel 2019, each window has its own ribbon and status bar.

To return to a single window, click the Close Window icon, which is the X in the top-right corner of window 2.

As shown in Figure 11.2, the goal is to have the values from cells F6:G6 on the Revenue tab carry forward to cells B5:C5 on the Summary tab. There are four ways to achieve this goal:

- Type a formula, such as **=Revenue!F6**, in cell B5.

- Build the formula using the mouse.

- Right-drag cells F6:G6 on the Revenue tab to the proper location on the Summary tab and then select Link Here.

- Copy cells F6:G6 on the Revenue tab. Paste to cells B5:C5 and then use the Paste Options fly-out menu to Link Here. This is the newest method and is discussed in the next section.

NOTE

Note that you have not created a second workbook. Instead, you have created a second camera looking at a different section of the same workbook. Any changes you make in one window appear in the other window.

Creating Links Using the Paste Options Menu

Follow these steps to set up a link using the new Paste Options fly-out menu:

1. Select the cells that have the figures you want to copy. For this example, select cells F6:G6 on the Revenue tab.

2. Press Ctrl+C to copy those cells.

3. Right-click the cell where the link should appear. For this example, right-click B5 on the Summary tab. In the menu that pops up, the sixth icon under Paste Options is Paste Link.

4. Choose Paste Link from the menu that appears (see Figure 11.3). Excel will insert formulas in B5:C5 on the Summary worksheet.

Figure 11.3 Copy the source cells to the target range.

Excel inserts a formula with the correct syntax to point to cells G6 on the Revenue tab (see Figure 11.4). Note that if data changes on the Revenue worksheet, the new results appear on the Summary worksheet.

Figure 11.4   After you choose Paste Link, a formula points to the other worksheet.

Creating Links Using the Right-Drag Menu

If you are adept with the mouse, there is an easier way to create links. This is particularly true if you have the two worksheets arranged side by side, which was presented previously in the Excel in Practice sidebar.

This method uses the Alternate Drag-And-Drop menu. This amazing menu, which has been hiding in Excel for several versions, offers a fast way to copy cells, link cells, change formulas to values, and more.

The Alternate Drag-and-Drop menu appears anytime you right-click the border of a selection, right-drag to a new location, and then release the mouse button.

In Figure 11.5, on the Expense Summary tab, select cells F3:G3. Hover over the edge of the selection rectangle until you see the four-headed arrow. Right-click and begin to drag to the other window.

CHAPTER 11

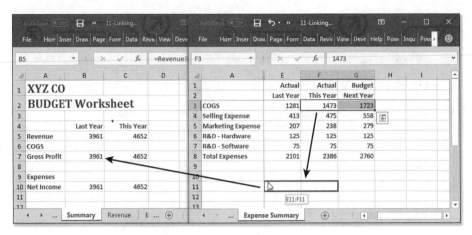

Figure 11.5   Right-click and drag the source cells.

When you have arrived at the new location, release the right mouse button and select Link Here, as shown in Figure 11.6. Excel builds a formula in the target location that has the proper syntax to link to the source cells. Note that because the worksheet name contains a space, Excel wraps the sheet name in apostrophes: =`'Expense Summary'!F3` (see Figure 11.7).

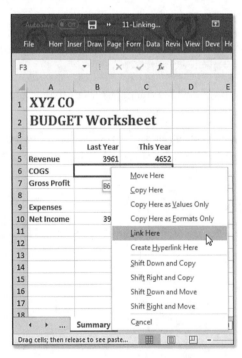

Figure 11.6   Release the mouse button to access this menu.

Figure 11.7 Excel builds the proper formula.

Inside OUT

The menu shown in Figure 11.6 has a wide variety of uses. My favorite is converting formulas to values without doing copy and paste values.

I do about 35 live all-day Excel seminars every year. The people who come to my seminars are there to earn Continuing Education credit hours, and they are almost always accountants who use Excel 40 hours a week. I've learned that someone in every room has some awesome trick that I have never seen before.

I first learned about the Right-Drag menu while doing a seminar in Columbus, Indiana. A fellow named Dave in the first row showed me how to replace formulas with values: Select the range of formulas. Hold down the right mouse button while you drag the range to the right one column. Keep holding down the right mouse button while you drag back to the original location. Then choose Copy Here As Values Only.

Given that the right-drag menu is not documented in Excel Help, you wonder how Dave ever accidentally discovered this technique.

Building a Link by Using the Mouse

Another method is to build a formula by pointing to the correct cell with the mouse. Start in a target cell, such as cell B9 on the Summary tab (see Figure 11.8).

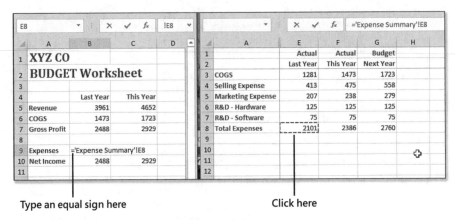

Figure 11.8   Type an equal sign and then click the source cell.

Instead of trying to remember the exact syntax, you can point to the correct cell. Type the equal sign and then click the desired worksheet tab. Using the mouse, click a cell to get the value from that cell. Excel builds the formula =`'Expense Summary'!F8` in the formula bar (see Figure 11.8). Excel waits for you to either press the Enter key to accept the formula or press another operator key to add other cells to the formula.

NOTE

The formula that Excel builds is a relative formula. You can copy B9 to B10 to retrieve the 2018 budget.

When you press the Enter key to accept the formula, Excel jumps back to the starting worksheet. The desired figure is carried through to the worksheet.

Links to External Workbooks Default to Absolute References

You can use any of the four methods described previously for building links to other worksheets when you want to build links to external workbooks. It is easiest if you open both workbooks.

Note that if you use any of the methods illustrated previously, Excel defaults to adding dollar signs into the external reference. The dollar signs create an absolute reference that makes it more difficult to copy.

Here is an example. When you use the mouse method described in Figure 11.8 to link to a worksheet in the same workbook, the cell reference is something like F8. If you use the same method to link to a worksheet in a different workbook, the cell reference created by Excel is automatically $F$8. The dollar signs make this an absolute reference, which is difficult to copy. If you need to copy this formula to other cells, you should press the F4 key three times to change from an absolute reference to a relative reference.

Building a Formula by Typing

You can always build the links by typing the formula. This is the least popular method because you need to understand an array of syntax rules. Keep in mind that these syntax rules change depending on whether the worksheet name contains a space, whether the link is external, and whether the linked workbook is open or closed.

Here are the syntax rules:

- For an internal link in which the worksheet name does not contain a space or special characters, use =SheetName!CellAddress. An example is =Result!B3.

- When the worksheet name contains a space or certain special characters, Excel automatically adds apostrophes around the workbook name and sheet name. An example is ='Result Sheet'!B3.

- For an external link, the name of the workbook is wrapped in square brackets and appears before the sheet name. An example is =[LinkToMe.xlsm]Sheet1!B3.

- If the workbook name or sheet name contains a space, add an apostrophe before the opening square bracket and after the sheet name. An example is ='[My File.xls] Income Statement'!B3.

- When Excel refers to a file such as [RegionTotals.xlsm], you can assume that the file is currently open. When you close the linked file, Excel updates the formula in the linking workbook to include the complete pathname. An example is =SUM('C:\[Region Totals.xlsm]Quota'!$B$2:$E$2).

Figure 11.9 illustrates examples of various formulas.

	A	B	C	D	E	F	G	H	I
1	**Link Syntax**								
2									
3	Type	Spaces?	Link Formula	Formula Text					
4	Internal	No	5	=Result!B3					
5	Internal	Yes	6	='Result Sheet'!B3					
6	External	No	1	='G:\2016InDepth\SampleFiles\[16LinkToMe.xlsm]Sheet1'!$B$3					
7	External	Yes	3	='[11-Link To Me.xlsm]Sheet3'!$B$4					
8	External Closed	No	7	='G:\2016InDepth\SampleFiles\[16Closed.xlsm]Sheet1'!$B$3					
9	External Closed	No	8	='G:\2016InDepth\SampleFiles\[16Closed.xlsm]Sheet 2'!$B$3					
10									

Figure 11.9 Syntax for various types of links.

Creating Links to Unsaved Workbooks

You can build a formula that links to a source workbook that has not been saved. This formula might point to Book1 or Book3 or the like. When you attempt to save the target workbook,

Excel presents a dialog box that asks, Save <filename> with References to Unsaved Documents? In general, you should cancel the save, switch to the unsaved source workbook, and then select File, Save As to save the file with a permanent name. Then you can come back to save the linking workbook.

Using the Links Tab on the Trust Center

By default, Excel applies security settings that frustrate your attempts to pull values from closed workbooks. Consider the following scenario using two workbooks labeled Workbook A and Workbook B:

1. Establish a link from Workbook A to Workbook B.

2. Save and close Workbook A.

3. Make changes to Workbook B. Save and close Workbook B.

4. Later, open Workbook B.

5. Open Workbook A.

In this case, the new values in Workbook B automatically flow through to Workbook A.

However, if you attempt to later open Workbook A before opening Workbook B, you see the following message: Automatic Update of Links Has Been Disabled (see Figure 11.10).

Figure 11.10   The link message initially appears in the info bar.

After you enable the content the first time, Excel marks the document as a trusted document. The next time you open the workbook, Excel displays a different cautionary message about links to external sources that could be unsafe, as shown in Figure 11.11.

Figure 11.11   Later, the Excel 2003–style link question appears.

You might wonder what could be unsafe about a link. I do, too. When I asked someone at Microsoft about this, they painted an incredibly convoluted scenario that I have never seen happen. The links that are described in this section are safe. Feel free to click Update.

Opening Workbooks with Links to Closed Workbooks

Suppose that you have saved and closed the linking workbook. You update numbers in the linked workbook. You save and close the linked workbook. Later, when you open the linking workbook, Excel asks if you want to update the links to the other workbook. If you created both workbooks and you have possession of both workbooks, it is fine to allow the workbooks to update.

Dealing with Missing Linked Workbooks

If you receive a linking workbook via email and you do not have access to the linked workbooks, Excel alerts you that the workbook contains links that cannot be updated right now. In this case, you should click Continue in the dialog box, as shown in Figure 11.12.

Figure 11.12   This message means that the linked workbook cannot be found. It shows up most often when someone emails you only the linking workbook.

You also get this message if the linked workbook was renamed, moved, or deleted. In that case, you should click the Edit Links button to display the Edit Links dialog box (see Figure 11.13). Then you should click the Change Source button to tell Excel that the linked workbook has a new name or location. Alternatively, you might need to click the Break Link button to change all linked formulas to their current values.

Figure 11.13   Manage or change links by using this dialog box.

TROUBLESHOOTING

Excel warns you about links when you open the workbook and offers an Edit Links button. If you skip that box and need to Edit Links later, how do you get back to the Edit Links dialog box?

Finding the Edit Links icon does not seem logical. I am old enough to remember that it used to be on the Excel 2003 Edit menu. Now, it turns out that Edit Links is in the Queries & Connections group on the Data tab of the ribbon.

Preventing the Update Links Dialog Box from Appearing

Suppose that you need to send a linking workbook to a co-worker. You want your co-worker to see the current values of the linking formulas without having the linked workbook. In this case, you want the co-worker to click Continue in Figure 11.12. However, some newer Excel customers think that every warning box is a disaster, so you might prefer to suppress that box for your co-worker. To do so, follow these steps:

1. On the Data tab, in the Connections group, select Edit Links.

2. In the lower-left corner of the dialog box that appears, click the Startup Prompt button. The Startup Prompt dialog box appears.

3. Select Don't Display The Alert And Don't Update Automatic Links (see Figure 11.14).

Figure 11.14   You can prevent others from seeing the Update Links message.

After emailing the workbook to your co-worker, you need to redisplay the Startup Prompt dialog box and change it back so that you will get the updated links.

CHAPTER 12

Array Formulas and Names in Excel

Long before Microsoft introduced tables and formulas such as =[@Revenue]-[@Cost], spreadsheets have offered the capability to assign a name to a cell, a range of cells, or a formula. The theory is that using a name for a range is easier to understand when used in a formula. For instance, =SUM(MyExpenses) makes formulas more self-documenting than =SUM(Sheet5!AB2:AB99). In Excel 2019, you use the Name Manager interface to assign and use names effectively.

Advantages of Using Names

Names have a variety of uses in a workbook. A name can be applied to any cell or range. Names are also useful for the following:

- Making formulas easier to understand and write. Defined names are offered in the Formula AutoComplete drop-down menu as you start to type a formula.

- Quick navigation.

- Forcing a formula reference to remain absolute—without having to use the dollar sign.

- Doing a two-way lookup with the intersection operator.

- Improving report results from Solver and Scenario Manager.

- Storing a value that will be used repeatedly but that might occasionally need to change, such as a sales tax rate.

- Storing formulas.

- Defining a dynamic range.

You have various ways to name a cell. The easiest way to define a name for a cell is to use the name box. To do so, select any cell in your worksheet. To the left of the formula bar is a box with the address of that cell. This box is known as the *name box* (see Figure 12.1). The quick way to assign a name is to click inside the name box and type the name, such as Revenue.

Name box

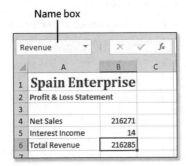

Figure 12.1   The name box is to the left of the formula bar.

When you press Enter, Excel tries to assign the name. If you get no message, the name is valid. If you get the message, "You must enter a valid reference you want to go to, or type a valid name for the selection," then the name is invalid. If you are taken to a new range, that name already exists.

NOTE

Excel offers the Table functionality. Although the Table feature enables you to create formulas using column names, the individual column names and table name are not considered named ranges.

The following are some basic rules for valid names:

- Names can be up to 255 characters long.

- Names can start with a letter, an underscore, or a backslash. Numbers can be used in a name, but they can't be the first character in the name.

- Names cannot contain spaces. However, you can use an underscore or a period in a name. For example, the names `Gross_Profit` and `Gross.Profit` are valid.

- Names cannot look like cell addresses. ROI2015 is already a cell address. The names R, r, C, and c cannot be used because these are the shorthand for selecting an entire row or column.

- Names cannot contain operator characters such as these:

    + - * / ( ) ^ & < > = %

- Names cannot contain special characters such as these:

    ! " # $ ' , ; : @ [ ] { } ` | ~

- Names cannot start with "c" or "r" followed by numbers and text. For example, r82hello or c123test are not valid. There is no longer a valid reason for this anomaly.

Table 12.1 provides some examples of valid and invalid names.

Table 12.1   Examples of Valid and Invalid Names

Valid Names	Invalid Names (and Reasons)
SalesTax	Sales Tax (includes a space)
Sales_Tax	XFD123 (valid cell address)
Sales.Tax	Tax2015 (valid cell address)
SalesTax2017	MyResults! (invalid special character)

Naming a Cell by Using the Name Dialog Box

The Formulas tab contains a group called Defined Names. The following example introduces the Name dialog box:

1. Select a cell that you would like to name. Click the Define Name icon from the Formulas tab. The New Name dialog box appears. In Figure 12.2, cell B8 is being assigned a name.

Figure 12.2   Choose a cell to be named and then select Define Name from the Formulas tab.

2. The New Name box uses IntelliSense to propose a name. Notice that in this particular example, Excel's IntelliSense was able to ascertain that this cell contains the text Cost

of Good Sold. Because that is not a valid name, Excel instead proposed naming the cell Cost_of_Good_Sold. You can either keep that name or override it with a name you prefer. In this case, override that name with the name COGS.

3. For now, leave the scope as Workbook. For a discussion of when to use a worksheet-level scope, see "Avoiding Problems by Using Worksheet-Level Scope," later in this chapter.

As you can see in Figure 12.3, the name was applied because the name box now shows COGS instead of B8.

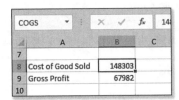

Figure 12.3   After you assign a name, the name box reflects the new name.

Using the Name Box for Quick Navigation

One advantage of using names is that you can use the drop-down menu in the name box to jump to any named cell. This includes cells that might be in distant sections of the worksheet or even on other sheets in the workbook.

If you plan to use the name box for navigation, assign a name to the upper-left corner of each section of your workbook. The name box drop-down menu then provides a mini table of contents, and people can use the name box to jump to any section of the workbook.

To illustrate this concept, follow these steps:

1. Click the New Sheet icon (next to the right-most sheet tab) to add a new sheet to the workbook.

2. On the new sheet, go to a distant cell. Give that cell a name, such as **SectionTwo**. Return to the original sheet in the workbook.

3. Click the name box's drop-down menu arrow to access a list of all names in the workbook, as shown in Figure 12.4.

4. Choose a name from the list to navigate quickly to that cell, even if it is on another worksheet.

Figure 12.4   The name box drop-down menu contains a list of all names in the workbook.

As you can see, named ranges are a great tool for quickly navigating a workbook. Note that names are presented in the name box alphabetically. If you want the names to appear sequentially, you can add names, such as Section1, Section2, Section3, and so on. You can also prefix the section names with letters, such as A-Income, B-Costs, C-Expense, D-Tax, E-Income. Then, you can jump to a section by choosing it from the alphabetical list in the name box. When used in this way, names in Excel are almost like bookmarks in Word.

TIP

If your names are too long to appear in the name box, you can widen the name box. Look for the three vertical dots between the name box and the formula bar. Drag to the right to expand the name box.

Avoiding Problems by Using Worksheet-Level Scope

Most names have a workbook-level scope. There are two specific reasons why you might want to use worksheet-level scope instead:

- You have many similar worksheets in a workbook, and you want to define the same names on each sheet. For example, you might want Revenue and COGS on each sheet from January through December.

- You routinely copy a worksheet from one workbook, and you want to avoid having phantom names with #REF! errors appear in the copied sheet. Note that this problem was prevalent before Excel 2013 but has now been corrected.

Defining a Worksheet-Level Name

To declare a name with worksheet-level scope, you can use one of these methods:

- Use Insert, Define Name. In the New Name dialog box, choose Worksheet from the Scope drop-down menu.

CHAPTER 12

- Click in the name box and type **Jan!Rev**, as shown in Figure 12.5. If the sheet name contains a space, wrap the sheet name in apostrophes: **'Budget 2018'!Rev**.

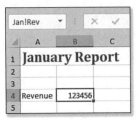

Figure 12.5   Create worksheet-level scope in the name box using this syntax.

- You will often inadvertently create a worksheet-level name by using a duplicate name. If you define Revenue on the January worksheet without declaring a scope, the name will have a workbook-level scope. If you then define Revenue on the February worksheet, it will automatically have a worksheet-level scope.

Referring to Worksheet-Level Names

If you want to refer to the Rev cell on the January worksheet from anywhere else on the January worksheet, simply use =Rev.

If you want to refer to the Revenue cell on the January worksheet from anywhere else in the workbook, use =Jan!Rev.

Using Named Ranges to Simplify Formulas

As introduced at the start of this chapter, the original reason for having named ranges was to simplify formulas. In theory, it is easier to understand a formula such as =(Revenue-COGS)/ Revenue.

Be sure to define the names before entering formulas that refer to those cells. When you create a formula using the mouse or arrow-key method, Excel automatically uses the names in the formula.

In the following example, the worksheet in Figure 12.6 has a name of Revenue assigned to B6 and a name of COGS assigned to B8. Rather than typing =**B6-B8** in cell B9, follow these steps to have Excel create a formula using names:

1. Select the cell where the formula should go. In this example, it is cell B9.

2. Type =.

3. Using the mouse, click the first cell in your formula. In this case, it is cell B6.

4. Type -.

5. Using the mouse, click the next cell in your formula. In this case, it is cell B8.

6. Press Enter.

7. Move the cell pointer back to the formula cell and look in the formula bar. You can see that Excel has built the formula =Revenues-COGS, as shown in Figure 12.6. In theory, this formula is self-documenting and easier to understand than =B6-B8.

	:	×	✓	*fx*	=Revenue-COGS

	A	B	C	D	E
4	Net Sales	216271			
5	Interest Income	14			
6	Total Revenue	216285			
7					
8	Cost of Good Sold	148303			
9	Gross Profit	=Revenue-COGS			
10					

Figure 12.6   New formulas created after names have been assigned reflect the cell names in the formula.

If you prefer to type your formulas, named ranges can also be a timesaver. Say that you start to type =**R**. Excel displays a drop-down menu offering many functions that start with R, such as RADIANS, RAND, and RANDBETWEEN. Your defined name of Revenue will be in this list of 20 items.

Keep typing. After you type **E**, the list shortens to four items: RECEIVED, REPLACE, REPT, and Revenue (see Figure 12.7). As you continue typing and type **V**, the only item in the list is your defined name of Revenue. You can now click Tab to insert this named range into your formula.

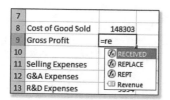

7		
8	Cost of Good Sold	148303
9	Gross Profit	=re
10		*RECEIVED*
11	Selling Expenses	*REPLACE*
12	G&A Expenses	*REPT*
13	R&D Expenses	*Revenue*

Figure 12.7   Type enough of the name to be unique, and then press Tab to insert the name in your formula.

Type the minus sign, type **COG**, and then press Tab to select COGS from the list.

Retroactively Applying Names to Formulas

When you learn the trick that was discussed in the "Using Named Ranges to Simplify Formulas" section, you might start naming all the input cells in your workbook, hoping that all the pre-existing formulas will take on the new names. Unfortunately, this does not work automatically.

To make the names become part of existing formulas, you have to use the Apply command. To do this, follow these steps:

1. On the Formulas tab, select the drop-down menu next to Define Name and select Apply Names. The Apply Names dialog box appears.

2. Choose as many names as you want in the Apply Names box. In this example, you should choose at least GrossProfit and TotalExpenses and then click OK. Existing formulas that point to these named cells change to include the cell names in the formula.

Using Names to Refer to Ranges

It is possible to define a name that refers to a larger range of cells. For example, you can select B11:B13 in Figure 12.8 and type a name such as **Expenses** into the name box.

If you later select Expenses from the name box, your cursor moves to cell B11, and the entire range is selected. Having a name apply to a range allows formulas such as =**Sum(Expenses)**.

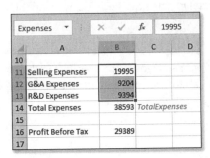

Figure 12.8   A name can refer to a rectangular range.

Adding Many Names at Once from Existing Labels and Headings

With Excel 2019, you can add many names in a single command, particularly if the names exist as labels or headings adjacent to the cells.

Suppose you have a worksheet with a series of labels in column A and values in column B. One example is shown in Figure 12.9. To do a wholesale assignment of names to the cells in column B, follow these steps:

1. Select the range of labels and the cells to which they refer. In this example, that range is A4:B16.

2. Select Formulas, Defined Names, Create From Selection. Excel displays the Create Names from Selected Range dialog box.

3. Because the row labels are in the left column of the selected range, select Left Column and then click OK, as shown in Figure 12.9.

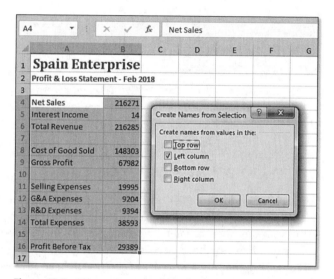

Figure 12.9   When you make this selection, Excel uses the text values in the left column to assign names to all the nonblank cells in column B of this range.

Excel does a fairly good job of assigning the names. Spaces are replaced with underscores to make the names valid. In this example, cell B4 is assigned the name Net_Sales. Cell C8 is assigned the name Cost_of_Good_Sold. In row 12, where the label contains an ampersand (&), Excel replaces the ampersand with an underscore, to form the name G_A_Expenses. Although this is not as meaningful as it could be if you wrote the name yourself, it is still pretty good.

In Excel 2019, you can apply names by using both the row labels and column headings at the same time. In Figure 12.10, the selections in the Create Names From Selected Ranges dialog box mean that nine new names will be added to the workbook. For example, Northeast refers to B2:F2, and Week5 refers to F2:F5.

NOTE

If a cell contained G & A Expenses, Excel would replace every space and ampersand with an underscore, creating the name G__A_Expenses.

Figure 12.10   In Excel 2019, you can create names based on the row labels and column headers at the same time.

Using Intersection to Do a Two-Way Lookup

After using Create from Selection in Figure 12.10, the name Southeast applies to the range B3:F3. The name Week5 applies to F2:F5. You can do a two-way lookup by using the intersection operator within the SUM function. The intersection operator is a space. A formula such as =SUM(Week5 Southeast) looks for the intersection of the two ranges and returns the value 1001 from cell F3 (see Figure 12.11). You can leave out the SUM() and simply type =Week5 Southeast.

The formula in Figure 12.11 is significantly easier than a traditional two-way lookup with the following:

=INDEX(B2:F5,MATCH("Southeast",$A$2:$A$5,0),MATCH("Week5",$B$1:$F$1,0))

	A	B	C	D	E	F	G	H	I	J
G7				fx	=SUM(Week5 Southeast)					
1		Week1	Week2	Week3	Week4	Week5				
2	Northeast	1048	1053	1031	1050	1078				
3	Southeast	1038	1015	1001	1055	1001				
4	Central	1094	1087	1091	1092	1017				
5	West	1034	1022	1065	1042	1050				
6										
7							1001 =SUM(Week5 Southeast)			
8										

Figure 12.11   This formula is asking for the intersection of two ranges.

NOTE

The intersection example works because you are hard-coding Southeast and Week5 into the formula. If those values were stored in other cells, you would have to use a pair of INDIRECT functions: =SUM(INDIRECT(E7) INDIRECT(E8)). Using INDIRECT makes the formula volatile, which forces that cell to recalculate more often, thus slowing down the worksheet.

Using Implicit Intersection

In Figures 12.10 through 12.12, the name "Northeast" applies to B2:F2. If you type =**Northeast** anywhere in columns B:F, Excel uses implicit intersection. Excel assumes that you want to refer only to the portion of the Northeast range that intersects the current column. Typing =**Northeast** in D7 returns 1031 because of the five values in the Northeast region: The 1031 in D2 intersects with the formula in D7. This is a cool shortcut method.

In Figure 12.12, an identical formula of =Southeast+Northeast is used in B8:F8.

Implicit intersections also work with vertical ranges. Week4 is defined as E2:E5. If you enter =**Week4** anywhere in rows 2 through 5, Excel returns the value from the Week4 range that intersects with the row that contains the formula. This allows identical formulas of =Week4+Week5, as shown in H2:H5 of Figure 12.12.

NOTE

You cannot use implicit intersection in an array formula. If you use =Southeast outside of columns B:F, it will refer to the entire range, so you would have to wrap it in a SUM or other function.

B8	▼	:	×	✓	fx	=Southeast+Northeast				
▲	A	B	C	D	E	F	G	H	I	J
1		Week1	Week2	Week3	Week4	Week5		W4+W5		
2	Northeast	1048	1053	1031	1050	1078		2128	=Week4+Week5	
3	Southeast	1038	1015	1001	1055	1001		2056	=Week4+Week5	
4	Central	1094	1087	1091	1092	1017		2109	=Week4+Week5	
5	West	1034	1022	1065	1042	1050		2092	=Week4+Week5	
6										
7								1001	=SUM(Week5 Southeast)	
8	East:	2086	2068	2032	2105	2079				
9		=Southeast+Northeast			=Southeast+Northeast					
10			=Southeast+Northeast			=Southeast+Northeast				
11				=Southeast+Northeast						
12										

Figure 12.12 Implicit intersection is changing for Office 365 customers in late 2018. You will have to wrap the cell reference inside a SINGLE() function. See the sidebar on the next page.

Inside OUT

The implicit intersection is changing for Office 365 customers.

Modern array functions are forcing a change to the syntax for the implicit intersection. The formula in B8 in the previous figure will have to be =SINGLE(Southeast)+SINGLE(Northeast).

If you are sharing the workbook with someone using the perpetual version of Office 365, Excel will automatically convert the old implicit intersection syntax to use SINGLE.

Using a Name to Avoid an Absolute Reference

A common scenario is when a formula such as VLOOKUP is used in a data set to look up data on another worksheet. You might enter a VLOOKUP formula in cell B2 and copy it to hundreds of records. The formula in cell B2 might be =VLOOKUP(A2,'Lookup Table'!A2:B25,2,False). As you copy this formula to row 3, the reference in the second argument incorrectly changes to 'Lookup Table'!A3:B26. When you need the reference to always point to A2:B25, you can add dollar signs to the reference: $A$2:$B$25.

If you will be frequently adding VLOOKUP formulas that will point to 'Lookup Table'!$A$2:$B$25, it can get tedious to continually use the syntax. After all, it is a confusing mix of dollar signs, apostrophes, and exclamation points.

To simplify the VLOOKUP formula, give A2:B25 a name such as ItemLookup. Then, the formula simply becomes =VLOOKUP(A2,ItemLookup,2,False). As you copy the formula down, it continues to point to A2:B25 on the Lookup Table worksheet. Figure 12.13 compares the formula without a name in B2 and the formula with a name in B3.

	A	B	C	D	E	F	G
	SKU	Title					
1	B2	Don't Fear the Spreadsheet	=VLOOKUP(A2,'Lookup Table'!$A$2:$B$25,2,FALSE)				
2	C9	VBA & Macros for Microsoft Excel 2013	=VLOOKUP(A3,ItemLookup,2,FALSE)				
3	C4	Excel Gurus Gone Wild	=VLOOKUP(A4,ItemLookup,2,FALSE)				
4	A4	Slaying Excel Dragons	=VLOOKUP(A5,ItemLookup,2,FALSE)				

B2 fx =VLOOKUP(A2,'Lookup Table'!$A$2:$B$25,2,FALSE)

Figure 12.13   The formula in B3 is easier to type because it uses a named range for the lookup table.

Using a Name to Hold a Value

So far, all the names defined in this chapter have referred to a cell or a range of cells. It is possible to assign a constant value to a name by using the New Name dialog box. You might do this to hold a value that could possibly change but would likely rarely change, such as a sales tax rate.

To use a name to hold a value, follow these steps:

1. Either click the Define Name icon or the Name Manager icon, and then click New. The New Name dialog box appears.

2. In the Name field of the New Name dialog box, type a name such as **Sales_Tax**.

3. In the Refers To box, remove any existing cell reference and type the new value, such as **=6.5%**.

4. Write formulas that refer to the new name, such as **Sales_Tax**. The formula might be something like **=C2*Sales_Tax**.

The advantage of using a name to refer to a constant is that if your tax rate changes, you can edit the value defined in the name, and all the formulas in the workbook recalculate. To edit an existing name, click the Name Manager, click the name, and then select Edit Name.

Assigning a Formula to a Name

Although names are traditionally used to refer to cells or constant values, you can use a name to refer to a formula. Look at any name in the Name Manager. The Refers To column starts with an equal sign, which means that named ranges always contain a formula.

A named formula enables you to replace a complicated formula with an easy-to-remember name. In this basic case, the formula does not contain cell references. For example, suppose you have discovered a fairly complex formula that would be difficult to remember, such as a formula to show the end of this month:

=EOMONTH(TODAY(),0)

In this case, you could assign the formula =EOMONTH(TODAY(),0) to a name such as MonthEnd, as shown in Figure 12.14. You could then use =MonthEnd in any cell to calculate the end of the current month.

CHAPTER 12

Figure 12.14   After a formula has been assigned to a name, you can use it as you would a constant.

Using Power Formula Techniques

Excel offers an amazing variety of formulas. This chapter covers some of the unorthodox formulas you can build in Excel. In this chapter, you discover the following:

- Using a formula to add the same cell across many sheets

- Using a formula to reference the previous sheet

- Editing multiple formulas into one

- Letting data determine the cell reference to use with the INDIRECT function

- Transposing relative column references to rows

- Using ROW() or COLUMN() to return an array of numbers

- Replacing thousands of formulas with one Ctrl+Shift+Enter (CSE) array formula

- Using one formula to return a whole range of answers

Using 3D Formulas to Spear Through Many Worksheets

It is common to have a workbook composed of identical worksheets for each month or quarter of the year. Every worksheet needs to have the same arrangement of rows.

If you want to total a particular cell across all the worksheets, you might try to write a formula with one term for each sheet—for example, =Sheet1!A1+Sheet2!A1+Sheet3!A1.... However, Excel supports a special type of formula that spears through several worksheets to add a particular cell from each worksheet. The syntax of the formula is =SUM(Sheet1:Sheetn!A1). If you use spaces in your worksheet names, add apostrophes around the pair of sheet names =SUM('Jan 2021:Dec2021'!A1).

As shown in Figure 12.15, Net Revenue is in row 4 on the January worksheet and is in the same row on the February worksheet. You cannot see this in Figure 12.15, but the arrangement of rows is identical on every worksheet.

	A	B	C
1	January		
2			
3		This Year	Prior Year
4	Net Revenue	9231	8049
5	Cost of Sales	4028	3269
6			
7	Gross Margin	5203	4780
8			
9	R&D	1176	1186
10	Mktg, G&A	1342	1170
11			
12	Operating Expenses	2518	2356
13			
14	Operating Income	2685	2424
15			
16	Interest	127	47
17			
18	Income Before Taxes	2812	2471
19			
20	Provision for Taxes	716	663
21			
22	Net Income	2096	1808
23			

	A	B	C
1	February		
2			
3		This Year	Prior Year
4	Net Revenue	9416	8210
5	Cost of Sales	4109	3335
6			
7	Gross Margin	5307	4875
8			
9	R&D	1200	1210
10	Mktg, G&A	1369	1193
11			
12	Operating Expenses	2569	2403
13			
14	Operating Income	2738	2472
15			
16	Interest	130	48
17			
18	Income Before Taxes	2868	2520
19			
20	Provision for Taxes	730	676
21			
22	Net Income	2138	1844
23			

Figure 12.15   The 12 workbooks, January through December, contain an identical arrangement of rows and columns.

When creating a worksheet, you might be tempted to write a formula such as =Jan!B4+Feb!B4+Mar!B4+Apr!B4, but doing so would be rather tedious.

Instead, you can write a formula that totals cell B4 from each worksheet, Jan through Dec. An example of the formula is =SUM(Jan:Dec!B4). After you enter this formula in cell B4, you can easily copy it to all the other relevant cells in the worksheet, as shown in Figure 12.16.

Excel 2013 introduced a new worksheet function called SHEETS(). You can use =SHEETS(Jan:Dec!A1) to learn that there are 12 sheets in the reference.

TIP

Sometimes you might need to sum a cell on all sheets that have a common naming convention. Perhaps you have worksheet names such as CostQ1, ExpensesQ1, CostQ2, ExpensesQ2, CostQ3, ExpensesQ3, CostQ4, and ExpensesQ4. To sum cell B4 on all of the cost sheets, type =SUM('Cost*'!B4). Remarkably, Excel converts this shorthand to a formula that points to each of the cost sheets:

=SUM(CostQ1!B4,CostQ2!B4,CostQ3!B4,CostQ4!B4)

I need to give a tip of the cap to Microsoft MVP Bob Umlas for this cool trick. Bob cautions that if you enter this formula on a worksheet that starts with Cost, the active sheet will be left out of the equation.

CHAPTER 12

		B4		▼	:	×	✓	*fx*	=SUM(Jan:Dec!B4)		

	A	B	C	D	E	F	G	H
1	Total Year							
2								
3		This Year	Prior Year			# of Sheets in references		
4	Net Revenue	119727	104394			12	=SHEETS(Jan:Dec!B4)	
5	Cost of Sales	49911	40508					
6								
7	Gross Margin	69816	63886					
8								
9	R&D	15253	15383					
10	Mktg, G&A	17406	15176					
11								
12	Operating Expenses	32659	30559					
13								
14	Operating Income	37157	33327					
15								
16	Interest	1648	610					
17								
18	Income Before Taxes	38805	33937					
19								
20	Provision for Taxes	9286	8599					
21								
22	Net Income	29519	25338					
23								

Figure 12.16   This formula spears through 12 worksheets to total cell B4 from each worksheet from January through December.

Inside OUT

The 3-D reference syntax is difficult to remember, particularly if you are not sure if you need apostrophes around the worksheet names.

There is an easy way to build these formulas using the mouse. Say that you want to total cells B5:N20 on all twelve sheets from Jan 2021 to Dec 2021. That total should appear on the Summary worksheet in cell B5. Follow these steps:

1. Start on the Summary worksheet, in cell B5.

2. Start typing =SUM(.

3. Using the mouse, click on the sheet tab for Jan 2021. Do not select any cells on that worksheet.

4. Hold down the shift key and click on the sheet tab for Dec 2021. At this point, the formula in the formula bar is:

   =SUM('Jan 2021:Dec 2021'!

5. Click on B5 and drag to N20.

6. Type the closing parenthesis and press Enter. You will end up with this formula:

   =SUM('Jan 2021:Dec 2021'!B5:N20)

Referring to the Previous Worksheet

When you have an arrangement of several sequential worksheets, you might want to keep a running total. This total would be calculated as the total on this sheet plus the running total from the previous sheet.

It is somewhat difficult to build a formula that always points to the previous sheet. Maybe you've tried the wrong approach shown in Figure 12.17: On the Feb worksheet, a formula refers to =Jan!B4. However, if you copy the formula to Mar or Apr, the formula still points to the Jan worksheet, which is not what you want.

Figure 12.17   You must rewrite this formula for each of the 11 other months.

Excel offers a very cool solution to this problem. The solution requires a few lines of VBA macro code. Don't be afraid. I can get you there and back without any problems. Here's what you do:

1. Press Alt+F11 to launch the VBA editor.

2. In the VBA editor, select Insert, Module.

3. Type the following lines into the blank module:

```
Function PrevSheet(ByVal MyCell As Range)
 Application.Volatile
 On Error Resume Next
 PrevSheet = Sheets(MyCell.Parent.Index - 1).Range(MyCell.Address)
End Function
```

4. Your screen should look similar to Figure 12.18.

```
Function PrevSheet(ByVal MyCell As Range)
    Application.Volatile
    On Error Resume Next
    PrevSheet = MyCell.Worksheet.Parent.Worksheets _
        (MyCell.Worksheet.Index - 1).Range(MyCell.Address).Value
End Function
```

Figure 12.18   The VBA editor screen should look like this.

5. Select File, Close, and Return to Microsoft Excel to return to Excel.

To realize the power of this function, you can put the workbook in Group mode and enter the function in 11 worksheets at once:

1. Select the Feb worksheet.

2. Hold down the Shift key while clicking the Dec worksheet tab. This highlights all 11 worksheets. Although you see the Feb worksheet, anything you do on that worksheet is also done to all 11 selected worksheets.

3. In cell E4, enter =*PrevSheet(B4)*. Press Enter to accept the formula. The Feb worksheet picks up the value from Jan, but each additional worksheet picks up the value from the previous sheet, as shown in Figure 12.19.

Figure 12.19   One formula using the custom function PrevSheet solves the prior month problem seamlessly across all the worksheets.

4. With the worksheets still in Group mode, copy cell B4 from the Feb worksheet to cells B5, B7, and so on.

5. Right-click any sheet tab and select Ungroup.

Combining Multiple Formulas into One Formula

With more than 460 functions available in Excel, it is possible to perform just about any calculation. Many times, however, it is easier to break the task down into many subformulas as you try to solve the problem.

For example, fellow Excel MVP and guru Bob Umlas taught me that I could use the Substitute function to locate the last space in a word. This is handy for finding the last word in a sentence or name. However, unlike Bob, I always need to build this formula over the course of several columns. It takes me seven columns to do a trick that Bob can do in one. Figure 12.20 shows all the formulas used to replicate the trick.

	A	B	C	D	E	F	G	H
						=SUBSTITUTE(A2," ","!",E2)		
1	NAME	No Spaces	Len A	Len B	# Spaces	Replace Last Space	Find !	MID
2	ALLISON GILMORE	ALLISONGILMORE	15	14	1	ALLISON!GILMORE	8	GILMORE
3	MARY ELLEN JELEN	MARYELLENJELEN	16	14	2	MARY ELLEN!JELEN	11	JELEN
4	FANNIE PERRY	FANNIEPERRY	12	11	1	FANNIE!PERRY	7	PERRY
5	JOE BOB BRIGGS	JOEBOBBRIGGS	14	12	2	JOE BOB!BRIGGS	8	BRIGGS
16								
17	Formulas used in Row 2:							
18	B2:	=SUBSTITUTE(A2," ","")						
19	C2:	=LEN(A2)						
20	D2:	=LEN(B2)						
21	E2:	=C2-D2						
22	F2:	=SUBSTITUTE(A2," ","!",E2)						
23	G2:	=FIND("!",F2)						
24	H2:	=MID(A2,G2+1,C2-G2)						
25								

Figure 12.20   It takes me seven formulas to isolate the last name.

If you've ever built a formula in small steps as shown previously, you can begin consolidating the formulas into one monster formula.

However, there's an easier way to combine many formulas into one formula. As an example, follow these steps:

1. Examine the final formula. It references cells that contain one or more subformulas. In Figure 12.21, cell H2 has a formula that references the value in A2 and subformulas in G2, C2, and G2. You remove the reference to G2 first.

	F	G	H
			=MID(A2,G2+1,C2-G2)
1	Replace Last Space	Find !	MID
2	ALLISON!GILMORE	8	GILMORE
3	MARY ELLEN!JELEN	11	JELEN
4	FANNIE!PERRY	7	PERRY
5	JOE BOB!BRIGGS	8	BRIGGS
16			

Figure 12.21   The goal is to replace G2 in this formula.

2. Move the cell pointer to the subformula in G2.

3. Press F2 to put the formula in edit mode.

4. With the mouse, highlight the formula in the formula bar, but do not highlight the equal sign in the subformula (see Figure 12.22).

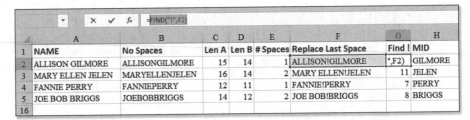

	A	B	C	D	E	F	G	H
1	NAME	No Spaces	Len A	Len B	# Spaces	Replace Last Space	Find !	MID
2	ALLISON GILMORE	ALLISONGILMORE	15	14	1	ALLISON!GILMORE	",F2)	GILMORE
3	MARY ELLEN JELEN	MARYELLENJELEN	16	14	2	MARY ELLEN!JELEN	11	JELEN
4	FANNIE PERRY	FANNIEPERRY	12	11	1	FANNIE!PERRY	7	PERRY
5	JOE BOB BRIGGS	JOEBOBBRIGGS	14	12	2	JOE BOB!BRIGGS	8	BRIGGS
16								

Figure 12.22   Copying characters from the formula bar is different from copying a cell.

5. Press Ctrl+C to copy this portion of the subformula to the Clipboard.

6. Go back to the final formula. Press F2 to put the formula in edit mode.

7. In the formula bar, using the mouse, highlight the first instance of G2, as shown in Figure 12.23.

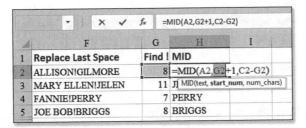

	F	G	H	I
1	Replace Last Space	Find !	MID	
2	ALLISON!GILMORE	8	=MID(A2,G2+1,C2-G2)	
3	MARY ELLEN!JELEN	11	J| MID(text, start_num, num_chars)	
4	FANNIE!PERRY	7	PERRY	
5	JOE BOB!BRIGGS	8	BRIGGS	

Figure 12.23   With the formula from cell G2 on the Clipboard, you select G2 in the final formula.

8. Press Ctrl+V to paste the subformula from cell G2 in place of the letters G2. The formula appears as shown in Figure 12.24. Note that you just added a new reference to the F2 subformula.

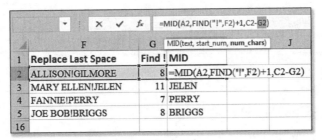

	F	G		J
1	Replace Last Space	Find !	MID	
2	ALLISON!GILMORE	8	=MID(A2,FIND("!",F2)+1,C2-G2)	
3	MARY ELLEN!JELEN	11	JELEN	
4	FANNIE!PERRY	7	PERRY	
5	JOE BOB!BRIGGS	8	BRIGGS	
16				

Figure 12.24   You can press Ctrl+V to paste the characters from the cell G2 formula instead of the reference to cell G2.

9. Because G2 appears again in this formula, repeat steps 7 and 8 for the second instance of G2.

10. Press Enter to accept this intermediate formula of =MID(A2,FIND("!",F2)+1, C2-FIND("!",F2)).

11. If there are additional references to a cell with a subformula in the new formula, repeat steps 1–10 for the next reference. In this case, you would replace the characters F2 with SUBSTITUTE(A2," ","!",E2). Continue working through the formula, replacing E2, then D2, then C2, then B2. Eventually, you end up with a monster formula, as shown in Figure 12.25. Your co-workers will look at that formula and assume you must be a spreadsheet wizard like Excel MVP Bob Umlas.

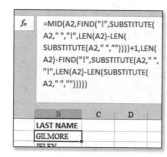

Figure 12.25   After several iterations of replacing references in the formula, you end up with one monster formula to replace the six subformulas.

Turning a Range of Formulas on Its Side

The Transpose option in the Paste Options dialog box is great for changing values that span across several columns into values that go down a column. Here's an example:

1. In Figure 12.26, you select B1:M1 and then press Ctrl+C.

A	B	C	D	E	F	G	H	I	J	K	L	M
1		Jan	Feb	Mar	Apr	May	Jun	Jul	Aug	Sep	Oct	Nov	Dec
2 Sales	1000	1090	1123	1213	1286	1350	1485	1530	1668	1701	1735	1891
3 Cost	530	545	618	631	694	689	728	796	867	833	850	927
4 Profit	470	545	505	582	592	661	757	734	801	868	885	964

Figure 12.26   Use the Transpose option to turn B1:M1 on its side.

2. Select the top-left cell where the range should be copied. In this example, select cell A7.

3. Right-click in the Paste Options section and select Transpose, as shown in Figure 12.26. The month names now go down the row. However, there's no good way to copy the calculation for profit from row 4 to the new table. You normally have to enter 12 different formulas in the range B7:B17, as shown in Figure 12.27.

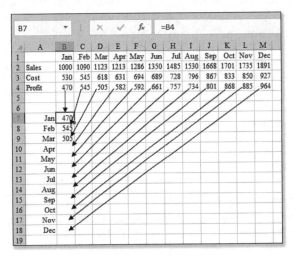

Figure 12.27   Transposing with a formula requires a different formula in each cell.

However, there are two ways to easily enter a single formula that turns those results on their side.

First, you can use the **INDEX** function in conjunction with **ROW**. Try it:

1. In cell B7, enter **=ROW(1:1)**. The result is the number 1.

2. Copy the formula from cell B7 down to B7:B18. The result returns a string of integers from 1 through 12.

3. Use the formula =ROW(A1) as the second argument in the INDEX function. A formula of =INDEX($B$4:$M$4,0,ROW(1:1)) achieves the perfect result, as shown in Figure 12.28.

Figure 12.28   You can use the ROW(1:1) trick as the second argument to the INDEX function to turn a range on its side.

One danger exists with just about every method described in this chapter: They produce results that the average person does not understand. So if you want to end up with straightforward formulas in B7:B18, you can use the following method:

1.   Enter a formula, such as **=B4**, in cell B5.

2.   Copy the first formula across row 5 for each month.

3.   Highlight the formulas in B5:M5.

4.   Use Home, Editing, Find & Select, Replace to display the Find And Replace dialog box. In the Find What box, enter an equal sign. In the Replace With box, enter an exclamation point. Click Replace All to change every occurrence of = to !. This converts the formulas to text, as shown in row 5 of Figure 12.29.

Figure 12.29   Converting the formulas to text allows them to be transposed.

5. Copy the range and highlight a new cell (in this example, cell B7).

6. Right-click and select Transpose. Because the cells are all text, they transpose perfectly, as shown in B7:B18 of Figure 12.29.

7. Use Ctrl+H or Home, Editing, Find & Select, Replace to display the Find And Replace dialog box. Type an exclamation point in Find What and an equal sign in Replace With. Click Replace All to change every ! back to =. It now looks as if you actually typed all 12 formulas individually.

Coercing a Range of Dates Using an Array Formula

A wildly powerful type of formula exists that most Excel users have never experienced. This single formula can do thousands of calculations. The formula is known as an *array formula*. You must use Ctrl+Shift+Enter when entering an array formula to tell Excel to evaluate the formula as an array.

Note: The Ctrl+Shift+Enter formula discussed in this section applies only to Excel 2019. Customers using Office 365 can use dynamic arrays to replace this formula. In a dynamic array, using SEQUENCE((C2-C1+1),1,C1,2) will replace using ROW(INDIRECT(C1&" "&C2)) in the following example. Ctrl+Shift+Enter will not be required.

Suppose you want to find out how many Wednesdays occurred between two dates. Enter the starting and ending dates in cells in an Excel worksheet, as shown in Figure 12.30.

B	C	D	E	F	G	H	I
					{=SUM(IF(WEEKDAY(ROW(INDIRECT(C1&":"&C2)))=4,1,0))}		
Start Date:	6/30/2015				6/30/2015	3	0
End Date:	9/15/2018				7/1/2015	4	1
Wednesdays:	168				7/2/2015	4	0
					7/3/2015	4	0

Figure 12.30 This single array formula replaces hundreds of intermediate calculations.

To start, the WEEKDAY function returns a number from 1 to 7 corresponding to the day of the week. =WEEKDAY(C1) returns the number 4 if the day is a Wednesday.

To check to see whether a particular day is a Wednesday, use the IF function:

=IF(WEEKDAY(C1)=4,1,0)

Using that formula, you could build a table showing all dates from the beginning date to the ending date as rows. The second column uses the IF/WEEKDAY function to test whether each date is a Wednesday. Sum that column to count the Wednesdays in the range. However, this table will contain hundreds of rows for every year in the data range.

Instead, use ROW(INDIRECT(C1&":"&C2)) to build an array in memory of all the dates. Although cell C1 is displaying 6/30/2015, it actually contains the number 42185. Similarly, cell C2 contains the number 43358. Concatenating C1 with a colon and C2 builds a text string of "42185:43358". This text is a valid reference, pointing to all the rows from 42185 to 43358. Asking for the ROW of that reference returns an array with the numbers 42185 to 43358.

To build the array formula, replace "C1" in the original IF/WEEKDAY function with the ROW/INDIRECT functions:

=IF(WEEKDAY(ROW(INDIRECT(C1&":"&C2)))=4,1,0)

That formula returns a series of zeroes and ones. Because you want to add up the ones in the resulting array, wrap the formula in a **SUM** function:

=SUM(IF(WEEKDAY(ROW(INDIRECT(C1&":"&C2)))=4,1,0))

After you type that formula, press Ctrl+Shift+Enter. Excel calculates hundreds of intermediate results and shows the answer in a single cell.

To learn more about Array formulas, check out Mike Girvin's *Ctrl+Shift+Enter* book (ISBN 978-1-61547-007-5). Office 365 customers will have access to new modern array functions such as SEQUENCE. You can simplify the above formula with =SUM(IF(WEEKDAY(SEQUENCE(C1,(C2-C1+1)))=4,1,0)), and this will require no Ctrl+Shift+Enter. Read about these in Chapter 1, under "New Array Functions in Office 365."

CHAPTER 12

TROUBLESHOOTING

Array formulas are difficult to paste. The paste area cannot overlap with the copy area. In the following figure, the array formula in D5 needs to be copied to D5:J35.

Normally, you would copy Cell D5 and then paste to cells D5:J35. With array formulas, this leads to an error. If you attempt to do this, you are told that you cannot move or change part of an array. The solution is to do the copy in two pieces:

1. Copy Cell D5 to D6:D35.
2. Copy D5:D35 and paste it to E5:J35.

	✓	fx	{=SUM((WEEKDAY(ROW(INDIRECT($B$1&":"&$B$2)))=D$3)*(DAY(ROW(INDIRECT($B$1&":"&$B$2)))=$C5))}									
C	D	E	F	G	H	I	J	K	L	M	N	
	1	2	3	4	5	6	7					
	Sun	Mon	Tue	Wed	Thu	Fri	Sat					
1	96											
2												
3												
4												
5												
6												
7												

Transforming Data

What if there was a tool that let you clean data 20 percent faster on day one? What if that tool accurately remembered all your steps so you could clean the data 99 percent faster on days two through two hundred? That tool has been hiding on the Data tab since Excel 2016.

Power Query is the best feature to arrive in Excel about which most people have never heard. After Excel 2013 was released, the Power Query add-in was released for Excel 2010 and Excel 2013. The Add-in was great, but many people in corporate environments don't ever see the add-ins. By the time that Excel 2016 shipped, Power Query was old news for the Excel team, and it was quietly slipped in to the Data tab of the ribbon. Unfortunately, most people never realize that the icons in the Get & Transform group are as powerful as they are.

Between Excel 2016 and Excel 2019, the tool continues to grow by leaps and bounds. You can now split by delimiter to rows, and you can combine a whole folder of Excel files.

This chapter introduces some of the tools available in Power Query as well as traditional tools such as Sort, Filter, Remove Duplicates, and Flash Fill.

Using Power Query

The Power Query tools were created to make it easier to clean ugly data. Suppose that your IT department provides a data set every day that has some problems. Rather than wait for the IT department to rewrite the query, you can use Power Query to memorize the steps needed to clean the data. When the IT department provides a new file, you simply refresh the query and Excel repeats all the data cleansing steps.

Figure 13.1 shows an ugly data set. Two different fields are in column A, separated by a comma. The customer column is in uppercase. Columns D through O are a repeating group with various month values going across. To pivot this data, you must unpivot D:O, creating an extra date column and then 12 times as many rows.

⊿	A	B	C	D	E	F	G
1	REGION, MARKET	PRODUCT	CUSTOMER	Jan-21	Feb-21	Mar-21	Apr-21
2	CENTRAL, CHICAGO	XYZ	SPRINGBOARD	13962	2401	13867	7132
3	EAST, ORLANDO	DEF	EXCEL LEARNING ZONE	2358	15104	5532	17757
4	SOUTH, HOUSTON	XYZ	RIBBON COMMANDER FRAMEW	7167	21456	17150	21708
5	CENTRAL, CHICAGO	DEF	DATASOLVERZ.COM	4380	7032	21357	13853
6	EAST, ORLANDO	ABC	NEW HOPE LAUNDRY	16784	7132	11430	2401
7	WEST, SEATTLE	DEF	MYSPREADSHEETLAB	13853	11220	7136	19539
8	CENTRAL, CHICAGO	XYZ	SURTEN EXCEL	5532	6714	14497	8876
9	EAST, BALTIMORE	ABC	NETCOM COMPUTER	4948	13206	5700	19288
10	SOUTH, HOUSTON	XYZ	WAC MODE DOC STORE SAN A	11550	17757	14497	9064

Placeholder

Figure 13.1   There are some problems in this data set created by the IT department.

Establishing a Workflow

Say that the IT department sends you this data every month. Your plan could be to save the workbook in the same folder with the same name, and you will build your query in a new workbook. This workbook will be designed always to open the file located at C:\Foo\Ugly-DataFromIT.xlsx.

Or, perhaps the file that they send each month must be combined with all of the previous monthly files. In that case, you should create a new folder to hold all of the workbooks from IT. Do not store anything else in this folder. A new workbook with the query would be saved in a different folder. In this case, you would choose Get Data, From File, From Folder.

Either of the above workflows will make it easier to refresh the query in the future. The "wrong" approach is to open the file from IT and then build the query in that file.

Loading Data Using Power Query

Power Query can load data from any of these sources:

- **Files**: Workbook, Text, CSV, XML, JSON, or from a folder

- **Database**: SQL Server, Access, Analysis Services, Oracle, IBM DB2, MySQL, PostgreSQL, Sybase, Teradata, and SAP HANA

- **Azure**: SQL Database, SQL Data Warehouse, HDInsight (HDFS), Blob Storage, Table Storage, and Data Lake Store

- **Online**: SharePoint, Exchange, Dynamics 365, Facebook, Salesforce Objects, and Salesforce Reports

- **Other**: Table, Range, Web, Microsoft Query, SharePoint List, OData Feed, Hadoop File, ActiveDirectory, Microsoft Exchange, ODBC, and OLEDB

All of the preceding items are found in the Get Data menu. This is the first icon on the Data tab. It is found in the Get & Transform Data group. A few of those choices are repeated in the Get & Transform Data group: From Text/CSV, From Web, and From Table/Range.

NOTE

You might have previously used the legacy connectors. In previous versions of Excel, the Data tab contained seven icons: From Access, From Web, From Text, From SQL Server, From OData Data Feel, From XML Data Import, and From Data Connection Wizard. While these seven commands still exist, they have been removed from the ribbon. If you need to access the old commands, go to File, Options, Data. The Show Legacy Data Import Wizards allows you to bring the icons back. Any icons you choose here will appear under Data, Get Data, Legacy Wizards.

Loading Data from a Single Excel Workbook

Create a new blank workbook. Save the workbook with a name such as PowerQueryToLoadUglyData.xlsx.

Choose Data, Get Data, From File, From Workbook, as shown in Figure 13.2.

Figure 13.2 Specify the source of the data to be transformed.

CHAPTER 13

Depending on the source, you will need to browse to the file, provide a connect string to the database, or provide a URL.

The Navigator dialog box will appear. Initially, nothing is shown in the Data Preview on the right. On the left side of the dialog box, click on the worksheet named Data. The Preview will appear on the right.

Below the Preview, you have choices to Load, Transform Data, or Cancel. You want to choose Transform Data so you can specify the data cleansing steps (see Figure 13.3).

Figure 13.3   Select the worksheet in the left pane to see a preview on the right pane.

Transforming Data in Power Query

The data appears in a new window called the Query Editor. Ribbon tabs appear for Home, Transform, Add Column, and View.

As shown in Figure 13.4, Power Query is treating the header row as a data row. Use Home, Use First Row As Headers to convert that row to a header row. If you ever had the opposite problem, in which Power Query assumed the first data row is headers, you could open the same drop-down menu and choose Use Headers As First Row.

Figure 13.4   The first edit is to identify the first row as headers.

Column A has both Region and Market in a single column, separated by a comma. Select that column by clicking on the REGION, MARKET header. Use Home, Split Column, By Delimiter.

Take a look at the Split by Delimiter dialog box in Figure 13.5, which feels like the Text To Columns Wizard in Excel. However, this version is far superior.

First, Power Query was able to guess that your delimiter is a comma. How did it do this? It looked at every cell in the first 20 rows and noticed a comma in each one. This is not rocket science. It makes me wonder why the Excel Text To Columns Wizard can't figure it out.

Second, Power Query will let you split at every comma or only the first and last comma. For anyone who ever had "Mary Ellen Walton," "Judy Norton Taylor," or "Billy Joe Jim Bob Briggs" overwrite adjacent data after Text To Columns, you will appreciate the ability to force the results into two columns.

Finally, Power Query offers the amazing ability to split each delimiter to a new row. Data in the other columns is copied down to the new rows.

Figure 13.5   Split by Delimiter is better than Text to Columns.

After you split a column, the new column names will be REGION, MARKET.1 and REGION, MAR-KET.2. Double-click each heading and type a new name such as Region for column A and Market for column B.

If you need to convert a column of uppercase words to proper case, select the column and select Transform, Format, Capitalize Each Word (see Figure 13.6).

Figure 13.6   The menu options for converting to proper case, uppercase, or lowercase.

Unpivoting Data in Power Query

It is very common to see data with months or years stretching across the columns. Pivot tables made from this structure are very difficult to use. In the past, fixing the data structure involved repeatedly copying and pasting, or using an obscure trick with Multiple Consolidation Ranges. Power Query makes this process amazingly simple.

In Figure 13.7, the first four columns are selected. Use Transform, Unpivot Columns, Unpivot Other Columns.

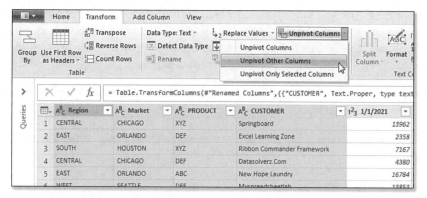

Figure 13.7   Select the label columns and choose to unpivot the other columns.

In this example, you go from 81 rows of 16 columns to 972 rows of six columns. As you can see in Figure 13.8, the fifth column is called Attribute, and the sixth column is called Value. You can use the Rename function to give these meaningful names, such as Month and Value or Month and Revenue.

	Region	Market	PRODUCT	CUSTOMER	Attribute	Value
1	CENTRAL	CHICAGO	XYZ	Springboard	1/1/2021	13962
2	CENTRAL	CHICAGO	XYZ	Springboard	2/1/2021	2401
3	CENTRAL	CHICAGO	XYZ	Springboard	3/1/2021	13867
4	CENTRAL	CHICAGO	XYZ	Springboard	4/1/2021	7132
5	CENTRAL	CHICAGO	XYZ	Springboard	5/1/2021	22810
6	CENTRAL	CHICAGO	XYZ	Springboard	6/1/2021	7167
7	CENTRAL	CHICAGO	XYZ	Springboard	7/1/2021	1819
8	CENTRAL	CHICAGO	XYZ	Springboard	8/1/2021	18264
9	CENTRAL	CHICAGO	XYZ	Springboard	9/1/2021	20408
10	CENTRAL	CHICAGO	XYZ	Springboard	10/1/2021	7167
11	CENTRAL	CHICAGO	XYZ	Springboard	11/1/2021	16936
12	CENTRAL	CHICAGO	XYZ	Springboard	12/1/2021	5532
13	EAST	ORLANDO	DEF	Excel Learning Zone	1/1/2021	2358
14	EAST	ORLANDO	DEF	Excel Learning Zone	2/1/2021	15104

Figure 13.8   Unpivoting creates a data set that is easy to pivot.

Select the Date column. Look at the Data Type value on the Transform tab. Power Query is treating these dates like text. With the Date column selected, choose Date from the Data Type dropdown menu.

If there are customers who had no revenue in a certain month, you could open the Filter dropdown menu on the Value column and uncheck 0 values to remove those records.

Adding Columns in Power Query

The new Column From Examples feature in Power Query for Excel 2019 is a nice improvement. Back in Excel 2016, you would have to write a new formula to create a column. The formula language is not like the Excel language. The formula to get a month name from a date is `Date.MonthName([Date])`. Power Query would not accept `date.monthname` or `Date.Monthname`. You had to type `Date.MonthName` with the three capital letters.

Every time that I had to create a formula in Power Query, I was always going out to the web to the Power Query Function Reference.

Today, the new Column From Examples features simplifies the process (see Figure 13.9). Follow these steps:

1. Select the Date column.

2. In Power Query, choose Add Column, Column From Examples. A new Column1 appears on the far-right side of the window.

3. Click the first cell of Column1 and type **January**.

4. Power Query will offer a choice of Month Name from Date. Click OK.

Power Query will add a new column called Month Name. The Formula bar shows the formula that you would use if you plan on learning Power Query formulas.

Figure 13.9   Add a new column to the query by typing an example.

Reviewing the Query

As shown in Figure 13.10, the right side of the Query Editor shows all the transformation steps that you've taken so far. You can see any settings associated with a step by clicking the gear icon. You can see the data at any point in the process by clicking the step. You can delete a step by using the X icon to the left of any step.

Figure 13.10   A list of transformation steps is saved with the query.

Power Query is writing an entire program in the M language behind the scenes. Go to View, Advanced Editor to see the M that was generated as you performed the data cleansing steps. Figure 13.11 shows an example.

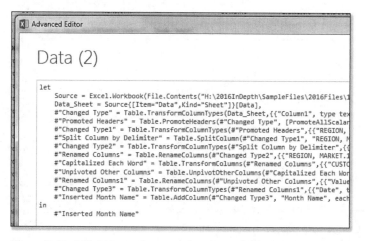

Figure 13.11   This M language query is written while you use the interface.

Loading and Refreshing the Data

After doing all the steps to clean the data, you can choose Home, Close & Load, as shown in Figure 13.12. You can either load to an Excel worksheet or directly to the Data Model. Obviously, if you are loading more than 1,048,576 records, you will want to load the data to the Data Model.

CHAPTER 13

Figure 13.12   Load the query and query definition to Excel or the Data Model.

Here is the beautiful feature: After you load the data to Excel, you can use Data, Refresh All to have the query go back to the data source, load the current data, and perform all the data cleansing steps automatically.

This is one example of the transformations available in Power Query. There is more functionality, and new functions are added monthly. You can use Power Query to consolidate all worksheets from a single file or one worksheet from multiple files.

Appending Worksheets from One Workbook

What if you have a workbook with monthly worksheets and you need to combine those records? In the Navigator dialog box, choose Select Multiple Items. Select each of the worksheet names, as shown in Figure 13.13.

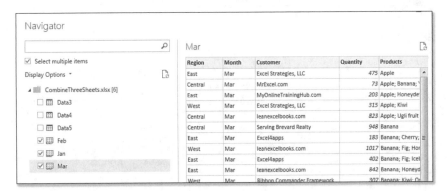

Figure 13.13   Choose to import each worksheet.

When you click Transform Data, the Power Query editor opens showing the first of several queries. On the Home tab, choose Append Queries. In the Append dialog box, choose Three Or More Tables and then move all the tables to the box on the right (see Figure 13.14).

The result will be a single query with records from all of the worksheets.

Figure 13.14   Append all the queries.

Splitting Each Delimiter to a New Row

Look at the second row of Figure 13.15. MyOnlineTrainingHub.com ordered 637 bundles of Apple; Cherry; Iceberg. You need to split those products to three rows. The customer name and all other information should be copied to the new rows.

Select the Product column. Select Split Column, By Delimiter. Power Query displays the Split Column By Delimiter dialog box and correctly guesses the delimiter is a semi-colon.

Click the Advanced Options, and you will see an option to Split Into either columns or rows; choose Rows.

A\u1d2e\u1d04 Customer	1²₃ Quantity	A\u1d2e\u1d04 Products
leanexcelbooks.com	144	Apple
MyOnlineTrainingHub.com	637	Apple; Cherry; Iceberg
Excel Strategies, LLC	391	Apple; Elderberry; Honeydew; Plum
leanexcelbooks.com	474	Apple; Jackfruit
Excel Strategies, LLC	985	Apple; Nectarine
Excel4apps	773	Banana; Elderber
DataSolverz.com	709	Banana; Iceberg;
leanexcelbooks.com	386	Banana; Jackfrui
Excel4apps	902	Banana; Kiwi; Ra
Excel Learning Zone	882	Cherry
WM Squared Inc.	576	Cherry; Elderber
MyOnlineTrainingHub.com	1027	Cherry; Fig; Lime
MyOnlineTrainingHub.com	943	Cherry; Fig; Ugli
Excel Strategies, LLC	662	Cherry; Jackfruit;
leanexcelbooks.com	969	Date; Elderberry
Serving Brevard Realty	116	Date; Iceberg; Ja
Serving Brevard Realty	706	Elderberry; Raspl
MyOnlineTrainingHub.com	296	Fig
XLYOURFINANCES, LLC	568	Fig

Split Column by Delimiter

Specify the delimiter used to split the text column.

Select or enter delimiter

Semicolon

Split at

○ Left-most delimiter
○ Right-most delimiter
● Each occurrence of the delimiter

▲ Advanced options
Split into
○ Columns
● Rows

Figure 13.15   Split each semi-colon to a new row.

...ou click OK to complete the split, the 126 rows transforms into 367 rows. Look how the ...tems for MyOnlineTrainingHub.com now appears on three separate rows in Figure 13.16.

AᴮC Customer	1²₃ Quantity	AᴮC Products
leanexcelbooks.com	144	Apple
MyOnlineTrainingHub.com	637	Apple
MyOnlineTrainingHub.com	637	Cherry
MyOnlineTrainingHub.com	637	Iceberg
Excel Strategies, LLC	391	Apple
Excel Strategies, LLC	391	Elderberry
Excel Strategies, LLC	391	Honeydew
Excel Strategies, LLC	391	Plum

Figure 13.16   Excel splits each product to a new row and copies the other information down.

Appending One Worksheet from Every Workbook in a Folder

While combining sheets from one workbook works, as described in the previous section, it will become unwieldy. You will have to re-create the query each month as new sheets are added. Power Query's best trick is to combine all of the single-sheet workbooks from a single folder.

From Excel, choose Get Data, From File, From Folder, then specify the folder. Power Query will show you a list of files in the folder. Choose Combine & Edit, as shown in Figure 13.17. In the Navigator screen, choose the correct worksheet.

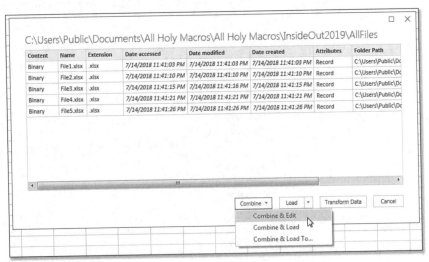

Figure 13.17   Choose to combine all of the workbooks in a folder.

Power Query is smart enough to promote the first row of the first file as headers. It will then discard all of the other headers in the remaining workbooks.

If you have extra columns in some files, those columns will appear in the final query, with the word "null" for the records that did not have the extra column.

Over time, if more workbooks are added to the folder, you simply have to click Refresh to have Excel reload everything from the folder.

Inside OUT

Power Query is evolving faster than Excel. New features will be due out in late 2018 or early 2019.

Power Query is built in to both Power BI and Power Excel. It is normal to see a new Power Query feature arrive in Power BI about a month before it arrives in Excel.

In July 2018, Microsoft blogged about a preview of new data profiling features coming to Power Query in Power BI. One would have to assume that these same features will appear in Office 365 by early 2019.

In the following figures, the data profiling reveals these facts about a Sales Representative column:

- There are 91 valid values in the column.

- There are 12 distinct values.

- Two values occur exactly once in the column. Power Query calls these "Unique Values," even though this seems misleading.

- A chart at the top of the column indicates a histogram of the 12 unique values.

- A chart at the bottom right indicates the length of the text entries.

These statistics will give you an overview of data before you import it. For example, an invoice number column might need to have 100 percent unique values. If there are duplicates, you can see this instantly and track down the problem.

Cleaning Data with Flash Fill

Suppose that you have data with first names in column A and last names in column B. The names are in uppercase. You would like to reshape the data, so you have the full names in proper case.

Add a heading in column C. Type the first and last name from A2 and B2 in cell C2. As soon as you type the first letter in the second cell, Excel springs into action and offers to fill the rest of the column for you (see Figure 13.18). Provided the preview looks right or even close, press Enter.

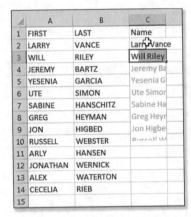

Figure 13.18   Type **W** in C3 and Excel offers to fill in the rest of the column.

In addition to filling the column, Excel provides two pieces of feedback. First, the status bar in the lower-left corner of the screen indicates that Flash Fill changed a certain number of cells.

Second, a tiny on-grid Flash Fill drop-down menu icon appears next to the first changed cell. The drop-down menu offers choices such as Undo and Accept. You can also choose to select all changed cells or all unchanged cells.

Coaching Flash Fill with a Second Example

After Flash Fill operates, look for any cells that don't fit the pattern. You might have a person with two first names (Mary Ellen Walton) or no last name (Pele). Type a new value in column C, and Flash Fill looks for other cells that match that pattern, correcting as it goes.

Flash Fill Will Not Automatically Fill in Numbers

With only 10 digits (in contrast to 26 letters), it is too likely that Excel could detect other patterns that are not the pattern you are intending. When Flash Fill sees a potential pattern, it temporarily "grays in" the suggestion but then removes the suggestion. Press Ctrl+E or click the Flash Fill icon on the Data tab to allow Flash Fill to work.

Flash Fill does not understand mathematical transformations. If the original number is 477 and you type **479** (add 2 to each cell) or **500** (round to the nearest hundred), Excel does not know how to Flash Fill the remaining cells.

Using Formatting with Dates

Dates are particularly troublesome. Suppose that you have a date of birth in column E with the format of YYYYMMDD. If you type **3/5/1970** in G2 and then press the Flash Fill icon, Excel does not correctly recognize the pattern. You get 3/5/ and the first four digits from E in each row, which is an interesting result. You can sort of understand how Excel was tricked into seeing the wrong pattern.

You can solve the date problem by formatting the column to show MM/DD/YYYY first.

Troubleshooting Flash Fill

The following are some tips for making Flash Fill work correctly:

- There can be no blank columns. It is not necessary to be in the column immediately to the right of the data, but you can't have any completely blank columns between where you want to Flash Fill and the source data.

- For the automatic Flash Fill to work, you should type the first value and then immediately type the second value. Do not perform any other commands between the first and second values. Don't type **G2**, go to Sheet 3, and then come back and type **G3**. By then, Flash Fill has stopped watching for patterns. The only exception is sorting. You could type **G2**, sort, type **G3**, and Flash Fill will work.

- Type a heading in the column that you are filling to prevent Flash Fill from filling your heading. Also, you could use bold for the other headings. Flash Fill follows the same rules that the Sort dialog box and the Ctrl+T Table dialog box use to detect whether there are headings. If Ctrl+T opens with the My Data Has Headings box checked, then Flash Fill does not overwrite your headings. This matters more than you might think because the headings don't usually follow the pattern of the data and they confuse Flash Fill if it is trying to find a pattern.

- Pressing Esc makes the Flash Fill preview go away. More than once, I've pressed Esc by mistake and lost the Flash Fill. Don't worry. Type the first one or two cells and then use Ctrl+E or click the Flash Fill icon on the Data tab to force Excel to run Flash Fill again.

- Flash Fill looks only for patterns. Flash Fill does not understand that AZ is the abbreviation for Arizona. It does not understand that Jan 23 is another way to write 1-23. Flash Fill doesn't have any opinions. Typing **Awesome** next to Bruce Springsteen does not cue Flash Fill that you are trying to classify musical acts.

CHAPTER 13

Flash Fill provides an easy way to solve many data problems. Even in the cases where an Excel pro knows a formula that can solve the problem, it is still easier to use Flash Fill.

TROUBLESHOOTING

Flash Fill can be fooled by ambiguous examples. It has an uncanny ability to see ambiguity where you could not detect it.

In the following example, you might type **Brian Alberts** in D2 and invoke Flash Fill from D3. Most rational human beings would assume that you wanted first name, a space, and last name.

Flash Fill, however, assumes that you want the first name from column A, the middle initial from column B, and then everything after the first letter of column C.

This leads to Flash Fill changing **David Bradley** to **David Mradley**. Always carefully examine the Flash Fill results to see if they make sense.

	A	B	C	D
1	First Name	M. I.	Last Name	Flash Fill
2	Brian	A	Alberts	Brian Alberts
3	David	M	Bradley	David Mradley
4	John	Y	Chen	John Yhen
5	Craig	M	Combel	Craig Mombel

Sorting Data

Sorting in Excel 2019 is handled in the Sort dialog box or by using the AZ and ZA buttons on the Data tab. In all, there are six entry points for sorting:

- Select the Home tab and then select Editing, Sort & Filter, Custom Sort.

- Right-click any cell and choose Sort.

- Select Sort from any filter drop-down menu.

- Select the Data tab and then select Sort & Filter, AZ or Sort & Filter, ZA.

- Open the Sort dialog box by going to the Data tab and selecting Sort & Filter, Sort.

The Sort dialog box in Excel 2019 offers up to 64 different sorting levels. If you get into sorting by color, you often have to specify several rules for one column, so the theoretical number of columns you can sort by is probably fewer than 64.

Sorting by Color or Icon

Excel can sort data by fill color, font color, or icon set. This also works with color applied through conditional formatting or color that you applied by using the cell format icons.

Because color is subjective, there is not a default color sequence. If one column contains 17 colors, you need to set up 17 rules in the Sort dialog box just to sort by that one column.

To sort by color, follow these steps:

1. Select a cell within your data.

2. Select the Sort icon on the Data tab. The Sort dialog box appears.

3. Select the desired field from the Sort By drop-down menu.

4. Change the Sort On drop-down menu to Cell Color.

5. In the Order drop-down menu, choose the color that should appear first.

6. In the final drop-down menu, select On Top.

7. To specify the next color, click the Copy Level button at the top of the Sort dialog box.

8. Choose the next color in the Order drop-down menu for the copied rule.

9. Repeat steps 7 and 8 for each additional color.

10. If you want to specify that values in another column should be used to break ties in the color column, select the Add Level button and specify the additional columns.

11. Click OK to sort the data.

Factoring Case into a Sort

Typically, an Excel sort ignores the case of the text. Values that are lowercase, uppercase, or any combination of the two are treated equally in a sort.

You can instead use a case-sensitive sort in Excel 2019 to sort lowercase values before uppercase values. For example, **abc** sorts before **ABC**. Similarly, **ABc** sorts before **ABC**.

If you want Excel to consider case when sorting, follow these steps:

1. Select a cell within your data.

2. Select the Sort icon on the Data tab. The Sort dialog box appears.

3. Choose the column from the Sort By drop-down menu.

CHAPTER 13

4. Click the Options button. The Sort Options dialog box appears.

5. Select the Case Sensitive check box.

6. Click OK to close the Sort Options dialog box.

7. Click OK to sort.

Reordering Columns with a Left-to-Right Sort

If you receive a data set from a colleague and the columns are in the wrong sequence, you could cut and paste them into the right sequence, or you could fix them all in one pass by using a left-to-right sort. To do this, follow these steps:

1. Insert a new blank row above the headings.

2. In the new row, type numbers corresponding to the correct sequence of the columns.

3. Make sure that one cell in the range is selected.

4. Select the Sort icon on the Data tab. The Sort dialog box appears.

5. Click the Options button. The Sort Options dialog box appears.

6. Select Sort Left to Right. Click OK to close the Sort Options dialog box.

7. The Sort By drop-down menu now contains a list of row numbers. Choose the first row.

8. The remaining drop-down menus should already include Values and Smallest to Largest.

9. Click OK to perform the sort.

10. Delete your temporary extra row at the top of the data set. The columns are then resequenced into the desired order.

TIP

Excel does not change the original column widths. Select all cells with Ctrl+A and then use Home, Format, AutoFit Column Width to resize all the columns.

Sorting into a Unique Sequence by Using Custom Lists

Sometimes company tradition dictates that regions or products should be presented in an order that is not alphabetic. For example, the sequence East, Central, West makes more sense geographically than the alphabetic sequence Central, East, West.

It is possible to set up a custom list to tell Excel that the region sequence is East, Central, West. You can then sort your data based on this sequence. You need to set up the custom list only once per computer. Follow these steps to do so:

1. Go to a blank section of any worksheet. Type the correct sequence for the values in a column.

2. Select this range.

3. Select File, Options. The Options dialog box appears.

4. Click the Advanced Group. Scroll down to the General section and then select Edit Custom Lists. The Custom Lists dialog box appears.

5. In the Custom Lists dialog box, the bottom section shows the range of cells you selected in step 2. If it is correct, click the Import button. Your new list, with the correct sequence, is added to the default custom lists.

6. Click OK to close the Custom Lists dialog box. Click OK to close the Options dialog box.

7. Clear your temporary data range from step 1.

To use the list with custom sorting, follow these steps:

1. Select one cell in your data.

2. Select the Sort icon on the Data tab. The Sort dialog box appears.

3. In the Sort By drop-down menu, choose the region with the custom sort sequence.

4. From the Order drop-down menu, select Custom List. You should now be back in the Custom Lists dialog box.

5. Click your custom list and then click OK. The Sort dialog box shows that the order is based on your custom list.

6. Click OK to sort into the custom sequence.

One-Click Sorting

All the examples discussed so far in this chapter have used the Sort dialog box, which is required for left-to-right sorting, custom sorting, and case-sensitive sorting. It also makes color sorting easier. You can accomplish all other sorts by using the AZ buttons on the various tabs.

It is important to select a single cell in the column to be sorted. When you select a single cell, Excel extends the selection to encompass the entire current region. If you select two cells or even the whole column, Excel warns you that it is about to sort part of your data and ignore the adjacent data. This is rarely what you want.

You can find the one-click sorting options on the Home and Data tabs. On the Home tab, they are buried in the Sort & Filter drop-down menu. On the Data tab, they are clearly visible as AZ and ZA buttons.

You can also find sorting options by right-clicking a cell in the column you want to sort and selecting Sort. Options in this menu enable you to sort in ascending or descending order. You can also put the cell color, font color, or icon on top.

Additional quick-sorting options are located in the Filter drop-down menus. You can use these options to sort in ascending order, in descending order, and by color.

Fixing Sort Problems

If it appears that a sort did not work correctly, check this list of troubleshooting tips:

- If the headers were sorted into the data, it usually means that one or more columns had a blank heading. Every column should have a nonblank heading. If you want the heading to appear blank, use an underscore in a white font to fool Excel. If you cannot insert a heading, you will have to use the Sort dialog box.

- Unhide rows and columns before sorting. Hidden rows are not resequenced in a sort.

- Use only one row for headings. If you need the headings to appear as if they are taking up several rows, put the headings in one row and wrap the text. To have control over where the text wraps, type the first line, press Alt+Enter, and then type the second line.

- Data in a column should be a similar type. For example, if you have a column of ZIP Codes, you might have numeric cells for ZIP Codes of 10001 through 99999 and text cells for ZIP Codes of 00001 through 09999. This is one common way to keep leading zeroes. Because text cells are sorted sequentially after numeric cells, sorting the ZIP Codes, in this case, will appear not to work. To fix this problem, convert the entire column to one data type to achieve the expected results.

- If your data has volatile formulas or formulas that point to cells outside the sort range, Excel calculates the range after sorting. If your sort sequence is based on this column, Excel accurately sorts the data, based on the information before the recalculation. If the values change after calculation, it will appear that the sort did not work.

- If your data must have blank columns or rows, be sure to select the entire sort range before starting the sort process.

Summarizing Data Using Subtotals or Filter

The Subtotal command was added way back in Excel 97. Not enough people realize that the command is in Excel, and those who have tried it often don't realize how powerful the command truly is. I used to have a regular gig as the Excel guy on Leo Laporte's *Call for Help* television show. During one appearance, I showed people how to use the Subtotal command. I figured it was probably the most boring six minutes of television in the history of the world. However, that one show generated more fan email than any other. People wrote to say that they had been spending two hours every day adding subtotals manually, and now they used the trick from the show to reduce the task to a minute.

Filtering enables you to quickly wade through waves of data and see only the records needed to answer an ad-hoc query. Excel continues to improve the AutoFilter feature with hopes that you will never have to venture into the complicated Advanced Filter feature. When it's combined with the Remove Duplicates command, you might never have to use the Advanced Filter.

The elusive Filter by Selection feature enables you to invoke filters even faster than before.

Duplicate data is a common problem in Excel. Beginning with Excel 2007, Microsoft provided tools to make finding and eliminating duplicates easier.

Adding Automatic Subtotals

When you have a database of detailed data, you might want to add subtotals to each group of records. If your data has one field that identifies the groups, you can use the Subtotals command to add the subtotals quickly. Figure 14.1 shows a data set that is suitable for this.

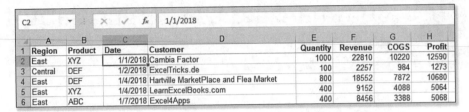

	A	B	C	D	E	F	G	H
					Quantity	Revenue	COGS	Profit
1	Region	Product	Date	Customer				
2	East	XYZ	1/1/2018	Cambia Factor	1000	22810	10220	12590
3	Central	DEF	1/2/2018	ExcelTricks.de	100	2257	984	1273
4	East	DEF	1/4/2018	Hartville MarketPlace and Flea Market	800	18552	7872	10680
5	East	XYZ	1/4/2018	LearnExcelBooks.com	400	9152	4088	5064
6	East	ABC	1/7/2018	Excel4Apps	400	8456	3388	5068

C2 = 1/1/2018

Figure 14.1 After sorting, you can quickly add subtotals to this data set.

Follow these steps to add subtotals to a data set:

1. Sort the data set by your group field. Select one cell in that column and then select Data, Sort & Filter, AZ.

2. Select one cell in your data set.

3. Select Data, Outline, Subtotal. Excel displays the Subtotal dialog box.

4. In the Subtotal dialog box, change the At Each Change In drop-down menu to reflect your group field.

5. Ensure that Use Function is set to Sum.

6. For each field you want to be totaled, select the field in the Add Subtotal To list, as shown in Figure 14.2.

Figure 14.2 You specify the fields to be totaled in the Subtotal dialog box.

7. If you want a page break after each group, select Page Break Between Groups.

8. Click OK to add subtotals. Excel adds a subtotal between each group, as shown in Figure 14.3.

Figure 14.3   Excel inserts extra rows between groups and adds subtotals.

At the very bottom of the data set, Excel has added a Grand Total row. This row is smart enough to ignore all the other subtotal rows in the data set (see Figure 14.4).

Figure 14.4   At the bottom of the data set, Excel inserted a Grand Total row.

Adding hundreds of subtotal rows is amazing in and of itself. However, the subtotals command offers so much more. You can go on to show only the subtotals, show the largest groups at the top, or copy the subtotals.

Working with the Subtotals

Take a close look at the left side of the worksheet in Figure 14.3. You see three new buttons to the left of column A labeled 1, 2, and 3. Those buttons are called Group and Outline buttons and were added automatically by the Subtotals command. They are the key to further analysis of the subtotals.

CHAPTER 14

Showing a One-Page Summary with Only the Subtotals

Click the #2 button that appears to the left of and just above cell A1. Excel hides all the detail rows, leaving only the customer subtotals and the Grand Total row.

After setting the print area, you would have a one-page summary of the 500+ rows of data (see Figure 14.5).

		C	D	E	F	G	H
	1	Date	Customer	Quantity	Revenue	COGS	Profit
+	6		Association for Computers & Taxation T.	2800	60299	27049	33250
+	11		Bits of Confetti Total	2300	50030	21612	28418
+	68		Cambia Factor Total	28900	622794	274978	347816
+	73		Construction Intelligence & Analytics, In	1400	31369	13730	17639
+	140		CPASelfStudy.com Total	33400	704359	311381	392978
+	145		Data2Impact Total	3300	72680	31946	40734
+	150		Excel Learning Zone Total	2600	54048	23780	30268
+	211		Excel4Apps Total	35700	750163	334614	415549
+	216		Excelerator BI Total	1400	31021	13745	17276
+	253		ExcelTricks.de Total	18600	390978	177281	213697
+	258		Fintega Financial Modelling Total	2700	59881	25913	33968
+	307		F-Keys Ltd. Total	29100	613514	275105	338409
+	348		Frontline Systems Total	23100	498937	219978	278959
+	353		Hartville MarketPlace and Flea Market T	1900	42316	18764	23552
+	358		IMA Houston Chapter Total	3300	71651	32471	39180
+	363		Juliet Babcock-Hyde CPA, PLLC Total	2000	46717	19961	26756
+	429		LaFrenier Sons Septic Total	40400	869454	382170	487284
+	434		Lake Local School District Total	2600	55251	24632	30619
+	439		LearnExcelBooks.com Total	1600	34364	15576	18788
+	444		MyOnlineTrainingHub.com Total	3000	62744	28644	34100
+	449		MySpreadsheetLab Total	2700	57516	26765	30751
+	454		New Hope Laundry Total	2000	39250	18614	20636
+	483		Profology.com Total	18700	406326	178585	227741
+	536		Serving Brevard Realty Total	26600	568851	252522	316329
+	581		Spain Enterprise Total	19700	427349	189331	238018
+	586		Vertex42 Total	2400	51240	22824	28416
+	591		WM Squared Inc. Total	1700	34710	16423	18287
−	592		Grand Total	313900	6707812	2978394	3729418
	593						

E592 = SUBTOTAL(9,E2:E590)

Figure 14.5   Click the #2 Group and Outline button to show a summary report.

If you click the #1 Group and Outline button, Excel hides everything except for the Grand Total. If you click the #3 button, Excel brings the detail rows back.

Sorting the Collapsed Subtotal View with the Largest Customers at Top

In Figure 14.5, you have the customers in alphabetical sequence. However, your manager is probably going to want to see the largest customers at the top of the report.

Think about this request, though. In row 211, the subtotal for Excel4Apps is one of the largest customers in the group, adding up data in rows 151 through 210. If you try to sort in descending order, and the data in row 211 comes up to row 3, the formula that looks at 60 rows of data will certainly evaluate to a #REF! error.

Amazingly, though, you can easily sort data when it is in the collapsed #2 view. Follow these steps:

1. Add subtotals as described earlier in this chapter.

2. Collapse the subtotals by clicking the #2 Group and Outline button.

3. Select one single cell in your revenue column.

4. Sort in descending order by clicking the ZA button on the Data tab.

The result is shown in Figure 14.6. The total for Excel4Apps flies out near the top of the data set, but it does not come to row 3. Instead, the total comes to row 128. The total for the largest customer is in row 67.

	C	D	E	F	G	H
F67		fx	=SUBTOTAL(9,F2:F66)			
			Quantity	Revenue	COGS	Profit
1	Date	Customer				
67		LaFrenier Sons Septic Total	40400	869454	382170	487284
128		Excel4Apps Total	35700	750163	334614	415549
195		CPASelfStudy.com Total	33400	704359	311381	392978
252		Cambia Factor Total	28900	622794	274978	347816
301		F-Keys Ltd. Total	29100	613514	275105	338409
354		Serving Brevard Realty Total	26600	568851	252522	316329
395		Frontline Systems Total	23100	498937	219978	278959
440		Spain Enterprise Total	19700	427349	189331	238018
469		Profology.com Total	18700	406326	178585	227741

Figure 14.6   Amazingly, you can sort data when it is collapsed.

Figure 14.7 shows the #3 view of Figure 14.6. You can see that Excel sorted groups of records when the data was collapsed. All the detail rows for a customer come along with the subtotal row, but the detail rows are not sorted by revenue.

	C	D	E	F	G	H
F67		fx	=SUBTOTAL(9,F2:F66)			
1	Date	Customer	Quantity	Revenue	COGS	Profit
119	11/9/2019	Excel4Apps	700	17059	7154	9905
120	11/17/2019	Excel4Apps	600	13680	6132	7548
121	11/21/2019	Excel4Apps	500	11330	4920	6410
122	11/28/2019	Excel4Apps	500	11470	5110	6360
123	12/1/2019	Excel4Apps	900	22887	9198	13689
124	12/7/2019	Excel4Apps	1000	23690	9840	13850
125	12/10/2019	Excel4Apps	1000	17410	8470	8940
126	12/10/2019	Excel4Apps	200	4492	1968	2524
127	12/29/2019	Excel4Apps	900	15363	7623	7740
128		Excel4Apps Total	35700	750163	334614	415549

Figure 14.7   Excel brings all the collapsed detail rows along with the subtotal row during a sort.

Copying Only the Subtotal Rows

A problem occurs when you try to copy the collapsed subtotal rows from Figure 14.6. If you select D1:H592, Copy, and then Paste the data to a new worksheet, you discover that Excel has copied all the hidden rows as well. Worse, the pasted data no longer has the group and outline symbols, so there is no way to collapse the data again.

The key to this task is to use a trick called Go To Special, Visible Cells Only. Excel still makes it hard to find this command.

Follow these steps:

1. Add subtotals to a data set as described previously.

2. Collapse to the subtotal-only view by clicking the #2 Group and Outline button.

3. Select the entire range of collapsed subtotals.

4. Open the Find and Select drop-down menu from the right side of the Home tab. Select the Go To Special command. Excel displays the Go To Special dialog box, as shown in Figure 14.8. This dialog box enables you to narrow a selection to only certain types of elements within your selection. This is a powerful dialog box.

Figure 14.8   The Go To Special dialog box enables you to reduce your selection to items meeting certain criteria.

5. In the Go To Special dialog box, select Visible Cells Only. Click OK. Excel deselects all the hidden rows.

TIP

You can replace steps 4 and 5 with a single keystroke. Hold down the Alt key while pressing the semicolon key. It turns out that Alt+; is the equivalent of selecting Home, Find & Select, Go To Special, Visible Cells Only, OK. Or, if you prefer to use the mouse, customize the Quick Access Toolbar (QAT) with an icon called Select Visible Cells.

6. Click Ctrl+C to copy those rows. As you can see in Figure 14.9, Excel has selected each visible row separately.

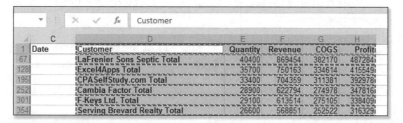

Figure 14.9   Excel copies only the visible rows.

7. Select a blank section of the workbook. Use Ctrl+V to paste only the subtotals. The subtotal formulas are converted to values. This is the only thing that would make sense.

Formatting the Subtotal Rows

When the Subtotal command adds subtotals, it inserts a new row for each subtotal. Excel copies your key field to the new row and appends the word *Total* after the key field. This text in the key field column appears in bold font. Unfortunately, Excel does not widen this column, so frequently the word *Total* appears to be truncated because it will not fit in the column.

The other subtotal columns get a formula that uses the SUBTOTAL function. Strangely, the cells containing the formulas in each subtotal row are not bold.

When I am doing my Power Excel seminars, I'm frequently asked how to bold the subtotal rows. Many people will try selecting E67:H592 in the collapsed #2 view and pressing Ctrl+B. Although this initially looks like it works, it actually fails.

The problem becomes apparent when you go back to the #3 view to see the detail rows. The detail rows up through row 66 are fine. The problem is that all the detail rows from row 68 through the end of the data set have been bolded. For some reason, Microsoft formats the rows that are hidden as a result of the Subtotal command.

CHAPTER 14

At this point, many people press Undo twice and start the process of manually formatting each subtotal row. There is, of course, an easier way. Follow these steps to format the subtotal rows:

1.   Add subtotals to a data set as described previously.

2.   Click the #2 Group and Outline button to collapse the data set to show only the subtotals.

3.   Select from the first subtotal row down to the grand total row. In the current data set, select from D67 through H592.

4.   Hold down Alt and press semicolon. Excel selects on the visible rows, which in this case are only the subtotal rows.

5.   Apply any desired formatting. In Figure 14.10, the cells are showing a mix of Cell Styles, Heading 4, and a light red background from the Fill drop-down menu.

		Date	Customer	Quantity	Revenue	COGS	Profit
	559	11/24/2018	Juliet Babcock-Hyde CPA, PLLC	100	2538	1022	1516
	560	7/21/2019	Juliet Babcock-Hyde CPA, PLLC	1000	22840	10220	12620
	561		Juliet Babcock-Hyde CPA, PLLC Total	2000	46717	19961	26756
	562	1/4/2018	Hartville MarketPlace and Flea Market	800	18552	7872	10680
	563	1/21/2018	Hartville MarketPlace and Flea Market	200	3552	1694	1858
	564	3/24/2019	Hartville MarketPlace and Flea Market	100	2484	1022	1462
	565	4/24/2019	Hartville MarketPlace and Flea Market	800	17728	8176	9552
	566		Hartville MarketPlace and Flea Market T	1900	42316	18764	23552
	567	11/15/2018	New Hope Laundry	1000	17250	8470	8780

Figure 14.10   Format only the subtotal rows.

6.   Click the #3 Group and Outline button to show all the detail rows.

Step 4 in this process is the key step. Using Alt+; selects only the visible rows in the collapsed subtotal view.

Removing Subtotals

After you add subtotals and copy those subtotal rows to another worksheet, you might want to remove the subtotals from the original data set. Follow these steps to remove the subtotals:

1.   Select one cell in the subtotaled data set.

2.   Go back to the Subtotals command on the Data tab of the ribbon.

3.   In the lower-left corner of the Subtotals dialog box, click the button for Remove All.

The subtotal rows are removed.

Subtotaling Multiple Fields

Suppose you want to add subtotals by region and product. You will add the subtotals twice. In the second Subtotal command, make sure you clear the Replace Current Subtotals check box.

Make sure that your data is sorted properly. You can either use the Sort dialog box to sort by region and then by product, or you can follow this set of steps, which requires only four clicks:

1. Select one cell in the Product column.

2. Click the AZ button on the Data tab.

3. Select one cell in the Region column.

4. Click the AZ button on the Data tab.

Because the sort in step 4 keeps the ties in the previous sequence, this set of steps effectively sorts by product within the region.

It is important that you add subtotals to the outer group first. Use the instructions earlier in this chapter in the "Adding Automatic Subtotals" section to add totals to the Region field.

Run the Subtotals command again. This time, specify Each Change In Product. Clear the Replace Current Subtotals check box.

You now have four Group and Outline buttons. If you press the #3 button, you see product totals and region totals, as shown in Figure 14.11. Note that Excel supports a maximum of eight Group and Outline buttons so that you could add up to six levels of subtotals.

Figure 14.11   Two sets of subtotals mean four Group and Outline buttons.

Subtotaling Daily Dates by Month

Say that you have daily dates and want to apply the subtotal after each month. Sort your data by the data field. Select the data column and apply a format that shows month and year as shown in Figure 14.12.

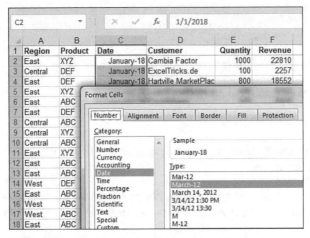

Figure 14.12   Format the date fields to show months.

Add the Subtotals for each change in Date. The subtotals will appear after each month. You can change the format for the date column back to a short date. The result, as shown in Figure 14.13, is daily dates with monthly subtotals.

	A	B	C	D	E	F	G	H
1	Region	Product	Date	Customer	Quantity	Revenue	COGS	Profit
17	West	ABC	1/23/2018	Excel4Apps	800	14592	6776	7816
18	East	ABC	1/24/2018	Spain Enterprise	600	12606	5082	7524
19	Central	ABC	1/25/2018	F-Keys Ltd.	1000	20770	8470	12300
20	East	ABC	1/26/2018	Spain Enterprise	400	8128	3388	4740
21	East	ABC	1/29/2018	LearnExcelBooks.co	400	7136	3388	3748
22	East	DEF	1/29/2018	Excel4Apps	700	17150	6888	10262
23	East	DEF	1/30/2018	LaFrenier Sons Sep	300	6714	2952	3762
24	East	ABC	1/31/2018	Excel4Apps	800	15640	6776	8864
25			January-18 Total		13000	273222	118420	154802
26	West	ABC	2/1/2018	LaFrenier Sons Sep	300	5532	2541	2991
27	West	DEF	2/3/2018	ExcelTricks.de	800	17160	7872	9288

Figure 14.13   After adding subtotals, change the date format back to a short date.

Filtering Records

The feature formerly known as AutoFilter is now called Filter. Along with the new name, the command has new features. Filtering works on any range of data with headings in the first row of the range. It works with ranges that have been defined as tables as well as regular ranges.

If you haven't visited the Filter since Excel 2003, the following features are new:

- The Search box enables you to search for values that match a wildcard. You can add the search results to a previous filter. Thus, you could quickly find all records that contain "bank" or "credit union."

- Multiselection is available in the Filter drop-down menu. If you need to select two, three, or ten values from the filter, it is easy to do now. On the flip side, it is slightly more difficult to filter to a single value because you first must uncheck the (Select All) box.

- You can filter by color or icon set.

- You can filter text columns based on cells that begin with a value, end with a value, or contain a value.

- You can filter number columns based on cells that are greater than, less than, or between values. You can choose Top 10, Above Average, or Below Average.

- You can filter date values by year or month. You can filter to conceptual values such as This Month, Last Quarter, or Year To Date.

- You can filter by selection. Rather than choosing from the Filter drop-down menu, you can select any value and use Filter By Selection to filter the data to that value.

The various features work great when one column contains values of the same type. For example, Excel expects that if you have dates in a column, all the cells except the header will be dates. Excel offers special text, number, or date formats based on what it sees in the column.

Using a Filter

The icon to turn on the filter drop-down menus toggles the feature on and off. To turn on the feature, click the icon once. To turn off the feature, click the icon again. You must select one cell in your data range before clicking the filter. You should have no blank rows or blank columns in the range to be filtered.

You can turn on the filter drop-down menus by using any of these methods:

- From the Data tab, select Filter.

- From the Home tab, open the Sort & Filter drop-down menu and choose Filter.

- Apply a table format to a range.

- Right-click any cell, select Filter, and then select one of the options under Filter. In addition to performing the filter, this will turn on the Filter feature if it was not previously turned on.

- Choose any value and then select the AutoFilter icon from the QAT. The Filter by Selection feature has been in Excel since Excel 2003, but the icon has never been included in the standard user interface. Also, this icon has always been mislabeled in the Customize dialog box. See "Filtering by Selection—Easy Way," later in this chapter, for more information.

When the filter is turned on, a drop-down menu arrow is added to each heading in the range.

Figure 14.14 shows the menu available for one drop-down menu. This particular column includes text values, so the special filter fly-out menu includes various special text filters.

Figure 14.14   The filter drop-down menu now features a multiselect list, as well as new special filters.

Inside OUT

There is a subtle difference between filtering using the Search box and filtering using the Contains Text filter.

If you needed to find all customers with Excel in their names in Figure 4.14, it would seem like typing **Excel** in the Search box is the best way.

However, if you plan on re-applying the filter later, either with the Reapply icon or by refreshing a pivot table, you should know that the Search box is a one-time snapshot of the current data. If the underlying data changes and you re-apply, the filter will not include new customers such as Turbo Excel.

To solve the problem, choose Text Filters, Contains.... In the Contains dialog box, type **Excel**. This creates a filter that can be re-applied.

Selecting One or Multiple Items from the Filter Drop-Down

In legacy versions of Excel, the filter drop-down menu included a simple list of items in the column, and you selected one of the values. The multiselect nature of filters included since Excel 2007 offers far more power, but you have to exercise special care in using the drop-down menu.

Follow these steps to select a single item:

1. When you initially select the drop-down menu, all the check boxes that appear in the column are selected, as shown in Figure 14.14.

2. To select a single value, click Select All. This clears all the items in the list, as shown in Figure 14.15.

Select All

Figure 14.15   Click Select All to clear the check boxes for all items.

3. Click the value on which you want to filter, as shown in Figure 14.16.

4. Click OK at the bottom of the drop-down menu to apply the filter.

Figure 14.16   When the check boxes have been cleared, select the one value of interest and click OK.

CHAPTER 14

The process you use to filter to multiple values is similar. First, click Select All to clear the check boxes for all items. You can then select the items that should be included in the filter.

TIP

With more than 1 million rows in Excel, you have the possibility for a long list of items in the Filter list—up to 10,000 items. Using the scrollbar to navigate through a list of 10,000 items will be inexact. However, there is a fast way to jump to a certain section of the list. Click any name in the list to activate the list. Then, type the first letter of your selection. Excel instantly jumps to the first item that starts with this letter. You can then use the PgDn or PgUp keys to move quickly through the items that start with that letter.

The multiselection capability is a vast improvement for filtering that can be completed in four clicks. Even though the old AutoFilter in legacy versions of Excel required only two clicks, the improvements are worth this hassle. For example, when you need to select everything except one certain value, you select the drop-down menu, clear the undesired value, and click OK.

Identifying Which Columns Have Filters Applied

Listed here are the visual clues in Excel 2019 you can use to identify columns in which a filter has been applied to a data set:

- The row numbers in the range appear in blue to indicate that the rows have a filter applied.

- The message area of the status bar in the lower-left corner of the screen shows a message similar to "2 of 34 records found."

- The drop-down menu for the filtered column changes from a simple drop-down menu arrow to a Filter icon, as shown in Figure 14.17.

Figure 14.17   After you apply a filter to column A, the icon on the filter drop-down menu changes.

Combining Filters

Filters are additive, which means that after you place a filter on a column, you can apply a filter to another column to show even fewer rows. You can apply two filters to the same column, such as when you want to select all the West region cells that are red.

Clearing Filters

After you apply a filter, you have several options for clearing it:

- From the filter drop-down menu, select Clear Filter from Column. This leaves filters on in other columns.

- From the filter drop-down menu, choose a different filter.

- From the Data tab, select Clear from the Sort & Filter group. This clears selected filters from any column but leaves the drop-down menus in place, so you can continue to select other filters.

- Select the Filter icon from the Data tab or the Home tab to clear all filters and turn off the filter feature.

Refreshing Filters

Keep in mind that when data in a range changes, the filters do not update automatically. This can happen when you add new rows or edit data. It can also happen if your data range has formulas that point to lookup tables in other parts of the workbook. In such a case, you need to have Excel calculate the filter again. Excel calls this feature *Reapply*. There are several ways you can reapply a filter:

- On the Data tab, select the Reapply icon.

- On the Home tab, select Sort & Filter, Reapply.

- Right-click a cell and then select Filter, Reapply.

Resizing the Filter Drop-Down

The filter drop-down menu always starts fairly small. If you have a long list of items, you might want the drop-down menu to be larger. To do this, hover your mouse over the three dots in the lower-right corner of the drop-down menu. When the mouse pointer changes to a two-headed diagonal arrow, click and drag down or to the right.

Filtering by Selection—Hard Way

You can filter without using the filter drop-down menus. Microsoft Access has offered a Filter by Selection icon in the toolbar for more than a decade. Excel includes this functionality, but it is hidden where most people will never find it.

To access the Filter by Selection feature, right-click any cell and then select Filter from the context menu. You then have an opportunity to filter based on the cell's value, color, font color, or icon, as shown in Figure 14.18.

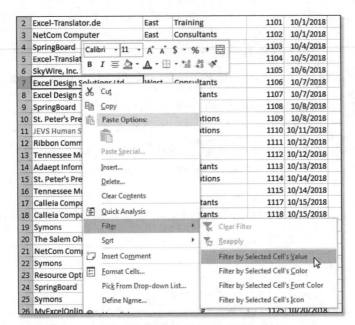

Figure 14.18   Although it is hidden, the Filter by Selection command provides a quick way to see all the other rows that match a single cell.

The Filter by Selection feature works even if the filter drop-down menus have not been activated previously. Using this feature turns on the filter drop-down menus for the data set.

It would be helpful if you could use this feature to select multiple values, such as selecting a cell that says East and then Ctrl+clicking a cell for West. You might think that filtering by selection would filter to both East and West, but that does not work in Excel 2019.

Filtering by Selection—Easy Way

The fast way to filter by selection is to add the AutoFilter icon to the Quick Access Toolbar.

To get one-click access to Filter by Selection, follow these steps:

1. Right-click the Quick Access Toolbar and select Customize Quick Access Toolbar.

2. In the Choose Commands From Drop-Down menu, select Commands Not In The Ribbon.

3. In the left list box, browse to and select AutoFilter, as shown in Figure 14.19. Click the Add button.

Figure 14.19 The icon labeled "AutoFilter" actually is Filter By Selection.

4. Click OK to close the Excel Options dialog box.

To use Filter by Selection, select a value in one of the data rows. Click the AutoFilter icon in the Quick Access Toolbar. If the data set did not previously have the filter drop-down menus, Excel turns on the Filter feature and filters the data set based on the value in the active cell.

Filter by Selection is additive, which means you can choose another value in another column and click the AutoFilter icon to filter the data set further.

In Figure 14.20, the data set is filtered to show Central region invoices for the Consultants market. This was accomplished in four mouse clicks:

1. Select a cell that contains Central, such as B4.

2. Click the AutoFilter icon in the Quick Access Toolbar.

3. Select Consultants in cell C17.

4. Click the AutoFilter icon.

CHAPTER 14

Figure 14.20   Filter by Selection is used twice to filter based on column C and then on column B.

Filtering by Color or Icon

The improved Conditional Formatting commands give you many ways to change the color of a cell. Filter by Color is a great way to find all of the records that match a color applied either through conditional formatting or the fill color or font color drop-down menu menus.

Imagine that you are tracking numerous projects in Excel. You manually highlight certain projects in red if you are missing key elements of the project information. You can use Filter by Color to show only the rows that have a red fill.

Filter by Color works for the cell color, font color, or the icon in the cell.

As shown in Figure 14.21, the Filter by Color fly-out menu offers to filter based on fill color, font color, or icon. Note that the sections of the fly-out menu appear only if you have used color or icons in the range. If all your cells contain black text, Filter by Font Color will not appear in the fly-out menu. If your range contains all black text on a white background, without icons, the Filter by Color menu will be disabled.

Figure 14.21   The Filter by Color fly-out menu offers to filter by icon, cell color, or font color.

Handling Date Filters

The filter drop-down menu for date columns automatically groups the dates into hierarchical groups.

In Figure 14.22, the underlying data contains daily dates. However, the default drop-down menu shows options for the years found in the data set.

Figure 14.22   Excel automatically groups dates up to years in the filter drop-down menu.

Click the plus sign next to any year to expand the list to show months within the year, as shown in Figure 14.23. You can then click the plus sign next to a month to see the days within the month.

TROUBLESHOOTING

You might hate the grouping of dates in the Filter menu. If your data set includes only a few scattered dates such as February 2, May 30, July 4, and September 4, wading through the grouped filters is annoying.

You can turn off the hierarchical grouping of dates in the filter drop-down menu. To do so, click the File menu and choose Options. In the Options dialog box, choose the Advanced category. Scroll down to the section for Display For This Workbook. Next, select a workbook, and then clear the check box for Group Dates in the AutoFilter Menu.

Figure 14.23   Expand the hierarchical view to see months within the years.

Using Special Filters for Dates, Text, and Numbers

Excel examines the data in a column to determine whether it contains mostly text, dates, or numeric values. Depending on which data type appears most often, Excel offers special filters designed for that data type.

For columns that contain mostly text, Excel offers the filters Begins With, Ends With, Contains, Does Not Contain, Equals, and Does Not Equal. You are allowed to use wildcard characters in these filters. For example, you can use an asterisk (*) for any number of characters or a question mark (?) to represent a single character. The Contains filter seems obsolete with the Search box in the Filter drop-down menu.

For columns with mostly numeric values, the special filters include Top 10, Above Average, Below Average, Between, Less Than, Greater Than, Does Not Equal, and Equals. For the Top 10 filter, you can specify the top or bottom values. You can also specify whether the results are based on the top 10 items or the top 10 percent of items. Finally, you can change the number 10 to any number. Thus, you can use this filter to show the bottom 20 percent or the top three items.

For columns with mostly dates, the special filters include Before, After, or Between a particular day, week, month, quarter, or year. The special filters also include Year To Date or All Dates In The Period, as shown in Figure 14.24.

Figure 14.24   Excel offers myriad date filters.

All the special filters offer a pathway to the legacy Custom AutoFilter dialog box. This filter enables you to combine two conditions by using an AND or OR clause. This feature solves your problems some of the time, but there are still complex conditions that require you to resort to using the advanced filter.

The Custom AutoFilter dialog box was nominally improved in Excel 2007. For example, a calendar control was added that can be used to select dates when you are filtering a date column. You can use the dialog box shown in Figure 14.25 to select dates that are within a certain range of dates.

CHAPTER 14

Figure 14.25   The custom filters allow you to build simple combinations of two conditions for filtering.

Totaling Filtered Results

After you have applied a filter, you might want to sum the visible cells in a column. This task is straightforward in Excel 2019. Select the first visible blank cell below the column and click the AutoSum button. Instead of inserting a SUM function, Excel inserts a SUBTOTAL function. The =SUBTOTAL(9,F2:F1874) function sums the visible rows from a data set that has been filtered. You can edit the first argument in the SUBTOTAL function to find the count, average, minimum, and maximum, as well as other calculations on the visible rows.

Formatting and Copying Filtered Results

When you apply a filter, some rows are hidden and other rows are visible. The rows hidden by the filter are different from rows hidden with the Hide Rows command. Rows that are hidden using Hide Rows are often included when you copy or format a range that contains those rows. When you have manually hidden rows, you must use Alt+; to narrow your selection to only the visible rows. It is not necessary to use Alt+; when the rows have been hidden by the Filter command. Alt+; is the shortcut for Go To Special, Visible Cells Only.

You can use this behavior to format or copy rows matching certain criteria. If you want to highlight all rows matching a criterion by changing the background color of the cell, follow these steps:

1. Select one cell in the unfiltered data set that matches the proper criterion.

2. Click the Filter by Selection icon in the Quick Access Toolbar. If you don't have this icon available, refer to Figure 14.17 and follow the instructions there.

3. Select the first visible cell below the headings.

4. Press Ctrl+Shift+Down Arrow and then Ctrl+Shift+Right Arrow to select all the cells below the heading.

5. Format the cells as desired.

6. Select Data, Filter to remove the filter and show all rows. You will find that only the rows that were visible during the filter have the new formatting.

Using the Advanced Filter Command

The Advanced Filter command is still present in Excel 2019. Microsoft should give this feature a new name because it is remarkably powerful and does much more than filtering. However, the Advanced Filter command is admittedly one of the more confusing commands in Excel. This is particularly true because you can use the Advanced Filter in eight ways, and each method requires slightly different steps.

> **TIP**
>
> **You can only copy filtered results to the active sheet, not to a new sheet. However, if you start on a blank sheet, you can specify that you want to filter data from another sheet and pull that data to the active sheet.**

The eight ways to use the Advanced Filter are derived by multiplying $2 \times 2 \times 2$. There are three options in the Advanced Filter dialog box, and depending on your choices for those three options, you can have possible combinations:

- You can choose either Filter In Place or Copy To A New Location.

- You can choose to filter with a criteria range or without any criteria.

- You can choose to return all matching values or only the unique values.

In reality, there are more than eight ways to use Advanced Filter. If you choose to copy records to a new location, you can either copy all the input columns in order or specify a subset of columns and/or a new sequence of columns.

You can build a simple filter for one column. You can combine any number of filters for multiple columns. You can build incredibly complex filters, using any formula imaginable. Alternatively, you can use no criteria at all. Using no criteria is common when you are using Advanced Filter to extract unique values or when you want to use Advanced Filter to reorder the sequence of columns.

To use Advanced Filter on a data set, follow these steps:

1. If you are using criteria, copy one or more headings from your data set to a blank section of the worksheet. Under each heading, list the value(s) you want to be included.

2. If you are using an output range and want to reorder the columns or include a subset of the columns, copy the headings into the appropriate order in a blank section of the worksheet. If you want all the original columns in their original sequence, the output range can be any blank cell.

3. Select a cell in your data range.

4. Select Data, Sort & Filter, Advanced.

5. Verify that the list range contains your original data set.

6. If you are using criteria, enter the criteria range.

7. If you want to copy the matching records to a new location, select Copy To Another Location. This enables the reference box for Copy To. Fill in the output range.

8. If you want the output range to contain only unique values, click Unique Records Only. If your output range contains a single field, a list of the values in that field is displayed that match the criteria. If your output range contains two or more fields, every unique combination of those two or more fields is displayed.

9. Click OK to perform the filter.

Excel in Practice: Using Formulas for Advanced Filter Criteria

Sometimes you might need to filter based on criteria that are too complex for any of Excel's built-in rules. For example, suppose you want to create an advanced filter to find all records in which one of 30 customers bought one of 20 products. The necessary criteria range would cover 601 rows and would take hours to build.

There is one obscure syntax of advanced filter criteria that enables you to filter to anything for which you can build a TRUE/FALSE formula. Use the following specifics to set up a filter that contains formulas:

1. This criteria range is two cells tall by one column wide.

2. The top cell is blank or contains text not found in the data range headers.

3. The second cell contains a formula that should have relative references pointing to the first data row of the input range.

4. The formula should evaluate to TRUE or FALSE. For example, to select all the West records where the invoice is above average for the West, use this:

```
=AND(B2="West",F2>AVERAGEIF($B$2:$B$1874,"West",$F$2:$F$1874))
```

When Excel sees that the first row of the criteria range is blank, it takes the formula in the second cell and applies it to all rows in the range. Any rows that would evaluate to TRUE are returned in the filter.

Advanced Filter Criteria

Even though it is not obvious from the instructions for using Advanced Filter, you can build advanced filter criteria that can ask for a range of values. For example, if you are using an advanced filter, it is unlikely you will want to filter to the customer with exactly $7,553 in sales. However, you might want to filter to invoices that are more than $5,000 in sales. To set up this criterion, type **Sales** into cell K1. In cell K2, type **>5000**. When you issue the Advanced Filter, Excel returns all invoices more than $5,000.

In Figure 14.26, the Advanced Filter operation extracts all East region sales in the Vehicles market. Three columns from the matching records will be copied to Columns L:N.

Figure 14.26   Advanced Filter is a powerful tool that can do much more than filter.

Note that criteria values that are in the same row are treated as if they were joined by AND. Because East and Vehicles are both in row 2, a record must be from the East region and have a market of vehicles to appear in the data set. If you move Vehicles from row 2 to row 3 and expand the criteria range to I1:J3, the two values are joined with an OR. All records that are from either the East region or the Vehicles market appear in the results.

Using Remove Duplicates to Find Unique Values

By its nature, transactional data has a lot of detail. You end up with transactional data in Excel because it is often the easiest to obtain. As you start to analyze transactional data, you often want to find the number of customers, number of products, or number of something in the data set.

For example, transactional data can tell you that there were 34 invoices issued last month, but that doesn't mean there were 34 customers. Some of those customers might have made repeat purchases. In this case, 20 customers could account for 34 invoices.

To find the number of unique customers, you need a way to eliminate the duplicate records in a data set. In legacy versions of Excel, this usually meant using Advanced Filter, some IF functions, or possibly a pivot table. However, in Excel 2019, the Remove Duplicates data tool makes it easier to remove duplicates.

The first thing to realize is that the Remove Duplicates tool is destructive because it really removes the duplicate records. If you want to keep the original transactional data intact, you should either make a copy of the customer column in a blank section of the workbook or make a backup copy of the workbook.

To find the unique values in a data set, follow these steps:

1. Copy the data set to a blank section of the worksheet. Make sure to leave a blank column between your real data and the copy of the data.

2. Select a single cell within the data set.

3. On the Data tab, in the Data Tools group, select Remove Duplicates. Excel expands the selection to include the entire range. In the Remove Duplicates dialog box, Excel predicts if your data has headers. This dialog box also shows a list of all the fields in the data set.

4. Because you are interested in a unique list of customers, click the Unselect All button to clear all check boxes, and then select the Customer field, as shown in Figure 14.27.

Figure 14.27   Choose which columns should be considered when analyzing duplicates.

5. Click OK to perform the action. Excel tells you how many duplicate values were found and removed. It also tells you how many unique values remain.

TIP

Remember that the Remove Duplicates command is destructive. For this reason, some-times you might want to find the duplicates and choose which version to remove. In that case, you Select Home, Conditional Formatting, Highlight Cell Rules, Duplicate Values.

Other times, you might want to send a copy of the unique values to a new location. In this case, use the Advanced Filter command discussed earlier in this chapter.

Finally, you might want to remove duplicates but add up the sales for all the removed records and then add them to the Customer field. Although this can be achieved with pivot tables, it can also be achieved using the Consolidate feature, which is discussed in the next section.

Combining Duplicates and Adding Values

In columns A:D of Figure 14.28, each customer appears one or more times in the list with sales, cost, and profit values. In addition to finding a unique list of customers, you would like to know the total sales and profit for each customer. You can use a pivot table to find the total sales for each customer. Alternatively, you can use the data tools to consolidate the table down to one record per customer.

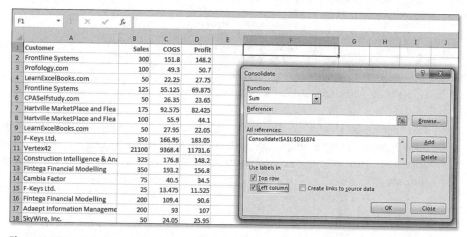

Figure 14.28   Start at a blank section of the workbook before invoking the Consolidate feature.

To use the Consolidate feature to total sales from all the records for that customer, follow these steps:

1. Instead of preselecting the data, move the cell pointer to a blank section of the worksheet.

2. Select Data, Data Tools, Consolidate. The Consolidate dialog box appears.

3. In the Consolidate dialog box, enter the reference to your data in the Reference box. The data will be combined based on the field in the left column of the range. If you have multiple lists of customers, you can click the Add button and enter additional ranges.

4. Make sure to select the Top Row and Left Column check boxes in the Use Labels In section.

5. Click OK.

Excel creates a new table. Each customer appears in the table just once. The sales associated with all the records of the customer appear in the new total, as shown in Figure 14.29.

F	G	H	I
	Sales	COGS	Profit
Frontline Systems	532675	263796.6	268878.4
Profology.com	946850	470308.7	476541.3
LearnExcelBooks.com	1228675	629414.6	599260.5
CPASelfstudy.com	2750	1376.4	1373.6
Hartville MarketPlace and Flea	658125	334804.7	323320.3
F-Keys Ltd.	702625	337767.2	364857.9
Vertex42	1124375	559745.1	564629.9
Construction Intelligence & Ana	17875	8945.95	8929.05
Fintega Financial Modelling	1265625	647611.6	618013.4
Cambia Factor	1233625	620172.9	613452.2
Adaept Information Manageme	620000	319127.8	300872.2
SkyWire, Inc.	609125	309001.4	300123.6
Data2Impact	648125	307050.8	341074.2
MyOnlineTrainingHub.com	755000	367083.2	387916.8
Surten Excel	33000	16735.3	16264.7
Wag More Dog Store, San Antor	17875	8984.95	8890.05

Figure 14.29 Excel consolidates all data by customer.

Two annoyances remain with this command. First, the heading for the leftmost column is never filled in. Second, the command leaves the results in the same sequence in which they originally appeared. In this example, you will probably want to add the heading above cell F2 and sort the data.

CHAPTER 15

Using Pivot Tables to Analyze Data

A pivot table enables you to summarize thousands or millions of records of data to a one-page summary in just a few clicks.

Suppose you have 400,000 records of transactional data. It is easy for some people to look at this and figure out that it represents $x million. But to learn some things about the data, you need to do some more analysis to spot trends in the data. A pivot table enables you to analyze trends in data without having to worry about formulas.

By using a pivot table, it is possible to create many views of your data, including the following:

- Breakdown of sales by product

- Sales by month, this year versus last year

- Percentage of sales by customer

- Customers who bought XYZ product in the East region

- Sales by product by month

- Top five customers with products

Of course, these are just examples. You can use pivot tables to slice and dice your data in almost any imaginable way.

Pivot tables were introduced in Excel 95 and have been evolving ever since:

- Excel 2019 introduces Pivot Table Defaults. A huge number of default settings in pivot tables are annoying. You can now fix these settings once, and all future pivot tables will have your favorite settings.

- Excel 2019 gives you the ability to turn off automatic date grouping, which was introduced in Excel 2016.

- Office 365 in 2018 has a new Artificial Intelligence feature (called either Insights or Ideas depending on your version of Office 365). Excel will use artificial intelligence to analyze your data and suggest up to 30 pivot tables or pivot charts.

- Excel 2016 includes a feature to automatically roll date fields up to months, quarters, and years.

- The add-in formerly known as Power Map is now built in to Excel as 3D Maps.

- Excel 2013 added a new entry point for pivot tables called Recommended Pivot Tables. This feature shows you various thumbnails of pivot tables before you begin creating one.

- Excel 2013 added the capability to create a data model from several different tables. You can create a relationship between tables without using VLOOKUPs and base pivot tables on the model.

- Timelines are a visual date filter introduced in Excel 2013. They join slicers, the visual filter introduced in Excel 2010. The best feature of timelines and slicers is the capability for them to drive multiple pivot tables built from the same data set.

- Power Pivot is a powerful add-in for Excel 2016 that enhances pivot tables. If you are using Excel 2016 Pro Plus or Office 365 Pro Plus or later, you have access to this add-in. Power Pivot enhances the ability to build multi-table models and provides key performance indicators (KPIs) and the DAX formula language.

- Excel 2010 introduced new calculations such as Rank, Percent Of Parent, and Running Percentage Of Total.

- Excel 2010 introduced the option to replace blanks in the outer row fields by repeating item labels from above.

- Excel 2007 simplified the pivot table interface and added new filters.

Creating Your First Pivot Table

Pivot tables are best created from transactional data—that is, raw data files directly from your company's IT department.

To create the best pivot tables, make sure your data follows these rules:

- Ensure each column has a one-cell heading. Keep the headings unique; don't use the same heading for two columns. If you need your headings to appear on two rows, type the first word, press Alt+Enter, and then type the second word.

- If a column should contain numeric data, don't allow blank cells in the column. Use zeros instead of blanks.

- Do not use blank rows or blank columns.

- If totals are embedded in your report, remove them.

- The workbook should not be in Compatibility mode. Many pivot table features from Excel 2007–2019 are disabled if the workbook is in Compatibility mode.

- If you add new data to the bottom of your data set each month, you should strongly consider converting your data set to a table using Ctrl+T. Pivot tables created from tables automatically pick up new rows pasted to the bottom of the tables after a refresh.

- If your data has months spread across many columns, go back to the source software program to see if a different view of the data is available with months going down the rows.

For most of this chapter, the pivot tables shown in the figures are from the data set in Figure 15.1. This data set has two years of transactional data. There is a single text column of Customer. There is a single date column. Numeric columns include Quantity, Revenue, COGS, and Profit.

	A	B	C	D	E	F	G	H
1	Region	Product	Date	Customer	Quantity	Revenue	COGS	Profit
2	East	XYZ	1/1/2024	MyOnlineTrainingHub.com	954	22810	10213	12597
3	Central	DEF	1/2/2024	WM Squared Inc.	124	2257	998	1259
4	East	XYZ	1/4/2024	SlinkyRN Excel Instruction	425	9152	4083	5069
5	East	DEF	1/4/2024	MrExcel.com	773	18552	7883	10669
6	East	ABC	1/7/2024	DataSolverz.com	401	8456	3389	5067
7	East	DEF	1/7/2024	Excel Design Solutions Ltd	1035	21730	9839	11891

Figure 15.1 This data set follows the rules of a good pivot table source.

Browsing Ten "Recommended" Pivot Tables

You can save a few mouse clicks by starting with the Recommended PivotTable dialog box.

Select a single cell in your data. On the Insert tab, choose Recommended PivotTables. Excel displays a dialog box with ten pivot tables down the left side. Click each pivot table to see a preview of the pivot table in the dialog box (see Figure 15.2). When you find one that is close, click OK to create that pivot table on a new worksheet.

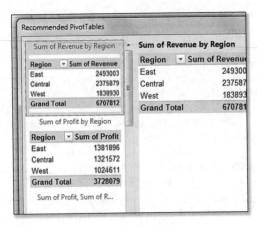

Figure 15.2   Excel uses heuristics to guess at ten pivot tables that make sense.

Is it worthwhile to use the Recommended PivotTables dialog box? The ten suggestions are not perfect, but many near the top of the list are a great starting point. Provided that you want your pivot table to appear on a new worksheet, and provided that you are building a pivot table from a single table, then you lose nothing by using Insert, Recommended PivotTable, OK instead of Insert, PivotTable, OK. At the very least, you start with two common fields in your pivot table and are usually two mouse clicks closer to being finished with the pivot table.

> ### NOTE
>
> The Excel 2013–era Recommended Pivot Table feature morphed into a much better artificial intelligence tool in 2018. The tool was initially called Insights but then changed to Ideas. The feature sends 250,000 cells to an artificial intelligence server and returns more than 30 recommended pivot charts. Unfortunately, this feature is exclusive to Office 365 and will not be available in Excel 2019.

The rules for choosing the recommended pivot tables are fairly complex. I believe some of the rules for deciding on the top 10 pivot tables are as follows:

- If you have a numeric field with a label of Revenue, that field is always given priority and appears in the first few pivot tables.

- If you use Sales instead of Revenue, Excel looks for a field called Profit.

- If Excel does not recognize any of the numeric field headings, it looks for the field with the largest total or the field on the right for the first few recommended pivot tables.

- Excel analyzes the text fields to determine the number of unique values for each field. The two fields with the fewest unique values are often suggested as the row fields in the first four pivot tables.

- Three of the ten pivot tables offer multiple numeric fields going across the report. At least one of those offers a Count or Average of one field.

- The final three pivot tables might contain an attempt to offer a cross-tab report, with fields in Row and Column, or with two fields in the row field. This logic is the weakest. In 50+ experiments, the logical combinations of Customers and Products or Region and Product only appeared in 6% of the trials. Hopefully, the Excel team can refine this logic over time.

Starting with a Blank Pivot Table

The traditional method for creating a pivot table is to create a blank one. Choose one cell in your data. Select PivotTable from the Insert tab. Excel displays the Create PivotTable dialog box, as shown in Figure 15.3.

Figure 15.3   Using the Create PivotTable dialog box, you can choose where to place the pivot table.

This dialog box box confirms the range of your data. Provided you have no blank rows or blank columns, Excel normally gets this right. In Figure 15.3, the underlying data has been made into a table using Ctrl+T and renamed as Data. You could instead choose to use an external data source.

Using the Create PivotTable dialog box, you have the choice of creating the pivot table on a new blank worksheet or in an existing location. You might decide to put the pivot table in J2 on this worksheet, or next to another existing pivot table or pivot chart if you plan on building a dash-board of several pivot tables.

You can build a pivot table from a relational model by checking the Add This Data to the Data Model check box. For details on building a pivot table from two or more tables, see Chapter 17, "Mashing Up Data with Power Pivot."

Adding Fields to Your Pivot Table Using the Field List

If you started with a blank pivot table, you see a PivotTable Fields panel that looks like Figure 15.4. The graphic shown in columns A:C is a placeholder to indicate where the pivot table will appear after you choose some fields. The PivotTable Fields area has a list of fields from your original data set at the top and four drop zones at the bottom. To build your report, you add fields to the drop zones at the bottom.

Figure 15.4   A blank pivot table and the PivotTable Fields list.

NOTE

The field list is generally docked to the right side of the Excel window. The figures in this book show the field list as undocked. To undock the field list, drag the title bar away from the edge of the window. It is hard to re-dock the field list. You must grab the left side of the title bar and drag the field list more than 50 percent off the right side of the Excel window.

If you built your pivot table using the Recommended PivotTables dialog box, you already see a few fields in the drop zones and a few fields in the report. Figure 15.5 shows the initial pivot table and field list when you choose Sum Of Revenue By Region.

Figure 15.5   If you choose a recommended pivot table, the first few fields are added to the pivot table.

Changing the Pivot Table Report by Using the Field List

If you are starting with Figure 15.4, check the Region, Product, and Revenue fields. If you are starting with Figure 15.5, check the Product field.

When you check a text or date field, that field automatically moves to the Rows drop zone in the PivotTable Fields list. When you check a numeric field, that field moves to the Values drop zone and is changed to Sum of *Field*.

By choosing Region, Product, and Revenue, you see Sum of Revenue by region and product, as shown in Figure 15.6.

Figure 15.6   Check fields in the top of the field list to build this report.

You can further customize the pivot table by moving fields around in the drop zones. For example, drag the Region field so it is below the Product field in the Rows drop zone. The report updates to show Region within Product, as shown in Figure 15.7.

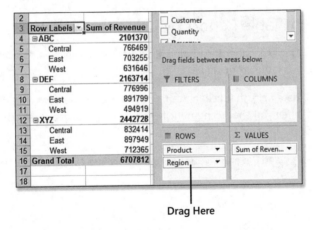

Drag Here

Figure 15.7   Drag the Region field to appear after the Product field in the Rows drop zone to change the report.

Drag the Region field from the Rows drop zone to the Columns drop zone, and you have a cross-tab report, as shown in Figure 15.8.

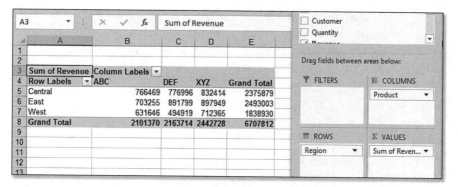

Figure 15.8   Pivot the Region field to the columns of the report.

Dealing with the Compact Layout

If you've been using pivot tables for many versions of Excel, you have to wonder about the bizarre layout of the pivot table shown previously in Figure 15.6. The totals appear at the top of each group instead of at the bottom. Two fields—Region and Product—appear in column A. Collapse buttons appear next to the regions.

This is a report layout called Compact Form. Introduced in Excel 2007, it is beautiful if you plan to present your pivot table in an interactive touch-screen kiosk complete with slicers. However, if you plan to reuse the results of the pivot table, the Compact Form is horrible. Every pivot table you create in the Excel interface starts with Compact Form. Here is how to go back to the Tabular Form layout:

1. Make sure that the active cell is inside the pivot table.

2. Go to the Design tab in the ribbon. Open the Report Layout drop-down. Select Show in Tabular Form. As shown in Figure 15.9, the totals move back to the bottom of each region. Also, Product moves to column B.

Figure 15.9   Change from Compact Form to Tabular Form to put each field in a new column.

3. Open the Report Layout drop-down and select Repeat All Item Labels. This eliminates the blanks in column A of the pivot table, as shown in Figure 15.10. This is a feature that has been badly needed in Excel for 15 years. It was finally added to Excel 2010.

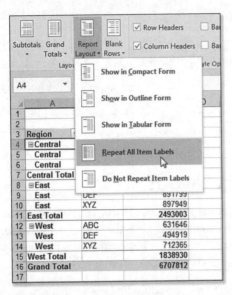

Figure 15.10   Using Repeat All Item Labels fills in blanks in the row area.

Rearranging a Pivot Table

The drop zone sections of the PivotTable Fields list box are as follows:

- **Filter**—You use this section to limit the report to only certain criteria. This section is virtually replaced by the slicer feature.

  ➤ *To learn more about filtering pivot tables, **see** Chapter 16, "Using Slicers and Filtering a Pivot Table."*

- **Rows**—This section is for fields that appear on the left side of the table. By default, all text fields move here when you select the check boxes in the top of the field list.

- **Columns**—This section is for fields that stretch along the top rows of columns of your table. Old database geeks refer to this as a *crosstab report*.

- **Values**—This section is for all the numeric fields that are summarized in the table. By default, most fields are automatically summed, but you can change the default calculation to an average, minimum, maximum, or other calculation.

You can add fields to a drop zone by dragging from the top of the PivotTable Fields list to a drop zone or by dragging from one drop zone to another. To remove a field from a drop zone, drag the field from the drop zone to outside of the PivotTable Fields list.

Finishing Touches: Numeric Formatting and Removing Blanks

After you arrange your data in the report, you want to consider formatting the numeric fields. For example, the pivot table in Figure 15.11 has Customer and Product in the Rows drop zone, Region in Columns, and Revenue in Values. It would be helpful if the numbers were formatted with commas as thousands separators. Also, consider changing the words "Sum of Revenue" to something less awkward, such as "Total Revenue" or even "Revenue."

▲	A	B	C	D	E	F
1						
2						
3	Sum of Revenue		Region ▼			
4	Customer	▼ Product ▼	Central	East	West	Grand Total
5	⊟ data2impact	ABC		5532		5532
6	data2impact	DEF	16784			16784
7	data2impact	XYZ		18264	16936	35200
8	data2impact Total		16784	23796	16936	57516
9	⊟ Data Solverz.com	ABC	124738	69040	87189	280967
10	Data Solverz.com	DEF	47373	132844	53218	233435
11	Data Solverz.com	XYZ	121922	58279	55560	235761
12	Data Solverz.com Total		294033	260163	195967	750163
13	⊟ Excel Design Solutions Ltd	ABC			13853	13853
14	Excel Design Solutions Ltd	DEF	4754	21730		26484
15	Excel Design Solutions Ltd	XYZ			19544	19544

Figure 15.11   You should add numeric formatting to this pivot table.

Follow these steps to apply a numeric format to the Revenue field:

1. Select cell A3 with the Sum Of Revenue heading. Type **Revenue** followed by a space and press Enter.

2. Right-click any number in the pivot table and choose Number Format. The familiar Format Cells dialog box appears.

3. Select the Number category. Select 0 decimal places, and add a thousands separator. Click OK to close the Format Cells dialog box. Click OK to close the Value Field Settings dialog box.

4. Right-click any cell in the pivot table and choose PivotTable Options.

5. On the Layout & Format tab of the PivotTable Options dialog box, type **0** next to For Empty Cells Show.

Figure 15.12 shows the new number format applied to the pivot table, along with the empty cells replaced with zero.

⊿	A	B	C	D	E	F
1						
2						
3	Revenue		Region ▼			
4	Customer ▼	Product ▼	East	Central	West	Grand Total
5	⊟ data2impact	ABC	5,532	0	0	5,532
6	data2impact	DEF	0	16,784	0	16,784
7	data2impact	XYZ	18,264	0	16,936	35,200
8	data2impact Total		23,796	16,784	16,936	57,516
9	⊟ Data Solverz.com	ABC	69,040	124,738	87,189	280,967
10	Data Solverz.com	DEF	132,844	47,373	53,218	233,435
11	Data Solverz.com	XYZ	58,279	121,922	55,560	235,761
12	Data Solverz.com Total		260,163	294,033	195,967	750,163

Figure 15.12   The finished pivot table has better numeric formatting.

Inside OUT

Sometimes, you might need to format a single cell in a pivot table.

For example, your manager might need the sales figures for bananas in the Central region to always be shown in blue.

A new feature appeared in Office 365 during 2018. Right-click the desired cell and choose Format Cells. The formatting will be applied in a new rule for the specific cell (in this example, the cell containing Central region banana sales). This formatting is sticky; if you rearrange the pivot table, the formatting will move to the new location, meaning if you move the location for Central region banana sales, the formatting moves with it. I can't imagine the overhead required for this simple feature.

In this example, you will notice if you remove "Banana" or "Central" from the pivot table via a slicer or a filter, the formatting will return when the item returns. However, if you completely remove "Region" or "Product" from the pivot table, the formatting is lost.

Three Things You **Must** Know When Using Pivot Tables

Pivot tables are the greatest invention in spreadsheets. However, you must understand the following three issues, presented in order of importance.

Your Pivot Table Is in Manual Calculation Mode Until You Click Refresh!

Most people are shocked to learn that changes to underlying data do not appear in a pivot table. After all, you change a cell in Excel, and all the formulas derived from the cell automatically change. You would think that the same should hold true for pivot tables, but it does not. Pivot tables are fast because the original data from the worksheet is loaded into a pivot cache in memory. Until you click the Refresh icon on the Analyze ribbon, Excel does not pick up the changes to the underlying data.

If You Click Outside the Pivot Table, All the Pivot Table Tools Disappear

If your field list disappeared and the Options and Design tabs are missing, it is likely that you clicked outside of the pivot table.

I've argued with Microsoft that because nothing is on the worksheet other than the pivot table, I am still looking at the pivot table even when I click outside of the pivot table. I continue to lose this argument, however. If the field list disappears and the tabs are gone, click back inside your pivot table.

You Cannot Change, Move a Part of, or Insert Cells in a Pivot Table

Many times, pivot tables get you very close to the final report you want, and you just want to insert a row or move one bit of the table. You cannot do this. If you try, you will be greeted with the ubiquitous message: "We can't make this change for the selected cells because it will affect a PivotTable." This is a fair limitation. After all, Excel needs to figure out how to redraw the table when you move something in the field list.

The solution is to copy the entire pivot table and then use Paste Values to convert the report to regular Excel data. You can either put this on a new worksheet or paste the entire table back over itself. If you go to a new worksheet, you can continue to modify the original pivot table. If you paste values over the original worksheet, the pivot table converts to a range, and you cannot pivot it further.

Calculating and Roll-Ups with Pivot Tables

Pivot tables offer many more calculation options than those shown so far in this chapter. One of the most amazing features is the capability to roll daily dates up to months, quarters, and years.

In Excel 2016, Excel could automatically create roll-ups from daily dates. If you have a data source with one or more years of dates, simply dragging the date field to the pivot table would create new virtual fields for Years, Quarters, and Months.

This new feature was not predictable and confusing. In Excel 2019, the feature is turned off by default, and you must go to File, Options, Data, and uncheck Disable Automatic Date Grouping Of Date/Time Columns In PivotTables to use the feature.

The example in the next section assumes the AutoGroup feature is disabled.

Grouping Daily Dates to Months, Quarters, and Years

Good pivot tables start with good transactional data. Invariably, that transactional data is stored with daily dates instead of monthly summaries.

To produce a summary by month, quarter, and year, follow these steps:

1. Start with data that contains daily dates. Build a pivot table with daily dates going down the row field, Region in the columns, and Sum Of Revenue in the value area.

2. Select one cell that contains a date. On the Analysis tab, choose Group Field.

3. In the Grouping dialog box, choose Months, Quarters, and Years. Click OK.

4. Figure 5.13 shows a pivot table with daily dates rolled up to months, quarters, and years.

Figure 15.13 Roll your daily dates up to months, quarters, and/or years.

For an interesting alternative to the report in Figure 15.13, follow these steps:

1. Uncheck the Region and Quarter fields to remove them from the report.

2. Drag the Years field from the Rows area to the Columns area.

You now have a pivot table that provides totals by month and quarter and compares years going across the report (see Figure 15.14). Notice that your pivot table field list includes three fields related to dates: The years and quarters fields are virtual fields. The original Date field includes the months. This was a brilliant design decision on Microsoft's part because it allows years and months to be pivoted to different sections of the pivot table.

	A	B	C	D	E
1					
2					
3	Revenue	Years			
4	Date	2024	2025	Grand Total	
5	Jan	273,222	264,691	537,913	
6	Feb	312,065	236,565	548,630	
7	Mar	275,166	216,561	491,727	
8	Apr	271,270	292,003	563,273	
9	May	332,076	287,443	619,519	
10	Jun	187,529	241,883	429,412	
11	Jul	363,807	295,851	659,658	
12	Aug	311,745	286,891	598,636	
13	Sep	261,306	217,076	478,382	
14	Oct	299,380	308,986	608,366	
15	Nov	251,216	301,880	553,096	
16	Dec	279,016	340,184	619,200	
17	Grand Total	3,417,798	3,290,014	6,707,812	
18					

Figure 15.14   Pivot years to the column area to show year over year.

Adding Calculations Outside the Pivot Table

Figure 15.15 shows % Growth instead of Grand Total in column D. However, after you group the dates in the pivot table, you are prevented from adding a calculated item inside the pivot table, so you must turn back to regular Excel to provide the % Growth column.

D5				f_x	=C5/B5-1

	A	B	C	D	E
1					
2					
3	Revenue	Years			
4	Date	2024	2025	% Growth	
5	Jan	273,222	264,691	-3.1%	
6	Feb	312,065	236,565	-24.2%	
7	Mar	275,166	216,561	-21.3%	
8	Apr	271,270	292,003	7.6%	
9	May	332,076	287,443	-13.4%	
10	Jun	187,529	241,883	29.0%	
11	Jul	363,807	295,851	-18.7%	
12	Aug	311,745	286,891	-8.0%	
13	Sep	261,306	217,076	-16.9%	
14	Oct	299,380	308,986	3.2%	
15	Nov	251,216	301,880	20.2%	
16	Dec	279,016	340,184	21.9%	
17	Grand Total	3,417,798	3,290,014	-3.7%	
18					

Figure 15.15   The % Growth column is a regular formula outside the pivot table, formatted to look like it is part of the pivot table.

CHAPTER 15

However, it is not simple for Excel to create that column. In particular, step 3 trips up most people. Follow these steps:

1. Right-click the Grand Total in D4 and choose Remove Grand Total.

2. Type a heading of % Growth in D5

3. In cell D5, type =**C5/B5-1**. You really have to type this formula! Do not touch the mouse or the arrow keys while you are building the formula, or you will be stung by the GetPivotData bug.

4. Format cell D5 as a percentage with one decimal place.

5. Double-click the fill handle in D5 to copy the formula down to all rows.

Changing the Calculation of a Field

By default, a numeric column will be added to the pivot table with a default calculation of Sum. Excel offers ten other calculations, such as Average, Count, Max, and Min.

For this section, the figures start with a completely new pivot table. You can follow along with these steps:

1. Delete the worksheet that contains the pivot table from the previous examples. This clears the pivot cache from memory.

2. Select one cell on the Data worksheet.

3. Choose Insert, PivotTable.

4. Add a check next to the Region, Product, and Revenue fields.

5. Drag Revenue to the Values area two more times. They will appear in the pivot table as Sum Of Revenue2 and Sum Of Revenue3.

6. On the Design tab, choose Report Layout, Show In Tabular Form.

7. You will have the pivot table shown in Figure 15.16.

	A	B	C	D	E
1					
2					
3	Region ▾	Product ▾	Sum of Revenue	Sum of Revenue2	Sum of Revenue3
4	⊟East	ABC	703255	703255	703255
5	East	DEF	891799	891799	891799
6	East	XYZ	897949	897949	897949
7	East Total		2493003	2493003	2493003
8	⊟Central	ABC	766469	766469	766469
9	Central	DEF	776996	776996	776996
10	Central	XYZ	832414	832414	832414
11	Central Total		2375879	2375879	2375879
12	⊟West	ABC	631646	631646	631646
13	West	DEF	494919	494919	494919
14	West	XYZ	712365	712365	712365
15	West Total		1838930	1838930	1838930
16	Grand Total		6707812	6707812	6707812
17					

Figure 15.16   This new pivot table starts with three numeric columns that default to Sum.

In column D, you would like a count of the number of records. Follow these steps to change column D to a count of the number of records:

1. Double-click the Sum Of Revenue2 heading in D3. This opens the Value Field Settings dialog box.

2. In the Value Field Settings dialog box, choose Count instead of Sum.

3. In the Custom Name field, type **Number of Orders** or any other name that makes sense to you.

4. Click OK. Column D now shows a count of records instead of a sum (see Figure 15.17).

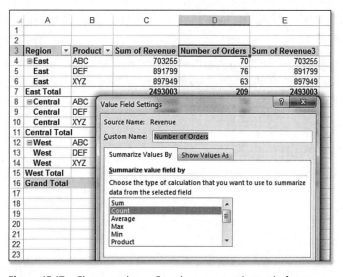

Figure 15.17   Change column C to show a count instead of a sum.

To change column E to show average revenue per order, follow these steps:

1. Double-click the Sum Of Revenue3 heading in E3. Change the calculation to Average.

2. Change the Custom Name field to "Avg Revenue."

3. Click the Number Format button.

4. Choose Currency with two decimal places.

5. Click OK twice to close the Format Cells and the Value Field Settings dialog box boxes. Excel now shows Avg Revenue in column E.

You can use a similar method to change to any of the 11 calculations offered in the Summarize Values By tab.

That's not all—there are more ways to show the values, as discussed in the next section.

Showing Percentage of Total Using Show Value As Settings

In addition to the 11 ways to summarize values, Excel 2019 offers 14 calculation options on the second tab of the Value Field Settings dialog box. To experiment with these 14 calculations, drag the Revenue field to the Values drop zone two more times. Follow these steps:

1. Double-click the heading in F3 to pen the Value Field Settings. Select the second tab in the Value Field Settings dialog box. Choose % Of Column Total from the drop-down. Change the Custom Name to % Of Total. Click OK.

2. Double-click G3, and select the second tab in the Value Field Settings dialog box. Choose % Of Parent Row Total from the drop-down. Change the Custom Name to % Of Parent and click OK.

Figure 15.18 shows the result. In row 4, the $703,255 of revenue in C4 is 10.48% of the grand total revenue. The calculation in G4 shows that the revenue in C4 is 28.21% of the East region revenue shown in C7.

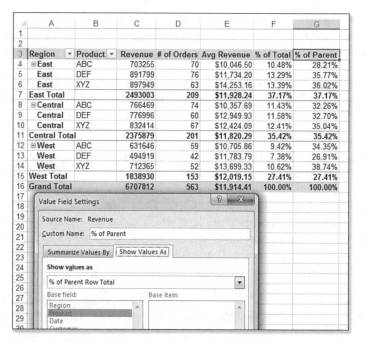

Figure 15.18   Use Show Values As for 14 additional calculations.

Showing Running Totals and Rank

Other options in the Show Values As drop-down include running totals and a ranking. These work best when there is only one field in the row area.

Delete the worksheet that contains the existing pivot table. Build a new pivot table with Customer in the Rows area. Drag Revenue six times to the Values area.

Initially, the customers are sorted alphabetically. Open the Row Labels drop-down in cell A3. Choose More Sort Options. In the Sort (Customer) dialog box, choose Descending (Z to A) By. In the drop-down, choose Sum Of Revenue. Click OK. The pivot table shows the largest customers at the top.

To change the calculation in each column, follow these steps:

1.   Select cell B3, and type the new name, **Revenue**, with a leading space. Choose Currency with 0 decimal places. Click OK.

2.   Double-click cell C3. On the Show Values As tab, choose Running Total In. In the Base Field list, choose Customer. Change the Custom Name to **Accum. Total**. Click Number Format. Choose Currency with 0 decimal places. Click OK twice.

3. Double-click cell D3. Click Field Settings. On the Show Values As tab, choose % Running Total In. In the Base Field list, choose Customer. Change the Custom Name to **Accum %**. Click Number Format. Choose Percentage with two decimal place. Click OK twice.

4. Double-click cell E3. Click Field Settings. On the Show Values As tab, choose Rank Largest To Smallest. In the Base Field list, choose Customer. Change the Custom Name to **Rank**. Click OK.

5. Double-click cell F3. Click Field Settings. On the Show Values As tab, choose % of Column Total. Change the Custom Name to **% of Total**. Click Percentage 1 decimal place. Click OK twice.

6. Double-click cell G3. Click Field Settings. On the Show Values As tab, choose % Of. In the Base Field list, choose Customer. In the Base Item field, you can choose (previous), (next), or a specific customer. Because the largest customer is leanexcelbooks.com, choose that customer as the Base Item setting. Change the Custom Name to **% of Top**. Choose the Number Format button. Click Percentage 1 Decimal Place. Click OK twice.

The resulting pivot table in Figure 15.19 shows examples of the 14 Show Values As options. Note that many of the options require the choice of a base field. A few also require that you select a base item.

	A	B	C	D	E	F	G
3	Customer	Revenue	Accum. Total	Accum. %	Rank	% of Total	% of Top
4	leanexcelbooks.com	$869,454	$869,454	12.96%	1	13.0%	100.0%
5	DataSolverz.com	$750,163	$1,619,617	24.15%	2	11.2%	86.3%
6	XLYOURFINANCES, LLC	$704,359	$2,323,976	34.65%	3	10.5%	81.0%
7	MyOnlineTrainingHub.com	$622,794	$2,946,770	43.93%	4	9.3%	71.6%
8	Serving Brevard Realty	$613,514	$3,560,284	53.08%	5	9.1%	70.6%
9	Excel4apps	$568,851	$4,129,135	61.56%	6	8.5%	65.4%
10	Mary Maids	$498,937	$4,628,072	69.00%	7	7.4%	57.4%
11	Excel Strategies, LLC	$427,349	$5,055,421	75.37%	8	6.4%	49.2%
12	MN Excel Consulting	$406,326	$5,461,747	81.42%	9	6.1%	46.7%
13	WM Squared Inc.	$390,978	$5,852,725	87.25%	10	5.8%	45.0%
14	LaFrenier Sons Septic	$72,680	$5,925,405	88.34%	11	1.1%	8.4%
15	Tennessee Moon	$71,651	$5,997,056	89.40%	12	1.1%	8.2%
16	Roto-Rooter	$62,744	$6,059,800	90.34%	13	0.9%	7.2%
17	Harvest Consulting	$60,299	$6,120,099	91.24%	14	0.9%	6.9%
18	Excel Design Solutions Ltd	$59,881	$6,179,980	92.13%	15	0.9%	6.9%
19	data2impact	$57,516	$6,237,496	92.99%	16	0.9%	6.6%
20	The Lab with Leo Crew	$55,251	$6,292,747	93.81%	17	0.8%	6.4%
21	Excel Learning Zone	$54,048	$6,346,795	94.62%	18	0.8%	6.2%
22	MAU Workforce Solutions	$51,240	$6,398,035	95.38%	19	0.8%	5.9%
23	Frontline Systems	$50,030	$6,448,065	96.13%	20	0.7%	5.8%
24	Resource Optimizer	$46,717	$6,494,782	96.82%	21	0.7%	5.4%
25	MrExcel.com	$42,316	$6,537,098	97.45%	22	0.6%	4.9%
26	Spain Enterprise	$39,250	$6,576,348	98.04%	23	0.6%	4.5%
27	University of North Carolina	$34,710	$6,611,058	98.56%	24	0.5%	4.0%
28	SlinkyRN Excel Instruction	$34,364	$6,645,422	99.07%	25	0.5%	4.0%
29	St. Peter's Prep	$31,369	$6,676,791	99.54%	26	0.5%	3.6%
30	Ribbon Commander Framework	$31,021	$6,707,812	100.00%	27	0.5%	3.6%
31	Grand Total	$6,707,812				100.0%	

Figure 15.19   Columns C:G are created using the Show Values As tab.

TROUBLESHOOTING

Excel offers many different ways of ranking ties. Pivot tables do not follow any of the existing methods and introduce a new method.

Say that you have five sales reps with sales of 1000, 800, 800, 400, and 200. The RANK.EQ function will rank two people in second place and no one in third place. The RANK.AVG function will rank both reps with sales of 800 with the tie in the 2.5 place. Pivot table ranks follow neither rule. In a pivot table, people would be ranked, 1, 2, 2, 3, 4; no one would be ranked fifth.

Using a Formula to Add a Field to a Pivot Table

The previous examples took an existing field and used the Show Values As setting to change how the data is presented in the pivot table. In this example, you learn how to add a brand-new calculated field to the pivot table. Follow these steps:

1. Select one of the numeric cells in the pivot table.

2. On the Analyze tab in the ribbon, choose Fields, Items & Sets. Choose Calculated Field from the drop-down. (If this option is not available, choose a cell in the value area of the pivot table.) Excel displays the Insert Calculated Field dialog box. The default field name of Field 1 and the default formula of =0 appear in the dialog box.

3. Type a new name, such as **GP%**.

4. The Formula field starts out as an equal sign, a space, and then a zero. You have to click in this field and press backspace to remove the zero.

5. Build the formula by double-clicking Profit, typing a slash, and then double-clicking Revenue. The dialog box should look like Figure 15.20. Click OK.

Figure 15.20   Build a calculated field.

6. The headings for calculated fields always appear strange. Select a cell in column H and choose Field Settings. Change the Custom Name from Sum of GP% to **GP%** with a leading or trailing space. Change the Number Format to Percentage with one decimal. Click OK twice. The final pivot table is shown in Figure 15.21.

Row Labels	Revenue	Accum. Total	Accum %	Rank	% of Total	% of Top	GP%
leanexcelbooks.com	$869,454	$869,454	13.0%	1	13.0%	100.0%	56.0%
DataSolverz.com	$750,163	$1,619,617	24.1%	2	11.2%	86.3%	55.4%
XLYOURFINANCES, LLC	$704,359	$2,323,976	34.6%	3	10.5%	81.0%	55.8%
MyOnlineTrainingHub.com	$622,794	$2,946,770	43.9%	4	9.3%	71.6%	55.8%
Serving Brevard Realty	$613,514	$3,560,284	53.1%	5	9.1%	70.6%	55.1%
Excel4apps	$568,851	$4,129,135	61.6%	6	8.5%	65.4%	55.6%
Mary Maids	$498,937	$4,628,072	69.0%	7	7.4%	57.4%	55.9%
Excel Strategies, LLC	$427,349	$5,055,421	75.4%	8	6.4%	49.2%	55.7%
MN Excel Consulting	$406,326	$5,461,747	81.4%	9	6.1%	46.7%	56.0%

Figure 15.21 This pivot table includes four value fields plus two calculated fields.

Formatting a Pivot Table

Excel offers a PivotTable Styles gallery on the Design tab. Instead, if you try to format individual cells in a pivot table, you will experience frustration. After you rearrange the pivot table, your manual formatting will be lost.

The PivotTable Styles gallery on the Design tab contains 73 built-in styles for a pivot table. The 73 styles are further modified by using the four check boxes for Banded Rows, Banded Columns, Row Headers, and Column Headers. Multiply that by the 20 color themes on the Page Layout tab, and you have 23,360 different styles. Multiply by the three report layouts, two options for blank rows, Grand Totals On or Off for Rows or Columns, Subtotals Above or Below, and you have more than a million styles available for your pivot table.

You can also build new styles. For example, if you would like the banded rows to be two rows tall, you can design a style for that.

To format a pivot table, select Banded Rows, Row Headers, and Column Headers from the Design tab of the ribbon. Then open the Styles gallery. Figure 15.22 shows some of the choices available in the gallery.

Figure 15.22   Select a style from the gallery on the Design tab.

Setting Defaults for Future Pivot Tables

Once you get some experience with pivot tables, you might find that you have favorite settings that you apply to every pivot table. A new feature in Excel 2019 lets you specify the defaults for future pivot tables.

To find the feature, choose File, Options, Data. The first choice is Edit Default Layout.

My favorite choices are:

- Change the Report Layout to Show In Tabular Form.

- Choose the checkbox for Repeat All Item Labels.

- I prefer Include Filtered Items In Totals, although this only affects pivot tables based on the Data Model.

These settings are shown in Figure 15.23.

CHAPTER 15

Figure 15.23 Specify your favorite pivot table settings as the default.

For settings not shown in the Edit Default Layout dialog box, click the PivotTable Options button in the Edit Default Layout dialog box. This can be confusing: if you click PivotTable Options from the Edit Default Layout dialog box, any changes you make to the PivotTable Options dialog box shown in Figure 15.24 will become the default pivot table. However, if you open the PivotTable Options by right-clicking a pivot table or using the Options button in the Design tab of the Ribbon, you will only change the current pivot table.

In Figure 15.24, I change the For Empty Cells Show setting to zero. Other people suggest using the Classic PivotTable Layout from the Display tab.

Figure 15.24 Anything beyond the settings in Figure 15.23 can be changed in this dialog box.

If you already have an existing pivot table with your favorite settings, you can import those settings as a default using the Import button in the Edit Default Layout dialog box.

> **NOTE**
>
> The Pivot Table Defaults feature shows how Excel.UserVoice.com can be an effective way to lobby for feature changes in Excel. I wrote up the idea for Pivot Table Defaults at Excel. UserVoice.com and asked others to vote. After getting several hundred votes, the Excel team added the feature. Note that I had been using my access as an Excel MVP to request this feature for five years, and I got nowhere. Once I posted it to Excel.UserVoice.com, and other people started agreeing with me, the Excel team was moved to act.

So, if you have something driving you crazy in Excel, write up your idea. Ask your co-workers to vote. It seems like 20 votes is enough to have your idea bubble up in the results, which means more people will see—and hopefully, vote—for your idea.

Figure 15.25 shows my original request.

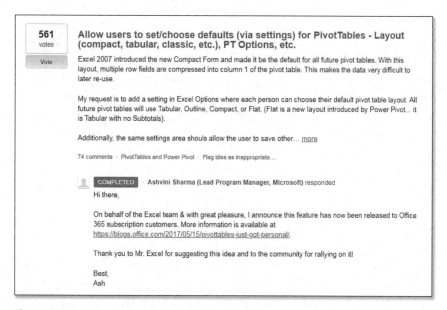

Figure 15.25   Anyone can submit an idea to Excel's suggestion box.

Finding More Information on Pivot Tables

More information about pivot tables is available in these locations:

- Chapter 16 covers slicers and other ways to filter a pivot table.

- Chapter 17 covers creating pivot tables from multiple tables using Power Pivot.

- Chapter 24, "Using 3D Maps," covers creating a pivot table on a map using 3D Maps.

For even more information on pivot tables, check out my upcoming new book on the subject: *Excel 2019 Pivot Table Data Crunching* (Que, ISBN 978-1-5093-0724-1), coauthored by Mike Alexander, in early 2019.

Using Slicers and Filtering a Pivot Table

Pivot table filters have been quietly evolving over the past several versions of Excel. Excel 2010 pivot tables introduced a visual filter called a *slicer*. Slicers enable you to perform ad-hoc analysis by choosing various items from various fields in the pivot table. Excel 2013 added a new date-centric visual filter called a *timeline*.

Filtering Using the Row Label Filter

To follow along, create a new pivot table from the 16-Slicers.xlsx file. Check the Customer, Date, Quantity, Revenue, COGS, and Profit fields. On the Design tab, open the Report Layout drop-down menu. Choose Tabular form and then choose Repeat All Item Labels. Choose the Banded Rows check box on the Design tab. You will end up with the pivot table shown in Figure 16.1. Drop-down lists in cells A3 and B3 lead to the row filter menus.

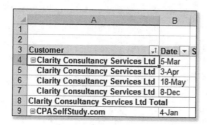

Figure 16.1 Drop-down lists in A3 and B3 lead to filters for Customer and Date.

Figure 16.2 shows the Filter menu for the Customer field. This drop-down menu contains four separate filter mechanisms:

- The Label Filters fly-out menu appears for fields that contain text values. You can use this fly-out to select customer names that contain certain words, begin with, end with, or fall between certain letters.

- The Value Filters fly-out menu enables you to filter the customers based on values elsewhere in the pivot table. If you want only orders over $20,000, or if you want to see the Top 10 customers, use the Value Filters fly-out.

417

- The Search box was added in Excel 2010 and is similar to using Label Filters, but faster.

- The check boxes enable you to exclude individual customers, or you can clear or select all customers by using Select All.

Figure 16.2   Four separate filter mechanisms exist in this drop-down menu.

Figure 16.3 shows the detail of the Value Filters fly-out. All these filters, except Top 10, were new in Excel 2007.

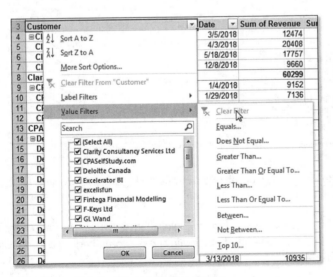

Figure 16.3   Detail of the Value Filters fly-out.

When you access the filter drop-down menu for a field that contains 100% dates, the Label Filters fly-out is replaced by a Date Filters fly-out, as shown in Figure 16.4. This fly-out offers conceptual filters, such as Last Month, Next Quarter, and This Year. The All Dates in Period choice leads to a second fly-out where you can choose based on month or quarter.

Figure 16.4   The Date Filters fly-outs appear when your field contains all date values.

Clearing a Filter

To clear all filters in the pivot table, use the Clear icon in the Sort & Filter group of the Data tab. To clear filters from one field in the pivot table, open the filter drop-down menu for that field and select Clear Filter from "Field."

Filtering Using the Check Boxes

The Customer drop-down menu includes a list of all the customers in the database. If you need to exclude a few specific customers, you can clear their check boxes in the filter list.

The (Select All) item restores any cleared boxes. If all the boxes are already selected, clicking (Select All) clears all the boxes.

Because it is easier to select three customers than to clear 27, if you need to remove most of the items from the list of customers, you can follow these steps:

1. If any customers are cleared, choose Select All to reselect all customers.

2. Choose Select All to clear all customers.

3. Select the particular customers you want to view, as shown in Figure 16.5.

Figure 16.5   Choose Select All to clear all customers and then select the few desired customers.

TROUBLESHOOTING

The Search box above the checkboxes does not get re-applied if you refresh the pivot table.

Perhaps you need to select all the customers with "Bank" in their names. You could do this with the Search box, and it would work. However, after adding more data to the source data and refreshing the pivot table, Excel will not pick up any new customers with "Bank" in their names.

A workaround is to use the Label Filters for Contains Bank. The Label Filter will be re-applied after a refresh.

Filtering Using the Label Filter Fly-Out

All the Label Filters choices shown previously in Figure 16.2 lead to the same dialog box. Suppose that you are interested in finding all customers whose name includes "Excel." Follow these steps:

1. Open the Customer filter drop-down menu.

2. Open the Label Filters fly-out.

3. Select Contains. Excel displays the Label Filter dialog box.

4. Type **Excel**. Click OK. The pivot table is filtered to customers whose name includes "Excel."

If you open the first drop-down menu in the Label Filter dialog box, you see the following choices:

- Equals

- Does Not Equal

- Is Greater Than

- Is Greater Than Or Equal To

- Is Less Than

- Less Than Or Equal To

- Begins With

- Does Not Begin With

- Ends With

- Does Not End With

- Contains

- Does Not Contain

- Is Between

- Is Not Between

You can use the wildcards * and ?, with * representing any character(s) and the ? wildcard representing a single character.

Filtering Using the Date Filters

When a field in the original data set contains only values formatted as dates, Excel offers the Date Filters fly-out shown previously in Figure 16.4.

Many of the date filters contain conceptual filters. If you filter a pivot table to Yesterday and then refresh the data set a week later, the dates returned by the filter will change.

The list of conceptual filters feels like it was borrowed from QuickBooks, but it is not quite as complete as those from QuickBooks. It would be nice to have choices such as Last 30 Days, Month to Date, and so on.

CHAPTER 16

The penultimate choice in the first fly-out is All Dates in the Period, which leads to a second fly-out. Choosing January or Quarter 1 is great when you have dates from several years, and you want to compare January from each year.

The last choice in the first fly-out is Custom Filter. As shown in Figure 16.6, you can use this filter to build a custom date range. Change the selection in the first drop-down menu to Is Between. Then use the date icons to choose your selected dates. The Whole Days check box was new in Excel 2013. Use this to truncate times from fields that contain date and time.

Figure 16.6   The Custom Filter in a date field offers to let you build any range of dates.

Filtering to the Top 10

Pivot tables offer a feature called Top 10. Despite the name, the filter is not just for finding the top 10 values. You can use the filter to find the top or bottom items. You can specify 5, 7, 10, or any number of items.

To start the filter, open the Customer filter drop-down menu. Open the Value Filters fly-out and select Top 10. Excel displays the Top 10 Filter dialog box. In Figure 16.7, the report has been filtered to show the top five customers based on revenue.

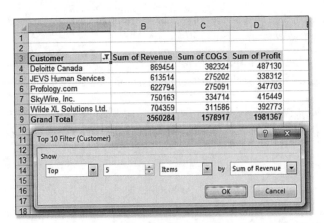

Figure 16.7   Filter to the top five customers based on revenue.

The Top 10 filter offers these options:

- The first drop-down menu in the dialog box offers a choice between Top and Bottom.

- The second field is a spin button and a text box. You can use the spin button to change from 5 to 10. If you need to get to 1,000,000, you should type that value into the text box instead of trying to hit the spin button 999,990 times.

- The next field is a drop-down menu with choices Items, Percent, and Sum. These three choices are discussed in the next sections.

- The final drop-down menu offers all the numeric fields in the VALUES area of the pivot table.

The Items/Percent/Sum drop-down menu offers a lot of flexibility. If you select Percent, the pivot table shows you enough customers so that you see *n*% of the value field. For example, you might ask for the top 80% of profit.

If you choose Sum, you can specify a large number as the second field in the dialog box. For example, you might want to see enough customers to reach $5 million in sales.

Filtering Using Slicers

Slicers are visual filters that make it easy to run various ad-hoc analyses. While slicers are easier to use than the Report Filter, they offer the added benefit that a slicer can filter multiple pivot tables and pivot charts created from the same data set.

Adding Slicers

To add default slicers, follow these steps:

1. Select one cell in your pivot table.

2. On the Analyze tab, select the Insert Slicer icon. Excel shows the Insert Slicers dialog box.

3. Choose any fields that would make suitable filter fields. In Figure 16.8, Region, Product, and Years are selected. Months, Quarters, and Date would also be effective, but you see how they can be filtered using a timeline later in this chapter. Click OK.

CHAPTER 16

Figure 16.8   Choose all fields that are suitable for visual filters.

Excel adds default filters, tiled in the center of your screen (see Figure 16.9).

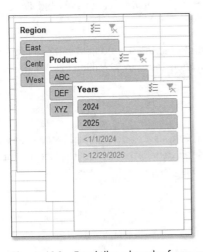

Figure 16.9   Excel tiles a bunch of one-column slicers.

Arranging the Slicers

You can reposition and resize the slicers. Choose a logical arrangement for the slicers. Following are some examples.

The Region and Product slicers contain short entries. Make each slicer wider and then use the Columns setting in the Slicer Tools Options tab to increase each slicer to three columns. See Figure 16.10 for the setting.

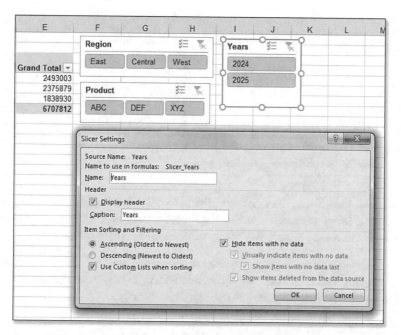

Figure 16.10   The Slicer Tools Options tab allows you to control the number of columns in a slicer. Further settings are in the Slicer Settings dialog box.

The Year slicer is wider than it needs to be. There are also two extra items (<1/1/2024 and >12/31/2025) in the slicer that are remnants of Auto Group. You can turn these off in the Slicer Settings dialog box. Select the slicer and choose Slicer Settings. Also, Hide Items with No Data is checked.

Inside OUT

Slicers can be configured to filter multiple pivot tables and pivot charts at the same time.

If both pivot tables are using the same data source, you can ensure that the slicers will affect both pivot tables.

If multiple pivot tables exist, follow these steps:

1. Select the slicer.
2. From the Slicer Tools Options tab of the ribbon, choose Report Connections.
3. Select each pivot table that should be filtered by the slicer.

To connect two pivot tables that came from two different data sets, the process is more complex. Say that you have a Region field in the Actuals table and in the Forecast table. The regions are similar, but the Forecast table has one extra region.

This method requires all the pivot tables to be based on the Data Model. If you have existing pivot tables, you will have to re-create them and use the selection for Add This Data To The Data Model in the Create PivotTable dialog box.

Follow these steps:

1. Make sure to format both the Actuals table and the Forecast table as a table using Ctrl+T.

2. Rename the tables as "Actuals" and "Forecast" instead of "Table1" and "Table2."

3. Copy the Region column from both tables into a new area (you don't need the heading from the second copy).

4. Use Data, Remove Duplicates on the new single-column region table so each region appears once.

5. Format this single-column table as a table. Rename it as Regions.

6. Choose Data, Relationships. Add a new relationship from Region in the Actuals table to Region in the Regions table. Repeat to create a relationship from Region in the Forecast table to Region in the Regions table.

7. Create a Forecast pivot table. Make sure to choose Add This Data To The Data Model when creating the pivot table. Use Revenue from the Forecast table but use Region from the Regions table.

8. Create an Actuals pivot table following the same guidance in step 7.

9. When you Insert, Slicer, choose the All tab at the top of the Insert Slicer dialog. Choose to create a slicer from the Region field in the Regions table.

This new Regions slicer will control both pivot tables.

Using the Slicers in Excel 2019

To select a single item from a slicer, choose that item. To multiselect in Excel 2019, first, choose the icon at the top of the slicer that has the three check marks. You can now click each item. You can also use the Ctrl key to select multiple nonadjacent items or drag the mouse to select adjacent items.

Selections in one slicer might cause items in other slicers to become unavailable. In this case, those items move to the end of the list. This gives you a visual indication that the item is not available based on the current filters.

To clear a filter from a slicer, click the Funnel-X icon in the top right of the slicer.

Filtering Dates

Excel 2013 added a Timeline control for filtering date fields. It is difficult to use. Instead of the Timeline, you could achieve more flexibility by arranging three slicers for Year, Quarter, and Month, as shown in Figure 16.11

Figure 16.11 shows a timeline. The timeline has been set to filter by quarter.

Figure 16.11   A timeline control lets you filter daily dates by month, quarter, or year without grouping.

Filtering Oddities

The next sections discuss a few additional features available for filtering pivot tables.

AutoFiltering a Pivot Table

I was doing a Power Excel seminar in Philadelphia when someone in the audience asked whether it is possible to AutoFilter a pivot table. The answer is no; the Filter field is not available when you are inside a pivot table.

There is a surprising bug, however. If you put the cell pointer to the right of the last heading of a data set and click the Filter icon, Excel turns on the AutoFilter drop-down menus. I call this cell the magic cell.

The guy at Microsoft in charge of making the AutoFilter icon unavailable when you are in a pivot table evidently forgot about that magic cell to the right of the headings. If you put the cell pointer in cell D1 in Figure 16.12, the Filter icon remains available.

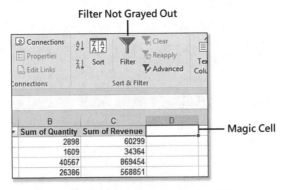

Figure 16.12   Although this works, the AutoFilters are not recalculated after a refresh.

What is the advantage of using the AutoFilters? The Top 10 AutoFilter works differently from the Top 10 PivotTable filter. In Figure 16.13, the Top 10 AutoFilter for the top six items returns the top five customers and the true grand total.

Figure 16.13 The AutoFilter Top 10 works differently from the pivot table filters.

If you try this method, remember that you have to go back to the magic cell to toggle off the AutoFilter. Also, if you change the underlying data and refresh the pivot table, the AutoFilter is not updated. After all, the Excel team believes that you can't AutoFilter a pivot table.

The AutoFilter lets you filter by one item along the Column field. In Figure 16.14, the report is showing the top five customers for product XYZ in column D. A regular pivot table filter would always be based on the Grand Total in column G.

Sum of Revenue	Product			
Customer	ABC	DEF	XYZ	Grand Total
CPASelfStudy.com	7136	4270	22958	34364
Harlem Globetrotters	13853	26484	19544	59881
Hartville Marketplace & Flea Market	99544	178254	149551	427349
Reports Wand	142412	182755	173770	498937
The Salem Historical Society, Salem, Ohio	15104	18064	18072	51240
Grand Total	3069797	3254120	383895	6707812

Figure 16.14 Use the AutoFilter to filter based on sales of one item.

Replicating a Pivot Table for Every Customer

This technique makes many copies of the pivot table, with a different Report Filter value in each copy. To use the feature, you have to move the field to the FILTERS drop zone in the PivotTable Fields list. To create a report for every customer, move the Customer field to the FILTERS drop zone. Select the Options drop-down menu from the Analyze tab. Select Show Report Filter Pages from the drop-down menu, as shown in Figure 16.15. Confirm which field should be used. Excel adds worksheets to your workbook. Each worksheet contains the original pivot table, with a different value chosen for the selected filter field.

CAUTION

Slicers are not visible on the copied pivot tables when you use this technique.

Figure 16.15 Replicate your pivot table for every value in a Report Filter field.

Sorting a Pivot Table

In all the pivot tables so far in this chapter, the customers are presented in alphabetical sequence. In each case, the report would be more interesting if it were presented sorted by revenue instead of by customer name.

Starting in Excel 2010, if you use the AZ or ZA icons on the Data tab, Excel automatically sets up rules in the Sort and More Sort Options dialog boxes.

To access these settings later, open a row field drop-down menu and choose More Sort Options. This opens the Sort (Customer) dialog box. Click the More icon to access More Sort Options (Customer).

Mashing Up Data with Power Pivot

The Power Pivot add-in debuted in Excel 2010. The add-in allowed you to:

- Load 100 million records in an Excel workbook

- Join data from Sheet1 and Sheet2 in a single workbook

- Create new calculated fields using a formula language called DAX

- Use time intelligence functions to handle fiscal years not ending in December

Power Pivot was not developed by the Excel team. It was developed by the SQL Server Analysis Services team. In Excel 2010, the add-in was free and mostly separate from Excel. It proved so popular that the Excel team slowly began incorporating Power Pivot into the core Excel product.

- In Excel 2013, Add This Data To The Data Model button was added to the Create Pivot-Table dialog box. This allowed you to create pivot tables from multiple sheets.

- In Excel 2016, the Add Measure choice was added to a right-click menu in the PivotTable Fields list. This allowed you to use DAX formulas.

- In Office 365, a new Relationships icon was added to the Data tab of the ribbon. This made it easier to define relationships between tables.

- In Excel 2016, the Power Query tools were added to the Data tab of the ribbon. This allows you to get more than 1,048,576 records into Excel.

- In Excel 2019, a Manage Data Model icon is added to the Data tab of the ribbon. This allows you to open the Power Pivot grid, define sort order, hide fields, define relationships using a diagram view, and more.

- With Excel 2019, the full benefits of Power Pivot are freely available to anyone using Windows versions of Excel. This is a great improvement over Excel 2013 and 2016 when only the Pro Plus and E3 versions of Office had full access to the Power Pivot grid.

Joining Multiple Tables Using the Data Model

When you see the term *Data Model* in Excel 2019, it's Microsoft's way of saying you are using Power Pivot without calling it Power Pivot.

Preparing Data for Use in the Data Model

When you are planning to use the Data Model to join multiple tables, you should always convert your Excel ranges to tables before you begin. You theoretically do not have to convert the ranges to tables, but it is far easier if you convert the ranges to tables and give the tables a name. If you don't convert the ranges to tables first, Excel secretly does it in the background and gives your tables meaningless names such as "Range."

Choose one cell in a data set and use Ctrl+T or Home, Format as Table. In the Create Table dialog box, make sure My Table Has Headers is selected. After you create a table, Excel gives your table a basic name, such as Table1, Table2, and so on. Go to the Table Tools Design tab of the ribbon and type a meaningful name, such as **Sales** or **Sectors**.

Figure 17.1 shows two ranges in Excel. Columns A:H contain a transactional data set named Sales. Columns J:K contain a customer lookup table called Sector. You would like to create a pivot table showing revenue by sector.

Customer	Quantity	Revenue	COGS	Profit		Customer	Sector
9 Wonderful Kettle Corp	901	21438	9209	12229		Fine Shingle Supply	Hardware
10 Matchless Hardware Traders	342	6267	2541	3726		Flexible Aerobic Co	Apparel
11 Cool Bottle Co	91	2401	1031	1370		Functional Eggbeater Co	Consumer
12 Vivid Edger Co	547	9345	4239	5106		Guaranteed Paint Co	Chemical
13 Excellent Doghouse Corp	558	11628	5093	6535		Improved Vegetable Inc.	Food
14 Vivid Edger Co	100	2042	983	1059		Inventive Door Inc.	Hardware
15 Powerful Edger Supply	250	3552	1696	1856		Magnificent Shingle Corp	Hardware
16 Supreme Clipboard Inc.	760	14440	6790	7650		Matchless Hardware Traders	Hardware
17 Improved Vegetable Inc.	810	14592	6781	7811		Mouthwatering Bicycle Corp	Consumer
18 Matchless Hardware Traders	606	12606	5090	7516		New Faucet Co	Hardware
19 Excellent Doghouse Corp	964	20770	8463	12307		Powerful Edger Supply	Hardware
20 Matchless Hardware Traders	365	8128	3400	4728		Rare Door Inc.	Hardware
21 Trendy Notebook Corp	389	7136	3403	3733		Savory Opener Inc.	Hardware
22 Improved Vegetable Inc.	652	17150	6888	10262		Special Luggage Inc.	Consumer
23 Wonderful Kettle Corp	338	6714	2967	3747		Supreme Clipboard Inc.	Consumer
24 Improved Vegetable Inc.	766	15640	6782	8858		Sure Linen Corp	Textiles
25 Wonderful Kettle Corp	346	5532	2541	2991		Tremendous Thermostat Partners	Electronics
26 Vivid Edger Co	817	17160	7864	9296		Trendy Notebook Corp	Consumer
27 Guaranteed Paint Co	902	21708	8866	12842		Vivid Edger Co	Hardware
28 Matchless Hardware Traders	985	19890	8467	11423		Wonderful Kettle Corp	Consumer
29 Excellent Doghouse Corp	116	1817	838	979			

Figure 17.1 You want to join these two tables together in a single pivot table.

Excel gurus are thinking, "Why don't you do a VLOOKUP to join the tables?" PowerPivot lets you avoid the VLOOKUP. In this case, the tables are small and a VLOOKUP would calculate quickly. However, imagine that you have a million records in the transactional table and 10 columns in the lookup table. The VLOOKUP solution quickly becomes unwieldy. The PowerPivot engine available in the Data Model can join the tables without the overhead of VLOOKUP.

Creating a Relationship Between Two Tables in Excel

Look in the Data Tools group of the Data tab of the ribbon for the new Relationships icon. Click the icon to open the Manage Relationships dialog box. Click on New... to open the Create Relationship dialog box.

Your relationship should start from the transactional data set. Open the Table drop-down menu and choose the Sales table. Open the Column (Foreign) drop-down menu and choose the Customer column. The Related Table is the Sectors table. The Related Column is also Customer. Figure 17.2 shows the completed dialog box. Click OK to create the relationship. Click Close to close the Manage Relationships dialog box.

Figure 17.2   Create a relationship between two tables.

Creating a relationship automatically loads both tables to the Data Model. This is a great way to accomplish two tasks with one action.

In the past, it was common to add the first table to the model by using Add This Data To The Data Model in the Create PivotTable dialog box. This method works fine, all except for the point where the pivot table shows the wrong numbers as it displays the A Relationship May Be Needed. I always cringed at that step. By building the relationship in advance, you avoid having wrong numbers in the pivot table.

Creating a Relationship Using Diagram View

If you see a Power Pivot tab in your ribbon, there is a quicker way to get the data in to the Data Model and create a relationship:

1. Select one cell in the first table. Use Power Pivot, Create Linked Table to add the data to the Data Model.

2. Repeat step 1 for the second table.

3. Click on the Manage icon in the Power Pivot tab or the Manage Data Model icon in the Data tab. The Power Pivot grid opens.

4. On the right side of the ribbon, choose Diagram View.

5. In Diagram View, click on the the Customer field in the Sales table and draw a line to the Customer field in the Sector table (see Figure 17.3).

6. Use the Switch To Workbook icon in the Power Pivot Quick Access Toolbar to return to Excel.

Figure 17.3   Create a relationship quickly with Diagram view.

Building a Pivot Table from the Data Model

Choose a blank cell where you want your pivot table to appear. Select Insert, PivotTable. Because you have already defined a relationship, the Create PivotTable dialog box will default to Use This Workbook's Data Model (see Figure 17.4).

Figure 17.4   Because you've created a relationship, the pivot table defaults to using the existing Data Model.

Look at the PivotTable Fields task pane. In the second line of the pane, you have a choice for Active or All and All is selected. You now see a list of each defined table in the Excel workbook. There is a triangle icon next to each table.

Click the triangle next to Sectors to see a list of the available fields in the Sectors table. Drag the Sector field to the Rows area. Click the triangle next to Sales to expand that table. Drag Revenue to the Values area.

As shown in Figure 17.5, you have successfully created a pivot table from two different data sets.

Figure 17.5   Without doing a VLOOKUP, you've successfully joined data from two tables in this report.

Unlocking Hidden Features with the Data Model

I do thirty-five live Excel seminars every year. I hear a variety of Excel questions in those seminars. Some questions are common enough that they pop up a couple times a year. When my answer starts with, "Have you ever noticed the box called 'Add This Data To The Data Model?'", people can't believe that the answer has been right there, hiding in Excel. A typical reaction from the audience member: "How was anyone supposed to know that 'Add This Data To The Data Model' means that I can create a Median in a pivot table?"

Counting Distinct in a Pivot Table

Consider the three pivot tables shown in Figure 17.6. The question is "How many unique customers are in each sector?". The pivot table in columns A and B allow you to figure out the answer. You can mentally count that there are two customers (B4 & B5) in the Associations sector. There are six customers listed in the Consultants sector.

But how would you present the top-left pivot table to your manager? You would have to grab some paper and jot down Associations: 2, Consultants: 6, Professional: 3, and so on.

When you try to build a pivot table to answer the question, you might get the wrong results shown in D3:D10. This pivot table says it is calculating a "Count of Customer," but this is actually counting the number of invoices in each sector.

The trick to solving the problem is to add your data to the Data Model.

	A	B	C	D	E
1					
2				Regular Pivot Table	
3	Sector	Customer		Sector	Count of Customer
4	Association	Association for Computers & Taxation		Associations	8
5	Association	IMA Houston Chapter		Consultants	85
6	Associations Total			Professional	36
7	Consultant	Andrew Spain Consulting		Retail	78
8	Consultant	Cambia Factor		Software	104
9	Consultant	Construction Intelligence & Analytics, Inc.		Training	252
10	Consultant	Data2Impact		Grand Total	563
11	Consultant	Excelerator BI			
12	Consultant	Fintega Financial Modelling		Data Model	
13	Consultants Total			Sector	Unique Customer
14	Profession	Juliet Babcock-Hyde CPA, PLLC		Associations	2
15	Profession	Serving Brevard Realty		Consultants	6
16	Profession	WM Squared Inc.		Professional	3
17	Professional Total			Retail	4
18	Retail	Bits of Confetti		Software	4
19	Retail	Hartville MarketPlace and Flea Market		Training	8
20	Retail	LaFrenier Sons Septic		Grand Total	27
21	Retail	New Hope Laundry			
22	Retail Total				

Figure 17.6   When you try to figure out the number of customers in a sector, it does not work.

The pivot table in D13:E20 in Figure 17.6 is somehow reporting the correct number of unique customers in each sector.

A regular pivot table offers 11 calculations: Sum, Count, Average, Max, Min, Product, Count Numbers, StdDev, StdDevP, Var, and VarP. These calculations have not changed in 33 years.

But if you create your pivot table and choose the box for Add This Data To The Data Model, a twelfth calculation option appears at the end of the Value Field Settings dialog box: Distinct Count.

Drag customer to the Values area. Double-click the Count Of Customer heading. Choose Distinct Count. Change the title, and you have the solution shown above. Figure 17.7 shows the Value Field Settings dialog box.

Figure 17.7   Distinct Count appears in Data Model pivot tables.

One oddity: the Product calculation is missing from the Value Field Settings for the Data Model. I've never met anyone who actually used the Product calculation. But if you were a person who loved Product, then having Excel swap out Product to make room for Distinct Count will not be popular. You can add a new Measure with =PRODUCT([Revenue]) to replicate the product calculation. See the example about creating Median later in this chapter.

Including Filtered Items in Totals

Excel pivot tables offer an excellent filtering feature called Top 10. This feature is very flexible: It can be Top 10 Items, Bottom 5 Items, Top 80%, or Top Records To Get To $4 Million In Revenue.

Shortening a long report to show only the top five items is great for a dashboard or a summary report.

But there is an annoyance when you use any of the filters.

In Figure 17.8, the top pivot table occupies rows 3 through row 31. Revenue is shown both as Revenue and as a % of Total. The largest customer is Andrew Spain Consulting with 869,000. In the top pivot table, the Grand Total is $6.7 Million and Andrew Spain is 12.96% of that total.

In the same figure, rows 34:40 show the same pivot table with the Top 5 selected in the Top 10 filter. The Grand Total now shows only $3.56 Million. Andrew Spain is 24% of the smaller total number.

This is wrong. Andrew should be 13% of the total, not 24%.

	A	B	C
3	**Customer**	**Sum of Revenue**	**% of Total**
25	CPASelfStudy.com	568851	8.48%
26	MySpreadsheetLab	613514	9.15%
27	599CD.com	622794	9.28%
28	Hartville MarketPlace and Flea Market	704359	10.50%
29	Excel4Apps	750163	11.18%
30	Andrew Spain Consulting	869454	12.96%
31	**Grand Total**	**6707812**	**100.00%**
32			
33	**Values Filters, Top 10, Top 5 Items**		
34	**Customer**	**Sum of Revenue**	**% of Total**
35	MySpreadsheetLab	613514	17.23%
36	599CD.com	622794	17.49%
37	Hartville MarketPlace and Flea Market	704359	19.78%
38	Excel4Apps	750163	21.07%
39	Andrew Spain Consulting	869454	24.42%
40	**Grand Total**	**3560284**	**100.00%**

Figure 17.8   Using the Top 10 Filter can change the Percentage of Total calculation.

On January 30, 2007, Microsoft released Excel 2007. A new feature was added to Excel called Include Filtered Items In Subtotals. This feature would solve the problem in Figure 17.8. However, as you can see, the feature is not available, as shown in Figure 17.9. It has been unavailable every day since January 30, 2007. I can attest to that because I check every day to see if it is enabled.

Figure 17.9   Include Filtered Items in Totals is not available.

To solve the problem? Choose Add This Data To The Data Model as you create the pivot table. Include Filtered Items In Subtotals is now enabled. The asterisk on the Grand Total in cell A49 means that there are rows hidden from the pivot table that are included in the totals.

More importantly, the % of Column calculation is still reporting the correct 12.96% for Andrew Spain Consulting in cell C48 of Figure 17.10.

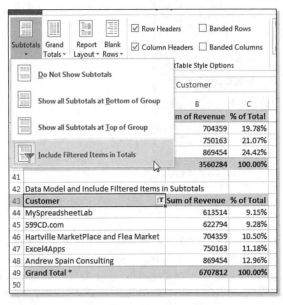

	A	B	C
		m of Revenue	% of Total
		704359	19.78%
		750163	21.07%
		869454	24.42%
		3560284	100.00%
41			
42	Data Model and Include Filtered Items in Subtotals		
43	**Customer**	**Sum of Revenue**	**% of Total**
44	MySpreadsheetLab	613514	9.15%
45	599CD.com	622794	9.28%
46	Hartville MarketPlace and Flea Market	704359	10.50%
47	Excel4Apps	750163	11.18%
48	Andrew Spain Consulting	869454	12.96%
49	**Grand Total ***	**6707812**	**100.00%**
50			

Figure 17.10   By choosing the Data Model, the calculation is correct.

Creating Median in a Pivot Table Using DAX Measures

Pivot tables still do not support the median calculation. But when you add the data to the Data Model, you can build any calculation supported by the DAX formula language. Between Excel 2016 and Excel 2019, the DAX formula language was expanded to include a Median calculation.

Calculations made with DAX are called *Measures*. Figure 17.11 shows different ways to start a DAX calculation. You can right-click the table name in the PivotTable Fields list and choose Add Measure. Or, you can use the Measures drop-down menu on the PowerPivot tab in Excel. Using the Measures drop-down menu is slightly better because any new measures are automatically added to the Values area of a pivot table.

Figure 17.11   Build a pivot table using the Data Model and then add a measure.

Figure 17.12 shows the Measure dialog box. There are several fields:

- The Table Name will be filled in automatically for you.

- Type a meaningful name for the new calculation in the Measure Name Box.

- You can leave the Description box empty.

- The *fx* button lets you choose a function from a list.

- The Check Formula button will look for syntax errors.

- Type =Median(Range[Revenue]) as the formula.

- In the lower-left, choose a number format.

As you type the formula, something that feels like AutoComplete will offer tool tips on how to build the formulas. When you finish typing the formula, click the Check Formula button. You want to see the result No Errors In Formula, as shown in Figure 17.12.

Figure 17.12   Build a measure to calculate Median.

Click OK. The Median Revenue will appear in the Fields list. Choose the field in the Fields list and it will be added to your pivot table.

Column E in Figure 17.13 shows the Median for each sector.

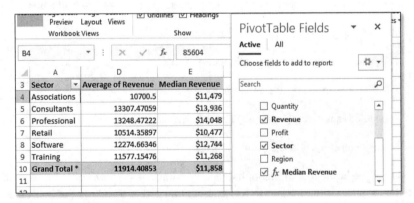

Figure 17.13   A pivot table with Medians.

> TROUBLESHOOTING
>
> **The Check Formula button in the Measure dialog box does ensure the formula will calculate correctly.**
>
> Shown previously in Figure 17.12, the Check Formula button will often return a message: `No Errors in Formula.` You add the measure to your pivot table and get a `#VALUE!` error.
>
> The `No Errors In Formula` error message means that you spelled all of the functions and field names correctly and that you are not missing any parentheses. It does not mean that the calculation will do what you want.
>
> There have been many times when I have struggled to finally get the `No Errors In Formula` message and then been crushed to find that the formula still does not work. This is when I head to the forums to see if someone can spot the logic error in my formula.

Calculations created by Measures are each to re-use. Change the pivot table from Figure 17.13 to show Regions in A instead of Sector. The measure is re-used and starts calculating statistics by Region (see Figure 17.14).

	A	D	E	F
3	Region	Average of Revenue	Median Revenue	
4	Midwest	12093.22222	$12,642	
5	Northeast	11301.12766	$10,624	
6	South	12333.29384	$12,360	
7	West	11972.55	$10,307	
8	Grand Total *	11914.40853	$11,858	
9				

Figure 17.14 The measure keeps working if you change the shape of the pivot table.

Time Intelligence Using DAX

The DAX formula language supports new functions for month-to-date, year-to-date, prior period, and so on.

Create a new `MTDSales` measure with the formula:

```
=CALCULATE([Sum of Revenue],DatesMTD(Sales[Date]))
```

The function CALCULATE is similar to SUMIFS, with one cool exception. Normally, a cell in a pivot table is filtered by the slicers, the row fields, and the column fields. In cell D21 of Figure 17.15, the row field is imposing a filter of 1/30/2018. The DAX measure is redefining the filter. By asking for all dates in DATESMTD(Sales[Date]), the MTDSales field returns all January 2018 dates up to and including the 30th of January.

CHAPTER 17

	A	B	C	D
3		Date	Sum of Revenue	MTDSales
16		1/23/2018	14,592	185,078
17		1/24/2018	12,606	197,684
18		1/25/2018	20,770	218,454
19		1/26/2018	8,128	226,582
20		1/29/2018	24,286	250,868
21		1/30/2018	6,714	257,582
22		1/31/2018	15,640	273,222
23		2/1/2018	5,532	5,532
24		2/3/2018	17,160	22,692
25		2/6/2018	21,708	44,400
26		2/7/2018	19,890	64,290
27		2/8/2018	1,817	66,107
28		2/9/2018	5,157	71,264
29		2/14/2018	13,867	85,131
30		2/16/2018	16,936	102,067
31		2/17/2018	11,430	113,497

Figure 17.15   The MTD calculation accumulates until a new month starts.

To calculate sales for the same day last year, use DATEADD to move back one year:

```
Prior Year Sales
=CALCULATE(Sales[Sum of Revenue],
ALL(Sales[Date (Year)]),
DATEADD(Sales[Date],-1,YEAR))
```

After you define a calculated field, you can use that field in future calculations:

```
Prior Year MTD Sales
=CALCULATE([PriorYearSales],
DATESMTD(Sales[Date]))
```

And then:

```
MTDChangeOverLastYear
=[MTDSales]-[PriorYearMTDSales]
```

Figure 17.16 shows the results of those calculations.

3	Date	Sum of Revenue	MTDSales	PriorYearSales	PriorYearMTDSales	MTDChangeOverLastYear
229	12/27/2018	9,460	277,825			277,825
230	12/28/2018	10,290	288,115			288,115
231	1/1/2019	10,245	10,245	22,810	22,810	-12,565
232	1/2/2019	11,240	21,485	2,257	25,067	-3,582
233	1/3/2019	9,204	30,689		25,067	5,622
234	1/4/2019	6,860	37,549	27,704	52,771	-15,222
235	1/6/2019	13,806	51,355		52,771	-1,416
236	1/8/2019	21,015	72,370		82,957	-10,587
237	1/9/2019	21,465	93,835	16,416	99,373	-5,538
238	1/11/2019	9,144	102,979		120,811	-17,832
239	1/12/2019	20,850	123,829		127,078	3,249

Figure 17.16   Each formula can build on a prior formula.

Here is the beautiful thing: If your goal is to show MTD sales growth, you can remove all the intermediate calculations from the pivot table and show only the final calculated field.

Overcoming Limitations of the Data Model

When you use the Data Model, you transform your regular Excel data into an OLAP model. There are annoying limitations and some benefits available to pivot tables built on OLAP models. The Excel team tried to mitigate some of the limitations for Excel 2019, but some are still present. Here are some of the limitations and the workarounds:

- **Less grouping**—You cannot use the Group feature of pivot tables to create territories or to group numeric values into bins. You will have to add calculated fields to your data with the grouping information.

- **Product is not a built-in calculation**—I've never created a pivot table where I had to multiply all the rows. That is the calculation that happens when you change Sum to Product. If you need to do this calculation, you can add a new Measure using the PRODUCT function in DAX.

- **Pivot tables won't automatically sort by custom lists**—It is eight annoying clicks to force a field to sort by a custom list: Open the field drop-down menu and choose More Sort Options. In the Sort Options dialog box, click More Options. In the More Sort Options dialog box, unselect Sort Automatically. Open the First Key Sort Order and choose your Custom List. Click OK to close More Sort Options dialog box. Click OK to close the Sort dialog box.

Inside OUT

The custom sorting solution mentioned previously requires eight mouse clicks. It works in the pivot table, but not in any slicers. There is possibly an easier way.

Check to see if all of these are true: If your Excel has a tab in the ribbon for Power Pivot. If you have a field with month name and another field with month number. Then, you can try these steps:

1. Select the Manage icon in the Power Pivot tab of the Excel ribbon to open the Power Pivot grid.

2. Use the tab icons in the bottom of the Power Pivot grid to find the correct sheet that contains your month names.

3. In the Power Pivot grid, select the column that contains the month names or month abbreviations.

4. In the Power Pivot ribbon, select Home, Sort By Column, as shown in the figure below.

5. In the resulting Sort By Column dialog box, specify that you want to sort Month By MonthNo. Click OK. From this point forward, the month name will appear correctly in both the pivot table and any slicers.

- **Strange drill-down**—Usually, you can double-click a cell in a pivot table and see the rows that make up that cell. This does work with the Data Model, but only for the first 1,000 rows.

- **No calculated fields or calculated items**—This is not a big deal, because DAX Measures run circles around calculated items.

- **Odd re-ordering items**—There is a trick in regular Excel pivot tables that you can do instead of dragging field names where you want them. Say that you go to a cell that contains the word *Friday* and type **Monday** there. When you press Enter, the Monday data moves to that new column. This does not work in Power Pivot pivot tables! You can still select Monday, hover over the edge, and drag the item to a new location.

- **No support for arrow keys in formula creation**—In the Excel interface, you might build a formula with =<LeftArrow>*<LeftArrow><LeftArrow><Enter>. This is not supported in Power Pivot. You will have to reach for the mouse to click on the columns that you want to reference.

- **Refresh will be slow**—The Refresh button on the Analyze tab forces Excel to update the data in the pivot table. Think before you do this in Excel 2019. In the current example, this forces Excel to go out and import the 1.7 million–row data set again.

- **February 29, 1900 does not exist in power pivot** —There was no February 29 in 1900. Lotus 1-2-3 had a bug: the date algorithms assumed that 1900 was a leap year. As Excel was battling for market share, they had to produce the same results as Lotus, so Excel repeated the February 29, 1900 bug. The SQL Server Analysis Team refused to perpetuate this bug and does not recognize February 29, 1900. In Excel, day 1 is January 1, 1900. In Power Pivot, day 1 is December 31, 1899. None of this matters unless you have sales that happened during January 1, 1900 through February 28, 1900. In that case, the two pivot tables will be off by a day. No one has data going back that far, right? It will never be an issue, right? Well, in 2018, I met a guy who had a column of quantities. He had values like 30 and 42 and 56. But that column was accidentally imported as a date. All the quantities were off by one.

- **32-Bit Excel is not enough**—I meet people who complain Excel is slow, even though they added more memory to their machine. Unfortunately, the 32-bit version of Excel can only access 3GB of the memory on your machine. To really use Power Pivot and the Data Model with millions of rows of data, you will need to install 64-Bit Excel. This does not cost anything extra. It does likely involve some pleading with the IT department. Also, there are some old add-ins that do not run in 64-bit Excel. If you happen to be using that add-in, then you must choose whether you want faster performance or the old add-in.

Enjoying Other Benefits of Power Pivot

Nothing in the previous list is a deal-breaker. In the interest of fairness, here are several more benefits that come from using Power Pivot and the Data Model:

- You can hide or rename columns. If your Database Administrator thinks `TextSlsRepNbr` is a friendly name, you can change it to `Sales Rep Number`. Or, if your data tables are littered with useless fields, you can hide them from the PivotTable Fields list. In the Power Pivot window, right-click any column heading and choose Hide From Client Tools.

- You can assign categories to fields, such as Geography, Image URL, and Web URL. Select the column in the Power Pivot window and choose a column. On the Advanced tab, choose a Data Category.

- You can define key performance indicators or hierarchies.

Learning More

Power Pivot and Power Query are powerful tools that are completely new for most Excellers. These are my favorite books to learn more:

- Mike Alexander and I cover more about Power Pivot in *Pivot Table Data Crunching Excel 2019* (ISBN 978-1-5093-0724-1).

- For Power Query, read *M Is for Data Monkey* by Ken Puls and Miguel Escobar (ISBN 978-1-61547-034-1).

- For DAX formulas in Power Pivot, read *Supercharge Excel* by Matt Allington (ISBN 978-1-61547-053-2).

- For Advanced Power Pivot, read *Power Pivot and Power BI* by Rob Collie and Avi Singh (ISBN 978-1-61547-039-6).

CHAPTER 17

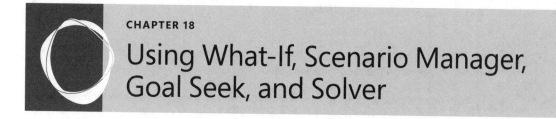

Using What-If, Scenario Manager, Goal Seek, and Solver

When Dan Bricklin invented VisiCalc in 1979, he was trying to come up with a tool that would let him quickly recalculate his MBA school case studies. Forty years later, spreadsheets are still used for the same functionality.

Newer spreadsheet tools such as Goal Seek and an improved Solver enable you to back directly into the assumptions that lead to a solution. This chapter discusses some of Excel 2019's features that are helpful when you are trying to find a specific answer.

Using What-If

After you have set up a model in Excel, you can make copies of the model side by side and then change the various input variables to test their impact on the final result. Because this type of analysis answers the question of what happens if a change is made, it is known generically as *what-if analysis*.

What-if analyses are the least formal method in this chapter. You copy the input variables and formulas multiple times. You can then vary the input variables until you reach a suitable solution.

For example, Figure 18.1 shows a worksheet to calculate the monthly payment on a car purchase. Cells E1, E2, and E3 are the known values: the price, term, and interest rate. Cell E4 calculates the monthly payment using the =PMT() function.

f_x	=PMT(E3/12,E2,-E1)	
D	**E**	**F**
Price	29900	
Term	60	
Interest	3.25%	
Payment	$540.59	

Figure 18.1 You might not like the answer in cell E4, but Excel makes the answer easy to find.

Cells E1:E4 are a self-contained mini-model. You can copy these cells several times over and perform what-if analysis on the car payment model.

Figure 18.2 shows a basic what-if worksheet that you can use to plug in different numbers manually. Each column uses a different combination of price, term, and interest rate.

D	E	F	G	H	I	J	K	L	M	N	O
Price	29900	29900	29900	29900	29900	29900	27500	27500	27500	25995	25995
Term	60	66	72	60	66	72	60	66	48	60	48
Interest	3.25%	3.50%	3.75%	4.50%	4.50%	4.50%	5.00%	5.00%	5.00%	5.00%	5.00%
Payment	$541	$499	$464	$557	$512	$475	$519	$477	$633	$491	$599

Figure 18.2 By making multiple copies of the table, you can create a what-if model.

There is nothing magic about this type of what-if analysis. There are no ribbon commands involved (other than applying Conditional Formatting, Color Scale to highlight the prices). You copy the model and plug in a few numbers. This is how most Excel worksheets use what-if analyses. The remaining topics in this chapter cover the What-If commands on the ribbon.

TROUBLESHOOTING

The Excel PMT function is great for calculating loan payments, but it frequently returns negative payments.

The PMT function shown in the previous figures has two annoying issues to make it work correctly.

When you go to the bank to get a loan, you will pay a specific interest rate to get that loan. In this example, let's say the interest rate is 4.5%. However, you cannot enter 4.5% as the first argument in PMT and get a correct answer. The Rate argument in the PMT function is expecting an interest rate per period for the loan. If you are making monthly payments, you will specify 4.5%/12.

Second, let's say you are buying a car that costs $25,000. The Present Value of the car is $25,000. If you enter =PMT(4.5%/12,60,25000) the formula will return a negative number. The logic here is that if a positive $25,000 pulls in to your garage, then a negative $466.08 will be leaving your checking account each month. However, you never write a check for -466.08. In order to get the PMT answer to return positive 466.08, you have to write the Present Value argument as negative: =PMT(4.5%/12,60,25000).

Because most people buy a car once every five years and a house once every ten years, the PMT function is particularly easy to forget between major purchases.

Creating a Two-Variable What-If Table

The analysis in Figure 18.2 is fairly ad hoc in that it basically enables you to try various combinations until you find one that is close to your target payment. If you have two variables to manipulate, you can use Excel's fairly powerful Data Table command. To use a data table, follow these steps to build the table shown in Figure 18.3:

1. Enter a formula in the upper-left corner of the table. This formula should point to at least two variable cells.

f_x	=PMT(E3/12,E2,-E1)				
D	**E**	**F**	**G**	**H**	**I**
Price	29900				
Term	60				
Interest	3.25%				
Payment	$540.59	48	54	60	6
	25900				
	26400				
	26900				

Figure 18.3   Preparing for a two-variable what-if analysis.

2. Along the left column of the table, enter various values for one of the input values. These values are substituted in a cell known as the *column input cell*.

3. Along the top row of the table, enter various values for the other input variable. These values are substituted in a cell that Excel calls the *row input cell*.

4. Select the entire table.

5. From the Data tab, select Data Tools, What-If Analysis, Data Table.

6. In the Data Table dialog, enter a row input cell and a column input cell.

7. Click OK to complete the table.

You can use the Data Table command to negotiate the price and term of the loan by following these steps:

1. Use the formula in cell E4 as the formula in the top-left corner of your table.

2. From E5:E21, fill in various possible values for purchase price.

3. From F4:K4, fill in various possible values for the term of the loan.

4. Select the entire table, E4:K21, as shown in Figure 18.4.

**Values along the top row
of the table are used in E2.**

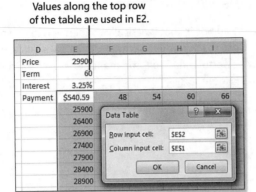

Figure 18.4   Setting up the Data Table dialog.

5.   Select Data Table from the Data tab to display the Data Table dialog, as shown in Figure 18.4. The dialog asks you for a row input cell and a column input cell. The Row Input Cell field offers to take each value from the top row of the table and plug it into a particular cell.

6.   Because the values in F4:K4 are loan terms, specify E2 for the row input cell.

7.   Similarly, the Column Input Cell field offers to take each value from the left column and replace that value in a particular cell. Because these cells contain vehicle prices, select E1 as the column input cell.

8.   Click OK. Excel fills in the intersection of each row and column with the monthly payment, based on the price in the left column combined with the loan term in the top row.

9.   Select just the interior of the table. You can see that Excel represents the table with the TABLE() array function. Figure 18.5 shows the table after a color scale has been applied.

$540.59	48	54	60	66	72	78
25900	576.15	516.21	468.27	429.07	396.42	368.81
26400	587.27	526.17	477.31	437.35	404.07	375.93
26900	598.39	536.14	486.35	445.64	411.73	383.05
27400	609.51	546.10	495.39	453.92	419.38	390.17
27900	620.64	556.07	504.43	462.20	427.03	397.29

Figure 18.5   The values in the table are calculated by a single TABLE() array formula. Oddly, you cannot enter the TABLE formula by typing it. You must use the Data Table command.

NOTE

You can use the Data Table command when only a single variable is changing. Enter values for the variable down the left column and enter a single cell with 1 in the top row. In the Data Table dialog, specify any blank cell as the row input cell. Alternatively, enter the changing values across the top row, and use a blank cell as the column input cell.

Modeling a Random Scenario Using a Data Table

The model shown in Figure 18.6 is known as a Random Walk Down Wall Street. In this simple model, a penny is flipped 25 times. If the penny comes up heads, you win a dollar. If the penny comes up tails, you lose $1. The model uses =IF(RAND()>.5,1,-1) to simulate the coin flip. The chart shows that the stock analyst running this model did well; he was always up and finished by making money (see Figure 18.6).

Figure 18.6   This hot-shot Wall Street analyst has been on a positive win streak.

Credit for this technique goes to Professor Simon Benninga. If you ever had a college class in financial modeling, you likely used Simon's textbook on the subject.

United States law requires financial firms to add the note that past results are not indicative of future returns. With the current model, press F9 to run the simulation again and you could see very different results. Same model. Same methods. Same guy pressing the F9 key, but the hot-shot stock analyst now loses someone's money—hopefully not yours (see Figure 18.7).

Figure 18.7 The same model loses money.

In my simple model, there are 25 coin flips. But it is possible to model 500 or 1,000 iterations with far more data points than a simple coin flip. After each run through the model, you might be interested in tracking the Max, the Min, the Standard Deviation, plus the most important statistic—did you make or lose money at the end?

In Figure 18.8, five formulas track the performance of one run of the model. It is possible to use Data, What-If Analysis, Data Table as shown in this figure. The top-left corner cell is blank. The Row Input Cell field is blank. The Column Input Cell field is pointing to a blank cell completely unrelated to the model.

Figure 18.8 This data table runs the entire model once for every row selected.

When you click OK to run the data table, every row returns the results of flipping the coin 25 times. Imagine if you had a model with many random variables and 1,000 iterations. You can use this technique to exercise the model hundreds of times (see Figure 18.9).

fx	{=TABLE(,H9)}				
H	**I**	**J**	**K**	**L**	**M**
Each row is cumulative result of 25 coin flips!					
Average	Highest	Lowest	StDev	Final	
0.2	3	-3	1.632993	3	
0.12	2	-2	1.16619	1	
3.56	7	1	1.733974	7	
-2.44	1	-7	1.87261	-7	
-5.56	-1	-13	3.536477	-13	
-0.68	3	-3	1.749286	-3	
-4.44	1	-10	3.267007	-9	

Figure 18.9   Each row in the resulting data table represents the results of dozens of coin flips.

Using Scenario Manager

The Data Table command is great for models with two variables that can change. However, sometimes you have models with far more variables that can change. In such a case, you could use the Scenario Manager, which enables you to create multiple scenarios, each changing up to 32 variables. With the added flexibility, it takes longer to create each scenario.

TIP

With up to 32 variables changing, it is best to use named ranges for all the input variables before you define your first scenario. One of the results of the Scenario Manager is a summary report. Using named ranges for all the input cells makes the report easier to understand.

➤ To learn how to use named ranges to your advantage, **see** "Using Named Ranges to Simplify Formulas," **p. 316.**

Figure 18.10 shows a sales model. Several input cells are highlighted in gray. The Scenario Manager dialog offers various scenarios that someone manually set up. Double-click any scenario to load those values into the model.

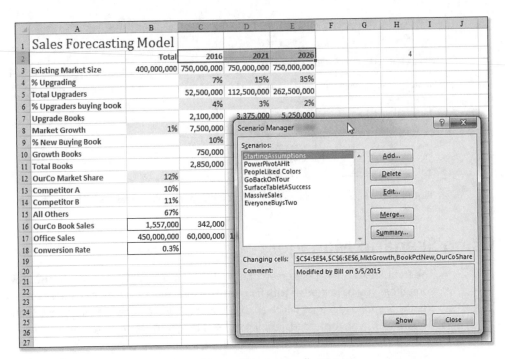

Figure 18.10   Choose any scenario to change all the input cells at once.

You can compare the results of all scenarios using either a regular summary report or a pivot table summary report. Figure 18.11 shows the regular summary report.

Scenario Summary		Current Values:	StartingAssumptions	PowerPivotAHit	PeopleLiked Colors	GoBackOnTour	SurfaceTabletASuccess
			Created by Bill Jelen	Assumes PowerPivot Drives Massive Growth	Assumes people reject office because of lack of color	Assumes World Tour in 2013-2014	Surface drives massive market growth, none buy books
Changing Cells:							
	UpgradePct14	7%	7%	8%	6%	7%	7%
	UpgradePct13	15%	15%	25%	4%	15%	15%
	UpgradePct08	35%	35%	55%	3%	35%	35%
	BookPct12	4%	4%	4%	4%	4%	4%
	BookPct13	3%	3%	4%	3%	3%	3%
	BookPct14	2%	2%	4%	2%	2%	80%
	MktGrowth	1%	1%	2%	-1%	1%	0%
	BookPctNew	10%	10%	10%	0%	10%	0%
	OurCoShare	12%	12%	12%	12%	18%	12%
Result Cells:							
	OurCoSalesForecast	1,557,000	1,557,000	3,708,000	378,000	2,335,500	1,503,000
	OurCoConversionPct	0.3%	0.3%	0.5%	0.5%	0.5%	0.1%

Notes: Current Values column represents values of changing cells at time Scenario Summary Report was created. Changing cells for each scenario are highlighted in gray.

Figure 18.11   After you identify the Results cells, Excel summarizes all scenarios.

Unfortunately, it is a tedious process to set up each scenario. To set up a scenario, use the following steps:

1. Select Data, Data Tools, What-If Analysis, Scenario Manager to display the Scenario Manager dialog. Initially, the Scenario Manager indicates that no scenarios are defined. Click the Add button to add a scenario. The Add Scenario dialog appears.

2. In the Add Scenario dialog, enter a name for this scenario and then choose which cells will be changing. Because the variable cells are not adjacent, select the first contiguous range and then Ctrl+click to add additional ranges (see Figure 18.12).

NOTE

It is best to add one scenario that represents your starting assumptions. Otherwise, those numbers will be lost.

Figure 18.12   Name your new scenario.

3. The Scenario Values dialog box appears, which can be used to edit the values for each starting cell (see Figure 18.13). Note that if you had previously named your input cells, the cell names appear in this dialog instead of addresses. Type new values. If you are finished creating scenarios, click OK. If you want to return to the Add Scenario dialog box to define another scenario, click OK.

Figure 18.13   Typing the input values is the tedious part.

CHAPTER 18

Creating a Scenario Summary Report

One powerful feature of Excel scenarios is the capability to create a Scenario Summary report. When you click the Summary button on the Scenario Manager dialog, Excel enables you to choose either a Scenario Summary report or a Pivot Table report. In either case, you should select one or more cells that represent the results of the model.

CAUTION

The Scenario Summary report is a snapshot in time. If you later change scenarios or add new scenarios, you must re-create and reformat the Scenario Summary report.

Adding Multiple Scenarios

You might want to share a workbook with others and have them add their own scenarios to get opinions from people in other areas of your company, such as sales, marketing, engineering, and manufacturing. To do this, follow these steps:

1. Save the workbook with just the starting scenario.

2. Route the workbook to each person. In a hidden field, Excel keeps track of who adds each scenario.

3. When you get the routed workbook back, open both the original workbook and the routed workbook.

4. Display the Scenario Manager in the original workbook.

5. Click the Merge button to display the Merge Scenarios dialog.

6. In the Book drop-down, select the name of the routed workbook.

7. Excel usually encounters identically named scenarios in the merge process. It differentiates any scenarios with identical names by adding a date or name to the incoming scenarios. If these scenarios are truly identical to the scenario that you originally sent out, delete them.

Using Goal Seek

On the television show *The Price Is Right*, one of the games is the Hi-Lo game. A contestant tries to guess the price of an item, and the host tells the player that the actual price is higher or lower. The process of homing in on a price of $1.67 might involve guesses of $2, $1, $1.50, $1.75, $1.63, $1.69, $1.66, $1.68, and finally $1.67. Using the techniques described so far in this chapter, you might play this game with Excel to try to hone in on an answer.

You might have an Excel worksheet set up that calculates a final value using several input variables. To solve the formula in reverse, you need to find input variables that generate a certain answer. There are several possible approaches:

- One difficult approach is to determine whether another Excel function reverses the calculation. For example, =ARCSIN() performs the opposite of =SIN(), and =NPER(), =RATE(), or =PV() back into a =PMT().

- Another approach is to use algebra to attempt to solve for one of the input variables.

- Most people simply play the Hi-Lo game by successively plugging in higher and lower answers to the input cell until they narrow in on an input variable that produces the desired result.

- If you play the Hi-Lo game, consider using the Goal Seek command. In effect, this command plays the Hi-Lo game at hyperspeed, arriving at an answer within a second.

Consider the car payment example at the beginning of the chapter. You want to find a price that yields a $475 monthly payment. You might find a =PV() function that can solve this. However, most people plug in successively higher or lower values for the price in cell E1 (see Figure 18.14).

Figure 18.14   Goal Seek lets you find one value by changing one other cell.

Excel's Goal Seek option, on the other hand, enables you to hone in quickly on a value. To use Goal Seek, follow these steps:

1. Select the answer cell. In this example, it would be the payment in cell E4.

2. From the Data Tools group of the Data tab, select the What-If Analysis drop-down, and then select Goal Seek. The Goal Seek dialog appears, as shown in Figure 18.14.

3. In the Goal Seek dialog, indicate that you want to set the answer cell to a particular value by changing a particular input cell. In this example, set cell E4 to the value of 475 by changing cell E1. Excel begins trying to home in on a value. When Excel gets to within a penny of the value, the results are presented. Behind the dialog, the worksheet shows the proposed price of 26272.12 in the worksheet.

4. Either accept this value by clicking OK or revert to the original value by clicking Cancel.

Goal Seek can be applied to other input cells. For example, in Figure 18.15, the Goal Seek in column F sought a $475 monthly payment by changing the term. If you are willing to make payments for 69 months, you can buy the desired car. However, when Goal Seek tried to get a $475 monthly payment by changing the interest rate, the result was the impossible negative interest rate.

	Original	Price	Term	Interest
Price	29900	26272.12	29900	29900
Term	60	60	69.10666	60
Interest	3.25%	3.25%	3.25%	-1.87%
Payment	$540.59	$475.00	$475.00	$475.00

Figure 18.15   Three different Goal Seek commands find how to yield a $475 payment by changing either the price, the term, or the rate.

Using Solver

It is possible to design problems that are far too complex for Goal Seek. These problems might have dozens of independent variables and various constraints. In such a case, you can use the Excel Solver add-in.

TIP

Solver was improved in Excel 2010. To get the old Solver to work, you had to have a good grasp on linear mathematics. Hence, the old Solver never worked for me. The new Solver offers advanced methodologies that find solutions to far more problems. If you had tried Solver before without success, it is time to try it again.

With Solver, you identify an output formula cell that you want to be maximized, minimized, or set to a particular value. You specify a range of cells that can be changed. You then specify a number of constraints on input cells or other formulas in the model.

The Solver add-in, which is free with Excel, was written by Dan Fylstra and Frontline Systems. History buffs might remember that Dan Fylstra was the president of VisiCorp—the world's first spreadsheet program. Frontline Systems offers more advanced versions of Solver plus an Excel Data Miner tool at www.Solver.com.

Installing Solver

To install Solver, follow these steps:

1. Press Alt+T and then press I to display the Add-Ins dialog.

2. In the Add-Ins dialog, make sure that Solver is checked.

Solving a Model Using Solver

To use Solver, your worksheet should contain one or more input variables. The worksheet should also contain one or more formulas that result in a solution within a single cell.

For each input variable, there might be certain constraints. For example, you might want to assume that a certain variable must be positive or that it should be in a certain range of values.

When using Solver, you identify the input range, the output cell, and the constraints. You can ask Solver to minimize or maximize the input cell. Alternatively, you can ask Solver to set the output cell to a particular value. Solver uses advanced algorithms to find input variables that meet your goal and fit within the constraints.

This might be easier to understand with a concrete example. Figure 18.16 shows a worksheet used to model the production of widgets. Cell B23 indicates that each worker in your factory can make 40 widgets per hour. Workers who work evenings, nights, or weekends are paid a shift differential. You can choose to keep your factory running for anywhere from five shifts a week (Monday through Friday, first shift) up to 21 shifts per week. You can sell as many widgets as you can produce, provided that the overall cost is less than $2 per widget. You have a skilled work-force of 100 workers available for first shift, 82 workers for second shift, and 75 workers for third shift. How many shifts should the plant be open to maximize production? Solver runs circles around Goal Seek in situations that deal with multiple constraints.

To use Solver to find the answer, use the following steps:

1. Note that cells B3 through B11 define how many shifts the factory will be open. All the remaining cells in the model calculate the total number of widgets produced and the average cost per widget. Your goal is to maximize the number of widgets produced (cell D22) while keeping the average cost per widget in F22 to less than $2.00.

2. Select Solver from the Data tab in the ribbon.

3. Enter D22 as the Objective. Choose to set this to a Max (see Figure 18.17).

A	B	C	D	E	F
Manufacturing Plant Productivity					
Day Shift M-F	5		Goals:		
Evening Shift M-F	5		*Maximize widget production*		
Night Shift M-F	5		*Keep cost of widgets < $2.00*		
Day Shift Saturday	1				
Evening Shift Saturday	1				
Night Shift Saturday	1				
Day Shift Sun	1				
Evening Shift Sun	1				
Night Shift Sun	1				
		Workers Avail per Shift	**Total Widgets**	**Total Cost**	
Labor Cost Per Shift					
Day Shift M-F	8.25	100	20000	38000	
Evening Shift M-F	8.75	82	16400	33700	
Night Shift M-F	9.25	75	15000	32750	
Day Shift Saturday	12.38	80	3200	8923.2	
Evening Shift Saturday	13.13	72	2880	8562.88	
Night Shift Saturday	13.88	65	2600	8217.6	
Day Shift Sun	16.5	50	2000	7600	
Evening Shift Sun	17.5	36	1440	6040	
Night Shift Sun	18.5	30	1200	5440	Per Widget
Overhead per shift	1000	Total	64720	149234	2.3058356
Widgets Per Worker Per Shift	40				

Figure 18.16   A worksheet to model widget production.

Figure 18.17   Define the model for Solver.

4. Define the input cells as B3:B11 in the By Changing Variable Cells box.

5. Use the Add button to add new constraints. One obvious constraint is that F22 must be less than a $2 cost. Cells B3:B5, which represent weekday shifts, cannot be higher than 5 per week because there are only 5 weekday shifts. There are other important constraints. You probably don't want an answer that says you work 0.329454 of a shift, so add a constraint that says B3:B11 must remain integers. Add a constraint that says those same cells cannot be negative. For the weekend shifts, the only valid values are 0 or 1. Use a constraint of Binary to allow only 0 or 1 as the input cells.

6. Three Solving Methods are available. Always start with GRG Nonlinear. If that doesn't work, try Evolutionary. If you are a math genius and have built a model with pure linearity, try Simplex LP.

7. Click the Solve button. Solver begins to iterate through possible solutions. If Solver finds a result, it reports success.

8. Click Save Scenario and give the scenario a solution such as SolverSolution. If you are going to define the solutions as a scenario, after doing this step, you can choose Restore Original Values and click OK. You can then use Data, What-If Analysis, Scenario Manager to add a scenario with your original values.

9. Select the Answer Report to have Excel provide a new worksheet that compares the original and final values.

NOTE

The GRG engine finds a solution that matches the constraints. However, it might not be the best solution. The LP Solver engine finds the best solution but only if you set up the model as a linear problem. The Evolutionary engine uses Monte Carlo to try random choices, hoping to home in on a better solution.

In the answer report, Solver tells you that you can produce 42,400 widgets by operating five day and evening shifts and two night shifts. The remaining shifts are not cost effective to keep the cost per widget in cell F22 less than $2.

With this current solution, the cost per widget is exactly $2.

TIP

Frontline Systems offer premium versions of their Solver products that can handle more input variables than the Solver in Excel. If you find that Solver cannot solve your problem, sign up for a free trial of Premium Solver at http://mrx.cl/solver77.

Inside OUT

Some problems cannot be solved in a single lifetime using Solver. Say that you have a billion possible input values and that the logic inside the model is not linear. Solver will often fail to come up with the best solution.

In this case, you can switch over to Monte Carlo analysis. Set up a model where you calculate the results a thousand or five thousand times. The Monte Carlo range would start with a column of =RANDBETWEEN(1,100000000). More columns in the Monte Carlo range would calculate the output of the model.

Let's say you are trying to find the largest possible output value. Add a =MAX(B1:B1000) off to the right of your model. Press F9 a few times and keep your eye on the result of the Max function. After a few presses of F9, you will start to notice the usual range for Max and the super-high range for Max. When you press F9 and get a large result for Max, scroll through the Monte Carlo range to find the input cell with the best output cell. Copy that row as values to a "Best Answer So Far" section (usually right near the Max result).

Now, keep pressing F9 until the Max function is larger than the Best Answer So Far. Copy that row and replace the Best Answer So Far.

After ten minutes of this process, you will usually have an answer better than Solver would have found.

CHAPTER 19

Automating Repetitive Functions Using VBA Macros

Every copy of Excel shipped since 1995 has included the powerful Visual Basic for Applications (VBA) lurking behind the grid. With VBA, you can do anything that you can do in the regular interface, and you can do it much faster. VBA shines when you have many repetitive tasks to undertake.

As Excel 2019 ships to the market, there are two emerging technologies that might eat into some of VBA's solutions. First, the Power Query tools on the Get & Transform group on the Data tab can automate routine data cleaning operations. You clean the data once using Power Query and then you can refresh the query when the underlying data changes. Read more about Power Query in Chapter 13, "Transforming Data with Power Query."

In May 2018, Microsoft announced support for JavaScript User Defined Functions. These functions rely on JavaScript instead of VBA. Their performance is still much slower than VBA, but, they offer one neat trick: They will work in Excel Online in addition to the desktop version of Excel. JavaScript is not covered in this book, but for an introduction to JavaScript in Excel, read Suat Ozgur's *Excel JavaScript UDFs Straight to the Point*.

Learning to use macros is a good news/bad news proposition. The good news is that Microsoft Office provides a macro recorder that can write a macro as you work. The bad news is that it is not easy to record a macro that works consistently with any data set. To unleash the power of macros, you need to understand how to edit recorded macro code. You can then record a macro that is close to what you want and edit that macro to create something that runs the way you want it to work.

Checking Security Settings Before Using Macros

Before you can use macros, you have to take some positive steps to affirm that you want to record or run a macro.

To enable VBA security, follow these steps:

1. Select File, Options to open the Excel Options dialog.

2. Select the Customize Ribbon category. In the right-side list box, select the Developer tab check box.

3. Click OK to exit the Excel Settings dialog. You now have a Developer tab on the ribbon.

4. On the Developer tab, click Macro Security in the Code group. The Security dialog appears.

5. In the Security dialog, change the Macro Settings option to Disable All Macros With Notification. With this setting, Excel alerts you whenever you open a workbook that has macros attached.

6. When you open a document and get the warning that the document has macros attached, if this is a document that you wrote and you expect macros to be there, click Enable Content to enable the macros. Otherwise, make sure the workbook came from someone you trust.

NOTE

In step 5, *with* is the operative word. You are choosing to disable macros and to display a notification to let you decide whether or not the macros should be enabled. Before choosing to enable macros, you can switch over to VBA and see what macros are in the workbook.

Recording a Macro

Plan your macro before recording it by thinking through the steps you need to perform. If you need to fix many items in a worksheet, you might want to select the first item first. This way, the macro can perform an action on cells relative to the original selection.

To record a macro, follow these steps:

1. On the Developer tab, select Record Macro.

2. In the Record Macro dialog box, type a name for the macro. The name cannot contain spaces. For example, instead of using Macro Name, you need to use MacroName.

3. Choose whether you want to store the macro in the current workbook, a new workbook, or a special Personal Macro Workbook. The personal macro workbook is a special

workbook designed to hold general-purpose macros that might apply to any workbook. If you are unsure, select to store the recorded macro in the current workbook.

4. Assign a shortcut key for the macro. Ctrl+J is a safe key because nothing is currently assigned to Ctrl+J. This shortcut key enables you to run the macro again.

5. Click OK to close the Record Macro dialog.

6. Turn on relative recording by clicking the Use Relative References icon in the Code group of the Developer tab. Relative recording records the action of moving a certain number of cells from the active cell.

7. Perform the actions you want to store in the macro.

8. Click the Stop Recording button on the left side of the status bar at the bottom of the Excel window.

9. Save the workbook before testing the macro.

10. Test the macro playback by typing the shortcut key assigned in step 4.

CAUTION

The alternative is an absolute recording. This method is extremely literal. The action of moving down three cells from A1 is recorded as "Select cell A4." That action is extremely limited—it would work only when the macro is played back with the active cell in A1.

Case Study: Macro for Formatting for a Mail Merge

Suppose that your co-worker has some names and addresses in Excel and she needs to do a mail merge in Word. Instead of teaching her how to do a mail merge, you offer to do the mail merge for her. In theory, this should take you a couple minutes. However, when the list of names arrives in the Excel worksheet, you realize the data is in the wrong format. In the Excel worksheet, the names are going down column A, as shown in Figure 19.1.

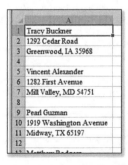

Figure 19.1 A simple task, such as doing a mail merge, is incredibly difficult when the data is in the wrong format.

To complete a mail merge successfully, the Excel worksheet should have fields for name, street address, and city+state+ZIP Code, as shown in Figure 19.2.

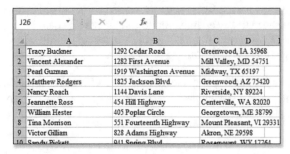

Figure 19.2 The goal is to produce data with fields in columns.

Before you start recording a macro, you need to think about how to break the task into easily repeatable steps.

It would be good to record a macro that can fix one name in the list. Assume that you start with the cell pointer on a person's name at the beginning of the macro, as shown in Figure 19.1. The macro would need to perform these steps to fix one record and end up on the name of the second person in the list:

1. Press the down-arrow key to move to the address cell.

2. Press Ctrl+X to cut the address.

3. Press the up-arrow key and then the right-arrow key to move next to the name.

4. Press Ctrl+V to paste the address.

5. Press the left-arrow key once and the down-arrow key twice to move to the cell for city, state, and ZIP Code.

6. Press Ctrl+X to cut the city.

7. Press the up-arrow key twice and the right-arrow key twice to move to the right of the street cell.

8. Press Ctrl+V to paste the city.

9. Press the left-arrow key twice and the down-arrow key once to move to the now blank row just below the name.

10. Hold down the Shift key while pressing the down-arrow key twice to select the three blank rows.

11. Press Ctrl+- to invoke the Delete command. Press R and then Enter to delete the row.

When you run a macro that goes through these steps, Excel deletes the three blank rows, but the selection now contains the three cells that encompass the next record, as shown in Figure 19.3. Ideally, the macro should end with only the name selected. Press Shift+Backspace to reduce the selection to the active cell.

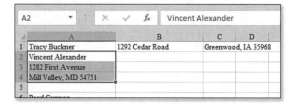

Figure 19.3   You need only one cell selected instead of three.

If the macro correctly performs all these steps, the first name and address are properly formatted. The blank rows left between the first and second names are deleted.

By making sure that the macro starts on a name and ends up on the next name, you allow the macro to be run repeatedly. If you assign this macro to the keyboard shortcut Ctrl+J, you can then hold down Ctrl+J and quickly fix records, one after the other.

How Not to Record a Macro: The Default State of the Macro Recorder

The default state of the macro recorder is a stupid state. If you recorded the preceding steps in the macro recorder, the macro recorder would take your actions literally. The English pseudo-code for recording these steps would say this:

1.   Move to cell A2.

2.   Cut cell A2 and paste to cell B1.

3.   Move to cell A3.

4.   Cut cell A3 and paste to cell C1.

5.   Delete rows 2 through 4.

6.   Select cell A2.

This macro works, but it works for only one record. After you've recorded this macro, your worksheet looks like the one shown previously in Figure 19.3.

When the default macro runs, it moves the name Vincent Alexander from cell A2 and pastes it on top of the address in cell B1. It then takes the address in cell A3 and pastes it on top of the city in cell C1. After that, it deletes rows 2, 3, and 4, removing the city and state. As shown in Figure 19.4, the macro provides the wrong result.

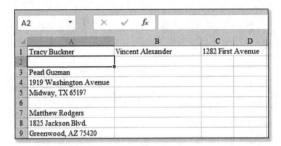

Figure 19.4   When the default macro runs, it ruins two records.

If you blindly ran this macro 100 times to convert 100 addresses, the macro would happily "eat" all 100 records, leaving you with just one record (and not even a correct record). To overcome this problem, use relative references, as discussed in the next section.

Relative References in Macro Recording

The key to recording a successful macro is to enable the Use Relative References setting in Excel. Had Microsoft made this the default, far more people would have success with their recorded macros. Locate the icon in the Code group on the Developer tab on the ribbon called Use Relative References. If you performed the steps described in the preceding section in relative recording mode, Excel would write code that does this:

1. Move down one cell.

2. Cut that cell.

3. Move up and over one cell and paste.

4. Move left and down two cells.

5. Cut that cell.

6. Move up and over two cells and paste.

7. Move left two cells, move down one cell, and delete three rows.

8. Move up and down one cell to select a single cell.

TIP

Ninety-eight percent of the time you are recording macros, you should have Use Relative Reference turned on.

These steps are far more generic than those recorded using the default state of the macro recorder. These steps work for any record, provided that you started the macro with the cell pointer on the first cell that contains a name.

For this example, you need to record the entire macro with relative recording turned on.

Starting the Macro Recorder

At this point, you have rehearsed the steps needed for a macro that puts data records into a format that is usable for a mail merge. After you make sure that the cell pointer is starting on the name in cell A1, you are ready to turn on the macro recorder.

You should not be nervous, but you need to perform the steps correctly. If you move the cell pointer in the wrong direction, the macro recorder happily records that for you and plays it back. It is annoying to watch the macro recorder play back your mistakes 100 times a day for the next 5 years. Therefore, follow these steps to create the macro correctly:

1. On the Developer tab, click the Record Macro icon from the Code group. The Record Macro dialog appears, as shown in Figure 19.5.

Figure 19.5 After making the needed selections, click OK to begin recording.

2. Excel suggests giving this macro the unimaginative name Macro1. Use any name you want, up to 64 characters and without spaces. For this example, name the macro FixOneRecord. Choose a shortcut key for the macro. The shortcut key is important. Because you have to run this macro once for each record in the present example, you might choose something like Ctrl+A, which is easy to press.

3. Make a selection from the Store Macro In drop-down. You have the option of storing the macro in this workbook, in a new workbook, or in the personal macro workbook. If this is a general-purpose macro that you will use every day on every file, it makes sense to store the macro in the personal macro workbook. However, because this macro will be used just to solve a current problem, store it in the current workbook.

4. Fill in a description if you think you will be using this macro long enough to forget what it does. When you are done making selections on the Record Macro dialog (refer to Figure 19.5), click OK. The Record Macro icon changes to a Stop Recording icon.

NOTE

Keep in mind that assigning a macro to Ctrl+A overwrites the usual action of that keystroke (selecting all cells). If you are writing a macro that will be used all day, every day, you should use a shortcut key that is not assigned to existing shortcuts, such as Ctrl+J. Although most of the letter keys are already assigned to a shortcut, you can always use the shifted shortcut keys. To assign a macro to Ctrl+Shift+A, press Shift+A into the shortcut field.

5. Click the Use Relative References icon in the Developer tab. The icon is highlighted.

6. Press the down-arrow key to move to the address cell.

7. Press Ctrl+X to cut the address.

8. Press the up-arrow key and then the right-arrow key to move next to the name.

9. Press Ctrl+V to paste the address.

10. Press the left-arrow key once and the down-arrow key twice to move to the cell for city, state, and ZIP Code.

11. Press Ctrl+X to cut the city.

12. Press the up-arrow key twice and the right-arrow key twice to move to the right of the street cell.

13. Press Ctrl+V to paste the city.

14. Press the left-arrow key twice and the down-arrow key once to move to the now-blank row just below the name.

15. Hold down the Shift key while pressing the down-arrow key twice to select the three blank rows.

16. Press Ctrl+- to invoke the Delete command. Press R and then Enter to delete the row.

17. Press the up-arrow key and the down-arrow key. Moving the cell pointer up a cell and then back to the name causes only a single cell to be selected.

18. When you are done, click the Stop Recording button.

This macro successfully fixes any record in the database, provided the cell pointer is on the cell containing the name when you run the macro. Try playing back the macro by pressing Ctrl+A to fix one record. To fix all records, hold down Ctrl+A until all records are fixed.

Running a Macro

To run a macro, follow these steps:

1. Click the Macros icon in the Code group of the Developer tab. The Macro dialog appears, as shown in Figure 19.6.

Figure 19.6   Playing back a macro by using the Macro dialog.

2. Select your macro and click the Run button. The macro fixes the first record.

3. Press Ctrl+A to run the FixOneRecord macro. The second record is fixed.

4. Hold down Ctrl+A to repeatedly run the macro. In a matter of seconds, all 100 names are in a format ready to use in a mail merge.

TIP
Displaying the Macro dialog every time you want to run a macro is not efficient. Try running the macro with a shortcut key.

CAUTION

When you run a macro, there is no undo. Therefore, you should save a file before running a new macro on it. It is easy to have accidentally recorded the macro in default mode instead of relative mode. You need to save the macro so that you can easily go back to the current state in case something does not work right.

This example represents an ideal use of a one-time macro. The process of fixing the data someone gave you involved mindless repetition. If there had just been four records, you could have mindlessly fixed them. However, because there were 100 records in this example, it made sense to record a macro and then run the macro repeatedly to solve the problem. You recorded the entire macro in relative mode, and you did not have to edit the macro. You probably run into a few situations a week in which a quick one-time-use macro would make your job easier.

Everyday-Use Macro Example: Formatting an Invoice Register

The macro recorder does not solve all tasks perfectly, however. Many times, you need to record a macro and then edit the recorded code to make the macro a bit more general. This example demonstrates how to do that.

In this example, a system writes out a file every day. This file contains a list of invoices generated on the previous day. The file predictably contains six columns—NAME, DATE, INVOICE, REVENUE, SALES TAX, and TOTAL—as shown in Figure 19.7. The file also looks horrible: The columns are the wrong width, there is no title, and there isn't a Total row at the bottom. You would like a macro that opens this file, makes the columns wider, adds a total row, adds a title, makes the headings bold, and saves the file with a new name. The following sections describe how to create this macro.

Figure 19.7 Create a macro to format this file every day.

Using the Ctrl+Down-Arrow Key to Handle a Variable Number of Rows

One of the inherent problems with this example is that your file will have a different number of rows every day. If you record a macro for this today to add totals in row 16, it will not work tomorrow, when you might have 22 invoices. The solution is to use the Ctrl+Down-Arrow key to navigate to the last row of your data.

You use Ctrl and any arrow key to move to the edge of a contiguous range of data. In Figure 19.7, if you press Ctrl+Down Arrow, you would move to cell A15. From cell A15, press Ctrl+Up Arrow to move back to cell A1. You can press the Ctrl+Right Arrow to move to cell F1.

You can also use the Ctrl+arrow key to jump over an abyss of empty cells. If you are currently at the edge of a range (for example, cell F1) and press Ctrl+Right Arrow, Excel jumps over all the blank cells and stops either at the next nonblank cell in row 1 or at the right edge of the worksheet, cell XFD1.

Making Sure You Find the Last Record

You might be tempted to start in cell A1, press Ctrl+Down Arrow, and then press the down-arrow key again to move to the first blank row in the data. However, that is not the safest method. This data file is coming from another system. Undoubtedly, one day a cashier will find a way to enter an order without a customer name. She will happen upon the accidental keystroke combination that causes the cash register to allow an order without a customer name. On that day, the Ctrl+Down-Arrow combination will stop at the wrong row and add totals in the middle of your data set. Thus, it is safer to use the Go To dialog to move to A1048576 and use Ctrl+Up Arrow to find the last record.

Recording the Macro in a Blank Workbook

Open a blank workbook, and save it with a filename such as MacroToImportInvoices.xlsm. You can record your macro in this blank workbook and save it. Then, each day, you can open the macro workbook. The macro will handle opening the data file and formatting it. Go through these steps while the macro recorder is running:

1. Open the file.

2. Press the F5 key to display the Go To dialog.

3. Go to cell A1048576 (the last cell in column A).

4. Turn on relative recording by clicking Use Relative References in the Developer tab. You use relative recording because you want to record the action of jumping to the last row, and that row will be in a different location each day.

5. Press End+Up Arrow to move to the last row that contains data.

6. Press the down-arrow key to move to the blank row below the last row for data.

7. Type the word **Total**.

8. Move right three cells.

9. Type the formula **=SUM(D$2:D15)**. Press Ctrl+Enter to stay in the current cell. Be sure to include a single dollar sign to lock the start of the range to row 2. Do not use the AutoSum icon to add this formula!

10. Drag the fill handle to the right two cells to copy the formula from D to E and F.

11. Select all cells with Ctrl+Shift+Home.

12. Select Home, Format, AutoFit Column Width to make all the columns wide.

13. Turn off relative recording by clicking the Use Relative References icon in the Developer tab. At this point, you always want to return to row 1 to format the headings. You don't want the recorder to record "Move up 15 rows." You always want to go to row 1.

14. Select row 1.

15. Open the Cell Styles gallery on the Home tab and choose Heading 4. Insert two rows using your favorite method. One method is to press Alt+I+R twice.

16. Move to cell A1.

17. Type the formula **="Invoices for "&TEXT(B4,"mmmm d, yyyy")**. Press Ctrl+Enter to accept the formula and stay in the cell.

18. Open the Cell Styles gallery and choose Title.

19. Use Save As to save the file with a new name to reflect today's date.

20. Click the Stop Recording button.

CHAPTER 19

In this macro example, you use a mix of relative and absolute recording to produce a macro that handles any number of rows of data. The macro will be somewhat useful, with two annoying limitations:

- If you saved the file as 2018-Feb-17Invoices.xls, the macro will attempt to overwrite that file every day.

- The macro will always want to open the same file. This is great if your cash register system always produces a file with the same name in the same folder. However, you might want the option to browse for a different file each day.

Both of these changes require you to edit the recorded macro. Before editing the macro, here is a look at how to open the Visual Basic Editor and at the syntax of VBA. To see the code to finish this example, refer to "Customizing the Everyday-Use Macro Example: GetOpenFileName and GetSaveAsFileName," later in this chapter.

Editing a Macro

To edit a macro, follow these steps:

1. Open the Macro dialog by pressing Alt+F8. The Macro dialog appears.

2. In the Macro dialog, select your macro and click Edit (refer to Figure 19.6). The Visual Basic Editor (VBE) is launched.

A number of panes are available in the VBE, but it is common to have three particular panes displayed, as shown in Figure 19.8:

- **Code pane**—The actual lines of the macro code are in the Code pane, which is usually on the right side of the screen.

- **Project pane**—This pane, which is in the upper left, shows every open workbook. Within the workbooks, you can see objects for each worksheet, an object for this workbook, and one or more code modules. If you cannot see the Project pane, press Ctrl+R or select View, Project Explorer to open it.

- **Properties pane**—This pane, in the lower left, is useful if you design custom dialogs. You can press F4 to display the Properties pane.

Project Pane   Code Pane

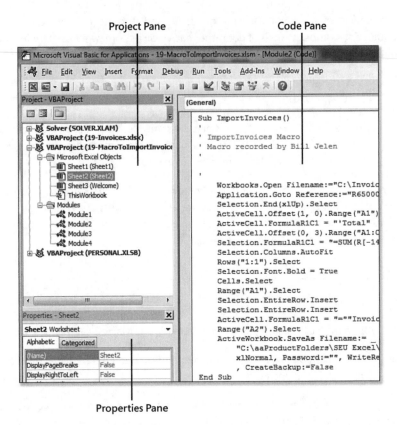

Properties Pane

Figure 19.8   The VBE allows editing of recorded macro code.

Understanding VBA Code—An Analogy

In the 1980s and early 1990s, many people going through school were exposed to an introductory class in a programming language called BASIC. Although Excel macros are written in Visual Basic for Applications, the fact that both languages contain the word *basic* does not mean that BASIC and VBA are the same or even similar. BASIC is a procedural language. VBA is an object-oriented language. In VBA, the focus is on objects. This can make VBA confusing to someone who has learned to program in BASIC.

The syntax of VBA consists of objects, methods, collections, arguments, and properties. If you have never programmed in an object-oriented language, these terms, and the VBA code itself, might seem foreign to you. The following sections compare these five elements to parts of speech:

● An object is similar to a noun.

● A method is similar to a verb.

- A collection is similar to a plural noun.

- An argument is similar to an adverb.

- A property is similar to an adjective.

Each of the following sections describes the similarity between the VBA element and a part of speech. These sections also describe how to recognize the various elements when you examine VBA code.

Comparing Object.Method to Nouns and Verbs

As an object-oriented language, the objects in VBA are of primary importance. Think of an object as any noun in Excel. Examples of objects are a cell, a row, a column, a worksheet, and a workbook.

A method is any action that you can perform on an object. This is similar to a verb. You can add a worksheet. You can delete a row. You can clear a cell. In Excel VBA, words such as *Add*, *Delete*, and *Clear* are methods.

Objects and methods are joined by a period, although in VBA, people pronounce the period as *dot*. The object is first, followed by a dot, followed by the method. For example, object.method, which is pronounced "object-dot-method," indicates that the method performs on the object. This is confusing because it is backward from the way English is spoken. If everyone spoke VBA instead of English, we would use sentences such as "car.drive" and "dinner.eat." When you see a period in VBA, it usually means that the word after the period is acting upon the word to the left of the period.

Comparing Collections to Plural Nouns

In an Excel workbook, there is not a single cell but rather a collection of many cells. Many workbooks contain several worksheets. Anytime you have multiple instances of a certain object, VBA refers to this as a *collection*.

The *s* at the end of an object may seem subtle, but it indicates you are dealing with a collection instead of a single object. Whereas ThisWorkbook refers to a single workbook, Workbooks refers to a collection of all the open workbooks. This is an important distinction to understand.

You have two main ways to refer to a single worksheet in a collection of worksheets:

- By its number, such as Worksheets(1)

- By its name, such as Worksheets("Jan")

Comparing Parameters to Adverbs

When you invoke a command such as the Save As command, a dialog pops up, and you have the opportunity to specify several options that change how the command is carried out. If the Save As command is a method, the options for it are parameters. Just as an adverb modifies a verb, a parameter modifies a method.

Most of the time, parameters are recorded by using this syntax:

```
ParameterName:=ParameterValue
```

One of the reasons that recorded code gets to be so long is that the macro recorder makes note of every option on the dialog, whether you select it or not.

Consider this line of code for SaveAs:

```
ActiveWorkbook.SaveAs Filename:="C:\Something.xlsx", _
    FileFormat:=xlOpenXMLWorkbook, CreateBackup:=False
```

In this recorded macro for SaveAs, the recorder noted parameter values for `Filename`, `FileFormat`, and `CreateBackup`. Figure 19.9 shows the Save As dialog. `Filename` and `FileFormat` are evident on the form. However, where is the option for Create Backup?

Figure 19.9   It seems like the macro recorder is making up options that are not on the dialog.

In the bottom center of the dialog is a Tools drop-down. If you select Tools, General Options, you see a dialog with four additional options, as shown in Figure 19.10. Even though you did not touch this Save Options dialog, Excel recorded the Backup value from the dialog for you.

Figure 19.10   Even though you did not touch the Save Options dialog, the macro recorder recorded the values from it.

Parameters have some potentially confusing aspects. Most of the time, there is a space following the method and then a list of one or more `ParameterName:=ParameterValue` constructs, separated by a comma and a space. However, there are a few exceptions:

- If the result of the method is acted upon by another method, the list of parameters is enclosed in parentheses, and there is no space after the method name. One example is when you add a shape to a worksheet and then Excel selects the shape. The code to insert the shape uses the AddShape method and five named parameters:

```
ActiveSheet.Shapes.AddShape Type:=msoShapeRectangle, _
  Left:=60, Top:=120, _
  Width:=100, Height:=100
```

- The macro recorder will record the process of adding the shape and then selecting the shape. Because the `.Select` method is acting upon the result of the `.AddShape` method, you see the parameters for the AddShape method surrounded by parentheses:

```
ActiveSheet.Shapes.AddShape(Type:=msoShapeRectangle, _
  Left:=60, Top:=120, _
  Width:=100, Height:=100).Select
```

- When you use the parameter name, you can specify the parameters in any sequence you like. The Help topic for the method reveals the official default order for the parameters. If you specify the parameters in the exact sequence specified in Help, you are allowed to leave off the parameter names. However, this is a poor coding practice. Even if you have memorized the default order for the parameters, you cannot assume that everyone else reading your code will know the default order. The problem is that sometimes the macro recorder will record code in this style. For example, here is the actual line of code that was recorded when I added a shape to a worksheet:

```
ActiveSheet.Shapes.AddShape(msoShapeRectangle, 60, 120, 100, 100).Select
```

CHAPTER 19

- It would be difficult to figure out this line of code without looking at the Help topic. To access Help, click anywhere in the method of AddShape and then press the F1 key. The Help topic reveals that the correct parameter order is Type, Left, Top, Width, Height.

NOTE

Keep in mind that parameters are like adverbs. They generally appear with a `Parameter Name:=Parameter Value` construct. However, there are times when the macro recorder lists the parameter values in their default order, without the parameter names or the `:=`.

Accessing VBA Help

You can click any object, method, argument, or parameter in VBA and press the F1 key to display a complete description of the item. The Help topic lists the valid properties associated with the object and the valid methods that can be used on the object. Often, the Help topic will include an example as well. To use the code in the example, you can highlight the code, press Ctrl+C to copy, and then paste this code directly into the Code pane of the Visual Basic Editor (also known as the VBE).

Comparing Adjectives to Properties

The final construct in VBA is the adjective used to describe an object. In VBA, adjectives are called *properties*. Think about a cell in Excel with a formula in it. The cell has many properties. These are some of the most popular properties:

- Value (the value shown in the cell)

- Formula (the formula used to calculate value)

- Font Name

- Font Size

- Font Color

- Cell Interior Color

In VBA, you can check on the value of a property, or you can set the property to a new value. To change several cells to be bold, for example, you would change their Bold property to True:

```
Selection.Font.Bold = True
```

You can also check to see whether a property equals a certain value:

```
If Selection.Value = 100 then Selection.Font.Bold = True
```

Properties are generally used with the dot construct, and they are almost always followed by =, as contrasted with the := used with parameters (for example, PropertyName = value).

Using the Analogy While Examining Recorded Code

When you understand that a period generally separates an object from a method or a property, you can start to make sense of the recorded code.

For example, the following line performs the Open method:

```
Workbooks.Open Filename:="C:\Invoices.xls"
```

In this example, the Filename parameter is shown with := after the parameter name. This first line in the following example performs the Select method on one particular member of the Rows collection:

```
Rows("1:1").Select
Selection.Font.Bold = True
```

The second line then sets the Bold property of the Font property of the selection to True. Using these two lines of code is equivalent to selecting row 1 and clicking the Bold icon. You notice that one property, such as Font, can have subproperties, such as Bold and Italic.

CHAPTER 19

TIP

In the Excel user interface, you generally need to select a cell before you can change something in it. In a macro, there is no need to select something first. For example, you can replace the two lines in the preceding example with this single line of code: Rows("1:1").Font.Bold = True.

Using Simple Variables and Object Variables

The macro recorder never records a variable, but you can add variables to a macro when you edit the code. Suppose that you need to do a number of operations to the row where the totals will be located. Instead of repeatedly going to the last row in the spreadsheet and pressing End+Up Arrow, you can assign the row number to a variable:

```
FinalRow = Range("A1048576").End(xlup).Row
TotalRow = FinalRow + 1
```

The words FinalRow and TotalRow are variables that each hold a single value. If you have data in rows 2 through 25 today, FinalRow will hold the value 25, and TotalRow will hold the value 26. This enables you to use efficient code, such as the following:

```
Range("A" & TotalRow).Value = "Total"
Range("C" & TotalRow).Formula = "=SUM(C2:C"& TotalRow & ")"
Range("D" & TotalRow).Formula = "=SUM(D2:D"& TotalRow & ")"
Range("E" & TotalRow).Formula = "=SUM(E2:E"& TotalRow & ")"
```

VBA also offers a powerful variable called an *object variable*. An object variable can be used to represent any object such as a worksheet, chart, or cell. Whereas a simple variable holds one value, an object variable holds values for every property associated with the object.

Object variables are declared using the `Dim` statement and then assigned using the `Set` statement:

```
Dim WSD as worksheet
Set WSD = Worksheets("Sheet1")
```

Using object variables offers the following advantages:

- It is easier to refer to `WSD` than to `ActiveWorkbook.Worksheets("Sheet1")`.

- If you define the object variable with a `DIM` statement at the beginning of the macro, as you type new lines of code, the VBE's AutoComplete feature shows a list of valid methods and properties for the object.

Using R1C1-Style Formulas

If you are a history buff of technology, you might know that VisiCalc was the first spreadsheet program for PCs. When Dan Bricklin and Bob Frankston invented VisiCalc, they used the A1 style for naming cells. In those early days, VisiCalc had competitors such as SuperCalc and a Microsoft program called MultiPlan. This early Microsoft spreadsheet used the notation of R1C1 to refer to cell A1. The cell that we know today as E17 would have been called R17C5, for row 17, column 5.

In 1985, Microsoft launched Excel version 1.0 for the Macintosh. Excel originally continued to use the R1C1 style of notation. During the next 10 years, Excel and Lotus 1-2-3 were locked in a bitter battle for market share. Lotus was the early leader, and it had adopted the A1 notation style familiar to VisiCalc customers. To capture more market share, Microsoft allowed Excel to use either A1-style notation or R1C1-style notation. Even today, in Excel 2016, you can turn on R1C1-style notation by selecting File, Options, Formulas, R1C1 Reference Style. In R1C1 reference style, column letters A, B, C are replaced with column numbers 1, 2, 3. Hardly anyone uses R1C1 reference style today; however, the macro recorder always records formulas in R1C1 style.

In R1C1 notation, the reference RC refers to the current cell. You can modify RC by adding a particular row number or column number. For example, R2C refers to the cell in row 2 of the current column. RC1 refers to the cell in this row that is in column 1.

If you put a row number or column number in square brackets, it refers to a relative number of cells from the current cell. If you have a formula in cell D16 and use the reference R[1]C[-2], you are referring to the cell one row below D16 and two columns to the left of D16, which would be cell B17.

You are probably wondering why the macro recorder uses this arcane notation style when recording formulas. It turns out that this style is fantastic for formulas. Whereas a column of formulas in A1 style will have a different formula in each cell, the same column of formulas in R1C1 style will be identical down the column. For example, enter a formula of =D2+E2 in cell F2. When you copy F2 to F3, Excel changes the references of E2 and D2 to be E3 and D3.

Now look at these same formulas in R1C1 style, as shown in Figure 19.11. Every formula in E2:E15 is identical. This makes sense because the formula is saying, "Add the sales tax one cell to the left of me to the merchandise amount that is two cells to the left of me." Every formula in F2:F15 is identical; even the total formulas in D16:F16 are identical.

	4	5	6
1	REVENUE	SALES TAX	TOTAL
2	252.11	=ROUND(0.06*RC[-1],2)	=RC[-1]+RC[-2]
3	68.67	=ROUND(0.06*RC[-1],2)	=RC[-1]+RC[-2]
4	111.4	=ROUND(0.06*RC[-1],2)	=RC[-1]+RC[-2]
5	151.47	=ROUND(0.06*RC[-1],2)	=RC[-1]+RC[-2]
6	131.71	=ROUND(0.06*RC[-1],2)	=RC[-1]+RC[-2]
7	221.62	=ROUND(0.06*RC[-1],2)	=RC[-1]+RC[-2]
8	225.02	=ROUND(0.06*RC[-1],2)	=RC[-1]+RC[-2]
9	261.84	=ROUND(0.06*RC[-1],2)	=RC[-1]+RC[-2]
10	195.08	=ROUND(0.06*RC[-1],2)	=RC[-1]+RC[-2]
11	72.31	=ROUND(0.06*RC[-1],2)	=RC[-1]+RC[-2]
12	168.12	=ROUND(0.06*RC[-1],2)	=RC[-1]+RC[-2]
13	79.54	=ROUND(0.06*RC[-1],2)	=RC[-1]+RC[-2]
14	258.73	=ROUND(0.06*RC[-1],2)	=RC[-1]+RC[-2]
15	248.44	=ROUND(0.06*RC[-1],2)	=RC[-1]+RC[-2]
16	=SUM(R2C:R[-1]C)	=SUM(R2C:R[-1]C)	=SUM(R2C:R[-1]C)
17			

Figure 19.11 In R1C1 style, every formula in F2:F15 is identical.

If you are forced to use A1-style formulas in a macro, you might try to enter the formula in cell F2 and then copy the formula from F2 to the remaining cells:

```
Range("F2").Formula = "=D2+E2"
Range("F2").Copy Destination:=Range("F3:F15")
```

On the other hand, you can enter all the formulas in one line of code when using R1C1-style formulas:

```
Range("F2:F15").FormulaR1C1 = "=RC[-2]+RC[-1]"
```

TIP

Although the macro recorder always records formulas in R1C1 style, you are allowed to write the macros using regular formulas. Change the FormulaR1C1 property to Formula. The following two lines of code are equivalent:

```
Range("F2:F15").FormulaR1C1 = "=RC[-2]+RC[-1]"
Range("F2:F15").Formula = "=D2-E2"
```

Fixing AutoSum Errors in Macros

Probably the most important reason to understand R1C1 formulas is to make sure that the macro recorder recorded the proper formula. This is important because the macro recorder does not do a good job of recording the intent of the AutoSum button. If your data set has numbers in D2:D15 today, pressing AutoSum from cell D16 will record the following line of macro code:

```
Selection.FormulaR1C1 = "=SUM(R[-14]C:R[-1]C)"
```

This formula adds a range from 14 rows above the selection to the cell just above the selection. This works only on days when you have exactly 14 rows of data. This is one of the most annoying bugs in a macro.

It is annoying because this type of logic error will not cause an actual error. If you run this macro on the invoice file you receive tomorrow that contains 20 invoices, the macro will happily total only the last 14 invoices instead of all 20. This means that you could distribute this report with a wrong total for several days before someone realizes that something is amiss.

However, you can correct this formula. You know that you have headings in row 1 and that the first invoice will appear in row 2. You need the macro to sum from row 2 to the row just above the current cell. Therefore, you need to change the formula to this:

```
Selection.FormulaR1C1 = "=SUM(R2C:R[-1]C)"
```

Customizing the Everyday-Use Macro Example: GetOpenFileName and GetSaveAsFileName

The everyday-use macro you recorded earlier in this chapter for formatting an invoice register is hard-coded to always open the same file and always save with the same filename. To make the macro more general, you can allow the person running the macro to browse for the file each morning and to specify a new filename during the Save As. Excel offers a straightforward way to display the File Open or File Save As dialog. Here is the code you need to use:

```
FileToOpen = Application.GetOpenFileName( _
  FileFilter:="Excel Files,*.xl*", _
  Title:="Select Today's Invoice File")
```

Note that this code displays the File Open dialog and allows a file to be selected. When you click Open, the dialog assigns the filename to the variable. It does not actually open the file. You then need to open the file specified in the variable:

```
Workbooks.Open Filename:=FileToOpen
```

When you want to ask for the filename to use in saving the file, use this code:

```
NewFileName = Application.GetSaveAsFilename( _
  Title:="Select File Name for Today")
ActiveWorkbook.SaveAs Filename:=NewFileName, _
  FileFormat:=xlOpenXMLWorkbookMacroEnabled
```

The following macro is the final macro to use each day:

```
Sub ImportInvoicesFixed()
' ImportInvoices Macro
' With Changes
 FileToOpen = Application.GetOpenFileName( _
  FileFilter:= _
  "Excel files (*.xls;*.xlsb;*.xlsx;*.xlsm)" & _
  ",*.xls;*.xlsb;*.xlsx;*.xlsm)", _
  Title:="Select Today's Invoice File")
 Workbooks.Open Filename:=FileToOpen
 Application.Goto Reference:="R1048576C1"
 Selection.End(xlUp).Select
 ActiveCell.Offset(1, 0).Range("A1").Select
 ActiveCell.FormulaR1C1 = "Total"
 ActiveCell.Offset(0, 3).Range("A1").Select
 Selection.FormulaR1C1 = "=SUM(R2C:R[-1]C)"
 Selection.AutoFill Destination:=ActiveCell.Range("A1:C1"), Type:= _
  xlFillDefault
 ActiveCell.Range("A1:C1").Select
 Range(Selection, Cells(1)).Select
 Selection.Columns.AutoFit
 Rows("1:1").Select
 Selection.Style = "Heading 4"
 Selection.Insert Shift:=xlDown
 Selection.Insert Shift:=xlDown
 Range("A1").Select
 Selection.FormulaR1C1 = "=""Invoices for ""&TEXT(R[3]C[1],""mmmm d, yyyy"")"
 Selection.Style = "Title"
 NewFileName = Application.GetSaveAsFilename( _
  Title:="Select File Name for Today")
 ActiveWorkbook.SaveAs Filename:=NewFileName, _
  FileFormat:=xlOpenXMLWorkbookMacroEnabled
End Sub
```

Of the 22 lines in the macro, you added two lines and corrected two lines. This is typical because between 10% and 20% of a recorded macro generally needs to be adjusted.

From-Scratch Macro Example: Loops, Flow Control, and Referring to Ranges

Suppose you work for a company that sells printers and scanners to commercial accounts. When you sell a piece of hardware, you also try to sell a service plan for that hardware. Customers in your state are taxed. Your accounting software provides a daily download that looks like columns A:D in Figure 19.12.

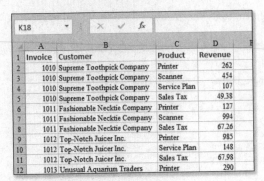

Figure 19.12 Your accounting software groups all hardware, service, and tax amounts into a single column.

You want to create a macro that examines each row in the data set and carries out a different action, based on the value in column C. You will probably want to write this macro from scratch. The following sections describe how to do this.

Finding the Last Row with Data

The recorded macro examples discussed earlier in this chapter suggested going to the last cell in column A and then pressing End followed by the up-arrow key to find the last row with data in column A.

In legacy versions of Excel, this would be accomplished with this code:

```
FinalRow = Range("A65536").End(xlUp).Row
```

This command became more complicated in Excel 2007. The last row in the worksheet is either 1048576 or 65536, depending on whether the workbook is in compatibility mode. The solution is to use Rows.Count, which is shorthand for `Application.Rows.Count`. This solution returns the total number of rows available in the current worksheet. Note that this property returns 65,536 in compatibility mode and 1,048,576 in regular mode.

The following line of code finds the last row in column A with a nonblank value:

```
FinalRow = Cells(Rows.Count, 1).End(xlUp).Row
```

TIP

Use XLUP as the argument for END. The lowercase "l" used in the code is often seen as the numeral 1. Using x1Up instead of xlUp causes an error.

Looping Through All Rows

The loop most commonly used in VBA is a For-Next loop. This is identical to the loop that you might have learned about in a BASIC class.

In this example, the loop starts with a For statement. You specify that on each pass through the loop, a certain variable will change from a low value to a high value. This simple macro will run through the loop 10 times. On the first pass through the loop, the variable x will be equal to 1. The two lines inside the loop will assign the value 1 to cells A1 and B1. When the macro encounters the Next x line, it returns to the start of the loop, increments x by 1, and runs through the loop again. The next time through the loop, the value of x is 2. Cell A2 is assigned the number 2, and cell B2 shows 4, which is the square of 2. Eventually, x will be equal to 10. At the Next x line, the macro will allow the loop to finish. The following is the code for this macro:

```
Sub WriteSquares()
 For x = 1 To 10
  Cells(x, 1).Value = x
  Cells(x, 2).Value = x * x
 Next x
End Sub
```

After you run this macro, you have a simple table that shows the numbers 1 through 10 and their squares, as shown in Figure 19.13.

Figure 19.13   This simple loop fills in ten rows.

After a loop is written, it can be adjusted easily. For example, if you want a table showing all the squares from 1 to 100, you can adjust the For x = 1 to 10 line to be For x = 1 to 100.

There is an optional clause in the For statement called the *step value*. If no step value is shown, the program moves through the loop by incrementing the variable by one each time through the loop. If you wanted to check only the even-numbered rows, you could change the loop to be For x = 2 to 100 in step 2.

If you are going to be optionally deleting rows from a range of data, it is important to start at the bottom and proceed to the top of the range. You would use −1 as the step value:

```
For x = 100 to 1 step −1
```

Referring to Ranges

The macro recorder uses the Range property to refer to a particular range. You might see the macro recorder refer to ranges such as Range("B3") and Range("W1:Z100").

The loop code shown in the preceding section emulates this style of referring to ranges. On the third time through the loop, this line of code would refer to cell B3:

```
Range("B" & x).value = x * x
```

However, how would you handle looping through each column? If you want to continue using the Range property, you need to jump through some hoops to figure out the letter associated with column 5:

```
For y = 1 to 26
 ThisCol = Chr(64+y)
 Range(ThisCol & 1).value = ThisCol
Next y
```

This method works fine if you are using 26 or fewer columns. However, if you need to loop through all the columns out to column XFD, you will spend all day trying to write the logic to assign the column label WMJ to column 15896.

The solution is to use the Cells property instead of the Range property. Cells requires you to specify a numeric row number and a numeric column number. For example, cell B3 is specified as follows:

```
Cells(3, 2)
```

If you need to refer to a rectangular range, you can use the Resize property. Resize requires you to specify the number of rows and the number of columns. For example, to refer to W1:Z100, use this:

```
Cells(1, 23).Resize(100, 4)
```

It is difficult to figure out that this refers to W1:Z100, but it enables you to loop through rows or columns.

You can use the following code to make every other column bold:

```
For y = 1 to 100 step 2
 Cells(1, y).Resize(200, 1).Font.Bold = True
Next y
```

Combining a Loop with `FinalRow`

Earlier in this chapter, you learned how to use the Ctrl+Up Arrow to find the final row in a data set. After finding the final row in the data set and assigning it to a variable, you can specify that the loop should run through `FinalRow`:

```
FinalRow = Cells(Rows.Count, 1).End(xlUp).row
For x = 2 to FinalRow
 ' Perform some action
Next x
```

Making Decisions by Using Flow Control

Flow control is the capability to make decisions within a macro. The following sections describe two commonly used flow control constructs: `If-End If` and `Select Case`.

Using the `If-End If` Construct

Suppose you need a macro to delete any records that say Sales Tax. You could accomplish this with a simple `If-End If` construct:

```
If Cells(x, 4).Value = "Sales Tax" Then
 Rows(x).Delete
End If
```

This construct always starts with the word `If`, followed by a logical test, followed by the word `Then`. Every line between the first line and the `End If` line is executed only if the logical test is `True`.

Now suppose that you want to enhance the macro so that any other amounts that contain service plan revenue are moved to column F. To do this, you use the `ElseIf` line to enter a second condition and block of lines to be used in that condition:

```
If Cells(x, 4).Value = "Sales Tax" Then
 Cells(x, 1).EntireRow.Delete
ElseIf Cells(x, 4).Value = "Service Plan" Then
 Cells(x, 5).Cut Destination:=Cells(x, 6)
End If
```

You could continue adding `ElseIf` statements to handle other situations. Eventually, just before the `End If`, you could add an `Else` block to handle any other condition you have not thought about.

Using the `Select Case` Construct

If you reach a point where you have many `ElseIf` statements all testing the same value, it might make sense to switch to a `Select Case` construct. For example, suppose you want to loop through all the records to examine the product in column C. If column C contains a printer, you want to move the amount in column D to a new column E. Scanner revenue should go to a new column F. Service plans go to a new column H. Sales tax goes to a new column I. You should also handle the situation when something is sold that contains none of those products. In that case, you would move the revenue to a new column G.

The construct begins with Select Case and then the value to check. The construct ends with End Select, which is similar to End If.

Each subblock of code starts with the word Case and one or more possible values. If you needed to check for Printer or Printers, you would enclose each in quotes and separate them with a comma.

After checking for all the possible values you can think of, you might add a Case Else subblock to handle any other stray values that might be entered in column C.

The following code checks to see what product is in column C. Depending on the product, the program copies the revenue from column D to a specific column:

```
Select Case Cells(x, 3).Value
 Case "Printer", "Printers"
 Cells(x, 4).Copy Destination:=Cells(x, 5)
 Case "Scanner", "Scanners"
 Cells(x, 4).Copy Destination:=Cells(x, 6)
 Case "Service Plan"
 Cells(x, 4).Copy Destination:=Cells(x, 8)
 Case "Sales Tax"
 Cells(x, 4).Copy Destination:=Cells(x, 9)
 Case Else
 ' Something unexpected was sold
 Cells(x, 4).Copy Destination:=Cells(x, 7)
End Select
```

Putting Together the From-Scratch Example: Testing Each Record in a Loop

Using the building blocks described in the preceding sections, you can now write the code for a macro that finds the last row, loops through the records, and copies the total revenue to the appropriate column. Now you need to add new headings for the additional columns.

The macro should use the End property to locate the final row and prefill columns E through I with zeros. Next, it should loop from row 2 down to the final row. For each record, the revenue column should be moved to one of the columns. At the end of the loop, the program alerts you that the program is complete, using a MsgBox command. The following is the complete code of this macro:

```
Sub MoveRevenue2()
 FinalRow = Cells(Rows.Count, 1).End(xlUp).Row
```

```
Range("E2", Cells(FinalRow, 9)).Value = 0
For x = 2 To FinalRow
Select Case Cells(x, 3).Value
Case "Printer", "Printers"
Cells(x, 4).Copy Destination:=Cells(x, 5)
Case "Scanner", "Scanners"
Cells(x, 4).Copy Destination:=Cells(x, 6)
Case "Service Plan"
Cells(x, 4).Copy Destination:=Cells(x, 8)
Case "Sales Tax"
Cells(x, 4).Copy Destination:=Cells(x, 9)
Case Else
' Something unexpected was sold - Accessory?
Cells(x, 4).Copy Destination:=Cells(x, 7)
End Select
Next x
MsgBox "Macro complete"
End Sub
```

CHAPTER 19

TIP

An alternative syntax of the Range property is to specify the top-left and bottom-right cells in the range, separated by a comma. In the macro described here, for example, you know you want to fill from cell E2 to the last row in column I. You can describe this range as follows:

```
Range("E2", Cells(FinalRow, 9))
```

This syntax is sometimes simpler than using `Cells()` and `Resize()`.

After you run this macro, you see that the revenue amounts have been copied to the appropriate columns, as shown in Figure 19.14.

A	B	C	D	E	F	G	H	I
Invoice	Customer	Product	Revenue	Printer	Scanner	Accessory	Service	Tax
1010	Supreme Toothpick Company	Printer	262	262	0	0	0	0
1010	Supreme Toothpick Company	Scanner	454	0	454	0	0	0
1010	Supreme Toothpick Company	Service Plan	107	0	0	0	107	0
1010	Supreme Toothpick Company	Sales Tax	49.38	0	0	0	0	49.38
1011	Fashionable Necktie Company	Printer	127	127	0	0	0	0
1011	Fashionable Necktie Company	Scanner	994	0	994	0	0	0
1011	Fashionable Necktie Company	Sales Tax	67.26	0	0	0	0	67.26
1012	Top-Notch Juicer Inc.	Printer	985	985	0	0	0	0
1012	Top-Notch Juicer Inc.	Service Plan	148	0	0	0	148	0
1012	Top-Notch Juicer Inc.	Sales Tax	67.98	0	0	0	0	67.98

Figure 19.14 After running the macro, you have a breakout of revenue by product.

A Special Case: Deleting Some Records

If a loop is conditionally deleting records, you will run into trouble if it is a typical For-Next loop. Suppose you want to delete all the sales tax records, as follows:

```
Sub ThisWontWork()
 FinalRow = Cells(Rows.Count, 1).End(xlUp).Row
 For x = 2 To FinalRow
  If Cells(x, 3).Value = "Sales Tax" Then
   Cells(x, 1).EntireRow.Delete
  Else
   Cells(x, 5).Value = "Checked"
  End If
 Next x
End Sub
```

Consider the data in Figure 19.15. The first time through the loop, x is equal to 2. Cell C2 does not contain sales tax, so cell E2 has the word checked. A similar result occurs for rows 3 and 4. The fourth time through the loop, cell C5 contains sales tax. The macro deletes the tax in row 5. However, Excel then moves the old row 6 up to row 5, as shown in Figure 19.16. The next time through the loop, the program inspects row 6, and the data that is now in row 5 will never be checked.

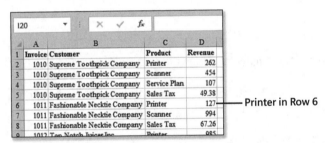

Figure 19.15   Before the macro deletes row 5, the Printer record is in row 6.

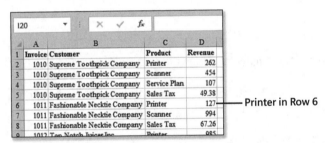

Figure 19.16   The old row 6 data moves up to occupy the deleted row 5. However, the macro blindly moves on to check row 6 next. The printer that moved to row 5 never gets checked.

The macro succeeds in deleting tax. However, several rows were not checked, as shown in Figure 19.17. Further, several extra blank rows at the bottom were likely checked needlessly.

	A	B	C	D	E
1	Invoice	Customer	Product	Revenue	
2	1010	Supreme Toothpick Company	Printer	262	Checked
3	1010	Supreme Toothpick Company	Scanner	454	Checked
4	1010	Supreme Toothpick Company	Service Plan	107	Checked
5	1011	Fashionable Necktie Company	Printer	127	
6	1011	Fashionable Necktie Company	Scanner	994	Checked
7	1012	Top-Notch Juicer Inc.	Printer	985	
8	1012	Top-Notch Juicer Inc.	Service Plan	148	Checked
9	1013	Unusual Aquarium Traders	Printer	290	
10	1013	Unusual Aquarium Traders	Scanner	555	Checked

Figure 19.17   Several rows were not checked in this loop.

The solution is to have the loop run backward. You need to start at the final row and proceed up through the sheet to row 2. When the macro deletes tax in row 31, it can then proceed to checking row 30, knowing that nothing has been destroyed (yet) in row 30 and above.

To reverse the flow of the loop, you have to tell the loop to start at the final row, but you also have to tell the loop to use a step value of -1. The start of the loop would use this line of code:

```
For x = FinalRow to 2 Step -1
```

The macro you need here represents a fairly common task: looping through all the records to do something conditionally to each record.

The following macro correctly deletes all the sales tax records:

```
Sub DeleteTaxOK()
 FinalRow = Cells(Rows.Count, 1).End(xlUp).Row
 For x = FinalRow To 2 Step -1
  If Cells(x, 3).Value = "Sales Tax" Then
   Cells(x, 1).EntireRow.Delete
  Else
   Cells(x, 5).Value = "Checked"
  End If
 Next x
End Sub
```

For the example described here, the macro recorder would be almost no help. You would have to write this simple macro from scratch. However, it is a powerful macro that can simplify tasks when you have hundreds of thousands of rows of data.

Inside OUT

Running a macro in slow motion is the key to successful debugging.

Seeing Figures 19.15 and 19.16 is the key in figuring out why your macro to delete some rows was not deleting all of the desired rows.

When you run a macro, the execution is so fast, you never can see those intermediate results. They key to getting those screenshots is to run the macro in debugging mode.

Switch to VBA. Click anywhere on any line of code in the macro that you want to debug. Press F8 to begin running the macro one line at a time. Each time you press F8, a line of code is highlighted in yellow. Press F8 to run the line of code in yellow.

Stepping through the code one line at a time allows you to see the code and the results of the code side-by-side. You can switch back and forth between Excel and VBA, or if you have two monitors, arrange the screens so VBA is on one monitor and Excel is on the other monitor.

Keep pressing F8 to run the next line of code. If you discover the problem, you can press F5 to run the rest of the macro at normal speed or select Run, Rest from the VBA editor to stop the macro.

TROUBLESHOOTING

Sometimes while debugging a macro, the code will work fine as you are stepping through the code. But it fails when you run the macro at full speed.

As you are stepping through the code, you are pressing F8 and then looking at the Excel screen. This might take you a few seconds between commands. Those few seconds often give Excel the time to complete the last command issued by the VBA macro.

In contrast, when you run the macro at full speed, Excel might not be done with one command before it tries to run the next command.

Consider the following pseudocode:

```
Add Error Bars to a Chart
Format the newly added Error Bars
```

If the second line tries to run before the error bars are added, then you will get an error. This never used to be a problem, but with Excel 2019, it happens more often.

You can add a few lines of code, as shown below, to encourage the Excel macro to slow down and allow pending events to complete. The hardest part is figuring out which lines of code need the DoEvents code. In the example described here, the following code might fix the problem:

```
Add Error Bars to a Chart
Application.DoEvents
Format the newly added Error Bars
```

Combination Macro Example: Creating a Report for Each Customer

Many real-life scenarios require you to use a combination of recorded code and code written from scratch. For example, Figure 19.18 shows a data set with all your invoices for the year. In this case, suppose you would like to produce a workbook for each customer that you can mail to the customer.

	A	B	C	D	E	F
1	Customer	Invoice	Date	Purchases	Paid	Open Balance
2	Hip Lawn Corporation	1001	1/4/18	8846	8846	0
3	Vivid Chopstick Traders	1002	1/4/18	1688	1688	0
4	Unusual Doorbell Company	1003	1/4/18	8415	8415	0
5	Excellent Utensil Corporatic	1004	1/4/18	2619	2619	0
6	Hip Lawn Corporation	1005	1/5/18	11476	11476	0
7	Fascinating Oven Supply	1006	1/5/18	4958	0	4958
8	Savory Glass Inc.	1007	1/5/18	11243	11243	0
9	Superior Bobsled Corporati	1008	1/5/18	4419	4419	0
10	Hip Lawn Corporation	1009	1/5/18	12562	12562	0
11	Savory Glass Inc.	1010	1/5/18	7409	7409	0

Figure 19.18   The goal is to provide a subset of this data to each customer.

One way to handle this task would be to use an advanced filter to get a list of all unique customers in column A. You would then loop through these customers, applying an AutoFilter to the data set to see only the customers that match the selected customer. After the data set is filtered, you can select the visible cells only and copy them to a new workbook. Then you can save the workbook with the name of the customer and return to the original workbook.

You can start by creating a blank procedure with comments to spell out the steps in the preceding paragraphs. Then you add code for the loop and other simple tasks, such as copying the selection to a new workbook. Whenever you encounter a step for which you have never written code, you can leave a comment with question marks. This enables you to go back and record parts of the process to finish the macro.

NOTE

It is common to indent each line of code with four spaces. Any lines of code inside an If-EndIf block or inside a For-Next loop are indented an additional four spaces. If you have typed a line of code that is indented eight spaces and then press Enter at the end of the line of code, the VBE automatically indents the next line to eight spaces. Each press of the Tab key indents by an additional four spaces. Pressing Shift+Tab removes four spaces of indentation. Although four is the default number of spaces for a tab, you can change this to any number of spaces using Tools, Options in the Visual Basic Editor.

Your first pass at a well-commented macro might look like this:

```
Sub ProduceReportForEachCustomer()
 ' Define object variables for new workbook
 ' Suffix of N means New
 Dim WBN As Workbook
 Dim WSN As Worksheet
 ' Define object variables for the current workbook
 ' Suffix of O means Old
 Dim WBO As Workbook
 Dim WSO As Worksheet
 Set WBO = ActiveWorkbook
 Set WSO = ActiveSheet
 ' Find the FinalRow in today's dataset
 FinalRow = Cells(Rows.Count, 1).End(xlUp).Row
 ' Use an Advanced filter to copy unique customers
 ' from column A to column H
 ' ???
 'Find the final customer in column H
 FinalCust = Cells(Rows.Count, 8).End(xlUp).Row
 ' Loop through each customer
 For x = 2 To FinalCust
  ' Turn on the AutoFilter for this customer
  ' ???
  ' Create a new workbook
  Set WBN = Workbooks.Add
  Set WSN = WBN.Worksheets(1)
  ' In the original workbook, select visible cells
  ' ???
  ' Copy the selection to the new workbook
  Selection.Copy Destination:=WSN.Cells(3, 1)
  ' AutoFit columns in the new workbook
  WSN.Columns.AutoFit
  ' Add a title to the new workbook
  WSN.Range("A1").Value = _
  "Recap of Purchases for " & WSN.Cells(4, 1).Value
  ' Save the new book
  WBN.SaveAs Filename:="C:\" & WSN.Cells(4, 1).Value & ".xlsx"
  WBN.Close SaveChanges:=False
  'Return to the original workbook
  WBO.Activate
  WSN.Select
 Next x
End Sub
```

The following sections explain that to create this macro, you need to figure out how to code the advanced filter to copy a unique list of customers to column H. You then need to figure out how to apply a filter to column A. Finally, you need to figure out how to select only the visible cells from the filter.

Using the Advanced Filter for Unique Records

You need to figure out how to use an advanced filter to finish the following section of code:

```
' Find the FinalRow in today's dataset
FinalRow = Cells(Rows.Count, 1).End(xlUp).Row
' Use an Advanced filter to copy unique customers
' from column A to column H
' ???
```

To use an advanced filter on this section of code, follow these steps:

1. Turn on the macro recorder.

2. On the Data tab, in the Sort & Filter group, click the Advanced icon to open the Advanced Filter dialog.

3. Select the option Copy to Another Location.

4. Adjust the list range to refer only to column A. The copy-to range will be cell H1.

5. Check the Unique Records Only box.

6. When the dialog looks as shown in Figure 19.19, click OK. The result is a new range of data in column H, with each customer listed just once, as shown in Figure 19.20.

Figure 19.19   Using an advanced filter to get a unique list of customers.

H	I	J
Customer		
Hip Lawn Corporation		
Vivid Chopstick Traders		
Unusual Doorbell Company		
Excellent Utensil Corporation		
Fascinating Oven Supply		
Savory Glass Inc.		
Superior Bobsled Corporation		
Steadfast Meter Inc.		
Sure Yardstick Corporation		
Magnificent Linen Partners		
Brilliant Chopstick Company		
Different Scooter Supply		
Mouthwatering Clipboard Corporation		
New Gadget Company		
Appealing Opener Partners		
Trouble-Free Bottle Inc.		
Wonderful Opener Supply		
Modular Tuner Corporation		
Magnificent Doghouse Inc.		
Stunning Freezer Inc.		

Figure 19.20 The advanced filter produces a list of customers for the macro to loop through.

7. On the Developer tab, click Stop Recording.

8. Use the Macros button to select Macro1 and then select Edit.

Even though the Advanced Filter dialog is still one of the most complicated facets of Excel 2016, the recorded macro is remarkably simple:

```
Sub Macro1()
'
' Macro1 Macro
'
'
 Range("A1:A1001").AdvancedFilter Action:=xlFilterCopy, CopyToRange:=Range( _
  "H1"), Unique:=True
 Range("H1").Select
End Sub
```

In your macro, there is no reason to select cell H1, so delete that line of code. The remaining problem is that the macro recorder hard-coded that today's data set contains 1,001 rows. You might want to generalize this to handle any number of rows. The following code reflects these changes:

```
FinalRow = Cells(Rows.Count, 1).End(xlUp).Row
Range("A1:A" & FinalRow) .AdvancedFilter Action:=xlFilterCopy, _
 CopyToRange:=Range("H1"), Unique:=True
```

Using AutoFilter

When you have a list of customers, the macro loops through each customer. The goal is to use an AutoFilter to display only the records for each particular customer. Next, finish this section of code as follows:

```
' Loop through each customer
For x = 2 To FinalCust
    ' Turn on the AutoFilter for this customer
    ' ???
```

To apply an AutoFilter to this section of code, follow these steps:

1. On the Developer tab, select Record Macro.

2. On the Home tab, select the icon Sort & Filter–Filter. Drop-down arrows are turned on for each field.

3. In the drop-down in cell A1, clear Select All and then select Hip Lawn Corporation.

4. Back on the Developer tab, stop recording the macro.

5. Use the Macros button to locate and edit Macro2 as follows:

```
Sub Macro2()
'
' Macro2 Macro
'
'
    Range("A2").Select
    Application.CutCopyMode = False
    Selection.AutoFilter
    Selection.AutoFilter Field:=1, Criteria1:="Hip Lawn Corporation"
End Sub
```

The macro recorder always does too much selecting. You rarely have to select something before you can operate on it. You can theorize that the only line of this macro that matters is the `Selection.AutoFilter` line. Because you will always be looking at the AutoFilter drop-down in cell A1, you can replace `Selection` with `Range("A1")`. Rather than continually ask for one specific customer, you can replace the end of the line with a reference to a cell in column H:

```
Range("A1").AutoFilter Field:=1, _ Criteria1:=Cells(x,8).Value
```

TIP

Even though you have an existing Module1 with your code, Excel chooses to record the new macro into a new module. Therefore, you need to copy recorded code from Module2 and then use the Project Explorer to switch to Module1 to paste the code into your macro.

Selecting Visible Cells Only

After you use the AutoFilter in the macro, you see records for only one customer. However, the other records are still there, but they are hidden. If you copied the range to a new worksheet, all the hidden rows would come along, and you would end up with 20 copies of your entire data set.

The long way to select only visible cells is to press F5 to display the Go To dialog. In the Go To dialog, click the Special button and then click Visible Cells Only. However, the shortcut is to press Alt+;.

To learn how to select only visible cells in VBA, record the macro by following these steps:

1. Select the data in columns A through F.

2. Turn on the macro recorder and press Alt+;.

3. Stop the macro recorder. You should see that the recorded macro has just one line of code:

```
Sub Macro5()
'
' Macro5 Macro
'
'
    Selection.SpecialCells(xlCellTypeVisible).Select
End Sub
```

In your original outline of the macro, you had contemplated selecting only visible cells and then doing the copy in another statement, like this:

```
' In the original workbook, select visible cells
' ???
' Copy the selection to the new workbook
Selection.Copy Destination:=WSN.Cells(3, 1)
```

Instead, copy the visible cells in one statement:

```
' In the original workbook, select visible cells
WSO.Range("A1:F" & FinalRow).SpecialCells(xlCellTypeVisible).Copy _
 Destination:=WSN.Cells(3, 1)
```

Combination Macro Example: Putting It All Together

The following macro started as a bunch of comments and a skeleton of a loop:

```
Sub ProduceReportForEachCustomerFinished()
 ' Define object variables for new workbook
 Dim WBN As Workbook
 Dim WSN As Worksheet
 ' Define object variables for the current workbook
```

```
Dim WBO As Workbook
Dim WSO As Worksheet
Set WBO = ActiveWorkbook
Set WSO = ActiveSheet
' Find the FinalRow in today's dataset
FinalRow = Cells(Rows.Count, 1).End(xlUp).Row
' Use an Advanced filter to copy unique customers
' from column A to column H
Range("A1:A" & FinalRow).AdvancedFilter Action:=xlFilterCopy, _
CopyToRange:=Range("H1"), Unique:=True
'Find the final customer in column H
FinalCust = Range("H1").End(xlDown).Row
' Loop through each customer
For x = 2 To FinalCust
 ' Turn on the AutoFilter for this customer
 Range("A1").AutoFilter Field:=1, Criteria1:=Cells(x, 8).Value
 ' Create a new workbook
 Set WBN = Workbooks.Add
 Set WSN = WBN.Worksheets(1)
 ' In the original workbook, select visible cells
 WSO.Range("A1:F" & FinalRow).SpecialCells(xlCellTypeVisible).Copy _
 Destination:=WSN.Cells(3, 1)
 ' AutoFit columns in the new workbook
 WSN.Columns.AutoFit
 ' Add a title to the new workbook
 WSN.Range("A1").Value = "Recap of Purchases for " & WSN.Cells(4, 1).Value
 ' Save the new book
 WBN.SaveAs Filename:="C:\" & WSN.Cells(4, 1).Value & ".xls"
 WBN.Close SaveChanges:=False
 'Return to the original workbook
 WBO.Activate
 WSO.Select
 Next x
End Sub
```

After doing three small tests with the macro recorder, you were able to fill in the sections to copy the customer records to a new workbook. After running this macro, you should have a new workbook for each customer on your hard drive, ready to be distributed via email.

VBA macros open up a wide possibility of automation for Excel worksheets. Anytime you are faced with a daunting, mindless task, you can turn it into a challenging exercise by trying to design a macro to perform the task instead. It usually takes less time to design a macro than it does to complete the task. You should save every macro you write. Soon you will have a library of macros that handle many common tasks, and they will enable you to develop macros faster. The next time you need to perform a similar task, you can roll out the macro and perform the steps in seconds instead of hours.

CHAPTER 19

More Tips and Tricks for Excel 2019

The chapters in this book are full of tips and tricks. This particular chapter is a catch-all for some of the tips that did not find a home elsewhere in the book.

Watching the Results of a Distant Cell

Sometimes you need to keep an eye on a single result on a worksheet other than the one you're currently in. For example, you might have a workbook in which assumptions on multiple worksheets produce a final ROI. As you change the assumptions, it would be good to know the effect on ROI.

It can be time consuming to constantly switch back and forth to the results worksheet after every change. Instead, you can set up a watch to show you the current value of the distant cell(s).

To set up a watch, follow these steps:

1. Select Formulas, Watch Window to display the floating Watch Window dialog box over the worksheet.

2. Click Add Watch in the Watch Window dialog box.

3. In the Add Watch dialog box, click the RefEdit button and then click the cells you want to watch.

4. Click Add to add the cell(s) to the Watch Window dialog box.

5. Repeat steps 2 through 4, as necessary.

6. Position the Watch Window dialog box in an out-of-the-way location above your worksheet so that you can continue to work.

Every time you make a change to the worksheet, the Watch Window dialog box shows you the current value of the watched cells, as shown in Figure 20.1.

Figure 20.1   The Watch Window dialog box shows you the results of key cells that you define. These cells can be in far-off cells or on other worksheets.

When the watch is defined, you can toggle the Watch Window dialog box by using the Watch Window icon in the Formulas tab.

TIP

You can double-click any entry in the Watch Window dialog box to scroll to that cell.

Calculating a Formula in Slow Motion

If you have a particularly complicated formula, you can watch how Excel calculates the formula in slow motion. This can help you locate any logic errors in the worksheet.

To evaluate a formula in slow motion, follow these steps:

1. Select the cell that contains the formula.

2. Select Formulas, Evaluate Formula. The Evaluate Formula dialog box appears, showing the formula. One element of the formula is underlined, indicating that this element will be calculated next.

3. To see the value of the underlined element immediately, click Evaluate.

4. If you want to see how that element is calculated, instead of clicking Evaluate, click Step In. Excel shows the formula for that element.

5. Eventually, the final level is evaluated to a number. Click Step Out to return one level up the dialog box.

6. Continue clicking Evaluate until you arrive at the answer shown in the cell.

Figure 20.2 shows an Evaluate Formula dialog box after Evaluate was clicked a few times.

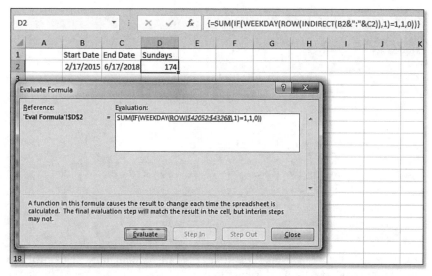

Figure 20.2   The Evaluate Formula dialog box enables you to watch the formula calculation in slow motion.

Inserting a Symbol in a Cell

Obscure key combinations are available to insert many symbols. However, you do not have to learn any of them. Instead, you can use the Symbol icon on the Insert tab to display the Symbol dialog box.

In the Symbol dialog box, you scroll through many subsets of the current font. When you find the desired symbol, select it and click the Insert button.

Editing an Equation

The Equation drop-down menu on the Insert tab offers eight prebuilt equations. If you happen to need one of these equations, you can select it from the drop-down menu.

If you need to build some other equation, insert a shape in the worksheet first. While the shape is selected, use Insert, Equation, Insert New Equation. A blank equation is added to the shape.

It seems very touchy, but you have to be inside the equation to have the Equation Tools Design tab showing. From the ribbon, you can open the various drop-down menus to insert a mathematical symbol. In Figure 20.3, some symbols have three placeholders. These are tiny text boxes where you can type various values.

Figure 20.3   You will build most equations using the drop-down menus on the Equation Tools
Design tab.

TROUBLESHOOTING

Although Excel can display equations, they are nothing more than drawing objects. You cannot have Excel solve the equations.

The Equation Editor originated in Word. I am sure the people writing for academic journals wanted a way to craft an equation in the papers, which led to the birth of the Equation Editor.

However, there is no actual mathematical ability built in to the Equation Editor. There is no magic button to have Excel actually integrate from x to y based on the equation.

Protecting a Worksheet

If you have many formulas in a worksheet, you might want to prevent others from changing them. In a typical scenario, your worksheet might have some input variables at the top. You might want to allow those items to be changed, but you might not want your formulas to be changed.

To protect a worksheet, follow these steps:

1. Select the input cells in your worksheet. These are the cells you want to allow someone to change.

2. Press Ctrl+1 or go to the Cells group of the Home tab and select Format, Format Cells. The Format Cells dialog box appears.

3. On the Protection tab of the Format Cells dialog box, clear the Locked check box. Click OK.

4. Select Review, Protect Sheet. The Protect Sheet dialog box appears.

5. Optionally, change what can happen in the protected workbook.

6. Click OK to apply the protection.

Inside OUT

A common scenario is to protect only the formula cells in a worksheet. While this is not as simple as clicking Protect Formulas, there is a buried command that can simplify the process.

First, unlock all cells as described in steps 2 and 3 in "Protecting a Worksheet."

Then, from any cell in your worksheet, select Home, Find & Select, Formulas. All the formula cells in the worksheet will be selected.

With the formulas selected, repeat step 2 above, but change the Locked status to Selected. Continue with steps 4 through 6 in "Protecting a Worksheet."

Repeat the Last Command with F4

Most people know that F4 is great for adding dollar signs to a reference when you are building a formula. When you are not editing a formula, the F4 key is used to repeat the previous command. Let's say that you had to change column widths of every other column to a width of 1. After you select cell B1 and press Alt+OCW1<Enter>, you can simply press the Right Arrow key twice and press F4 to repeat the Column Width command on column D. Keep pressing Right Arrow, Right Arrow, F4 until all the column widths are fixed.

Bring the Active Cell Back in to View with Ctrl+Backspace

Sometimes, you end up at the bottom of a data set while the active cell is at the top. Press Ctrl+Backspace and Excel will scroll the active cell back into view.

Separating Text Based on a Delimiter

Depending on the source of your data, you might find that information is loaded into Excel with many fields in one cell. If the fields are separated by a character, you can separate the data into multiple columns. To do so, follow these steps:

1. Select the one-column range that contains multiple values in each cell.

2. Select Data, Data Tools, Convert Text to Column. Excel displays the Convert Text to Columns Wizard dialog box.

3. In step 1 of the wizard, select Delimited and click Next.

4. In step 2 of the wizard, choose your delimiter. Excel offers check boxes for Tab, Semicolon, Comma, and Space. If your delimiter is something different, select the Other box and type the delimiter. Click Next (see Figure 20.4).

Figure 20.4   Identify the delimiter in step 2 of the wizard.

5. In step 3 of the wizard, indicate whether any of your columns are dates. Click the column in the Data Preview section and then select Date in the Column Data Format section. By default, Excel replaces the selected column and uses adjacent blank columns. To write the results to a different output area, enter a destination in step 3 of the wizard.

6. Click Finish to parse the column.

7. Excel does not automatically make the columns wide enough, so select the Cells section of the Home tab and then select Format, Width, AutoFit to make the output columns wide enough for the contents.

Auditing Worksheets Using Inquire

If you have Office 2019 Pro Plus or higher, you can enable the Inquire add-in. The add-in enables tools for discovering potential problems in workbooks. You can see a visual map of relationships, mark cells that contain certain potential problems, or compare two versions of the same workbook.

To enable Inquire, do both of these steps:

1. Press Alt+T followed by I to display the Add-Ins dialog box. Choose Inquire and click OK.

2. Select File, Options, Add-Ins. At the bottom of the screen, choose Manage Com Add-Ins and click Go. Choose Inquire and click OK. A new Inquire tab appears in the ribbon.

Suppose that you have a workbook that you send to a co-worker for review. When you receive the changed version of the workbook from the co-worker, you would like to see if any changes were made to the workbook.

Rename one or both workbooks so you can tell which is the original and which is the changed version. Open both workbooks. From the Inquire tab, choose Compare Files. Specify the newer, changed version of the workbook in the Compare drop-down menu. Specify the original work-book in the To drop-down menu. This might seem backward from the way that you would think the files should be specified.

After you click Compare, the results show in the Spreadsheet Compare tool.

If you don't care about cell formatting changes, uncheck that category in the lower left of the window.

The top of the window shows a view of the two workbooks. Any changes are color coded to match the color legend shown in the lower left.

CHAPTER 20

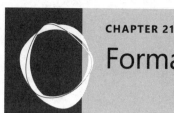

Formatting Worksheets

Formatting adds interest and readability to documents. If you have taken time to create a spreadsheet, you should also take the time to make sure that it is eye catching and readable.

You can format documents in Excel 2019 with any of these three methods:

- **Use table styles**—You can use table styles to format a table with banded rows, accents for totals, and so on.

- **Use cell styles**—You can use cell styles to identify titles, headings, and accent cells. The advantage of using cell styles is that you can quickly apply new themes to change the look and feel of a document.

- **Use formatting commands**—You can use traditional formatting commands to change the font, borders, fill, numeric formatting, column widths, and row heights. The usual formatting icons are on the Home tab as well as in the Format Cells dialog box.

Why Format Worksheets?

You can open a blank worksheet and fill it with data without ever touching any of Excel's formatting commands. The result is functional, but not necessarily readable or eye catching. Figure 21.1 contains an unformatted report in Excel.

	A	B	C	D	E	F	G	H
1	Astonishing Treadmill Inc.							
2	Sales Forecast							
3	2018							
4								
5	Line	Product	Jan	Feb	Mar	Q1	Apr	May
6	Consumer	A451	278	285	271	834	291	332
7		A636	357	334	387	1078	456	358
8		A686	161	144	244	549	165	225
9		B416	428	443	425	1296	448	432
10		B519	711	706	764	2181	697	789
11		D553	128	116	104	348	147	194
12		D555	376	405	378	1159	471	450
13		D801	353	352	377	1082	366	354
14		D914	296	274	279	849	394	315
15		E196	625	611	724	1960	700	651
16		E476	458	471	479	1408	484	463
17		Subtotal	4171	4141	4432	12744	4619	4563
18	Professio	K121	174	244	149	567	193	259

Figure 21.1 After typing data into a spreadsheet, you have an unformatted report.

Figure 21.2 contains the same data but with formatting applied. The formatted report in Figure 21.2 is more interesting and easier to read than the unformatted one for the following reasons:

- The reader can instantly focus on the totals for each line.

- Headings are aligned with the data.

- Borders break the data into sections.

- Accent colors highlight the subtotals and totals.

- The title is prominent, in a larger font, and a headline typeface is used.

- Numeric formatting has removed the extra decimal places and added thousands separators.

- Quarterly totals appear in italic.

- The column widths are adjusted properly.

- A short row adds a visual break between the product lines.

- Headings for each product line are rotated, merged, and centered.

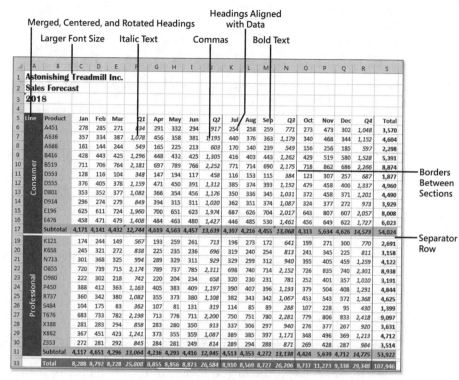

Figure 21.2   Readability is improved after formatting the report.

The formatting applied to Figure 21.2 takes a few extra minutes, but it dramatically increases the readability of the report. Because you have taken the time to put the worksheet together, it is worth a couple of extra minutes to make the worksheet easier for the consumer to read.

Using Traditional Formatting

Formatting is typically carried out in the Format Cells dialog box or using the formatting icons located on the Home tab.

In Excel 2019, the traditional formatting icons are in the Font, Alignment, and Number groups on the Home tab, as shown in Figure 21.3. Additional column- and row-formatting commands are available in the Format drop-down menu in the Cells group on the Home tab.

Figure 21.3   Most icons from the former Formatting toolbar are in the Font, Alignment, and Number groups on the Home tab.

If your favorite setting is not on the Home tab, you can take one of the four entry paths to the Format Cells dialog box, which provides access to additional settings, such as Shrink to Fit, Strikethrough, and more border settings:

- Press Ctrl+1, which is Ctrl and the number 1. You can press Ctrl+Shift+F to display the Font tab on the same dialog box.

- Click the dialog box launcher icons in the lower-right corner of the Font, Alignment, or Number groups. Each icon opens the dialog box, with the focus on a different tab.

- Right-click any cell and select Format Cells.

- Select Format Cells from the Format drop-down menu on the Home tab.

As shown in Figure 21.4, the Format Cells dialog box includes the following six tabs:

- **Number**—Gives you absolute control over numeric formatting. You can choose from 96,885 built-in formats or use the Custom category to create your own.

- **Alignment**—Offers settings for horizontal alignment, vertical alignment, rotation, wrap, merge, and shrinking to fit.

- **Font**—Controls font, size, style, underline, color, strikethrough, superscript, and subscript.

- **Border**—Controls line style and color for each of the four borders and the diagonals on each cell.

- **Fill**—Offers 16 million fill colors and patterns.

- **Protection**—Used to lock or unlock cells.

Figure 21.4   The Format Cells dialog box offers complete control over cell formatting. You can visit this dialog box when the icons on the ribbon do not provide enough detail.

Changing Numeric Formats by Using the Home Tab

If you ever shop for hardware at a general-purpose store, you have probably experienced how it can have almost what you need, but never exactly what you need. At this point, you probably curse your decision to stop at the general-purpose retailer and drive another mile down the road to Home Depot or Lowe's, where you can always find exactly what you need.

Using the Number group on the Home tab is like shopping at a general-purpose retailer. It has many settings for numeric formatting, but often they are not exactly what you need. When this happens, you end up visiting the Number tab on the Format Cells dialog box.

To start, there are three icons—for currency, percentage, and comma style. The Percentage icon is useful. Unfortunately, the Currency and Comma icons apply an Accounting style to a cell, and the Accounting style is inappropriate for everyone except accountants. Furthermore, these three icons are not toggle buttons, which means that when you use one of them, there is not an icon to go back quickly to a general style, other than Undo.

The Increase and Decrease Decimal icons are useful. Each click of one of these buttons forces Excel to show one more or one fewer decimal place. If you have numbers showing two decimal places in all cells, two clicks on the Decrease Decimal icon solves the problem.

Figure 21.5 shows the Currency, Percentage, Comma, Increase Decimal, and Decrease Decimal buttons in the Number group of the Home tab. The Currency button offers a drop-down menu with choices based on your regional settings.

TIP

Excel uses the value in the active cell for each of the formats inside the drop-down menu, and no sample if the cell is blank.

Figure 21.5   The Currency and Comma icons both use an Accounting style. This is wonderful for accountants, but others should resist using them.

Above the five buttons in the Number group is a drop-down menu that has a dozen popular number styles. Figure 21.6 shows the styles in the drop-down menu. The range A2:F12 shows these styles applied to four numbers.

	A	B	C	F	G	H
1						
2	General	1234.567	0.625	-1		
3	Number	1234.57	0.63	-1.00		
4	Currency	$1,234.57	$0.63	-$1.00		
5	Accounting	$ 1,234.57	$ 0.63	$ (1.00)		
6	Short Date	5/18/1903	1/0/1900			
7	Long Date	Monday, May 18, 1903	Saturday, January 00, 1900			
8	Time	1:36:29 PM	3:00:00 PM			
9	Percentage	123456.70%	62.50%	-100.00%		
10	Fraction	1234 4/7	5/8	-1		
11	Scientific	1.23E+03	6.25E-01	-1.00E+00		
12	Text	1234.567	0.625	-1		

Drop-down menu list:

- ABC 123 General — No specific format
- 12 Number — 1234.57
- Currency — $1,234.57
- Accounting — $1,234.57
- Short Date — 5/18/1903
- Long Date — Monday, May 18, 1903
- Time — 1:36:29 PM
- % Percentage — 123456.70%
- 1/2 Fraction — 1234 4/7
- 10^2 Scientific — 1.23E+03
- ABC Text — 1234.567
- More Number Formats...

Figure 21.6   Excel 2019 offers 11 popular number styles in this drop-down menu.

The following list provides some comments and cautions about using the number styles from the drop-down menu in the Home tab:

- General format is a number format. Decimal places are shown if needed. No thousands separator is used. A negative number is shown with a minus sign before the number.

- Number does not use a thousands separator. It forces two decimal places, even with numbers that do not need decimal places, such as in cell F3.

- Currency is a useful format for everyone. The currency symbol is shown immediately before the number. All numbers are expressed with two decimal places. Negatives are shown with a hyphen before the number.

- Accounting is great for financial statements and annoying for everything else. Negative numbers are shown in parentheses. Currency symbols are left-aligned with the edge of the cell. Positive numbers appear one character from the right edge of the cell to allow them to line up with negative numbers.

- Percentage uses two decimal places when selected from the drop-down menu. This is one format for which it is actually better to use the icon on the ribbon than the Format Cells dialog box.

- Fraction defaults to showing a fraction with a one-digit divisor. If you have a number such as 0.925, some Excel number formats correctly show this as 15/16. Unfortunately, the Fraction setting in this drop-down menu rounds it to one-digit divisors.

Changing Numeric Formats by Using Built-in Formats in the Format Cells Dialog Box

The Format Cells dialog box offers more number formats than the Home tab. My favorite number format can be accessed only through the Format Cells dialog box. I find that I avoid the buttons in the Number group in the Home tab and go directly to the Format Cells dialog box.

You can display the Format Cells dialog box by clicking the dialog box launcher icon in the lower-right corner of the Number group of the Home tab. When you open the Format Cells dialog box this way, the Number tab is the active tab.

Twelve categories appear on the left side of the Number tab. The General and Text categories each have a single setting. The Custom category enables you to use formatting codes to build any number format. The remaining nine categories each offer a collection of controls to customize the numeric format.

Using Numeric Formatting with Thousands Separators

Using numeric formatting with thousands separators is my favorite format. The thousands separators make the number easy to read. You can suppress the decimal places from the numbers. Microsoft does not offer buttons on the Home tab to select this format. The comma button is a perfect place for it, but instead Microsoft assigns that to the accounting format.

To format cells in numeric format, follow these steps:

1.   Press Ctrl+1 to display the Format Cells dialog box.

2.   Select the Number category from the Number tab.

3.   Select the Use 1000 Separator check box.

4.   Optionally, adjust the Decimal Places spin button to 0.

5.   Optionally, select a method for displaying negative numbers.

Figure 21.7 shows the Number category of the Format Cells dialog box.

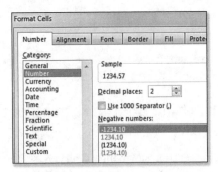

Figure 21.7   The Number category is the workhorse in Excel.

Displaying Currency

Two categories are used for currency: Currency and Accounting. The Currency category is identical to the Number category shown in Figure 21.7, with the addition of a currency symbol drop-down menu. This drop-down menu offers 409 different currencies from around the world.

The second category is Accounting. With this category, the currency symbol is always left aligned in the cell. The last digit of positive numbers appears one character from the right edge of the cell so that positive and negative numbers line up. In addition, negative numbers are always shown in parentheses.

Displaying Dates and Times

The Date category offers 17 built-in formats for displaying dates, and the Time category offers nine built-in formats for displaying time. Each category has two formats that display both date and time.

The date formats vary from short dates such as 3/14 to long dates such as Wednesday, March 14, 2012. You should pay particular attention to the Date formats and the Sample box. Some formats show only the month and the day. Other formats show the month and the year. For example, the values in the Type box are for March 14, 2012. Other types such as March-01 display month-year. Types, such as 14-Mar, display day-month.

An interesting format near the bottom of the list is the M type. This displays month names in JFMAMJJASOND style, as shown in Figure 21.8. Readers of the *Wall Street Journal*'s financial charts will instantly recognize that each month is represented by the first letter of the month in this style. This style works great when used as the labels along the x-axis of a chart.

Figure 21.8 A variety of date and time formats is available.

In the Time category, pay attention to an important distinction between the 1:30 p.m., 13:30, and 37:30:55 types. The first type displays times from 12:00 a.m. through 11:59 p.m. The second type displays military time. In this system, midnight is 0:00, and 11:59 p.m. is 23:59. Neither of these types displays hours exceeding 24 hours. If you are working on a weekly timesheet or any application in which you need to display hours that total to more than 24 hours, you need to use the 37:30:55 type in the Time category. This format is one of a few that displays hours exceeding 24.

Displaying Fractions

The Fractions category rounds a decimal number to the nearest fraction. Types include fractions in halves, quarters, eighths, sixteenths, tenths, and hundredths. In addition, the first three types specify that the decimal should be reduced to the nearest fraction with up to one, two, or three digits in the denominator.

Figure 21.9 shows a variety of decimals formatted with five different fractional types. In row 14, notice that this random number can appear as 1/2, 49/92, or 473/888 when using the Up To *N* Digit types. Excel rounds the number to the closest fraction.

Figure 21.9   Excel can display decimals as fractions in a variety of formats.

In column E, note that if you ask Excel to show the number in eighths, Excel uses 4/8 and 2/8 instead of 1/2 or 1/4.

You probably feel as if you spent too much time in junior high math learning how to reduce fractions. The good news is that the first three fraction types of number formatting in Excel eliminate the need for manually reducing fractions.

Displaying ZIP Codes, Telephone Numbers, and Social Security Numbers

Spreadsheets were invented in Cambridge, Massachusetts. However, if you enter the ZIP Code for Cambridge (02138) in a cell, Excel does not display the ZIP Code correctly. It truncates the leading zero, giving you a ZIP Code of 2138.

To combat this problem, Excel provides four special formatting types, all of which are U.S. centric:

- The Zip Code and Zip Code + 4 styles ensure that East Coast cities do not lose the leading zeros in their ZIP Codes.

- The Phone Number type formats a telephone number with parentheses around the area code and a hyphen after the exchange.

- The Social Security Number type groups the digits into groups of three, two, and four numbers that are separated by hyphens.

Figure 21.10 shows cells formatted with the four types available in the Special category.

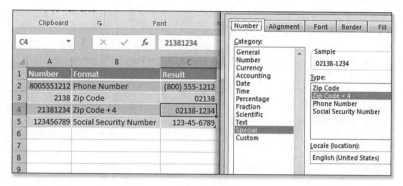

Figure 21.10   United States customers will appreciate the Special category in the Format Cells dialog box.

NOTE

If you happen to live in one of the 195 countries in the world besides the United States, you will undoubtedly need other formatting for your postal codes, telephone numbers, or national ID numbers. You can create number formats such as the ones shown in the Special category as well as the other formats you might need by using the Custom category, as discussed in the next section.

Changing Numeric Formats Using Custom Formats

Custom number formats provide incredible power and flexibility. Although you do not need to know the complete set of rules for them, you will probably find a couple of custom number formats that work perfectly for you.

TIP

A good way to learn custom number formatting codes is to select a format and then click Custom to see the code for the selected format. For example, click Fraction and then click As Quarters (2/4). When you click Custom, you learn that the custom number code is # ?/4. Using this knowledge, you could build a new custom format code to show data in 17ths: # ?/17.

To use a custom number format, follow these steps:

1. Select the cells to be highlighted.

2. Display the Format Cells dialog box by pressing Ctrl+1.

3. Select the Number tab.

4. Select the Custom category.

5. Type the formatting codes into the Type box. Excel shows you a sample of the active cell with this format in the Sample box.

6. After you make sure this format looks correct, click OK to accept it.

Using the Four Zones of a Custom Number Format

A custom number format can contain up to four different formats, each separated by a semicolon. The semicolons divide the format into as many as four zones. Excel allows different formatting, depending on whether a cell contains a positive number, a negative number, a zero, or text. You need to keep in mind the following:

- Separate formatting codes for zones by using semicolons.

- If you type only one number format, it applies to all numbers.

- If you type only two formats, the first format applies to positive and zero. The second format is used for negative.

- If all four formats are used, they refer to positive, negative, zero, and text values, respectively.

In Figure 21.11, a custom number format uses all four zones. The table in rows 11:14 shows how various numbers are displayed in this format. Notice that cell B12 appears in red type.

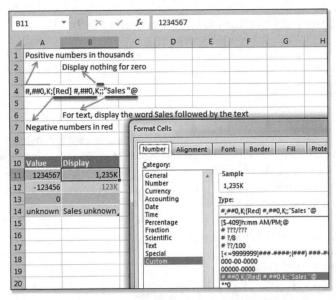

Figure 21.11 The four zones of a custom number format can cause positive, negative, zero, and text values to display differently.

Controlling Text and Spacing in a Custom Number Format

You can display a mix of text and numbers in a numeric cell by including the text in double quotation marks. For example, "The total is "$#,##0 precedes the number with the text shown in quotes.

If you need a single character, you can omit the quotation marks and precede the character with a backslash (\). For example, the code $#,##0,,\M displays numbers in millions and adds an M indicator after the number. The letters BDEGHMNSY require a backslash. The rest of the letters can be used without a backslash.

Some characters require neither a backslash nor quotation marks. These special characters are $ - + / ( ) : ! ^ & ' ~ { } = < > and the space character.

To add a specific amount of space to a format, you enter an underscore followed by a character. Excel then includes enough space to include that particular character. One frequent use for this is to include _) at the end of a positive number to leave enough space for a closing parenthesis. The positive numbers then line up with the negative numbers shown in parentheses.

To fill the space in a cell with a repeating character, use an asterisk followed by the character. For example, the format **0 fills the leading space in a cell with asterisks. The format 0*- fills the trailing space in a cell with hyphens.

If you are expecting numbers but think you might occasionally have text in the cell, you can use the fourth zone of the format. You use the @ character to represent the text in the cell. For example, 0;0;0;"Unexpected entry of "@ highlights the text cells with a note. If someone types a number, she gets the number. If someone types **hello**, she gets "Unexpected entry of hello."

Controlling Decimal Places in a Custom Number Format

Use a zero as a placeholder when you want to force the place to be included. For example, 0.000 formats all numbers with three decimal places. If the number has more than three places, it is rounded to three decimal places.

Use a pound sign (#) as a placeholder to display significant digits but not insignificant zeros. For example, 0.### displays up to three decimal places, if needed, but can display "1." for a whole number.

Use a question mark to replace insignificant zeros on either size of the decimal point with enough space to represent a digit in a fixed-width font. This format was designed to allow decimal points to line up, but with proportional fonts, it may not always work.

To include a thousands separator, include a comma to the left of the decimal point. For example, #,##0 displays a thousands separator.

To scale a number by thousands, include a comma after the numeric portion of the format. Each comma divides the number by a thousand. For example, 0, displays numbers in thousands, and 0,, displays numbers in millions.

Using Conditions and Color in a Custom Number Format

The condition codes available in numeric formatting predate conditional formatting by a decade. You should consider the flexible conditional formatting features for any new conditions. However, in case you encounter an old worksheet with these codes, it is valid to use colors in the format: red, blue, green, yellow, cyan, black, white, magenta, Color 1, ..., Color 56. You include the color in square brackets. It should be the first element of any numeric formatting zone.

You can include a condition in square brackets after the color but before the numeric formatting. For example, [Red][<=100];[Color 17][>100] displays numbers under 100 in red and other numbers in blue. The United States telephone special format uses this custom condition:

```
[<=9999999]###-####;(###) ###-####
```

Using Dates and Times in a Custom Number Format

Although many of these settings are arcane, I still regularly use many of the date and time formats shown in Table 21.1. The various m and d codes allow flexibility in expressing dates.

Table 21.1   Date and Time Formats

To Display This:	Use This Code:
Months as 1–12	m
Months as 01–12	mm
Months as Jan–Dec	mmm
Months as January–December	mmmm
Months as the first letter of the month	mmmmm
Days as 1–31	d
Days as 01–31	dd
Days as Sun–Sat	ddd
Days as Sunday–Saturday	dddd
Years as 00–99	yy
Years as 1900–9999	yyyy
Hours as 0–23	h
Hours as 00–23	hh
Minutes as 0–59	m
Minutes as 00–59	mm

Seconds as 0–59	s
Seconds as 00–59	ss
Hours as 4 AM	h AM/PM
Time as 4:36 PM	h:mm AM/PM
Time as 4:36:03 P	h:mm:ss A/P
Elapsed time in hours such as 25:02	[h]:mm
Elapsed time in minutes such as 63:46	[mm]:ss
Elapsed time in seconds	[ss]
Fractions of a second	h:mm:ss.00

The custom number format m/d/yy or m/d/y displays the month and day numbers as one digit if possible. For example, dates formatted with this code display as 1/9/08, 1/31/08, 9/9/09, and 12/31/08. Note that you cannot display the year as a single digit.

A custom number format of mm/dd/yy always uses two digits to display the month and day. Examples are 01/09/08 and 01/31/08.

The remaining date and time codes can display months as Jan, January, or J and days as 1, 01, Fri, or Friday.

NOTE

Note that the letter m can be used either as a month or as a minute. If the m is preceded by an h or followed by an s, Excel assumes you are referring to minutes. Otherwise, the month is displayed instead.

Displaying Scientific Notation in Custom Number Formats

To display numbers in scientific format, you use E- or E+ exponent codes in a zone.

If a format contains a zero (0) or pound sign (#) to the right of an exponent code, Excel displays the number in scientific format and inserts an E. The number of zeros or pound signs to the right of a code determines the number of digits in the exponent. E- or e- places a minus sign by negative exponents. E+ or e+ places a minus sign by negative exponents and a plus sign by positive exponents.

Take the following, for example:

- 1450 formatted with 0.00E+00 displays as 1.45E+03.

- 1450 formatted with 0.00E-00 displays as 1.45E03.

- 0.00145 formatted with either code displays as 1.45E-03.

Aligning Cells

Worksheets look best when the headings above a column are aligned with the data in the column. Excel's default behavior is to left align text and right align values and dates.

In Figure 21.12, the month heading in F1 is left aligned, and the numeric values starting in row 2 are right aligned. This makes the worksheet look haphazard. To solve the problem, you can right align the headings cells.

To right align cells, select the cells and click the Right Align icon in the Alignment group of the Home tab.

NOTE

The Alignment tab of the Format Cells dialog box offers additional alignment choices, such as justified and distributed.

Figure 21.12   In column F, the left-aligned heading appears out of alignment with the numbers. Columns G and H show the headings after the Right Align icon is clicked.

Changing Font Size

There are three icons in the Font group of the Home tab for changing font size:

- The Increase Font Size A icon increases the font size in the selected cells to the next larger setting.

- The Decrease Font Size A icon decreases the font size in the selected cells to the next smaller setting.

- The Font Size drop-down menu offers a list of font sizes. You can hover over any font size to see the Live Preview of that size in the selected cells of the worksheet (see Figure 21.13).

NOTE

If you need a font size that is not in the drop-down menu, you can type a new value in the drop-down menu. For example, although the drop-down menu jumps from 12 to 14, you can click the value and type 13.

Font Size drop-down menu

Increase Font Size
Decrease Font Size

Figure 21.13   When you use the Font Size drop-down menu, Live Preview shows you the effect of an increased font size before you select the font.

Changing Font Typeface

Since Excel 2007, changing the font typeface has been vastly improved over earlier versions of Excel. In some legacy versions of Excel, the Font drop-down menu showed the font names in the style of each font. However, beginning with Excel 2007, Live Preview shows how the font will look as you hover over the font in the selected cells (see Figure 21.14). Notice that the Font name drop-down menu is in the Font group of the Home tab.

NOTE

By using the Font tab of the Format Cells dialog box, you can also apply strikethrough, superscript, and subscript.

Figure 21.14   The Font drop-down menu in the Home tab shows the look of each font, and Live Preview shows how individual cells will look with the font applied.

CHAPTER 21

Applying Bold, Italic, and Underline

Three icons in the Font group in the Home tab enable you to change the font to apply bold, italic, and underline. Unlike the icons in the Number group, these icons behave properly, toggling the property on and off. The Bold icon is a bold letter *B*. The Italic icon is an italic letter *I*. The Underline icon is either an underlined *U* or a double-underlined *D*. The Underline icon is actually a drop-down menu. As shown in Figure 21.15, you can select the drop-down menu to change from Single Underline to Double Underline.

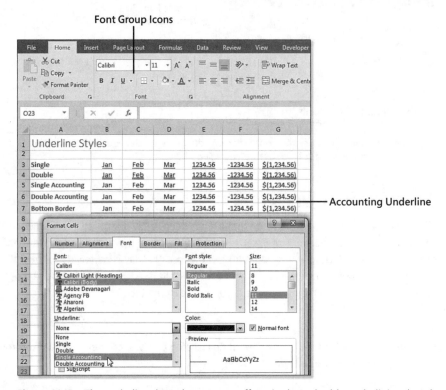

Figure 21.15   The underline drop-down menu offers single or double underlining, but the extra choices in the Format Cells dialog box solve some text underlining issues.

The underline style applies to the characters in the cell. If you have a cell that contains 123, the underline is three characters wide. If you have a cell with 1,234,567.89, the underline is 12 characters wide.

The Format Cells dialog box offers more choices. Settings for Single Accounting underline create an underline that extends nearly to the edges of the cell, but leaves a gap between the underline in the next cell. This often looks better than using a bottom border across the cells.

Using Borders

There are 1.7 billion unique combinations of borders for any four-cell range. The Borders drop-down menu in the Font group of the Home tab offers 13 popular border options plus five border tools. If you must draw nonstandard borders, explore the Draw Borders tool in this drop-down menu.

You must understand an important concept when applying borders to a range. Suppose you select 20 rows by 20 columns, such as cells A1:T20. If you apply a top border by using the drop-down menu, only the top row of cells A1:T1 have the border. Often, this is not what you were expecting. For example, you might have wanted a border on the top of all 400 cells.

Notice that in the Format Cells dialog box, there is a representation of a 2×2 cell range. The border style drawn in the top edge of this box affects only the top edge of the range. The border style drawn in the middle horizontal line of the box affects all the horizontal borders on the inside of the selected range.

The fastest way to select all horizontal and vertical borders in the range is to click the Outline button and then the Inside button in the Presets section of the dialog box.

Coloring Cells

Excel allows you to use a gradient to fill a cell. This can provide an interesting look for a title cell. Gradient formatting is available only in the Format Cells dialog box.

The Font group on the Home tab offers a paint bucket drop-down menu and an A drop-down menu. The paint bucket is a color chooser for the background fill of the cell. The A drop-down menu is a color chooser for the font color in the cell. Both drop-down menus offer six shades of the 10 theme colors, 10 standard colors, and the More Colors option. The paint bucket drop-down menu also offers the menu choice No Fill, as shown in Figure 21.16.

Figure 21.16   The paint bucket drop-down menu offers theme colors, 10 standard colors, and the link More Colors.

The More Colors link offers the two-tabbed Colors dialog box. You can either choose a color from the Standard tab or enter an RGB value on the Custom tab.

The ability to use a two-color gradient in a cell was a new feature beginning with Excel 2007. To activate this feature, follow these steps:

1. Select one or more cells. If you select a range of cells, Excel repeats the gradient for each cell in the range.

2. Press Ctrl+1 to display the Format Cells dialog box.

3. Select the Fill tab.

4. Click the Fill Effects button.

5. In the Color 1 and Color 2 drop-down menus, choose two colors or choose one color and white.

6. In the Shading Styles section, choose a shading style.

7. In the Variants section, choose one of the three variations. A sample is shown in the Sample box.

8. Click OK to close the Fill Effects dialog box.

9. Click OK to close the Format Cells dialog box.

Figure 21.17 shows the Fill Effects dialog box. Cell A1 contains a vertical shading, from left to right. Cell A4 shows the opposite variant of vertical shading. Cell A9 shows the from-the-center variant of the vertical shading. Cell A13 shows a diagonal-down shading style.

In all versions except Excel 2007, pattern fills are available. Use the Pattern Color and Pattern Style drop-down menus in the Fill tab of the Format Cells dialog box to add a pattern shading to a cell. A15 of Figure 21.17 shows a pattern.

Figure 21.17   You can add gradients as the fill within cells.

Adjusting Column Widths and Row Heights

You can adjust the width of every column in a worksheet. In many cases, narrowing the columns to reduce wasted space can allow a report to fit on one page.

Most tasks in Excel can be accomplished in three or more ways. In most cases, I have a favorite method to perform any task and use that method exclusively. However, setting column widths and row heights is a task where I actively use many methods, depending on the circumstances.

You can use the following seven methods to adjust column width (each method applies equally well to adjusting row heights):

- **Click the border between the column headings**—As shown in Figure 21.18, you can drag to the left to make the column narrower. You can drag to the right to make the column wider. A ToolTip appears, showing the width in points and pixels. The advantage of this method is that you can drag until the column feels like it is the right width. The disadvantage is that this method fixes one column at a time.

Figure 21.18   The right border between one cell letter and the next is the key to adjusting column widths.

- **Double-click the border between column headings**—Excel automatically adjusts the left column to fit the widest value in the column. The advantage of this method is that the column is exactly wide enough for the contents. The disadvantage is that a very long title in cell A1, for example, makes this method ineffective. You might have been planning to allow the title in cell A1 to spill over to B1, C1, and D1. However, the double-click method makes the column wide enough for the long title. In this case, you want to use the last method in this list.

- **Select many columns and drag the border for one column**—When you do this, the width for all columns is adjusted. The advantage of this method is that you can adjust all columns at once, and they are all a uniform width.

- **Select many columns and double-click one of the borders between column letters**—When you do this, all the columns adjust to fit their widest value.

- **Use the ribbon**—Select one or more columns. From the Cells group of the Home tab, select Format, Column Width. Then enter a width in characters and click OK.

- **Apply one column's width to other columns**—If one column is a suitable width, and you want all other columns to be the same width, you should use this method. Select the column with the correct width and then press Ctrl+C to copy. Next, select the columns to be adjusted. Select the Clipboard section of the Home tab and select Paste, Paste Special, Column Widths. Finally, click OK.

- **AutoFit a column to all the data below the title rows**—If you have a long title in the first few rows and need to AutoFit the column to all the data below the title rows, use this method. Click the first cell in the data range and then press the End key. Next, hold down the Ctrl and Shift keys while pressing the down-arrow key. This selects a contiguous range from the starting cell downward. Now select the Cells section of the Home tab and then select Format, AutoFit Selection. If you were a power user in Excel 2003 or earlier, you might remember this method as Alt+O+C+A. This legacy keyboard shortcut still works.

Using Merge and Center

In general, merged cells are bad. If you have a merged cell in the middle of a data table, you will be unable to sort the data. You will be unable to cut and paste data unless the same cells are merged. However, it is okay to use merged cells as a title to group several columns together.

In Figure 21.19, the Consumer and Professional headings correspond to the columns B:F and G:K, respectively. It is appropriate to center each heading above its columns.

CAUTION

Merging cells brings some negative side effects. Suppose that you had merged B100:G100. You start in cell B1, hold down the Shift key, and start pressing PgDn to select cells in column B. When you reach or pass the merged cell B100, your selection size will automatically expand to be six columns wide because this is the width of the merged cell. To prevent this problem, you might use Center Across Selection, found in the Home tab. This gives the same look as the merged cell, without the problems caused by the merge.

	A	B	C	D	E	F	G	H	I	J	K
1											
2		Consumer					Professional				
3	Month	A451	A636	A686	B416	B519	K121	K658	N713	O855	O980
4	Jan	167	198	168	139	153	145	144	198	195	168
5	Feb	166	132	135	150	183	170	198	103	195	194
6	Mar	191	103	112	190	136	124	151	108	167	182
7	Apr	125	147	175	150	190	182	154	140	173	178
8	May	121	160	147	169	170	183	147	138	196	181
9	Jun	131	166	548	179	196	165	140	177	191	177
10	Jul	182	118	144	116	172	171	158	141	149	170
11	Aug	137	129	183	163	105	188	103	116	195	102
12	Sep	130	108	124	177	170	108	168	168	142	138
13	Oct	146	197	180	177	143	180	152	177	188	123
14	Nov	154	153	180	158	129	110	118	179	151	155
15	Dec	107	162	151	145	158	178	180	159	129	188
16											

CHAPTER 21

Figure 21.19   Because the row 2 categories are not part of the data table and will never need to be sorted, it is okay to merge and center those cells.

To merge and center cells, follow these steps:

1. Click in the cell that contains the value that is to be centered, and then drag to select the entire range to be merged. In this example, click in cell B2 and drag to cell F2. The result is that B2 is the active cell, and B2:F2 is selected.

2. From the Home tab, select Alignment, Merge & Center, and then select Merge & Center again, as shown in Figure 21.20.

Figure 21.20   Select Merge & Center from the drop-down menu.

3. Repeat steps 1 and 2 for any other column headings.

4. Optionally, apply an outline border around the merged cells.

Note that after you merge the cells, the entire range becomes one cell. In Figure 21.21, the word *Consumer* is in an ultra-large cell B2. In this worksheet, cells C2, D2, E2, and F2 no longer exist. If you attempt to use the Go To dialog box to move to cell C2, you will be taken to cell B2 instead.

▲	A	B	C	D	E	F	G	H	I	J	K
1											
2		Consumer					Professional				
3	Month	A451	A636	A686	B416	B519	K121	K658	N713	O855	O980
4	Jan	167	198	168	139	153	145	144	198	195	168
5	Feb	166	132	135	150	183	170	198	103	195	194
6	Mar	191	103	112	190	136	124	151	108	167	182

(cell reference box: P19, with f_x)

Figure 21.21 Columns are visually grouped into product lines by the merged cells.

TROUBLESHOOTING

While selecting cells, if you touch a merged cell, your selection will instantly become as wide as the merged cell.

In the figure below, you might try selecting A1:A99 by pressing Ctrl+Shift+Up Arrow. That would usually be a great way to select the cells with data in the column.

▲	A	B	C	D	E
1	This title is a merged cell				
2	Product	Rep	Sales		
94	Date	Chris	940		
95	Date	Barb	950		
96	Fig	Barb	960		
97	Elderberry	Chris	970		
98	Elderberry	Andy	980		
99	Date	Andy	990		
100					

However, the merged cell in A1 causes your selection to become as wide as the merged cell. You end up selecting A1:E99 instead of A1:A99.

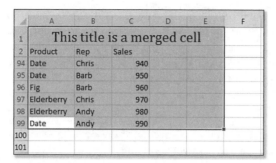

To prevent the problem, you could add a blank Row 2 to separate the merged cell from your data.

Or, you could stop using merged cells. Select A1:E1 and then select, Home, Format, Format Cells, Alignment, and then open the Horizontal drop-down menu and choose Center Across Selection. This creates the same look as Merge & Center, but the selection rectangle will not widen when you touch A1.

To fix the problem shown in the figure, hold down the Shift key while you press the down arrow key. You will have A2:E99 selected. Now that the merged cell is no longer part of the selection, hold down Shift while pressing the left arrow key four times.

Rotating Text

Vertical text is difficult to read. However, at times space considerations make it advantageous to use vertical text. In Figure 21.22, for example, the names in row 5 are much wider than the values in the rest of the table. If you use Format, AutoFit Selection, the report is too wide.

	A	B	C	D	E	F	G
5		Product	Blankenship	Cunningham	Fitzpatrick	Hamilton	Hernderson N
6		A451	339	258	293	316	252
7		A636	438	332	377	408	325
8		A686	218	166	188	203	162
9		B416	513	389	442	477	380
10		B519	844	640	727	786	626
11	Consumer	D553	178	135	154	166	132
12		D555	472	358	407	439	350
13		D801	427	324	368	397	317
14		D914	374	283	322	348	277
15		E196	761	578	656	709	564
16		E476	573	434	494	533	425
17		Subtotal	5,137	3,897	4,428	4,782	3,810

Figure 21.22   The headings are much wider than the data. Vertical text can solve the problem.

In the Alignment tab of the Home group, an Orientation drop-down menu offers five variations of vertical text. Figure 21.23 compares the five available options. Although the Angle options look great, they reduce the column width by only 12%. Vertical Text reduces the column width by 75% but takes far more vertical space. The option Rotate Text Up reduces the column width by 73% and takes up less than half the vertical space of the Vertical Text option.

NOTE

After you rotate the text, select the Cells section of the Home tab and then select Format, AutoFit Selection again to narrow the columns.

Figure 21.23 Of the five options, the Rotate Text options take up the least space.

If you need more control over the text orientation, you can select the Alignment option in the drop-down menu to display the Alignment tab of the Format Cells dialog box. This tab allows rotation from 90 degrees to –90 degrees, in 1-degree increments, as shown in the bottom right of Figure 21.23.

Formatting with Styles

Instead of using the settings in the Font group of the Home tab, you can format a report by using the built-in cell styles. Cell styles have been popular in Word for more than a decade. They have been available in legacy versions of Excel, but because they were not given a spot on the Formatting toolbar, few people took advantage of them.

Figure 21.24 shows the styles available when you select Styles, Cell Styles in the Home tab.

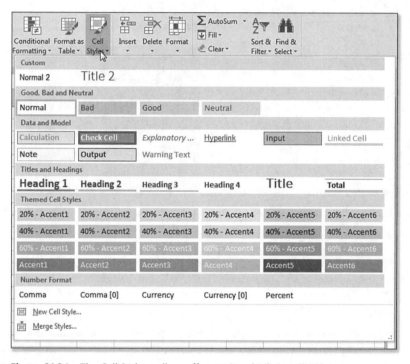

Figure 21.24   The Cell Styles gallery offers various built-in cell styles.

An advantage to using cell styles is that you can convert the look and feel of a report by choosing from the themes on the Page Layout tab. Figure 21.25 shows one of the several themes applied to the report.

CHAPTER 21

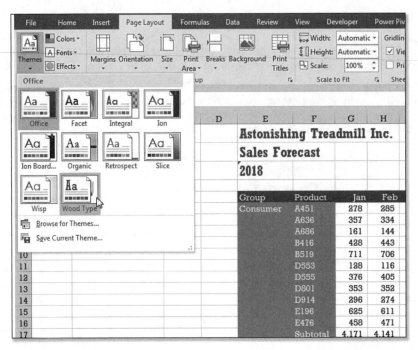

Figure 21.25   When you choose a new theme, a report formatted with cell styles takes on a new look.

The Cell Styles gallery offers a menu item to add additional styles to a workbook. Using cell styles provides an interesting alternative to the traditional method of formatting.

NOTE

You might wonder why Excel 2019 suggests that calculated cells should be in orange font or why Notes should have a yellow background. I spent the first two years of working with Excel 2007 wondering why calculated cells should be orange. However, the better question is, "Why not orange?" When I receive worksheets from others who use this convention, it is easy to understand that they are using the built-in cell styles, which makes it easier to follow the logic of the worksheet. In Figure 21.26, the forecasting model was formatted using Cell Styles from the Data and Model section of the Cell Styles menu. If everyone in your company used these styles, it would be easier to spot the input cells in any model.

Figure 21.26   Adopt the cell styles suggestions for input cells, calculated cells, and so on to make it easier to see the logic in the model.

Understanding Themes

A *theme* is a collection of colors, fonts, and effects. Office 2019 has 20 built-in themes. If you've upgraded your computer from a previous version, you can also download new themes from Office Online or design your own themes.

TIP

The Office theme is the default theme in Excel 2019. In an effort to look modern, Microsoft changed the Office theme starting in Excel 2013. If you had previously embraced themes in Excel 2007 or Excel 2010, you might have become a fan of the old Office theme. The Title cell style in the old Office theme was better than the Title cell style in the new Office theme. Worse, if you open an old document created with Excel 2007 or Excel 2010, the old Office theme will still be available. New workbooks have the new Office theme. It is annoying that they used the same name for two different themes.

Here is how to get the old Office theme back. On the Page Layout tab, open three drop-down menus for color, font, and effects. In each drop-down menu, choose Office 2007–2010 theme. After choosing from those three drop-down menus, choose Themes, Save Current Theme. Save the theme with a name such as OfficeReal or aaaOffice. Custom themes appear at the top of the Themes drop-down menu, so it will be relatively easy to go back to the old theme, even in new workbooks.

Themes are shared in simple XML files, which means they can be propagated throughout a company. A theme has the following components:

- **Fonts**—A theme has two fonts: one for body text and one for titles. The fonts come into play more often in PowerPoint and Word than in Excel. However, styles in Excel also use fonts.

- **Colors**—There are 12 colors: four for text and backgrounds, six accent colors that are used in charts and table accents, and two for hyperlinks. One of the two colors for hyperlinks indicates followed hyperlinks, whereas the other color indicates hyperlinks that have not been followed. The colors shown here appear in the top of the Color Chooser shown previously in Figure 21.16.

- **Effects**—Each theme includes several object effects, such as bevel and line style.

Choosing a New Theme

Themes are managed on the Page Layout tab. Listed next are the four drop-down menus available in the Themes group:

- **Themes**—Allows you to switch among the built-in themes.

- **Colors**—Allows you to change the color scheme to use the colors from another theme.

- **Fonts**—Allows you to use the fonts from another theme.

- **Effects**—Allows you to use the effects from another theme.

NOTE

Note that you can use only one theme per workbook. If you are changing the theme on Sheet33, the same changes are made on all the other worksheets in the workbook.

Changing a theme affects charts, tables, SmartArt diagrams, and inserted objects.

To switch to another theme, follow these steps:

1. Arrange your worksheet so that you can see any themed elements, such as tables or charts, on the right side of the screen.

2. From the Page Layout tab, select the Themes drop-down menu from the Themes group.

3. Hover over the various themes. The worksheet updates to show the new colors, fonts, and effects.

4. When you identify a theme you like, click the theme to apply it to the workbook.

If you are strictly interested in the accent colors, you can select the Colors drop-down menu from the Themes group to see the accent colors used in each theme. Note that this drop-down menu offers a grayscale option that is not available in the Themes drop-down menu.

Inside OUT

One common request is to go back to the theme used in Excel 2007 and 2010. People had six years to create documents with the bold colors introduced in Excel 2007.

The colors used in the Office theme changed in Excel 2013. When you open the Themes drop-down menu, there is nothing offering you to go back to the Office 2007–2010 colors.

However, each theme is defined by colors, fonts, and effects. If you skip the Theme drop-down menu and head directly to each of the three component drop-downs, you will find a theme called Office 2007 – 2010.

It seems just a bit rotten that Microsoft hid the old theme in the Color/Fonts/Effects drop-down menus when most people would think to look in the Themes drop-down menu.

Creating a New Theme

You might want to develop a special theme, which is fairly easy to do. First, you need to select two fonts and six accent colors. For example, suppose you want to create a theme to match your company's color scheme. The hardest part is finding six colors to represent your company, because most company logos have two or three colors. Use a tool such as colorschemedesigner.com to find complementary colors for your company colors.

Specifying a Theme's Colors

To specify new theme colors, follow these steps:

1. Select Page Layout, Themes, Colors, Create New Theme Colors. The Create New Theme Colors dialog box appears.

2. To change any accent color, select the drop-down menu next to Accent 1 through Accent 6. The Color Chooser appears. Select More Colors. Enter the color codes for Red, Green, and Blue. Repeat for the other accent colors.

3. In the Name box, give the theme a name, such as your company name.

4. Click Save to accept the theme.

Specifying a Theme's Fonts

To specify new theme fonts, follow these steps:

1. Select Page Layout, Themes, Fonts, Create New Theme Fonts.

2. Select a font from the Heading Font drop-down menu. If a custom font is used in your company's logo, using it might be appropriate.

3. Select a font from the Body Font drop-down menu. This should be a font that is easy to read. Avoid stylized fonts for body copy.

4. Give the theme a name. It is okay to reuse the same name from the color theme.

5. Click Save to accept the theme changes.

TIP

In June 2009, famed font designer Erik Spiekermann released the Axel font family, which he designed specifically for showing tables of numbers in Microsoft Excel. You can purchase Axel from https://www.fontshop.com/families/axel.

Reusing Another Theme's Effects

There is no dialog box to choose the effects associated with a theme. Other than editing the XML by hand, you are limited to using the effects from one of the built-in themes.

To select effects for a theme, from the Page Layout tab, select Themes, Effects. Then choose one of the existing themes.

The Effects drop-down menu is initially vexing. There are only subtle clues about the effects used in the theme. Each effects icon consists of a circle, an arrow, and a rectangle. The circle represents effects for Simple shapes. The arrow represents Moderate effects. The rectangle represents Intense effects. These roughly correspond to rows in the Shape Styles gallery found on the Drawing Tools Format tab. Row 1 in the gallery is simple, row 4 is moderate, and row 6 is intense.

Saving a Custom Theme

To reuse a theme, you must save it. To save a theme, from the Page Layout tab, select Themes, Save Current Theme.

By default, themes are stored in the Document Themes folder. In Windows Vista and Windows 7, the folder is in `C:\Users\user name\AppData\Roaming\Microsoft\Templates\Document Themes`.

Be sure to give your theme a useful name and then click Save.

Using a Theme on a New Document

When you open a new document on the same computer, the Custom theme is in the Themes drop-down menu on the Page Layout tab. You can use this theme on all future documents.

Sharing a Theme with Others

If you want to share a theme with others, you need to send them the .thmx file from the theme folder.

The people you share the theme with can either copy the .thmx file to their equivalent folder or save the .thmx file to their desktop and use the Browse for Themes option, by choosing Page Layout, Themes, Browse for Themes.

Other Formatting Techniques

Now that you have the basics for formatting cells and worksheets, the rest of this chapter provides an overview of various formatting tips and tricks. These techniques discuss how to mix formatting within a single cell, wrap text in several cells, and use cell comments.

TIP

After selecting characters in the cell, move the mouse pointer to the right and up to activate a shortened version of the mini toolbar. You can use icons on this floating toolbar to format the selected characters.

Formatting Individual Characters

Occasionally, you might find yourself entering a short memo on a worksheet. This might occur as an introduction or as instructions to a lengthy workbook. Although Excel is not a full-featured word processor, it can do a few word processing tricks.

One trick is to highlight individual characters in a cell to add emphasis or to make them stand out. You can do this to any cell that does not contain a formula. In Figure 21.27, for example, text has been typed in column A and allowed to extend over the edge of the column into columns A:J. One word in row 4 is in a bold, underlined, red font.

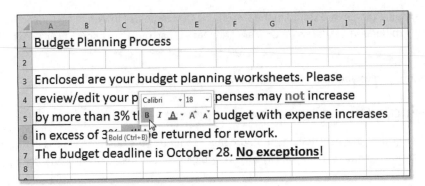

Figure 21.27 Formatting for individual characters in a cell can be changed by selecting those characters while in Edit mode.

To format individual characters, follow these steps:

1. Display the Home tab.

2. Select the cell that contains the characters to be formatted.

3. Press the F2 key to edit the cell.

4. Using the mouse, highlight the characters in the cell. Move up and to the right to display the mini toolbar.

5. Although most of the ribbon is grayed out, the options for font size, color, underline, bold, italic, and font name are available in the Font group of the Home tab. Apply any formatting, as desired, from this group.

6. If the changes are not visible in the formula bar, press Enter to accept the changes to preview them.

Changing the Default Font

Excel offers a default font setting to be used for all new workbooks. With the Excel 2019 paradigm of themes, the default font for new workbooks is initially the generic value of BODY FONT. However, this is not an actual font; instead, it refers to the main font used by the current theme.

To change your default font for all new workbooks, follow these steps:

> NOTE
>
> If you like the concept of using themes to change the look and feel of a document, you should leave the default font setting as BODY FONT and change the font used in the theme.

1. The menu for changing the default font does not offer Live Preview of the fonts. Therefore, go to the Font section of the Home tab and select the Font drop-down menu to inspect the available fonts in their actual styles. Find the name of the font you want to use.

2. From the File menu, select Excel Options. The Excel Options dialog box appears.

3. Click the Popular category in the left margin.

4. In the second section, When Creating New Workbooks, select the Use This Font drop-down menu. Select the font name you chose in step 1.

5. Click OK to close the Excel Options dialog box.

6. Close and restart Microsoft Excel for the changes to take effect.

The default font setting has an effect only in new workbooks. It does not affect workbooks previously created.

Wrapping Text in a Cell

You might have one column in a table that contains long, descriptive text. If the text contains several sentences, it would be impractical to make the column wide enough to include the longest value in the column. Excel offers the capability to wrap text on a cell-by-cell basis to solve this problem.

When you wrap text, one annoying feature of Excel becomes evident. All cells in Excel are initially set to have their contents aligned with the bottom of the cell. You probably do not notice this because most cells in Excel are the same height. However, when you wrap text, the cell heights double or more. When this occurs, it becomes evident that the bottom alignment looks strange. To correct this problem, follow these steps:

> ### NOTE
> If the rows are too tall, you will have a tendency to grab the right edge of the column and drag it outward to make the description column wider. A long-standing bug causes Excel not to resize the row heights automatically after this step. Instead, you need to select the Cells section of the Home tab and then select Format, AutoFit Row Height to resize the row height after adjusting the column width.

1. Decide on a reasonable column width for the column that contains the descriptive text. If you try to wrap text in a column that is only 8 points wide, you will be lucky to fit one word per line. If you have the space, a width of at least 24 allows suitable results for the text wrapping.

2. From the Cells section of the Home tab, select Format, Column Width. Choose a width of 24 or greater.

3. Choose the cells in the column to be wrapped.

4. From the Home tab, select Alignment, Wrap Text.

5. Select all cells in the range.

6. From the Home tab, select Alignment, Top Align. The values in the other columns now align with the top of the descriptive text.

Figure 21.28 shows a table where the descriptions in column B have had their text wrapped and all the cells are top aligned.

	A	B	C	D	E
1	Product	Description	Jan	Feb	Mar
	A451	Run up to six preset programs and two customizable workout programs. Other safety features include a large stop switch, starts from only .05 mph and low-profile running hood. A great value. Additional features include cooling fans and speed and incline controls on the arm rests.	278	285	271
2					
	A636	Folding treadmill frame design originated from the demand of hotels for a treadmill as mobile as a room	357	334	387

Figure 21.28   After wrapping text in a column, you should top align all columns.

Justifying Text in a Range

When using Excel as a word processor to include a paragraph of explanatory body copy in a worksheet, you usually have to decide where to break each line manually. Otherwise, Excel offers a command that reflows the text in a paragraph to fit a certain number of columns.

For this reason, you should do some careful preselection work before invoking the command by following these steps:

1. Ensure that your text is composed of one column of cells that contain body copy. It is fine if the sentences extend beyond one column, but the text should be arranged so that the left column contains text and the remaining columns are blank.

2. Ensure that the upper-left cell of your selection starts with the first line of text.

3. Ensure that the selection range is as wide as you want the finished text to be.

4. If your sentences currently extend beyond the desired width, Excel requires more rows to wrap the text. Include several extra rows in the selection rectangle. Figure 21.29 shows a suitable-sized selection range.

Figure 21.29   You need to select more rows than necessary. The number of columns selected determines the width of the final text.

5. From the Home tab, select Editing, Fill, Justify. Excel flows the text so that each line is shorter than the selection range. Figure 21.30 shows the result.

Figure 21.30   Excel flows the text to fit the width of the original selection.

Adding Cell Comments

Cell comments can contain a few sentences or paragraphs to explain a cell. Although the default is for all comments to use a yellow sticky-note format, you can customize comments with colors, fonts, or even pictures.

In the default case, a comment causes a red triangle to appear in a cell. If you hover over the triangle, the comment appears. Alternatively, you can request that comments be displayed all the time. This creates an easy way to add instructions to a worksheet.

Follow these steps to insert a comment, format it, and cause it to be displayed continuously:

1. Select a cell to which you want to add a comment.

2. Select Review, Comments, New Comment, or right-click the cell and select New Comment or press Shift+F2.

3. The default comment starts with your name in bold on line 1 and the insertion point on line 2. To remove your name from the comment, backspace through your name and then press Ctrl+B to turn off the bold.

4. Type instructions to the person using the worksheet. You can make the instructions longer than the initial size of the comment.

   NOTE

   Keep in mind that a comment can contain more than 2,000 words of body copy.

5. After entering the text, click the resize handle in the lower-right corner of the comment. Drag to allow the comment to fit the text.

6. The selection border around the comment can be made of either diagonal lines or dots. If your selection border is diagonal lines, click the selection border to change it to dots.

7. Right-click the selection border and select Format Comment. The Format Comment dialog box appears.

8. In the Format Comment dialog box, change the font, alignment, colors, and so on, as desired. The Transparency setting on the Colors and Lines tab allows the underlying spreadsheet to show through the comment. If you choose the Fill Color drop-down menu, you can select Fill Effects and insert a picture as the background in the comment.

9. Click OK to return to the comment.

10. Right-click in the cell and select Show/Hide Comments. This causes the comment to be permanently displayed on the worksheet.

11. To reposition the comment, click the comment. Drag the selection border to a new location.

Figure 21.31 shows a comment that has been formatted, resized, and set to be displayed.

Figure 21.31   Cell comments can provide instructions or tips for people who use your spreadsheet.

Copying Formats

Excel worksheets tend to have many similar sections of data. After you have taken the time to format the first section, it would be great to be able to copy the formats from one section to another section. The next sections in this chapter discuss the two methods offered in Excel 2019 for doing this: pasting formats and using the Format Painter icon.

Pasting Formats

An option on the Paste Options menu allows you to paste only the formats from the Clipboard. The rules for copying and pasting formats are as follows:

●   If your original selection is one cell, you can paste the formats to as many cells as you want.

●   If your original selection is one row tall and multiple cells wide, you can paste the formats to multiple rows, and the final paste area will be as wide as the original copied range.

●   If your original selection is one column wide and multiple cells tall, you can paste the formats to multiple columns, and the final paste area will be as tall as the original copied range.

Follow these steps to copy formats:

1. Select a formatted section of a report. This might be one cell, one row of cells, or a rectangular range of cells.

2. Press Ctrl+C to copy the selected section to the Clipboard.

3. Select an unformatted section of your worksheet. If your selection in step 1 is a rectangular range, you can select just the top-left cell of the destination range.

4. Press Ctrl+V to paste. Press Ctrl again to open the Paste Options menu. Press R to paste only the formats. The formats from the original selection are copied to the new range. Although the amounts initially changed after you pressed Ctrl+C, the original amounts are restored after you press R.

5. If you have multiple target destinations to format, repeat step 4 as needed.

The disadvantage of using the Paste Formats method is that it does not change column widths. To copy column widths without pasting values, on the Home tab, click the Paste drop-down menu and then select Paste Special, Column Widths, OK.

CAUTION

Do not attempt to use the Column Widths icon in the Paste Options menu to solve this problem. The Column Widths icon always pastes the values along with the column widths. Because you are only trying to copy formats and column widths in this example, this is not a suitable result.

Pasting Conditional Formats

Starting with Excel 2010, the rules changed when you paste a range with one conditional formatting onto another range with a different conditional formatting. The copied conditional format replaces the existing conditional formatting. There might be times when you want to merge the existing icon set in the source range with the existing color scale in the target range. In this case, choose All Merging Conditional Formats from the Paste Special dialog box, or the elusive icon in the second row, fourth column of the Paste Options menu. Note that this pastes formats, formulas, and borders as well as merges the conditional formats.

Using the Format Painter

The Format Painter icon appears in the Clipboard group of the Home tab. The prominent location of the icon might encourage you to attempt to use this feature. The Format Painter is still tricky to use.

To copy a format from a source range to a destination range, follow these steps:

1.   Select the source range. If you want to copy column widths, the source range must include complete columns.

2.   Click the Format Painter icon once in the Clipboard group of the Home tab. The mouse icon changes to a plus and a paintbrush.

3.   Immediately use the mouse to click and drag to select a destination range. If the source range was five columns wide, the destination range should also be five columns wide.

4.   If you accidentally click somewhere else or click the wrong size range, undo and start over.

The ToolTip for the Format Painter icon advertises a little-known feature. This feature enables you to copy a format to many ranges. To do this, follow these steps:

1.   Select the source range.

2.   Double-click the Format Painter icon.

3.   Click a new destination range. The format is copied. Alternatively, you can drag to paint a different size range.

4.   Repeat step 3 as many times as you want.

5.   When you are done formatting ranges, press Esc or single-click the Format Painter icon to turn off the feature.

Copying Formats to a New Worksheet

You can use a straightforward way to make a copy of a worksheet. This method is better than creating a new worksheet and copying formats from the original sheet to the new sheet. Among its advantages are that column widths and row heights are copied and page setup settings are copied.

To copy a worksheet within the current workbook, follow these steps:

1.   Activate the worksheet to be copied.

2.   Hold down the Ctrl key. Click the worksheet tab and drag it to a new location. A new sheet is created with a strange name, such as Sheet3 (2).

3.   Right-click the sheet tab and select Rename. The cursor moves to the tab, which is now editable.

4.   Type a new name and press Enter. The tab has a new name.

CHAPTER 21

To copy a worksheet to a new workbook, follow these steps:

1. Activate the worksheet to be copied.

2. Right-click the sheet tab. Select Move Or Copy to display the Move Or Copy dialog box.

3. In the To Book drop-down menu, select (new book).

4. Click Create A Copy.

Using Data Visualizations and Conditional Formatting

Many people feel their eyes glaze over when they encounter a screen full of numbers. Fortunately, Microsoft offers data-visualization features to Excel that make those screens full of numbers easier to interpret.

The following are some of the possibilities in data visualization:

- Adding data bars (that is, tiny, in-cell bar charts) to cells based on the cell value. In Excel 2019, data bars can be negative, include an axis, and have new scaling options.

- Adding color scales to cells based on the cell value. This is often called a *heat map*. Whereas the old conditional formatting would allow you to apply one color if a value exceeds a certain amount, a color scale applies a range from a gradient based on how high the value is.

- Adding icon sets (think traffic lights) to cells based on the cell value.

- Adding color, bold, italic, strikethrough, number formatting, and so on to cells based on the cell values.

- Quickly identifying cells that are above average.

- Quickly identifying the top *n* or bottom *n*% of cells.

- Quickly identifying duplicate values.

- Quickly identifying dates that are today or yesterday or last week.

- Sorting by color or by icon (after you've added icons or color).

Although it is easy to set up basic conditional formatting, you need to know a few tricks, which you discover later in this chapter, for creating better conditional formatting than most people will figure out on their own.

Using Data Bars to Create In-Cell Bar Charts

A *data bar* is a swath of color that starts at the side of a cell and extends into the cell based on the value of the cell. Small numbers get less color. The largest numbers might be 100% filled with color. This creates a visual effect that enables you to visually pick out the larger and smaller values. Figure 22.1 shows many examples of data bars.

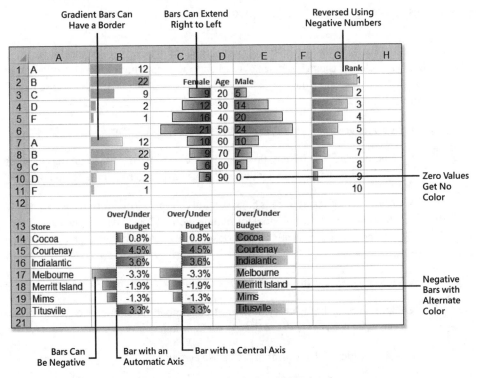

Figure 22.1   Examples of many of the properties in Excel 2019 data bars.

Many options are available in Excel 2019 data bars:

- Data bars can be solid or a gradient.

- Values of zero get no data bar, as shown in cell E10.

- Data bars can be negative. Negative bars are shown in a different color and usually extend to the left of a central axis. You have three choices in where to place the zero axis. In cells B14:B20, the setting is Automatic. Because the largest positive number is further from zero than the smallest negative number, the axis appears slightly to the left of center. This allows the bar for 4.5% in B15 to appear larger than the bar for −3.3% in B17. You can also force the axis to appear in the center, as in cells C14:C20. Or, in a bizarre setting, you can force the negative bars to extend in the same direction as the positive values, but with a different color. There are two philosophical ways to show the negative bars. You can assign −3.3% the most color because it is farthest from zero, or you could assign −1.3% the most color because it is the mathematically the largest of the negative numbers (−1.3% > −3.3%). Excel 2019 uses the latter method.

- To "reverse" a data bar—to show the most color for the largest number—multiply the numbers by −1 to make them negative. Use a custom number format of "0;0;0;" to display the negative numbers as positive. Make the negative bars extend in the same direction as positive. You end up with the surprising results shown in G1:G11.

- You can control the color of the positive bar, the positive bar border, the negative bar, the negative bar border, and the axis color.

- Bars can now extend right to left, as shown in cells C3:C10. This allows comparative histograms as in C2:E10.

- You can specify the scale of the data bars. Although the scale is initially set to automatic, you can specify that the min or max is set to a certain number or to the lowest value, a percentage, a percentile, or a formula.

- You can choose to show only the data bar and to hide the number in the cell. This is how I managed to get words in cells E14:E20. The numbers are hidden by the conditional formatting dialog box, and then a linked picture of the words is pasted over the cells. Because the data bars are on a drawing layer above the regular drawing layer, this works.

- All data bars in a group have the same scale. This is unlike sparklines, where the scale is allowed to change from graphic to graphic.

NOTE

If you don't like the six basic colors Excel offers for data bars, you can choose any other color, as described in the next section.

CHAPTER 22

Creating Data Bars

Creating data bars requires just a few clicks. Follow these steps:

CAUTION

In step 1, if you attempt to select a range that contains both units sold and revenue dollars, the size of the revenue numbers overpowers the units sold numbers, and no color appears in the units sold cells.

1. Select a range of numeric data. Do not include the total in this selection. If the data is in noncontiguous ranges, hold down the Ctrl key while selecting additional areas. This range should be composed of numbers of similar scale. For example, you can select a column of sales data or a column of profit data.

2. From the Home tab, select Conditional Formatting, Data Bars. You see six built-in colors for the data bars: blue, green, red, orange, bright blue, and pink. The colors appear in both solid and gradient forms. Select one of them. The result is a swath of color in each cell in the selection, as shown in Figure 22.2.

Figure 22.2   After applying a data bar, you can easily see that California is a leading exporter of agriculture products.

Customizing Data Bars

By default, Excel assigns the largest data bar to the cell with the largest value and the smallest data bar to the cell with the smallest value. You can customize this behavior by following these steps:

1. From the Conditional Formatting drop-down list on the Home tab, select Manage Rules.

2. From the Show Formatting Rules drop-down list, select This Worksheet. You now see a list of all rules applied to the sheet.

3. Click the Data Bar rule.

4. Click the Edit Rule button. Alternatively, you could double-click the rule in step 3. You see the Edit Formatting Rule dialog box, as shown in Figure 22.3.

Figure 22.3   You customize data bars by using the Edit Formatting Rule dialog box.

A number of customizations are available in this dialog box:

- Select the Show Bar Only setting to hide the numbers in the cells and to show only the data bar.

- For the Minimum and Maximum values, you can choose from Automatic, Number, Percent, Percentile, Formula, and Smallest/Largest Number. If you select Automatic, Excel chooses a minimum and maximum value. You can override this by setting one value to a specific number.

- In the Bar Appearance section, you can specify gradient or solid fill for the bar. You can specify a solid border or no border. Two color chooser drop-down lists enable you to change the color of the bar and the border.

- The Bar Direction drop-down list enables you to select Context, Left to Right, or Right to Left. The default choice of Context is always left to right, unless you are in an international edition of Excel in which the language reading order is right to left.

When you choose Negative Values and Axis, you have new settings to adjust the color of the bar and the border for negative bars. You can also control whether the zero axis is shown at the cell midpoint or at an automatic location based on the relative size of the negative and positive numbers. If the axis is shown, you can adjust the color as well.

Showing Data Bars for a Subset of Cells

In the data bars examples given in the previous sections, every cell in the range receives a data bar. But what if you just want some of the values (for example, the top 20% or the top 10) to have data bars? The process for making this happen isn't intuitive, but it is possible. You apply the data bar to the entire range. Then you add a new conditional format (a very plain format) to all the cells that you don't want to have data bars. For example, you might tell Excel to use a white background on all cells with values outside of the top 10.

The final important step is to manage the rules and tell Excel to stop processing more rules if the white background rule is met. This requires clever thinking. If you want to apply data bars to cells in the top 10, you first tell Excel to make all the cells in the bottom 21 look like every other cell in Excel. Turning on Stop If True (in the Conditional Formatting Rules Manager dialog box) is the key to getting Excel to not apply the data bar to cells with values outside of the top 10.

Figure 22.4 shows data bars applied to only the top 10 states.

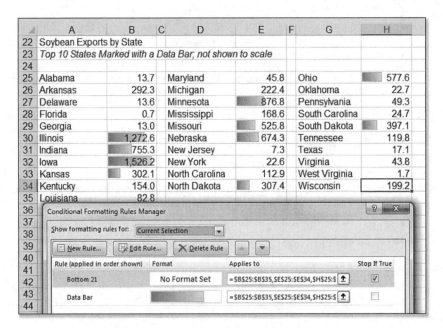

Figure 22.4   Using Stop If True after formatting the lower 21 with no special formatting allows the data bars to appear only for the top states.

Using Color Scales to Highlight Extremes

Color scales are similar to data bars. Instead of having a variable-size bar in each cell, however, color scales use gradients of two or three different colors to communicate the relative size of each cell. Here's how you apply color scales:

1. Select a range that contains numbers. Be sure not to include headings or total cells in the selection.

2. Select Conditional Formatting, Color Scales from the Home tab.

3. From the Color Scales fly-out menu, select one of the 12 styles to apply the color scale to the range. (Note that this fly-out menu offers subtle differences that you should pay attention to. The first six options are scales that use three colors. These are great onscreen or with color printers. The last six options are scales that use two colors. These are better with monochrome printers.)

In a two-color red/white color scale, the largest number is formatted with a dark red fill. The smallest number has a white fill. All the numbers in between receive a lighter or darker shade of pink based on their position within the range (see Figure 22.5).

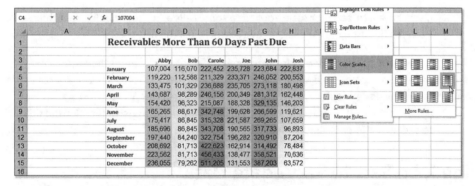

Figure 22.5   Excel provides a range of shading, depending on the value. You can see that Carole's and John's receivables have been increasing throughout the year.

You are not limited to the color scales shown in the fly-out menu. If you select Home, Conditional Formatting, Manage Rules, Edit Rule, you can choose any two or three colors for the color scale.

You also can choose where to assign the smallest, largest, and midpoint values (see Figure 22.6). Column E and the Edit Formatting Rule show how to highlight central values. Using a three-color scale, the minimum and maximum are set to white, whereas the middle numbers are assigned a color.

Figure 22.6 You can choose any colors to use in the color scale.

You should be aware of one strange situation: Normally, Excel lets you mix conditional formatting in the same range. You might apply both a color scale and an icon set.

If you have a three-color scale applied to some cells and choose a different three-color scale from the fly-out menu, the latter choice overwrites the first choice.

However, Excel treats two-color scales as a different visualization than three-color scales. If you have a three-color scale applied and you then try to switch it to a two-color scale using the fly-out menu, Excel creates two rules for those cells. The latter two-color scale is the only one to appear in Excel 2019, but you might be confused when you go to the Manage Rules dialog box to see two different rules applied to the cells.

Using Icon Sets to Segregate Data

Icon sets, which were popular with expensive management reporting software in the late 1990s, have now been added to Excel. An icon set might include green, yellow, and red traffic lights or another set of icons to show positive, neutral, and negative meanings. With icon sets, Excel automatically applies an icon to a cell, based on the relative size of the value in the cell compared to other values in the range.

Excel 2019 ships with 20 icon sets that contain three, four, or five different icons. The icons are always left-aligned in the cell. Excel applies rules to add an icon to every cell in the range:

- **Three-icon sets**—For the three-icon sets, you have a choice between arrows, flags, two varieties of traffic lights, signs, stars, triangles, and two varieties of what Excel calls 3 Symbols. This last group consists of a green check mark for the good cells, a yellow exclamation point for the middle cells, and a red X for the bad cells. You can get the symbols either in a circle—that is, 3 Symbols (Circled)—or alone on a white background (that is, 3 Symbols). One version of the arrows is available in gray. All the other icon sets use red, yellow, and green.

- **Four-icon sets**—For the four-icon sets, there are two varieties of arrows: a black-to-red circle set, a set of cell phone power bars, and a set of four traffic lights. In the traffic light option, a black light indicates an option that is even worse than the red light. The power bars icons seem to work well on both color displays and monochromatic printouts.

TIP

After creating several reports with icon sets, I have started to favor the cell phone power bars, which look good in both color and black and white.

- **Five-icon sets**—For the five-icon sets, there are two varieties of arrows, boxes, a five-power bar set, and an interesting set called 5 Quarters. This last set is a monochromatic circle that is completely empty for the lowest values, 25% filled, 50% filled, 75% filled, and completely filled for the highest values.

Setting Up an Icon Set

Icon sets require a bit more thought than the other data visualization offerings. Before you use icon sets, you should consider whether they will be printed in monochrome or displayed in color. Several of the 20 icon sets rely on color for differentiation and look horrible in a black-and-white report.

To set up an icon set, follow these steps:

1. Select a range of numeric data of a similar scale. Do not include the headers or total rows in this selection.

2. From the Home tab, select Conditional Formatting, Icon Sets. Select one of the 20 icon sets. Figure 22.7 shows the five-power bar set selected.

Figure 22.7   You can choose from the 20 icon sets.

Moving Numbers Closer to Icons

In the top rows of Figure 22.8, the icon set has been applied to a rectangular range of data. The icons are always left aligned. Numbers are typically right-aligned. This can be problematic. Someone might think that the icon at the left side of cell G3 is really referring to the right-aligned number in F3, for example.

You might try centering the numbers to get the numbers closer to the icons in rows 7–9 in Figure 22.8. This drives purists crazy because the final digit of the 100 in cell H8 doesn't line up with the final digits of cells H7 and H9.

A better solution is shown in rows 12–14. Keep the numbers right aligned, and use the Increase Indent icon to move the numbers closer to the icon.

If you don't want to show numbers at all, you can edit the conditional formatting rule and select Show Icon Only. Rows 17–19 show this solution. Ironically, when the numbers are no longer displayed, you can position the icons by using the Left Align, Center Align, and Right Align icons.

The over-the-top solution in rows 22–24 involves using Show Icon Only and then pasting a linked picture of the numbers from other cells.

D	E	F	G	H
Normal	Speed	Quality	Satisfaction	Efficiency
Akron	◑ 85 ●	95 ◐	82 ◕	89
Boise	● 95 ◔	76 ●	95 ●	100
Chicago	○ 67 ○	65 ◔	75 ●	95
Centered	Speed	Quality	Satisfaction	Efficiency
Akron	◑ 85	● 95	◐ 82	◕ 89
Boise	● 95	◔ 76	● 95	● 100
Chicago	○ 67	○ 65	◔ 75	● 95
Indented	Speed	Quality	Satisfaction	Efficiency
Akron	◑ 85	● 95	◐ 82	◕ 89
Boise	● 95	◔ 76	● 95	● 100
Chicago	○ 67	○ 65	◔ 75	● 95
Icon Only	Speed	Quality	Satisfaction	Efficiency
Akron	◑	●	◐	◕
Boise	●	◔	●	●
Chicago	○	○	◔	●
Tricky	Speed	Quality	Satisfaction	Efficiency
Akron	◑ 85	● 95	◐ 82	◕ 89
Boise	● 95	◔ 76	● 95	◕100
Chicago	○ 67	○ 65	◔ 75	● 95

Figure 22.8   Changing the alignment of the numbers moves them closer to the icon.

Here are the steps to create rows 22 through 24:

1. Select one of the cells with the icon set formatting.

2. From the Home tab, select Conditional Formatting, Manage Rules.

3. In the Conditional Formatting Rules Manager dialog box, click the Icon Set rule and then click Edit Rule.

4. In the middle of the Edit Formatting Rule dialog box, select Show Icon Only. Click OK twice to close the two dialog boxes.

5. Select all the cells that contain icons and click the Align Center button on the Home tab.

6. Page down so that you are outside of the printed range. Stay in the same column. Set up a formula to point to the number in the top-left corner of the icon set range. Copy this formula down and over to be the same size as your icon set range. This gives you a range of just the numbers.

7. Format this range of numbers to be right-aligned with an indent of 1.

8. Copy this range of numbers.

9. Go back to the original set of icons and select Paste, Picture Link. A picture of the original numbers appears behind the icons.

Mixing Icons or Hiding Icons

As of Excel 2010, it became possible to mix icons from different sets. In Figure 22.9, A2:C7 is a five-icon set with a mix of icons—gold star, green flag, yellow caution sign, and so on. You start with any five-icon set. Edit the rule and change the icon for each position.

Figure 22.9 Mix icons to create unusual sets.

In A11:D17, scores of 95 and higher receive a gold star, and all other scores get no icon. The open dialog box shows how this is done; the lower two rules show No Cell Icon.

Using the Top/Bottom Rules

The top/bottom rules are a mix of the old- and new-style conditional formatting. They are similar to the old conditional formatting because you must select one formatting scheme to apply to all the cells that meet the rule. However, they are new because rather than specifying a particular number limit, you can ask for any of these conditions:

- **Top 10 Items**—You can ask for the top 10, top 20, or any number of items.

- **Top 10%**—If 20% of your records account for 80% of your revenue, you can highlight the top 20% or any other percentage.

- **Bottom 10 Items**—To highlight the lowest-performing records, select Bottom 10.

- **Bottom 10%**—To highlight the records in the lowest 5%, select Bottom 10%.

- **Above Average**—You can highlight the records that are above the average. As with all the other rules, the average is recalculated as the numbers in the range change.

- **Below Average**—You can highlight the records that are below the average.

To set up any of these conditional formatting rules, follow these steps:

1. From the Home tab, select Conditional Formatting, Top/Bottom Rules, and then choose one of the six rule types shown in Figure 22.10.

Figure 22.10   You can choose one of these six rule types.

2. The dialog box for above/below average does not require you to select a threshold value, but for the other four rule types, Excel asks you to enter the value for N. As you change the spin button, the Live Preview feature keeps updating the selection with the appropriate number of highlighted cells.

3. The drop-down list portion of the dialog box initially shows Light Red Fill with Dark Red Text. When you select the drop-down list, you have six default styles and the powerful Custom Format option. If one of the six styles is suitable, choose it. Otherwise, proceed to step 4.

4. If you choose Custom Format, you are taken to a special version of the Format Cells dialog box. This version has Number, Font, Border, and Fill tabs. You can choose settings on one or more of these tabs. Click OK to close the Format Cells dialog box.

5. Click OK to close the dialog box for your particular rule.

Excel adds the rule to the list of rules. By default, rules added most recently are applied first.

Using the Highlight Cells Rules

The traditional conditional formatting rules appear in the Highlight Cells Rules menu item of the Conditional Formatting drop-down list, along with several new rules. The traditional rules include Greater Than, Less Than, Between, and Equal To. Note that slightly obscure rules such as Greater Than or Equal To are hidden behind the More Rules option. The following are the traditional rules:

- **Text That Contains**—This rule enables you to highlight cells that contain certain text.

- **A Date Occurring**—With this rule, you can define conceptual rules such as yesterday, today, tomorrow, last week, this week, next week, last month, this month, next month, or in the last seven days.

- **Duplicate Values**—With this rule, you can highlight both records of a duplicate or highlight all the records that are not duplicated.

TROUBLESHOOTING

Excel's definition of unique values does not match what you likely mean by unique values.

To the Excel team, a unique value is a value that occurs exactly once in the range. It does not seem helpful in most situations. Would Amazon care about the products that sold exactly one time? Outside of someone trying to find one-hit wonders from the Billboard music charts, I am not sure when finding values that occur exactly once is useful.

Instead, I would prefer that Excel highlight the cells that would be left after using Remove Duplicates. Highlight the first occurrence of each product whether it occurs once or 100 times.

To highlight the first occurrence of a value in C2:C100, use a formula-based condition where =COUNTIF(C$1:C2,C2)=1. Be cautious to use only one dollar sign in that formula. This formula creates an expanding range that looks from C1 down to the current row.

To create a formula-based conditional format, use Home, Conditional Formatting, New Rule, Use A Formula To Determine Which Cells To Format.

The options for Highlight Cells Rules are shown in Figure 22.11.

Figure 22.11   Many powerful and easy conditions are available in the Highlight Cells Rules menu.

Highlighting Cells by Using Greater Than and Similar Rules

You might think that Greater Than and the similar rules for Less Than, Equal To, and Not Equal To are some of the less powerful conditional formatting rules. In fact, these are the first rules described in this chapter that you can use to base the conditional format threshold on a particular cell or cells. This enables you to build some fairly complex rules without having to resort to the formula option of conditional formatting.

To set up a rule to highlight values greater than a threshold, follow these steps:

1. Select a range of data. Unlike with the other rules, you might choose to include totals in this selection.

2. Select Home, Styles, Conditional Formatting, Highlight Cell Rules, Greater Than to display the Greater Than dialog box.

3. Enter a threshold value in the Greater Than dialog box.

4. Choose one of the six formats from the With drop-down list. Or choose Custom Format from the With drop-down list to have complete control over the number format, font, borders, and fill.

5. Click OK to apply the format.

By way of example, let's look at several options for filling in the threshold value in the Greater Than dialog box. Figure 22.12 shows the conditional formatting rule for all cells greater than 200,000. This is a simple threshold value.

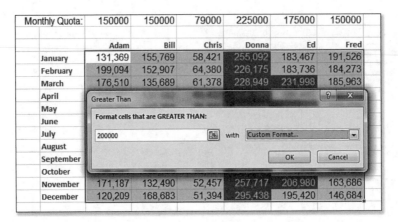

Figure 22.12 You can format all cells greater than a certain value, such as 200,000.

You can specify a cell as the threshold value. You can either use the reference icon at the right side of the box or type an equal sign and the cell reference. In Figure 22.13, the formula highlights any cell that does not exceed the quota in row 1 above the current cell using =D$1.

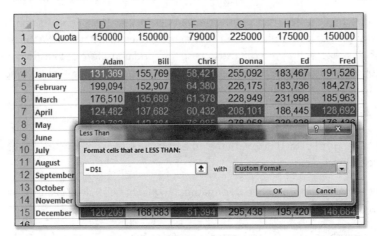

Figure 22.13 You can format all cells less than a certain cell. Prefix the cell reference with an equal sign.

The formula in Figure 22.13 has to be written for the active cell. Although D4:I15 is the selected range, the name box shows that D4 is the active cell. The formula of =D$1 is compared to the active cell of D4. The threshold cell then becomes the cell in row 1 that is in the same column as each cell in the selection.

The Greater Than concepts discussed here apply equally well to the Less Than, Equal To, and Between rules. If you need to access other rules, such as Less Than or Equal To, you can follow these steps:

1. Set up the rule by using Less Than.

2. From the Conditional Formatting icon, select Manage Rules.

3. Select the Less Than rule and click Edit Rule.

4. Use the drop-down list shown in Figure 22.14 to select Less Than or Equal To.

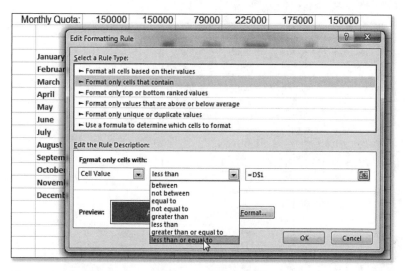

Figure 22.14   After using a quick format with Less Than, you can go to the Manage Rules option to access Less Than or Equal To.

Comparing Dates by Using Conditional Formatting

The date feature was added in Excel 2007. If you are familiar with the reporting engine in Quicken or QuickBooks, the list of available dates will seem similar. A nice feature is that Excel understands the dates conceptually. If you define a feature to highlight dates from last week, the rule automatically updates based on the system clock. If you open the workbook a month from now, new dates are formatted, based on the conditional formatting.

Some of the date selections are self-explanatory, such as Yesterday, Today, and Tomorrow. Other items need some explanation:

•   A Week is defined as the seven days from Sunday through Saturday. Choosing This Week highlights all days from Sunday through Saturday, including the current date.

- In The Last 7 Days includes today and the six days before today.

- This Month corresponds to all days in this calendar month. Last Month is all days in the previous calendar month. For example, if today is May 1 or May 31, the period Last Month applies to April 1 through April 30.

Figure 22.15 shows the various formatting options, with a system date of June 22, 2018.

◢	A	B	C	D	E	F	G
1	Today is Friday, Jun 22, 2018						
2	**This Week**		**Last Week**		**Next Week**		**Last 7 Days**
3	Wed 6/20		Thu 6/14		Wed 6/27		Thu 6/14
4	Thu 6/21		Fri 6/15		Thu 6/28		Fri 6/15
5	Fri 6/22		Sat 6/16		Fri 6/29		Sat 6/16
6	Sat 6/23		Sun 6/17		Sat 6/30		Sun 6/17
7	Sun 6/24		Mon 6/18		Sun 7/1		Mon 6/18
8	Mon 6/25		Tue 6/19		Mon 7/2		Tue 6/19
9	Tue 6/26		Wed 6/20		Tue 7/3		Wed 6/20
10	Wed 6/27		Thu 6/21		Wed 7/4		Thu 6/21
11	Thu 6/28		Fri 6/22		Thu 7/5		Fri 6/22
12	Fri 6/29		Sat 6/23		Fri 7/6		Sat 6/23
14	**Today**		**Yesterday**		**Tomorrow**		
15	Wed 6/20		Wed 6/20		Wed 6/20		
16	Thu 6/21		Thu 6/21		Thu 6/21		
17	Fri 6/22		Fri 6/22		Fri 6/22		
18	Sat 6/23		Sat 6/23		Sat 6/23		
19	Sun 6/24		Sun 6/24		Sun 6/24		
21	**This Month**		**Last Month**		**Next Month**		
22	Sun 4/22		Sun 4/22		Sun 4/22		
23	Thu 5/31		Thu 5/31		Thu 5/31		
24	Sat 6/30		Sat 6/30		Sat 6/30		
25	Tue 7/31		Tue 7/31		Tue 7/31		
26	Fri 8/31		Fri 8/31		Fri 8/31		

Figure 22.15   Note that Last 7 Days includes today and the previous six days.

The date formatting option would be particularly good for highlighting the items in a to-do list that are due, overdue, or about to be due.

Identifying Duplicate or Unique Values by Using Conditional Formatting

Conditional formatting claims that it can mark either duplicate or unique values in a list of values. It seems that Microsoft missed an opportunity to include a different version of unique values than the one that it included. It would be very useful if Microsoft had included an option to mark only the first occurrence of each unique item.

In column A of Figure 22.16, Excel has marked the duplicate values. Both Adam and Bill appear twice in the list, and Excel has marked both occurrences of the values. You might be tempted to sort by color to bring the red cells to the top, but you still have to carefully go through to delete one of each pair.

Figure 22.16   Marking duplicates or unique values with the built-in conditional formatting choices requires additional work to decide which of the duplicates to keep to produce a unique list.

In column C of Figure 22.16, Excel has applied a conditional format to the unique values in the list. In Excel parlance, this means that Excel marks the items that appear only once in a list. If you would keep just the marked cells as a list of the unique names in the list, you would effectively miss any name that was duplicated.

In a perfect world, this feature would have the logic to include one of each name in the conditional format. The conditional formatting in column E resorts to using the fairly complex formula of =COUNTIF(E$1:E1,E2)=0 to highlight the unique values.

➤ To learn more about using formulas to mark cells, see "Using a Formula for Rules," p. 570.

Using Conditional Formatting for Text Containing a Value

The Text That Contains formatting rule is designed to search text cells for cells that contain a certain value.

Figure 22.17 contains a column of cells. Each cell in the column contains a complete address, with street, city, state, and ZIP. It would normally be fairly difficult to find all the records for a particular state. However, this is easy to do with conditional formatting. Follow these steps:

1. Select a range of cells that contains text.

2. From the Home tab, select Conditional Formatting, Highlight Cell Rules, Text That Contains.

3. In the Refers To box, enter a comma, a space, and the state you want to find. Note that this test is not case sensitive (for example, searching for ", pa" is the same as searching for ", PA").

4. Choose an appropriate color from the drop-down list.

5. Click OK to apply the format.

Figure 22.17   Without having to use a wildcard character, you can use the Text That Contains dialog box to mark cells based on a partial value.

As with the Find dialog box, you can use wildcard characters. You can use an asterisk (*) to indicate any number of characters and a question mark (?) to indicate a single character.

Tweaking Rules with Advanced Formatting

All the formats available from icons on the Conditional Formatting group are referred to as *quick formatting*. According to legend, the Excel team bought and read a number of Excel books, and if the author spent a page trying to explain a convoluted way to format something using formulas in conditional formatting, then that option became a quick formatting icon.

Every quick formatting item has an option at the bottom called More Rules. When you click this option and get to the New Formatting Rule dialog box, you find options that didn't make it as quick formatting icons.

The next section of this chapter discusses using the formula option for conditional formatting. Almost anything is possible by using the formula option, but it is harder to use than the quick formatting icons. If Excel offers a built-in, advanced option, you should certainly use it instead of trying to build a formula to do the same thing.

The lists shown in Tables 22.1 and 22.2 are organized to show all the options for specific rule types. The six rule types are in the top of the New Formatting Rule dialog box. Items listed in the right column are advanced options that are available only by clicking More Rules.

Table 22.1   Options for Formatting Cells Based on Content

Option	Advanced Options Available Using More Rules
Cell value between x and y	Cell value not between x and y
Cell value equal to x	Cell value not equal to x
Cell value greater than x	Cell value less than x
Cell value greater than or equal to x	Cell value less than or equal to x
Specific text containing x	Specific text not containing x
	Specific text beginning with x
	Specific text ending with x
Dates occurring yesterday	
Dates occurring today	
Dates occurring tomorrow	
Dates occurring in the last 7 days	
Dates occurring last week	
Dates occurring next week	
Dates occurring last month	
Dates occurring this month	
Dates occurring next month	
More Rules	Blanks
	No Blanks
	Errors
	No Errors

Table 22.2   Options for Formatting Values That Are Above or Below Average

Option	Advanced Options Available Using More Rules
Above the average for the selected range	One standard deviation above the average for the selected range
	Two standard deviations above the average for the selected range
	Three standard deviations above the average for the selected range
Below the average for the selected range	One standard deviation below the average for the selected range
	Two standard deviations below the average for the selected range
	Three standard deviations below the average for the selected range

Using a Formula for Rules

Excel has three dozen quick conditional formatting rules and twice as many advanced conditional formatting rules. What if you need to build a conditional format that is not covered in the quick or advanced rules? As long as you can build a logical formula to describe the condition, you can build your own conditional formatting rule based on a formula.

Some basic tips can help you successfully use formulas in conditional formatting rules. When you understand these rules, you can build just about any rule you can imagine.

Starting in Excel 2007, a formula is allowed to refer to cells on another worksheet. This enables you to compare cells on one worksheet to a worksheet from a previous month or to use a VLOOKUP table on another worksheet.

Getting to the Formula Box

To set up a conditional format based on a rule, follow these steps:

1.   Select a range of cells.

2.   In the Style group of the Home tab, select Conditional Formatting, Add New Rule.

3.   In the New Formatting Rule dialog box, choose the rule type Use a Formula to Determine Which Cells to Format. You now see the New Formatting Rule dialog box.

The following sections give you some tips for building a successful formula.

Working with the Formula Box

Following are the key concepts involved in writing a successful formula:

- The formula must start with an equal sign.

- The formula must evaluate to a logical value of TRUE or FALSE. The numeric equivalents of 1 and 0 are also acceptable results.

- When you use the mouse to select a cell or cells on a worksheet, Excel inserts an absolute reference to the cell. This is rarely what you need for a successful conditional formatting rule. You can immediately press the F4 key three times to toggle away the dollar signs in the formula.

- You probably have many cells selected before starting the conditional formatting rule. You need to look at the left of the formula bar to see which cell in the selection is the active cell. If you write a relative formula, you should write the formula that will appear in the active cell. Excel applies the formula appropriately to all cells. This is a key point.

- If the dialog box is in the way of cells you need to select, you can drag the dialog box out of the way by dragging the title bar. If you absolutely need to get the dialog box out of the way, you can use the Collapse Dialog box button at the right side of the formula box. This collapses the dialog box to a tiny area. To return it to full size, you click the Expand Dialog box button at the right side of the collapsed dialog box.

- The formula box is one of the evil sets of controls that have three possible statuses: Enter, Point, and Edit. Look in the lower-left corner of the Excel screen. The status initially says that you are in Enter mode. This means that Excel is expecting you to type characters such as the equal sign. If, instead, you use the mouse or arrow keys to select a cell, Excel changes to Point mode. In Point mode, the selected cell's address is added to the formula box.

CAUTION

The annoying thing about the formula box is that you always start in something called Enter mode. When you are in Enter mode, if you use any of the navigation keys (that is, Page Down, Page Up, left arrow, right arrow, down arrow, up arrow), Excel changes to Point mode and starts inserting random cell addresses at inappropriate places in your formula. Press F2 until you see Edit in the lower-left corner of the Excel window. You can now use the left and right arrows to move through the formula.

The following sections describe several useful conditional formatting rules. This list only scratches the surface of the possible rules you can build. It is designed to generate ideas of what you can accomplish by using conditional formatting.

CHAPTER 22

Finding Cells Within Three Days of Today

The quick formatting feature offers to highlight yesterday or today or tomorrow, but what if you need to find any cells within three days of today, either plus or minus? If the active cell is B2, use a formula of =ABS(TODAY()-B2)<4.

Finding Cells Containing Data from the Past 30 Days

The Excel quick formatting option offers to highlight this month or last month. However, highlighting this month or last month can mean a number of vastly different things. Highlighting this month on the second of the month shows a lot of the future and only one day of the past. The same rule on the 29th of the month highlights a lot of the past and only a few days of the future. It would be more predictable to write a rule that shows the past 30 days.

You create this rule similarly to the way you created the Next Three Days rule in the preceding section. You first compare the date in the cell by using TODAY() to make sure the date in the cell is less than today. If the active cell is F4, you use the following formula:

=AND(F4<TODAY(),(TODAY()-F4)<=30)

To generalize this formula for other periods, such as the past 15 days or the past 45 days, you change the 30 to a different number.

Highlighting Data from Specific Days of the Week

The WEEKDAY() function converts a date to a number from 1 through 7. When used without additional arguments, the value of WEEKDAY(date) for a Sunday is 0 and for Saturday is 7.

Suppose the active cell is H4. If you needed to highlight all the Wednesdays, for example, you could check to see whether WEEKDAY(H4)=4. To find all the Fridays, you would check to see whether WEEKDAY(H4)=6. To find either date, you would use =OR(WEEKDAY(H4)=4, WEEKDAY(H4)=6).

To generalize this formula, you could substitute any number from 1 through 7 to highlight Sundays, Mondays, and so on.

Highlighting an Entire Row

Most conditional formatting highlights a cell based on the value in that cell. In this case, you would like to highlight the entire row for the row with the largest product sale.

In Figure 22.18, cell A2 is the active cell. You need to select the entire range of A2:G14. Your goal is to write a rule for all those cells that will always look at column D, but the row will vary based on the cell being evaluated. In this case, and in any case in which you want to highlight the entire row based on one column, you use the mixed reference with a dollar sign before the column letter. You want to see whether =$D2 is equal to the largest value in the range.

	A	B	C	D	E	F
1	Invoice	Customer	Product	Tax	S&H	Total
2	8422	Ideal Linen Corpora	181	10.86	7.95	199.81
3	8423	Effortless Luggage (	361	21.66	15.95	398.61
4	8424	Dependable Sprayer	319	19.14	15.95	354.09
5	8425	Amazing Adhesive	245	14.7	11.95	271.65
6	8426	Guaranteed Thermo	275	16.5	11.95	303.45
7	8427	Unique Utensil Corp	341	20.46	15.95	377.41
8	8428	Effortless Wax Inc.	215	12.9	11.95	239.85
9	8429	Supreme Kettle Inc.	273	16.38	11.95	301.33
10	8430	Different Utensil Inc	363	21.78	15.95	400.73
11	8431	Cool Gadget Inc.	267	16.02	11.95	294.97
12	8432	Superior Linen Inc.	279	16.74	11.95	307.69
13	8433	Vivid Paint Compan	174	10.44	7.95	192.39
14	8434	Leading Chopstick I	172	10.32	7.95	190.27
15						

Figure 22.18   The combination of a mixed reference and the absolute reference enables you to highlight an entire row.

To find the largest value in column D, you use an absolute reference to D2:D14—that is, `=MAX($D$2:$D$14)`. The conditional formatting formula for this specific case is `=$D2=MAX($D$2:$D$14)`.

To change this rule to highlight the smallest value in column D, you change MAX to MIN. To base the test on another column, change D to the other column in three places in the formula.

Highlighting Every Other Row Without Using a Table

You might find yourself using the Format as Table feature only to add alternating bands of color to a table. If you don't need the other table features, using a conditional format can achieve the same effect.

Do you remember when you were first learning to do division? You would express the quotient as an integer and then a remainder. For example, 9 divided by 2 is 4 with a remainder of 1, sometimes written as 4R1.

The trick to formatting every other row is to check the remainder of the row number after dividing by 2. Excel has functions that make this easy. First, `=ROW()` returns the row number of the given cell. Next, `=MOD(ROW(),2)` divides the row number by 2 and tells you the remainder. The task is then simply to highlight the rows where the remainder is equal to 1 or equal to zero.

NOTE

The Excel table formatting enables you to create alternate formatting in which every other two rows are formatted. To duplicate this with conditional formatting, you have to divide the row number by 4 and examine the remainder. There are four possible remainders: 0, 1, 2, and 3. You can look for results greater than 1 or less than 2 to be formatted. To do this, you change the preceding formula to `=MOD(ROW(),4)<2`.

In Figure 22.19, the active cell is A2. The formula to achieve the banding effect is
`=MOD(ROW(),2)=0`.

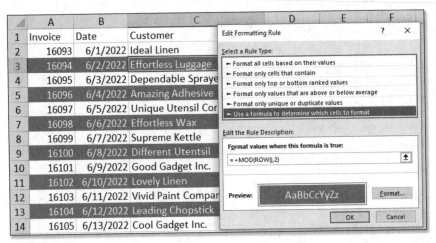

Figure 22.19   It is possible to create a row-banding effect without using the Excel table formatting.

To generalize this formula for your particular data set, you could change A2 to be the active cell's address.

Combining Rules

Excel allows multiple conditions to evaluate to TRUE. In legacy versions of Excel, when a condition was met, Excel quit evaluating additional conditions. For each rule in Excel 2019, you can decide whether Excel should stop evaluating additional rules or whether Excel can continue evaluating rules.

For example, one rule might set the font color to blue. Another rule might set the font style to bold. Cells meeting both rules can be formatted in blue bold. Cells meeting one rule can be either blue or bold. Cells meeting neither rule will be in normal font style.

If two rules attempt to create conflicting formatting, Excel uses the first rule in the list. For example, if Rule 1 turns the font red and Rule 7 turns the font blue, the font is red.

Ten types of formatting can be changed in each cell. Naturally, each type conflicts with others of the same type. Only the first rule that evaluates to TRUE can change the fill color.

Very few formatting styles conflict with each other. Only the cell fill and the color scale are mutually exclusive. Otherwise, you can have up to nine rules evaluate to TRUE for any given cell. Table 22.3 illustrates the interplay between the ten formatting styles.

Table 22.3   Cell Formatting Styles

Style	Effect
Font color	Changes the font color for cells meeting a condition.
Font style	Applies normal, bold, italic, or bold italic to cells meeting a condition.
Underline	Adds or removes single or double underlining for cells meeting a condition.
Strikethrough	Applies strikethrough for cells meeting a condition.
Number format	Changes the number format for cells meeting a condition.
Border	Alters the borders for cells meeting a condition. You might think that you could combine two rules that both affect the border. For example, you might want to make the top border blue for cells that meet Rule 1 and the right border red for cells that meet Rule 2. Even though this conceptually makes sense, Excel allows only the first true rule to change the borders.
Cell fill	Changes the cell background for cells meeting a condition. Amazingly, this works fine in combination with data bars. (The cell fill appears to the right of the data bar.) It also works fine with icon sets, and it works fine with all the preceding options. However, cell fill and color scales cannot coexist. Only the first true rule appears in the cell.
Color scale	Changes the cell background for all cells in the range, with the color being determined by the value of one cell in relation to the other cells in the range. This rule can coexist with everything but itself and the cell fill formatting.
Data bar	Adds an in-cell bar chart in each cell. This rule can coexist with any other type of rule.
Icon set	Adds an icon in the left side of the cell. This rule can coexist with any other type of rule.

You can use a number of ways to clear conditional formats. A few quick options are available from the ribbon:

- You can highlight the entire range with conditional formatting and then use Home, Styles, Conditional Formatting, Clear, Selected Cells. This removes all conditions from the current selection.

- To clear all the conditional formats from the current worksheet, you can use Home, Styles, Conditional Formatting, Clear, Entire Sheet. This is handy if you have only one set of rules set up on the sheet. You can delete all the rules without having to select the entire range.

NOTE

Deleting columns or rows deletes the rules associated with those columns or rows. Selecting Home, Editing, Clear, All or Home, Editing, Clear, Formats removes the rules.

- If you have rules assigned to a pivot table or a table, you can select one cell in the pivot table or table. This enables new options for Home, Styles, Conditional Formatting, Clear, This Table or Home, Styles, Conditional Formatting, Clear, This PivotTable.

If you have multiple rules assigned to a range and you need to delete just a portion of those rules, you can use Home, Styles, Conditional Formatting, Manage Rules. In the Conditional Formatting Rules Manager dialog box, you should use the top drop-down list to display rules in the current selection, this worksheet, or any other worksheet. You can then highlight a specific rule and click the Delete Rule button.

Extending the Reach of Conditional Formats

In every example in this chapter, you have been advised to highlight the entire range before setting up the conditional format. It is also possible to assign a conditional format to one cell and then extend the rule to other cells. There are three ways to copy a conditional format:

- You can select a cell with the appropriate rule and then press Ctrl+C to copy it. Then you select the new range and select Home, Clipboard, Paste, Paste Special, Formats, OK to copy the conditional formatting from the one cell to the entire range.

- Select a cell with the appropriate rule. Click the Format Painter icon in the Home tab. Select a new range to paste the conditional format to the new range.

- You can select Home, Styles, Conditional Formatting, Manage Rules. Then you select a rule. In the Applies To column, you see the list of cells that have this rule. You can type a new range there or use the collapse button to make the dialog box smaller so that you can highlight the new range.

When you are using conditional formats that compare one cell to the entire range, using the second method is safer to ensure that Excel understands your intention.

Special Considerations for Pivot Tables

This section talks about the special conditional formatting options that are available for pivot tables.

➤ See Chapter 15, "Using Pivot Tables to Analyze Data," to review the detailed discussion of pivot tables.

A typical pivot table might contain two or more levels of summary data. In the pivot table in Figure 22.20, for example, cells H4:J16 contain sales data. However, if you tried to create a data bar for this entire range, the subtotal values in rows 9 and 15 would make the data bars in the other rows look too small.

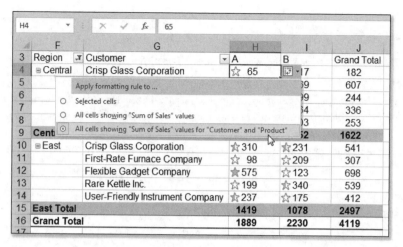

	F	G	H	I	J
3	Region	Customer	A	B	Grand Total
4	⊟ Central	Crisp Glass Corporation	☆ 65	▾17	182
5		Apply formatting rule to ...		39	607
6	○ Selected cells			99	244
7	○ All cells showing "Sum of Sales" values			54	336
8				03	253
9	Cent ⦿ All cells showing "Sum of Sales" values for "Customer" and "Product"			52	1622
10	⊟ East	Crisp Glass Corporation	☆ 310	☆ 231	541
11		First-Rate Furnace Company	☆ 98	☆ 209	307
12		Flexible Gadget Company	★ 575	☆ 123	698
13		Rare Kettle Inc.	☆ 199	☆ 340	539
14		User-Friendly Instrument Company	☆ 237	☆ 175	412
15	**East Total**		**1419**	**1078**	**2497**
16	**Grand Total**		**1889**	**2230**	**4119**

Figure 22.20   The trick to a successful conditional format in a pivot table is to apply the format only to items at the same detail level.

To set up a data bar for the detail items in a pivot table, follow these steps:

1. Select a detail cell in the pivot table. In Figure 22.20, a cell such as H4 will do.

2. Choose any visualization from the Conditional Formatting drop-down list. In Figure 22.20, the 3-stars icons set is shown.

3. A tiny pivot icon appears to the right of the cell. Click this drop-down list to access three conditional formatting settings for pivot tables. The choices are the following:

   a. **Selected Cells**—You can apply the rule to just the one cell. This is not what you want in this case.

   b. **All Cells Showing Sum Of Sales Values**—You can apply the rule to cells including the total column, grand total row, and all the subtotal rows. Remember that the size of the grand total causes all the detail items to have data bars that are too small.

   c. **All Cells Showing Sum Of Sales Values for "Customer" and "Product"**—This is the option you use most of the time. The meaning of this option is dependent on careful selection of a detail cell in step 1. If you selected a subtotal row instead, this option would apply the data bars only to the subtotal rows.

The actual words in the second and third options vary, depending on the fields displayed in your pivot table. For successful pivot table formatting, select the third option.

Inside OUT

There is a great trick for showing data bars in two different colors. It was documented once on the Excel team blog in 2007 but has since been deleted and lost forever.

This obscure trick has been posted in the Microsoft Excel team blog. It turns out that every conditional formatting rule has a formula value that determines whether the rule is shown. Microsoft exposed this rule in the user interface for some conditional formatting rules but not for the data bars. You can, however, access it in the VBA editor!

Suppose that your goal is to add a data bar to a range of cells. If the value is 90 or greater, you would like the bars to be green. If the value is 89 or less, you would like the bars to be red. Here's how you accomplish this:

1. Select the range of cells to be formatted.
2. Use the Conditional Formatting quick options to add to the range of a data bar that is red.
3. Select Conditional Formatting, Add New Rule to add a second rule that applies a green data bar. You see only the most recent rule, so all the data bars are green.
4. In the Name box, note cell is the active cell because you need this information in step 7.
5. Press Alt+F11 to switch to the VBA editor.
6. Press Ctrl+G to display the Immediate pane.
7. Type `Selection.FormatConditions(1).Formula = "=if(A2>89, TRUE, FALSE)"` and then press Enter. Cell A2 should be changed to the name of the active cell from step 4.
8. The result is that the green bars are visible only when the value is 90 or greater. In all other cases, the bars appear red.

CHAPTER 23

Graphing Data Using Excel Charts

Between Excel 2016 and Excel 2019, two new charts were added to Excel: the Funnel chart and the Filled Map chart. There was an announcement at a Microsoft conference in May 2018 that Excel would soon start supporting the Power BI Custom Visuals. This functionality is exclusive to Office 365. Take a look at three examples at the end of this chapter.

Before getting to the new charts, the chapter covers general techniques for creating graphs.

After you have the chart, a paintbrush icon offers 10 to 15 ways to style the chart. Styles range from minimalist to intense. If you are a disciple of Professor Edward R. Tufte and you believe every bit of ink on the chart has to have a meaning, you will prefer minimalist styles.

Choosing from Recommended Charts

The data in Figure 23.1 is a simple trend of monthly sales. Headings for the months appear in B1:M1. Sales appear in B2:M2. A label of "Sales" appears in A2. The label in A1 is optional. To create a chart, follow these steps:

1. Select A1:M2.

2. On the Insert tab, choose Recommended Charts. Excel displays the Insert Chart dialog box. The Recommended Charts tab shows four thumbnails on the left side. Click each thumbnail to see a larger chart on the right side. A description below the chart explains why this chart is appropriate.

3. Click OK to insert the chart in the center of the visible window. Grab the border of the chart and drag to the appropriate place. (See the following Troubleshooting Tip if you have to move the chart more than a screenful of data away.)

4. Notice the three icons to the right of the chart and the two contextual ribbon tabs that appear while the chart is selected. The following sections show you how to use those tools to polish the chart.

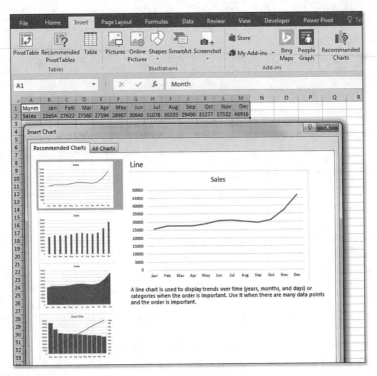

Figure 23.1 Select the data, and Excel suggests possible chart styles.

TROUBLESHOOTING

Excel plots the chart in the middle of the visible screen. By selecting your data, the visible portion of the window is often at the bottom of the worksheet instead of the top.

Suppose you have data in A1:C500 that should appear on a chart. You would probably start in A1, press Ctrl+Shift+Down Arrow, and then press Ctrl+Shift+Right Arrow. You would end up with rows 490 through 520 visible on your screen. However, if you insert a chart, it would appear at the bottom of your data instead of at the top of your data. Instead, press Ctrl+Backspace before creating the chart, which brings the active cell back into view.

Using the Paintbrush Icon for Styles

Click the paintbrush icon to reveal a flyout menu with 12 to 15 professionally designed chart styles for the selected chart (see Figure 23.2).

Figure 23.2   The paintbrush icon leads to these professionally designed chart styles.

The chart styles in this menu look new and stylish. Consider the style shown in Figure 23.2. You have fading drop lines extending from a data label down toward the baseline of the chart. The chart area and plot area are dark blue, and all chart elements are white. The marker is really the data label. The actual line appears only between October and December because of the jump in sales. I went back to Excel 2010 to see whether it's possible to create the identical chart. You can. It takes 26 separate steps, most of which require at least two mouse clicks. And that is 26 steps when you are trying to mimic an existing chart. If you were to try to come up with those steps without having a pattern to follow, it would be very time consuming. Excel 2019 makes it available with just a few clicks.

Deleting Extraneous Data Using the Funnel

The data in Figure 23.3 includes quarterly totals and an annual total. Accidentally including this data in the chart is a common mistake. The size of the subtotals and total columns makes all the other columns indistinguishable from each other.

Open the Funnel icon. You can unselect the Quarterly and Annual Totals.

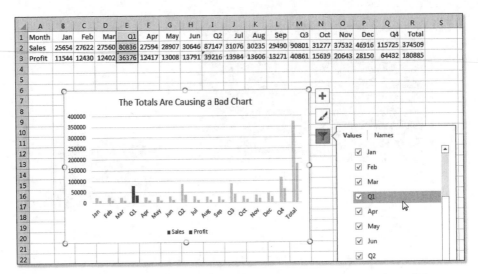

	A	B	C	D	E	F	G	H	I	J	K	L	M	N	O	P	Q	R	S
1	Month	Jan	Feb	Mar	Q1	Apr	May	Jun	Q2	Jul	Aug	Sep	Q3	Oct	Nov	Dec	Q4	Total	
2	Sales	25654	27622	27560	80836	27594	28907	30646	87147	31076	30235	29490	90801	31277	37532	46916	115725	374509	
3	Profit	11544	12430	12402	36376	12417	13008	13791	39216	13984	13606	13271	40861	15639	20643	28150	64432	180885	

Figure 23.3   This chart is doomed because the selected data includes quarterly totals.

Changing Chart Options Using the Plus Icon

All the chart settings that used to be on the Excel 2010 Layout tab in the ribbon have moved to a plus icon to the right of a selected chart. As shown in Figure 23.4, click the plus icon. Hover over Legend to have a flyout appear to the right with choices of Right, Top, Left, Bottom, and More Options. If you decide you don't need a legend, simply uncheck the option from the initial menu.

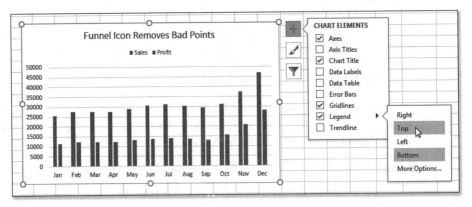

Figure 23.4   Use the plus icon to reach settings for major chart elements.

Easy Combo Charts

These charts are great when you have two different orders of magnitude in the same chart. Combo charts appeared in the Excel 2003 Chart Wizard. They were hidden on a back tab in the wizard, but at least they were there. In Excel 2007–2010, they weren't in the wizard, but charting gurus could figure out how to create them. Now, you have an incredibly flexible interface for creating combo charts.

Figure 23.5 shows a perfect example of data in need of a combo chart. Row 2 shows monthly sales. Row 3 shows the YTD number and accumulates all the monthly sales. The problem, again, is that the height of the December YTD number forces the monthly sales line to be too small for you to actually notice any variability. Choose Insert, Recommended Chart, All Types, Combo. The new interface for combo charts enables you to identify which series should be plotted on the secondary axis.

Figure 23.5   Choose a combo chart to move the line to the secondary axis.

Creating a Frequency Distribution with a Histogram Chart

Creating a frequency distribution using the FREQUENCY array function is difficult and confusing. The Histogram chart in Excel 2019 makes it easy. In Figure 23.6, you want to summarize thousands of points. Select the points. Choose Insert, Recommended Chart, and choose Histogram.

Excel creates bins along the bottom of the chart. Because the chart doesn't use round numbers when establishing groups, the automatic bins will be chaotic. Double-click the bins along the bottom to display the Format Axis task pane. Choose Axis Options, then the Chart icon, and specify a round number for the Bin Width. In Figure 23.6, the Bin Width is 10. Control the starting bin by using the Underflow Bin.

Figure 23.6   Excel easily turns thousands of data points into a histogram.

The Pareto chart rearranges the bins from the histogram so the bins with the most values appear on the left side of the chart. The Pareto line is tied to the secondary axis and shows what percentage of the population is to the left of the bin (see Figure 23.7).

Figure 23.7   A Pareto chart shows the most popular categories on the left.

In Figure 23.7, it is difficult to get an exact reading of the Pareto line. What percentage of the data points falls within the first two columns? You must mentally draw a vertical line up the center of the second column. When it intersects the Pareto line, extend that point to the right axis. About 39 percent of the points fall in the first two columns.

Showing Financial Data with a Waterfall Chart

Figure 23.8 shows a profit waterfall chart that analyzes a pricing proposal. The total list price of the deal is $10 million. The sales team is offering two discounts to get the total revenue down to $6 million. Various cost components take the deal down to $1.2 million of gross profit. Sales commissions take the net profit to $1.1 million.

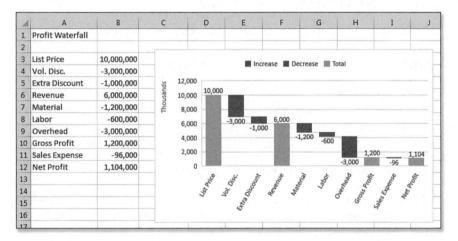

Figure 23.8   Waterfall charts show increases or decreases.

In Figure 23.8, four columns are marked as totals and will touch the zero axis. The other markers are either increases or decreases from the previous value. Set up your data so that the increases are positive, and the decreases are negative.

The chart will always initially look wrong because Excel cannot tell which columns should touch the zero axis.

After creating the chart, double-click the first column that should touch the axis. Check the Set as Total box. From there, single-click the other total columns and choose the same box.

Changing the colors in the chart is particularly hidden in the Ivy charts. To change the color, follow these steps:

1.   Click once on the legend to select the whole legend.

2.   Click a second time on one individual legend entry to select one type of data point.

CHAPTER 23

3.   Right-click the legend entry and a Fill drop-down list appears, as shown in Figure 23.9.

Figure 23.9   Changing the colors in a waterfall can only be done through the legend.

Saving Time with Charting Tricks

Here are some charting techniques that have been in Excel for several versions.

Adding New Data to a Chart by Pasting

Even though this next trick has existed in Excel since 1997, not many people know about it—you can add new data to a chart by pasting. Suppose you have a chart showing data for several months. You have nicely formatted and customized the chart. You now have new data available. Instead of re-creating the chart, you can paste the new data to the existing chart.

Follow these steps to expand the chart by pasting new data on it:

1.   Make sure the new data has a heading consistent with the old data. Note that if you accidentally enter the heading as Text instead of Date, or vice versa, the trick has unexpected results.

2.   Select the new data, including the heading.

3.   Press Ctrl+C to copy the new data.

4.   Select the chart.

5.   Press Ctrl+V to paste the new data on the chart.

Inside OUT

Building X Y Scatter charts with two series is particularly difficult. You can create the chart using a Paste Special.

In the first image below, a scatter chart has been created from B1:C21. Follow these steps to add the second population:

1. Select the X and Y values with headings from G1:G7.

2. Copy that data to the Clipboard.

3. Click the chart to select it.

4. From the ribbon, select Home and open the Paste Options drop-down menu by clicking the bottom of the Paste icon. Do not choose the icon for Paste; instead, click Paste Special.

5. The Paste Special dialog offers to Add Cells As New Series. The Values (Y) In option is already set to Columns, and Series Names In First Row is already checked. However, you will need to choose Categories (X Values) in First Column. Leave Replace Existing Categories unchecked.

6. Click OK to add the second series to the chart.

7. Use the plus icon at the top right of the chart to add Legend and Axis Titles.

CHAPTER 23

Two series appear on a scatter chart. One shows tenure earnings versus earnings for hourly workers. A second series shows the tenure earnings versus earnings for salaried workers.

Note that if you are willing to reorient your data so you have adjacent pairs of columns, you can create the chart by using the All Charts tab of the Insert Chart dialog box. Choose X Y (Scatter) category from the left navigation bar and then choose the top-right tile in the preview area. The tile does not have a name, but it will show two series of dots instead of three series.

The Insert Charts dialog box offers three preview tiles for X Y Scatter charts. Choose the top-right tile to treat each pair of columns as a series.

Dealing with Small Pie Slices

In many data series, a few pie slices take up 80% of the pie, and many tiny slices account for the rest of the pie. Typically, the last pie slices end up at the back of the pie, where it is impossible to fit the labels, so no one can make out what they are.

When you have several small data points at the end of a pie chart series, and you need to see all the smaller segments, you can change the chart type to a special type called Bar Of Pie. In this type, the smallest few categories are exploded out and shown as a columns chart next to the pie.

To change an existing pie chart to a Bar of Pie chart, follow these steps:

1. Select the chart.

2. From the Type group of the Design tab, select Change Chart Type. The Change Chart Type dialog box appears.

3. In the Change Chart Type dialog box, select the last option for pie charts: Bar Of Pie.

4. Click OK to close the dialog box.

5. Double-click the bar chart. The Format Data Series task pane appears. Choose the chart icon.

6. In the Format Data Series task pane, you have control over the number of values in the bar chart. You can indicate to Split Series By Percentage Value and specify that any items less than 10 percent should end up in the bar portion of the chart. The result is shown in Figure 23.10.

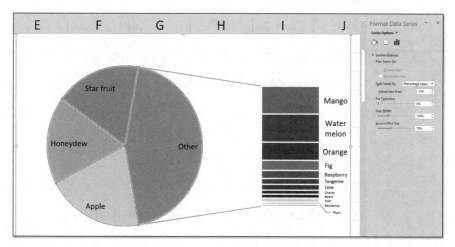

Figure 23.10   A series has been split by percentage with items less than 10% appearing in the bar portion of the chart.

Saving a Favorite Chart Style as a Template

Although Microsoft has provided great-looking built-in charts, you will likely design some great-looking charts of your own. After you have designed a chart, you can save it as a template. When you build new charts based on that template, all the settings for colors, fonts, effects, and chart elements are applied to the new data.

For all the power and glitz of Excel's built-in chart styles, the chart templates feature can save you massive amounts of time, such as if you routinely customize your charts to meet company standards.

Follow these steps to create a template:

1. Build a chart and customize it as necessary.

2. Right-click the chart. Choose Save as Template. Give the chart template a name. Excel saves the template with a .crtx file extension.

To create a chart by using your template, follow these steps:

1. Select the data you want to chart.

2. From the Insert tab, choose any of the Chart drop-down lists and then select All Chart Types. The Create Chart dialog box appears.

3. In the Create Chart dialog box, select the Templates category.

4. Click the desired template if there is more than one.

5. Click OK. Excel creates the chart with all the custom formatting from the saved template.

If you like your template so much that you want all future charts to be based on the template, follow these steps to make the template your default style:

1. Select a chart based on the desired template.

2. From the Design tab, select Change Chart Type. The Create Chart dialog box appears.

3. In the Create Chart dialog box, select the Templates category.

4. Select the desired template.

5. In the lower-left corner of the Change Chart Type dialog box, select Set as Default Chart.

In the future, you can create a chart that uses this template by following these steps:

1. Select the data you want to chart.

2. Press Alt+F1 to apply your default template.

Office 365 Will Soon Support the Custom Visuals from Power BI

The Power BI product from Microsoft offered support for open-source visuals submitted by developers. These custom visuals have become popular in Power BI. As of September 2018, Microsoft is encouraging developers to start preparing for these visualizations to be available in Excel.

Think of each visualization as an add-in. You will use the Excel Store on the Insert tab to find and download custom visuals to your computer.

Once the visualizations are downloaded, you can access them using the plus icon in the Insert Charts area, as shown in Figure 23.11. First, select your data for the visualization, and click the plus icon. Choose a visualization from the Custom Visuals tab on the Insert Chart dialog box.

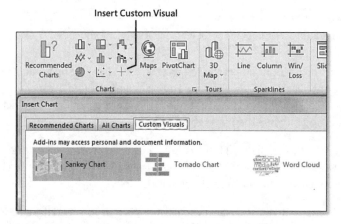

Figure 23.11   Use the Plus icon to add a custom visualization.

One example of a custom visualization is a Word Cloud. In Figure 23.12, the words from the table of contents for this book are arranged in a visualization.

CHAPTER 23

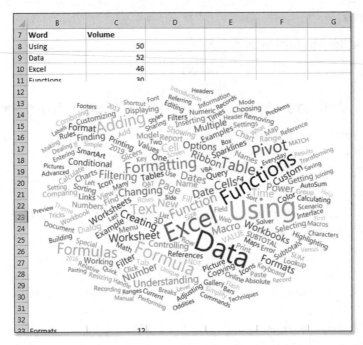

Figure 23.12   A Word Cloud uses a larger font for words that appear frequently.

A Charts pane appears on the right side of the screen when the visualization is selected. The formatting tools will be specific to each visualization. For example, the Word Cloud visualization in Figure 23.12 changed the default settings to specify a minimum angle of -30 degrees, maximum angle of +30 degrees, and no more than seven orientations.

A Sankey chart shows the flow of material from various cities to another (see Figure 23.13). This type of chart, with two sets of labels, would be very hard to build into the current Excel chart model. However, by allowing custom visualizations, it is possible.

One inherent complication with these custom visualizations is that you need the add-in installed on your computer to display the chart. If you send the workbook to others, they might not have the same add-in. If you click the top-right of the visualization as shown in Figure 23.14, you can access a menu to show the visualization as an image.

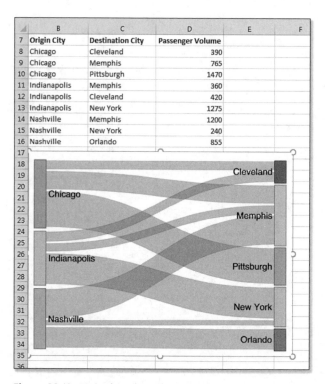

	B	C	D	E	F
7	Origin City	Destination City	Passenger Volume		
8	Chicago	Cleveland	390		
9	Chicago	Memphis	765		
10	Chicago	Pittsburgh	1470		
11	Indianapolis	Memphis	360		
12	Indianapolis	Cleveland	420		
13	Indianapolis	New York	1275		
14	Nashville	Memphis	1200		
15	Nashville	New York	240		
16	Nashville	Orlando	855		

Figure 23.13   A Sankey chart shows the flow from one set of locations to another.

Figure 23.14   Embed an image of the current chart in case someone else opens the workbook and does not have the add-in.

You can build a pivot table and display the results on an animated map using the 3D Map feature. This functionality debuted as the Power Map add-in for Excel 2013. The functionality was renamed 3D Map and built in to Excel starting with Excel 2016.

Examples of 3D Maps

The first three figures represent corn acreage by state for the year 2014. Figure 24.1 shows a shaded area map. Iowa and Illinois are the leading producers of corn.

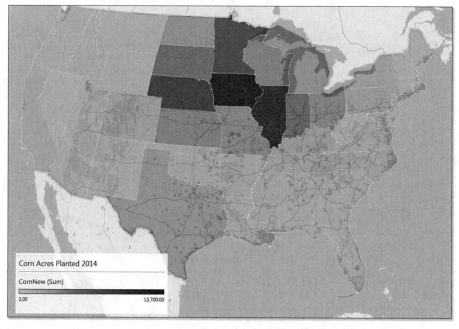

Corn Acres Planted 2014

CornNew (Sum)

2.00   13,700.00

Figure 24.1 In a shaded area map, a darker color indicates a higher value.

Figure 24.2 shows a column chart. The height of each column correlates to acres of corn planted. Note that this visualization looks best when you tip the map to look at it closer to ground level.

Figure 24.2   A column chart in each state indicates the amount of corn planted.

Figure 24.3 shows a heat map. The points with the highest value are shown in a red/yellow/green/blue circle, whereas smaller points might appear in just blue.

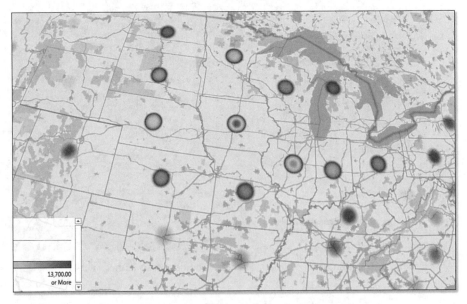

Figure 24.3   A heat map uses red and yellow to indicate the highest values.

Adding Color Information for Categories

The next figures are based on data from FlightStats.com. Figure 24.4 shows the position and altitude of a Southwest Airlines flight from Akron, Ohio, to Orlando, Florida. By using a Category field, the columns are a different color based on whether the flight is below 10,000 feet, climbing, level, or descending.

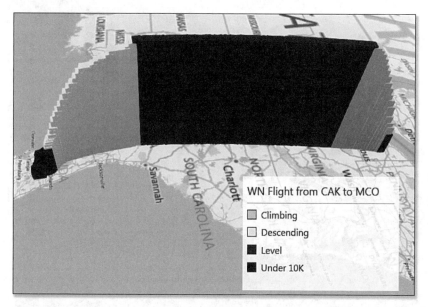

Figure 24.4   Different colors indicate different stages of this aircraft flight.

Zooming In

FlightStats provides new data every minute. Although the flight in Figure 24.4 looks like a solid line, when you zoom in, as in Figure 24.5, you can see the gaps between the columns. While landing, this flight flew west of downtown Orlando, flew four minutes south of the airport, turned, and landed four minutes later.

When you pan to the beginning of the flight as in Figure 24.6, you see the first four minutes of the flight as viewed southwest of Akron, Ohio. By changing the theme to use a satellite photograph of the ground, you can see that the plane took off to the northeast from runway 5 and began turning south three minutes into the flight.

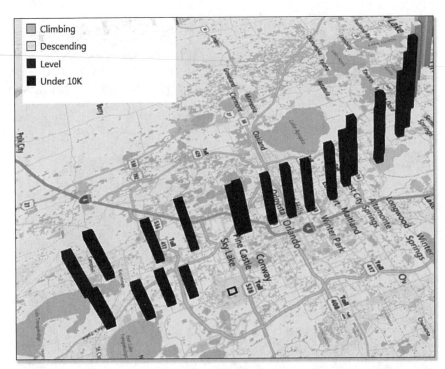

Figure 24.5   You can zoom in on any portion of the map.

Figure 24.6   Using the satellite theme, you can make out individual streets, buildings, and runways.

Animating Over Time

If your data set includes a date or time field, you can animate the data over time. A time scrubber appears at the bottom of the map. Click the Play button to the left of the scrubber to play the entire sequence or grab the scrubber and drag to any particular day or time.

In Figure 24.7, the flight has reached Columbus, Ohio, by 8:47 a.m. In Figure 24.8, the flight crosses through the northeast corner of Tennessee by 9:15 a.m.

Scrubber

Figure 24.7   Animate the map over time to watch events unfold.

Figure 24.8   Either allow the scene to play the entire time span or drag the scrubber to a specific time.

Going Ultra-Local

The previous example showed a 1,000-mile journey that spanned more than two hours. This example shows a 2-mile story that spans 50 years. Figure 24.9 shows Merritt Island, Florida, in November 1967. Engineers who work at Kennedy Space Center on the Apollo program had started building houses on the canals of Merritt Island. Each tiny square is a house.

Figure 24.9 Each tiny square is a house on a canal.

Figure 24.10 shows the same area at the end of the Apollo program in 1972. More houses have been built.

Figure 24.11 shows the area as the first Shuttle mission took off in 1981.

Figure 24.10   You can see which neighborhoods developed during the Apollo years.

Figure 24.11   By the Space Shuttle era, more neighborhoods had filled in.

Figure 24.12 shows the detail of two neighborhoods. The height of the column is the last sale amount. When you animate this data over time, you can see the run-up of sale prices in 2009 leading up to the housing bubble.

Figure 24.12   Zoom in and change to a satellite photo to see individual houses.

Getting Your Data into 3D Map

The mapping engine is always using data from the PowerPivot data model. You don't have to load your data to the data model. Just choose one cell in the data set and select Insert, 3D Map. Excel loads the data to the data model for you.

However, if your data is in multiple tables, and if you have the full version of PowerPivot, you can load your tables to PowerPivot and define relationships between the tables.

3D Map requires one or more geographic fields, such as City, County, Country, State or Province, Street, Postal or ZIP Code, or Full Address. If you have data that already has latitude and longitude, the program can use that. If you are using a custom map, the X, Y coordinates will work. If you are using custom shapes, Power Map can accept .kml or .shp files.

Figure 24.13 shows a simple data set. Columns A and B provide enough geography with City and State. Column C is a Category column to provide different colors on the map. It rounds the population from column D to the nearest 25,000. Column D contains the population. This data will be plotted at the city level. For some cities, it would be possible to get by with only column A. However, without the FL qualifier in column B, it is likely that Melbourne would appear in Australia instead of Florida. When in doubt, add extra geography fields, even if every value in column B is FL.

			×	✓	*fx*	=MROUND(D2,25000)	

	B	C	D
City	State	Category	Population
Jacksonville	FL	825000	821784
Miami	FL	400000	399457
Tampa	FL	325000	335709
St. Petersburg	FL	250000	244769
Orlando	FL	250000	238300
Hialeah	FL	225000	224669
Tallahasee	FL	175000	181376
Fort Lauderdale	FL	175000	165521
Port St. Lucie	FL	175000	164603
Pembrooke Pines	FL	150000	154750
Cape Coral	FL	150000	154305
Hollywood	FL	150000	140768
Gainesville	FL	125000	124354
Miramar	FL	125000	122041
Coral Springs	FL	125000	131096
Clearwater	FL	100000	107685
Miami Gardens	FL	100000	107167

Figure 24.13   Select one cell in your data and choose Insert, 3D Map.

With one cell in your data selected, choose Insert, 3D Map. It takes several seconds for the data to be loaded to the PowerPivot data model. You are then presented with the 3D Maps window. A Field List is hovering above the map. The Location box on the right shows the fields that Excel detected as being geography. Pay particular attention that this is correct. A field that contains values such as "123 Main Street" should be classified as Street and not Address. The Address data type is reserved for values that contain a complete address, such as "30 Rockefeller Plaza, New York, NY 10112."

In Figure 24.14, the Location box has a 93% hyperlink on the right side. You can see many blue columns already appearing in Florida. The hyperlink indicates that geocoding is finished and 93% successful, but there were some places that Bing was unsure of.

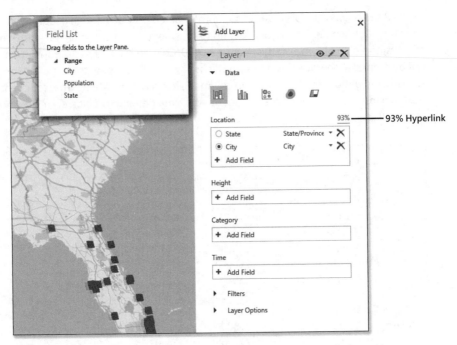

Figure 24.14   Things look good, but only 93% of points were correctly located.

Click the 93% hyperlink for a report of the places with low mapping confidence. As shown in Figure 24.15, everything is actually correct. If something was not correct, you would have to go back to the original data in Excel, add more geography, and then refresh the data in 3D Map.

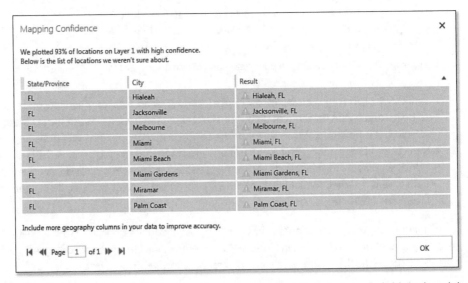

Figure 24.15   Currently, the only way to improve accuracy is to include more fields in the original data set.

TROUBLESHOOTING

When 3D Map cannot find a location, there is no way to specifically point to it on a map.

I've seen data sets where Excel thinks Paris is in Kentucky and Melbourne is in Florida. In these cases, adding a new column named "Country" with the appropriate country can help.

Also, when assigning your fields to a geography category, understand the difference between "Street" and "Address." If your data has a column with values such as "123 Main Street," this should be classified as a street. If you have values such as "123 Main Street, New York, NY," this should be classified as an address.

If you refer to "123 Main Street" as an address, there will be many points misplaced.

After the records are assigned to the correct geography, you can move fields from the Field List to the drop zones. In Figure 24.16, the population is the height. The columns are different colors thanks to a new field added to the category area. Note that to add a new field, you would return to Excel and insert a new column in the middle of the data. Add a formula, such as =MROUND(D2,25000). Return to 3D Map and click Refresh.

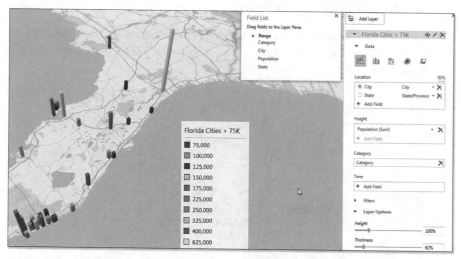

Figure 24.16 A map showing the largest cities in Florida.

3D Map Techniques

Here are some useful techniques when using 3D Map.

Tipping, Rotating, and Zooming the Map

There are clickable navigation icons on the map. But master these mouse techniques for faster navigation:

- Hold down Alt. Left-click and drag the mouse left or right to rotate the map. In most of the Florida examples in this chapter, the map looks best when you are viewing it from the Atlantic Ocean. I made that happen by dragging the mouse left while holding down Alt.

- Hold down Alt. Left-click and drag the mouse up or down to tip the map. Dragging down gives you a view looking straight down on the map. Dragging up gives you a view from ground level.

- Hold down Ctrl. Scroll the wheel on your mouse to zoom in or out. Note that you often have to click the map once before the wheel mouse will start to work.

Adding a Photo to a Point

Right-click any column and choose Add Annotation. In the Description field, choose Image and browse to the location of the image. Choose a size and a placement. The image appears next to the column with an arrow (see Figure 24.17).

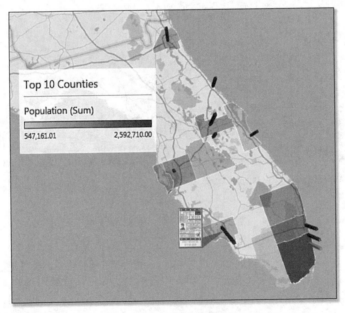

Figure 24.17   This map shows two map types on two different layers.

Combining Layers

Figure 24.17 shows a map made from two different tables. This is easy if you have the Power Pivot tab displayed in your ribbon. Follow these steps:

1. Format both data sets in Excel as a table.

2. On the PowerPivot tab, choose Create Linked Table from both tables.

3. On the Insert tab, choose 3D Map.

4. Both tables appear in the field list. Drag County and State from the first table to the Location box. Choose a shaded area map. Add Population as the Value for the map.

5. Click Add Layer. You get a new Location box. Drag City and State from the second table. Build a column chart from this layer.

If you are using Excel 2016 and do not have the Power Pivot tab in the ribbon, there are two alternate ways to get the tables into the data model:

- One simple method is to create a pivot table from each data set. In the Insert PivotTable dialog box, choose the box for Add This Data To The Data Model. It does not matter what you put in the pivot table; simply creating the pivot table is enough.

- The other method is to use Power Query. From each table, choose Data, From A Table/ Range. When the Power Query window opens, you will see Close & Load icon on the left side. Open the drop-down menu below that icon and choose Close & Load To. In the Close & Load dialog box, choose Only Create A Connection and choose Add This Data To The Data Model.

The result: Figure 24.17 shows a map in which the top 10 Florida counties are highlighted. The columns indicate places where I have done my live Power Excel seminar. Any county that is shaded without a column indicates a market I have been overlooking.

Changing Column Size or Color

The thickness of a column is more than one city block. If you want to show multiple houses on a street, you won't be able to tell one point from the others. In the right panel, choose Layer Options. Change the Thickness slider to 10% or less.

To change the colors used on the map, go to Layer Options. Use the 60 colors in the color drop-down menu or define your own color.

Resizing the Various Panes

Almost every legend or information pane takes up too much room. If you are working on a small laptop, your inclination will be to close all panes because they are covering up the map. If you have a large monitor, you can resize each pane. Click on the pane, and then use one of the two resize handles. To move a pane, click and drag the pane to a new location.

When you have a Time panel on the map, right-click and choose Edit. You can control the Time Format.

Adding a Satellite Photograph

Use the Themes drop-down menu in the ribbon. The second theme offers a satellite image. Outside of the first two themes, I rarely find anything that looks acceptable.

Showing the Whole Earth

What if you have data points in America and Australia? There is no way to see both halves of the globe at the same time. Use the Flat Map option in the ribbon. When you zoom out, you can see the entire world map.

Understanding the Time Choices

When you add a field to the Time drop zone, a small clock icon appears above the right side of the field. This icon offers three choices, as shown in Figure 24.18:

- **Data Shows for an Instant**—The point appears when the scrubber reaches the date associated with that record. As the scrubber moves to the next day, the point disappears.

- **Data Accumulates Over Time**—Suppose you are showing ticket sales over time. After a ticket has been purchased, it should stay on the map. Choose Data Accumulates Over Time.

- **Data Stays Until It Is Replaced**—One map that I frequently use shows the last sale price for various houses in a neighborhood. A house might sell once every 7 years. In this case, you want the last sales price to remain until the house is sold at a different price.

Figure 24.18   Three choices are available near the Time field.

Note that there is no good way to change a category as time progresses. You might want to show Chicago as red from 2013 to 2015 and then as green from 2019 to 2020. There currently is no good way to do this in 3D Map.

Inside OUT

Is it possible to animate a line between two points in a 3D Map?

The capability to show movement along a path is not built-in to 3D Map, but you can fake it. Find the latitude and longitude of both points. Build a new table in Excel with 1,000 rows. Add a date field that increments by an hour or a day in each row. For the latitude and longitude, add 1/1000 of the difference between the start and end point in each row. Set the time value that each point shows for an instant. When you press the Play button, the points will rapidly appear, then disappear, giving the illusion of a point racing from the start point to the end point.

Controlling Map Labels

You have only one option with map labels—either show them or do not. After you turn them on, they seem to have a mind of their own. If you zoom way out, you see large labels for each continent and map labels for some countries (see Figure 24.19).

Figure 24.19   Some countries are labeled, and others are not.

As you zoom in, more countries are labeled, and some city labels appear.

Zoom in to a city, as in Figure 24.20. Some streets are labeled and others are not. What if an important street is one that is not named? You have no explicit control over which items are labeled and which are not. Your only hope is to zoom out, recenter the map slightly, and then zoom back in. Keep doing this until luck falls on your side and the particular street is labeled.

Figure 24.20   Some streets are labeled, and others are not. You have little control over which get labels.

Building a Tour and Creating a Video

A tour is composed of multiple scenes. You can use the New Scene drop-down menu to duplicate the current scene as a new scene.

Your first scene might start out with a view of the entire country. Your next scene might zoom in on one portion of the country. Then a scene might add an annotation to one point. The next scene might fly to another part of the country. Each scene has a duration and an Effects duration. The various effects are designed to add visual interest.

CAUTION

You rarely want a Time field in more than one scene. If your first scene shows the data growing over time, and then the next scene zooms in on one portion of the map, you must remove the Time field in the second scene or you will watch the data repopulate in each scene.

After building several scenes, use the Play Tour icon to test the timing of the scenes. When you have a tour that looks good, use the Create Video icon to build a video of the tour. Note that this step can take up to an hour, so it makes sense to test the tour before building a video.

Using an Alternate Map

You can use 3D Map to show data on something other than a globe. For example, a retail store might have transaction data showing sales by time and item. If you can map the item number to a location in the store map, you can plot sales by location.

Preparing the Store Image

First, find (or create) a map of the store. Figure out the height and width of the image in pixels. When you look at your store map, the lower-left corner has a coordinate of X=0, Y=0. As you move from left to right across the image, the X values increase. As you move from bottom to top, the Y values increase.

The process of locating each item in the store can be tedious. If you have Photoshop, open the image in Photoshop and press F8 to display a panel showing the X,Y coordinates of the mouse. Make sure to change the measurement units from inches to pixels. You can hover your mouse over a location on the store map. The X value reported by Photoshop is correct. The Y value is the distance from the top edge of the image, so you have to subtract the reported Y value from the height of the image. Or, if it is easier, key the reported Y values into Excel and then use a formula to change.

Specifying a Custom Map

After launching 3D Map, move your X and Y field to the Location box. Choose X Coordinate and Y Coordinate as the field type. You see a question asking whether you want to change to a custom map (see Figure 24.21). Choose Yes.

Figure 24.21   Specify X and Y as the location type.

In the Change Map Type dialog box, choose New Custom Map, as shown in Figure 24.22.

Figure 24.22   Specify a custom map.

Although I appreciate the team who built 3D Map, the Custom Map Options dialog box always requires a lot of tweaking. Unless you managed to sell something at the X=0, Y=0 position in your store map, the default settings will always be wrong. Use the following steps to change the settings:

1. For the X Max, specify the width of the image in pixels.

2. For the Y Max, specify the height of the image in pixels.

3. Click the Picture icon and browse to the image of your store map.

4. Change from Auto Fit to Pixel Space.

Figure 24.23 shows the settings.

Figure 24.23   Change the settings for converting X,Y locations to a position in your image.

Your data is plotted on the store map. You can use the Alt and Ctrl navigation keys to rotate, tip, and zoom in on the map (see Figure 24.24).

Figure 24.24   Data animates over time on a map of your retail store floor plan.

Using Sparklines

Edward Tufte wrote about small, intense, simple datawords in his 2006 book, *Beautiful Evidence*. Tufte called them *sparklines* and produced several examples where you could fit dozens of points of data in the space of a word. Tufte's concepts made it into Excel 2010.

Fitting a Chart into the Size of a Cell with Sparklines

Excel's implementation of sparklines offers line charts, column charts, and a Win/Loss chart. Figure 25.1 shows an example of each:

- **Win/Loss**—The 1951 Pennant Race (in rows 7 and 8) shows two examples of a Win/Loss chart. Each event (in this case, a baseball game) is represented by either an upward-facing marker (to indicate a win) or a downward-facing marker (to indicate a loss). This type of chart shows winning streaks. The final three games were the playoffs between the Dodgers and the Giants, with the Giants winning two games to one.

- **Line**—The sparkline in row 12 shows 120 monthly points of the Dow Jones Industrial Index, indicating the closing price for each month in one decade.

- **Column**—Rows 16 through 21 compare monthly high temperatures for various cities using sparkcolumns. The minimum and maximum values for each city are marked in a contrasting color. Curitiba, in the southern hemisphere, has its warmest month in February.

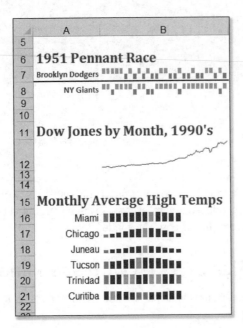

Figure 25.1   Excel 2019 offers three types of sparklines.

Sparklines can exist as a single cell (the Dow Jones example) or as a group of sparklines (the temperature example). When sparklines are created as a group, you can specify that all the sparklines should have the same scale or that they should be independent. There are times where each is appropriate.

The Sparkline feature offers the capability to mark the high point, the low point, the first point, the last point, or all negative points.

There is no built-in way to label sparklines. However, sparklines are drawn on a special drawing layer that was added to Excel 2007 to accommodate the data visualizations discussed in Chapter 22, "Using Data Visualizations and Conditional Formatting." This layer is transparent, so with some clever formatting, you can add some label information in the cell behind the sparkline.

Understanding How Excel Maps Data to Sparklines

Contrary to most examples that you see in the Microsoft demos, sparklines do not have to be created adjacent to the original data set.

Suppose that you have the 4-row-by-12-column data set shown in Figure 25.2. This data shows four series of economic data. It can be used to create four sparklines.

	2003	2004	2005	2006	2007	2008	2009	2010	2011	2012	2013	2014
Unemployment	6	5.5	5.1	4.6	4.6	5.8	9.3	9.6	8.9	8.1	7.4	6.2
GDP	11142	11853	12623	13377	14029	14292	13939	14527	15518	16163	16768	17419
New Construction	1848	1956	2068	1801	1355	906	554	586.9	608.8	780.6	924.9	1003
Consumer Credit	2077	2192	2291	2462	2616	2651	2553	2647	2756	2924	3098	3317

Figure 25.2   Four series of economic indicators for a duodecennial.

You can create the sparklines in a four-row-by-one-column range, as shown in D3:D6 of Figure 25.3, or in a one-row-by-four-column range, as shown in A1:D1 of the same figure. When you specify a sparkline, you specify the source data and the target range. Given a 4×12 cell source data and a 1×4 or 4×1 target range, Excel figures out that it should create four sparklines.

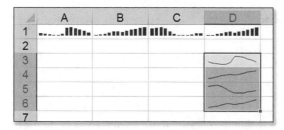

Figure 25.3   The sparklines can be plotted in a row or a column, regardless of whether the original data was in rows or columns.

What if your original data set is perfectly square? This occurs when you have four rows by four columns, as shown in Figure 25.4.

	2011	2012	2013	2014
Unemployment	8.9	8.1	7.4	6.2
GDP	15518	16163	16768	17419
New Construction	608.8	780.6	924.9	1003
Consumer Credit	2756	2924	3098	3317

Figure 25.4   The original data set has the same number of rows and columns.

You then have the chance that Excel will choose to create the sparklines along the wrong axis (see Figure 25.5).

Figure 25.5   Excel might choose the wrong way to draw the sparklines.

While those sparklines are selected, go to the Sparkline Tools Design tab of the ribbon, open the Edit Data drop-down menu, and select Switch Row/Column (see Figure 25.6). The sparkline is reversed.

Figure 25.6   Excel offers a way to reverse the row and column.

TROUBLESHOOTING

Sparklines are scaled independently. Because there are no labels along the left axis, it is hard to see the magnitude of each line.

This is by design and allows you to see unemployment in percentages compared to GDP in trillions. There are cases where each sparkline is showing items that can be compared to each other.

In these cases, use the Axis settings in the Sparkline Tools. Change the Minimum Value and the Maximum Value to the Same For All Sparklines.

Creating a Group of Sparklines

The worksheet in Figure 25.7 includes more than a decade of leading economic indicators. Use the following steps to add sparklines to the table.

	A	B	C	D	E
3	Economic Indicators 2003-2014				
4			2003	2004	2005
5	Unemployment		6	5.5	5.1
6	GDP		11142	11853	12623
7	New Construction		1848	1956	2068
8	Consumer Credit		2077	2192	2291

Figure 25.7   Add space in your table for the sparklines.

1. Insert a blank column between columns A and B. This provides room for the sparklines to appear next to the labels in column A.

2. Select the data in C4:N8. Note that you should not include any headings in this selection.

3. On the Insert tab, select Column from the Sparkline group. Excel displays the Create Sparklines dialog box. This dialog box is the same for all three types of sparklines. You have to specify the location of the data and the location where you want the sparklines. Because your data is 4 rows by 12 columns, the Location Range must be a four-cell vector. You can either specify one row by four columns or four rows by one column.

TIP

In step 1, you might find that you don't need to print the table of numbers; just the labels and sparklines will suffice.

4. Select B5:B8 as the location range, as shown in Figure 25.8.

5. Click OK to create the default sparklines.

Figure 25.8   Preselect the data range and then specify the location range.

As shown in Figure 25.9, the sparklines have no markers. They are scaled independently of each other. The unemployment max of 9.6 reaches nearly to the top of cell B5, indicating the maximum for Unemployment is probably about 10. By contrast, the maximum for GDP in B6 is closer to 17,500.

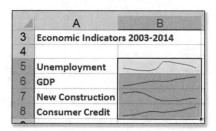

Figure 25.9   Default sparklines have no markers and are autoscaled to fit the cell.

The Show group of the Sparkline toolbar enables you to mark certain points on the line. In Figure 25.10, the high point is marked with a dot. This one change adds a lot of information to the sparklines. New Construction peaked in 2005. Unemployment peaked in 2010, and GDP and Consumer Credit both hit a new high in 2014.

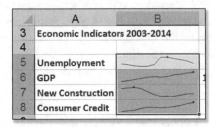

Figure 25.10   Placing a marker at the high point adds key information to the sparkline.

Built-In Choices for Customizing Sparklines

The Sparkline Tools Design tab offers five groups of choices for customizing sparklines: Edit Data, Type, Show, Style, and Group. Each is discussed in this section.

The Edit Data drop-down menu enables you to redefine the data range for the source data and the location. If you have to add new data to existing sparklines, you can do so here. Generally, you would edit the location for the whole group, but the drop-down menu enables you to edit data for a single sparkline.

The Type group enables you to switch between Line, Column, and Win/Loss charts.

The Show group offers the second-most useful settings in the tab. The six check boxes here control which points should display markers in the sparkline:

- High Point

- Low Point

- First Point

- Last Point

- Negative Points

- All Points

Here, you can choose to highlight the high point, the low point, the first point, or the last point. Note that if there is a tie for high or low point, both points in the tie are marked. You can also choose to highlight all points and/or the negative points.

For sparklines, any item you choose in the Show group is drawn as a marker on the line. You can control the color for each of the six options using the Marker Color drop-down menu, discussed next.

For sparkcolumns, the markers are always shown for All Points, so the All Points check box is grayed out. Choosing any of the five other check boxes in the Show group causes those particular columns to be drawn in a different color.

For Win/Loss, you'll generally choose Markers and Negative. This is how the losses show in a contrasting color from the wins.

In Figure 25.11, examples of the various options are shown:

- In cell B3, the high, low, first, and last points are shown.

- In cell B5, all markers are shown in the same color.

- When you choose Markers and Negative, all points appear, but you can change the negative points to another color, as shown in cell B7.

- In cells B11 and B13, the chosen markers are shown in a contrasting color.

- Cells B9 and B15 are examples where the horizontal axis is shown. This helps to differentiate positive from negative. Note that the axis always appears at a zero location.

Figure 25.11   Use the Show group to highlight certain points.

The Style gallery seems to be a huge waste of real estate. In the Office theme, it offers 36 ugly alternatives for sparkline color. This group also offers the Sparkline Color drop-down menu, which is the standard Excel 2016 color chooser. The color chosen here controls the line in a

CHAPTER 25

sparkline. You use the Marker Color drop-down menu to control the color of the high, low, first, last, and negative points, as well as the default color for regular markers.

You use the Group group to ungroup a group of sparklines. Any changes that you make on the Design tab apply to all the sparklines in the group. This is usually a desired outcome. However, if you needed to mark the high point in one line and the low point in another line, you would ungroup the sparklines.

NOTE

For sparklines, the sparkline color controls the color of the line. For sparkcolumns or the Win/Loss chart, the sparkline color controls the color of the columns.

You can also group sparklines or clear sparklines using icons in the Group group. The Axis drop-down menu appears in this group and contains the most important settings for sparklines. You learn how to use the Axis drop-down menu in the next example.

Controlling Axis Values for Sparklines

Figure 25.12 presents a group of sparkcolumns showing the average high temperatures for several cities. These cities are a mix of tropical and frigid locales.

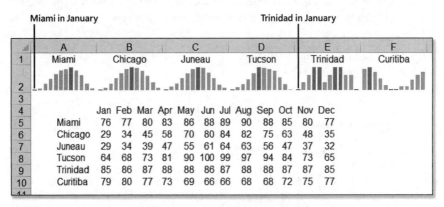

Figure 25.12   The automatic vertical scale assigned to each sparkline doesn't work in this example.

The default behavior is that each sparkline in the group gets its own scale. This worked for the varying economic indicators in Figure 25.7. However, it does not work here.

When the vertical axis scale is set to Automatic, you can never really know the high and low of the scale in use. If you study the data and the sparkline for Trinidad, it appears as if Excel has chosen a min point of 84.8 and a max point of 89. Without any scale, you might think that Trinidad in January is as cold as Chicago in January.

Figure 25.13 shows the options available in the Axis drop-down menu on the right end of the Sparkline Tools Design tab. The important settings here are the options for the minimum value and maximum value.

Figure 25.13   Control the vertical axis using this drop-down menu.

If you change the minimum and maximum values to the setting Same for All Sparklines, then all six sparklines in this group have the same min and max scale. The sparklines in Figure 25.14 initially look better. Juneau is never as warm as Tucson, but you still do not know the min and max values.

Figure 25.14   Force all sparklines to have the same vertical scale.

Take a close look at Chicago. It appears that the January high temperature is about zero, but the data table shows that the average high temperature in January is 29. You can estimate that these columns run from a minimum of 28 to a maximum of 101, based on looking through the data.

My suggestion is to always visit the Axis drop-down menu and set custom min and max values. For example, in the temperature example, you would set a minimum of 0 and a maximum of 100.

Setting Up Win/Loss Sparklines

The data for a Win/Loss sparkline is simple: Put a 1 (or any positive number) for a win and put a –1 (or any negative number) for a loss. Put a zero to have no marker.

In Figure 25.15, you can see the data for a pair of Win/Loss sparklines. The 2 in cell F3 does not cause the marker to appear any taller than any of the 1s in the other cells. However, it does cause that marker to be shown as the max point.

Figure 25.15   Data sets for wins and losses are composed of 1s and –1s.

The data for the Win/Loss sparkcolumn chart does not have to be composed of 1s and –1s. Any positive and negative numbers will work.

In Figure 25.16, the data shows the closing price for the Dow for a period of a few months. Column D calculates the daily change. The Win/Loss chart in rows 4 and 5 does not show the magnitude of the change but instead focuses on how many days in a row had market gains versus market losses.

	A	B	C	D	E
1	**Dow Jones 30 Industrials**				
2	**Jan - Apr 2015**				
3					
4					
5					
6					
7					
8		Date	Adj Close*	Change	
9		27–Jan-15	17,387.21		
10		28–Jan-15	17,191.37	-195.84	
11		29–Jan-15	17,416.85	225.48	
12		30–Jan-15	17,164.95	-251.90	

Figure 25.16   This chart focuses on how many days in a row were gains or losses. The magnitude of the change is not factored in.

The following are some notes about the chart in Figure 25.16:

- Cells B4:E5 are merged to show a larger sparkline.

- If you stretch out a sparkcolumn or a Win/Loss chart wide enough, gaps eventually show up between the columns. This helps to quantify the number of events in a streak.

- One up marker in B and one down marker in C are a darker color. These represent the largest negative change and largest positive change.

Inside OUT

Sparklines do not officially support stacked column charts, but you can create one with a little trickery.

(This method was discovered by long-time Excel MVP Ingeborg Hawighorst of Teylyn.com.)

To create a stacked column chart sparkline from two series, follow these steps:

1. Start two series, white and black.
2. Add a White+Black helper series. This sparkline will be as tall as the white and black series combined.
3. Create three column sparklines from the three series.

4. Click each sparkline and use the Ungroup command on the Sparkline Tools Design tab of the ribbon. From this point on, you only need to work with the White sparkline and the Helper sparkline. You can ignore the Black sparkline.
5. For each sparkline, go to Sparkline Tools, Axis. Set the Minimum Axis to zero for both sparklines. Set the Maximum Axis to the same number for both sparklines.
6. Copy the cell containing the Helper sparkline.

7. Go to a new location and click Home, select the Paste drop-down menu, and choose Linked Picture.

8. Copy the cell containing the White sparkline.

9. Paste a Linked Picture in the same vicinity of the White sparkline using the same steps. Drag the White sparkline over the Helper sparkline and nudge carefully until they line up.

Provided you pasted the Helper sparkline picture before the White sparkline picture, the White sparkline should be on top. If not, right-click the White sparkline picture and choose Bring To Front.

As shown in the image below, the White sparkline in front of the Black sparkline gives the illusion that you have a stacked column.

Showing Detail by Enlarging the Sparkline and Adding Labels

The examples of sparklines created by Tufte in *Beautiful Evidence* almost always label the final point. Some examples include min and max values or a gray box to indicate the normal range of values.

Professor Tufte's definition of sparklines includes the word *small*. If you are going to be showing sparklines on a computer screen, there is no reason they have to stay small.

When you increase the height and width of a cell, the sparkline automatically grows to fill the cell. If you merge cells, the sparkline fills the complete range of merged cells.

In Figure 25.17, the height of row 2 is set to 56.25. This height allows for five rows of 8-point Calibri text to appear in the cell. To determine the optimum height for your font, type 1 and press Alt+Enter, type 2 and press Alt+Enter, type 3 and press Alt+Enter, type 4 and press Alt+Enter, and then type 5 in a cell. Then select Home, Format, AutoFit Row Height.

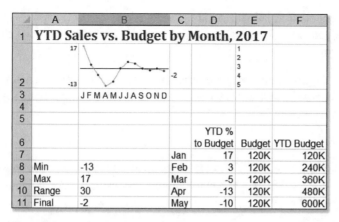

⊿	A	B	C	D	E	F
1	**YTD Sales vs. Budget by Month, 2017**					
2				-2		
3		J F M A M J J A S O N D				
4						
5						
6				YTD % to Budget	Budget	YTD Budget
7			Jan	17	120K	120K
8	Min	-13	Feb	3	120K	240K
9	Max	17	Mar	-5	120K	360K
10	Range	30	Apr	-13	120K	480K
11	Final	-2	May	-10	120K	600K

Figure 25.17   This sparkline has many labels, but they are all manually added outside the sparkline.

The sparkline in cell B2 is set to have a custom minimum and a custom maximum that match the minimum and maximum of the data set.

The label in cell A2 is right-justified 8-point Calibri font. The formula in A2 is =B9&REPT(CHAR(10),4)&B8. This formula concatenates the maximum value, four line feeds, and the minimum value. Ensure the Wrap Text icon is selected on the Home tab.

The labels in B3 are 10-point Calibri. Type **J F M A M J J A S O N D** in cell B3 and adjust the column width to fit the text. (Note: Be sure to place spaces between each of the letters.)

Formulas in B10 and B13 calculate the range from min to max as well as the quintile where the final value falls. The formula in C2 uses =REPT(CHAR(10),B13-1)&B11 to put the final label at about the right height to match the final point.

In Figure 25.18, the city labels are values typed in the same cell as the sparkcolumns. The max scale is set to 120 to make sure there is room for the city name to appear. The Month abbreviations below the charts are **J F M A M J J A S O N D** in 6.5-point Courier New font.

Figure 25.18   Labels are created by typing in a small font in the cell.

If you set a row height equal to 110, you can fit 10 lines of text in the cell using Alt+Enter. Even with a height of 55, you can fit five lines of text. This enables the label for the final point to get near to the final point.

In Figure 25.19, a semitransparent gray box indicates the acceptable limits for a measurement. In this case, anything outside of 95% to 105% is sent for review. These gray boxes are shapes from the Insert tab.

TIP

After trying both 6-point and 7-point font and not having the labels line up with the bars, I ended up using 6.5-point font and adjusting the column widths until the columns lined up with the labels.

Figure 25.19   A gray box shows the acceptable range to help the reader locate items outside of this range.

Use the following tips when setting up the box:

1. Temporarily change the first two points in the first cell to be at the min and max for the box.

2. Increase the zoom to 400%.

3. Draw a rectangle in the cell.

4. Use the Drawing Tools Format tab to set the outline to None.

5. Under Shape Fill, select More Fill Colors. Choose a shade of gray. Because shapes are drawn on top of the sparkline layer, drag the transparency slider up to about 70% transparent.

6. Use the resize handles to make sure the top and bottom of the box go through the first and second points of the line.

7. After getting the box sized appropriately, reset the first two data points back to their original values.

8. Copy the cell that contains the first box. Paste onto the other sparkline cells. Because the sparklines are not copied, only the box is pasted.

TIP

It is possible to copy sparklines. You have to copy both the sparkline and the data source in a single copy. If your copy range includes both elements, the sparkline is pasted.

Other Sparkline Options

You can choose how to deal with gaps in the data. Select Sparkline Tools Design, Edit Data, Hidden and Empty Cells to display the Hidden and Empty Cell Settings dialog box, shown in Figure 25.20.

Figure 25.20   Choose how to deal with missing points.

By default, any missing data in the source range is plotted as a gap, as shown in the top chart in Figure 25.20. Alternatively, you can choose to plot the missing values as zero (center chart) or have Excel connect the data points with a straight line (bottom chart). Also, by default, any data in hidden rows or columns is removed from the sparkline. To keep the hidden data in the chart, select the Show Data in Hidden Rows and Columns check box in Figure 25.20.

CHAPTER 26

Formatting Spreadsheets for Presentation

Images and artwork provide an interesting visual break from tables of numbers in Excel 2019. Office 2019 provides eight elements that you can use to illustrate a workbook:

- **SmartArt**—SmartArt is a collection of similar shapes, arranged to imply a process, groups, or a hierarchy. You can add new shapes, reverse the order of shapes, and change the color of shapes. SmartArt includes a text editor that allows for Level 1 and Level 2 text for each shape in a diagram. Many styles of SmartArt include the capability to add a small picture or logo to each shape.

- **Shapes**—You can add interesting shapes to a document. Shapes can contain words. In fact, shapes are the only art objects in which the words can come from a cell on the worksheet. You can add glow, bevel, and 3D effects to shapes.

- **WordArt**—WordArt enables you to present ordinary text in a stylized manner. You can use WordArt to bend, rotate, and twist the characters in text.

- **Text Boxes**—With text boxes, you can flow text in a defined area. The text box feature is excellent if you need to include paragraphs of body copy in a worksheet. Text boxes support multiple columns of text.

- **Pictures**—Excel worksheets tend to be dominated by numbers. Add a picture to liven up a spreadsheet and add interest. Excel offers an impressive number of ways to format your picture.

- **Online Pictures**—Insert a Creative Commons cartoon or image from a Bing Image Search.

- **Icons**—Insert an icon from a selection of 505 icons.

- **3D Models**—Insert a 3D model file and rotate it along all axes.

Using SmartArt

You use SmartArt to show a series of similar shapes, in which each shape represents a related step, concept, idea, or grouping. You build SmartArt by typing Level 1 text and Level 2 text in a text pane. Excel automatically updates the diagram, adding shapes as you add new entries in the text pane.

The goal of SmartArt is to enable you to create a great-looking graphic with a minimum of effort. After you define a SmartArt image, you can change to any of the other 221 layouts by choosing the desired layout from the gallery. Text is carried from one layout to the next. Figure 26.1 shows four SmartArt styles:

- **Chevron Accent Process**—In this layout, all text is typed as Level 1.

- **Pie Process**—A pie chart advances to show more and more of the process complete.

- **Hexagon Cluster**—Each shape has a corresponding accent picture. Small hexagons indicate the picture and text pair.

- **Continuous Picture List**—Used to show groups of interconnected information. Includes a round accent picture.

Figure 26.1   Subtle differences in four of the 195 possible SmartArt layouts give more weight to either Level 1 or Level 2 text.

Elements Common in Most SmartArt

A SmartArt style is a collection of two or more related shapes. In most styles, you can add additional shapes to illustrate a longer process. However, a few styles are limited to only a certain number of items.

Each shape can contain a headline (Level 1 text). Most shapes allow for body copy (Level 2 text). A few shapes allow for a picture. Some of the 199 layouts show only Level 1 text. If you switch to a style that does not display Level 2 text and then back, the shape remembers the Level 2 text it originally included. After you save and close the file, the hidden text is removed.

While you are editing SmartArt, a text pane that is slightly reminiscent of PowerPoint appears. You can type some bullet points into the text pane. If you demote a bullet point, the text changes from Level 1 text to Level 2 text. If you add a new Level 1 bullet point, Excel adds a new shape to the SmartArt.

Inserting SmartArt

Although there are 195 different layouts of SmartArt, you follow the same basic steps to insert any SmartArt layout:

1. Select a cell in a blank section of the workbook.

2. From the Insert tab, select SmartArt from the Illustrations group. The Choose a SmartArt Graphic dialog box appears.

3. Choose a category in the left side of the Choose a SmartArt Graphic dialog box.

4. Click a SmartArt type in the center of the Choose a SmartArt Graphic dialog box.

5. Read the description on the right side. This description tells you whether the layout is good for Level 1 text, Level 2 text, or both.

6. Repeat steps 4 and 5 until you find a style suitable for your content. Click OK. Figure 26.2 shows an outline of the SmartArt drawn on the worksheet. When you type text in the text pane, it is added to the selected shape.

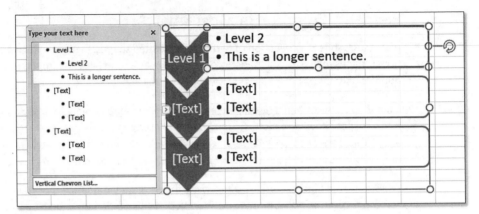

Figure 26.2   When you type in the text pane, the text is added to the selected element of the SmartArt.

7. Fill in the text pane with text for your SmartArt. You can add, delete, promote, or demote items by using icons in the SmartArt Tools Design tab. Or, use the tab key to demote an item and Shift+Tab to promote an item. The SmartArt updates as you type more text. In most cases, adding a new Level 1 item adds a new shape element to the SmartArt.

8. Add longer text to the SmartArt, and Excel shrinks the font size of all the elements to make the text fit. You can make the entire SmartArt graphic larger at any time by grabbing the resize handles in the corners of the SmartArt and dragging to a new size. After you resize the graphic, Excel resizes the text to make it fit in the SmartArt at the largest size possible.

9. The color scheme of the SmartArt initially appears in one color. To change the color scheme, use the Change Colors drop-down menu in the SmartArt Tools Design tab. Excel offers several versions of monochrome styles and five styles of color variations for each diagram.

10. Choose a basic or 3D style from the SmartArt Styles gallery. The first three 3D styles (Polished, Inset, or Cartoon) have a suitable mix of effects but are still readable.

11. Move the SmartArt to the proper location. Position the mouse over the border of the SmartArt, avoiding the eight Resize handles. The cursor changes to a four-headed arrow. Click and drag the SmartArt to a new location. If you drag the SmartArt to the left side of the worksheet, the text pane moves to the right of the SmartArt.

12. Click outside the SmartArt. Excel embeds the SmartArt graphic in the worksheet and hides the SmartArt tabs, as shown in Figure 26.3.

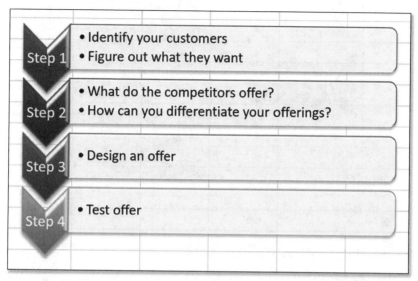

Figure 26.3   Click outside the SmartArt boundary to embed the completed SmartArt.

Changing Existing SmartArt to a New Style

You can change SmartArt to a new style in a couple of ways:

- Left-click the SmartArt and then select SmartArt Tools, Layouts from the Design tab to choose a new layout. The Layouts drop-down menu initially shows only the styles that Excel thinks are a close fit to the current style. If you want to access the complete list of styles, you have to select More Layouts. Hover over layouts to preview how the message will appear in the new layout. Figure 26.4 shows the same message from Figure 26.3 in four different layouts.

- A faster way to access the complete list of styles is to right-click between two shapes in the SmartArt and select Change Layout from the context menu. This step is a little tricky because you cannot click an existing shape. Instead, you must click inside the SmartArt border, but on a portion of the SmartArt that is empty.

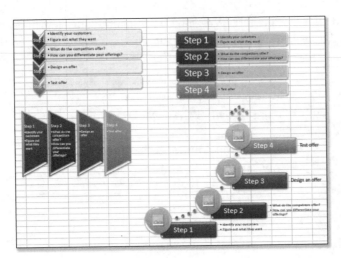

Figure 26.4 The same words are shown in four different layouts.

Adding Images to SmartArt

Thirty-six SmartArt layouts in the Picture category are designed to hold small images in addition to the text. In some of these styles, the picture is emphasized. However, in other pictures, the focus is on the text, and the picture is an accent.

When you select one of these styles, you can add text using the text pane and then specify pictures by clicking the picture icon inside each Level 1 shape.

You can click a picture icon to display the Insert Picture dialog box. Then you can choose a picture and click Insert. Repeat this process to add each additional picture. The pictures are cropped automatically to fit the allotted area.

After adding pictures, you can use all the formatting tools on the Picture Tools Format tab.

Special Considerations for Organizational Charts and Hierarchical SmartArt

Hierarchical SmartArt can contain more than two text levels. As you add more levels to the SmartArt, Excel continues to intelligently add boxes and resize them to fit.

Figure 26.5 shows a diagram created in the Hierarchy layout. In this layout, each level is assigned a different color.

Figure 26.5   Hierarchical SmartArt can contain more than two levels.

Four styles in the Hierarchical category are organization charts. These layouts are used to describe reporting relationships in an organization. There are a few extra options in the ribbon for organization charts. For example, if you select the SmartArt Tools Design tab, the Add Shape drop-down menu includes the option Add Assistant. You can select this option to add an extra shape immediately below the selected level.

In the Create Graphic group of the Design tab, the Org Chart drop-down menu offers four options for showing the boxes within a group. First, you select the manager for the group. Then you select the appropriate type from the drop-down menu to affect all direct reports for the manager. Figure 26.6 illustrates the four options for Org Chart:

- **VP of Sales**—Shows a standard organization chart. The regions are arranged side by side.

- **VP of Manufacturing**—Includes a Right Hanging group that enables departments to be arranged vertically to the right of the line.

- **VP of Engineering**—Includes a Left Hanging group that enables departments to be arranged vertically to the left of the line.

- **CFO**—Includes a Both group that lists direct reports in two columns under the manager on both sides of the vertical line.

In each group, the assistant box is set off from the other boxes.

Figure 26.6 Organization charts include additional options to control the arrangement of direct reports.

Using Shapes to Display Cell Contents

In legacy versions of Excel, shapes were known as AutoShapes. Today, Excel shapes have some new formatting options, such as shadow, glow, and bevel.

Perhaps the best part of shapes is that you can tie the text on a shape to a worksheet cell. For example, in Figure 26.7, the shape is set to display the current value of cell B2. Every time the worksheet is calculated, the text on the shape is updated.

Figure 26.7 You can set shapes to display the current value of a cell.

Follow these steps to insert a shape into a worksheet:

1. Select a blank area of the worksheet.

2. From the Insert tab, open the Shapes drop-down menu.

3. Select one of the 147 basic shapes.

4. The mouse pointer changes to a small crosshair. Click and drag in the worksheet to draw the shape.

5. Choose a color scheme from the Shapes Styles drop-down menu.

6. Select Shape Effects, Preset, and select an effect.

7. Look for a yellow handle on the shape, which enables you to change the inflection point for the shape. For example, on the rounded rectangle, sliding the yellow handle controls how wide the rounded corners are.

8. Look for a gray circle on the outside of the shape. If necessary, drag this circle to rotate the shape.

9. To include static text in the shape, click in the middle of the shape and type the text. You can control the style by using the WordArt Styles drop-down menu. You can control text size and color by using the formatting buttons on the Home tab. The shape can include text from any cell, but it cannot perform a calculation.

NOTE

If you want the shape to include a calculated value, skip step 9 and follow steps 10 through 12.

10. If desired, add a new cell that formats a message for the shape. As shown in Figure 26.8, add the formula `="We are at "&TEXT(B13,"0%")&" of our goal with "&DOLLAR(B12)&" collected to date!"` to an empty cell to convert the calculation in cell B13 to a suitable message.

Figure 26.8 This shape picks up the formula from cell B14 to show how a message changes with the worksheet.

11. Click in the middle of the text box as you would if text was being added.

12. Click in the formula bar, type **=B14**, and then press Enter. As shown in Figure 26.8, the shape displays the results from the selected cell.

Working with Shapes

The Drawing Tools section of the Format tab contains sections to change the shape style, fill, outline, effects, and WordArt effects.

In the Insert Shapes dialog box, use the Edit Shape, Change Shape command to choose another shape style.

If you right-click a shape and select Format Shape, Excel displays the Format Shape dialog box, with the fine-tuning settings Fill, Line, Line Style, Shadow, 3D Format, 3D Rotation, and Text Placement.

Using WordArt for Interesting Titles and Headlines

Even though WordArt was redesigned in Excel 2007, it is still best to use it sparingly, such as for a headline or title at the top of a page. It is best to use it for impressive display fonts to add interest to a report. However, you would not want to create an entire 20-page document in WordArt.

To use WordArt, follow these steps:

1. Select a blank section of the worksheet.

2. From the Insert tab, select the WordArt drop-down menu.

3. Choose from the 20 WordArt presets in the drop-down menu. Do not worry that these presets seem less exciting than the WordArt in legacy versions of Excel. You can customize the WordArt later.

4. Excel adds the generic text "Your Text Here" in the preset WordArt you chose. Select this default text and then type your own text.

5. Select the text. Choose a new font style by using either the mini toolbar that appears or the Home tab.

6. Use the WordArt Styles group on the Drawing Tools Format tab to color the WordArt. To the right of the Styles drop-down menu are icons for text color and line color and a drop-down menu for effects. The Effects drop-down menu includes the fly-out menus Shadow, Reflection, Glow, Soft Edges, Bevel, and 3D Rotation.

7. To achieve the old-style WordArt effects, from the Format tab, select Drawing Tools, WordArt Styles, Text Effects, Transform, and then select a shape for the text. Figure 26.9 shows the WordArt with a Curve Down transformation.

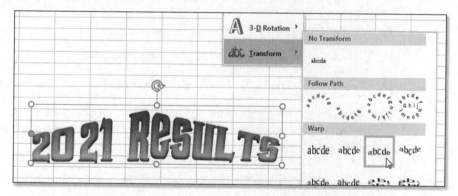

Figure 26.9   WordArt includes the Transform menu to bend and twist type.

CHAPTER 26

Using Text Boxes to Flow Long Text Passages

WordArt is perfect for short titles. However, it is not suitable for long text passages that you want to fit in a range. Whereas the Home, Fill, Justify command works for text that is less than 256 characters, a text box allows long paragraphs of text to flow.

To use a text box object to create two columns of text, follow these steps:

1. Select a blank section of the worksheet.

2. From the Insert tab, select Text, Text Box.

3. Drag in your document to draw a large text box on the worksheet.

4. Either type your text here or switch to Word, copy the text, and then switch back to Excel and paste the text.

5. Right-click the text box and select Exit Edit Mode.

6. Use the Font group on the Home tab to adjust the font size and face.

7. Right-click the text box and select Format Shape. The Format Shape task pane appears.

8. In the headline of the task pane, choose Text Options.

9. Choose the third icon below the headline to display the Text Box options.

10. Adjust the margins and alignment, if desired.

11. Click the Columns button. The Columns dialog box appears.

12. Choose two columns with nonzero spacing between them, as shown in Figure 26.10.

13. Click the X at the top right of the task pane to close the task pane. The result is a text box that has two columns of text. As you change the size of the text, it automatically reflows to fit the desired columns.

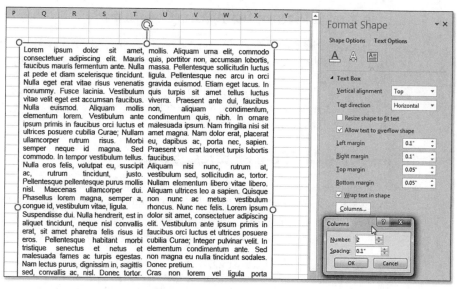

Figure 26.10 You can change the number of columns.

Using Pictures and Clip Art

Excel 2019 offers 28 quick picture styles and the tools to create thousands of additional effects.

When the spreadsheet was invented in 1979, accountants were amazed and thrilled with the simple black-and-white, numbers-only spreadsheets. The image processing tools available in Excel 2019 elevate spreadsheets from simple tables of numbers to beautiful marketing showpieces.

Getting Your Picture into Excel

For reasons unknown, you cannot simply drag and drop photographs into Excel. Drag and drop works in Word, PowerPoint, and even OneNote, but not Excel. In Excel, you have to use the Insert tab and choose either Pictures or Pictures Online:

- Use the Pictures icon for pictures stored on your PC or network.

- Use Online Pictures for pictures stored in your OneDrive, on your Flickr account, in the Office Online clip art collection, or to do a Bing Image search.

- Use Screenshot to capture a picture already displayed in a browser or other application on your computer.

Inserting a Picture from Your Computer

When you choose the Picture icon, you can browse to any folder on your computer or network. Use the Views drop-down menu to display thumbnails so you can browse by picture instead of picture name.

Excel inserts the picture so that the top-left corner of the picture is aligned with the active cell. The picture usually extends and covers hundreds of cells.

Inserting Multiple Pictures at Once

If you multiselect pictures using the Ctrl key while browsing, Excel inserts all the pictures, over-laps them, and selects all the pictures. If the size of the entire stack of pictures seems too large, you can resize them all by using the Height and Width settings in the ribbon. But soon, you have to rearrange the pictures so you can actually see them. Follow these steps:

1. Click outside the picture stack, on the Excel grid, to deselect the pictures.

2. Click the top photo in the stack to select that one single photo.

3. Drag the photo to a new location on the worksheet.

4. Repeat steps 2 and 3 for the remaining pictures in the stack.

Inserting a Picture or Clip Art from Online

When you choose the Online Pictures icon, you can load pictures from your OneDrive, Flickr, Office Online, or you can search Bing Images for pictures with a Creative Commons license.

If options for OneDrive or Flickr are not showing, you need to add a connection to those ser-vices. Visit Profile.Live.Com to connect Flickr to your Microsoft account. Open the File menu and choose Account from the left navigation area. Your connected services appear in the center portion of the screen. Click the Add Service button, then Microsoft Account, Flickr to connect to an existing Flickr account.

Even if you don't have a lot of photos stored online, you can access the royalty-free images and clip art at Office Online. Follow these steps:

1. Select a cell where you want the picture to start.

2. Choose Insert, Online Pictures.

3. In the Insert Pictures dialog box, type a keyword next to Bing Image Search, as shown in Figure 26.11.

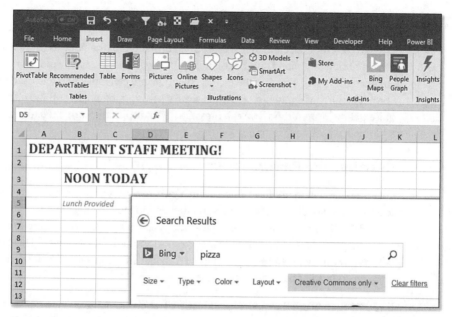

Figure 26.11   Enter a keyword to search.

4. Click the magnifying glass icon to search. In a few moments, a wide variety of choices are presented in a gallery.

5. Choose an image and click Insert. Excel pauses briefly while the image is downloaded and then inserts the image in the worksheet.

CAUTION

You can also search Bing Images. Initially, the results will show only images that Bing believes to be licensed under Creative Commons, which clearly is not a perfect system. In my first search, the first set of results included a trademarked Pizza Hut logo from some random website. Just because that site's webmaster stole the image and slapped a Creative Commons license on his website does not protect you if you use the image illegally. Therefore, use caution when distributing worksheets that contain images sourced from Bing (and even more so if you click the Show All Web Results button to broaden the Bing search to include copyrighted images). For free images, check out Unsplash.com.

TIP

Office 365 introduced a setting for Picture Transparency on the Picture Tools, Format tab. If you need to see the values in cells behind the picture, you easily can adjust the transparency.

Adjusting the Picture Using the Ribbon Tab

When a picture is selected, the Picture Tools Format tab of the ribbon is available. The choices on this ribbon tab offer a number of presets that will save you time in adjusting the picture. For example, a single click in the Picture Styles gallery can replace 16 micro-adjustments in the Format Picture task pane. To save time, always try using the presets on the ribbon. If you can't quite get the right setting, you can press Ctrl+1 to display the Format Picture task pane to reach additional adjustment settings.

Resizing the Picture to Fit

One problem you might have when using a picture on a worksheet is that the image may be too large. As digital cameras improve, it is becoming increasingly common for digital images to be 9, 10, 11, or more megapixels. These images are very large. For example, an image from a 3-megapixel camera occupies the area from A1 through Q41. You would have to zoom out before you can even see the whole photo. Your first step is usually to reduce the picture size so it fits on your cover page or report.

If you frequently use the mouse, your first inclination would be to drag the lower-right corner of the picture up and to the left to reduce the picture size. If the picture is too large for the window, you can zoom out to 1 percent%. Instead, use the spin buttons for Height and Width located in the Size group of the Picture Tools Format tab of the ribbon. Reduce the height or width, and the other setting reduces proportionally. Click and hold the "down" icon next to height until you can see the entire image in the Excel window.

When the entire picture is visible in the window, you can use the resize handle in any corner to change the picture size.

NOTE

When you use the mouse or the ribbon tools to resize a photo, Excel ensures that the picture stays proportional. If you want to change a landscape picture to portrait, you can either use the Crop tool or turn off the Lock Aspect Ratio setting. Figure 26.12 compares these methods. The original picture is too large. A proportional resize keeps everything from the original picture while changing the size. If you need the picture to be taller than wide, you can unlock the aspect ratio and change the width. This creates a funny-looking picture, such as trees that are skinny and too tall. A better choice might be using the Crop tool to remove unnecessary parts of the photograph.

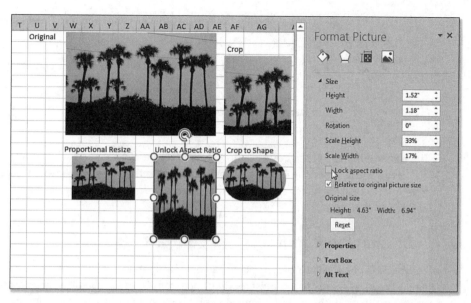

Figure 26.12   Resize proportionally or use the cropping tool to avoid distortion in the photograph.

To unlock the aspect ratio for a photograph, follow these steps:

1. Select the photograph by clicking it.

2. Press Ctrl+1 to display the Format Picture task pane.

3. Four icons appear at the top of the task pane. Click the third icon to display the Size, Properties, Text Box, and Alt Text categories.

4. Click the Size heading to open the size choices.

5. Uncheck the Lock Aspect Ratio check box. You can now stretch or compress the height or width alone.

Cropping a picture involves removing extraneous parts of the picture while in Crop mode. To crop a picture, follow these steps:

1. Select a picture.

2. Click the top half of the Crop icon in the Size group of the Picture Tools section of the Format tab. Eight crop handles appear on the edges and corners of the picture. Use the handles as follows:

    ■   To crop out one side of a picture, drag the center handle on that side inward toward the middle of the picture.

- To crop both sides equally, hold down Ctrl while you drag the center handle on either side inward.

- To crop equally on all four sides, hold down Ctrl while dragging one of the corner handles inward.

3. When the picture is cropped appropriately, click the Crop icon in the Picture Tools Format tab to exit Crop mode.

The rounded corners of the bottom-right photo in Figure 26.13 are achieved by cropping the photo to a shape. Open the Crop drop-down menu and choose Crop to Shape. You can choose from the 135 built-in shapes and then further change the shape using the yellow inflection handles on the shape.

Adjusting the Brightness and Contrast

You might capture a photograph in less than optimal lighting conditions. I went out one evening to capture photos of the latest rocket launch from Cape Canaveral when an osprey came flying by with his freshly caught dinner. The photograph was a cool action shot but was too dark because I did not have time to adjust the camera settings. Excel offers 201 choices each for Brightness, Contrast, and Sharpness. With 201 choices each, you have 8.1 million ways to adjust a photo, which is overwhelming.

Starting in Excel 2010, Microsoft began offering 25 thumbnails in the Corrections drop-down menu (see Figure 26.13). Select the picture, open the drop-down menu, and choose the thumbnail that gives the best light to the picture. You can also choose from the five thumbnails at the top to soften or sharpen the image. Most people will be able to tell which of these 25 thumbnails makes the picture look the best. If you are a professional photographer, you can access the Format Picture task pane to micromanage the settings.

For more adjustments, the Color drop-down menu offers Sepia, Black and White, and various other settings.

Figure 26.13 One of the presets rescued this photograph.

Adjusting Picture Transparency So Cell Values Show Through

Any inserted picture appears on top of the cells. If you want to see the cell values behind the picture, use the Transparency drop-down menu. This new feature debuted in Office 365 in September 2018. You can find it just to the right of the Artistic Effects drop-down menu.

Adding Interesting Effects Using the Picture Styles Gallery

For a quick way to make a picture look interesting, you can use one of the 28 presets in the Picture Styles gallery. These presets include various combinations of rotation, bevel, lighting, surface, shadow, frame, and shape. Here's how you use them:

1. Select a picture. The Picture Tools Format tab appears.

2. To the right of the Picture Styles icon, select the drop-down menu arrow.

3. Hover over the 28 built-in styles until you find one that is suitable.

4. To apply the style, click the style in the gallery.

Figure 26.14 shows the gallery and several varieties of built-in picture styles.

Figure 26.14 The Picture Styles gallery offers many quick alternatives for formatting pictures.

The 28 styles in the Picture Styles gallery were professionally chosen by graphic design experts. There is nothing in here that you could not do using the settings in the Format Picture task pane. However, choosing a style is much faster and requires less experimentation. To illustrate, two similar pictures appear in Figure 26.15. The top picture was formatted in two clicks using the Picture Styles gallery. The bottom picture was formatted by adjusting 16 different settings in the Format Picture task pane. The list of settings is shown in column L.

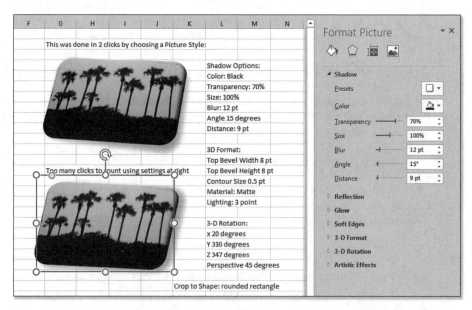

Figure 26.15 You can replicate the styles in the gallery by combining 16 different settings.

By using the Format Picture task pane, you could expand the 28 styles to millions of styles. However, it takes much longer to find the right combination of shadow, reflection, and so on when you opt to use the task pane instead of the Picture Styles gallery.

Applying Artistic Effects

Figure 26.16 shows the Artistic Effects fly-out menu. All these effects were new in Excel 2010. You can make your photo look like a pencil sketch, a mosaic, a photocopy, and more. Figure 26.16 shows some of the more interesting artistic effects.

The original photo is in the top left. Artistic effects make the photo look like an illustration.

Figure 26.16   These artistic effects were added in Excel 2019.

Removing the Background

Legacy versions of Excel offered a Set Transparent Color setting that would never work. However, Microsoft added impressive logic to Excel 2010 to help you remove the background from a picture. A few simple tweaks will make the tool even better. Follow these steps:

1.   Select the photo.

2.   Click the Remove Background icon. A new Background Removal tab appears in the ribbon. Excel also takes a first guess at which portions of the photo are background. You can improve this guess dramatically in step 3.

3. Excel draws a bounding box around the area it believes is the subject of the photograph. It often misses a corner of the subject; for example, a foot or an arm is outside of the box. When you resize the bounding box to exactly include 100 percent of the subject, Excel recalculates which portions of the photograph are background. Anything deemed to be background is shown in purple. I usually find that the first guess in step 2 is about 50 percent correct, and that the second guess after step 3 is about 95 percent correct.

4. If there are tiny areas of background to which Excel failed to apply purple shading, use the Areas To Remove icon and click those areas. If there are tiny areas of the subject that are erroneously shaded in purple, click the Mark Areas To Keep icon and click those areas (see Figure 26.17).

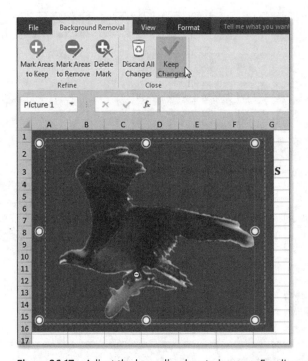

Figure 26.17   Adjust the bounding box to improve Excel's prediction of the background.

5. When the image looks correct, click Keep Changes. The grid now shows through the background of the photograph.

6. To edit cells behind the photograph, you cannot click on the cells. Click outside of the photograph and use the arrow keys to move underneath the photograph. You can then add text or titles (see Figure 26.18).

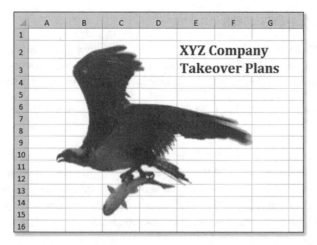

Figure 26.18   Use the arrow keys to reach cells behind the photograph.

Inside OUT

When you import pictures into a workbook, the file size of the workbook can increase dramatically.

If you plan to view the image onscreen only, you can reduce the size of the picture to reduce the size of the workbook. Here's how you do it:

1. Select the picture.

2. In the Picture Tools Format tab, select Compress Pictures from the Adjust group. Excel displays the Compress Pictures dialog box. Based on your choices here, Excel reduces the file size and removes the cropped areas of the photo.

To globally reduce the size of all images in a workbook, select File, Options, Advanced, and change the Default Resolution from 220 ppi to 96 ppi.

Inserting Screen Clippings

If you need to grab an image of a web page, a PDF file, or a PowerPoint slide, you can grab a screen capture of the entire window or a portion of the window. I use this feature frequently and find the technique for inserting a portion of a window is more useful most of the time.

1. In Excel, position the cell pointer at the point where you want to insert the screen clipping.

2. If you have two monitors, get the other application visible in the other monitor. If you have a single monitor, switch to the other application and then immediately back to Excel. The screen clipping tool is going to hide the current Excel window, revealing the previously active application. Thanks to the Single Document Interface, you can now use this trick to capture a picture of another Excel workbook.

3. Select Insert, Screenshot. You see a thumbnail of each open window. Skip all those big icons and go to the words Screen Clipping at the bottom of the menu (see Figure 26.19). The current Excel screen disappears, and the remaining window's screen stays visible but dims.

Figure 26.19 Choose Screen Clipping to copy a portion of another window.

4. Using the mouse, draw a rectangle around the portion of the application window that you want to capture. As you drag, that portion of the screen brightens.

5. Release the mouse. The original Excel window reappears, and a picture of the clipped screen is inserted in the workbook.

Selecting and Arranging Pictures

You will sometimes have two pictures that overlap. Excel maintains an order for the pictures. Typically, the picture inserted most recently is shown on top of earlier pictures. You can haphazardly resequence the pictures using the Send Backward or Send Forward command on the Picture Tools Format tab. Suppose that you've inserted 12 pictures. Picture 1 and Picture 12 are overlapping, and you want Picture 1 to be on top of Picture 12. You would have to choose Send Backward 11 times before they appear correctly. Next to Send Backward is a drop-down menu with a choice called Send to Back. This moves the selected picture to the back of the stack.

Even easier is the Selection pane. Use Home, Find & Select, Selection Pane to list all shapes and pictures in the sheet. You can drag a picture to a new location in the list, as shown in Figure 26.20. Pictures at the top of the list appear on top of pictures at the bottom of the list. You can also choose to hide a picture by clicking the Eye icon.

Figure 26.20   Picture 7 has been hidden, and Picture 3 is in the process of being moved within the stack.

TROUBLESHOOTING

Worksheets with an excessive number of images can slow down dramatically. Using the Hide All button allows you to quickly scroll through the workbook without the delays from rendering images.

I once received a call from someone who said his workbook had been getting progressively slower and was now running at a crawl even though it was just a simple worksheet containing 12 images.

However, I learned that the creator of the worksheet had been copying data from another workbook and pasting it into this worksheet each time he had to generate a new work order.

The person did not realize that he was pasting the same 12 images with each workorder. The images were nicely stacked right on top of each other. Although only 12 images were visible, there were more than 1,400 images in the worksheet.

If someone tried to scroll one row down the worksheet, Excel would re-draw the 1,400 images, which meant scrolling just a short distance could take more than a minute.

The fix was simple. Clicking Hide All made the worksheet responsive. Note that pressing Ctrl+6 will toggle the visibility of all objects.

If you need to select many pictures at once, choose Home, Find & Select, Select Objects. Draw a large rectangle around many objects, and they all will be selected.

The Align option enables you to make sure that several images line up. To make Picture 3 and Picture 2 line up with Picture 1, follow these steps:

1. Select Picture 3.

2. Ctrl+click Picture 2 and then Ctrl+click Picture 1.

3. Select Align, Align Left. The left edges of Picture 2 and Picture 3 move so they line up with the left edge of Picture 1.

CAUTION

After you use Select Objects, the mouse pointer remains a white arrow, and you will be unable to select cells. Press the Escape key to exit this mode.

If you select multiple images and group them together by using the Group drop-down menu, you can then move the images, and their location relative to each other remains the same.

Inserting Icons

Excel 2019 offers a series of royalty-free icons that can be added to your worksheet. To start, use the Icons button on the Insert tab of the ribbon. Provided you are connected to the Internet, a series of icons in 26 categories will appear in the Insert Icons dialog box, as shown in Figure 26.21.

Figure 26.21 More than 200 royalty-free icons are available.

To insert an icon, select the icon and then press Insert.

Once inserted into your worksheet, you can use the Graphic Tools Format tab of the ribbon to change the color, outline, and bevel. Handles on the icon allow you to change the size and rotations. Figure 26.22 shows some of the effects.

Figure 26.22   After inserting an icon, change the size, rotation, color, and outline.

Examining 3D Models

There are a large number of 3D Models available on the Internet. Excel 2019 can import files saved with any of these extensions: *.fbx, .obj, .3mf, .ply, .stl, and .glb. A large number of 3D Model files are available from NASA. Point your favorite search engine at NASA 3D Models to find them.

Select, Insert, 3D Models, From File, and select a model. Initially, the model appears in the worksheet as shown in Figure 26.23.

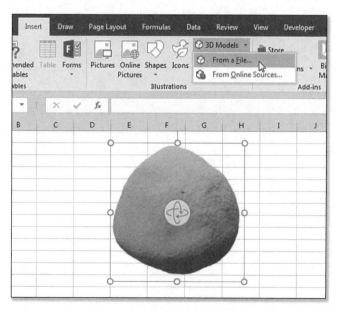

Figure 26.23   The icon in the middle of this asteroid means that you can rotate it in several dimensions.

With the object selected, click the 3D Rotation icon and drag it in any direction.

- Dragging right and left will rotate sideways.

- Dragging up and down will rotate vertically.

- Dragging diagonally will rotate diagonally.

- If you drag far enough, the object will rotate so you can see the back side of the object.

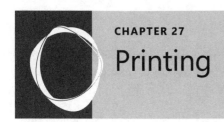

You've finished your workbook model and now it is time to print. In reality, you are most likely going to email the workbook or export it to a PDF. But there are still some workbooks that you will print on real paper. This chapter gives you some tips to making that printout look great.

Printing in One Click

If you're a keyboard enthusiast, you might be upset that in Excel 2019, Ctrl+P takes you to the Print panel instead of performing a quick print. In a few steps, you can bring Quick Print back to Excel 2019.

The Quick Access Toolbar (QAT) is the row of small icons that appears just above or just below the ribbon. At the right edge of this toolbar is a drop-down menu menu. Open the drop-down menu at the right edge of the Quick Access Toolbar to display a short list of popular commands. Choose Quick Print, as shown in Figure 27.1.

Figure 27.1 Add Quick Print to the Quick Access Toolbar.

When you click the Quick Print icon, one copy of the current worksheet is sent to the last printer you used in Excel. If you have not previously printed in this Excel session, the worksheet is sent to the default printer.

Although this brings the Quick Print back as a mouse click, it still isn't great for keyboard-centric people. If you press and release the Alt key in Excel, you see a row of shortcuts for the first nine items in the Quick Access Toolbar. Because Quick Print is the eighth icon in Figure 27.1, Alt+8 does a Quick Print.

Finding Print Settings

There are at least nine places in Excel where you can change the print settings or page setup. The most common tasks are found in multiple places. For example, you can change margins in five of the nine places. You can change paper size and orientation in four of the nine places.

As you move down to the obscure settings, you might be able to find them in only one or two places. Figure 27.2 shows a cross-reference. For any given task, you can locate where you might be able to change the setting.

Nine places are listed across the top of Figure 27.2. Here is where to find each place:

- **File, Print**—Open the File menu and choose Print to display the Print panel. This panel has a mix of Printer and Page Setup settings in the center and a large Print Preview on the right. Introduced in Excel 2010, it aims to be a one-stop place for getting your printout to look right.

- **Page Layout Tab of the Ribbon**—Click the Page Layout tab in the ribbon. You find three groups related to printing: Page Setup, Scale to Fit, and Sheet Options.

- **Page Setup Dialog**—Click the diagonal arrow icon in the lower-right corner of the three groups in the Page Layout ribbon tab to launch the legacy Page Setup dialog box. This dialog box contains four tabs. The superscript next to each bullet in Figure 27.2 identifies the tab: 1 for Page, 2 for Margins, 3 for Header/Footer, 4 for Sheet. You can also reach this dialog box by clicking the Print Titles icon in the Page Layout tab of the ribbon.

- **Page Layout View**—Choose Page Layout on the View tab. This icon also appears in the lower right of the Excel screen.

Task	File, Print	Page Layout Tab	Page Setup Dialog	Page Layout View	Header & Footer Tab	Page Break Preview View	Printer Properties Dialog	Excel Options	Print Preview Full Screen
Get the Report to Fit On the Page									
Set the Paper Size	•	•	•[1]					•	
Select Portrait or Landscape Orientation	•	•	•[1]					•	
Adjust the Margins on the Printed Page	•	•	•[2]	•					•
Repeat titles and headings on each printed page			•[4]						
Add a page number and other header/footer items			•[3]	•	•				
Exclude part of your worksheet from the print range		•	•[4]						
Add manual page breaks to the document		•				•			
Display page breaks	•							•	•
Hide page breaks								•	
Force more data to fit on a page	•	•	•[1]			•			
Preview the printed page	•			•	•	•			•
Print the Report									
Choose which printer to use	•								
Control settings specific to that printer	•		•[2]				•		
Print multiple worksheets at once	•								
Other Print Settings									
Center the report on the page			•[2]						
Collate multiple printed sets	•						•		
Control the first page number			•[1]						
Print the Excel gridlines		•	•[4]						
Print the A, B, C column headings and row numbers		•	•[4]						
Print comments			•[4]						
Replace error values when printing			•[4]						
Print on both sides of the page	•						•		
Control the order in which pages print			•[4]						
Adjust the print quality			•[1]						
Force the printout to greyscale			•[4]					•	
Print in draft quality			•[4]					•	

Figure 27.2   Various printing tasks are spread throughout the Excel interface. The superscript in the Page Setup Dialog column refers to the tab within the dialog box.

- **Header & Footer Tools Design Tab**—When you are in Page Layout view, click one of the three header or three footer zones on any page to have the Header & Footer tools Design tab appear in the ribbon. Note that you have to click away from the header or footer zone to exit Page Layout view. Although this tab is the most hidden, it offers an easier way to control headers and footers (see Figure 27.3).

CHAPTER 27

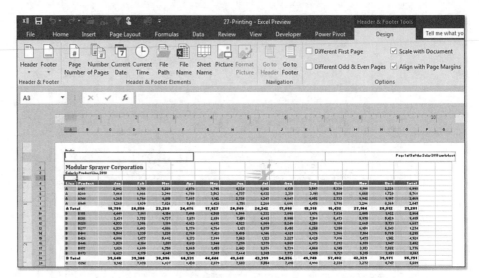

Figure 27.3   After you click into a header in Page Layout view, you can access the Header & Footer Tools tab in the ribbon.

- **Page Break Preview View**—Click Page Break Preview on the View tab. This icon also appears at the bottom right of the Excel window.

- **Printer Properties Dialog**—Use Ctrl+P to display the Print panel. A Printer Properties link appears just below the printer name.

- **Excel Options**—Open the File menu and then choose Options, Advanced. This is the only place to turn off the display of automatic page breaks after you've done a Print Preview.

- **Print Preview Full Screen**—Add this icon to the Quick Access Toolbar to reach a full-screen version of Print Preview similar to older versions of Excel.

The rest of this chapter covers most of the tasks along the left side of Figure 27.2.

Previewing the Printed Report

Before you start adjusting the page settings, you can take a quick look at how the worksheet currently will print.

Using the Print Preview on the Print Panel

One method to view the printed document is to use File, Print or Ctrl+P. For now, ignore the settings in the middle panel and look at the Print Preview pane on the right.

If your document is larger than one page, you have a vertical scrollbar to the right of the Print Preview. Use this scrollbar to move to other pages.

Four icons are available at the bottom of the Print Preview window (see Figure 27.4):

- To navigate to a new page, use the left-arrow or right-arrow icon in the lower left. You can also type a new page number in the page number text box and press Enter or Tab. The PgDn and PgUp keys still work, but only when you click the preview first.

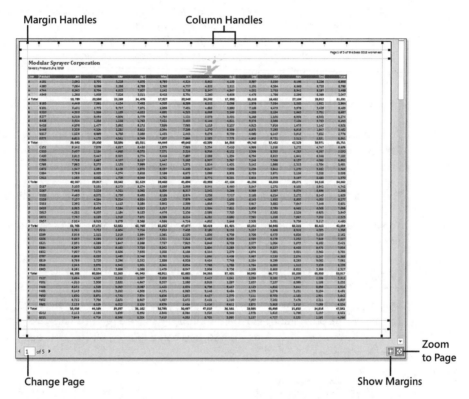

Figure 27.4   Print Preview controls.

- The Zoom check box feels like it is reversed. If you clear this check box, Excel zooms in to a smaller section of your printout.

- Select the Show Margins check box to have Excel draw draggable margins in the page. Drag any of the margin lines to change the page margins. Drag any of the column handles to resize columns.

When you first look at the print preview, check for these obvious problems:

- Does one column or a few rows spill over to a second page when you want everything to fit on one page? See "Repeating the Headings on Each Page," later in this chapter.

- On a multipage report, go to page 2 of the document. Are the titles and headings appearing on pages after the first page? If not, see "Repeating the Headings On Each Page," later in this chapter.

- Are page numbers appearing where you want them? If not, see the "Adding Headers or Footers to the Printed Report" section, later in this chapter.

To close the File menu and return to your document, click the large left-pointing arrow in the top-left corner of the File menu.

Using Full-Screen Print Preview

Some people develop macros in Excel where they want someone to preview a report in Print Preview. The new Print Preview on the Print panel doesn't work with these macros, so the Excel team added a command that gets you to a full-screen Print Preview.

The full-screen Print Preview works particularly well with wide reports in a landscape orientation.

You must add the Print Preview Full Screen to your ribbon or Quick Access Toolbar. For instructions, see Chapter 3, "Customizing Excel."

Making the Report Fit on the Page

Before you print, you want to make sure your data is going to fit on the page. You can control the paper size, orientation, and margins. You can make a few heading rows print at the top of each page. You can add information such as page number, file location, date, and time in the header or footer.

TROUBLESHOOTING

Page numbers always start at 1 each time you print. This can be frustrating if you want to number a worksheet named "Sheet1" as pages 1 to 5 and a worksheet named "Sheet2" as pages 6 to 8.

The workaround is to print both worksheets in a single print command. Follow these steps:

1. Start with the first sheet selected.

2. Ctrl+click on each additional worksheet tab to be included. This puts those worksheets in group mode. Be careful not to edit any cells on the visible worksheet because similar changes will happen on all the worksheets.

3. Select File, Print. In the first drop-down menu below the Settings heading, choose Print Active Sheets. The sheets will print and use consecutive page numbers.

4. Right-click any of the selected sheets and choose Ungroup Sheets.

Setting Worksheet Paper Size

You can choose from a variety of paper size options in the Size drop-down menu in the Page Layout tab, as shown in Figure 27.5. When you encounter a report that is too wide for a regular sheet of paper, you can switch to a larger page size, such as Legal paper. You can choose one paper size or select More Paper Sizes from the bottom of the list to specify a new size.

TIP

Some paper sizes, such as 11"×17", are available only if your selected printer offers that size. If your default printer cannot print large-format paper, you should change the printer selection in the Print panel and then return to the Page Setup dialog box to select the larger-format paper.

Figure 27.5   Choose a paper size.

Adjusting Worksheet Orientation

Changing a report to print sideways, which is also referred to as *landscape*, takes just a couple of mouse clicks. From the Page Layout tab, select Page Setup to see the Orientation drop-down menu, which offers Portrait and Landscape options.

Adjusting Worksheet Margins

When you are trying to squeeze an extra column into a report, you can tweak the report to have smaller margins. Figure 27.2 shows that there are five different places you can adjust the margins for your worksheet. Here are my favorite three methods:

- **Choose Page Layout, Margins**—This drop-down menu offers three settings: Normal, Wide, and Narrow. If you have previously used custom margins, another setting appears with the last custom margins you used. To apply one of these standard setups, choose the setup you want to use from the Margins drop-down menu. To apply a different custom margin, select Custom Margins from the bottom of this menu. Selecting Custom Margins takes you to the Page Setup dialog box, discussed next.

- **Use the Page Setup dialog box**—When you click the dialog box launcher icon in the bottom right of the Page Setup group, Excel displays the Page Setup dialog box. Use the Margins tab to adjust the margins at the top, left, right, and bottom, as well as the margins for the footer and header. This dialog box offers precise control of the six margin settings.

- **Choose View, Page Layout View**—When you use this option, gray margins appear on each edge of the ruler. You can drag the gray margins in or out to decrease/increase the margin.

Either version of the Print Preview window has a Show Margins setting. After you've displayed the margins in Print Preview, you can move the margins in or out.

Repeating the Headings on Each Page

For reports that span more than one page, you might want the headings from the report to print at the top of each page. Although the Print Titles icon was promoted to a large icon on the Page Layout tab in the ribbon, this command leads back to the somewhat confusing Page Setup dialog box, as shown in Figure 27.6. Suppose that you have a report that is two pages wide and several pages long. However, you notice that the printed page 2 of the printed report does not include title or column headings. If you want to have the titles and column headings repeat at the top of each row, you need to select 1:4 in the Rows to Repeat at Top option and A:B in the Columns to Repeat at Left option. When you return to the Page Setup dialog box later, Excel will have added dollar signs to these settings. You don't need to type the dollar signs; Excel will add them.

NOTE

To specify rows to repeat at the top, you can indicate either a single row using 1:1 or a range of rows using 1:4. Similarly, columns to repeat at left might be a single column (A:A) or a range of columns (A:B).

Figure 27.6 Use the Page Setup dialog box to specify print titles to repeat on each page.

Excluding Part of Your Worksheet from the Print Range

By default, Excel prints all the nonblank cells on a worksheet. Sometimes, you have a nicely formatted table of data to print, but the spreadsheet also includes some work cells in an out-of-the-way location that you do not want to print. To prevent the work cells from being printed, follow these steps:

1. Select the range of cells to be included in the print range, such as cells A1:Z99. Alternatively, you can print everything in certain columns. For example, you might select columns C:X to be printed.

2. From the Page Layout tab, select Page Setup, Print Area, Set Print Area.

To clear the print area and to print everything on the worksheet, you can use the Clear Print Area option from the Set Print Area drop-down menu.

Occasionally, you will want to ignore the print areas and print everything on the worksheet. As described in the "Choosing What to Print" section later in this chapter, you can use the Ignore Print Areas setting to temporarily override the print area. Alternatively, you can print a certain range by selecting the range and then using Selection in the Print panel.

Forcing More Data to Fit on a Page

You will often have worksheets in Excel that are a few columns too wide or a few rows too long to fit on a page.

The Scale to Fit group on the Page Layout tab provides options for width, height, and a percentage scale. In most cases, you change the height, width, or both to achieve the desired effect.

If your worksheet is a few columns too wide, change the Width drop-down menu to specify that the worksheet should fit on one page. If you have a report that is too tall, change the Height drop-down menu to specify that the worksheet should be one page tall. When you select either of these options, the Scale option is grayed out, but it still shows the scaling percentage used to make the report fit.

Sometimes, a report cannot fit into one page and still be readable. This is when you can make intelligent decisions about the best location for page breaks.

Working with Page Breaks

The two varieties of page breaks are automatic and manual. An *automatic page break* occurs when Excel reaches the bottom or right margin of a physical page. These page breaks change automatically as you adjust margins, add rows, delete rows, or even change the height of certain rows on the page.

Initially, automatic page breaks are not shown in the worksheet. However, after you go to Print Preview and return to Normal view, automatic page breaks are shown using a thin dashed line in the document. Automatic page breaks are also evident in Page Layout view and Page Break Preview mode. To turn off the page breaks, use File, Options, Advanced, Display Options for This Worksheet to find a check box for Show Page Breaks.

You can manually insert page breaks at rows or columns where you want to start a new page. For example, you might want to insert a manual page break at the start of a new section in a report. A manual page break does not automatically change in response to changes in the worksheet rows.

Manually Adding Page Breaks

To add a page break manually at a certain row, follow these steps:

1. Select an entire row by clicking the row number that should be the first row on the new page. Alternatively, select the cell in column A in that row.

2. From the Page Layout tab, select Page Setup, Breaks, Insert Page Break.

To add a page break manually at a certain column, follow these steps:

1. Select an entire column by clicking the letter above the column that should be the first column on the new page. Alternatively, select row 1 in that column.

2. From the Page Layout tab, select Page Setup, Breaks, Insert Page Break.

CAUTION

If you insert a page break while the cell pointer is outside row 1 or column A, Excel simultaneously inserts a row page break and a column page break. This is rarely what you want. Make sure to select a cell in column A to insert a row break or to select a cell in row 1 to insert a column break.

Manual Versus Automatic Page Breaks

In Normal view, a subtle visual difference exists between manual and automatic page breaks. The dashed line used to indicate a manual page break is more pronounced than the line used to indicate an automatic page break.

To see a better view of page breaks, you can select View, Page Break Preview to switch to Page Break Preview mode. In this mode, automatic page breaks are shown as dotted blue lines. Manual page breaks are shown as solid lines.

Using Page Break Preview to Make Changes

An advantage of Page Break Preview mode is that while you are in this mode, you can move a page break by dragging the line associated with the page break. If you drag an automatic page break to expand the number of rows or columns on a page, Excel automatically changes the Scale percentage for all pages.

Removing Manual Page Breaks

To remove a manual page break for a row, follow these steps:

1. Position the cursor in the row below the page break.

2. From the Page Layout tab, select Page Setup, Breaks, Remove Page Break.

3. To remove a manual page break for a column, follow these steps:

4. Position the cursor in the column to the right of the page break.

5. From the Page Layout tab, select Page Setup, Breaks, Remove Page Break.

To remove all manual page breaks, from the Page Layout tab, select Page Setup, Breaks, Reset All Page Breaks. Note that clearing the page breaks also resets the scaling back to 100%.

Adding Headers or Footers to the Printed Report

Although you might describe the row of labels that appear at the top of the report as "headings," in this section "headers" are elements that are not in the cells of the worksheet but print at the top of the page. Excel offers three header areas: left, center, and right. Similarly, there are three footer areas.

You can build headers and footers using the third tab of the legacy Page Setup dialog box, but Excel now offers a graphical method for building your headers.

The only entry point for the new Header & Footer Tools Design tab of the ribbon is in Page Layout view. From the View tab, select Page Layout View. Excel displays the worksheet with white space for margins.

At the top of each page, you see gray Click to Add Header text. Hover the mouse in this area, and you see that there are three header zones. Click in the Left, Center, or Right header to display the Header & Footer Tools Design tab in the ribbon.

You can either type a static header in the box or use the icons on the ribbon tab to add text that will change at print time. For example, if you insert the code for Date or Time, the printed header reflects the date or time that the report was printed. You can use the formatting tools on the Home tab to format the text in the header.

To exit Header/Footer mode, click in any cell of the worksheet.

Adding an Automatic Header

For a quick header or footer, you can click the Header or Footer drop-down menu in the Header & Footer Tools Design tab. The drop-down menu offers 16 different automatic headers, including various page-numbering styles, the system date, your name, your company name, the sheet name, and the file path and filename.

Some of the Header entries include values separated by commas. These entries put header values into the left, center, and right header sections.

> TIP
>
> **Although you cannot add to the automatic Header list, you can select an automatic header that is close to what you want and then customize it.**

NOTE

The process for adding footers is to the same as the process for adding headers. Throughout the rest of this chapter, several sections include additional information about headers. Keep in mind that the identical instructions apply to footers as well.

Adding a Custom Header

You can type any text you want into the three header areas. One of the automatic headers reads Confidential, but you can customize this in any way dictated by your company. No matter what type of header you need, you can add it by clicking in any header area and then typing the desired text. To start a new line, press Enter.

Icons for dynamic fields are located in the Header & Footer Tools Design tab. To add an element, click in a header or footer area, position the cursor in the proper place, and click the appropriate icon in the ribbon. As long as the insertion cursor is in the header area, the screen displays the code for that field, such as &[Date] or &[Time].

TIP

To include an ampersand in the header or footer, you must use the code &&. For example, to add the header Profit & Loss, type `Profit && Loss`.

You can mix static text and dynamic text. For example, you could type **Page**, and then click the Page Number icon. Type **of** and then click the Number of Pages icon. Type **of the**, and then click the Sheet Name icon. Type **Worksheet**. The resulting text shows Page &[Page] of &[Pages]

of the &[Tab] Worksheet. When you print, the actual text might be Page 3 of 5 of the Sales 2018 Worksheet.

Inserting a Picture or a Watermark in a Header

You can add a picture to a header or footer. It can be either a small picture that prints in the header area or a large picture that extends below the header area and acts as a watermark behind the worksheet.

To add a picture to a header, follow these steps:

1. Select View, Page Layout View.

2. Click in the header area of the document.

3. From the Header & Footer Tools Design tab, select Header & Footer Elements, Picture. Excel displays the Insert Online Picture dialog box.

4. Select the picture to include in the header. Select a picture and click Insert. Excel adds the text &[Picture] to the header. You cannot tell how large the picture will print at this point.

5. Click in the spreadsheet to see the size of the picture.

6. If you discover that the picture is too large, click in the header area.

7. From the Header & Footer Tools Design tab, select Header & Footer Elements, Format Picture. The Format Picture dialog box appears.

TIP

Keep in mind that you won't see how large the picture will be until you click outside the header.

8. In the Format Picture dialog box, use the Size section to reduce the scale of the picture.

9. If you want your picture to appear as a watermark behind the spreadsheet, you need to lighten the picture. To do so, click the Picture tab of the Format Picture dialog box. Change the Color drop-down menu to Washout.

10. None of the picture items in the header features Live Preview. To preview your picture, close the dialog box and then click outside the header. If the picture is not the way you want it, repeat steps 6 through 9 as necessary.

NOTE

If you use the spin button to change the height in the Scale section, the width is automatically changed as well, to keep the scale proportional.

Using Different Headers and Footers in the Same Document

Excel 2019 allows the following four header and footer scenarios:

- The same header/footer on all pages

- One header/footer on page 1 and a different header/footer on all other pages

- One header/footer on all odd pages and a different header/footer on all even pages

- One header/footer on page 1, a second header/footer on even pages, and a third header/footer on all odd pages from 3 and up

Excel manages these scenarios by storing three headers for each worksheet. The first header is variously called the odd page header or just the header. As you select and clear the options' check boxes, the contents of each header remain constant, even though they might be used on different pages. Table 27.1 shows the details of each header option.

Table 27.1 Header Options

Different First Page	Different Odd and Even Pages	Odd Page Header	Even Page Header	First Page Header
Cleared	Cleared	Called the header and used on all pages	Not used	Not used
Cleared	Selected	Called the odd page header and used for pages 1, 3, 5, and so on	Called the even page header and used for pages 2, 4, 6, and so on	Not used
Selected	Cleared	Called the header and used for pages 2, 3, 4, and so on	Not used	Called the first page header and used for page 1
Selected	Selected	Called the odd page header and used for pages 3, 5, 7, and so on	Called the even page header and used for pages 2, 4, 6, and so on	Called the first page header and used for page 1

If you add a header in Page Layout view, it is known as the odd page header. In the default configuration, Excel displays the odd page header on all pages of the printout.

Excel has two other sets of headers that are initially hidden. One set is called the First Page Header. The other set is called the Different First Page, which you can select from the Options group on the Header & Footer Tools Design tab. When this option is used, Excel displays the first page header above page 1 and uses the odd page header everywhere else.

CHAPTER 27

TIP

To minimize confusion, it is best to select the Options section check boxes **Different First Page** and **Different Odd & Even** before entering headers.

Scaling Headers and Footers

Settings in the Page Layout tab allow you to force a worksheet to fit a certain number of pages. If the scaling options require a 75 percent scale on Sheet1 and a 95 percent scale on Sheet2, your headings are scaled as well. This causes your page numbers to appear at a different point size in various sections of the report.

Excel offers an option to force all headers and footers to print at 100 percent scale, regardless of the zoom for the sheet. To select this option, from the Header & Footer Tools Design tab, select Options and clear the Scale with Document check box.

Printing from the File Menu

To access the Print panel, you can either select File, Print or press Ctrl+P. The panel merges settings from the Print and Page Setup dialog boxes in the middle of the screen and the Print Preview on the right side of the screen. As you update settings in the middle of the screen, the Print Preview updates, which enables you always to see the current preview (see Figure 27.7).

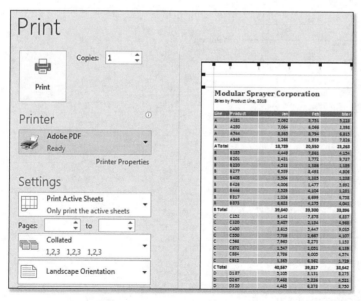

Figure 27.7   Print Preview and Print Settings are combined in a single screen.

The left side of the screen starts with a very large Print button. Click this button to print the document. The spin button next to the Print button enables you to control the number of copies to print.

The rest of the left panel contains a new kind of gallery. You can see the current choice of the gallery without opening the gallery. If the correct printer is already selected, there is no need to open the drop-down menu.

Choosing a Printer

When you open the Printer drop-down menu, Excel displays all the current printers and indicates if the printer is currently online and/or available. This handy improvement enables you to detect if the department printer is in a Paper Jam condition so you can print to a different printer.

Choosing What to Print

As shown in Figure 27.8, the Print What gallery offers Active Sheets, Entire Workbook, and Selection settings. You can further modify these settings by choosing Ignore Print Area.

Figure 27.8 Choosing what to print.

If you choose the Active Sheets option, the currently selected sheet prints. If you have specified a print area, only that range prints; otherwise, Excel prints the entire used range of the document. However, if you select multiple sheets in Group mode, all the selected sheets print.

If you choose the Entire Workbook option, all the nonhidden worksheets in the workbook print. One advantage to this option is that the pages are numbered consecutively as the printout moves from Sheet1 to Sheet2.

Choosing the Selection option enables you to override the print area temporarily. However, if you need to print one small range of a large report, select that range and then choose the Selection option in the Print What gallery. This prevents you from having to change the Print Area twice.

The Ignore Print Area option causes Excel to ignore any print areas specified previously. This causes the entire used area of the worksheet to be printed.

You can select specific pages to print using the Pages spin buttons. To print a single page, enter that page number in both the Pages and To boxes.

Changing Printer Properties

After you choose a printer, the remaining galleries on the left side of the Print panel are redrawn. If you are printing to an office printer that supports collating and stapling, use the galleries to select each of these options. If you are printing to a home printer that does not have these options, Excel does not show those galleries.

> ### TIP
> If a specific property does not appear, you can click the Printer Properties hyperlink at the bottom of the left panel to access the vendor-supplied Printer Property dialog box.

Changing Some of the Page Setup Settings

Even though it might seem like they are out of place, the last settings on the left side of the Print panel are used to control portrait versus landscape, paper size, and margins. If you change a setting here, it will also change in the Page Setup dialog box.

If your initial reaction is to wonder why these settings are repeated here, you might also wonder why your favorite Page Setup settings are not also repeated. Even though it is nice to switch from portrait to landscape here, it would also be nice to be able to change the Page Scaling or Rows to Repeat at Top settings here. However, this cannot be done because those settings require you to close the Print panel and to use the Page Layout tab of the ribbon.

Using Page Layout View

When you open Excel, the default view is called Normal view. In legacy versions of Excel, your only choices were Normal view and Page Break Preview mode. However, beginning with Excel 2007, Microsoft added the Page Layout view, which works well when you are preparing a document for printing.

In Excel 2019, the three views are available either in the View tab or on the right side of the status bar.

In Page Layout view, you have a fully functioning worksheet. For example, the formula bar works, and you can scroll around the worksheet. However, listed next are the differences between Page Layout and Normal view:

- White space appears to show the margins on each page. This is usually an advantage because you have a clear view of any page breaks between columns or rows. If you want to hide the white space, you can click the white space and choose Hide White Space.

- A ruler appears below the formula bar that you can use to change margins by dragging the gray areas of the ruler.

- Areas are marked Click to Add Header and Click to Add Footer. Whereas headers and footers are buried in legacy versions of Excel, in the Page Layout view of Excel 2019, it is obvious that headers and footers are available.

- Areas outside the data area of a worksheet are marked with Click to Add Data. One of the problems with Page Break Preview mode is that areas outside the data area were grayed out. However, the Click to Add Data labels option invites you to continue adding pages to your worksheet.

- The only disadvantage to Page Layout view is that Excel turns off your Freeze Panes settings in Page Layout view. Excel warns you that this is happening. Excel does this to emphasize that Print Titles are different from Freeze Panes.

TIP
Keep in mind that Excel does not restore the Freeze Panes settings when you return to Normal view.

Exploring Other Page Setup Options

Other page setup options are scattered throughout the various interface areas. Although some of these are fairly obscure, you might need to use them in certain situations.

Printing Gridlines and Headings

To print the gridlines on a worksheet, from the Page Layout tab, select Sheet Options, Gridlines, Print.

You can also print the A-B-C column headings and 1-2-3 row headings. To do this, from the Page Layout tab, select Sheet Options, Headings, Print. This option is helpful when you are printing formulas using the FORMULATEXT function, and you need to see the cell address of each cell.

Centering a Small Report on a Page

Small reports can look out of place printed in the upper-left corner of a page. Rather than increasing margins, you can choose to center the report horizontally or vertically on a page.

Select Page Layout, Margins, Custom Margins to display the Page Setup dialog box. Two check boxes at the bottom of the dialog box center the report on the page.

Replacing Error Values When Printing

Excel calculations sometimes result in various errors such as #N/A! or DIV/0. Although these error values help you determine how to fix the errors, they look out of place on a printed page. You can choose to replace any error cells with a blank or two hyphens.

Choose View, Print Titles to open the Sheet tab of the Page Setup dialog box. Open the Cell Errors As drop-down menu and choose <blank> or --.

Printing Comments

Cell comments often appear as a tiny red triangle in a cell. You can print a table of all the comments at the bottom of your report. Use the Comments drop-down menu in the Sheet tab of the Page Setup dialog box and choose At End of Sheet.

Excel prints your report and then starts a new page listing each comment. The new page shows the cell and the comment content.

The other option for printing comments is to print any visible comments where they are currently displayed. To show all comments, choose Review, Show All Comments. When comments are displayed, you can drag them to a new location, so they are not covering up important cells.

Controlling the First Page Number

You might be inserting a printed Excel worksheet in the middle of a printed Word document. If the Excel worksheet is appearing as the tenth page in the Word report, for example, you would want the Excel page numbers to start at 10 instead of 1.

From the Page Layout tab, choose the dialog box launcher at the bottom right of the Page Setup group. Excel displays the Page tab of the Page Setup dialog box. The last setting is First Page Number and is initially set to Auto. Type **10** in this box, and Excel prints the Excel worksheet using page numbers 10, 11, 12, and so on.

Inside OUT

Exporting a worksheet as a PDF is really like printing.

You can create a PDF from any workbook in Excel 2019. Think of creating a PDF as if you are "printing" to a special printer that makes PDF files. Thus, it is important that you set the print ranges before you begin. If you want multiple worksheets in your PDF, select those worksheets in Group mode before creating the PDF. (For example, select Sheet1 and then Ctrl+click the tabs for Sheet3 and Sheet7 to put those three sheets in Group mode.)

To save a worksheet as a PDF file, select File, Export, Create PDF/XPS. You have the option to save the file in a high-resolution format suitable for printing or a low-resolution format that is suitable for viewing onscreen.

If you frequently work with PDF files, you might have noticed that some PDFs contain data that can be selected, copied, and pasted to Excel. Other PDFs contain strange formatting that causes the content pasted back to Excel to render horribly. You would think that a PDF file created by the Excel team would have the capability to paste back into Excel, but this is not the case. Try opening the PDF in Word and then copying the data from Word to Excel.

Power BI Desktop is a new application that lets you share interactive dashboards based on your Excel data. Authoring of dashboards is quick; you are basically building pivot charts by dragging fields to a PivotTable Fields list.

Charts are automatically interactive; if you select something in one chart, all the other charts will filter to the selected item. You can create hierarchies to allow people to drill down into the data.

With a monthly subscription, you can publish your dashboards to the Power BI servers. You can invite others in your company to consume your reports on their computers or mobile devices.

Getting Started with Power BI Desktop

Getting started with Power BI Desktop is free. You will need a work email account. Hotmail or Gmail will not qualify. Start at PowerBI.Microsoft.com, and sign up and download Power BI Desktop for free.

When you first open Power BI, you will sign in with the account credentials that you created. You are then presented with a start screen with a number of tutorials, as shown in Figure 28.1.

Figure 28.1 Power BI Desktop is the authoring tool for Power BI.

Preparing Data in Excel

Before you can use Power BI, you need to prepare the data you want to use in it. To do this, build an Excel workbook with each of your data sets formatted as a table. Using the sample files for this book, you would perform the following steps to create a data model in PowerBIData.xlsx:

1. Select each of the three data sets and format as a table using Ctrl+T.

2. Name the tables Sales, Geography, and Calendar.

CAUTION

It is tempting to do a lot of pre-work in Excel, such as defining relationships, marking data categories, creating synonyms, and defining hierarchies. However, it is best to do this work in Power BI Desktop because all of these settings are lost when you select Home, Get Data, From Excel. If you choose File, Import, Excel Workbook Contents, more of your Excel work will get imported, but the hierarchies will still be lost.

TIP

If you do already have queries and relationships defined in your Excel file, you should choose File, Import, Excel Workbook Contents as described below instead of choosing Get Data, Excel.

Importing Data to Power BI

The most obvious way to get Excel data into Power BI is not the best. If you choose Home, Get Data, from Excel, you can import the data, but any queries, relationships, KPIs, and Synonyms will be lost.

First, Power BI Desktop has an icon where the File menu should be. It is good to see the Power BI team learned nothing from the mistakes in Office 2007. Click on the File icon to the left of the Home tab. Choose Import, Excel Workbook Contents. Browse to and select your Excel workbook.

An oddly old message appears that reads, "We don't work directly with Excel workbooks, but we know how to extract the useful content from them." Click Start.

At the end of the importing process, a message will show you the migration is complete and report what has been imported (see Figure 28.2).

Figure 28.2   Power BI can import queries and tables from Excel.

TROUBLESHOOTING

There are multiple ways to get Excel data into Power BI Desktop, and the most obvious way is not always best.

A large Get Data icon appears on the Home tab. If you open the drop-down menu associated with this icon and choose Excel, Power BI will import only the data from the Excel file, ignoring the data model and any Power Query queries.

If you choose File, Import, Excel Workbook Contents, then Power BI will import the Data Model, Power Query definitions, Data Model calculated columns, measures, KPIs, Data Categories, and Relationships.

Again, keep in mind that the File menu is to the left of the Home tab and does not read, "File." Instead, the File menu appears with an icon that looks like a piece of notebook paper.

NOTE

Power BI Desktop offers a full version of Power Query. Use the Home, Edit button to launch Power Query.

Getting Oriented to Power BI

Welcome to a new, unfamiliar world. Power BI opens with a vast expanse of white nothing covering the middle 80 percent of your screen. A common reaction is: "What do I do now?"

Let's take a look at various elements in the Power BI screen.

In the top right are two panels called Visualizations and Fields (see Figure 28.3).

The Fields panel is essentially like the top part of the PivotTable Field list. If you import the workbook associated with this chapter, you start out seeing table names Calendar1, Geography, and Sales; you can use the triangle icon to expand any table and see the fields in that table.

NOTE

Note that Power BI automatically renames an Excel table named "Calendar" as "Calendar1" because there is already a DAX **function named** CALENDAR.

The Visualizations panel starts with about 30 built-in data visualizations. You can add more visualizations using the icon with three dots. Below the panel of visualizations is the Values area. This is like the bottom half of the PivotTable Fields list. You will drag fields here to create a visualization. The Paint Roller icon leads to various formatting choices that are available for a visualization.

Figure 28.3   Create new visualizations using these tools in the top right.

In the lower left of the Power BI Desktop screen is a tab labeled Page 1 and a plus sign, which allows you to add more pages (see Figure 28.4). These are like worksheet tabs in Excel; you can build a report with multiple pages of dashboards.

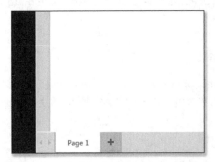

Figure 28.4   Add more pages in the lower left.

In the top left of the screen, there are three icons labeled Report, Data, and Relationships (see Figure 28.5).

- The Report view is where you will build your dashboard.

- The Data view shows you the data loaded in Power BI and is very similar to the Manage Data Model screen in Power Pivot.

- The Relationships view is similar to the Diagram view in Power Pivot.

Figure 28.5   Where is your data? Click the second icon along the left.

Preparing Data in Power BI

To create effective reports in Power BI, you want to create some relationships and further customize your data.

Click on the Relationships icon. (See the bottom icon in Figure 28.6.)

In the Relationships view, you will see that Power BI Desktop automatically detected a relationship between the Sales table and the Geography table. Hover over the line between the tables and Power BI Desktop will show you that the Customer field is used to create the relationship in both tables.

You will also note that Power BI could not figure out that the Calendar1 table should be related to the Sales table.

And, if you resize the tables, you will see the Sigma icon next to Quantity, Revenue, COGS, and Profit. This is correct and means that Power BI will summarize those fields. However, Power BI is also planning on totaling the MonthNo and Year fields in the Calendar table. This is not correct.

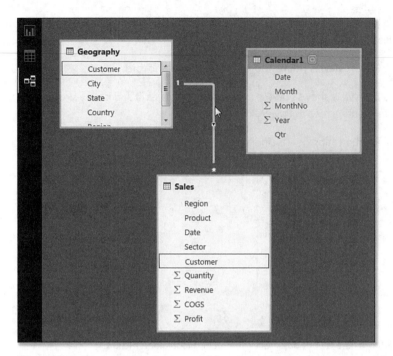

Figure 28.6   Power BI Desktop detected the relationship between Sales and Geography.

You need to define a relationship between the Sales and Calendar1 table. Click on Date in the Sales table. Drag and drop that field on the Date field in Calendar1 to create the relationship.

To prevent the Year field from showing up as a Sum Of Year, follow these steps:

1. Click on the Data icon, which is the second of three icons along the left side of the screen. In the Data view, you will see the values from one of your tables. To switch to another table, select the table from the Fields panel on the right side of the screen. As an Excel pro, looking on the right side of the screen seems foreign. You would think that there should be tabs at the bottom of the screen for the three data tables.

2. Click on the heading for MonthNo to select that column.

3. Go to the Modeling tab in Power BI. Change the Default Summarization from Sum to Don't Summarize (see Figure 28.7).

4. Repeat Steps 2 and 3 for any other numeric columns that should not be summarized. In the current data, it is the Year field. In other data, you might find numeric account numbers, cost centers, or item numbers.

Figure 28.7   By default, Power BI Desktop wants to sum any field that is completely numeric. Override this behavior for years, months, account numbers, and so on.

Assign categories to any geography or image URL fields. Power BI Desktop can plot your data on a map if you have fields like city, zip code, or state. Using the Data view, display the Geography table. Click on each heading for City, State, Country, and choose the appropriate data type using the Data Category drop-down on the Modeling tab (see Figure 28.8).

If you want to display images in your report, include a column with the URL for each image. Choose the Image URL category for that column. When you display the field in a table, the image from that URL will appear.

Figure 28.8   Categorize any geographic fields.

Building an Interactive Report with Power BI Desktop

Now that your data has been set up in Power BI Desktop, it is time to begin creating charts and tables that will appear in the dashboard.

Building Your First Visualization

Click the Report icon (this is the top of the three icons along the left side of Power BI Desktop). The large empty white canvas appears in the center of your screen.

Look in the Visualizations panel. There are many built-in tools available. To get your feet wet, choose the first item—a stacked bar chart (see Figure 28.9).

Notice that the field areas changes from Values to Axis, Legend, and Value. Every time that you choose a visualization type, the list of field types will change.

Figure 28.9   To start, choose any visualization from the Visualizations panel.

When you choose a Bar Chart from the visualizations panel, a tile placeholder appears on the canvas, as shown in Figure 28.10. You can resize this tile using any of the eight resize handles. Or, drag by the Title Bar area (it is in the vicinity of the two horizontal bars near the top center) to move it to a different location.

Figure 28.10   Before you add fields to a visualization, it starts as a blank tile.

To add fields to the visualization, choose Revenue from the Sales table, and choose Region from the Geography table. Region will move to the Axis drop zone. Revenue will move to the Values drop zone (see Figure 28.11).

Figure 28.11   Choose fields for the chart.

At the top of the drop zones, you will see a paint roller icon; click it to find formatting options for the chart. These options will be different depending on the type of visualization.

In Figure 28.12, the data labels have been turned on. The remaining options in the figure let you customize the appearance of the data labels.

Figure 28.12   Use the Paint Roller section to format your chart.

You might experiment with the Show Background options. You can color the tile with any theme color and set the transparency for the color.

The third icon is the Analysis icon. This looks like a search box with a chart trend line in the magnifying glass. For the Bar Chart visualization, the only choice is to add a Constant Line. Some companies might have the need to show a line at an arbitrary position. In Figure 28.13, the settings to draw a dotted line at $1.5 Million is shown.

With the settings in Figures 28.11 through Figures 28.13, you will get the chart shown in Figure 28.14.

Figure 28.13   Set up a Constant Line.

Figure 28.14   A Bar Chart with data labels and a Constant Line at $1.5 Million.

There are two different ways to sort this chart. Use the Three Dots icon in the top right of the chart to choose if regions should be sorted alphabetically or by revenue. (See Figure 28.15.)

The other icon to the left of the Ellipsis icon is a Full-Screen icon. Instead, you can use the Spot-light selection in the menu, which causes all other charts to fade into the background and keeps the current chart as the focus.

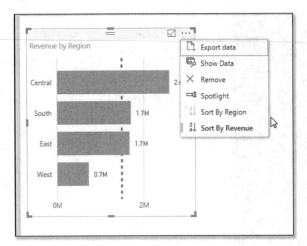

Figure 28.15   Settings for the chart are in a menu accessed through the ellipsis.

Building Your Second Visualization

This will seem very simple, but it trips me up every time. In order to create a second tile in your report, you must click away from the first tile. It is easy; simply click anywhere in the white noth- ingness of the report canvas.

However, if you forget to click away and click the Column Chart visualization, you will change the current chart from a bar chart to a column chart. I don't know why I constantly forget this step, but I constantly forget this step.

Click in the white space of the report. Choose a Column chart from the Visualization panel. Drag Revenue to the Values area. Drag Customer to the Axis area. Drag Product to the Legend area.

The result shown in Figure 28.16 is a column chart with customers along the bottom. The three product lines are stacked for each column. In this particular data set, there are ten big custom- ers and a bunch of tiny customers. You could resize the column chart to be very wide and show the long tail of small customers. Also, you can drag the right edge of the chart in to show only the ten largest customers. A scrollbar would let someone drag over to see the small customers.

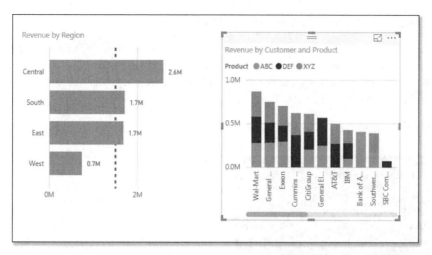

Figure 28.16   A second visualization is a column chart showing customer and product.

Cross-Filtering Charts

Here is where the magic of Power BI starts to kick in. Let's face it, you could have created both of the previous charts in Excel. The Constant Line would have required some Andy-Pope-style charting tricks, but it could have been done. The magic is how every chart in Power BI can filter the other charts.

Click on the bar for Central region in the first chart. The second chart will update. Central region customers will stay bright. Other customers will fade to a lighter color (see Figure 28.17).

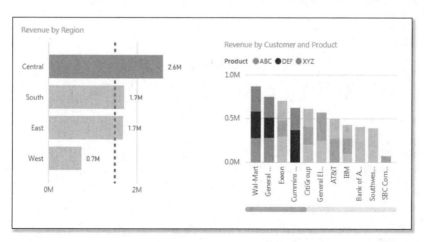

Figure 28.17   By choosing the Central region from the Bar Chart, the customer chart reacts.

Creating a Drill-Down Hierarchy

Interactive hierarchies are very easy to set up in Power BI Desktop. Click the first bar chart to select it. Display the Fields section in the Visualizations pane. The Axis contains the Region field. Drag three more fields from the geography table and drop them beneath Region: State, City, and Customer (see Figure 28.18).

Nothing appears to change in the chart, but you have set up a cool drill-down feature.

Figure 28.18   Stack four fields in the Axis area to create a drill-down.

Once the hierarchy has been created, a new Drill Down icon appears in the top right of the chart. Click the icon shown in Figure 28.19 to enable Drill Down mode.

Figure 28.19   Click to turn on Drill Down mode.

Once Drill-Down mode is active, click on Central in the bar chart to see a new chart of all of the states in the Central region.

Notice how the column chart updates to show only customers in the Central region (see Figure 28.20).

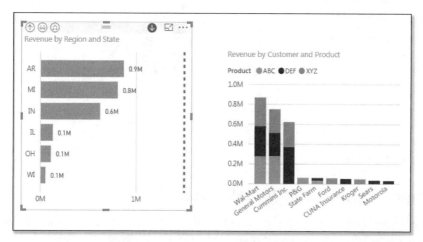

Figure 28.20   Click on the Central bar in the bar chart, and the chart drills down to show states in the Central region.

From Figure 28.20, you could continue to click on Arkansas and drill-down to Bentonville. Click Bentonville and drill-down to Wal-Mart. Because that is not very interesting, click the Drill-Up icon in the top left of the chart to return to all regions.

Then, click South. Click on Texas. The results in Figure 28.21 show the City level: Dallas, Irving, and Houston.

The choices from the point shown in Figure 28.21 are very subtle. You could click on one of the three cities to show the customers in that city. Or, you could decide you want to see all of the customers in any of the three cities. The second icon in the top left appears as two down-arrows. Click that icon to move one level down the hierarchy without any further filtering. You will see Exxon, AT&T, Southwest, SBC, and Compaq.

To return to the Region level, press the Drill Up icon several times.

CHAPTER 28

Figure 28.21   Drill down to the City level.

Importing a Custom Visualization

You can add new visualizations to Power BI Desktop. The last icon in the Visualizations area is three dots. Click those dots and choose Import From Marketplace.

You can browse a variety of free visualizations. In Figure 28.22, click the Add button next to the Enlighten Aquarium.

Figure 28.22   Power BI visualizations are open source, so you will find a wide array of useful and not-so-useful visualizations.

After adding the Enlighten Aquarium visualization, you will see a new fish icon in the Visualizations pane (see Figure 28.23).

Figure 28.23   Installing new visualizations from the Marketplace is a hassle-free experience.

Click a blank area of your report canvas. Add a new visualization by clicking the fish icon in the Visualizations pane.

The field drop zones are now labeled Fish and Fish Size. Drag Customer to the Fish area and Revenue to the Fish Size area.

An aquarium appears in your report with various-sized fish swimming back and forth (see Figure 28.24). Click on the biggest fish; it will stop swimming, and an information panel appears with Wal-Mart and 869,454.

The aquarium will respond to cross-filtering. If you filter the bar chart to just South, only the five fish from the South region will be swimming.

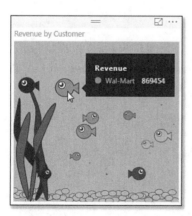

Figure 28.24   A fish chart in Power BI.

NOTE

In May 2018, Microsoft announced that you would soon be able to add the Power BI Custom Visuals to Office 365 versions of Excel. I cannot wait for the day when all of my column charts will be replaced with aquarium charts.

Publishing to Power BI

Now that your data has been set up in Power BI Desktop, you can share it with others by publishing to Power BI.

Power BI runs in any modern browser. There are dedicated apps for the iPad, iPhone, and Android phones. The default report is designed for a computer screen.

Publishing to a Workspace

On the Home tab in Power BI, choose Publish. The Publish To Power BI dialog will ask you which workspace to use (see Figure 28.25).

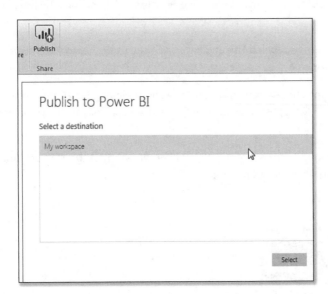

Figure 28.25   A report must be published to a workspace.

After publishing, you can choose to view in Power BI or to see Insights. Figure 28.26 shows your report running in Chrome.

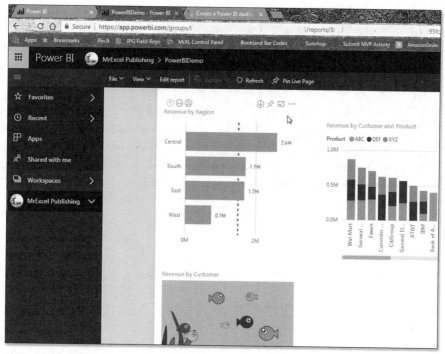

Figure 28.26   View the report in a browser.

Inside OUT

What ever happened to Power View? It seems to have disappeared from Excel.

Back in Excel 2013 Pro Plus, Microsoft debuted a new interactive dashboard product called Power View. It could use the Power Pivot data model. It offered interactive dashboards.

Although the Power View dashboard appeared as a sheet in your Excel workbook, it was clearly not a regular Excel sheet. It was a foreign body masquerading as an Excel worksheet.

When I wrote *Excel 2013 Inside Out*, I dedicated half a chapter to this new interactive dashboard tool.

By Excel 2016, you could no longer find any mention of Power View in Excel. They hid the icon. Only people who already knew about Power View and were using it could find how to bring the Power View icon back.

Once Microsoft took such drastic steps to keep people from discovering Power View, I knew that Power View was doomed.

Power BI is a re-imagined version of Power View. Your Power BI reports are not stored in the Excel file. It is far easier to share them with others on mobile devices.

However, if you were an early adopter and have a bunch of Power View workbooks in your possession, you can import the workbooks into Power BI and they will attempt to simulate a similar dashboard in Power BI. Some visualizations are not supported. The awesome animated scatter chart made famous by TED Talk superstar Hans Rosling is not supported. However, basic charts will import just fine.

Appendixes

APPENDIX A
DAX Functions

As an Excel pro, you probably have a fairly good handle on the calculation functions used in Excel. Today, you might need to dabble in the Data Analysis Expressions (DAX) formula language when creating a new measure in a pivot table. This appendix is a categorized list of the DAX functions with the syntax and a short description.

The first table is an alphabetical list of Excel functions and the equivalent DAX function. If the Excel function is not in Table A.1, then there is no direct DAX equivalent.

If you compare Table A.1 below to Table B.1 in Appendix B, you will note that in 90% of the cases, the function names are the same. That is likely thanks to Rob Collie, and Excel Project Manager who moved over to the Power Pivot team. In Appendix B, there are hardly any similarities between the Power Query functions and their Excel equivalents.

Excel Functions and DAX Equivalents

Table A.1 shows an alphabetical list of Excel functions with their DAX equivalents.

Table A.1   Excel Functions with DAX Equivalents

Excel Function	DAX Equivalent	Category
ABS	ABS	Math & Trig (Table A.7)
ACOS	ACOS	Math & Trig (Table A.7)
ACOSH	ACOSH	Math & Trig (Table A.7)
AND	AND	Logical (Table A.6)
ASIN	ASIN	Math & Trig (Table A.7)

ASINH	ASINH	Math & Trig (Table A.7)
ATAN	ATAN	Math & Trig (Table A.7)
ATANH	ATANH	Math & Trig (Table A.7)
AVERAGE	AVERAGE	Statistical (Table A.10)
AVERAGEA	AVERAGEA	Statistical (Table A.10)
BETA.DIST	BETA.DIST	Statistical (Table A.10)
BETA.INV	BETA.INV	Statistical (Table A.10)
CEILING	CEILING	Math & Trig (Table A.7)
CEILING.MATH	ISO.CEILING	Math & Trig (Table A.7)
CHISQ.INV	CHISQ.INV	Statistical (Table A.10)
CHISQ.INV.RT	CHISQ.INV.RT	Statistical (Table A.10)
CODE	CODE	Text (Table A.11)
COMBIN	COMBIN	Math & Trig (Table A.7)
COMBINA	COMBINA	Math & Trig (Table A.7)
CONCATENATE	CONCATENATE	Text (Table A.11)
CONFIDENCE.NORM	CONFIDENCE.NORM	Statistical (Table A.10)
CONFIDENCE.T	CONFIDENCE.T	Statistical (Table A.10)
COS	COS	Math & Trig (Table A.7)
COSH	COSH	Math & Trig (Table A.7)
COUNT	COUNT	Statistical (Table A.10)
COUNTA	COUNTA	Statistical (Table A.10)
COUNTBLANK	COUNTBLANK	Statistical (Table A.10)
DATE	DATE	Date & Time (Table A.2)
DATEDIF	DATEDIFF	Date & Time (Table A.2)
DATEVALUE	DATEVALUE	Date & Time (Table A.2)
DAY	DAY	Date & Time (Table A.2)
DEGREES	DEGREES	Math & Trig (Table A.7)
DIVIDE	DIVIDE	Math & Trig (Table A.7)
EDATE	EDATE	Date & Time (Table A.2)
EOMONTH	EOMONTH	Date & Time (Table A.2)
EVEN	EVEN	Math & Trig (Table A.7)
EXACT	EXACT	Text (Table A.11)
EXP	EXP	Math & Trig (Table A.7)
EXPON.DIST	EXPON.DIST	Statistical (Table A.10)
FACT	FACT	Math & Trig (Table A.7)

FALSE	FALSE	Logical (Table A.6)
FILTER	FILTER	Filter (Table A.4)
FIND	FIND	Text (Table A.11)
FIXED	FIXED	Text (Table A.11)
FLOOR.MATH	FLOOR	Math & Trig (Table A.7)
GCD	GCD	Math & Trig (Table A.7)
GEOMEAN	GEOMEAN	Statistical (Table A.10)
HOUR	HOUR	Date & Time (Table A.2)
IF	IF	Logical (Table A.6)
IFERROR	IFERROR	Logical (Table A.6)
INT	INT	Math & Trig (Table A.7)
INT	INT	Math & Trig (Table A.7)
ISBLANK	ISBLANK	Information (Table A.5)
ISERROR	ISERROR	Information (Table A.5)
ISEVEN	ISEVEN	Information (Table A.5)
ISLOGICAL	ISLOGICAL	Information (Table A.5)
ISNONTEXT	ISNONTEXT	Information (Table A.5)
ISNUMBER	ISNUMBER	Information (Table A.5)
ISTEXT	ISTEXT	Information (Table A.5)
LCM	LCM	Math & Trig (Table A.7)
LEFT	LEFT	Text (Table A.11)
LEN	LEN	Text (Table A.11)
LN	LN	Math & Trig (Table A.7)
LOG	LOG	Math & Trig (Table A.7)
LOG10	LOG10	Math & Trig (Table A.7)
LOWER	LOWER	Text (Table A.11)
MAX	MAX	Statistical (Table A.10)
MAXA	MAXA	Statistical (Table A.10)
MEDIAN	MEDIAN	Statistical (Table A.10)
MID	MID	Text (Table A.11)
MIN	MIN	Statistical (Table A.10)
MINA	MINA	Statistical (Table A.10)
MINUTE	MINUTE	Date & Time (Table A.2)
MONTH	MONTH	Date & Time (Table A.2)
MROUND	MROUND	Math & Trig (Table A.7)

NORM.DIST	NORM.DIST	Statistical (Table A.10)
NORM.INV	NORM.INV	Statistical (Table A.10)
NORM.S.DIST	NORM.S.DIST	Statistical (Table A.10)
NORM.S.INV	NORM.S.INV	Statistical (Table A.10)
NOT	NOT	Logical (Table A.6)
NOW	NOW	Date & Time (Table A.2)
ODD	ODD	Math & Trig (Table A.7)
OR	OR	Logical (Table A.6)
PERCENTILE.EXC	PERCENTILE.EXC	Statistical (Table A.10)
PERCENTILE.INC	PERCENTILE.INC	Statistical (Table A.10)
PI	PI	Math & Trig (Table A.7)
POISSON.DIST	POISSON.DIST	Statistical (Table A.10)
POWER	POWER	Math & Trig (Table A.7)
PRODUCT	PRODUCT	Math & Trig (Table A.7)
QUOTIENT	QUOTIENT	Math & Trig (Table A.7)
RADIANS	RADIANS	Math & Trig (Table A.7)
RAND	RAND	Math & Trig (Table A.7)
RANDBETWEEN	RANDBETWEEN	Math & Trig (Table A.7)
RANK.EQ	RANK.EQ	Statistical (Table A.10)
REPLACE	REPLACE	Text (Table A.11)
REPT	REPT	Text (Table A.11)
RIGHT	RIGHT	Text (Table A.11)
ROUND	ROUND	Math & Trig (Table A.7)
ROUNDDOWN	ROUNDDOWN	Math & Trig (Table A.7)
ROUNDUP	ROUNDUP	Math & Trig (Table A.7)
SEARCH	SEARCH	Text (Table A.11)
SECOND	SECOND	Date & Time (Table A.2)
SIGN	SIGN	Math & Trig (Table A.7)
SIN	SIN	Statistical (Table A.10)
SINH	SINH	Statistical (Table A.10)
SQRT	SQRT	Math & Trig (Table A.7)
SQRTPI	SQRTPI	Statistical (Table A.10)
STDEV.P	STDEV.P	Statistical (Table A.10)
STDEV.S	STDEV.S	Statistical (Table A.10)
SUBSTITUTE	SUBSTITUTE	Text (Table A.11)

SUM	SUM	Math & Trig (Table A.7)
SUMIFS	CALCULATE	Filter (Table A.4)
SWITCH	SWITCH	Logical (Table A.6)
T.DIST	T.DIST	Statistical (Table A.10)
T.DIST.2T	T.DIST.2T	Statistical (Table A.10)
T.DIST.RT	T.DIST.RT	Statistical (Table A.10)
T.INV	T.INV	Statistical (Table A.10)
T.INV.2T	T.INV.2T	Statistical (Table A.10)
TAN	TAN	Statistical (Table A.10)
TANH	TANH	Statistical (Table A.10)
TEXT	FORMAT	Text (Table A.11)
TEXTJOIN	CONCATENATEX	Text (Table A.11)
TIME	TIME	Date & Time (Table A.2)
TIMEVALUE	TIMEVALUE	Date & Time (Table A.2)
TODAY	TODAY	Date & Time (Table A.2)
TRIM	TRIM	Text (Table A.11)
TRUE	TRUE	Logical (Table A.6)
TRUNC	TRUNC	Math & Trig (Table A.7)
UNICHAR	UNICHAR	Text (Table A.11)
UNIQUE	DISTINCT	Filter (Table A.4)
UNIQUE	VALUES	Filter (Table A.4)
UPPER	UPPER	Text (Table A.11)
VALUE	VALUE	Text (Table A.11)
VAR.P	VAR.P	Statistical (Table A.10)
VAR.S	VAR.S	Statistical (Table A.10)
VLOOKUP	RELATED	Filter (Table A.4)
WEEKDAY	WEEKDAY	Date & Time (Table A.2)
WEEKNUM	WEEKNUM	Date & Time (Table A.2)
XIRR	XIRR	Statistical (Table A.10)
XNPV	XNPV	Statistical (Table A.10)
YEAR	YEAR	Date & Time (Table A.2)
YEARFRAC	YEARFRAC	Date & Time (Table A.2)

APPENDIX A

Date and Time Functions in DAX

Table A.2 lists Date and Time Functions in DAX.

Table A.2   Date and Time Functions in DAX

Function	Description
CALENDAR(<start_date>, <end_date>)	Returns a table with a single column named "Date" that contains a contiguous set of dates. The range of dates is from the specified start date to the specified end date, inclusive of those two dates.
CALENDARAUTO([fiscal_year_end_month])	Returns a table with a single column named "Date" that contains a contiguous set of dates. The range of dates is calculated automatically based on data in the model.
DATE(<year>, <month>, <day>)	Returns the specified date in datetime format. Similar to Excel function DATE.
DATEDIFF(<start_date>, <end_date>, <interval>)	Returns the count of interval boundaries crossed between two dates. Similar to Excel function DATEDIF.
DATEVALUE(date_text)	Converts a date in the form of text to a date in datetime format. Similar to Excel function DATEVALUE.
DAY(<date>) -	Returns the day of the month, a number from 1 to 31. Similar to Excel function DAY.
EDATE(<start_date>, <months>)	Returns the date that is the indicated number of months before or after the start date. Use EDATE to calculate maturity dates or due dates that fall on the same day of the month as the date of issue. Similar to Excel function EDATE.
EOMONTH(<start_date>, <months>)	Returns the date in datetime format of the last day of the month, before or after a specified number of months. Use EOMONTH to calculate maturity dates or due dates that fall on the last day of the month. Similar to Excel function EOMONTH.
HOUR(<datetime>)	Returns the hour as a number from 0 (12:00 A.M.) to 23 (11:00 P.M.). Similar to Excel function HOUR.
MINUTE(<datetime>)	Returns the minute as a number from 0 to 59, given a date and time value. Similar to Excel function MINUTE.

MONTH(<datetime>)	Returns the month as a number from 1 (January) to 12 (December). Similar to Excel function MONTH.
NOW()	The NOW function is useful when you need to display the current date and time on a worksheet or calculate a value based on the current date and time, and have that value updated each time you open the worksheet. Similar to Excel function NOW.
SECOND(<time>)	Returns the seconds of a time value, as a number from 0 to 59. Similar to Excel function SECOND.
TIME(hour, minute, second)	Converts hours, minutes, and seconds given as numbers to a time in datetime format. Similar to Excel function TIME.
TIMEVALUE(time_text)	Converts a time in text format to a time in datetime format. Similar to Excel function TIMEVALUE.
TODAY()	Returns the current date. Similar to Excel function TODAY.
WEEKDAY(<date>, <return_type>)	Returns a number from 1 to 7 identifying the day of the week of a date. By default, the day ranges from 1 (Sunday) to 7 (Saturday). Similar to Excel function WEEKDAY.
WEEKNUM(<date>, <return_type>)	Returns the week number for the given date and year according to the return_type value. The week number indicates where the week falls numerically within a year. Similar to Excel function WEEKNUM.
YEAR(<date>)	Returns the year of a date as a four-digit integer in the range 1900-9999. Similar to Excel function YEAR.
YEARFRAC(<start_date>, <end_date>, <basis>)	Calculates the fraction of the year represented by the number of whole days between two dates. Use the YEARFRAC worksheet function to identify the proportion of a whole year's benefits or obligations to assign to a specific term. Similar to Excel function YEARFRAC.

APPENDIX A

Time Intelligence Functions in DAX

Table A.3 shows Time Intelligence Function in DAX.

Table A.3   Time Intelligence Functions in DAX

Function	Description
CLOSINGBALANCEMONTH(<expression>,<dates>[,<filter>])	Evaluates the expression at the last date of the month in the current context.
CLOSINGBALANCEQUARTER(<expression>,<dates>[,<filter>])	Evaluates the expression at the last date of the quarter in the current context.
CLOSINGBALANCEYEAR(<expression>, <dates>[,<filter>][,<year_end_date>])	Evaluates the expression at the last date of the year in the current context.
DATEADD(<dates>, <number_of_intervals>,<interval>)	Returns a table that contains a column of dates, shifted either forward or backward in time by the specified number of intervals from the dates in the current context.
DATESBETWEEN(<dates>, <start_date>,<end_date>)	Returns a table that contains a column of dates that begins with the start_date and continues until the end_date.
DATESINPERIOD(<dates>, <start_date>, <number_of_intervals>,<interval>)	Returns a table that contains a column of dates that begins with the start_date and continues for the specified number_of_intervals.
DATESMTD(<dates>)	Returns a table that contains a column of the dates for the month to date, in the current context.
DATESQTD(<dates>)	Returns a table that contains a column of the dates for the quarter to date, in the current context.
DATESYTD(<dates> [,<year_end_date>])	Returns a table that contains a column of the dates for the year to date, in the current context.
ENDOFMONTH(<dates>) -	Returns the last date of the month in the current context for the specified column of dates.
ENDOFQUARTER(<dates>)	Returns the last date of the quarter in the current context for the specified column of dates.
ENDOFYEAR(<dates> [,<year_end_date>])	Returns the last date of the year in the current context for the specified column of dates.
FIRSTDATE(<dates>)	Returns the first date in the current context for the specified column of dates.
FIRSTNONBLANK(<column>, <expression>)	Returns the first value in the column, column, filtered by the current context, where the expression is not blank.
LASTDATE(<dates>)	Returns the last date in the current context for the specified column of dates.

LASTNONBLANK(<column>, <expression>)	Returns the last value in the column, column, filtered by the current context, where the expression is not blank.
NEXTDAY(<dates>)	Returns a table that contains a column of all dates from the next day, based on the first date specified in the dates column in the current context.
NEXTMONTH(<dates>)	Returns a table that contains a column of all dates from the next month, based on the first date in the dates column in the current context.
NEXTQUARTER(<dates>)	Returns a table that contains a column of all dates in the next quarter, based on the first date specified in the dates column, in the current context.
NEXTYEAR(<dates>[,<year_end_date>])	Returns a table that contains a column of all dates in the next year, based on the first date in the dates column, in the current context.
OPENINGBALANCEMONTH(<expression>,<dates> [,<filter>])	Evaluates the expression at the first date of the month in the current context.
OPENINGBALANCEQUARTER(<expression>,<dates>[,<filter>]) -	Evaluates the expression at the first date of the quarter, in the current context.
OPENINGBALANCEYEAR(<expression>, <dates>[,<filter>][,<year_end_date>])	Evaluates the expression at the first date of the year in the current context.
PARALLELPERIOD(<dates>, <number_of_intervals>,<interval>)	Returns a table that contains a column of dates that represents a period parallel to the dates in the specified dates column, in the current context, with the dates shifted a number of intervals either forward in time or back in time.
PREVIOUSDAY(<dates>)	Returns a table that contains a column of all dates representing the day that is previous to the first date in the dates column, in the current context.
PREVIOUSMONTH(<dates>)	Returns a table that contains a column of all dates from the previous month, based on the first date in the dates column, in the current context.
PREVIOUSQUARTER(<dates>)	Returns a table that contains a column of all dates from the previous quarter, based on the first date in the dates column, in the current context.
PREVIOUSYEAR(<dates> [,<year_end_date>])	Returns a table that contains a column of all dates from the previous year, given the last date in the dates column, in the current context.
SAMEPERIODLASTYEAR(<dates>)	Returns a table that contains a column of dates shifted one year back in time from the dates in the specified dates column, in the current context.
STARTOFMONTH(<dates>)	Returns the first date of the month in the current context for the specified column of dates.

STARTOFQUARTER(<dates>)	Returns the first date of the quarter in the current context for the specified column of dates.
STARTOFYEAR(<dates>)	Returns the first date of the year in the current context for the specified column of dates.
TOTALMTD(<expression>,<dates> [,<filter>])	Evaluates the value of the expression for the month to date, in the current context.
TOTALQTD(<expression>,<dates> [,<filter>])	Evaluates the value of the expression for the dates in the quarter to date, in the current context.
TOTALYTD(<expression>,<dates> [,<filter>][,<year_end_date>])	Evaluates the year-to-date value of the expression in the current context.

Filter Functions in DAX

Table A.4 shows Filter Functions in DAX.

Table A.4   Filter Functions in DAX

Function	Description
ADDMISSINGITEMS(<showAllColumn> [, <showAllColumn>]..., <table>, <groupingColumn> [, <groupingColumn>]...[,	The ADDMISSINGITEMS function will return BLANK values for the IsSubtotal columns of blank rows it adds.
ALL({<table>|<column> [,<column>[,<column>[,...]]]})	Returns all the rows in a table, or all the values in a column, ignoring any filters that might have been applied. This function is useful for clearing filters and creating calculations on all the rows in a table.
ALLEXCEPT(<table>,<column> [,<column>[,...]])	Removes all context filters in the table except filters that have been applied to the specified columns.
ALLNOBLANKROW({<table>|<column> [,<column>[,<column>[,...]]]})	From the parent table of a relationship, returns all rows but the blank row, or all distinct values of a column but the blank row, and disregards any context filters that might exist.
ALLSELECTED([<tableName> | <columnName>])	The ALLSELECTED function gets the context that represents all rows and columns in the query, while keeping explicit filters and contexts other than row and column filters. This function can be used to obtain visual totals in queries.
CALCULATE(<expression>,<filter1>, <filter2>...)	Evaluates an expression in a context that is modified by the specified filters. Similar to Excel function SUMIFS*.
CALCULATETABLE(<expression>, <filter1>,<filter2>,...)	Evaluates a table expression in a context modified by the given filters.

CROSSFILTER(<columnName1>, <columnName2>, <direction>)	Specifies the cross-filtering direction to be used in a calculation for a relationship that exists between two columns.
DISTINCT(<column>)	This function cannot be used to return values into a cell or column on a worksheet; rather, you nest the DISTINCT function within a formula, to get a list of distinct values that can be passed to another function and then counted, summed, or used for other operations. Similar to Excel function UNIQUE.
EARLIER(<column>, <number>)	EARLIER is mostly used in the context of calculated columns.
EARLIEST(<column>)	Returns the current value of the specified column in an outer evaluation pass of the specified column.
FILTER(<table>,<filter>)	Returns a table that represents a subset of another table or expression. Similar to Excel function FILTER.
FILTERS(<columnName>)	Returns the values that are directly applied as filters to columnName.
HASONEFILTER(<columnName>)	Returns TRUE when the number of directly filtered values on columnName is one; otherwise returns FALSE.
HASONEVALUE(<columnName>)	Returns TRUE when the context for columnName has been filtered down to one distinct value only. Otherwise is FALSE.
ISCROSSFILTERED(<columnName>)	Returns TRUE when columnName or another column in the same or related table is being filtered.
ISFILTERED(<columnName>)	Returns TRUE when columnName is being filtered directly. If there is no filter on the column or if the filtering happens because a different column in the same table or in a related table is being filtered, then the function returns FALSE.
KEEPFILTERS(<expression>)	Modifies how filters are applied while evaluating a CALCULATE or CALCULATETABLE function.
RELATED(<column>)	Returns a related value from another table. Similar to Excel function VLOOKUP.
RELATEDTABLE(<tableName>)	Evaluates a table expression in a context modified by the given filters.
SELECTEDVALUE(<columnName> [, <alternateResult>])	Returns the value when the context for columnName has been filtered down to one distinct value only. Otherwise returns alternateResult.
SUBSTITUTEWITHINDEX(<table>, <indexColumnName>, <indexColumnsTable>, [<orderBy_expression>,[<order>] [,<orderBy_expression>, [<order>]]...])	The index starts at 0 (0-based) and is incremented by one for each additional row in the right/second join table supplied. The index is based on the sort order specified for the right/second join table.

USERELATIONSHIP(<columnName1>, <columnName2>)	Specifies the relationship to be used in a specific calculation as the one that exists between columnName1 and columnName2.
VALUES(<TableNameOrColumnName>)	This function cannot be used to return values into a cell or column on a worksheet; rather, you use it as an intermediate function, nested in a formula, to get a list of distinct values that can be counted, or to filter or sum other values. Similar to Excel function UNIQUE.

Information Functions in DAX

Table A.5 shows Information Functions in DAX.

Table A.5   Information Functions in DAX

Function	Description
CONTAINS(<table>, <columnName>, <value> [, <columnName>, <value>]...) -	Returns true if values for all referred columns exist, or are contained, in those columns; otherwise, the function returns false.
CUSTOMDATA()	Returns the content of the CustomData property in the connection string.
ISBLANK(<value>)	Checks whether a value is blank and returns TRUE or FALSE. Similar to Excel function ISBLANK.
ISERROR(<value>)	Checks whether a value is an error and returns TRUE or FALSE. Similar to Excel function ISERROR.
ISEVEN(number)	Returns TRUE if number is even, or FALSE if number is odd. Similar to Excel function ISEVEN.
ISLOGICAL(<value>)	Checks whether a value is a logical value (TRUE or FALSE), and returns TRUE or FALSE. Similar to Excel function ISLOGICAL.
ISNONTEXT(<value>)	Checks if a value is not text (blank cells are not text) and returns TRUE or FALSE. Similar to Excel function ISNONTEXT.
ISNUMBER(<value>)	Checks whether a value is a number and returns TRUE or FALSE. Similar to Excel function ISNUMBER.
ISONORAFTER(<scalar_expression>, <scalar_expression>, sort_order, [,scalar_expression>, <scalar_expression>, [sort_order][,...])	Based on the sort order, the first parameter is compared with the second parameter. If the sort order is ascending, the comparison to be done is first parameter greater than or equal to second parameter. If the sort order is descending, the comparison to be done is second parameter less than or equal to first parameter.

ISTEXT(<value>)	Checks if a value is text and returns TRUE or FALSE. Similar to Excel function ISTEXT.
LOOKUPVALUE(<result_columnName>, <search_columnName>, <search_value> [,<search_columnName>, <search_value>]...)	Returns the value in result_columnName for the row that meets all criteria specified by search_columnName and search_value.
USERNAME()	Returns the domain name and username from the credentials given to the system at connection time.

Logical Functions in DAX

Table A.6 shows Logical Functions in DAX.

Table A.6   Logical Functions in DAX

FUNCTION	DESCRIPTION
AND(<logical1>,<logical2>)	Checks whether both arguments are TRUE and returns TRUE if both arguments are TRUE. Otherwise returns false. Similar to Excel function AND.
FALSE()	Returns the logical value FALSE. Similar to Excel function FALSE.
IF(logical_test>,<value_if_true>, value_if_false)	Checks if a condition provided as the first argument is met. Returns one value if the condition is TRUE, and returns another value if the condition is FALSE. Similar to Excel function IF.
IFERROR(value, value_if_error)	Evaluates an expression and returns a specified value if the expression returns an error; otherwise returns the value of the expression itself. Similar to Excel function IFERROR.
NOT(<logical>)	Changes FALSE to TRUE, or TRUE to FALSE. Similar to Excel function NOT.
OR(<logical1>,<logical2>)	Checks whether one of the arguments is TRUE to return TRUE. The function returns FALSE if both arguments are FALSE. Similar to Excel function OR.
SWITCH(<expression>,<value>, <result>[,<value>,<result>]... [, <else>])	Evaluates an expression against a list of values and returns one of multiple possible result expressions. Similar to Excel function SWITCH.
TRUE()	Returns the logical value TRUE. Similar to Excel function TRUE.

Math and Trig Functions in DAX

Table A.7 shows Math and Trig Functions in DAX.

Table A.7   Math and Trig Functions in DAX

Function	Description
ABS(<number>)	Returns the absolute value of a number. Similar to Excel function ABS.
ACOS(number)	Returns the arccosine, or inverse cosine, of a number. The arccosine is the angle whose cosine is number. The returned angle is given in radians in the range 0 (zero) to pi. Similar to Excel function ACOS.
ACOSH(number)	Returns the inverse hyperbolic cosine of a number. The number must be greater than or equal to 1. The inverse hyperbolic cosine is the value whose hyperbolic cosine is number, so ACOSH(COSH(number)) equals number. Similar to Excel function ACOSH.
ASIN(number)	Returns the arcsine, or inverse sine, of a number. The arcsine is the angle whose sine is number. The returned angle is given in radians in the range -pi/2 to pi/2. Similar to Excel function ASIN.
ASINH(number)	Returns the inverse hyperbolic sine of a number. The inverse hyperbolic sine is the value whose hyperbolic sine is number, so ASINH(SINH(number)) equals number. Similar to Excel function ASINH.
ATAN(number)	Returns the arctangent, or inverse tangent, of a number. The arctangent is the angle whose tangent is number. The returned angle is given in radians in the range -pi/2 to pi/2. Similar to Excel function ATAN.
ATANH(number)	Returns the inverse hyperbolic tangent of a number. Number must be between -1 and 1 (excluding -1 and 1). The inverse hyperbolic tangent is the value whose hyperbolic tangent is number, so ATANH(TANH(number)) equals number. Similar to Excel function ATANH.
CEILING(<number>, <significance>)	Rounds a number up, to the nearest integer or to the nearest multiple of significance. Similar to Excel function CEILING.
COMBIN(number, number_chosen)	Returns the number of combinations for a given number of items. Use COMBIN to determine the total possible number of groups for a given number of items. Similar to Excel function COMBIN.
COMBINA(number, number_chosen)	Returns the number of combinations (with repetitions) for a given number of items. Similar to Excel function COMBINA.

COS(number)	Returns the cosine of the given angle. Similar to Excel function COS.
COSH(number)	Returns the hyperbolic cosine of a number. Similar to Excel function COSH.
CURRENCY(<value>)	Evaluates the argument and returns the result as currency data type.
DEGREES(angle)	Converts radians into degrees. Similar to Excel function DEGREES.
DIVIDE(<numerator>, <denominator> [,<alternateresult>])	Performs division and returns alternate result or BLANK() on division by 0. Similar to Excel function DIVIDE.
EVEN(number)	Returns number rounded up to the nearest even integer. You can use this function for processing items that come in twos. For example, a packing crate accepts rows of one or two items. The crate is full when the number of items, rounded up to the nearest two, matches the crate's capacity. Similar to Excel function EVEN.
EXP(<number>)	Returns e raised to the power of a given number. The constant e equals 2.71828182845904, the base of the natural logarithm. Similar to Excel function EXP.
FACT(<number>)	Returns the factorial of a number, equal to the series 1*2*3*...* , ending in the given number. Similar to Excel function FACT.
FLOOR(<number>, <significance>)	Rounds a number down, toward zero, to the nearest multiple of significance. Similar to Excel function FLOOR.MATH.
GCD(number1, [number2], ...)	Returns the greatest common divisor of two or more integers. The greatest common divisor is the largest integer that divides both number1 and number2 without a remainder. Similar to Excel function GCD.
INT(<number>)	Rounds a number down to the nearest integer. Similar to Excel function INT.
ISO.CEILING(<number>[, <significance>])	Rounds a number up, to the nearest integer or to the nearest multiple of significance. Similar to Excel function CEILING.MATH.
LCM(number1, [number2], ...)	Returns the least common multiple of integers. The least common multiple is the smallest positive integer that is a multiple of all integer arguments number1, number2, and so on. Use LCM to add fractions with different denominators. Similar to Excel function LCM.
LN(<number>)	Returns the natural logarithm of a number. Natural logarithms are based on the constant e (2.71828182845904). Similar to Excel function LN.

APPENDIX A

LOG(<number>,<base>)	Returns the logarithm of a number to the base you specify. Similar to Excel function LOG.
LOG10(<number>)	Returns the base-10 logarithm of a number. Similar to Excel function LOG10.
INT(<number>)	Rounds a number down to the nearest integer. Similar to Excel function INT.
MROUND(<number>, <multiple>)	Returns a number rounded to the desired multiple. Similar to Excel function MROUND.
ODD(number)	Returns number rounded up to the nearest odd integer. Similar to Excel function ODD.
PI()	Returns the value of Pi, 3.14159265358979, accurate to 15 digits. Similar to Excel function PI.
POWER(<number>, <power>)	Returns the result of a number raised to a power. Similar to Excel function POWER.
PRODUCT(<column>)	To return the product of an expression evaluated for each row in a table, use PRODUCTX Function (DAX). Similar to Excel function PRODUCT.
PRODUCTX(<table>, <expression>)	To return the product of the numbers in a column, use PRODUCT Function (DAX).
QUOTIENT(<numerator>, <denominator>)	Performs division and returns only the integer portion of the division result. Use this function when you want to discard the remainder of division. Similar to Excel function QUOTIENT.
RADIANS(angle)	Converts degrees to radians. Similar to Excel function RADIANS.
RAND()	Returns a random number greater than or equal to 0 and less than 1, evenly distributed. The number that is returned changes each time the cell containing this function is recalculated. Similar to Excel function RAND.
RANDBETWEEN(<bottom>,<top>)	Returns a random number in the range between two numbers you specify. Similar to Excel function RANDBETWEEN.
ROUND(<number>, <num_digits>)	Rounds a number to the specified number of digits. Similar to Excel function ROUND.
ROUNDDOWN(<number>, <num_digits>)	Rounds a number down, toward zero. Similar to Excel function ROUNDDOWN.
ROUNDUP(<number>, <num_digits>)	Rounds a number up, away from 0 (zero). Similar to Excel function ROUNDUP.
SIGN(<number>)	Determines the sign of a number, the result of a calculation, or a value in a column. The function returns 1 if the number is positive, 0 (zero) if the number is zero, or -1 if the number is negative. Similar to Excel function SIGN.

SQRT(<number>)	Returns the square root of a number. Similar to Excel function SQRT.
SUM(<column>)	Adds all the numbers in a column. Similar to Excel function SUM.
SUMX(<table>, <expression>)	Returns the sum of an expression evaluated for each row in a table.
TRUNC(<number>,<num_digits>)	Truncates a number to an integer by removing the decimal, or fractional, part of the number. Similar to Excel function TRUNC.

Other Functions in DAX

Table A.8 lists other functions in DAX.

Table A.8   Other Functions in DAX

Function	Description
DATATABLE(ColumnName1, DataType1, ColumnName2,DataType2..., {{Value1, Value2...}, {ValueN, ValueN+1...}...})	Provides a mechanism for declaring an inline set of data values.
ERROR(<text>)	Raises an error with an error message.
EXCEPT(<table_expression1>, <table_expression2>	Returns the rows of one table which do not appear in another table.
GENERATESERIES(<startValue>, <endValue> [, <incrementValue>])	Returns a single column table containing the values of an arithmetic series—that is, a sequence of values in which each differs from the preceding by a constant quantity. The name of the column returned is Value.
GROUPBY(<table>, [<groupBy_columnName1>], [<name>, <expression>]...)	The GROUPBY function is similar to the SUMMARIZE function. However, GROUPBY does not do an implicit CALCULATE for any extension columns that it adds. GROUPBY permits a new function, CURRENTGROUP(), to be used inside aggregation functions in the extension columns that it adds. GROUPBY attempts to reuse the data that has been grouped making it highly performant.
INTERSECT(<table_expression1>, <table_expression2>)	Returns the row intersection of two tables, retaining duplicates.
ISEMPTY(<table_expression>)	Checks if a table is empty.
NATURALINNERJOIN(<leftJoinTable>, <rightJoinTable>)	Performs an inner join of a table with another table. The tables are joined on common columns (by name) in the two tables. If the two tables have no common column names, an error is returned.

NATURALLEFTOUTERJOIN(<leftJoinTable>, <rightJoinTable>)	Performs an inner join of a table with another table. The tables are joined on common columns (by name) in the two tables. If the two tables have no common column names, an error is returned.
SUMMARIZECOLUMNS(<groupBy_columnName> [,< groupBy_columnName >]..., [<filterTable>]... [, <name>, <expression>]...)	Returns a summary table over a set of groups.
TREATAS(table_expression, <column>[, <column> [, <column>[,...]]]})	Applies the result of a table expression as filters to columns from an unrelated table.
UNION(<table_expression1>, <table_expression2> [,<table_expression>]...)	Creates a union (join) table from a pair of tables.
VAR <name> = <expression>	Stores the result of an expression as a named variable, which can then be passed as an argument to other measure expressions. Once resultant values have been calculated for a variable expression, those values do not change, even if the variable is referenced in another expression.

Parent and Child Functions in DAX

Table A.9 lists Parent and Child Functions in DAX.

Table A.9   Parent and Child Functions in DAX

Function	Description
PATH(<ID_columnName>, <parent_columnName>)	Returns a delimited text string with the identifiers of all the parents of the current identifier, starting with the oldest and continuing until current.
PATHCONTAINS(<path>, <item>)	Returns TRUE if the specified item exists within the specified path.
PATHITEM(<path>, <position>[, <type>])	Returns the item at the specified position from a string resulting from evaluation of a PATH function. Positions are counted from left to right.
PATHITEMREVERSE(<path>, <position>[, <type>])	Returns the item at the specified position from a string resulting from evaluation of a PATH function. Positions are counted backwards from right to left.
PATHLENGTH(<path>)	Returns the number of parents to the specified item in a given PATH result, including self.

Statistical Functions in DAX

Table A.10 lists Statistical Functions in DAX.

Table A.10   Statistical Functions in Dax

Function	Description
ADDCOLUMNS(<table>, <name>, <expression>[, <name>, <expression>]...)	Adds calculated columns to the given table or table expression.
AVERAGE(<column>)	Returns the average (arithmetic mean) of all the numbers in a column. Similar to Excel function AVERAGE.
AVERAGEA(<column>)	Returns the average (arithmetic mean) of the values in a column. Handles text and non-numeric values. Similar to Excel function AVERAGEA.
AVERAGEX(<table>,<expression>)	Calculates the average (arithmetic mean) of a set of expressions evaluated over a table.
BETA.DIST(x,alpha,beta,cumulative, [A],[B])	Returns the beta distribution. The beta distribution is commonly used to study variation in the percentage of something across samples, such as the fraction of the day people spend watching television. Similar to Excel function BETA.DIST.
BETA.INV(probability,alpha,beta, [A],[B])	If probability = BETA.DIST(x,...TRUE), then BETA.INV(probability,...) = x. The beta distribution can be used in project planning to model probable completion times given an expected completion time and variability. Similar to Excel function BETA.INV.
CHISQ.INV(probability,deg_freedom)	The chi-squared distribution is commonly used to study variation in the percentage of something across samples, such as the fraction of the day people spend watching television. Similar to Excel function CHISQ.INV.
CHISQ.INV.RT(probability,deg_freedom)	If probability = CHISQ.DIST.RT(x,...), then CHISQ.INV.RT(probability,...) = x. Use this function to compare observed results with expected ones in order to decide whether your original hypothesis is valid. Similar to Excel function CHISQ.INV.RT.

CONFIDENCE.NORM(alpha,standard_dev,size)	The confidence interval is a range of values. Your sample mean, x, is at the center of this range and the range is x ± CONFIDENCE.NORM. For example, if x is the sample mean of delivery times for products ordered through the mail, x ± CONFIDENCE.NORM is a range of population means. For any population mean, μ0, in this range, the probability of obtaining a sample mean further from μ0 than x is greater than alpha; for any population mean, μ0, not in this range, the probability of obtaining a sample mean further from μ0 than x is less than alpha. In other words, assume that we use x, standard_dev, and size to construct a two-tailed test at significance level alpha of the hypothesis that the population mean is μ0. Then we will not reject that hypothesis if μ0 is in the confidence interval and will reject that hypothesis if μ0 is not in the confidence interval. The confidence interval does not allow us to infer that there is probability 1 − alpha that our next package will take a delivery time that is in the confidence interval. Similar to Excel function CONFIDENCE.NORM.
CONFIDENCE.T(alpha, standard_dev,size)	Returns the confidence interval for a population mean, using a Student's t distribution. Similar to Excel function CONFIDENCE.T.
COUNT(<column>)	The COUNT function counts the number of cells in a column that contain numbers. Similar to Excel function COUNT.
COUNTA(<column>)	The COUNTA function counts the number of cells in a column that are not empty. It counts not just rows that contain numeric values, but also rows that contain nonblank values, including text, dates, and logical values. Similar to Excel function COUNTA.
COUNTAX(<table>,<expression>)	The COUNTAX function counts nonblank results when evaluating the result of an expression over a table. That is, it works just like the COUNTA function, but is used to iterate through the rows in a table and count rows where the specified expressions results in a nonblank result.
COUNTBLANK(<column>)	Counts the number of blank cells in a column. Similar to Excel function COUNTBLANK.
COUNTROWS(<table>)	The COUNTROWS function counts the number of rows in the specified table, or in a table defined by an expression.
COUNTX(<table>,<expression>)	Counts the number of rows that contain a number or an expression that evaluates to a number, when evaluating an expression over a table.
CROSSJOIN(<table>, <table> [, <table>]...)	Returns a table that contains the Cartesian product of all rows from all tables in the arguments. The columns in the new table are all the columns in all the argument tables.

DATATABLE(ColumnName1, DataType1, ColumnName2, DataType2…,	Provides a mechanism for declaring an inline set of data values.
DISTINCTCOUNT(<column>)	The DISTINCTCOUNT function counts the number of distinct values in a column.
EXPON.DIST(x,lambda,cumulative)	Returns the exponential distribution. Use EXPON.DIST to model the time between events, such as how long an automated bank teller takes to deliver cash. For example, you can use EXPON.DIST to determine the probability that the process takes at most 1 minute. Similar to Excel function EXPON.DIST.
GENERATE(<table1>, <table2>)	Returns a table with the Cartesian product between each row in table1 and the table that results from evaluating table2 in the context of the current row from table1.
GENERATEALL(<table1>, <table2>)	Returns a table with the Cartesian product between each row in table1 and the table that results from evaluating table2 in the context of the current row from table1.
GEOMEAN(<column>)	To return the geometric mean of an expression evaluated for each row in a table, use GEOMEANX Function (DAX). Similar to Excel function GEOMEAN.
GEOMEANX(<table>, <expression>)	To return the geometric mean of the numbers in a column, use GEOMEAN Function (DAX).
MAX(<column>)	Returns the largest numeric value in a column, or between two scalar expressions. Similar to Excel function MAX.
MAXA(<column>)	Returns the largest value in a column. Logical values and blanks are counted. Similar to Excel function MAXA.
MAXX(<table>,<expression>)	Evaluates an expression for each row of a table and returns the largest numeric value.
MEDIAN(<column>)	To return the median of an expresssion evaluated for each row in a table, use MEDIANX Function (DAX). Similar to Excel function MEDIAN.
MEDIANX(<table>, <expression>)	To return the median of numbers in a column, use MEDIAN Function (DAX).
MIN(<column>)	Returns the smallest numeric value in a column, or between two scalar expressions. Ignores logical values and text. Similar to Excel function MIN.
MINA(<column>)	Returns the smallest value in a column, including any logical values and numbers represented as text. Similar to Excel function MINA.
MINX(<table>, < expression>)	Returns the smallest numeric value that results from evaluating an expression for each row of a table.
NORM.DIST(X, Mean, Standard_dev, Cumulative)	Returns the normal distribution for the specified mean and standard deviation. Similar to Excel function NORM.DIST.

NORM.INV(Probability, Mean, Standard_dev)	The inverse of the normal cumulative distribution for the specified mean and standard deviation. Similar to Excel function NORM.INV.
NORM.S.DIST(Z, Cumulative)	Returns the standard normal distribution (has a mean of zero and a standard deviation of one). Similar to Excel function NORM.S.DIST.
NORM.S.INV(Probability)	Returns the inverse of the standard normal cumulative distribution. The distribution has a mean of zero and a standard deviation of one. Similar to Excel function NORM.S.INV.
PERCENTILE.EXC(<column>, <k>)	To return the percentile number of an expression evaluated for each row in a table, use PERCENTILEX.EXC Function (DAX). Similar to Excel function PERCENTILE.EXC.
PERCENTILE.INC(<column>, <k>)	To return the percentile number of an expression evaluated for each row in a table, use PERCENTILEX.INC Function (DAX). Similar to Excel function PERCENTILE.INC.
PERCENTILEX.EXC(<table>, <expression>, k)	To return the percentile of numbers in a column, use PERCENTILE.EXC Function (DAX).
PERCENTILEX.INC(<table>, <expression>, k)	To return the percentile of numbers in a column, use PERCENTILE.INC Function (DAX).
POISSON.DIST(x,mean,cumulative)	Returns the Poisson distribution. A common application of the Poisson distribution is predicting the number of events over a specific time, such as the number of cars arriving at a toll plaza in 1 minute. Similar to Excel function POISSON.DIST.
RANK.EQ(<value>, <columnName>[, <order>])	Returns the ranking of a number in a list of numbers. Similar to Excel function RANK.EQ.
RANKX(<table>, <expression> [, <value>[, <order>[, <ties>]]])	Returns the ranking of a number in a list of numbers for each row in the table argument.
ROW(<name>, <expression>[[, <name>, <expression>]...])	Returns a table with a single row containing values that result from the expressions given to each column.
SAMPLE(<n_value>, <table>, <orderBy_expression>, [<order> [, <orderBy_expression>,	Returns a sample of N rows from the specified table.
SELECTCOLUMNS(<table>, <name>, <scalar_expression> [, <name>,	Adds calculated columns to the given table or table expression.
SIN(number)	Returns the sine of the given angle. Similar to Excel function SIN.
SINH(number)	Returns the hyperbolic sine of a number. Similar to Excel function SINH.

STDEV.P(<ColumnName>)	Returns the standard deviation of the entire population. Similar to Excel function STDEV.P.
STDEV.S(<ColumnName>)	Returns the standard deviation of a sample population. Similar to Excel function STDEV.S.
STDEVX.P(<table>, <expression>)	Returns the standard deviation of the entire population.
STDEVX.S(<table>, <expression>)	Returns the standard deviation of a sample population.
SQRTPI(number)	Returns the square root of (number * pi). Similar to Excel function SQRTPI.
SUMMARIZE(<table>, <groupBy_columnName> [, <groupBy_columnName>]... [, <name>, <expression>]...)	Returns a summary table for the requested totals over a set of groups.
T.DIST(X,Deg_freedom,Cumulative)	Returns the Student's left-tailed t-distribution. Similar to Excel function T.DIST.
T.DIST.2T(X,Deg_freedom)	Returns the two-tailed Student's t-distribution. Similar to Excel function T.DIST.2T.
T.DIST.RT(X,Deg_freedom)	Returns the right-tailed Student's t-distribution. Similar to Excel function T.DIST.RT.
T.INV(Probability,Deg_freedom)	Returns the left-tailed inverse of the Student's t-distribution. Similar to Excel function T.INV.
T.INV.2T(Probability,Deg_freedom)	Returns the two-tailed inverse of the Student's t-distribution. Similar to Excel function T.INV.2T.
TAN(number)	Returns the tangent of the given angle. Similar to Excel function TAN.
TANH(number)	Returns the hyperbolic tangent of a number. Similar to Excel function TANH.
TOPN(<n_value>, <table>, <orderBy_expression>, [<order> [, <orderBy_expression>,	Returns the top N rows of the specified table.
VAR.P(<columnName>)	Returns the variance of the entire population. Similar to Excel function VAR.P.
VAR.S(<columnName>)	Returns the variance of a sample population. Similar to Excel function VAR.S.
VARX.P(<table>, <expression>)	Returns the variance of the entire population.
VARX.S(<table>, <expression>)	Returns the variance of a sample population.
XIRR(<table>, <values>, <dates>, [guess])	Returns the internal rate of return for a schedule of cash flows that is not necessarily periodic. Similar to Excel function XIRR.
XNPV(<table>, <values>, <dates>, <rate>)	Returns the present value for a schedule of cash flows that is not necessarily periodic. Similar to Excel function XNPV.

APPENDIX A

Text Functions in DAX

Table A.11 lists Text Functions in DAX.

Table A.11   Text Functions in DAX

Function	Description
BLANK()	Returns a blank.
CODE(text)	Windows ANSI code for the first character of text. Similar to Excel function CODE.
CONCATENATE(<text1>, <text2>)	Joins two text strings into one text string. Similar to Excel function CONCATENATE.
CONCATENATEX(<table>, <expression>, [delimiter])	Concatenates the result of an expression evaluated for each row in a table. Similar to Excel function TEXTJOIN.
EXACT(<text1>,<text2>)	Compares two text strings and returns TRUE if they are exactly the same, FALSE otherwise. EXACT is case-sensitive but ignores formatting differences. You can use EXACT to test text being entered into a document. Similar to Excel function EXACT.
FIND(<find_text>, <within_text> [, [<start_num>] [, <NotFoundValue>]])	Returns the starting position of one text string within another text string. FIND is case-sensitive. Similar to Excel function FIND.
FIXED(<number>, <decimals>, <no_commas>)	Rounds a number to the specified number of decimals and returns the result as text. You can specify that the result be returned with or without commas. Similar to Excel function FIXED.
FORMAT(<value>, <format_string>)	Converts a value to text according to the specified format. Similar to Excel function TEXT.
LEFT(<text>, <num_chars>)	Returns the specified number of characters from the start of a text string. Similar to Excel function LEFT.
LEN(<text>)	Returns the number of characters in a text string. Similar to Excel function LEN.
LOWER(<text>)	Converts all letters in a text string to lowercase. Similar to Excel function LOWER.
MID(<text>, <start_num>, <num_chars>)	Returns a string of characters from the middle of a text string, given a starting position and length. Similar to Excel function MID.
REPLACE(<old_text>, <start_num>, <num_chars>, <new_text>)	REPLACE replaces part of a text string, based on the number of characters you specify, with a different text string. Similar to Excel function REPLACE.

REPT(<text>, <num_times>)	Repeats text a given number of times. Use REPT to fill a cell with a number of instances of a text string. Similar to Excel function REPT.
RIGHT(<text>, <num_chars>)	RIGHT returns the last character or characters in a text string, based on the number of characters you specify. Similar to Excel function RIGHT.
SEARCH(<find_text>, <within_text> [, [<start_num>] [,<NotFoundValue>]])	Returns the number of the character at which a specific character or text string is first found, reading left to right. Search is case-insensitive and accent sensitive. Similar to Excel function SEARCH.
SUBSTITUTE(<text>, <old_text>, <new_text>, <instance_num>)	Replaces existing text with new text in a text string. Similar to Excel function SUBSTITUTE.
TRIM(<text>)	Removes all spaces from text except for single spaces between words. Similar to Excel function TRIM.
UNICHAR(number)	Returns the Unicode character referenced by the numeric value. Similar to Excel function UNICHAR.
UPPER(<text>)	Converts a text string to all uppercase letters Similar to Excel function UPPER.
VALUE(<text>)	Converts a text string that represents a number to a number. Similar to Excel function VALUE.

Power Query M Functions

When using the Get & Transform tools, you might need to create a formula. The formula language used in the Power Query editor is the Power Query M language. This appendix is a categorized list of the Power Query M functions with the syntax and a short description.

The first table is an alphabetical list of Excel functions and the equivalent Power Query M function. If the Excel function is not in Table B.1, then there is no direct Power Query M equivalent.

TROUBLESHOOTING

Power Query M functions are case sensitive.

In the Excel formula bar, you can enter =max(or =Max(or =MAX(or even =MAX (. In Power Query, you must enter the function with the exact case shown in the tables included in this appendix.

Excel Functions with Power Query M Equivalents

Table B.1 shows an alphabetical list of Excel functions with their Power Query M equivalents.

Table B.1   Excel Functions and Power Query M Equivalents

Excel Function	Power Query	Category
ABS	Number.Abs	Number Operations (Table B.28)
ACOS	Number.Acos	Number Trigonometry (Table B.31)
ASIN	Number.Asin	Number Trigonometry (Table B.31)
ATAN	Number.Atan	Number Trigonometry (Table B.31)
AVERAGE	List.Average	List Averages (Table B.14)
BITAND	Number.BitwiseAnd	Number Bytes (Table B.24)
BITLSHIFT	Number.BitwiseShiftLeft	Number Bytes (Table B.24)
BITOR	Number.BitwiseOr	Number Bytes (Table B.24)
BITRSHIFT	Number.BitwiseShiftRight	Number Bytes (Table B.24)
BITXOR	Number.BitwiseXor	Number Bytes (Table B.24)
CEILING	Number.RoundAwayFromZero	Number Rounding (Table B.30)
CEILING.MATH	Number.RoundUp	Number Rounding (Table B.30)
CHAR	Character.FromNumber	Text Text Comparisons (Table B.47)
CLEAN	Text.Clean	Text Transformations (Table B.48)
CODE	Character.ToNumber	Text Text Comparisons (Table B.47)
COMBIN	Number.Combinations	Number Operations (Table B.28)
CONCAT	Text.Combine	Text Transformations (Table B.48)
COS	Number.Cos	Number Trigonometry (Table B.31)
COSH	Number.Cosh	Number Trigonometry (Table B.31)
COVARIANCE.P	List.Covariance	List Numerics (Table B.18)
DATEVALUE	Date.FromText	Date (Table B.6)
DAY	Date.Day	Date (Table B.6)
DEC2BIN	Text.ToBinary	Text Text Comparisons (Table B.47)
ENCODEURL	Uri.EscapeDataString	URI (Table B.51)
EOMONTH	Date.EndOfMonth	Date (Table B.6)
EXP	Number.E	Number Constants (Table B.25)
EXP	Number.Exp	Number Operations (Table B.28)
FACT	Number.Factorial	Number Operations (Table B.28)
FLOOR	Number.RoundTowardZero	Number Rounding (Table B.30)

FLOOR.MATH	Number.RoundDown	Number Rounding (Table B.30)
HOUR	Duration.Hours	Duration (Table B.9)
HOUR	Time.Hour	Time (Table B.49)
ISEVEN	Number.IsEven	Number Information (Table B.27)
ISODD	Number.IsOdd	Number Information (Table B.27)
ISOWEEKNUM	Date.WeekOfYear	Date (Table B.6)
LEFT	Text.Start	Text Extraction (Table B.43)
LEN	Text.Length	Text Information (Table B.44)
LN	Number.Ln	Number Operations (Table B.28)
LOG	Number.Log	Number Operations (Table B.28)
LOG10	Number.Log10	Number Operations (Table B.28)
LOWER	Text.Lower	Text Transformations (Table B.48)
MAX	List.Max	List Ordering (Table B.19)
MEDIAN	List.Median	List Ordering (Table B.19)
MID	Text.Middle	Text Extraction (Table B.43)
MIN	List.Min	List Ordering (Table B.19)
MINUTE	Duration.Minutes	Duration (Table B.9)
MINUTE	Time.Minute	Time (Table B.49)
MOD	Number.Mod	Number Operations (Table B.28)
MONTH	Date.Month	Date (Table B.6)
PERMUT	Number.Permutations	Number Operations (Table B.28)
PI	Number.PI	Number Constants (Table B.25)
POWER	Number.Power	Number Operations (Table B.28)
PRODUCT	List.Product	List Numerics (Table B.18)
PRODUCT	Value.Multiply	Value (Table B.52)
PROPER	Text.Proper	Text Transformations (Table B.48)
QUOTIENT	Value.Divide	Value (Table B.52)
RAND	Number.Random	Number Random (Table B.29)
RANDBETWEEN	Number.RandomBetween	Number Random (Table B.29)
REPLACE	Text.Replace	Text Modification (Table B.46)
REPT	Text.Repeat	Text Transformations (Table B.48)
RIGHT	Text.End	Text Extraction (Table B.43)
ROUND	Number.Round	Number Rounding (Table B.30)
SECOND	Duration.Seconds	Duration (Table B.9)
SECOND	Time.Second	Time (Table B.49)

APPENDIX B

SIGN	Number.Sign	Number Operations (Table B.28)
SIN	Number.Sin	Number Trigonometry (Table B.31)
SINH	Number.Sinh	Number Trigonometry (Table B.31)
SORT	List.Sort	List Ordering (Table B.19)
SQRT	Number.Sqrt	Number Operations (Table B.28)
STDEV	List.StandardDeviation	List Averages (Table B.14)
SUM	List.Sum	List Averages (Table B.14)
SUM	Value.Add	Value (Table B.52)
TAN	Number.Tan	Number Trigonometry (Table B.31)
TANH	Number.Tanh	Number Trigonometry (Table B.31)
TEXT	Date.ToText	Date (Table B.6)
TEXT	Number.FromText	Number Conversion and Formatting (Table B.26)
TEXT	Number.ToText	Number Conversion and Formatting (Table B.26)
TEXT	Text.From	Text Text Comparisons (Table B.47)
TEXT	Time.ToText	Time (Table B.49)
TEXTJOIN	Combiner.CombineTextByDelimiter	Combiner (Table B.4)
TRIM	Text.Trim	Text Transformations (Table B.48)
UNIQUE	List.Distinct	List Selection (Table B.20)
UPPER	Text.Upper	Text Transformations (Table B.48)
VALUE	Number.From	Number Conversion and Formatting (Table B.26)
VALUE	Value.FromText	Text Text Comparisons (Table B.47)
WEEKDAY	Date.DayOfWeek	Date (Table B.6)
YEAR	Date.Year	Date (Table B.6)

Accessing Data Functions in Power Query M

Table B.2 lists how to access data functions in Power Query M.

Table B.2 Accessing Data Functions in Power Query M

Access.Database(database,[options])	Returns a structural representation of an Microsoft Access database.
ActiveDirectory.Domains([forestRootDomainName])	Returns a table with Domain information available in the current domain or optional Active Directory forest.

AdobeAnalytics.Cubes([options])	Returns a table of multidimensional packages from Adobe Analyics.
AdoDotNet.DataSource(providerName, connectionString,[options])	Returns the schema collection for an ADO.NET data source.
AdoDotNet.Query(providerName, connectionString, query,[options])	Returns the result of running a native query on an ADO.NET data source.
AnalysisServices.Database(server, database, [options])	Returns a table of multidimensional cubes or tabular models from the Analysis Services database.
AnalysisServices.Databases(server,[options])	Returns the Analysis Services databases on a particular host.
AzureStorage.BlobContents(url,[options])	Returns the content of the specified blob from an Azure storage vault.
AzureStorage.Blobs(account,[options])	Returns a navigational table containing all containers found in the Azure Storage account. Each row has the container name and a link to the container blobs.
AzureStorage.Tables(accountName)	Returns a navigational table containing a row for each table found at the account URL from an Azure storage vault. Each row contains a link to the azure table.
Csv.Document(source, [columns], [delimiter], [extraValues], [encoding])	Returns the contents of a CSV document as a table using the specified encoding.
Cube.AddAndExpandDimensionColumn(cube, dimensionSelector, attributeNames, [newColumnNames])	Merges the specified dimension table, dimensionSelector, into the cube's, cube, filter context and changes the dimensional granularity by expanding the specified set, attributeNames, of dimension attributes.
Cube.AddMeasureColumn(cube, column, measureSelector)	Adds a column with the name column to the cube that contains the results of the measure measureSelector applied in the row context of each row.
Cube.ApplyParameter(cube, parameter, [arguments])	Returns a cube after applying parameter with arguments to cube.
Cube.AttributeMemberId(attribute)	Returns the unique member identifier from a member property value.
Cube.AttributeMemberProperty(attribute, propertyName)	Returns the property propertyName of dimension attribute attribute.
Cube.CollapseAndRemoveColumns(cube, columnNames)	Changes the dimensional granularity of the filter context for the cube by collapsing the attributes mapped to the specified columns columnNames.
Cube.Dimensions(cube)	Returns a table containing the set of available dimensions within the cube.

Cube.DisplayFolders(cube)	Returns a nested tree of tables representing the display folder hierarchy of the objects (e.g., dimensions and measures) available for use in the cube.
Cube.MeasureProperties(cube)	Returns a table containing the set of available properties for measures that are expanded in the cube.
Cube.MeasureProperty(measure, propertyName)	Returns the property of a measure.
Cube.Measures(cube)	Returns a table containing the set of available measures within the cube.
Cube.Parameters(cube)	Returns a table containing the set of parameters that can be applied to the cube.
Cube.Properties(cube)	Returns a table containing the set of available properties for dimensions that are expanded in the cube.
Cube.PropertyKey(property)	Returns the key of property property.
Cube.ReplaceDimensions(cube, dimensions)	Replaces dimensions in a cube.
Cube.Transform(cube, transforms)	Applies the list cube functions, transforms, on the cube.
DB2.Database(server, database,[options])	Returns a table with data relating to the tables in the specified DB2 Database.
Excel.CurrentWorkbook()	Returns the tables in the current Excel workbook.
Excel.Workbook(workbook, [useHeaders], [delayTypes])	Returns a table representing sheets in the given Excel workbook.
Exchange.Contents()	Returns a table of contents from a Microsoft Exchange account.
Facebook.Graph(url)	Returns a table containing content from the Facebook graph .
File.Contents(path)	Returns the binary contents of the file located at a path.
Folder.Contents(path)	Returns a table containing the properties and contents of the files and folders found at a path.
Folder.Files(path)	Returns a table containing a row for each file found at a folder path, and subfolders. Each row contains properties of the folder or file and a link to its content.
GoogleAnalytics.Accounts()	Returns the Google Analytics accounts for the current credential.

Hdfs.Contents(url)	Returns a table containing a row for each folder and file found at the folder url, {0}, from a Hadoop file system. Each row contains properties of the folder or file and a link to its content.
Hdfs.Files(url)	Returns a table containing a row for each file found at the folder url, {0}, and subfolders from a Hadoop file system. Each row contains properties of the file and a link to its content.
HdInsight.Containers(accountName)	Returns a navigational table containing all containers found in the HDInsight account. Each row has the container name and table containing its files.
HdInsight.Contents(accountName)	Returns a navigational table containing all containers found in the HDInsight account. Each row has the container name and table containing its files.
HdInsight.Files(accountName, containerName)	Returns a table containing a row for each folder and file found at the container URL, and subfolders from an HDInsight account. Each row contains properties of the file/folder and a link to its content.
Informix.Database(server, database,[options])	Returns a table of SQL tables and views available in an Informix database on server server in the database instance named database.
Json.Document(jsonText, [encoding])	Returns the contents of a JSON document. The contents may be directly passed to the function as text, or it may be the binary value returned by a function like File.Contents.
Json.FromValue(value, [encoding])	Produces a JSON representation of a given value value with a text encoding specified by encoding.
MySQL.Database(server, database,[options])	Returns a table with data relating to the tables in the specified MySQL Database.
OData.Feed(serviceUri, [headers],[options])	Returns a table of OData feeds offered by an OData serviceUri.
Odbc.DataSource(connectionString,[options])	Returns a table of SQL tables and views from the ODBC data source specified by the connection string connectionString.
Odbc.InferOptions(connectionString)	Returns the result of trying to infer SQL capabilities for an ODBC driver.
Odbc.Query(connectionString, query,[options])	Connects to a generic provider with the given connection string and returns the result of evaluating the query.

APPENDIX B

OleDb.DataSource(connectionString,[options])	Returns a table of SQL tables and views from the OLE DB data source specified by the connection string.
OleDb.Query(connectionString, query,[options])	Returns the result of running a native query on an OLE DB data source.
Oracle.Database(server,[options])	Returns a table with data relating to the tables in the specified Oracle Database.
PostgreSQL.Database(server, database,[options])	Returns a table with data relating to the tables in the specified PostgreSQL Database.
RData.FromBinary(stream)	Returns a record of data frames from the RData file.
Salesforce.Data([loginURL],[options])	Connects to the Salesforce Objects API and returns the set of available objects (i.e., Accounts).
Salesforce.Reports([loginURL],[options])	Connects to the Salesforce Reports API and returns the set of available reports.
SapBusinessObjects.Universes(url)	Connects to the SAP BusinessObjects BI Universe at the specified URL and returns the set of available universes.
SapBusinessWarehouse.Cubes(server, systemNumberOrSystemId, sclientIds, [soptionsOrLogonGroups], [soptionss])	Returns the InfoCubes and queries in an SAP Business Warehouse system grouped by InfoArea.
SapHana.Database(server,[options])	Returns the packages in an SAP HANA database.
SharePoint.Contents(url, [options])	Returns a table containing a row for each folder and document found at the SharePoint site url. Each row contains properties of the folder or file and a link to its content.
SharePoint.Files(url,[options])	Returns a table containing a row for each document found at the SharePoint site url, and subfolders. Each row contains properties of the folder or file and a link to its content.
SharePoint.Tables(url,[options])	Returns a table containing the result of a SharePoint List as an OData feed.
Soda.Feed(url)	Returns the resulting table of a CSV file that can be accessed using the SODA 2.0 API. The URL must point to a valid SODA-compliant source that ends in a .csv extension.
Sql.Database(server, database,[options])	Returns a table containing SQL tables located on a SQL Server instance database.
Sql.Databases(server,[options])	Returns a table with references to databases located on a SQL Server instance. Returns a navigation table.

Sybase.Database(server, database,[options])	Returns a table with data relating to the tables in the specified Sybase Database.
Teradata.Database(server,[options])	Returns a table with data relating to the tables in the specified Teradata Database.
Web.Contents(url,[options])	Returns the contents downloaded from a web url as a binary value.
Web.Page(html)	Returns the contents of an HTML webpage as a table.
WebAction.Request(method, url,[options])	Creates an action that, when executed, will return the results of performing a method request against url using HTTP as a binary value.
Xml.Document(contents,[options], [encoding])	Returns the contents of an XML document as a hierarchical table (list of records).
Xml.Tables(contents,[options], [encoding])	Returns the contents of an XML document as a nested collection of flattened tables.

Binary Functions in Power Query M

Table B.3   List of Binary Functions in Power Query M

Binary.Buffer(binary)	Buffers the binary value in memory. The result of this call is a stable binary value, which means it will have a deterministic length and order of bytes.
Binary.Combine(binaries)	Combines a list of binaries into a single binary.
Binary.Compress(binary, compressionType)	Compresses a binary value using the given compression type.
Binary.Decompress(binary, compressionType)	Decompresses a binary value using the given compression type.
Binary.From(Value, [encoding])	Returns a binary value from the given value.
Binary.FromList(list)	Converts a list of numbers into a binary value.
Binary.FromText(text, encoding)	Decodes data from a text form into binary.
Binary.InferContentType(source)	Returns a record with field Content.Type that contains the inferred MIME-type.
Binary.Length(binary)	Returns the length of binary values.
Binary.ToList(binary)	Converts a binary value into a list of numbers.
Binary.ToText(binary, encoding)	Encodes binary data into a text form.
BinaryFormat.7BitEncodedSigned Integer(binary)	A binary format that reads a 64-bit signed integer that was encoded using a 7-bit variable-length encoding.
BinaryFormat.7BitEncodedUnsigned Integer(binary)	A binary format that reads a 64-bit unsigned integer that was encoded using a 7-bit variable-length encoding.

BinaryFormat.Binary([length])	Returns a binary format that reads a binary value.
BinaryFormat.Byte(binary)	A binary format that reads an 8-bit unsigned integer.
BinaryFormat.ByteOrder(binaryFormat, byteOrder)	Returns a binary format with the byte order specified by a function.
BinaryFormat.Choice(binaryFormat, choice, [type])	Returns a binary format that chooses the next binary format based on a value that has already been read.
BinaryFormat.Decimal(binary)	A binary format that reads a .NET 16-byte decimal value.
BinaryFormat.Double(binary)	A binary format that reads an 8-byte IEEE double-precision floating point value.
BinaryFormat.Group(binaryFormat, group, [extra], [lastKey])	Returns a binary format that reads a group of items. Each item value is preceded by a unique key value. The result is a list of item values.
BinaryFormat.Length(binaryFormat, length)	Returns a binary format that limits the amount of data that can be read. Both BinaryFormat.List and BinaryFormat.Binary can be used to read until end of the data. BinaryFormat.Length can be used to limit the number of bytes that are read.
BinaryFormat.List(binaryFormat, [countOrCondition])	Returns a binary format that reads a sequence of items and returns a list.
BinaryFormat.Null(binary)	A binary format that reads zero bytes and returns null.
BinaryFormat.Record(record)	Returns a binary format that reads a record. Each field in the record can have a different binary format.
BinaryFormat.SignedInteger16(binary)	A binary format that reads a 16-bit signed integer.
BinaryFormat.SignedInteger32(binary)	A binary format that reads a 32-bit signed integer.
BinaryFormat.SignedInteger64(binary)	A binary format that reads a 64-bit signed integer.
BinaryFormat.Single(binary)	A binary format that reads a 4-byte IEEE single-precision floating point value.
BinaryFormat.Text(length, [encoding])	Returns a binary format that reads a text value. The optional encoding value specifies the encoding of the text.
BinaryFormat.Transform(binaryFormat, transform)	Returns a binary format that will transform the values read by another binary format.
BinaryFormat.UnsignedInteger16(binary)	A binary format that reads a 16-bit unsigned integer.
BinaryFormat.UnsignedInteger32(binary)	A binary format that reads a 32-bit unsigned integer.
BinaryFormat.UnsignedInteger64(binary)	A binary format that reads a 64-bit unsigned integer.
Table.PartitionValues(table)	Returns information about how a table is partitioned.

Combiner Functions in Power Query M

Table B.4   List of Combiner Functions in Power Query M

Combiner.CombineTextByDelimiter (delimiters, [quoteStyle])	Returns a function that combines a list of text into a single text using the specified delimiter. Similar to Excel function TEXTJOIN.
Combiner.CombineTextByEachDelimiter (delimiters, [quoteStyle])	Returns a function that combines a list of text into a single text using each specified delimiter in sequence.
Combiner.CombineTextByLengths(lengths, [template])	Returns a function that merges a list of text into a single text.
Combiner.CombineTextByPositions (positions, [template])	Returns a function that merges a list of text into a single text.
Combiner.CombineTextByRanges(ranges, [template])	Returns a function that merges a list of text into a single text.

Comparer Functions in Power Query M

Table B.5   List of Comparer Functions in Power Query M

Comparer.Equals(comparer, x, y)	Returns a logical value based on the equality check over the two given values.
Comparer.FromCulture(culture, [ignoreCase])	Returns a comparer function given the culture and a logical value for case sensitivity for the comparison. The default value for ignoreCase is false. The value for culture are well-known text representations of locales used in the .NET framework.
Comparer.Ordinal(x, y)	Returns a comparer function which uses Ordinal rules to compare values.
Comparer.OrdinalIgnoreCase(x, y)	Returns a case-insensitive comparer function which uses Ordinal rules to compare the provided values x and y.

APPENDIX B

Date Functions in Power Query M

Table B.6   List of Date Functions in Power Query M

Date.AddDays(dateTime, days)	Returns a Date/DateTime/DateTimeZone value with the day portion incremented by the number of days provided. It also handles incrementing the month and year portions of the value as appropriate.
Date.AddMonths(dateTime, numberOfMonths)	Returns a DateTime value with the month portion incremented by n months.
Date.AddQuarters(dateTime, quarters)	Returns a Date/DateTime/DateTimeZone value incremented by the number of quarters provided. Each quarter is defined as a duration of three months. It also handles incrementing the year portion of the value as appropriate.
Date.AddWeeks(dateTime, weeks)	Returns a Date/DateTime/DateTimeZone value incremented by the number of weeks provided. Each week is defined as a duration of seven days. It also handles incrementing the month and year portions of the value as appropriate.
Date.AddYears(dateTime, years)	Returns a DateTime value with the year portion incremented by n years.
Date.Day(dateTime)	Returns the day for a DateTime value. Similar to Excel function DAY.
Date.DayOfWeek(dateTime, [firstDayOfWeek])	Returns a number between 0 and 6 representing the day of the week from a DateTime value. Similar to Excel function WEEKDAY.
Date.DayOfWeekName(date, [culture])	Returns the day of the week name.
Date.DayOfYear(dateTime)	Returns a number that represents the day of the year from a DateTime value.
Date.DaysInMonth(dateTime)	Returns the number of days in the month from a DateTime value.
Date.EndOfDay(dateTime)	Returns a DateTime value for the end of the day.
Date.EndOfMonth(dateTime)	Returns a DateTime value for the end of the month. Similar to Excel function EOMONTH.
Date.EndOfQuarter(dateTime)	Returns a Date/DateTime/DateTimeZone value representing the end of the quarter. The date and time portions are reset to their terminating values for the quarter. The timezone information is persisted.
Date.EndOfWeek(dateTime, [firstDayOfWeek])	Returns a DateTime value for the end of the week.
Date.EndOfYear(dateTime)	Returns a DateTime value for the end of the year.
Date.From(value, [culture])	Returns a Date value from a value.

Date.FromText(date, [culture])	Returns a Date value from a set of date formats and culture value. Similar to Excel function DATEVALUE.
Date.IsInCurrentDay(dateTime)	Indicates whether the given DateTime value dateTime occurs during the current day, as determined by the current date and time on the system.
Date.IsInCurrentMonth(dateTime)	Returns a logical value indicating whether the given Date/DateTime/DateTimeZone occurred during the current month, as determined by the current date and time on the system.
Date.IsInCurrentQuarter(dateTime)	Returns a logical value indicating whether the given Date/DateTime/DateTimeZone occurred during the current quarter, as determined by the current date and time on the system.
Date.IsInCurrentWeek(dateTime)	Returns a logical value indicating whether the given Date/DateTime/DateTimeZone occurred during the current week, as determined by the current date and time on the system.
Date.IsInCurrentYear(dateTime)	Returns a logical value indicating whether the given Date/DateTime/DateTimeZone occurred during the current year, as determined by the current date and time on the system.
Date.IsInNextDay(dateTime)	Indicates whether the given DateTime value dateTime occurs during the next day, as determined by the current date and time on the system.
Date.IsInNextMonth(dateTime)	Returns a logical value indicating whether the given Date/DateTime/DateTimeZone occurred during the next month, as determined by the current date and time on the system.
Date.IsInNextNDays(dateTime, days)	Indicates whether the given DateTime value dateTime occurs during the next number of days, as determined by the current date and time on the system.
Date.IsInNextNMonths(dateTime, months)	Indicates whether the given DateTime value dateTime occurs during the next number of months, as determined by the current date and time on the system.
Date.IsInNextNQuarters(dateTime, quarters)	Indicates whether the given DateTime value dateTime occurs during the next number of quarters, as determined by the current date and time on the system.
Date.IsInNextNWeeks(dateTime, weeks)	Indicates whether the given DateTime value dateTime occurs during the next number of weeks, as determined by the current date and time on the system.

APPENDIX B

Date.IsInNextNYears(dateTime, years)	Indicates whether the given DateTime value dateTime occurs during the next number of years, as determined by the current date and time on the system.
Date.IsInNextQuarter(dateTime)	Returns a logical value indicating whether the given Date/DateTime/DateTimeZone occurred during the next quarter, as determined by the current date and time on the system.
Date.IsInNextWeek(dateTime)	Returns a logical value indicating whether the given Date/DateTime/DateTimeZone occurred during the next week, as determined by the current date and time on the system.
Date.IsInNextYear(dateTime)	Returns a logical value indicating whether the given Date/DateTime/DateTimeZone occurred during the next year, as determined by the current date and time on the system.
Date.IsInPreviousDay(dateTime)	Indicates whether the given DateTime value dateTime occurs during the previous day, as determined by the current date and time on the system.
Date.IsInPreviousMonth(dateTime)	Returns a logical value indicating whether the given Date/DateTime/DateTimeZone occurred during the previous month, as determined by the current date and time on the system.
Date.IsInPreviousNDays(dateTime, days)	Indicates whether the given DateTime value dateTime occurs during the previous number of days, as determined by the current date and time on the system.
Date.IsInPreviousNMonths(dateTime, months)	Indicates whether the given DateTime value dateTime occurs during the previous number of months, as determined by the current date and time on the system.
Date.IsInPreviousNQuarters(dateTime, quarters)	Indicates whether the given DateTime value dateTime occurs during the previous number of quarters, as determined by the current date and time on the system.
Date.IsInPreviousNWeeks(dateTime, weeks)	Indicates whether the given DateTime value dateTime occurs during the previous number of weeks, as determined by the current date and time on the system.
Date.IsInPreviousNYears(dateTime, years)	Indicates whether the given DateTime value dateTime occurs during the previous number of years, as determined by the current date and time on the system.

Date.IsInPreviousQuarter(dateTime)	Returns a logical value indicating whether the given Date/DateTime/DateTimeZone occurred during the previous quarter, as determined by the current date and time on the system.
Date.IsInPreviousWeek(dateTime)	Returns a logical value indicating whether the given Date/DateTime/DateTimeZone occurred during the previous week, as determined by the current date and time on the system.
Date.IsInPreviousYear(dateTime)	Returns a logical value indicating whether the given Date/DateTime/DateTimeZone occurred during the previous year, as determined by the current date and time on the system.
Date.IsInYearToDate(dateTime)	Returns a logical value indicating whether the given Date/DateTime/DateTimeZone occurred in the period starting January 1st of the current year and ending on the current day, as determined by the current date and time on the system.
Date.IsLeapYear(dateTime)	Returns a logical value indicating whether the year portion of a DateTime value is a leap year.
Date.Month(dateTime)	Returns the month from a DateTime value. Similar to Excel function MONTH.
Date.MonthName(date, [culture])	Returns the name of the month component.
Date.QuarterOfYear(dateTime)	Returns a number between 1 and 4 for the quarter of the year from a DateTime value.
Date.StartOfDay(dateTime)	Returns a DateTime value for the start of the day.
Date.StartOfMonth(dateTime)	Returns a DateTime value representing the start of the month.
Date.StartOfQuarter(dateTime)	Returns a DateTime value representing the start of the quarter.
Date.StartOfWeek(dateTime, [firstDay])	Returns a DateTime value representing the start of the week.
Date.StartOfYear(dateTime)	Returns a DateTime value representing the start of the year.
Date.ToRecord(date)	Returns a record containing parts of a Date value.
Date.ToText(date, [format], [culture])	Returns a text value from a Date value. Similar to Excel function TEXT.
Date.WeekOfMonth(dateTime)	Returns a number for the count of week in the current month.
Date.WeekOfYear(dateTime, [firstDayOfWeek])	Returns a number for the count of week in the current year. Similar to Excel function ISOWEEKNUM.
Date.Year(dateTime)	Returns the year from a DateTime value. Similar to Excel function YEAR.

DateTime Functions in Power Query M

Table B.7   List of DateTime Functions in Power Query M

DateTime.AddZone(dateTime, timezoneHours, [timezoneMinutes])	Adds the timezonehours as an offset to the input DateTime value and returns a new DateTimeZone value.
DateTime.Date(dateTime)	Returns a date part from a DateTime value.
DateTime.FixedLocalNow()	Returns a DateTime value set to the current date and time on the system.
DateTime.From(value, [culture])	Returns a DateTime value from a value.
DateTime.FromFileTime(fileTime)	Returns a DateTime value from the supplied number.
DateTime.FromText(dateTime, [culture])	Returns a DateTime value from a set of date formats and culture value.
DateTime.IsInCurrentHour(dateTime)	Indicates whether the given DateTime value occurs during the current hour, as determined by the current date and time on the system.
DateTime.IsInCurrentMinute(dateTime)	Indicates whether the given DateTime value occurs during the current minute, as determined by the current date and time on the system.
DateTime.IsInCurrentSecond(dateTime)	Indicates whether the given DateTime value occurs during the current second, as determined by the current date and time on the system.
DateTime.IsInNextHour(dateTime)	Indicates whether the given DateTime value occurs during the next hour, as determined by the current date and time on the system.
DateTime.IsInNextMinute(dateTime)	Indicates whether the given DateTime value occurs during the next minute, as determined by the current date and time on the system.
DateTime.IsInNextNHours(dateTime, hours)	Indicates whether the given DateTime value occurs during the next number of hours, as determined by the current date and time on the system.
DateTime.IsInNextNMinutes(dateTime, minutes)	Indicates whether the given DateTime value occurs during the next number of minutes, as determined by the current date and time on the system.
DateTime.IsInNextNSeconds(dateTime, seconds)	Indicates whether the given DateTime value occurs during the next number of seconds, as determined by the current date and time on the system.
DateTime.IsInNextSecond(dateTime)	Indicates whether the given DateTime value occurs during the next second, as determined by the current date and time on the system.

DateTime.IsInPreviousHour(dateTime)	Indicates whether the given DateTime value occurs during the previous hour, as determined by the current date and time on the system.
DateTime.IsInPreviousMinute(dateTime)	Indicates whether the given DateTime value occurs during the previous minute, as determined by the current date and time on the system.
DateTime.IsInPreviousNHours(dateTime, hours)	Indicates whether the given DateTime value occurs during the previous number of hours, as determined by the current date and time on the system.
DateTime.IsInPreviousNMinutes(dateTime, minutes)	Indicates whether the given DateTime value occurs during the previous number of minutes, as determined by the current date and time on the system.
DateTime.IsInPreviousNSeconds(dateTime, seconds)	Indicates whether the given DateTime value occurs during the previous number of seconds, as determined by the current date and time on the system.
DateTime.IsInPreviousSecond(dateTime)	Indicates whether the given DateTime value occurs during the previous second, as determined by the current date and time on the system.
DateTime.LocalNow()	Returns a DateTime value set to the current date and time on the system.
DateTime.Time(dateTime)	Returns a time part from a DateTime value.
DateTime.ToRecord(dateTime)	Returns a record containing parts of a DateTime value.
DateTime.ToText(dateTime, [format], [culture])	Returns a text value from a DateTime value.

DateTimeZone Functions in Power Query M

Table B.8   List of DateTimeZone Functions in Power Query M

DateTimeZone.FixedLocalNow()	Returns a DateTimeZone value set to the current date, time, and timezone offset on the system.
DateTimeZone.FixedUtcNow()	Returns the current date and time in UTC (the GMT timezone).
DateTimeZone.From(value, [culture])	Returns a DateTimeZone value from a value.
DateTimeZone.FromFileTime(fileTime)	Returns a DateTimeZone from a number value.
DateTimeZone.FromText(dateTimeZone, [culture])	Returns a DateTimeZone value from a set of date formats and culture value.

DateTimeZone.LocalNow()	Returns a DateTime value set to the current system date and time.
DateTimeZone. RemoveZone(dateTimeZone)	Returns a DateTime value with the zone information removed from the input DateTimeZone value.
DateTimeZone. SwitchZone(dateTimeZone, timezoneHours, [timezoneMinutes])	Changes the timezone information for the input DateTimeZone.
DateTimeZone.ToLocal(dateTime)	Returns a DateTime value from the local time zone.
DateTimeZone.ToRecord(dateTimeZone)	Returns a record containing parts of a DateTime value.
DateTimeZone.ToText(dateTimeZone, [format], [culture])	Returns a text value from a DateTime value.
DateTimeZone.ToUtc(dateTime)	Returns a DateTime value to the Utc time zone.
DateTimeZone.UtcNow()	Returns a DateTime value set to the current system date and time in the Utc timezone.
DateTimeZone.ZoneHours(dateTime)	Returns a time zone hour value from a DateTime value.
DateTimeZone. ZoneMinutes(dateTimeZone)	Returns a time zone minute value from a DateTime value.

Duration Functions in Power Query M

Table B.9 List of Duration Functions in Power Query M

Duration.Days(duration)	Returns the day component of a Duration value.
Duration.From(value)	Returns a Duration value from a value.
Duration.FromText(duration)	Returns a Duration value from a text value.
Duration.Hours(duration)	Returns an hour component of a Duration value. Similar to Excel function HOUR.
Duration.Minutes(duration)	Returns a minute component of a Duration value. Similar to Excel function MINUTE.
Duration.Seconds(duration)	Returns a second component of a Duration value. Similar to Excel function SECOND.
Duration.ToRecord(duration)	Returns a record with parts of a Duration value.
Duration.TotalDays(duration)	Returns the total magnitude of days from a Duration value.
Duration.TotalHours(duration)	Returns the total magnitude of hours from a Duration value.
Duration.TotalMinutes(duration)	Returns the total magnitude of minutes from a Duration value.

Duration.TotalSeconds(duration)	Returns the total magnitude of seconds from a Duration value.
Duration.ToText(duration, [format])	Returns a text value from a Duration value.

Error Functions in Power Query M

Table B.10   List of Error Functions in Power Query M

Diagnostics.ActivityId()	Returns an opaque identifier for the currently-running evaluation.
Diagnostics.Trace(traceLevel, message, value, [delayed])	Writes a trace message, if tracing is enabled, and returns value.
Error.Record(reason, message, detail)	Returns a record containing fields "Reason", "Message", and "Detail" set to the provided values. The record can be used to raise or throw an error.

Expression Functions in Power Query M

Table B.11   List of Expression Functions in Power Query M

Expression.Constant(value)	Returns a constant text literal from a value.
Expression.Evaluate(expression, [environment])	Evaluates a text expression and returns the evaluated value.
Expression.Identifier(name)	Returns a text value that can be used as an identifier from a text value.

Function Functions in Power Query M

Table B.12   List of Function Functions in Power Query M

Function.From(functionType, function)	Takes a unary function and creates a new function with the type functionType that constructs a list out of its arguments and passes it to function.
Function.Invoke(function, args)	Invokes the given function using the specified and returns the result.
Function.InvokeAfter(function, delay)	Returns the result of invoking function after duration delay has passed.
Function.IsDataSource(function)	Returns whether or not function is considered a data source.

Lines Functions in Power Query M

Table B.13   List of Lines Functions in Power Query M

Lines.FromBinary(binary, [quoteStyle], [includeLineSeparators], [encoding])	Converts a binary value to a list of text values split at lines breaks.
Lines.FromText(text, [quoteStyle], [includeLineSeparators])	Converts a text value to a list of text values split at lines breaks.
Lines.ToBinary(lines, [lineSeparator], [encoding], [includeByteOrderMark])	Converts a list of text into a binary value using the specified encoding and lineSeparator. The specified lineSeparator is appended to each line. If not specified, then the carriage return and line feed characters are used.
Lines.ToText (lines, [lineSeparator])	Converts a list of text into a single text. The specified lineSeparator is appended to each line. If not specified, then the carriage return and line feed characters are used.

List Functions

The List functions are separated into these categories: List Generators, List Information, List Membership, List Numerics, List Ordering, List Selection, List Set Operations, and List Transformation.

List Averages Functions in Power Query M

Table B.14   List of List Averages Functions in Power Query M

List.Average(list)	Returns an average value from a list in the datatype of the values in the list. Similar to Excel function AVERAGE.
List.Mode(list, [equationCriteria])	Returns an item that appears most commonly in a list.
List.Modes(list, [equationCriteria])	Returns all items that appear with the same maximum frequency.
List.StandardDeviation(list)	Returns the standard deviation from a list of values. List.StandardDeviation performs a sample-based estimate. The result is a number for numbers, and a duration for DateTimes and Durations. Similar to Excel function STDEV.
List.Sum(list)	Returns the sum from a list. Similar to Excel function SUM.

List Generators Functions in Power Query M

Table B.15   List of List Generators Functions in Power Query M

List.Dates(start, count, step)	Returns a list of date values from size count, starting at start and adds an increment to every value.
List.DateTimes(start, count, step)	Returns a list of DateTime values from size count, starting at start and adds an increment to every value.
List.DateTimeZones(start, count, increment)	Returns a list of of DateTimeZone values from size count, starting at start and adds an increment to every value.
List.Durations(start, count, step)	Returns a list of durations values from size count, starting at start and adds an increment to every value.
List.Generate(initial, condition, next, [selector])	Generates a list from a value function, a condition function, a next function, and an optional transformation function on the values.
List.Numbers(start, count, [increment])	Returns a list of numbers from size count starting at initial and adds an increment. The increment defaults to 1.
List.Random(count, [seed])	Returns a list of count random numbers, with an optional seed parameter.
List.Times(start, count, step)	Returns a list of time values of size count, starting at start.

List Information Functions in Power Query M

Table B.16   List of List Information Functions in Power Query M

List.Count(list)	Returns the number of items in a list.
List.IsEmpty(list)	Returns whether a list is empty.
List.NonNullCount(list)	Returns the number of items in a list excluding null values.

APPENDIX B

List Membership Functions in Power Query M

Table B.17   List of List Membership Functions in Power Query M

List.AllTrue(list)	Returns true if all expressions in a list are true.
List.AnyTrue(list)	Returns true if any expression in a list in true.
List.Contains(list, value, [equationCriteria])	Returns true if a value is found in a list.
List.ContainsAll(list, values,[equationCriteria])	Returns true if all items in values are found in a list.
List.ContainsAny(list, values,[equationCriteria])	Returns true if any item in values is found in a list.
List.PositionOf(list, value, [occurrence], [equationCriteria])	Finds the first occurrence of a value in a list and returns its position.
List.PositionOfAny(list, values, [occurrence], [equationCriteria])	Finds the first occurrence of any value in values and returns its position.

List Numerics Functions in Power Query M

Table B.18   List of List Numerics Functions in Power Query M

List.Covariance(list1, list2)	Returns the covariance from two lists as a number. Similar to Excel function COVARIANCE.P.
List.Product(list)	Returns the product from a list of numbers. Similar to Excel function PRODUCT.

List Ordering Functions in Power Query M

Table B.19   List of List Ordering Functions in Power Query M

List.Max(list, [default], [comparisonCriteria], [includeNulls])	Returns the maximum item in a list, or the optional default value if the list is empty. Similar to Excel function MAX.
List.MaxN(list, countOrCondition, [comparisonCriteria], [includeNulls])	Returns the maximum values in the list. After the rows are sorted, optional parameters may be specified to further filter the result.
List.Median(list, [comparisonCriteria])	Returns the median item from a list. Similar to Excel function MEDIAN.
List.Min(list, [default], [comparisonCriteria], [includeNulls])	Returns the minimum item in a list, or the optional default value if the list is empty. Similar to Excel function MIN.

List.MinN(list, countOrCondition, [comparisonCriteria], [includeNulls])	Returns the minimum values in a list.
List.Sort(list, [comparisonCriteria])	Returns a sorted list using comparison criterion. Similar to Excel function SORT.

List Selection Functions in Power Query M

Table B.20   List of List Selection Functions in Power Query M

List.Alternate(list, count, [repeatInterval], [offset])	Returns a list with the items alternated from the original list based on a count, optional repeatInterval, and an optional offset.
List.Buffer(list)	Buffers the list in memory. The result of this call is a stable list, which means it will have a deterministic count, and order of items.
List.Distinct(list, [equationCriteria], criteria)	Filters a list down by removing duplicates. An optional equation criteria value can be specified to control equality comparison. The first value from each equality group is chosen. Similar to Excel function UNIQUE.
List.FindText(list, text)	Searches a list of values, including record fields, for a text value.
List.First(list, [defaultValue])	Returns the first value of the list or the specified default if empty. Returns the first item in the list, or the optional default value, if the list is empty. If the list is empty and a default value is not specified, the function returns.
List.FirstN(list, countOrCondition)	Returns the first set of items in the list by specifying how many items to return or a qualifying condition provided by countOrCondition.
List.InsertRange(list, offset, values)	Inserts items from values at the given index in the input list.
List.IsDistinct(list, [equationCriteria])	Returns whether a list is distinct.
List.Last(list, [defaultValue])	Returns the last set of items in the list by specifying how many items to return or a qualifying condition provided by countOrCondition.
List.LastN(list, [countOrCondition])	Returns the last set of items in a list by specifying how many items to return or a qualifying condition.
List.MatchesAll(list, condition)	Returns true if all items in a list meet a condition.
List.MatchesAny(list, condition)	Returns true if any item in a list meets a condition.
List.Positions(list)	Returns a list of positions for an input list.
List.Range(list, offset, [count])	Returns a count items starting at an offset.

APPENDIX B

List.Select(list, condition)	Selects the items that match a condition.
List.Single(list)	Returns the single item of the list or throws an Expression.Error if the list has more than one item.
List.SingleOrDefault(list, [default])	Returns a single item from a list.
List.Skip(list, [countOrCondition])	Skips the first item of the list. Given an empty list, it returns an empty list. This function takes an optional parameter countOrCondition to support skipping multiple values.

List Set Operations Functions in Power Query M

Table B.21   List of List Set Operations Functions in Power Query M

List.Difference(list1, list2,[equationCriteria])	Returns the items in list 1 that do not appear in list 2. Duplicate values are supported.
List.Intersect(list, [equationCriteria])	Returns a list from a list of lists and intersects common items in individual lists. Duplicate values are supported.
List.Union(list,[equationCriteria])	Returns a list from a list of lists and unions the items in the individual lists. The returned list contains all items in any input lists. Duplicate values are matched as part of the Union.
List.Zip(lists)	Returns a list of lists combining items at the same position.

List Transformation Functions in Power Query M

Table B.22   List of List Transformation Functions in Power Query M

List.Accumulate(list, seed, accumulator)	Accumulates a result from the list. Starting from the initial value seed, this function applies the accumulator function and returns the final result.
List.Combine(list)	Merges a list of lists into single list.
List.RemoveFirstN(table, [countOrCondition])	Returns a list with the specified number of elements removed from the list starting at the first element. The number of elements removed depends on the optional countOrCondition parameter.
List.RemoveItems(list1, list2)	Removes items from list1 that are present in list2 and returns a new list.

List.RemoveLastN(list, offset, [count])	Returns a list with the specified number of elements removed from the list starting at the last element. The number of elements removed depends on the optional countOrCondition parameter.
List.RemoveMatchingItems(list, values, [equationCriteria])	Removes all occurrences of the given values in the list.
List.RemoveNulls(list)	Removes null values from a list.
List.RemoveRange(list, offset, [count])	Returns a list that removes count items starting at offset. The default count is 1.
List.Repeat(list, count)	Returns a list that repeats the contents of an input list count times.
List.ReplaceMatchingItems(list, replacements,[equationCriteria])	Replaces occurrences of existing values in the list with new values using the provided equationCriteria. Old and new values are provided by the replacements parameters. An optional equation criteria value can be specified to control equality comparisons.
List.ReplaceRange(list, index, count, replaceWith)	Returns a list that replaces count values in a list with a replaceWith list starting at an index.
List.ReplaceValue(list, oldValue, newValue, replacer)	Searches a list of values for the value and replaces each occurrence with the replacement value.
List.Reverse(list)	Returns a list that reverses the items in a list.
List.Split(list, pageSize)	Splits the specified list into a list of lists using the specified page size.
List.Transform(list, transform)	Performs the function on each item in the list and returns the new list.
List.TransformMany(list, collectionTransform, resultTransform)	Returns a list whose elements are projected from the input list.

APPENDIX B

Logical Functions in Power Query M

Table B.23   List of Logical Functions in Power Query M

Logical.From(value)	Returns a logical value from a value.
Logical.FromText(text)	Returns a logical value of true or false from a text value.
Logical.ToText(logical)	Returns a text value from a logical value.

Number Functions

The Number category is split into Number Constants, Number Conversion and Formatting, Number Information, Number Operations, Number Random, Number Rounding, and Number Trigonometry.

Number Bytes Functions in Power Query M

Table B.24   List of Number Bytes Functions in Power Query M

Number.BitwiseAnd(number1, number2)	Returns the result of a bitwise AND operation on the provided operands. Similar to Excel function BITAND.
Number.BitwiseNot(x, y)	Returns the result of a bitwise NOT operation on the provided operands.
Number.BitwiseOr(x, y)	Returns the result of a bitwise OR operation on the provided operands. Similar to Excel function BITOR.
Number.BitwiseShiftLeft(x, y)	Returns the result of a bitwise shift left operation on the operands. Similar to Excel function BITLSHIFT.
Number.BitwiseShiftRight(x, y)	Returns the result of a bitwise shift right operation on the operands. Similar to Excel function BITRSHIFT.
Number.BitwiseXor(x, y)	Returns the result of a bitwise XOR operation on the provided operands. Similar to Excel function BITXOR.

Number Constants Functions in Power Query M

Table B.25   List of Number Constants Functions in Power Query M

Number.E	Returns 2.7182818284590451, the value of e up to 16 decimal digits. Similar to Excel function EXP.
Number.Epsilon	Returns the smallest possible number.
Number.NaN	Represents 0/0.
Number.NegativeInfinity	Represents -1/0.
Number.PI	Returns 3.1415926535897931, the value for Pi up to 16 decimal digits. Similar to Excel function PI.
Number.PositiveInfinity	Represents 1/0.

Number Conversion and Formatting Functions in Power Query M

Table B.26   List of Number Conversion and Formatting Functions in Power Query M

Byte.From(value, [culture], [roundingMode])	Returns a 8-bit integer number value from the given value.
Currency.From(value, [culture], [roundingMode])	Returns a currency value from the given value.
Decimal.From(value, [culture])	Returns a decimal number value from the given value.
Double.From(value, [culture])	Returns a double number value from the given value.
Int16.From(value, [culture], [roundingMode])	Returns a 16-bit integer number value from the given value.
Int32.From(value, [culture], [roundingMode])	Returns a 32-bit integer number value from the given value.
Int64.From(value, [culture], [roundingMode])	Returns a 64-bit integer number value from the given value.
Int8.From(value, [culture], [roundingMode])	Returns a signed 8-bit integer number value from the given value.
Number.From(value, [culture])	Returns a number value from a value. Similar to Excel function VALUE.
Number.FromText(text, [culture])	Returns a number value from a text value. Similar to Excel function TEXT.
Number.ToText(number, [format], [culture])	Returns a text value from a number value. Similar to Excel function TEXT.
Percentage.From(value, [culture])	Returns a percentage value from the given value.
Single.From(value, [culture])	Returns a single number value from the given value.

Number Information Functions in Power Query M

Table B.27   List of Number Information Functions in Power Query M

Number.IsEven(value)	Returns true if a value is an even number. Similar to Excel function ISEVEN.
Number.IsNaN(value)	Returns true if a value is Number.NaN.
Number.IsOdd(value)	Returns true if a value is an odd number. Similar to Excel function ISODD.

APPENDIX B

Number Operations Functions in Power Query M

Table B.28   List of Number Operations Functions in Power Query M

Number.Abs(number)	Returns the absolute value of a number. Similar to Excel function ABS.
Number.Combinations(setSize, combinationSize)	Returns the number of combinations of a given number of items for the optional combination size. Similar to Excel function COMBIN.
Number.Exp(number)	Returns a number representing e raised to a power. Similar to Excel function EXP.
Number.Factorial(number)	Returns the factorial of a number. Similar to Excel function FACT.
Number.IntegerDivide(number1, number2,[precision])	Divides two numbers and returns the whole part of the resulting number.
Number.Ln(number)	Returns the natural logarithm of a number. Similar to Excel function LN.
Number.Log(number, [base])	Returns the logarithm of a number to the base. Similar to Excel function LOG.
Number.Log10(number)	Returns the base-10 logarithm of a number. Similar to Excel function LOG10.
Number.Mod(number, divisor,[precision])	Divides two numbers and returns the remainder of the resulting number. Similar to Excel function MOD.
Number.Permutations(setSize, permutationSize)	Returns the number of total permutatons of a given number of items for the optional permutation size. Similar to Excel function PERMUT.
Number.Power(number, power)	Returns a number raised by a power. Similar to Excel function POWER.
Number.Sign(number)	Returns 1 for positive numbers, -1 for negative numbers, or 0 for zero. Similar to Excel function SIGN.
Number.Sqrt(number)	Returns the square root of a number. Similar to Excel function SQRT.

Number Random Functions in Power Query M

Table B.29   List of Number Random Functions in Power Query M

Number.Random()	Returns a random fractional number between 0 and 1. Similar to Excel function RAND.
Number.RandomBetween(bottom, top)	Returns a random number between the two given number values. Similar to Excel function RANDBETWEEN.

Number Rounding Functions in Power Query M

Table B.30   List of Number Rounding Functions in Power Query M

Number.Round(value, digits, roundingMode)	Rounds a number to a certain number of digits. Similar to Excel function ROUND.
Number.RoundAwayFromZero(value)	Returns Number.RoundUp(value) when value >= 0 and Number.RoundDown(value) when value < 0. Similar to Excel function CEILING.
Number.RoundDown(value)	Returns the largest integer less than or equal to a number value. Similar to Excel function FLOOR.MATH.
Number.RoundTowardZero(value)	Returns Number.RoundDown(x) when x >= 0 and Number.RoundUp(x) when x < 0. Similar to Excel function FLOOR.
Number.RoundUp(value)	Returns the larger integer greater than or equal to a number value. Similar to Excel function CEILING.MATH.

Number Trigonometry Functions in Power Query M

Table B.31   List of Number Trigonometry Functions in Power Query M

Number.Acos(angle)	Returns the arccosine of a number. Similar to Excel function ACOS.
Number.Asin(angle)	Returns the arcsine of a number. Similar to Excel function ASIN.
Number.Atan(angle)	Returns the arctangent of a number. Similar to Excel function ATAN.
Number.Atan2(y, x)	Returns the arctangent of the division of two numbers.
Number.Cos(angle)	Returns the cosine of a number. Similar to Excel function COS.
Number.Cosh(angle)	Returns the hyperbolic cosine of a number. Similar to Excel function COSH.
Number.Sin(angle)	Returns the sine of a number. Similar to Excel function SIN.
Number.Sinh(angle)	Returns the hyperbolic sine of a number. Similar to Excel function SINH.
Number.Tan(angle)	Returns the tangent of a number. Similar to Excel function TAN.
Number.Tanh(angle)	Returns the hyperbolic tangent of a number. Similar to Excel function TANH.

Record Functions

The Record functions are split into these categories: Record Selection, Record Serialization, Record Transformations, Table Construction, Table Conversions, Table Information, and Table Row Operations.

Record Information Functions in Power Query M

Table B.32   List of Record Information Functions in Power Query M

Record.FieldCount(record)	Returns the number of fields in a record.
Record.HasFields(record, fields)	Returns true if the field name or field names are present in a record.

Record Selection Functions in Power Query M

Table B.33   List of Record Selection Functions in Power Query M

Record.Field(record, field)	Returns the value of the given field. This function can be used to dynamically create field lookup syntax for a given record. In that way, it is a dynamic verison of the record[field] syntax.
Record.FieldNames(record)	Returns a list of field names in order of the record's fields.
Record.FieldOrDefault(record, field, [defaultValue])	Returns the value of a field from a record, or the default value if the field does not exist.
Record.FieldValues(record)	Returns a list of field values in order of the record's fields.
Record.SelectFields(record, fields, [missingField])	Returns a new record that contains the fields selected from the input record. The original order of the fields is maintained.

Record Serialization Functions in Power Query M

Table B.34   List of Record Serialization Functions in Power Query M

Record.FromList(list, fields)	Returns a record given a list of field values and a set of fields.
Record.FromTable(list)	Returns a record from a table of records containing field names and values.
Record.ToList(record)	Returns a list of values containing the field values of the input record.
Record.ToTable(record)	Returns a table of records containing field names and values from an input record.

Record Transformations Functions in Power Query M

Table B.35   List of Record Transformations Functions in Power Query M

Record.AddField(record, fieldName, value, [delayed])	Adds a field from a field name and value.
Record.Combine(list)	Combines the records in a list.
Record.RemoveFields(record, fields, [missingField])	Returns a new record that reorders the given fields with respect to each other. Any fields not specified remain in their original locations.
Record.RenameFields(record, renames, [missingField])	Returns a new record that renames the fields specified. The resultant fields will retain their original order. This function supports swapping and chaining field names. However, all target names plus remaining field names must constitute a unique set or an error will occur.
Record.ReorderFields(record, fieldOrder, [missingField])	Returns a new record that reorders fields relative to each other. Any fields not specified remain in their original locations. Requires two or more fields.
Record.TransformFields(record, transformOperations, [missingField])	Transforms fields by applying transformOperations. For more information about values supported by transformOperations, see Parameter Values.

Replacer Functions in Power Query M

Table B.36   List of Replacer Functions in Power Query M

Replacer.ReplaceText(text, old, new)	This function is provided to List.ReplaceValue or Table.ReplaceValue to replace text in list or table.
Replacer.ReplaceValue(value, old, new)	This function is passed List.ReplaceValue or Table.ReplaceValue to replace values in a list or table.

Splitter Functions in Power Query M

Table B.37   List of Splitter Functions in Power Query M

Splitter.SplitByNothing()	Returns a function that does no splitting, returning its argument as a single element list.
Splitter.SplitTextByAnyDelimiter (delimiters, [quoteStyle])	Returns a function that splits text by any supported delimiter.

Splitter.SplitTextByDelimiter(delimiter, [quoteStyle])	Returns a function that will split text according to a delimiter.
Splitter.SplitTextByEachDelimiter (delimiters, [quoteStyle])	Returns a function that splits text by each delimiter in turn.
Splitter.SplitTextByLengths(lengths)	Returns a function that splits text according to the specified lengths.
Splitter.SplitTextByPositions(positions)	Returns a function that splits text according to the specified positions.
Splitter.SplitTextByRanges(ranges)	Returns a function that splits text according to the specified ranges.
Splitter.SplitTextByRepeatedLengths (length, [startAtEnd])	Returns a function that splits text into a list of text after the specified length repeatedly.
Splitter.SplitTextByWhitespace ([quoteStyle])	Returns a function that splits text according to whitespace.

Table Functions

This category is split into Table Construction, Table Conversions, and Table Information.

Table Column Operations Functions in Power Query M

Table B.38   List of Table Column Operations Functions in Power Query M

Table.Column(table, column)	Returns the values from a column in a table.
Table.ColumnNames(table)	Returns the names of columns from a table.
Table.ColumnsOfType(table, listOfTypes)	Returns a list with the names of the columns that match the specified types.
Table.DemoteHeaders(table)	Demotes the header row down into the first row of a table.
Table.DuplicateColumn(table, columnName,newColumnName, [columnType])	Duplicates a column with the specified name. Values and type are copied from the source column.
Table.HasColumns(table, columns)	Returns true if a table has the specified column or columns.
Table.Pivot(table, pivotValues, attributeColumn, valueColumn, [aggregationFunction])	Given a table and attribute column containing pivotValues, creates new columns for each of the pivot values and assigns them values from the valueColumn. An optional aggregationFunction can be provided to handle multiple occurrence of the same key value in the attribute column.

Table.PrefixColumns(table, prefix)	Returns a table where the columns have all been prefixed with a text value.
Table.PromoteHeaders(table,[options])	Promotes the first row of the table into its header or column names.
Table.RemoveColumns(table, columns, [missingField])	Returns a table without a specific column or columns.
Table.RenameColumns(table, renames, [missingField])	Returns a table with the columns renamed as specified.
Table.ReorderColumns(table, columnOrder, [missingField])	Returns a table with specific columns in an order relative to one another.
Table.SelectColumns(table, columns, [missingField])	Returns a table that contains only specific columns.
Table.TransformColumnNames(table, nameGenerator,[options])	Transforms column names by using the given function.
Table.Unpivot(table, pivotColumns, attributeColumn, valueColumn)	Given a list of table columns, transforms those columns into attribute-value pairs.
Table.UnpivotOtherColumns(table, pivotColumns, attributeColumn, valueColumn)	Translates all columns other than a specified set into attribute-value pairs, combined with the rest of the values in each row.

Table Construction Functions in Power Query M

Table B.39 List of Table Construction Functions in Power Query M

ItemExpression.From(function)	Returns the AST for the body of a function.
RowExpression.Column(columnName)	Returns an AST that represents access to a column within a row expression.
RowExpression.From(function)	Returns the AST for the body of a function.
RowExpression.Row(function)	An AST node representing the row in a row expression.
Table.FromColumns(lists, [columns])	Returns a table from a list containing nested lists with the column names and values.
Table.FromList(list, [splitter], [columns], [default], [extraValues])	Converts a list into a table by applying the specified splitting function to each item in the list.
Table.FromRecords(records, [columns], [missingField])	Returns a table from a list of records.
Table.FromRows(rows, [columns])	Creates a table from the list where each element of the list is a list that contains the column values for a single row.

Table.FromValue(value)	Returns a table with a column containing the provided value or list of values.
Table.Split(table, pageSize)	Splits the specified table into a list of tables using the specified page size.
Table.View(table, handlers)	Creates or extends a table with user-defined handlers for query and action operations.
Table.ViewFunction(function)	Creates a function that can be intercepted by a handler defined on a view (via Table.View).

Table Conversions Functions in Power Query M

Table B.40   List of Table Conversions Functions in Power Query M

Table.ToColumns(table)	Returns a list of nested lists each representing a column of values in the input table.
Table.ToList(table, [combiner])	Returns a table into a list by applying the specified combining function to each row of values in a table.
Table.ToRecords(table)	Returns a list of records from an input table.
Table.ToRows(table)	Returns a nested list of row values from an input table.

Table Information Functions in Power Query M

Table B.41   List of Table Information Functions in Power Query M

Table.ColumnCount(table)	Returns the number of columns in a table.
Table.IsEmpty(table)	Returns true if the table does not contain any rows.
Table.Profile(table)	Returns a profile of the columns of a table.
Table.RowCount(table)	Returns the number of rows in a table.
Table.Schema(table)	Returns a table containing a description of the columns (i.e., the schema) of the specified table.
Tables.GetRelationships(tables, [dataColumn])	Returns the relationships among a set of tables.

Table Row Operations Functions in Power Query M

Table B.42   List of Table Row Operations Functions in Power Query M

Table.AlternateRows(table, offset, skip, take)	Returns a table containing an alternating pattern of the rows from a table.
Table.Combine(tables, [columns])	Returns a table that is the result of merging a list of tables. The tables must all have the same row type structure.

Table.FindText(table,text)	Returns a table containing only the rows that have the specified text within one of their cells or any part thereof.
Table.First(table,[default])	Returns the first row from a table.
Table.FirstN(table, [countOrCondition])	Returns the first row(s) of a table, depending on the countOrCondition parameter.
Table.FirstValue(table, [default])	Returns the first column of the first row of the table or a specified default value.
Table. FromPartitions(partitionColumn, partitions, [partitionColumnType])	Returns a table that is the result of combining a set of partitioned tables into new columns. The type of the column can optionally be specified; the default is any.
Table.InsertRows(table, offset, rows)	Returns a table with the list of rows inserted into the table at an index. Each row to insert must match the row type of the table.
Table.Last(table, [default])	Returns the last row of a table.
Table.LastN(table, countOrCondition)	Returns the last row(s) from a table, depending on the countOrCondition parameter.
Table.MatchesAllRows(table, condition)	Returns true if all of the rows in a table meet a condition.
Table.MatchesAnyRows(table, condition)	Returns true if any of the rows in a table meet a condition.
Table.Partition(Table. FromRecords({[A=1], [A=2], [A=3], [A=4], [A=5], [A=6]}),"A", 2, each _)	Partitions the table into a list of groups number of tables, based on the value of the column of each row and a hash function. The hash function is applied to the value of the column of a row to obtain a hash value for the row. The hash value modulo groups determines in which of the returned tables the row will be placed.
Table.Range(table, offset, [count])	Returns the specified number of rows from a table starting at an offset.
Table.RemoveFirstN(table, [countOrCondition])	Returns a table with the specified number of rows removed from the table starting at the first row. The number of rows removed depends on the optional countOrCondition parameter.
Table.RemoveLastN(table, [countOrCondition])	Returns a table with the specified number of rows removed from the table starting at the last row. The number of rows removed depends on the optional countOrCondition parameter.
Table.RemoveRows(table, offset, [count])	Returns a table with the specified number of rows removed from the table starting at an offset.
Table. RemoveRowsWithErrors(table, [columns])	Returns a table with all rows removed from the table that contain an error in at least one of the cells in a row.

Table.Repeat(table, count)	Returns a table containing the rows of the table repeated the count number of times.
Table.ReplaceRows(table, offset, count, rows)	Returns a table where the rows beginning at an offset and continuing for count are replaced with the provided rows.
Table.ReverseRows(table)	Returns a table with the rows in reverse order.
Table.SelectRows(table, condition)	Returns a table containing only the rows that match a condition.
Table.SelectRowsWithErrors(table, [columns])	Returns a table with only the rows from table that contain an error in at least one of the cells in a row.
Table.SingleRow(table)	Returns a single row from a table.
Table.Skip(table, [countOrCondition])	Returns a table that does not contain the first row or rows of the table.

Text Functions

The text functions are split into Text Information, Text Membership, Text Modification, Text Comparisons, and Text Transformations.

Text Extraction Functions in Power Query M

Table B.43   List of Text Extraction Functions in Power Query M

Text.At(value, index)	Returns a character starting at a zero-based offset.
Text.End(string, numChars)	Returns the number of characters from the end of a text value. Similar to Excel function RIGHT.
Text.Middle(text, start, [count])	Returns the substring up to a specific length. Similar to Excel function MID.
Text.Range(text, offset, [count])	Returns a number of characters from a text value starting at a zero-based offset and for count number of characters.
Text.Start(string, count)	Returns the count of characters from the start of a text value. Similar to Excel function LEFT.

Text Information Functions in Power Query M

Table B.44   List of Text Information Functions in Power Query M

Text.Length(text)	Returns the number of characters in a text value. Similar to Excel function LEN.

Text Membership Functions in Power Query M

Table B.45   List of Text Membership Functions in Power Query M

Text.Contains(string, substring, [comparer])	Returns true if a text value substring was found within a text value string; otherwise, false.
Text.EndsWith(string, substring, [comparer])	Returns a logical value indicating whether a text value substring was found at the end of a string.
Text.PositionOf(text, substring, [occurrence], [comparer])	Returns the first occurrence of substring in a string and returns its position starting at startOffset.
Text.PositionOfAny(string, list, [occurrence])	Returns the first occurrence of a text value in list and returns its position starting at startOffset.
Text.StartsWith(string, substring, [comparer])	Returns a logical value indicating whether a text value substring was found at the beginning of a string.

Text Modification Functions in Power Query M

Table B.46   List of Text Modification Functions in Power Query M

Text.Insert(text, offset, newText)	Returns a text value with newValue inserted into a text value starting at a zero-based offset.
Text.Remove(text, removeChars)	Removes all occurrences of a character or list of characters from a text value. The removeChars parameter can be a character value or a list of character values.
Text.RemoveRange(text, offset, count)	Removes count characters at a zero-based offset from a text value.
Text.Replace(text,old,new)	Replaces all occurrences of a substring with a new text value. Similar to Excel function REPLACE.
Text.ReplaceRange(text, offset, length, newText)	Replaces length characters in a text value starting at a zero-based offset with the new text value.
Text.Select(text, selectChars)	Selects all occurrences of the given character or list of characters from the input text value.

Text Comparisons Functions in Power Query M

Table B.47   List of Text Comparisons Functions in Power Query M

Character.FromNumber(number)	Returns a number to its character value. Similar to Excel function CHAR.
Character.ToNumber(character)	Returns a character to its number value. Similar to Excel function CODE.
Guid.From(value)	Returns a Guid.Type value from the given value.
Json.FromValue(value, [encoding])	Produces a JSON representation of a given value.
Text.From(value, [culture])	Returns the text representation of a number, date, time, datetime, DateTimeZone , logical, duration, or binary value. If a value is null, Text.From returns null. The optional culture parameter is used to format the text value according to the given culture. Similar to Excel function TEXT.
Text.FromBinary(binary, [encoding])	Decodes data from a binary value into a text value using an encoding.
Text.NewGuid()	Returns a Guid value as a text value.
Text.ToBinary(text, [encoding], [includeByteOrderMark])	Encodes a text value into binary value using an encoding. Similar to Excel function DEC2BIN.
Text.ToList(text)	Returns a list of characters from a text value.
Value.FromText(value, [culture])	Decodes a value from a textual representation, value, and interprets it as a value with an appropriate type. Value.FromText takes a text value and returns a number, a logical value, a null value, a DateTime value, a Duration value, or a text value. The empty text value is interpreted as a null value. Similar to Excel function VALUE.

Text Transformations Functions in Power Query M

Table B.48   List of Text Transformations Functions in Power Query M

Text.AfterDelimiter(text, delimiter, [index])	Returns the portion of text after the specified delimiter.
Text.BeforeDelimiter(text, delimiter, [index])	Returns the portion of text before the specified delimiter.
Text.BetweenDelimiters(text, startDelimiter, endDelimiter, [startIndex], [endIndex])	Returns the portion of text between the specified startDelimiter and endDelimiter.
Text.Clean(string)	Returns the original text value with non-printable characters removed. Similar to Excel function CLEAN.

Text.Combine(text, separator)	Returns a text value that is the result of joining all text values with each value separated by a separator. Similar to Excel function CONCAT.
Text.Lower(string)	Returns the lowercase of a text value. Similar to Excel function LOWER.
Text.PadEnd(text, length, pad)	Returns a text value padded at the end with pad to make it at least length characters.
Text.PadStart(text, length, [pad])	Returns a text value padded at the beginning with pad to make it at least length characters. If pad is not specified, whitespace is used as pad.
Text.Proper(string)	Returns a text value with first letters of all words converted to uppercase. Similar to Excel function PROPER.
Text.Repeat(string, repeatCount)	Returns a text value composed of the input text value repeated a number of times. Similar to Excel function REPT.
Text.Reverse(text)	Reverses the provided text.
Text.Split(string, separator)	Returns a list containing parts of a text value that are delimited by a separator text value.
Text.SplitAny(string, separator)	Returns a list containing parts of a text value that are delimited by any separator text values.
Text.Trim(text, [trimChars])	Removes any occurrences of characters in trimChars from text. Similar to Excel function TRIM.
Text.TrimEnd(text, [trimChars])	Removes any occurrences of the characters specified in trimChars from the end of the original text value.
Text.TrimStart(text, [trimChars])	Removes any occurrences of the characters in trimChars from the start of the original text value.
Text.Upper(string)	Returns the uppercase of a text value. Similar to Excel function UPPER.

Time Functions in Power Query M

Table B.49   List of Time Functions in Power Query M

Time.EndOfHour(dateTime)	Returns a DateTime value from the end of the hour.
Time.From(value, [culture])	Returns a time value from a value.
Time.FromText(time, [culture])	Returns a time value from a set of date formats.
Time.Hour(dateTime)	Returns an hour value from a DateTime value. Similar to Excel function HOUR.
Time.Minute(dateTime)	Returns a minute value from a DateTime value. Similar to Excel function MINUTE.

Time.Second(#datetime(2011, 12, 31, 9, 15, 36.5))	Returns a second value from a DateTime value Similar to Excel function SECOND.
Time.StartOfHour(datetime)	Returns the first value of the hour from a time value.
Time.ToRecord(time)	Returns a record containing parts of a date value.
Time.ToText(time, [format], [culture])	Returns a text value from a time value. Similar to Excel function TEXT.

Type Functions in Power Query M

Table B.50   List of Type Functions in Power Query M

Type.AddTableKey(table, columns, isPrimary)	Add a key to a table type.
Type.ClosedRecord(#"type")	The given type must be a record type and returns a closed version of the given record type (or the same type, if it is already closed).
Type.Facets(type)	Returns the facets of a type.
Type.ForFunction(signature, parameter, min)	Creates a return type for a function and specifies the minimum number of arguments required to invoke the function.
Type.ForRecord(fields, open)	Returns a record type from a fields record.
Type.FunctionParameters(functionType)	Returns a record with field values set to the name of the parameters of a function type, and their values set to their corresponding types.
Type.FunctionRequiredParameters(#"type")	Returns a number indicating the minimum number of parameters required to invoke the type of function.
Type.FunctionReturn(type)	Returns a type returned by a function type.
Type.Is(type1, type2)	Returns True or False if the column is of type1 or type2.
Type.IsNullable(#"type")	Returns true if a type is a nullable type; otherwise, false.
Type.IsOpenRecord(#"type")	Returns whether a record type is open.
Type.ListItem(#"type")	Returns an item type from a list type.
Type.NonNullable(#"type")	Returns the non nullable type from a type.
Type.OpenRecord(#"type")	Returns an opened version of a record type, or the same type, if it is already open.
Type.RecordFields(#"type")	Returns a record describing the fields of a record type with each field of the returned record type having a corresponding name and a value that is a record of the form [Type = type, Optional = logical].

Type.ReplaceFacets(type, facets)	Replaces the facets of a type.
Type.ReplaceTableKeys(tableType, keys)	Replaces the keys in a table type.
Type.TableColumn(tableType, column)	Returns the type of a column in a table.
Type.TableKeys(tableType)	Returns keys from a table type.
Type.TableRow(table)	Returns a row type from a table type.
Type.TableSchema(tableType)	Returns a table containing a description of the columns (i.e., the schema) of the specified table type.
Type.Union(types)	Returns the union of a list of types.

URI Functions in Power Query M

Table B.51   List of URI Functions in Power Query M

Uri.BuildQueryString(query)	Assemble a record into a URI query string.
Uri.Combine(baseUri, relativeUri)	Returns a Uri based on the combination of the base and relative parts.
Uri.EscapeDataString(data)	Encodes special characters in accordance with RFC 3986. Similar to Excel function ENCODEURL.
Uri.Parts(absoluteUri)	Returns a record value with the fields set to the parts of a Uri text value.

Value Functions in Power Query M

Table B.52   List of Value Functions in Power Query M

DirectQueryCapabilities.From(value)	DirectQueryCapabilities.From
Embedded.Value(value, path)	Accesses a value by name in an embedded mashup.
SqlExpression.SchemaFrom(schema)	SqlExpression.SchemaFrom
SqlExpression.ToExpression(sql, environment)	SqlExpression.ToExpression
Value.Add(value1, value2,[precision])	Returns the sum of the two values. Similar to Excel function SUM.
Value.As(value, type)	Value.As is the function corresponding to the as operator in the formula language. The expression value as type asserts that the value of a value argument is compatible with type as per the is operator. If it is not compatible, an error is raised.

Value.Compare(value1, value2,[precision])	Returns 1, 0, or -1 based on value1 being greater than, equal to, or less than the value2. An optional comparer function can be provided.
Value.Divide(value1, value2,[precision])	Returns the result of dividing the first value by the second. Similar to Excel function QUOTIENT.
Value.Equals(left, right, equater)	Returns whether two values are equal.
Value.Firewall(key)	Value.Firewall
Value.Is(value, type)	Value.Is is the function corresponding to the is operator in the formula language. The expression value is type returns true if the ascribed type of vlaue is compatible with type, and returns false if the ascribed type of value is incompatible with type.
Value.Metadata(value)	Returns a record containing the input's metadata.
Value.Multiply(value1, value2,[precision])	Returns the product of the two values. Similar to Excel function PRODUCT.
Value.NativeQuery(target, query, [paremeters],[options])	Evaluates a query against a target.
Value.NullableEquals(value1, value2)	Returns a logical value or null based on two values.
Value.RemoveMetadata(value)	Removes the metadata on the value and returns the original value.
Value.ReplaceMetadata(value, newMeta)	Replaces the metadata on a value with the new metadata record provided and returns the original value with the new metadata attached.
Value.Replacetype(value, replacedType)	A value may be ascribed a type using Value.ReplaceType. Value.ReplaceType either returns a new value with the type ascribed or raises an error if the new type is incompatible with the value's native primitive type.
Value.Subtract(value1, value2,[precision])	Returns the difference of the two values.
Value.Type(value)	Returns the type of the given value.
Variable.Value(identifier)	Returns the value of the variable stored in identifier.

Index

Symbols

3D formulas
- building with mouse, 330
- spearing through worksheets, 328-330

3D Maps
- animating over time, 607
- color categories in, 605
- columns
  - changing colors, 615
  - resizing, 615
- custom maps, 619
  - creating, 619-621
  - image preparation, 619
- data, inserting, 610-613
- Flat Map option, 616
- labels, viewing, 617-618
- layers, combining, 615
- panes, resizing, 616
- photos, adding to points, 614
- points, animating line between, 617
- rotating, 614
- satellite photos in, 616
- time in, 616-617
- tipping, 614
- tours, creating, 618
- troubleshooting, 613
- types of
  - column charts, 604
  - heat maps, 604
  - shaded area maps, 603
- ultra-local, 608-610
- zooming, 605-606, 614

3D models, 17-18, 639, 665-666

32-bit Excel, 447

64-bit Excel, 447

1904 date system, 85

& (ampersand) operator, joining text, 141-142

* (asterisk) wildcard character, 188

#CALC! error message, 139

#DIV/0! error message, 138

=+ (equal plus), in formulas, 129

error message, 139

#FIELD! error message, 139

#N/A! error message, 138

#NULL! error message, 139

? (question mark) wildcard character, 188

#REF! error message, 138

#SPILL! error message, 40, 139

[ ] (square brackets), in date/time formatting, 194

#VALUE! error message, 138

A

N

Q

QUARTILE.EXC() function, 296

QUARTILE.INC() function, 296

queries. *See* Power Query

question mark (?) wildcard character, 188

Quick Access Toolbar (QAT), 63

commands

adding, 63-64

removing, 64

customizing, 64-66

settings (Excel Options dialog box), 80

touch mode, 69

quick formatting, 576

QUOTIENT() function, 165

R

R1C1 style

A1 style versus, 484-485

fixing AutoSum errors in, 485-486

RADIANS() function, 299

RANDARRAY function, 45, 53-54

RANDBETWEEN() function, 165, 180-182

RAND() function, 165, 180-182

random numbers, generating, 53-54, 180-182

random scenario modeling, 453-455

random sorts, 45

Range property, syntax, 493

ranges

conditional formatting, 185

criteria ranges

creating, 275

headings for, 272

miracle version, 277-278

of dates, creating with array formulas, 338-339

describing, 263-265

formatting, 53

of formulas, transposing, 335-338

justifying text in, 550-551

names

advantages of, 315

avoiding absolute references, 326

defining, 316, 322

defining multiple names from labels, 322-324

defining with New Name dialog box, 317-318

in formulas, 320-322

implicit intersection, 325

navigation with Name dialog box, 318-319

in Scenario Manager, 455

two-way lookups with, 324

valid characters for, 316-317

worksheet-level scope, 319-320

rectangular ranges, toggling references with F4, 125-126

referencing in macros, 490

selecting, shortcut keys for, 102

as tables, defining, 132

values based on, 249-250, 387

RANK.AVG() function, 296, 411

RANK.EQ() function, 296, 411

rankings in pivot tables, 409-410

RATE() function, 288

realigning numbers in icons sets, 566-567

reapplying filters, 374

rearranging pivot tables, 400-401

RECEIVED() function, 288

Recent File List command (Backstage), 67

recent workbooks list

changing number to view, 84

clearing, 68

Recommended PivotTable dialog box, 393-395

direct precedents, 146

Evalute Formula dialog box, 149

Excel as calculator, 150

F9 key, 149-150

highlighting formula cells, 146

implicit intersection, 126

Show Formulas mode, 145

Trace Error feature, 140

Watch Window feature, 148

FORMULATEXT() function, 262

importing data into Power BI Desktop, 689

inserting cells with shortcut keys, 21

keyboard accelerators, 90

macros, debugging mode, 496

manual page breaks, 676

OFFSET() function, 265

page numbers on printed documents, 672

performance, 663

pivot tables

  changing pivot tables, 403

  missing tools, 403

  rankings in, 411

  refreshing data, 402

  viewing contextual tabs, 60

PMT function, 450

selecting cells bug, 23-24

selecting merged cells, 538-539

solving equations, 508

sorting data, 362

sparkline axis settings, 626

TRIM() function, 215

unique values, 570

TRUE() function, 232, 249-250

TRUNC() function, 166

Trust Center links, creating, 312-313

Trust Center settings (Excel Options dialog box), 80

Trusted Document settings, 84

trusted locations, folders as, 85

two-variable what-if analysis, 451-452

two-way lookups with intersection operator, 324

TYPE() function, 233

Type Power Query M functions, 774-775

typing links to worksheets, 311

U

ultra-local 3D Maps, 608-610

unary minus example (order of operations), 136

underline format, 532

undo, macros and, 474

undocking pivot table field list, 396

UNICHAR() function, 170, 216-217

UNICODE() function, 170, 217-218

UNIQUE function, 48-50

unique records, advanced filters in macros, 499-500

unique values

  conditional formatting, 570, 574-575

  consolidating and adding, 389-390

  extracting with formulas, 48-50

  finding, 387-389

unlocking aspect ratio for pictures, 655

unpivoting data in Power Query, 349-350

unsaved workbooks

  creating links to, 311

  recovering, 67

unselecting cells with Ctrl+click, 24

Update Links dialog box, suppressing, 314

updating links in worksheets

  to closed workbooks, 313

  to missing linked workbooks, 313

  suppressing Update Links dialog box, 314

Plug into learning at

microsoftpressstore.com

The Microsoft Press Store by Pearson offers:

- Free U.S. shipping

- Buy an eBook, get three formats – Includes PDF, EPUB, and MOBI to use with your computer, tablet, and mobile devices

- Print & eBook Best Value Packs

- eBook Deal of the Week – Save up to 50% on featured title

- Newsletter – Be the first to hear about new releases, announcements, special offers, and more

- Register your book – Find companion files, errata, and product updates, plus receive a special coupon* to save on your next purchase

 Pearson